**PENGUIN BOOKS**
# SHOTS FROM THE HIP

Charles Shaar Murray was born in London in 1951, and began his career in 1970 as one of the participants in the notorious 1970 *Oz Schoolkids' Issue*. He joined *New Musical Express* two years later and eventually became *NME's* Associate Editor before returning to a freelance career in 1981. He is the author of *Crosstown Traffic* (1989), an internationally acclaimed critical study of the life and work of Jimi Hendrix, which he subsequently adapted into a radio series for the BBC World Service and which won a Gleason Award in 1991, and (with Roy Carr) of *David Bowie: The Illustrated Record* (1981). His journalism and criticism have also appeared in the *Daily Telegraph, Observer, Q, Vogue, The Face, Times Literary Supplement, Literary Review, New Statesman, Guardian, Time Out* and *MacUser*. In collaboration with Brooklyn-based artist Floyd Hughes, he has created *Purple Days*, a fantasy biography of Jimi Hendrix in comic-strip form.

Charles Shaar Murray's favourite cult objects are the Fender Stratocaster, the Apple Macintosh and the Zippo lighter. He lives in North London with his wife, and is currently nervously gearing up to commence writing his first novel.

# Shots from the Hip

Charles Shaar Murray

PENGUIN BOOKS

PENGUIN BOOKS

Published by the Penguin Group
Penguin Books Ltd, 27 Wrights Lane, London W8 5TZ, England
Penguin Books USA Inc. 375 Hudson Street, New York, New York 10014, USA
Penguin Books Australia Ltd, Ringwood, Victoria, Australia
Penguin Books Canada Ltd, 2801 John Street, Markham, Ontario, Canada L3R 1B4
Penguin Books (NZ) Ltd, 182–190 Wairau Road, Auckland 10, New Zealand

Penguin Books Ltd, Registered Offices: Harmondsworth, Middlesex, England

The articles in this book were first published in *Cream, IT, New Hi Fi Sound,
New Musical Express*, the *Observer, Oz, Q*, the *Daily Telegraph* and *Vogue*,
between 1971 and 1990
This collection first published 1991
1 3 5 7 9 10 8 6 4 2
Copyright © Charles Shaar Murray, 1971, 1972, 1973, 1974, 1975, 1976, 1977,
1978, 1979, 1980, 1981, 1982, 1983, 1984, 1985, 1986, 1987, 1988, 1989, 1990, 1991
Preface copyright © Neil Spencer, 1991
All rights reserved

Printed in England by Clays Ltd, St Ives plc
Filmset in 10/11½ pt Monophoto Bodoni Light 504

# Contents

# Preface

JOURNALISM isn't written for books. At least it shouldn't be, and the column composed with one eye on eventual compilation is a stilted, false thing which history invariably finds less interesting than the impassioned dispatch.

Ideally, journalism should be clacked out on a battered Remington typewriter by a hack with sweat stains below his armpits, bags beneath his eyes and an overflowing ashtray in front of him. It is torn out of the typewriter carriage by a hatchet faced sub-ed wearing a green eyeshade and stainless-steel armbands and rushed for typesetting while a small army of printers oil presses humming in anticipation of a front-page exclusive. Journalism may also be barked down payphones by reporters with pencils poised and trilbys tipped back, murmured into tape recorders while on the prowl in a Watergate basement, or declaimed into a radio microphone by a wide-eyed commentator.

The scenario – hilariously explored by director Billy Wilder in *The Front Page* – may vary, but it remains journalism's abiding myth, the scene which rolls through the mind of any cub reporter entering journalism college or scribbling the first page of their fanzine. Technology may have altered its incidentals, but word-processors, computerized presses and non-smudge ink still require a hapless hack somewhere along the line, even though his or her words often enter a grinding mill of sub-editors and re-write teams, to be tweaked into final shape by editors and proprietors. Despite this, the writers remain the stars of any journal. National tabloid or trade monthly, the reporter is the messenger from the front line of events, and often their interpreter. The much despised critic likewise remains an arbiter of reality. And the deadline still hangs like a guillotine blade over hacks of all persuasions.

Britain's weekly rock press, that mutant genre that lies halfway between newspaper and magazine, has long had its own variant of the *Front Page* scenario, with anxious editors hovering while spotty hacks squeeze out a breathless review of the opening night of the Bowie tour, preview the illegally obtained white-label copy of the latest Solitary Brick album, or transcribe the meandering, 'exclusive' Keith Richards interview.

Such excitations are nowadays widespread through the media. In Britain, the music industry is served not only by its traditional youthful allies in the music press, but by journals from the *Daily Telegraph* to the *Tatler*, by all four TV channels and by any number of pirate radio stations operating alongside the legal stations. Satellites orbit the earth specifically to supply twenty-four-hour pop television. Pop's anthems sell jeans, beer, washing powder and banks. In North America, *Rolling Stone*, the cultural lodestone of the Woodstock generation, has become as august as the *Wall Street Journal* (well, almost), while rock, the idiot bastard son itself, is as often to be found living in a Bel Air mansion as in a New York crash pad, and now hawks a traditionalism as self-conscious and phony as Ralph Lauren's ranch.

It is sometimes hard to remember that even in the mid-seventies, when rock was arguably at its most self-inflated and pompous and there was certainly no shortage of fortunes being made, pop's entire coverage on British TV was two weekly shows — *Top of the Pops* and *Old Grey Whistle Test* (for teenyboppers and twenties rockers respectively). Fleet Street (as then was) was only marginally more interested. There was the occasional Stones or Who article in one of the Sunday colour supplements. The tabloids bothered only with Donny Osmond mania, drug overdoses and the ritual busting of Paul McCartney and Keith Richards (for pot and heroin respectively).

Otherwise, popular music was left to the music press. This was staffed by a peculiar blend of Tin Pan Alley era hacks, enthusiastic young music fans graduated from the provincial press, over-earnest college kids and assorted crazies looking for a way into the music industry. The collapse of the 'underground press' in the early seventies had propelled many of its staff into mainstream journalism, and *New Musical Express* — at that time an ailing pop sheet looking to refurbish itself in the rock era — became home for several of the best underground press writers, and helped fill the vacuum created by the disappearance of *Oz*, *I.T.*, *Friends* and others. Britain's independent monthly *Cream*, not to be confused with the US *Creem*, was another important source of talent.

The quality of the *NME*'s writing team, which included Charles Shaar Murray, Nick Kent, Ian MacDonald and Andrew Tyler, together with its abrasive humour and willingness to bite the hand of the music industry which fed it, soon saw it eclipse its rivals. As in rock itself, the USA was the aspirational role model; everyone had their copy of Tom Wolfe's *New Journalism* collection, and US writers like Lester Bangs were avidly read. As well as in-depth reportage and tough-minded criticism, the *NME* writers brought an innovative dexterity to the language of musical journalism. In particular Murray, or CSM as his soubriquet had it, became celebrated for a style and vocabulary that slammed together street argot and punctilious grammar, critical lucidity with gut-level honesty. *NME*'s reputation as 'a writers' paper' ensured that numerous talented scribblers would subsequently pass through its pages. The paper also brought with it an awareness of the wider culture within which popular music operated: there was coverage of film, comics, books and a strong political subtext.

The collision between hippie idealism and corporate zest applied to both the music industry and to its journals, and just as record companies were forced occasionally to apologize for the misdemeanours of their musicians (lyrics celebrating drug use or a sexist record cover, for example), so *NME*'s owners, IPC, were occasionally embarrassed by their wayward, if highly profitable, charge and its exotic use of the vernacular. 'Must we fling this filth at our pop kids?' trumpeted the *Sunday People*, alongside a revelation that Cliff Richard 'wouldn't have *NME* in the house'. The answer seemed to be yes.

The music industry had, by the turn of the sixties, come to regard itself as something approaching the new Hollywood, a wide-open boomtown, a fantasy playground of lotus-eaters and overnight fortunes, the real creator of the popular icons of the day. Record company launches for the feeblest of records became increasingly lavish, and it was a standing gag that any lowly rock hack could eat, drink, be dressed and funded at the expense of record companies. Despite its increasingly evident multi-national muscle and the celebrated debauches of the musicians themselves, the industry remained caught up in a backwash of hippie idealism that still saw music as a transformational force. Though the dreamweaver incarnate, John Lennon, had told everyone as early as 1970 that 'the dream is over', few faced up to the truth.

Before I joined *NME* in the mid-seventies I was in awe of the volume and quality of wordage produced by its principal writers, particularly Murray and Kent. First-hand knowledge of the deadlines under which they laboured served only to heighten my admiration; deadlines which were met only by a commitment that far exceeded its material rewards. The *modus operandi* of the two couldn't have been more different; Kent's manuscripts came scrawled in rococo biro, with numerous amendments etched between the lines, Murray's came hammer-typed into the page. Both, though, were united by their belief in spontaneity and rarely second-guessed themselves.

The demented atmosphere in the cramped *NME* offices in Covent Garden were scarcely conducive to orderly copy flow, but against all odds the paper appeared each week and prospered. The paper's critical tone veered between uncritical fan worship, satire and gleeful cynicism, its prose from the dull to the glittering. When what the paper had been campaigning for musically − a revitalization of pop from the roots − actually came along in the form of punk, it was as initially as shocked as everyone else. But punk and the music press were made for each other. Banned from venues and airplay, 'the music press was the only place left for punk to happen,' as Bob Geldof put it ('Modest Bob' was himself an ex-*NME* contributor).

Such is the context of many of the pieces collected in *Shots from the Hip*. It is a volume that should delight the author's many admirers, gathering as it does numerous pieces acclaimed at the time of their publication and fondly recalled subsequently (and cited in numerous music books) but available only via the vintage magazine racks. Aside from the fluidity of their language, their portraits of mega and minor luminaries from the pop firmament and their critical insight and humour, hopefully the assembled pieces also give some idea of the wider dialogue of which they were a part. They certainly offer a singular history of pop's evolution over the last two decades.

Given that the pieces in *Shots from the Hip* span some twenty years and half a dozen different publications, their continuity of critical thought and evenness of tone are remarkable. Charles rumbled in his teens that if white boys couldn't quite play the blues, they could certainly get them, and just as the blues is the bedrock of twentieth-century popular music, so Charles's abiding love for all things R&B permeates his writing. Those inescapable twelve bars have always been the blueprint (forgive the pun) of his critique, and the transformation of the blues at the hands of Jimi Hendrix, recasting those old bordello moans into a music of space-age splendour, remains for CSM rock's highest achievement.

Charlie's appalled fascination for the Frankenstein's monster of heavy metal likewise stems from his R&B roots; there are several apologies here to the blues for rock's invention of metal. The glam school of Bolan and Bowie provided another key element in the Murray overview ... but then there are also comic-book superheroes climbing in the window, tough-guy private eyes kicking down his door, and The Ramones droning on the record deck. You figure it out. As editor of *NME* for several years, many of the pieces in *Shots from the Hip* brought me delight. I hope they do the same for readers new and old.

Neil Spencer
London
May 1990

# Acknowledgements

RESPECT is due to every editor I've ever learned from. In order of appearance, I was taught my trade by Richard Neville, Felix Dennis and particularly Jim Anderson at *Oz*, Charlie Gillett and Bob Houston at *Cream* and a whole *New Musical Express* posse including Tony Tyler, Nick Logan, Ian MacDonald, Neil Spencer, Alan Smith, Bob Woffinden and Jack Scott. All along the way, I've sharpened and developed ideas by arguing the toss with a whole slew of colleagues, adversaries and friends; most prominent among many being Nick Kent, Andrew Tyler, the aforementioned MacDonald, Spencer and Tyler T., Roy Carr, the late Peter Erskine, Tony Parsons, Julie Burchill, Paul Morley, Ian Penman, Jon Savage, Lloyd Bradley, Mark Ellen, Andy Gill, Mat Snow, Paul duNoyer, Dave Marsh, Ed Ward and Mick Farren.

Special thanks are due to Alan Lewis, current Editor of *NME*, and to IPC Magazines for permission to reprint some of the material here.

For setting in motion the events which led to the compilation of this book, thanks to Chris Barstow for sowing the seed, plus a special tip of the hat and an honours degree in Advanced Networking to Karen Krizanovich; for being an abnormally creative and patient editor, Spencer and I wish to thank – with an unbecoming degree of slobbering effusiveness – Jonathan Riley at Penguin Books.

Plus I'd like to thank my parents, Agnes Schaar Murray and the late Henry M. Murray, and my wife Ruth King, and to wish cool runnings to Joseph 'Captain Snaps' Stevens, photographer and raconteur supreme, with whom I shared some of my best adventures.

CSM
June 1990

# Yes: 'The Yes Album'
(Atlantic)

*Oz* 33, 1971

YES? Maybe.

# Isaac Hayes: 'Black Moses' (Stax);
# Roland Kirk: 'Natural Black Inventions' (Atlantic);
# Jimi Hendrix: 'Hendrix In The West' (Polydor);
# Curtis Mayfield: 'Roots' (Buddah)

*Oz* 41, 1972

THANKS to Don McLean, rock and roll is moving uneasily into a state of manic nostalgia. 'Back to the roots!!' is the cry, and everybody is frantically ploughing the fields in search of wherever their roots happen to be hiding. Every closet in sight is being combed for skeletons, and we vicariously rediscover everything from traditional British folk music to fifties rock, country and bluegrass to music-hall. Ray Davies and Martin Carthy ransack the English past, and The Band and all their country cousins from LA point us towards the Golden West. Some of us are even starting to get back to black music.

To claim to have found a representative selection of black music on four records is patently absurd, but as a random cross-section of what's approximately happening, the above clutch of recent issues give rise to some interesting conclusions. With one exception, the 'blacker' the music is, the more powerful it is.

1

Thus Rahsaan Roland Kirk, supposedly an esoteric, isolated *jazz* figure, far removed from the current musical spectrum, is playing music that emits far more energy, more power, more *soul* than the amazingly turgid Isaac Hayes, currently being touted as the leading figure in contemporary black music.

The Hayes phenomenon poses some fascinating questions about demographics, musical sociology and the politics of assimilation. A much respected Stax backroom boy for some ten years, Hayes was responsible as producer, composer, arranger and keyboards player for some of the finest examples of Stax studio soul, notably for most of Sam and Dave's better records. A couple of years ago, he came out of his shell and began to issue a series of solo albums, featuring attenuated, heavily orchestrated versions of popular songs, mainly drawn from the repertoires of 'standard' singers. These included long monologues and sold startlingly well. Hayes worked a deft line in personality hype, capitalizing on his imposing personal appearance. He's a big man with a full beard and a shaven head, and he was photographed bare-chested, wearing gold chains and huge shades. His latest album, like the others, a heavy money-maker, shows to what proportions his cult has expanded.

The album is called 'Black Moses', and the cover is a literal interpretation of that title. The outer cover unwraps to form a four-foot-by-three cross, in which Isaac stands, arms outstretched in a Messianic pose, swathed in DeMille robes and his famous shades. The sleeve note, printed in indecipherable Gothic lettering and impenetrable Biblical prose, tells Isaac's life story, referring to him throughout as a prophet of his people. Once inside the lavish packaging, one finds that the records are conspicuously lacking in the aggressive blackness of their surrounding hype. Hayes' thick-tongued basso voice is cloaked in a gentle funky rhythm section and great clouds of Hollywood strings as he meanders through a selection of songs that would not be out of place on a Tony Bennett album, material like 'Brand New Me', 'I'll Never Fall In Love Again' and 'They Long To Be Close To You'. He doesn't even perform Curtis Mayfield's 'Man's Temptation' as well as Al Kooper and his 'Part Time Love' is certainly no threat to Johnnie Taylor. The 'hard funky raps that sermonize the sometimes bittersweet relationship between man and wo-man' have all the depth and honesty of the talking bits on fifties vocal group records, and only 'Good Love 699–69' has any life to it. Strangely enough, it's the only Hayes composition in the two-record set, and the only one resembling his early work.

The point is: who's buying this shit? To my ears, Isaac Hayes is a monstrous shuck. His nightclub schmaltz is soul aimed at those audiences, both black and white, who like to think that they're into soul music but who cannot cope with the reality and energy of true black cultural spokesmen like Ray Charles and Aretha Franklin. It's music for Sidney Poitier to ball Diahann Carroll to, and is probably selling to airline stewardesses and executives all over the States. There was more power in his *Shaft* theme than in this entire package.

After Isaac Hayes, it's a tremendous relief to turn to an authentic black genius. Rahsaan Roland Kirk. Kirk is one of this planet's master musicians, and while 'Natural Black Inventions' (subtitled 'Root Strata') is at least as aggressively 'black' as the Hayes album, it means what it says. 'I accept the fact that a lot of people are still asleep and will stay asleep on these sounds that are a part of my life – my black experience,' writes Kirk in the notes, but I hope he's wrong. This album features Kirk unaccompanied except by percussion, and piano on one cut. He plays an infinite number of horns, many of them simultaneously. This unbelievable multiple virtuosity generally leaves his audiences so shattered that they fail to realize that he'd be amazing even if he only played one all night. He has seemingly limitless supplies of breath, and can power three horns indefinitely. Maybe he breathes through his ears, through the top of his head, through the end of his cock, fuck knows, but he's totally on his own. In person, he's compulsive watching whether lurching all over the stage at the Ronnie Scott Club chanting 'B-L-A-C-K-N-U-S-S, BLACKNUSS' or blowing the minds of a Roundhouse audience, fighting his way through the power cuts to give the people more excitement, intense communal involvement and just more sheer music than any four rock bands combined. Roland Kirk gives proof, it any were needed, that so-called *jazz* still has the power to communicate in a real and direct way with a young mass audience. If you want to hear a *real* genius, not one of rock's sensitive-and-observant Genius-of-the-Month Club fresh from Laurel Canyon and a Carole King session, check out 'Natural Black Inventions: Root Strata' and

3

prepare for one hell of a shock. If you're a mainstream rock freak, you'll never think of jazz in quite the same way again.

The man who always neatly knocked a huge hole in my theory that the value of black music was proportionate to the artist's involvement with the black audience/community – what Roland Kirk refers to as 'the black experience' – was Jimi Hendrix. Though jazz musicians (like Kirk and Miles Davis) saw him in a black perspective, the mass black audience found his music intolerable. Like the Motown artists who it is so hip to despise, Hendrix was a white man's black man, though admittedly there was a world of difference in the circumstances. The latest instalment in the continuing Jimi Hendrix market onslaught is for some reason entitled 'Hendrix In The West', and though saddled with a sleeve apparently designed during a ten-minute dope break by the dregs of Polydor's Art Department, is the finest of all the posthumous Hendrix records. It not only includes his epic performance of 'Johnny B. Goode', second only to Berry's, but an incredibly delicate version of 'Little Wing', a stunning group improvisation on 'Red House', jokey interpretations of 'God Save The Queen' and 'Sgt Pepper' from the IoW complete with Jeff Dexter's introduction now appearing on record for the *third* time (Christ, it's boring) and a new cut of 'Voodoo Chile'. I have no new superlatives to apply to the work of Jimi Hendrix, but if your collection has a deficit in the Hendrix department, this is the one to get.

While the mass black audience never appreciated Jimi Hendrix, it ate up Isaac Hayes, and another old studio pro who sells a lot of records, Curtis Mayfield. Mayfield is a lot more likeable than Hayes, lacking all that Messianic hype and general self-importance. He sings in a light falsetto, writes gentle, earnest, unimpeachable liberal songs about getting down to the funky, funky roots, his beautiful black brothers and sisters, relating to the underground, and so on. Unfortunately, on 'Roots', he has, like Hayes, sent out to the candy store for a double scoop of cloying marshmallow strings and wrapped everything up in them. Mayfield's mellow sweetness is bearable only in a small-group situation, where the relative prominence of the guitars and percussion sharpens up the sound, and allows you to listen to his lyrics without choking on the arrangements. His live album is far more enjoyable than 'Roots' but even there I find Mayfield's unremitting cuteness rather wearing. Despite his preoccupation with social issues, he comes on like a black John Sebastian. He's even featured on the enclosed poster skipping about merrily in a field. You'd never catch Hayes doing that. He'd fall over his robes.

Against the larger picture, it's sadly clear that few black artists have yet become real, bona-fide gilt-edged superstars without capturing a white audience, either like Nat 'King' Cole, Louis Armstrong or B.B. King. Or like Jimi Hendrix. But now, at last, we can listen to black music, and evaluate it ourselves. We no longer need Pat Boone to be the middleman between us and Fats Domino, Mick Jagger to run relay between us and Chuck Berry, Mike Bloomfield to prepare us for B.B. King. The Roundhouse audience heard Rahsaan Roland Kirk, and he played them his natural black inventions, and they heard them loud and clear and hot and close. If the sixteen-year-olds are ready for meat as strong as Roland Kirk, then that is in itself a cause for optimism. If enough people have the ears and the devotion, then the next couple of years should hear some mighty music indeed.

# I'm all right Smackwater Jack!

*Cream*, February 1972

JUST in case you'd forgotten, Brian Jones, Jimi Hendrix, Janis Joplin, Alan Wilson, Duane Allman (maybe), Johnny Winter (almost). And going back a little further, there's Charlie Parker, Billie Holiday and Lenny Bruce, not forgetting Frankie Lymon. And on top of that there are all those who just got through, and those who didn't who we don't know the names of.

Once upon a time we thought we were too far advanced to let death into our culture. Our ways were ways of righteousness and all our paths were peace. In 1967 we marched against the representatives of The Man armed to the teeth with tulips and chrysanthemums. We smoked our shit and sat giggling in our headphones, we dropped acid and wandered out into the sunlight to look for butterflies. 'There was so much love around that a whole generation almost died of an overdose of it,' said Richard Neville at the *Oz* trial. We were so much older then, we're younger than that now. Because now the cool four hundred are being immensely hip about cocaine and machine guns, neither of which are particularly good for children and other living things. Because now we're well and truly out of the garden.

In the last few years, heroin and cocaine have begun sliding their way back into hip vocabularies. We read of how the jazzmen of the forties and fifties blew themselves to pieces in slow motion and asked ourselves incredulously how anyone could let themselves get fucked up on that stuff. Timothy Leary wrote in *The Politics of Ecstasy* that people who'd taken acid were in fact *more* aware of the destructive effects of so-called hard drugs than others, and we all nodded wisely and incorporated that statement into our armoury of rebuttals to any suggestion that smoking shit and dropping acid led to anything else. All the underground papers came out strongly against heavy dope and nobody really thought anything of it again until we started losing a few rock and roll stars here and there.

Of course, heroin ('smack', when it's at home) wasn't dormant between 1956 and 1970. In the States it's been a fact of life all along. The peculiarly vicious thing about the smack epidemic there is that the principal victims are those whose social and economic positions render them least able to cope with it. The comfortably off middle-class freaks smoke shit ($24.30 the ounce) or drop acid ($1.50 a hit), but it's in the Black and Puerto Rican parts of town, where prices and rents are higher and wages are lower than anywhere else, that you find men with daily $50 and $100 habits to feed. To raise this kind of money, and make no mistake, raise it they must, they have to turn to what is referred to as 'crime' when it's performed on whites. In the closed environment of the ghettoes, the only sources are from the brothers and sisters themselves. So to pay The Man for their life-giving poison – yes, The Man, it's always the same Man – they have to brutalize, harass and rip off their own, which keeps revolutionary action off the streets. The Man couldn't have worked out a neater system of pacification if he'd tried.

*You can always tell a junkie by the way his machine gun
shakes.*

**Yossarian**, East Village Other

*Seems that everybody whose heart is still thumpin'
Is snortin', smokin' or shootin' or somethin' . . .
And Nixon sayin' don't worry . . .*

*Curtis Mayfield*

But, of course, we were too hip to fall for that one. After all,
heroin is the ultimate anaesthetic for those whose lives have
become completely unendurable, and we were all happy hippies,
doing up shit and acid to dig on what was happening — we were
into *life*, as far into life as we could possible get, so we used
whatever was needed to psychedelize suburbia, and looned about
giggling in the streets. I once came home on acid, and couldn't
believe it when my parents didn't notice. Rock and roll bands had
only just stopped singing coy, cliquey songs about shit, like
'Itchycoo Park' and 'Along Comes Mary', and the only group to
come really up front about smack were The Velvet Underground.
The BBC, of course, got splendidly paranoid about the whole
thing, banned everything even vaguely druggy, and even when
Steppenwolf came out with 'The Pusher', and 'Snow Blind Friend'
and John Lennon with 'Cold Turkey', pointedly ignored the fact
that all these were anti-hard-drug songs and went right ahead and
banned them anyway. How we laughed.

*Well I smoked a lotta grass, I popped a lotta pills.
But I never took nothin' that my spirit couldn't kill.
God damn, God damn, God damn the pusher man . . .*

*Hoyt Axton*

*He said he wanted heaven, but praying was too slow.
So he bought a one-way ticket on an airline made of snow.
He said that it was different flyin' low, dyin' slow, flyin'
    low.*

*Hoyt Axton*

Then the deaths started. They'd been a long time coming, but
they were easy to explain. 'They say that you never need uppers if
you lead a natural and healthy life,' says Nickey Barclay of Fanny,
'but going on the road with a rock group is not a normal, healthy
life.' To put it mildly. 'Touring,' to quote Frank Zappa, 'can
make you crazy.' Brian Jones knew that well enough. Many of The

Stones' records in fact featured Keith Richards playing several overdubbed guitar parts because Brian Jones would come into the studio (if he turned up at all) too fucked up to play and nod out, fall on the floor with his guitar still strapped to him. The road did that to Brian Jones until they found him face down in his swimming pool.

In 1967, Jimi Hendrix told an interviewer from the now-defunct *Music Maker*, 'I don't see how anyone could use a needle on themselves. When I was little and they took me to the doctor I used to scream and cry when they tried to put that needle in me.' Jimi eventually found out, though. Jimi, who told a Toronto court that he'd 'grown out of drugs'. Jimi, who claimed to have taken grass and hash twice each, acid four times and coke and smack once each. Jimi, who snorted coke five minutes before he went on at the Isle of Wight. Jimi, who choked on his own vomit in a London hotel after accidentally taking nine sleeping pills.

Alan Wilson, gentle tree freak, Blind Owl, who went out into his beloved redwood forests with a sleeping bag and a handful of downers because a groupie he loved wouldn't come to a concert with him. Janis Joplin, who could even juice Pigpen McKernan of The Dead under the table, and who shouted, 'I don't know why these kids take drugs when they could have a drink of Southern Comfort.' Janis hit the floor so hard that she had a broken nose when they found her, locked in her motel room still holding the change from her last packet of cigarettes.

'Bogus rock and roll stars added to the mystique about smack – it wasn't enough that they were shooting dope themselves, but their example allowed them to be used by the vampires to get thousands of kids strung out on death drugs so they could be more easily controlled,' wrote White Panther John Sinclair in an agonized, raging piece of polemics which appeared recently in *Oz* under the title 'And Then Along Came Jones'. Sinclair, recently released, was jailed for nine and a half years for giving two joints to a narco. 'Heroin is the ultimate commodity of all time, and the ironic thing is that the kids who called themselves free, getting away from the slavery their parents were trapped in, have been turned into even bigger slaves with even less to show for it than the most brainwashed honky. Jones (heroin) has simply perverted everything we ever set out to do, and if we're ever going to get back to where we were, we're going to have to eliminate this poison from our community. Skag ain't dope, it's death!'

> *The only dope worth shooting is Richard Nixon.*
> *Abbie Hoffman*

But like it or not, even now people still emulate their favourite rock and roll stars, and right now their favourite rock and roll stars have some expensive habits. It's fashionable to simulate vomiting when reading about Engelbert Humperdinck ordering sixty-five suits at a throw, but who mutters 'Pig!' when reading about the Allman Brothers snorting coke through hundred-dollar bills? Or about Stephen Stills' famous suitcase which travelled with him everywhere on his last tour with Crosby, Stills, Nash and Young? It contained smack and coke to the value of ten thousand dollars. Statistic of the month: at £350 per ounce, your fave rave rock star can spend more on coke in one week than even a fairly prosperous family would lay out on food in a year. *POWER TO THE PEOPLE ! ! !* It makes one wonder what the hip community's reaction would have been if Manson ('Charlie' to all his mates in the alternative press) had done his number in Laurel Canyon, if the house he chose had belonged to Graham Nash and if the corpse had been Joni Mitchell. Would a spokeswoman of the women's unit of the Weathermen have still come out and stated, 'Oh man, it was so groovy to think of them eating a meal right there with those *stuck pigs*'? Peace, brother, and don't forget the meat-axe on your way out.

All of which may give you some idea why I cannot listen to The Velvet Underground. The outside edge of my dope experience is (at the time of writing) acid, and unless you're strongly masochistic, an acid experience and the Velvets are mutually exclusive. One good friend told me, referring to his days as a needle freak, that there are very few records that you can jack up to. He mentioned The Velvet Underground, Leonard Cohen. At first, I thought he said 'jack off to', remembering what Jeff Nuttall had written in *Bomb Culture*: 'Watching someone take a fix is like watching them masturbate.' 'People like Johnny Winter,' he said, 'are like closet queens, they're closet junkies. They don't come up front about it in their songs.'

Johnny Winter. Now there's an interesting case. As you may have read in this magazine a few issues back, Winter has been in a Texas mental home since June, getting off smack. Over Christmas he jammed with his brother Edgar's band, White Trash, for a live album. After the tumultuously successful sets, Winter's manager, Steve Paul, told the press that 'Johnny is going back for another five months so that he can get even better.' Afterwards, Edgar reminisced, 'Johnny's band used to hold contests to see who could go onstage the most fucked up.'

> *I put a needle in my arm,*
> *It did some good, it did some harm.*
>
> > Leonard Cohen

> *I'll die young, but it's like kissing God.*
>
> > Lenny Bruce

Basically, anyone who used smack is, by definition, fucked up. To take smack is a virtual admission that large areas of your life are so horrible that they must be totally obliterated. James Taylor was clinically addicted all the time that he was recording his first album. Again, in the fifties we almost lost Miles, Trane and Mingus, to name but three. Cocaine is simply the best buzz going – total euphoria at 15 dollars a minute. Phil Spector's Christmas cards contained the celebrated *Easy Rider* still of him snorting, captioned 'A little snow at Christmas never hurt anyone!' Not with your money, Phil. You can even afford disposable silver spoons.

In these circumstances, it's almost a relief to hear from the juicers, the Faces and Whos of this world. 'I was drinkin' port wine 'til I fell off the stage. Right off. The band kept on without a bass player. That was good wine,' Berry Oakley of the Allman Brothers Band told *Rolling Stone*. Then you remember that Janis was a juicer, and Jim Morrison. Pigpen has been too sick and weak to work for some time now, with a fucked-up liver and a perforated ulcer 'just from juicing'. 'I mean it's incredible,' said Jerry Garcia. 'I gave him a pint of blood. We all did.'

Rock and roll stars are forced into vicious, self-destructive behaviour simply because of the vicious self-destructive lives they lead. None of them were turned on to smack at the age of fifteen as was Charlie Parker and as yet none of them has tried to hold up a store to get the bread to score, as has Stan Getz. Still, it's early days yet.

*My pappa he told me, whiskey's a curse.*
*But to be on cod'ine is a million times worse,*
*An' it's real, an' it's real, one more time . . .*

*Buffy Sainte-Marie*

One of the most frightening experiences I've ever had was to see Davy Graham play. Graham was the Big Daddy of British folk guitar, the man who laid down the guide-lines for Bert Jansch, John Renbourn *et al.* Last June he was booked into the club where I worked as disc-jockey on the rock nights, and as one of a duo called Gyf on the folk nights. The lunchtime before the gig we saw this weird guy with short frizzy red hair and beard standing outside the club. He had a guitar case in one hand and a holdall in the other and he was just *standing* there in the noonday crowds, not moving, hardly blinking, just standing there growing out of the pavement. We decided it couldn't be Davy Graham, and as we passed out of sight, he was still there, unmoving.

When we got to the gig that night, we found it *was* Davy Graham. He'd changed into a suit, and when he got up to play, his movements were jerky and uncoordinated. He'd sit there, never speaking, with a strange grin on his face. If he blew a line, instead of covering up and carrying on, why, he'd go back and play the line a couple of times until he was happy with it, and *then* he'd carry on. The audience were mystified, but after all he *was* playing some beautiful things. In the second half, he suddenly sat up, blinked and announced clearly, 'This song is in a modal tuning, over a cycle of eight beats . . .' and went into a long, involved technical explanation that was incomprehensible to anybody who wasn't a guitarist with a strong grounding in Indian music. He did another ten minutes, put down his guitar, packed it despite cries of 'More' and 'Anji' (which he hadn't played), picked up his holdall (which he'd kept on the stage), took half a step, and stayed there with one leg in the air.

For five minutes he stood like that, then he walked to the manager's office to get his bread. 'He's better than he was last time I saw him,' said the other half of Gyf. 'He couldn't play "Anji" last time.'

'Anji', Davy Graham's most famous composition, every budding folk guitarist's beginner piece, the standby of every floorsinger in every club in the land. Davy Graham couldn't play it.

*Well a nickel is a nickel an' a dime is a dime,*
*I snort cocaine any old time,*
*Hey hey baby have a whiff on me,*
*Whatever happened to the friends I know,*
*Who needs friends when you can have snow,*
*Hey hey people have a whiff on me ...*

*Leadbelly*

Perhaps the last words should go to a man who has played on one album and two gigs in the last year or so, a man in whose continued career we each and every one of us have a vested interest, a man whose music we all miss very much.

'The bigger you are, the more pressure, the more loneliness, the more fear. I feel I'm almost continually on trial. Every time I step on stage now, I know I am expected to give more than I possibly can. The strain is terrifying. Jimi and Janis phased themselves out of a situation that had become intolerable. The demands made on them both by a cynical and insensitive milieu and by an unthinking and adulatory public proved too much. All we want to do is to be left alone and make music. But because we are called "rock stars", a whole different set of expectancies are thrust upon us – that we should have instant opinions about almost everything, that we should set an example to the young people of today by making public statements about drugs, that we should dress and behave like the freaks we're supposed to be.

'The pressure today is so much greater than when I started out in jazz. We used to play in clubs before maybe 200 people. Today the groups perform for anywhere between 40,000 and 200,000 people. You've always got to be up, always smiling. By the end of the night, or after a long trip, you need something to give you a life. For some people it's liquor. For others it's drugs. We're all hooked on something. Take the drugs away from many rock musicians and blues players and you'd be left with only half a man. Ours is a universal problem: how to find peace in a society which we feel to be hostile. We want to express that search in our music since that is our most eloquent voice. We need the drugs to help us, to free our minds and our imaginations from the prejudices and snobbery that have been bred into us. And there is no one who doesn't pray for that.'

Eric Clapton said that.

*And you can't argue with a man,*
*When he don't want to understand . . .*
*And all in all it was a pretty good year for the undertaker*

Gerry Goffin

Yeah, god damn the pusher man, baby – and mind how you go.

# 'Hello. I'm Marc Bolan. I'm a superstar. You'd better believe it.'

*Cream*, May 1972

**T**YRANNOSAURUS *Rex rose out of the sad and scattered leaves of an older summer. During the hard grey winter they were tended and strengthened by those who love them. They blossomed with the coming of spring, children rejoiced and the earth sang with them. It will be a long and ecstatic summer.*

John Peel, 1968,
*sleeve note to first 'Tyrannosaurus Rex' album*

*T. Rex are the new Beatles, the teen idols of the seventies, and the biggest pop sensation in years. Now they are verged on international success, following the most exciting succession of chart hits since the days of Bill Haley and Lennon and McCartney.*

**Blurb to** Melody Maker *special* Bolan!

Once again, rock and roll madness has settled over the nation, and someone has reintroduced frenzy and hysteria into a section of the musical environment ruled almost exclusively by the Middle of the Road, Dawn, the balladeers and the Jonathan King Karma Squad. People had realized that it was close on ten years since 'Love Me Do' and the psychological need for a new Beatles had become so bad that they were even touting The Bay City Rollers for the part. After all, they went down well in Scotland. A stronger child was required, and despite initial disbelief, what we got was Marc Bolan.

Marc Bolan, superstar. A star is someone who we know about, but a superstar is someone *everybody* knows about – your parents, the milkman, your bank manager, everybody. With a double-page spread in the *Daily Mirror*, Marc Bolan is property as public as no one has really been since those halcyon days of 1964, when we all waited, tense and nervous, on the verge of some great discovery, conscious that Jones and Jagger and Lennon and McCartney were about to lead us to some new places.

To the most important group of people in the country – the adolescents and pre-adolescents – Bolan is more than a superstar, he's a superhero. He's not even a symbol of some force or power or concept; he *is* it, he's the main man. And it makes me laugh, because I can remember 1968 when Tyrannosaurus Rex was a £15 acoustic guitar and a pair of ripped-off bongos, something John Peel kept rambling on about and who couldn't get on TV.

> *Tyrannosaurus Rex should be stamped out, along with their gaseous aider and abetter, John Peel.*
>
> *Reader's letter to* Melody Maker, *1968*

Bolan's improbable journey from the most esoteric of the esoteric to the very toppermost of the poppermost seems logical when viewed through the lens of hindsight, but if you had said four years ago that Marc Bolan would be the biggest thing in British rock you would have been advised to have a good lie down until you felt better. The only person who would not have laughed himself sick was Marc Bolan.

From acoustic freebies in Hyde Park to Wembley's Empire Pool in four years, flat. A rags-to-riches story in the best Horatio Alger tradition. All that happened was that Bolan added more and more technology, more and more instruments, more and more sounds and production, and when the necessary level of electrical energy had been built up, all hell broke loose. Rock and roll madness, verily.

What's more, hardly anyone saw it coming. 1968 was the year of the heavy electric summer. 'Wheels Of Fire', Joe Cocker, Julie Driscoll, Brian Auger, Arthur Brown, and the blues boom, and the music of Bolan and bongo player Steve Peregrine Took was a welcome clearing in the thick, heavy electric jungle. ' "Deborah" sold 750 the first day and it blew my mind,' said Bolan. Any gentle freak who believed that Nostradamus and King Arthur were alive and well in a UFO hovering somewhere over Glaston-bury Tor, or who read Tolkien and Moorcock over his brown rice and apple juice, just had to own the Tyrannosaurus Rex albums, they were essential. 'My People Were Fair And Had Sky In Their Hair, But Now They're Content To Wear Stars On Their Brows' and 'Prophets Seers And Sages, The Angels Of The Ages', in terms of heroics and headlines they mattered not at all, but they sold enough to keep Marc and Steve Took warm and functioning. Eventually they started going out for £150 a night on the college circuit (one social sec. told the *MM* 'We book anyone John Peel likes') and they got bagged with the Incredible String Band.

'What happened was that when we started, "Layers Of The Onion" had come out and they were considered to be something very funky, and they were getting a lot of press. No one had ever heard of us, so I immediately said to people, hey man, don't compare us with the Incredible String Band, who were beginning to be big and no one had ever heard of us. So I in fact cultivated a battle between the two and in fact we did become bigger, but it was very deliberate, and I was very aware of the two things. I only did it because we *weren't* similar.'

So, as time went on, Bolan got more and more involved with the complexities of electric rock. After the departure of Steve Peregrine Took, Bolan linked up with Micky Finn, percussionist, painter, former leader of a Mod band called The Blue Men and one-time Pill King. The resulting single, 'The King Of The Rumbling Spires', and album, 'Beard Of Stars', backed up Bolan's mythological speculations with the tougher support of newly acquired Fenders and Gibsons – and a £12 chord organ from Woolworth's. Finally, the abbreviation from Tyrannosaurus Rex to plain T. Rex so that even Tony Blackburn could pronounce it, the big hit single that made the charts with a bullet and all manner of pandemonium. The cream on the cake was the addition of a bassist and drummer. That's how it's done.

I've never seen so many beautiful fourteen-year-old girls in my life as at the T. Rex Wembley concert. You go through into that big, concrete slaughterhouse and they're all milling around buying Bolan books, Bolan posters, 'official Marc Bolan sashes' whatever *they* are, rip-offs of every description, fake programmes, greasy old creeps touting tickets at only twice the regular price, rock and roll madness. And all Marc's children are there – weekend dropout hippieboppers meticulously dressed in Early Roundhouse; a sprinkling of skinheads; bemused mums firmly clutching their primary-school-age tots by the wrists; a few older groovers come to check it all out and maybe get laid, looking incredibly uneasy; some short-haired Members Of The Public, and most self-conscious of all, the kids in the white shirts and dark trousers and bulging duffle bags that indicate they've come *straight from school* – the shame of it all! The biggest and best gig yet and they can't even dress up.

It's a whole new world and I feel like a sixth-former sitting at the second-year dinner table. I'm fascinated by Marc's children – is that skinhead *really* wearing glitter under his eyes? – and I'm wandering about digging the people when suddenly this kid, who's no way over fourteen, is standing next to me looking down at my boots and mumbling 'Got any speed?' I send him away with the proverbial flea in his ear, but five minutes later there's three others with the same request. I ask why they think I'm a dealer, and the spokesman points to my briefcase, left over from schooldays and plastered with promotional stickers. 'They all carry cases, man . . .' If I look so suspicious I feel I'd better split before The Man gets interested, because dope dealing is no way for a nice Jewish boy like me to make a living.

Possibly one of the most encouraging aspects of Bolanoia is that T. Rex's audience comes from right across the board – skinheads, straights, freaks alike, and this is what makes him anathema to the cultural elitist division of the rock audience. Heavy rock sociology decrees that if you don't like the audience, you can't like the band, and to sit in the same audience as turns up for a Bolan gig is only fractionally less odious than to *play* to them.

Also, there ain't 'arf a lot of 'em, and if that many people dig a band, there must be something wrong with them, which is why any luckless 'underground' band who attempt to raise the standard of radio rock are branded as teenybopper sell-outs by the kind of people who had to wait until 1968, when it became chic to say that Brian Wilson was a genius, before they could admit that they liked The Beach Boys. It should be superfluous to point out that The Beatles, The Stones, The Who, Jimi Hendrix, The Yardbirds, Phil Spector and if you want to get technical, Bessie Smith,

Robert Johnson and all the others who recorded before the invention of the long-playing record, began their careers (and changed quite a few heads into the bargain) on singles. But that makes no difference to the kind of oneupman so brilliantly caricatured on the Cheech and Chong album: 'No, man, I'm not into . . . AM.'

Inside, the stage is dominated by a ten-foot-high cut-out of the Electric Warrior tearing into his Les Paul, and two posters of him waving his white Strat. Onstage, Rosko is rapping away at a fantastic rate of watts, fast AM nonsense, unstoppable flow of words. He plays The Drifters' 'Saturday Night At The Movies' and the people sing along. He brings on Quiver, who play a pleasant set, laid-back and funky, Cal Batchelor and Tim Renwick playing some of the sweetest interlocking double lead you ever heard in your life. Bolan will later become indignant at any suggestion that the cut-out is inhibiting or distasteful to Quiver, but it seems a cheap and nasty gesture on someone's part, an unnecessary way to ensure that Bolan's presence hangs over the stage even with him still in the dressing-room.

I'm having difficulty coping with the local geography of the Empire Pool, and by the time I reach my seat, I find a clump of little girls – very young, subteenyboppers – in and around it. When I request them to move, they glance at one another and then unanimously shake their heads. I'm gratified that the younger generation has such an admirable disrespect for the property/territory ethic, but annoyed that my steely-eyed demeanour and casual authority meet with nothing but a flurry of giggles. Dignity outraged, I stick around until Quiver quit the stage to a polite rustle of friendly applause. They have acquitted themselves well tonight, but they'd be kidding themselves if they think that the audience will remember them when they leave, or even recognize the name the day after. But for now, they've pleased a tough and callous audience, if only momentarily.

Interval time. A bit of prowling around in the grimy corridor and a quick hit of alcohol in the bar. Back in the bullring, Rosko is playing Betty Wright's 'Cleanup Woman' and explaining that he was asked to play it by Marc himself. He then announces that the next time you see him he'll be introducing T. Rex. *Yeeek!*

The stage is swarming with roadies and lesser minions. When a roadie scuttles on with an armful of guitars, there's a mass intake of breath from all over the hall. Even for a heretic, the tension is extraordinary. The air is humming with nine thousand people hardly daring to breathe because any second now . . .

Yes! There's Rosko and you can't even hear him because they're all screaming, and I needn't have worried about regaining my seat because the three little girls and half the others surrounding us have all hugged each other, squealed and rushed the stage. Bill Legend behind the drum kit, Steve Currie strolling on casually with his Fender Precision bass and his bright red pants, Micky Finn leaping at his battery of conga drums as if it were a month since he'd seen them and not the two hours since he'd beaten them into submission at the 5.30 house, and then on bops the man of the moment, the little guy who used to sit on the floor going 'Oochie-coochie-tie-dye, do the one inch rock.' It's only Marc Bolan whom Chris Welch used to call the Bopping Imp and the National Elf, and here's what looks like half the jailbait in London rushing the stage as he picks up a well-worn Les Paul and launches into – what?

Much has been written about Bolan's sexual status with his fans (and T. Rex are one of the very few bands today that really have 'fans'). Michael Watts has written that Bolan is a romantic rather than a sexual figure, but some of Bolan's lyrics indicate otherwise. Personally, I rather dig the idea of a very young female audience taking home records with lyrics like 'I'm gonna suck you' (from 'Jeepster'), 'Girl I really dig your breasts' (from 'Raw Ramp', the B-side of 'Get It On') and 'Let's do it like we're friends' (from 'Jewel' on the T. Rex album), not to mention 'She ain't no witch and I love the way she twitch' (from 'Hot Love') and all the assorted orgasmic gasps and sighs of 'Take me!' that crop up all over 'Electric Warrior'. It bodes well for the future, despite the fact that a significant proportion of Marc's young Bolanoids wouldn't really know what to do with him if they found him one night tucked up in their beds.

The only parts of Bolan's repertoire which had then reached my ears were the old stuff I used to hear on the radio in 1968 and the big hit singles exposed via Radio One, *Top of the Pops* and the jukebox of my local boozer. His first number is unfamiliar to me, but I'm having difficulty hearing it anyway. The kids are being loud, the PA is shitty, and, besides, I'm not really listening, I'm watching. I've never been to a gig even remotely like this and yet it all seems familiar. Racial memory. Then it hits me, it's the Shea Stadium movie all over again. Seated high up in the stands, with fifty-seven varieties of total hysteria all around me, I feel a strange sense of peace like standing on the top of a Cornish cliff watching the waves roll in . . . 'sittin' on the dock of the bay . . .'.

So I sit and watch finely formed little rivulets and currents of people coalesce into breakers, to surge up to the cliff top on which Bolan and his buddies are grinding their way through 'Cadillac', shatter, retreat and reform, return. Rock and roll madness. And with that sense of utter stillness. I realize that rock has reached its third stage, that with Bolan and T. Rex and all these weird little children, the circle game has begun again. Rock and roll lives, stands, continues. The circle is unbroken.

> *We can't go back we can only look behind from where we*
> *came, going round and round and round in the circle game.*
>
> *Joni Mitchell*

The number ends. Bolan surveys all that he has mastered. 'Rock on,' he says. He announces 'Jeepster' and we're all off again. One guy in the next row is having a bad time. He's tall and skinny and fair-haired, physically totally unsuited to being a Bolan, so he's cut his hair short on top and let it grow into long, thin wisps onto his shoulders, turned into a passable Rod Stewart, the next best thing. He's hopelessly pissed or on downers or just overcome by the occasion, and can't stand up, he's falling about all over the place, and his mates, all of whom look as if they'd be more at home in the Shed, are trying to help him, hold him up, but he just mutters something incomprehensible and turns over and I move my briefcase, my dope dealer's briefcase, in case he falls on it, and Marc's children are storming the stage again.

Between numbers they clap rhythms, and when the band play the crowd have to adjust their beat to Bolan's ('It's terrible, it really is, you just have to shut your ears to it'). When he sends the other three offstage and sits, cross-legged, on the stage to pick his Epiphone jumbo, the mood changes to one of awe and expectancy. The little girls are quiet now as Bolan plays 'Cosmic Dancer', one of his better new songs. Though the PA makes his acoustic strumming sound tinny and scratchy and his voice floats out over the congregation:

*I was dancing when I was twelve . . .*
*I danced myself right out the womb*
*Is it strange to dance so soon*
*I danced myself into the tomb . . .*

A strange, circular, reincarnation song, its protagonist forever dancing himself from womb to tomb to womb. In Empire Pool, I'm impressed. Whenever Bolan does one of his little gasps or sighs, the little girls squeal. He does another song, and then Finn joins him with a pair of bongos for one more. Then it's back to the electricity and Legend and Currie return to get their teeth into 'Telegram Sam' and 'Hot Love'. By now I'm focused enough to start evaluating the playing and they sound rough. Without Bolan's multiple guitars and Tony Visconti's strings, it's all bare and thin, but Marc's children don't mind. As long as they can shriek along with him during the middle part of 'Hot Love', what do they care? Later they will begin to evolve standards and perceptions as we did with The Beatles and The Stones or Hendrix and Cream or Berry and Holly or Coltrane and Parker. But right now it's enough to shriek. And why not?

And now it's time for the big finish, folks! as T. Rex unveil the extended version of 'Get It On'. Again, without Ian McDonald's saxes and Rick Wakeman's piano and Tony Visconti's strings and Bolan's other two guitars, it's not up to expectations and Finn and Currie's backup vocals ain't no way as good as Howard Kaylan and Mark Volman, but Bolan rushes through the song and then freaks out, he drops into a squat, puts a white Stratocaster – *a white Stratocaster*, Marc, you tamper with powerful ghosts doing that – between his legs and belabours it with a tambourine. It sounds horrible and meanwhile Finn is leaping about at stage front throwing little plastic tambourines into the throng, which devours them with a terrible hunger.

When it's over, Bolan and the boys split to an aggrieved howl. The sound of T. Rex's audience is something new and frightful to me. When Rod Stewart struts out to sing it's "Ello mate – 'ave a drink and give us a song then'; for Chuck Berry it's love and affection and gratitude; for The Dead it's a sense of real joy, and sure it's vociferous, but it's a friendly admiration, a collaboration with Dead and people working together to produce the best possible mutual high. But the Bolan audience have a different cry, *Iwannit-Iwannit-Iwannit* they yell, *Gimme gimme gimme!*

20

So Rosko comes back out and does his showbiz thing and T. Rex troop back out for their encore. They do 'Summertime Blues', which was on the 'White Swan' maxi-single. On its release, Mick Farren reviewed it in *I.T.* as follows: 'A while back I made a terrible recording of "Summertime Blues." Now T. Rex have made a really horrible version. *"Can't help you son cos you're too young to vote."* Of course he can't help you, you're five years old and mentally retarded.'

They don't play it very well. Of course they're shagged out after a hard set, but only Bolan's unmistakable voice distinguishes it from a church hall support band. 'The reason I do it is because once you've done . . . um . . . your own thing and you've hit a peak which . . . I hate encores, and it's like a non-encore, it's like a vehicle for the kids to really hang out, it gives them something that they know, that's the only reason I use it . . . I don't like encores, and I don't always do them either, because I consider like we end with "Get It On" normally, and I consider that a great ender, and I don't know how to top that man. Visually I can't do any more than that. Probably the only way to top it is to come out and play on my own. In fact the impact . . . but that would kill . . . it's like concert two, you've got to do another concert after that, which is twelve encores, which is three hours in. No, it does, because you want to play more, you see, so "Summertime Blues" I use as a thing for the kids to get off on, they don't have to think too much about it, which is cool. I don't have to think . . . and it allows me . . . each time we always play it differently, and they know it . . . it's just a title of a song, a sequence and a riff that people know automatically. It's just a vehicle . . . we used to do "Honey Don't" at one point . . . encores are a drag. Hendrix never did an encore in his life.'

Finally the house lights go on and the Pool disgorges its prey, some of whom buy, on the way out, the Bolan paraphernalia that they rejected on the way in. The place is full of cute little people looking for other cute little people, and as I don't in the wildest stretches of anybody's imagination classify as a cute little person, I wave one of my magic bits of paper and waft myself past the massed OAPs who act as security and I'm . . . backstage.

In the pressroom I see clustered round the bar and outlying tables a variety of journalists and celebrities. Bernie Taupin striding around in his latest pair of earrings. Bolan's parents, the subjects earlier that week of an excruciatingly banal *Record Mirror* interview by Valerie Mabbs, are there looking faintly bemused but ecstatically proud and happy. Chris Charlesworth from the *MM*, the first man to spot that famous pair of pink panties being flung at the stage, is holding forth at the bar. 'Did he eat them then or later?' asks a disgruntled colleague. Valerie Mabbs doesn't seem to want to talk to me, so I engulf some chicken sandwiches, do my best to exhaust the bar's supplies of rum and swap reactions with Steve Peacock from *Sounds* and Tony Tyler from *NME*. Drink drink talk talk.

Enter Bolan sweaty and grinning. He's stockier than I would have imagined, stubbly, harder looking than that almost frightening androgynous beauty he had on the 'Beard Of Stars' album cover. With him is B.P. Fallon, known to all as 'Beep', Bolan's right-hand man and 'information roadie'. The Electric Warrior hugs his parents and begins to circulate. I am buttonholed by a quietly demented painter who has some crazed notion of getting the government to sponsor a cartoon film he's working on by getting Bolan to appear in it to preach against drug-taking among the young. 'Tell me,' he asks, 'is Marc and the group on drugs?'

So, in the days that followed I did a lot of thinking about the forces that had been revealed to me. I set about obtaining all the Tyrannosaurus Rex and T. Rex records and I took them home and listened to them all repeatedly, much to the fury of the people I live with. Armed with these, photostats of most of Bolan's recent reviews and cuttings, and the *MM* special (terrible production, embarrassingly bad) and *RM* special (long on information, short on good writing), I moved into the cans to investigate the gradual process of change that led from 'Deborah' to 'Electric Warrior'.

What's apparent right from the start is that Bolan's claim that he has always been a rock and roller is not as absurd as it first sounds. Even on the very first album there are rock and roll songs, or what would be rock and roll songs if played by an electric rock band. 'Hot Rod Mama' played electrically would sound like a speeded-up version of Dylan's 'From A Buick Six', for instance. 'Say something like "Chateau On Virginia Waters" or one of those tracks, "Mustang Ford". If Led Zeppelin did "Mustang

Ford" it would sound just like Led Zeppelin. I mean like "Chateau On Virginia Waters" done by Elton John would sound like an Elton John song. The only thing was that my tempos were out with traditional music — you know, rock and roll. I had no backbeat to what I did, it was all jangly. But I didn't have — you got to state if for people, man, and I didn't because I'd never played with a drummer.'

Bolan had, in fact, done an abortive stint in John's Children, which produced the legendary 'Desdemona'. Tyrannosaurus Rex was an acoustic band simply because John's Children's record company, Track, had taken back Bolan's guitars and amps when he left the band. 'With John's Children I had my shit together so we only ever did four songs on stage. We only did a tour of Germany with The Who, we did a twenty-minute spot. It was total smash-up media . . . I used to drag amplifiers across the stage. All that John's Children were at that period were what I am now. I'm only doing the same thing I wanted to do then.'

Mick Farren once wrote of Bob Dylan that he'd always wanted to be Elvis Presley, but as there was a vacancy for a Woody Guthrie he took the gig. Marc Bolan wanted to be Jimi Hendrix, but found himself cast as a Robin Williamson.

Those first two Tyrannosaurus Rex albums weren't really very good. Only a few of the songs stand out (like the brilliant 'Strange Orchestras' and 'Child Star' which had a good tune), but due to Bolan's enunciation (or lack of it) and the absence of a lyric sheet, it's hard to tell what he's going on about, and the drabness of the production makes it tiresome to listen to just as sound. In 1969 Bolan told Peter Frame of *Zigzag* that the production was indeed 'very bad. It was the first album Tony Visconti had ever produced and it was done at Advision on an 8-track — the first in the country — and they didn't know how to use it. The stereo was awful. When we were doing it, it sounded good, but when it was on a record, it sounded very thin and nasty.'

The first turning point came with 'Unicorn'. Between them Bolan and Took handled vocals, guitars, harmonium, lip organ, fonofiddle, bongos, African talking drums, bass guitar, piano, drum kit, assorted percussion, pixiephone and gong, a far cry from the simple guitar and bongos they started out with. 'I'm really into Phil Spector. When we did 'Unicorn', the whole of 'Unicorn', it was in fact technically a cross between 'Pet Sounds' all the Phil Spector things. And nobody got it, man, at the time. You listen to the drum sound on 'She Was Born To Be My Unicorn', it's totally a Phil Spector drum sound. It's all Phil Spector, the whole album, and no one knew what I was doing at the time.'

'Unicorn' was the first Tyrannosaurus Rex album that I could comfortably listen to. Bolan and Visconti had learned to use the studios properly; 'Romany Soup' had twenty-two tracks on it and took five hours to mix. The album's opening cut, 'Chariots Of Silk', is, to this day, one of the best things Bolan has ever done, drum riff straight out of The Ronettes' 'I Wonder' contrasting strangely with its strange landscape, full of Mages and Bards and the Huntress: 'Chariots of silk she rode/stallions of gold she owned'. Depending on how seriously you take such things, Bolan's lyrics were improving. 'Catblack' featured Tony Visconti playing what Bolan described as a 'Runaround Sue' piano backup, teenage chord progression and all, but with lyrics that were finely constructed as well as evocative:

> *Catblack the wizard's hat*
> *Spun in lore from Dagamoor*
> *The skull of jade*
> *Was pearl inlaid*
> *The silks, skin spun, repelled the sun . . .*

Like the first album, 'Unicorn' featured John Peel reading a children's story. It was Steve Took's last album with the band, and Bolan was at his wits' end because promoters assumed that the Tyrannosaurus was extinct and therefore stopped offering him gigs. Eventually he joined up with Finn and the next album, 'A Beard Of Stars', featured Bolan's reintroduction to the electric guitar. He hung out at Eric Clapton's Surrey mansion copping licks. 'Because I've spent some time with him lately, the guitar on the new record sounds like Eric to me, because his whole vibe is within me,' he told Pete Frame.

Bolan's technical command of his instrument was shaky, and therefore he could not and cannot to this day rely on being Captain Speedfingers, dazzling the punters with absolutely nothing played at fantastic velocity. Bolan's electric guitar leads are, like those of nearly every other contemporary player, strongly Hendrix influenced, but unlike all those who copy the screams and the feedback and the electronic holocausts, he uses the sweet, melodic, 'Little Wing' style. His leads, when he's playing good, concentrate on tonal and melodic content, simple, clean, elegant lines which twist and curl and end up in unexpected places.

On the other hand, when he does his practising in public and gets into long jams, he's quite appalling, because when he's out of ideas, there's absolutely nothing happening. 'Elemental Child', the last cut on 'Beard', is a fine example of Bolan wanking away at great length. The song is fine ('Torch girl of the marshes/her kiss is a whip of the moon') but the guitar solo is interminable and sounds like any young guitarist in his local music shop going to town on the Les Paul and Marshall 100 until the assistant comes back.

The music was, however, getting better and the lyrics becoming less flowery. In 'Organ Blues', musically a forerunner of 'Hot Love', he wrote, 'We make feasties of the beasties, but the beasties just live in the wild/You know you're slower now and you were faster when you were a child.'


'For three years I didn't do anything visually. I played sitting down all the time, never moved, didn't move a muffle! But we had big albums and things and were what I thought was successful at the time till all this happened. You spoke of media earlier, and the credibility of the band was lessened by the fact that people associated us with Flower Power, and that was a long gone era, and I wanted people to look at the thing in a new light, and the only way to do that was to have a label change, and change the music, and change the name, but not lose any identity either way.

'I make it sound very controlled, but it wasn't at all, it all happened in three days, and I got put on Fly Records. I didn't choose to be there. Legally that happened because the company I was with signed with those people, who formed Fly Records. The music grew through three albums to what it is now, and people did all that bullshit about instant overnight electricity, which was ludicrous because it had taken two and a half years. From 'Unicorn' upwards, it's very obvious.'

> *As God-like I strode the forecourt a small voice hailed from*
> *a vehicle which lay mute and lifeless beneath the harsh*
> *lights. Drawing my noble sword, Renshaw, I was across*

*the concrete in a trice to find that my tiny friends, T.
Rex, were becalmed. Chuckling, I scooped them up in the
palm of my hand and laid them gently on top of a soft
pile of Green Stamps and bore them so to London town.
As we sped straight and true to that fair city they told
me of their concert tour and of the new record 'Ride A
White Swan' on Fly Records. Doubtless you'll own it
before long – if you don't by Christmas, my flock of
highly trained hedgehogs will fan out through the land
and retribution will be swift and terrible – indeed it
will . . .*

*John Peel*, Disc, *1970*

*Ten pounds is a lot of money, man . . . it's a bus fare
and strings for your guitar.*

*Marc Bolan, 1969*

'Ride A White Swan' made a number two and won a Silver Disc.
The rhythm section of bassist Steve Currie and drummer Bill
Legend were added, and the hard-rock T. Rex couldn't go wrong.
For more than two years, the singles chart had been tepid and
boring except for the odd Jethro Tull single, and T. Rex made
consistently excellent singles. 'I see no reason why freaks shouldn't
be in the charts, but then they turn around and resent you for it,'
Bolan told Peter Frame in mid-'71, with 'Hot Love' at the top for
six weeks and 'Get It On' awaiting release.

It's easy to tell what sound Bolan is aiming for by the tracks he
leaves behind. T. Rex's music is not derivative in the sense that,
say, Grand Funk's is, because though you can see where it's
coming from, it is a synthesis, and all creative rock music has
been a synthesis. In Bolan's head, Tolkien and Berry are collaborat-
ing on songs, which are taken to Sam Phillips' Sun Studios in
Memphis with Phil Spector at the board, Eddie Cochran playing
rhythm guitar, Jimi Hendrix lead, Buddy Holly up front to sing
and The Ronettes somewhere at the back and Brian Wilson,
David Bowie and Syd Barrett all hanging around offering
advice . . .

Does it work? Make up your own mind. It's worked in that
someone has revived the single as an art form. Any imbecile can
furzle around for seventeen minutes and come up with some good
licks, but to lay it all down in 2.15 or 3.38 or whatever is a dying trade.

The album boom was a reaction against constricting, formula singles, but as anyone who has to wade through more than a dozen new albums a week will tell you, right now we're suffering from a surfeit of amazingly tedious long-players, so anyone with a gift for producing listenable music in a concise form is very welcome, and now that singles from The Stones and The Who are few and far between, events rather than regular, punctual occurrences, T. Rex are the best singles band we've got. The art of making singles as opposed to albums is no more odious than that of the short-story writer as opposed to the novelist.

John Fogerty of Creedence Clearwater Revival is another musician who understands this: 'A single means you've got to get it across in a very few minutes. You don't have twenty minutes on each side of an LP. All it means is that you've got to think a little harder about what you're doing. We learned from the singles market not to put a bunch of padding on your album. Each song's got to go someplace. Most of this is a built-in uptightness. Singles are what I dug when I was little, therefore I have to change now. I've grown up, I don't like Top 40 . . . which is dumb. Why not change Top 40?'

Marc Bolan has changed Top 40, but it's a shame that not all of his 'Electric Warrior' album is up to the standard of the singles. 'Cosmic Dancer', a fine song, is spoilt by incongruously heavy-handed drumming from Legend and Visconti's saccharine string writing. 'The Motivator' is an inferior version of 'Get It On' and 'Lean Woman Blues' is unbelievably clumsy, though Bolan raises a smile by counting the band in by yelling, 'One – two and BUCKLE MY SHOE!!' 'Planet Queen' is an indifferent song rescued only by a fine chorus and the excellent vocal backup by Howard Kaylan and Mark Volman. After all, who could sing a line like 'Give me your daughter' better than The Mothers Of Invention?

'Rip Off' is a mess, but entertaining. The structure is like a one-chord 'Tutti-Frutti', but every so often Bolan sends a reflective minor chord drifting across the chaos. It ends with Ian McDonald improvising mantrically against a long electronic chord. As the chord changes he plays a beautiful bubbling, looping turnaround and then vanishes into the texture of the sustained chord. It might even turn some people onto Coltrane.

Bolan's new-style lyrics blend cars and chicks into the old

sword and sorcery scenes, emphasizing yet again that it's all a matter of technology, that it doesn't matter whether you use a silken chariot or a Cadillac as long as it gets you there on time. Despite its Eddie Cochran guitar riffs, 'Ride A White Swan' was, lyrically, mainstream Bolan: 'Wear a tall hat just like in the old days/ride a white swan with a tattooed gown/Take a black cat and put it on your shoulder/ and in the morning you'll know all you know.' 'Hot Love' had lyrics that *sounded* right, whether you consciously listened to them or not: 'She's faster than most and she lives on the coast/She ain't no witch an' I love the way she twitch/She's my woman of gold and she's not very old' and a guitar solo that merely sent two or three random notes floating across the changes – but it worked.

Like many another performer, Bolan capitalizes on his limitations – he doesn't so much sing as manipulate his vocal mannerisms, and his simple lead guitar style is born of necessity. He only seems to have one rhythm guitar lick, but he knows his rock and roll, and he makes it count. Just at the fade of 'Get It On', he murmurs, 'And meanwhile, I was *still* thinkin'' ' . . . the pay-off line of Chuck Berry's 'Little Queenie'.

'I wanted to record "Little Queenie", but it wouldn't have worked again, so I wrote my own song to it, and I put that on the end so that someone like you would know and wouldn't say What a cunt, Bolan, ripping off "Little Queenie" because in the end, it's only the feel of the song.'

Subjectively, Bolan singles sound fine when they slide into your head during the course of the day. On *Top of the Pops* or Radio One or my local pub jukebox, T. Rex's records shine out like diamonds in the mud. But in the more competitive environment of an evening at home playing records, they suffer by comparison with The Who or The Dead, or The Stones or The Byrds, or Steeleye Span, or whoever your own best friends may be. But it's good bopping music, and there'll never be too much of that.

*Interviewer: Where's Steve Took these days?*
*Bolan: Oh, I don't know . . . in the gutter somewhere.*

*John Peel awarded an MBE for his services to Tyrannosaurus Rex.*

*Bob Dawbarn's New Year Predictions,*
Melody Maker, *Christmas 1968*

*I went to Newcastle with John Peel to see Beefheart at the*
*weekend, and he said that he'd had no social contact*
*with Bolan since they had their first hit. Every time he*
*phones the office someone tells him that Marc's tied up*
*right now, man, can he call back on Saturday, far out.*

*Richard Neville*

*See a tin can at my feet/think I'll kick it down the street,*
*That's the way to treat a friend . . .*

*Randy Newman*

At the Republican convention in Miami four years ago, Norman
Mailer, working on the principle that you can tell as much from a
man's circle as from the man himself, declined to watch Nixon's
speech and went to have a look at his elephant. In the rock and
roll business you can judge a star not only by his groupies (and
vice versa) but by his organization (and vice versa). When the new
Jeff Beck Group went on the road, I tried to get an interview with
Beck, but his management spewed out endless miles of red tape,
which would be too boring to talk about, and so Beck went off on
an American tour uninterviewed. It is still unclear as to whether
an interview with Beck will appear in these pages or not, but if it
doesn't it is neither Beck's fault nor ours, but that of his boring
management.

By contrast, when I went to the T. Rex office the day before
Wembley to collect my ticket, everyone was friendly, helpful and
cooperative despite being out of their minds 'trying to get this
boogie together' as B.P. Fallon put it. Beep also gave me an apple
and a lift back to the West End. When I called to ask for an
interview with Bolan, I was told that he was going to the States,
but that I could talk to him for as long as I wanted after the 17th.
I said that I had to deliver copy by then. All right, said Beep, come
round tomorrow at one and you can have an hour or so. No
problem.

So the evening before the interview I went down to the Grove
to talk to Steve Peregrine Took. He was watching *Callan* on his
colour set in the flat he shares with Russ of The Pink Fairies, and
various mutual friends were dotted around the room. We all got
blasted, and then we talked about the good old days. Took,
formerly the London and Home Counties Mandrax Champion,
now works as a solo singer-guitarist, 'Ladbroke Grove's answer to

29

James Taylor', and he is working on a single with the former bass player from Curved Air. A tall, skinny, immensely friendly guy, his stubble and leather and shades make him look more like a biker than a former flower-child. He'll probably go down in rock mythology as the Pete Best of the seventies.

'It's really strange,' he said. 'Little girls come up to me and touch me and squeal and run away. The other day at the Aldermaston gig all these little girls started screaming "Marc Bolan, Marc Bolan" at me, so I screamed back, "Steve Took, Steve Took," till they went away.'

He has one or two memories of his one American tour with Tyrannosaurus Rex. 'We were staying at the Chelsea in New York and Marc didn't like it. He kept running his finger under shelves and going, "Oh! *Grubby!*" and so we had to move to this big fuckin' hotel where they kept staring at us all the time. So I said to June, Marc's wife, that I didn't want to be a part of no fuckin' freak show. She said, "I like to be surrounded by *nice* things." ' Took puts a world of scorn into the word 'nice'.

So the following day I went out for the interview. I gave myself too much time in which to find the place, with the result that I had to kill thirty-five minutes in a grimy caff in Gray's Inn Road, drinking abominable coffee and reading about Todd Rundgren and Pete Seeger in *Rolling Stone*. Eventually I stumbled into the office tired, wasted and bleary, all my carefully prepared, tough, hard-hitting questions melting away. Chelita Secunda, ex-wife of Bolan's former manager Tony Secunda, ousted the previous week with a blaze of publicity, smooths my passage, indicates the bored-looking black velvet figure perched on the desk and says, somewhat superfluously, 'This is Marc Bolan.'

Black velvet suit with diamond shapes embroidered out of sequins. 'See if his eyes are pinned,' Took had said the previous night, but he wears heavy shades. His head and his hands seem marginally too large for his frame. We shake hands, say hello, and Chelita ushers us into another part of the office.

'What can I do for you?' he asks.

'Tell me things.'

'What kind of things?'

'Whatever's on your mind.'

'I've got lawsuits on my mind right now. Do you want anything to drink?' I ask for a coffee and he goes out. I deposit my case and coat, get out the cassette machine and turn my attention to the Aria jumbo leaning against a chair. I'm just taking a wrong turning on an Albert King run when Bolan comes back in, sipping a Scotch and Coke. 'Rock on,' he says and we sit down.

Effectively, I blow the interview. Nothing of consequence really gets discussed, and we just sit and talk about rock and roll for an hour or so. Bolan has this very hard, dry, precise little voice, his pronunciation almost BBC except for the slang. He sits there like a little jewelled snake, very poised, very elegant, and we talk about Chuck Berry and Bo Diddley and Nik Cohn and Jeff Beck and John Lennon and Phil Spector and Uriah Heep and whether there are wizards in Tooting Bec and Neasden. He's studied his rock and roll for more than fifteen years with maniacal devotion. 'There's very little that I don't know about rock and roll,' he says, 'on any level. Or pop music, for that matter.

'I'm very erratic,' he says, 'but that's part of art and I consider myself to be an artist, and I don't feel any compunction to be professional if I don't feel like it or play if I don't want to. It's my right. If I'm committed to do a gig, I'll *be* there and I'll play, if people have paid to see me. Whether or not I can get myself together to play well is totally up to my head. I tend to be able to do it, because that's what I'm here for, and it's karmically very bad for me not to do it. It's also very selfish, not to do numbers, but to allow oneself not to go to bed the night before and be maybe drugged out or whatever, and have to do a concert when you know you're in no condition to. It's a stupid thing to do. Every rock and roller's done it, and it's the sort of thing you only do once. Some people do it all the time, which is sad, but it's the sort of thing one learns not to do. I've seen Sly being carried on, but that's cool as long as . . . he has personal pain, man . . . it's hard, it's very hard. I won't ever judge. I've given up judging people as I've given up criticizing people for no other reason that the more I learn about rock and roll, about the sort of success that I've had to experience and probably always wanted . . . the amount of pain and aggravation and heartbreak that's gone with it has in fact not been worth it. It has musically, because I love the music, I mean this is what I do, but the pain is so fucking great, man, and it's the sort of thing that you can't express, which is how, lyrically, Berry leads into "Tulane" or one of those things. The man has got a lot of soul, and the one thing that people can't deny me — I don't care if they agree, they can't deny me. I've made my point, you know what I mean? Now whether they can relate to it is . . . I'm not going to say I'm a gas, or that I deserve to be as successful. People have *made* me successful. Without the people, there is no success. And also if my head was different it wouldn't have happened.'

Finally Bolan split to go to court. 'Write whatever pleases you, man, I don't mind,' he said as he closed the door behind me.

I didn't like Marc Bolan. I had enjoyed talking to him immensely, but something in his vibration disagreed with me. He had seemed like a tiny, elegant steamroller, riding over all obstacles, buffeting people with the wind of his passage.

Michael Alfandary, promoter: 'We've all heard of the T. Rex ten bob concerts. How many of you have ever been to one? No one, because that's all a bloody hype. I've been on to Chrysalis agency for years saying I will do a concert at Hemel Hempstead and charge ten bob and I will pay T. Rex the fee that justifies ten bob and I will make zero money if T. Rex will do it. The reply from Chrysalis is "You might not like cash but we do and T. Rex dig it too."'

Bolan: 'Maybe that's why we don't have an agency any more.'

> '*I only do it for the madness.*'
> '*What kind of madness, Marc?*'
> '*Rock and roll madness.*'

So the four-man group which is actually a two-man group with two salaried employees which is actually a solo act has sold sixteen million records in fourteen months. In their first fourteen chart months, The Beatles had sold five million. Bolan sells three out of every hundred singles in this country. Rock and roll madness.

But finally, Marc, I have to salute you, because you've made millions of kids who never listened to rock and roll begin listening. They copy your hair and your clothes and those Anello and Davide girls' strap shoes you wear are now advertised in Oxford Street as 'Bolan Shoes' with your picture underneath. Whether people like me dig you is irrelevant. You have kept the circle unbroken, you have ensured our survival, you've postponed the day the music died. So go 'head on, Marc. Rock on. But remember all your passengers. These weird kids may not be The Children Of

Rarn, but take good care of them, man, because right now at this stage of the game, you hold the keys.

Get it on.

## Elvis Presley: 'Elvis Now' (RCA)

*I.T.*, 6 July 1972

THAT snoring sound you hear is Elvis Presley recording 'Elvis Now'. After his renaissance at the end of the sixties, he's gone right back to sleep again, and for the most part he sounds just like any paunchy pub baritone mumbling his way through a selection of more or less contemporary material from the pens of Paul McCartney, Kris Kristofferson, Gordon Lightfoot and Les Reed. The album's worst moments are a song entitled 'Miracle Of The Rosary' and his hideous version of Buffy Sainte-Marie's beautiful 'Until It's Time For You To Go'. If Buffy were to dismember Elvis with a meataxe, this recording would, if played in court, result in an acquittal from any jury comprised of human beings. The album's final section, 'I Was Born About Ten Thousand Years Ago', is fifth-rate Presley that nevertheless stands head-and-shoulders above anything else on 'Elvis Now'. He wrote it himself, and it sounds as if they woke him up to sing it. Elvis, repeat one hundred times every night before going to bed, 'Youcandoanythingbutgetoffmabluesuedeshoes'.

## Edgar Winter's White Trash: 'Roadwork' (Epic); 'The Jeff Beck Group' (Epic)

*Oz* 43, July 1972

EDGAR Winter's White Trash are advanced cases of the Live Album Syndrome. Their line-up allows them to tackle soul, gospel, blues and rock, depending on whether Jerry Lacroix, Rick

Derringer or Edgar himself happens to be out front. However, their endless posturing prevents them from sounding like the real professional soul or blues band they so desperately want to be. It's like the difference between Albert King and Alvin Lee; ballet becomes extravagance. The entire ensemble sings and plays as if it is getting paid by the note.

On the plus side, every number displays White Trash's enormous technical facility, but in every instance they are undermined by their self-indulgence. The singers are all very distinctive: Lacroix has a beefy, funky voice reminiscent of Otis Redding and David Clayton-Thomas, Winter sounds like an enraged bee attempting to impersonate Mose Allison, and Derringer (who plays lead guitar throughout and also produced) is a fine exponent of that punk-rock stance which says: *I got this big fuckin' amplifier, man, so I wanna see some rock and roll out there* . . . but his six-minute bravura performance of Berry's 'Back In The USA' is flatulent and over-blown. Despite their infinite musical superiority, White Trash could learn a lot about rock and roll interpretation from those veteran punks, the MC5.

Most of this album is a waste of time. However, on three or four occasions it really comes to life. Halfway through the first side, Lacroix does a three-minute soul original called 'Jive, Jive, Jive' which, with its flaring, blazing brass riffs, conjures up the ghost of Otis Redding far better than the rather tired version of his 'I Can't Turn You Loose' which follows, and is the band's new single. At the end of the second side, Winter says, 'We got a little surprise for you here tonight . . . people keep asking me "Where's yer brother?"' . . . the crowd roars, and on comes Johnny Winter to roar through a sloppy but powerful version of 'Rock And Roll Hoochie Koo', the song Derringer wrote for him when they were in Johnny Winter And together. It's messy, but it's so good to hear Johnny Winter again that I've got my blind ear to the speakers.

During the marathon version of 'Tobacco Road' that takes up most of side three, Derringer takes a long acappella guitar solo that is probably the most rapid piece of electric guitar playing that I can remember hearing. It'll probably become a set-piece for aspiring Claptons to have to master in some horrific Rock Conservatory of the future. Edgar also acquits himself impressively on saxophone and piano, though the second half of his piano solo is marred by his insistence on scatting along with it. Derringer is a speedy little punk with an awesome command of his instrument and a lot of neat tricks, but all the really great rock guitarists have either a demon or an angel inside them. With the exception of Garcia, most of them are demons and none more so than Jeff Beck.

Since his last album, Beck has brought in an outside producer, Steve Cropper, no less. Unlike 'Rough And Ready', this one features some real songs, like Don Nix's 'Going Down', Dylan's 'Tonight I'll Be Staying Here With You', and a couple of Motown standards. 'Going Down' cuts Nix's own version to pieces and comes very near to equalling the version Stone The Crows use for their encore. The trouble is still in the vocal department. In performance, Bob Tench's rasping, tuneless soul vocals fit in with the rest of the band, but in the more sober environment of the home, he sounds very uncomfortable. Max Middleton's lucid, jazzy piano serves as a most effective contrast to all the mayhem and brutality that surrounds it.

Jeff Beck is the subject of many unprintable anecdotes centring around his groupies and fellow musicians. After about three bars of his performance on 'Highways', you know that they are all true. Anyone who'd play that is clearly capable of stopping at nothing. His instrumental version of Syreeta Wright's hit 'I Can't Give Back The Love I Feel For You', though, is astonishing for its lyricism and unabashed sentiment, as is the final instrumental 'Definitely Maybe', a lovely improvisation on the guitar lick Jimmy Page used for Cocker's 'Help For My Friends'. There's also a Dr John-ish Cropper/Beck song called 'Sugar Cane', and if that wasn't enough they also trash all over Dave Clark's old hit 'Glad All Over'. Words fail me.

# A Concerned Young Person looks at the Longford Report

*Cream*, November 1972

IT is becoming increasingly obvious that a censorship boom is upon us. Every other newspaper poster tells of some politico or other ranting on about stemming the tide of filth.

Within twelve days of the publication of the Longford Report, a photographer earning a weekly salary of £23 had been sentenced to pay £10 a week in fines until some time in 1995. His crime was importing dirty books. Even Paul Raymond, the Allen Klein of tits 'n' ass, got busted, and *Men Only* is about as subversive as the *Radio Times* and as left wing as the *Daily Telegraph*. That estimable gentleman Mr Robert Carr, fresh from his industrial triumphs, vows to liberate Britain from smut.

The Longford Report, incidentally, had the best publicity campaign of any paperback for a long time. And through it all, the tabloids kept up a constant and adroit barrage of tough and righteous editorials about the corruption of the young while making sure that none of their readers went without their regular diet of nipples and navels.

So nowadays when you go to buy your cigarettes in London's Charing Cross Road, you can see 'Maiden's Prayer' dildoes stacked up next to the Gitanes and absurd fetishist magazines on every other West End newstand. Not long ago a copy of this very magazine was spotted in an Islington porn shop; to be misunderstood is indeed a terrible thing. Berwick Street's invaluable sci-fi bookshop 'Dark They Were And Golden Eyed' feels constrained to hang a sign in the window stating that they don't sell pornography, a disclaimer which may not do them much good if the police decide to start busting American monster magazines — which could well happen.

Meanwhile the BBC which, as all right-thinking, Christian, lion-hearted Anglo-Saxons will agree, is dominated by a pack of Leftists, continues to deprave the nation with Alf Garnett and *Late Night Line Up*. At any moment I expect Malcolm Muggeridge to issue a statement informing the world that *Playboy* causes hijackings and that pre-, post- and extra-marital sex leads directly to refusal to watch *Stars on Sunday*.

Possibly the most outstanding characteristic of the Longford Report, Mary Whitehouse's hilarious autobiography *Who Does She Think She Is?*, and the speeches of most major politicians on this subject is the fact that they are all terrified. In the oft-quoted words of Stephen Stills, they are scared shitless.

They are the most astounding bunch of paranoid hysterics this side of the American underground press. In their cosmography, a weird assembly of Little Red Schoolkids, Russian Communists.

American glossy tit millionaires, Australian iconoclasts and Swedish pornographers, with Joan Bakewell and Alice Cooper thrown in for good measure, are conspiring to flood this green and pleasant land with photographs of girls called Inger being fucked by pigs, dogs, goats, horses, battery-powered vibrators and Mick Jagger.

Lord Longford has changed the course of English history by the simple act of assembling his motley inquiry team, letting them froth at the mouth, editing it all into (just about) readable prose, and passing it off on the public and the media as a serious study of pornography. Incidentally, the cover of the paperback edition of the report contains the word 'Pornography' in huge red letters, and if I had the bread I would be delighted to prosecute the publishers under the Trade Descriptions Act.

The report shows its true colours in its selections from its expert testimony, and from the unsolicited statements from members of the public. In one extraordinary paragraph, the report states that abortion, contraception, homosexual clubs and Women's Lib were 'aspects of the permissive society which ... may have some connection with pornography'.

It goes on: 'Many writers, predominantly in older age groups, were deeply distressed by the national image they felt to be widely disseminated outside Britain. Historical precedents of Rome and Weimar were quoted to illustrate the consequences of "over-indulgence" in sexuality ... There was noticeable bitterness among many who felt that they had fought against Hitler to preserve freedom, but that England was now no longer "a land fit for heroes".' Was it ever?

They move in a world where the *Schoolkids' Oz* is 'moral manure', where vast masses of people are bewildered and terrified by the media's incompatibility with the Christian view of love and marriage, young minds are buffeted and sent reeling by endless tides of boobs and buttocks, where 'moral pollution' lurks, leering and tumescent between the *Beano* and *Woman's Own* in every newsagents.

As one who spent much of his time hanging out with dopers and writing for *Oz* and *I.T.*, I was instilled with police paranoia, most of which turned out to be entirely justified. Thus it came as a real revelation to learn that the Realm is as terrified of us as we are of them. They may harass us and bust us, but we'll fuck their children silly in a hundred and four different positions, stone them out of their gourds with cannabis resin (thank you, Lord) and befoul their minds with Communist propaganda set to hard rock. Or so an over-credulous perusal of *Play Power* might have one think.

But the most telling passages in the Longford document are statements such as this: 'Our society has always worked on the assumption that the weak need protecting not only from the strong, but from themselves and their own weaknesses. Here, if ever, is an area where this sort of protection is long overdue.' Yeah, relax, baby, you're safe – just leave the driving to us.

It's the same old paternalistic routine – first you characterize people as being unfit to make their own decisions, and then it becomes the simplest thing in the world to get them to accept your right to make those decisions for them. And all in the name of protection. Ever heard of protection rackets? A Mr C.H. Rolph is quoted as saying, 'There is a need for some people to be protected and even more for their right to privacy to be protected.' Again, that's great if you happen to be Mr C.H. Rolph, but who decides whose privacy must be protected – and by whom?

A recurring lament is the dissociation of sex from love. When *Love Story* smashed cinema attendance records everywhere, there was much rejoicing by those who favoured the romantic revival. They ecstatically proclaimed that this was final proof that the public did not want any more sex and violence. Then along came *Clockwork Orange* and *The Godfather* which broke all the records all over again, and neither of those movies are exactly *Mary Poppins*. So what about love and personal relationships?

One close friend once told me that he particularly liked one of his girlfriends because 'she knows I don't like 'em there when I wake up.' I, on the other hand, have never enjoyed sex so much as with a girl who I really loved, and if she'd been gone when I awoke, I would have been totally emotionally destroyed. So who's right? It all comes down to what the Festival of Light have always refused to admit: different strokes for different folks. Or you boogie and I'll choogle.

Across the water, that great statesman Richard M. Nixon recently rejected the findings of the US Presidential Commission on Obscenity and Pornography, characterizing their findings as 'morally bankrupt' because he disagreed with them. Well, it was during an election campaign.

In part, Nixon said: 'If the level of filth rises in the adult community, the young people in our society cannot help but also be inundated by the flood. Pornography can corrupt a society and a civilization. The people's elected representatives have the right and the obligation to prevent that corruption. The warped and brutal portrayal of sex in books, plays, magazines and movies, if not halted and reversed, could poison the well-springs of American and Western culture and civilization. The pollution of a culture, the pollution of our civilization with smut and filth is as serious a situation for the American people as the pollution of our once pure air and water.'

Fine, stirring stuff. How the morality of a nation founded on genocide and sustained by repression can be trifled with is slightly beyond my comprehension but no doubt it went down well in Baltimore, Maryland.

The society we live in has crippled the emotional responses of a number of people to the extent that they can only derive pleasure from fantasies of sadism, masochism, sodomy and rape. To proceed to condemn such people as evil is a monstrous perversion, a greater crime against nature than every hard porn book ever printed.

The revolution is upon us. Those of us who pray for the revolution may well get their prayers answered in a way they never expected – the Festival of Light. If that happens, then we'd better start evolving a coherent philosophy before the Whitehouse–Muggeridge–Longford axis gets there first.

# David Bowie:
# 'Pin Ups' (RCA)

*Oz* 48, 1973

CURIOUSER and curiouser. It took until 1968 for people to start getting nostalgic about the fifties, but lo and behold, it ain't even 1974 yet and already there's a hankering for the sixties in the air. And who should be leading the New Wave of sixties nostalgia but David Bowie. Curiouser and still curiouser.

'Pin Ups' brings together songs by The Who ('I Can't Explain' and 'Anyway Anyhow Anywhere'), The Pretty Things ('Rosalyn' and 'Don't Bring Me Down'), The Yardbirds ('I Wish You Would' and 'Shapes Of Things'), Them ('Here Comes The Night'), The Pink Floyd ('See Emily Play'), The Kinks ('Where Have All The Good Times Gone'), The Merseys ('Sorrow'), The Easybeats ('Friday On My Mind') and The Mojos ('Everything's All Right'). So far, critical reaction has veered from the lukewarm to the downright contemptuous. On certain levels, the adverse criticisms have been justified, but it all comes down to this: what criteria are appropriate for dealing with this particular venture?

All right, first the bad news. Bowie has failed to differentiate between songs he likes and songs that he can sing without modifying his basic vocal approach. Basically, Bowie's vocal style has been developed to express lyrics, and in some cases even act them out. Therefore, this approach only works with good lyrics. Since only 'See Emily Play' and 'Where Have All The Good Times Gone' have anything even approaching what are generally regarded as good lyrics, most of the songs collapse under the weight of what Bowie puts into them. In addition, most of the songs are R&B (albeit R&B once removed) and Bowie really isn't an R&B singer, though he can sing in the appropriate style if he thinks he ought to. Therefore 'Rosalyn', 'I Wish You Would' and 'Everything's All Right' are well sung, and 'Anyway Anyhow Anywhere' picks up remarkably well after an initially disastrous opening where he tries to sing like Presley (Elvis, not Reg).

With the exception of 'I Can't Explain', where an attempt to do a Vanilla Fudge slowdown collapses almost instantly, most of the tracks are very neatly arranged and played. Mick Ronson (guitar), Mike Garson (piano), Trevor Bolder (bass) and Aynsley Dunbar (drums) carry themselves like officers and gentlemen throughout.

If you were into all this stuff first time around then you probably won't touch this with a ten-foot dildo, unless someone tries to talk you into it. Allow me to try, however. If you approach it as a fairly charming piece of nostalgic self-indulgence, then you're not going to encounter any major barriers.

On the other hand, if all these songs are new to you, then you're really going to dig it. Listen to 'Pin Ups' in the spirit in which it was made and it's mostly an OK album, and on occasion (particularly 'Where Have All The Good Times Gone') it's considerably better than that.

One problem remains. What the hell is going on in the seventies that people are going to want to get nostalgic about in the eighties? You gotta think ahead, y'know.

# The man who ate Alice Cooper

*NME*, 15 February 1974

THE trouble with Alice Cooper is that he never really understood what tastelessness was all about.

Ostensibly, the *raison d'être* of the Alice Cooper assault on public credulity, gullibility and excess income was founded on the assumption that the public enactment of the American Nightmare was a ritual of liberation and purification – plus the entirely logical belief that said assault would garner a whole lotta green ones for all concerned.

The method employed would consist of a show that was the ultimate in tastelessness.

The litany of furnishings in Cooper's chamber of horrors is by now long since mutated into the stuff of legend: baby-killing, necrophilia, the use of powerfully emotive death-symbols such as electric chairs, gallows and guillotines, a couple of gallons of sour-mash sex-role ambiguity, a plague of pythons, several dozen dead chickens and a lot of enthusiastically aggressive rock and roll.

All of which merely proves how little Cooper knows about tastelessness. What he's into is *bad taste*, which is a totally different ball game, and in an infinitely lower league. Tastelessness is an arrogant rejection of the obsolete and restrictive concepts of both good *and* bad taste; bad taste is an acknowledgement of the existence merely of good taste and a conscious attempt to defy it.

One would place The Stones and all other great pulp artists in the first category; Alice Cooper belongs firmly in the second.

The first mass public manifestation of the man/organism generally known as Alice Cooper was in 1969, when something answering to this description was announced as an early signing to Frank Zappa's Straight label.

41

Straight, it will be recalled, was the companion to Bizarre in F.V.Z.'s Warner-Reprise-backed campaign to demolish the world with an exquisitely orchestrated barrage of esoteric tastelessness (see above). The something turned out to be Alice Cooper; or to put it another way: Alice Cooper (vocal/harp), Glen Buxton (lead guitar), Michael Bruce (guitar/piano), Dennis Dunaway (bass) and Neil Smith (drums).

Alice Cooper was a preacher's son from Phoenix, Arizona.

His real name was Vincent Furnier, a fact which he successfully managed to keep a secret until he'd been a superstar for nearly two years. He also used to be in a group called The Spiders (not *the* Spiders), and also in a group called The Nazz (not *the* Nazz, either). After these blinding successes, he worked his way from Phoenix to Detroit to LA, by which time he was conjoined with those other guys as Alice Cooper (moving fast tonight, folks).

As documented on their first album 'Pretties For You' (Straight), the Alice Cooper of that time were a vastly pretentious and laughably inept psychedelic punk garage band, distinguished from platoons of similar oafish combos by a kind of low-budget Theatre-of-Cruelty presentation and a primitive gesture in the direction of sex-role ambiguity. The reason that they got signed is that most audiences found the band actively *repulsive*.

Legend hath it that their emergence on record was due to the fact that they had snuck into Frank Zappa's Laurel Canyon basement in the small hours of the morning and commenced to churn out some absurdly ugly music, thereby provoking Uncle Frank to stumble in, clad in bedsocks and nightcap, mumbling something to the effect that if youse guys will kindly shut the hell up and get the hell out and let me get the hell to sleep I will sign you and your absurdly ugly music to my label (which is *extremely heavy duty* and is incorporated in my *corporate logo*). See my manager, Herbie Cohen. Apocryphal though it may be, it seems as plausible and generally true-to-life as any other possible explanation for the appearance of 'Pretties For You'.

The cover of this particular product depicted a young girl lifting her skirt and revealing her panties to a less than fascinated older man in a lumpy overcoat, which was all part of the Cooper aesthetic of being as offensive as was humanly possible – i.e. pretending to be a fag act, throwing chickens at the audience and like that. The album itself is a rather pitiful collection of tattered clichés disinterred from old Yardbirds, Beatles and Stones LPs coupled with earnest attempts to mimic the more obvious effects handed down to posterity by Big Guys like Iron Butterfly, The Moody Blues and The Mothers.

1970 brought a second album on Straight, entitled 'Easy Action', which found the Coopers slightly more proficient and slightly less pretentious, but still by no means either impressive or interesting. Lester Bangs (at that time still two Deep Purple albums away from entering his punk phase) described the first Cooper album in *Rolling Stone* as being 'totally dispensable'. On the evidence of 'Pretties For You' and 'Easy Action' he was dead right.

Incidentally, they are both now available for your inspection, reincarnated as a Warners double album entitled 'School Days'. Central Quality Control recommends that they be investigated only for reasons of research.

Things commenced to get mildly interesting once the band split (or were split, as the case may be) from Zappa and Cohen, and eventually found themselves ensconced with a gent named Shep Gordon (who did the managing) and a Canadian geezer named Bob Ezrin (who did the producing).

The first album to come from this exciting combination of talents was 'Love It To Death' (Warner Bros), and it was clear that Ezrin had earned every letter of his production credit. Why, the band sounded almost tight, they had magically learned the gentle art of pacing and dynamics and they had even managed to write A Classic.

Said Classic was a song called 'I'm Eighteen', and coming from a zero-quality band like the Coopers, it was nothing less than phenomenal. Side one, track two on the album, it was a pleasant cross between punk introspection and teen ballad, all about how confused the narrator felt to have reached the age of eighteen.

'Lines form on my face and hands/lines form from the ups and downs/I'm in the middle without any plans/I'm a boy and I'm a man,' sings Cooper. 'I'm eighteen and I don't know what to do,' before getting to his punch line 'I'm eighteen and I like it.'

In many ways, it was the long-delayed answer to that popular musical question of the fifties: 'Why Must I Be A Teenager In Love?'

43

Basically, it was a masterstroke of audience identification. Alternatively, it was a genuinely sensitive exploration of the eternal dilemma of the adolescent. Your choice will count for 3 per cent of your total final mark.

The cover of 'Love It To Death' displayed the Coopers in pouts and make-up sleazing it up for all they were worth (which was comparatively little until 'I'm Eighteen' went monstrous) but looking rather too butch to carry it off with the total *élan* of a Bowie. The cover pictures established that they were a bunch of twerps trying to look like street punks trying to look like drag queens.

The music contained in this particular *objet d'art* in no way outshone 'I'm Eighteen', but it was solid, competent and could even be suspected of having been in recent close contact with an idea. 'Is It My Body?' presented Cooper rather coyly posing that very question soulfully adding, 'Or do you want to find out who I really am?' which could put *anybody* off heavy petting.

An early significant homage to old movies was paid by 'The Ballad Of Dwight Frye'. As any fool knows, Dwight Frye is the name of the actor who played Henry Frankenstein's hunchbacked assistant Fritz in Boris Karloff's first Frankenstein movie for Universal Pictures in 1931.

The album's principal triumph of kitsch was the inclusion of Rolf Harris's 'Sun Arise', which is performed with a touching degree of reverence for the original. There was also a slight but catchy little song called 'We Sure Got A Long Way To Go', which Cooper was later to use at the climax of his concerts to rebuke audiences whose bloodlust got too ludicrous.

So the Ezrin-augmented Coopers came virtually out of nowhere with a good album and the first of their two all-time classic singles.

Until 'I'm Eighteen', they had been a minor cult band (with what little reputation they possessed based almost entirely on their associations with Zappa and fancifully embellished gossip about some of their more ridiculous concerts), but suddenly they'd made it with a big hit single, thereby becoming public property.

Given the higher budget that comes with fame, they got seriously into the theatrics; and the next step was to take as razed such pettifogging social problems as adolescent traumas and sexual identity, and get into big stuff, like psychopathy, execution and baby-killing.

Having done their collective best to mess around with America's sexuality, the next major section of its soul that they were going to go down on was America's Massive Collective Death Wish.

The next album was 'Killer', and the presentation of their next tour was built around it.

'Killer' merits some serious attention because it's probably Alice Cooper's best album, and though it contained nothing as epic as 'I'm Eighteen', it consolidated Cooper's claim to being an outstanding seventies act. Under Ezrin's guidance, the band sounded like an excellent second division act with a first division singer and first division songs.

Cooper himself was indeed an excellent singer; his voice was light but rough and he'd clearly heard enough Jim Morrison to know how to exploit a lyric to its fullest. He didn't play very good harp, though.

The songs, mostly written by Cooper and Michael Bruce, were flash, arrogant, pointed and reasonably inventive, plus they showed an advanced awareness of the techniques of persona manipulation.

Cooper's lifestyle included getting himself blurred around the edges on beer at grotesquely early hours of the morning, and staying that way all day while subjecting himself to a permanent barrage of the pernicious nonsense that serves America for day-time television. (In all fairness, American TV is not significantly more pernicious than British TV, but at least there are three times as many different kinds of perniciousness to choose from.)

Anyway, anybody who watched non-stop daytime TV while mildly drunk for any significant period of time would probably turn into a psychopath – or at least a good imitation of one, which latter fate overtook our Mr Cooper.

Due to the added sensitivity lent him by his phenomenal intake of beer and his intensive study of the insights imparted him through his TV set, he was able to chart the major American phobias with unerring accuracy. He was living proof that a man who spends most of his life pissed in front of a TV set can still make a million dollars.

So at one moment he was the arrogant rock star of 'Under My

Wheels' and 'Be My Lover', next time you looked he was the phantom jetset poisoner of the truly surreal 'Halo Of Flies' (complete with oh-so-macabre quote of the melody of 'My Favourite Things') and then the leather-clad gun-slinger of 'Desperado', which (courtesy of Ezrin) was blessed with an orchestral arrangement worthy of Dmitri Tiomkin himself and (courtesy of Cooper and Bruce) a lyrical ambiguity which oscillates between the Old West and modern times. Cooper trotted out his most Morrisonian intonations for lines like 'I'm a killer and . . . I'm a clown', which folded back out of the song into his own basic persona.

'Killer's' most notorious piece of unpleasantness came on the second side with the justly celebrated 'Dead Babies'. The sheer calculatedness of the whole Cooper trip was more than a little apparent, but the tongue-in-cheek arrangement (complete with backing voice doing French horn impressions in a determinedly Beatlesque way that actually owed more to 'Little Soldier Boy', a thoroughly horrendous song from The Yardbirds' 'Little Games' album), was extremely pretty, and that confused people considerably.

The ubiquitous Bangs, who'd been converted to the Cooper cause, allowed that he found the song pretty repulsive himself, but that was in the days when Cooper was still pretending to be a serious artist. Later, his overt opportunism and total cynicism was automatically to defuse the raw gut-reactions that his manipulation of the world's subconscious produced, but in 1971 he hadn't been sussed yet and so other otherwise rational people owned up to having been shaken and terrified by him.

The stage act that went with 'Killer' was certainly impressive, though.

Cooper cut a figure more tragic than glamorous: alternately puzzled, tormented kid confused by his own sexuality, demoniacal Jack the Ripper in semi-drag.

The band mooched around the stage like a herd of rather unintelligent bison under the influence of some amphetamine or other, bludgeoning out extremely loud Who and Yardbirds pastiches between the set-pieces, which included such Heavy Numbers as Cooper straitjacketed by a uniformed nurse during 'Dwight Frye' and fried to death in a glowing electric chair after the baby-killing antics.

Plus the goddam snake, of course. The snake became a Cooper

trade-mark, along with the torn black clothes, ratty hair and sloppy make-up.

As Cooper got further and further into Grand Guignol, he abandoned the remaining shreds of his original androgyny stance in favour of further explorations of the joys of sadism and necrophilia – far more American topics.

Though the band were monstroso in their native land, it took 'School's Out' to break them over here.

They'd done a gig at the Rainbow in late 1971, but their reputation rested mainly on reports filtering back from the colonies. Cooper liked trotting out raps about everybody-is-bisexual (though he himself had had the same girlfriend for nearly five years and would probably have been totally freaked out if any fags had actually tried anything on him) and how-his-violence-exorcized-the-violence-of-the-audience – not to mention putting forward the theory that Alice was some kind of Mr Hyde figure who possessed him onstage, whereas in reality he was just a good ol' boy who was nice to his mother and liked to drink a lot of beer and watch TV.

On top of that, he coyly revealed that he really enjoyed telling lies.

It was his latter admission that I found most endearing. Though many of the more serious and committed American critics started to regard Alice Cooper as 'a threat to our beloved rock and roll', I found him far more palatable as an outrageous fake-out artist than I ever did as a theoretically genuine psycho.

The less integrity and credibility he had, the more I admired him, because all that high-flown garbage about sexuality and violence was irritatingly pretentious, the worst kind of sanctimonious inflated pap.

I began to observe Cooper's antics with a perverse kind of admiration. Once in on the joke, it became a real pleasure to watch him putting everybody else on so brilliantly. Why, the guy should have been a politician.

So in the summer of 1972, unto us was delivered 'School's Out'.

Hailed by many as the 'My Generation' of the seventies, it had a manic bombast which lent a kind of spurious dignity, and even from Cooper it was epic.

It meant that the Coopers had produced no less than two classic

singles (two more than most people), and even though it was later
discovered that it had been none other than Li'l Rick Derringer
who'd played that galvanic guitar part, it was still a rousing piece
of pseudo-revolutionary rock, at least as good as either of Slade's
best singles and four solar systems ahead of cheap nonsense like
'Teenage Rampage'.

And of course it was safe as milk, because after all it was only
good ol' Alice, who was about as revolutionary as Bob Hope.
After all, Alice's thing was showbiz first, rock second, and revolution a poor seventeenth on the priority list. You knew without
having to be told that the Coop was one natural-born golfer.

The 'School's Out' album is pretty much disposable.

A street-punk fantasia about gang-fights and high-school utiliz-
ing massive borrowed chunks of *West Side Story*, it was principally designed as a sound track for the band's latest touring
extravaganza, and Ezrin made the elementary mistake of assuming
that it would work without the visuals.

Never having seen that particular show (it only played one
British gig – in Glasgow), I'm here to testify that it doesn't. The
Hammer Films horror show tactics were shelved completely, the
Cooper persona underwent its first real degree of softening and in
general, only the single is worth the vinyl it's printed on.

Summer '73 brought 'Billion Dollar Babies', which spawned no
less than three hit singles.

'Hello Hooray' was written by a Canuck songwriter named Rolf
Kempf, 'Elected' was a rewrite of 'Reflected', a rather dire tune
from their first album rejigged around the theme of Cooper
running for President, and 'No More Mr Nice Guy' was an almost
inspired piece of persona-juggling about how he and his folks
were mistreated and ostracized because the Blue Meanies thought
he was sick and obscene. Real poor-old-Alice stuff.

The visual motif of the album was money.

The band were depicted clad in white satin posing in front of a
real billion dollars in real cash holding a baby with Cooperesque
eye make-up smeared across his chubby dial. The sleeve was
designed to look like a giant wallet made of green snakeskin, and
folded inside was – you guessed – a billion dollar bill.

The band and their entourage toured in a jet painted black and
embossed with gold dollar signs; fake money was sprinkled over

the audience at one point – get it? After sex, death and street violence, the nearest remaining totem in the American pantheon was money. Christ, he'd sure made enough of it, and so had a sweet kind of logic.

The Coopers, y'see, were one of the first post-hippie superstar bands. Zeppelin, for example, can't make it into that category as long as Robert Plant continues to ride his current lyrical obsessions.

Therefore, it was perfectly natural and not in the least bit incongruous for them to glorify violence, perversion (and I don't care how liberated you are, bub, necrophilia is perversion unless you're a vampire) and materialism – and no more so for their audience (to whom 'hippies' meant being bored to death by their elder brothers' and sisters' Grateful Dead albums) to respond to these stimuli.

'Billion Dollar Babies' included a return to Grand Guignol with two of Cooper's all-time nasties, 'I Love The Dead' (which is self-explanatory) and 'Sick Things' (ditto). It even featured Donovan mumbling along on the title track, sung either by or about an inflatable dolly (see 'Heartache, In Every Dream Home A') – and if that ain't degenerate then I don't know what is.

'I Love The Dead', though, was really the outside edge in Cooperian grotesquerie. I crave your indulgence, therefore, for this lyrical sentiment:

> *While friends and neighbours mourn your silly grave*
> *I have other uses for you, darling . . .*
>
> © *Essex Music, 1973*

Pervy, ain't it? In actual fact, it's just good, solid teenage entertainment, about as relevant as a platypus and based solidly on the ethos of the cheap thrill. Me, I wouldn't have it any other way.

'Billion Dollar Babies' contained more than its fair share of utter crap, but it was definitely an improvement on the abysmal 'School's Out'.

The show that went with it was a stunning presentation, the ultimate in exploitative pulp theatre, every single trash fantasy coming to life befo' yo' very eyes. Guillotines, whips, the band in cages, a beheading, the ritual beating-up of a Nixon lookalike,

'God Bless America' as an encore, no less than *three* reflector balls, dentistry . . . everything but a tactical nuclear missile aimed at the audience.

The audience were the stars, though. They came in Cooper make-up, they stomped and gouged each other to get at the fake money and cheap posters, they howled for fake blood. When Cooper told them that they were crazier than he was, he for once wasn't lying. He isn't Alice Cooper – they are.

Cooper hasn't played live since then.

Their last album, 'Muscle Of Love', was a return to hard rock without trimmings, and showed the band playing better than they ever did before.

Trouble was, it was rather unmemorable, and sadly lacking in presence. On its release I reviewed it favourably and then stuck it on the shelf and forgot about it. It was only when I started to prepare this piece that I realized that I hadn't listened to it for a year, and playing it found that I hadn't missed much, which just about sums it up.

Cooper's solo album, 'Welcome To My Nightmare', is set for release within the near future. It'll be interesting to see where he goes with it.

Alice Cooper is the quintessential American artist of the seventies. In a decade when straight America has discovered that it can't trust the cops, it can't trust the FBI, it can't trust the CIA and it can't even trust its own goddam government, it is only fitting that the youth of America discover that they can't trust rock and roll either.

You can't even weasel out of it with that 'don't-trust-the-artist-trust-the-art' spiel either, because Cooper's art is so blatantly exploitative, opportunistic and cynical that it's even less trustworthy than he is. After the way that Dylan and Bowie (to name but two) copped out on their audiences the lesson should have been obvious, but if it took Cooper to really drive it home, then it's all been worthwile.

Cooper is a master charlatan; indeed, he has elevated charlatanry to a higher artistic plane than anybody else in rock and roll had ever dreamed of. In fact, he's such an outrageous phoney that he isn't even genuinely tasteless.

Real tastelessness is intrinsically liberating because it throws off the shackles of conventional definitions of good or bad taste.

Cooper, on the other hand, has demonstrated the strength of his conditioning by his patent inability to cast aside these chains. By remorselessly and slavishly playing up to the existing definitions of ultimo bad taste (and committing the colossal tactical blunder of admitting that it's bad taste), he has irrefutably demonstrated his allegiance to the old order, to the old standards. As a liberationist, he's a bad joke.

What Alice Cooper represents, in the final analysis, is a more insidious form of conformity than the Osmonds ever dreamed of.

# Tom Jones:
# Hammersmith Odeon

*NME*, 16 March 1974

HAD a nightmare long ago. Imagine a crowd in the grip of Osmond-type hysteria – all rushing the stage, trying to grope the performer, howling at him out of the balcony, doing all that stuff.

The only weird thing about them is that many of them are good stolid mums, all dressed in leather waistcoats, trying to look like teenyboppers. The man on the stage is neither a squeaky-voiced pubescent nor a skinny androgyne, but a hefty-looking dude with heavy shoulders and thick sideboards. Is there sex after forty?

Watching Tom Jones last Thursday it all came back. Before we got the Pontypridd Powerpack in person, though, we had to wade through an orchestra playing 'Eye Level' and 'Spanish Eyes' and a competent but underwhelming soul trio called the Blossoms, plus the repulsive Ted Rogers telling anti-woman, anti-Irish, anti-rock ('Have you seen Mott The Hoople? They shouldn't be making records, they should be fighting Dr Who') and anti-hippie jokes ('They're all on LSD – Last Summer's Dirt') to howls of appreciative laughter.

Good solid professionalism – he knows his audience's prejudices perfectly and reinforces them, laying it on with a trowel. It was exactly like a bad TV variety show.

So then we had Big Tom himself, backed by the Johnny Spence Orchestra and his own admirably tight but generally inaudible rhythm section plus the Blossoms doing a fair approximation of The Sweet Inspirations' contribution to the Elvis Presley Show.

The guy really does have a great voice – powerful, well controlled, flexible – and his phrasing is gorgeous, though he is overfond of taking the easy way out and hitting the vibrato button too hard and too often.

He struts out onto the stage doing the funky barnyard fowl and roaring through 'Turn On Your Lovelight'. The band almost kick. Feet tap.

Then he comes down the front to be hugged and kissed by middle-aged women and to swap tired stud jokes with the audience before lumbering gracelessly through a ballad.

Tom Jones is infuriating. Somewhere inside him is a guy who obviously digs country, funk and soul music, blues and rock and roll, and who can sing all that stuff like a master when he wants to, and sometimes that inner Jones pokes his head out and rocks like a muthuh, but that canned virility persona is on top most of the time.

During the sequence where he introduces the rhythm section, his guitarist (Big Jim Sullivan's stand-in) played an excellent solo and Tom did a great from-Cardiff-to-Memphis jive routine, but then the bump-and-grind bits and boring *doubles entendres* took over again.

Still, I really dug 'She's A Lady' (by far the best of his numerous singles), and his encore was genuinely funky.

Sometimes I wonder what would have happened if he'd got himself a kick-ass little five-piece band, stuck to blues, rock, soul and country and really worked out. He would have made some amazing records (he should do an album of Jerry Reed songs), but he wouldn't be nearly so rich and famous.

Another good man gone down.

Yes, Matilda, there *is* sex after forty. Hey – do their daughters know they're out?

# Elton John: The short hello

*NME*, 6 July 1974

**O**L' Coconut Bonce is back. Elton Schmelton himself in the too, too solid flesh, still opening up interview sessions by walking into the room at exactly eleven-oh-four-ack-emma and saying, 'Good evening,' just like he thought it was funny. Still, he's pretty good-humoured considering that he's talking to somebody who panned the peanuts out of 'Caribou', his latest assault on the record racks of the nation.

Anyway he's just (surprise!) taken a holiday, and both his waistline and his scalp-coating are thinner than ever, so after the compliments of the season have been ritually exchanged, we tie Elt to his chair, shine bright lights into his eyes and start asking all them tough, hard-hitting questions.

'All right, punk – talk and talk fast 'cuz if ya don't tell me yer gonna haveta tell it to Homicide!' I flipped a butt out of the crumpled pack in my pocket, bought myself a drink from the office bottle and waited for Bugsy to spill.

'Now – whydja put out another album so soon after "Goodbye Yellow Brick Road"?' I asked softly, waiting for that yellow gleam of fear to light up behind his small, piggy eyes.

They all break – eventually. Some break easy and some break hard. But this mug didn't have what it takes.

I knew he'd talk.

'It wasn't so soon – it was practically a year after,' he replied, the words spilling from his mouth in an obscene torrent. I moved the lighter a little further away from his nose. 'We have to do – under our commitment to MCA and Dick James Music – two albums a year, and that means doing one every six months right from the word Go.'

'Now waiddaminute, creep,' I whispered, spitting the butt from my mouth and crushing it to the bare concrete of the floor, 'didn't "Yellow Brick Road" count as two?'

That shook him. He licked his lips a couple times, but he managed to come back from it. 'No. That was the tragic part, y'see. If it had counted as two I wouldn't have had to do another one. I was really distressed that it didn't count as two because it was such an effort to make it. We're off to do another one in August, but hopefully that won't come out for a year.

'We have to do two albums a year until the contract comes up in February. We've just signed a new one which means that we can just do one a year – or no albums a year – and take it easy for a bit, which I'm sure will come as a great relief to everybody, especially the band.

'The live work's been cut down too. All the live work we've

done this year has been Australia, Japan and New Zealand and two dates in England, so it's halfway through the year and we've only done four weeks of gigs. We've just had two months off, which is great.'

He seemed to be a little off his guard, so I figured it was time to throw in a sneaky one. 'So whaddya do in yer time off?' I asked him. He shifted a little in his chair.

Those ropes had probably cut off the circulation in his hands and feet by now, so I loosened them.

But not too much.

'You go to a lotta superstar parties – right?'

He wasn't too happy with that one. 'I really get annoyed about that. I hardly every go to those things at all. When I do, I always get my picture taken. I went to Kiki's party in New York, but . . . I went to a tennis ranch in Arizona for two weeks because I had to get away from everything. I was screaming . . . I just couldn't loon. Very depressed, very overweight – I was really blimpish at Watford – so I went away and lost about twenty-eight pounds. It's all discipline.'

My ears perked up. Elton a fladge? But no, it was not to be. 'I just played tennis for seven hours a day and dieted a lot. Hopefully I'm going to be the new sylph-like E.J. by the time the American tour starts. My guitarist Davey's like Bowie – he's got a hollow gut. It makes me sick. I've only got to look at a doughnut and I put on about six pounds. Yeah, I'm just a sports groupie now. Won the mixed doubles two weeks running, had my picture taken with Billie Jean King. I've just been relaxing and having a good time – which I needed to do, since I was getting really distraught what with five years of schlepping all over the world.'

He was getting relaxed again. I hit him with another tough one. 'You dropped everybody from Rocket except Maldwyn Pope and Kiki Dee – right?' He nodded.

Smart boy.

'So why doncha get yourself a real street-level rock and roll band?'

He swallowed – hard. I grabbed him by his hair (which wasn't easy) and tilted the chair back. I was gonna get an answer if I hadda pistol-whip the bastard.

'We tried,' he whined. 'That's what we've been looking for for a year and a half, but it's so bloody hard.' I let go of the chair and he woulda fallen off it if it hadn't been for the rope. 'We turned down Queen and Cockney Rebel, so we're pretty good judges of character.' He burst out laughing and I let him have it with the butt of the Luger. 'No, no, they wanted a lot of money and we just couldn't afford it. I'd love to get someone like Iggy and the Stooges, but they've broken up.' He spat out a few fragments of tooth. I mopped the blood off his chin before it could get to his shirt. 'I've got my spies out in Detroit trying to find James Williamson. He's so good. The Dolls – they're just not good at carrying out what they preach. But Iggy and the Stooges – that band are just so hot. We were staying in Atlanta and they were playing Richard's Club – which is a great club – I went down to see them one night with Davey and we thought they were incredible, so we flew back to Atlanta and went to see them another night. I thought it would be great to jam with them dressed as a gorilla, so I rented this gorilla suit and walked onstage in the middle of their set. He thought it was some fuckin' maniac 'cuz he's always getting attacked by maniacs. A couple of roadies loomed up and I thought I was getting chucked off. Mind you, the gorilla costume stunk, it was about a hundred and ninety degrees in there and I nearly got thrown off for my troubles. I sort of jigged around for a couple of minutes feeling like a prat and then walked off, and then Iggy announced, "Da guy in da gorilla suit wuz Elton John," and the audience were going, "Awww, c'mon." I mean it coulda been Bob Dylan in there.'

Now that would've been something, I thought. Bob Dylan and Elton John in the same gorilla suit. But I wasn't gonna tell him that.

'You mean you're still talking to him after that review?' asked Stevens. 'You're a really civil guy.' John smiled weakly. 'A really Sybil Thorndyke.' 'You're the most Sybil Thorndyke I've met for a long time,' I cracked back. 'The most civil dyke you've met for a thorn-time,' he replied.

I hadda hand it to him. Getting grilled by two mugs like us and still making with the funnies. The punk was tougher than I thought. It was time for another question – a tough one. We gotta break this guy by twelve before Julie Webb gets here. 'Seen *The Exorcist*?' I snarled.

'Oh yes – I really liked it. Laughed all the way through. I saw it about three days after it opened and the whole audience was in hysterics. I read the book, which petrified the life out of me, it really did. So I laughed nervously all the way through. A couple of scenes were a bit gory, and I was a bit shaky when I left. So I went and had an Indian meal, ran into Gary Glitter and my tooth fell out . . .'

'Hold it, punk,' I said softly. 'What was that?'

'Actually it was half a tooth, because I hadn't been to a dentist for ages. I went to the Tandoori in Fulham Road, half a tooth fell out and Gary Glitter gave me a big kiss — right there in the middle of the restaurant.'

Stevens was shocked. 'Twenty years on the force and I ain't never heard anything like it.' I was pretty shook up myself. Elton John didn't seem to think that he'd said anything outa line. I wanted to tear him apart, but I couldn't do anything with Stevens there. So I gave myself another butt, lit it with a shaky hand. 'You're gonna give the rock and roll business a bad name,' muttered Stevens.

'Bunch'a poofters,' smirked John. He started talking about movies again, and we let him ramble while we pulled ourselves together. 'I saw *That's Entertainment* in New York. It's a montage of old MGM musicals. It's two-and-a-quarter hours long and they have the most incredible bits of old Fred Astaire and Busby Berkeley and Esther Williams.

'She's so outrageous. If she'd lived today she would have been Suzi Quatro. Diving off these boards with 800,000 people diving in after her in the shape of the Empire State Building — it was just incredible. It was so camp — I mean she came out of the water with fireworks around her head. The things some people will do — Elton John starts tour coming out of the water with fireworks coming out of his head.'

He went on to give us a spiel about how Bowie had sold out the Amphitheatre in LA for six days, despite a top price of fifteen dollars, ahead of even such well-known creeps as John Denver. I came back with a snappy quote from an old Marc Bolan interview in which the Little Caesar had said sump'n along the lines of, 'David doesn't have anywhere near the balls and charisma that I have — he ain't no way gonna make it.'

'Marc used to sit in my house,' croaked back John, 'and tell me how many records he'd sold – and I know how many he'd sold and his figures were just ludicrous. It's sad, because he's only fooling himself. It's easy to say, "I've sold 84 million records." I've seen him say that to the music press so many times, and it's a wonder that no one's ever followed it up.

'Also his quote about "Get It On" going gold in the States – well, it wasn't. I like the little bloke, actually. I think he's an idiot to say those things, but that's just him. He's just signed a new record deal, so that might help him out. He's just gone to Casablanca – Neil Bogert's company, the guy who used to run Buddah. They've got Fanny as well – and Kiss. The music's not as bad as the pictures. Actually.'

I mashed the stub of the cigarette out on the right lens of his glasses – the other one had somehow gotten cracked – and hissed, 'Ray Cooper isn't really playing much on "Caribou", is he?' from about an inch away.

'It was just a feeler for him,' moaned John. 'He did a couple of vibes things and some percussion. The next time we record, he'll be playing drums, he'll be playing keyboards. He'd only just joined the band. Now we're getting him organized with ARPs and things like that. I'm gonna give up playing piano. I'm gonna become a rock and roll suicide, take my nasty out and piddle all over the front row, just to get rid of my staid old image.'

Now we were getting somewhere. I flicked a glance over at Stevens. 'I think we can help you there, kid. It'd better become known that you're taking dope. I mean, you don't have to actually take any, but as long as we can say you are . . .'

He got the message.

'When I said that Billie Jean King was my heroine what I *meant* was that she *had* my heroin. Elton John scores at Wimbledon . . .' he was getting the idea. 'I was going to go to Wimbledon as a nun 'cuz I kept getting pestered by all these Bjorn Borgs. You've heard of hamburgers, now we've got bjornburgers. Anyway, I was going to go dressed as a nun – with a big pair of sparkly glasses that said "Elton John".'

'How different d'you think your career would've been if you'd had great eyesight?' I snapped.

'I don't think people buy my records because of my spectacles – or because of my testicles,' he riposted. He was getting his breath back. 'I'm quite pleased for Buddy Holly and all his compatriots.

There's not many women singers who wear glasses, apart from Nana Mouskouri. There's Bonnie Bramlett — Dory Previn, she's like a female Randy Newman. Bette Midler said my new album should be called "Fat Reg From Pinner". I wanted to call it "Ol' Pink Eyes Is Back", but I had a rebellion on my hands, the band didn't like it. Charlie Watts' wife had the best one. She wanted to call it "Ol' Four Eyes Is Back".'

That was good, I mean, we laughed at that one. Someone even suggested that Stevie Wonder call his next album, 'Ol' No-Eyes Is Back'. We didn't laugh at that one. Then I remembered that he was from Homicide, so I laughed just a little bit. There was a silence. To fill it, I decided to ask a question.

'Why d'ya pick weird places to record?' I asked. My voice sounded a bit funny, so I splashed down some rye to loosen my tonsils. 'Where ya gonna do the next one? Iceland?'

'We're doing the next one at Caribou again. We've taken five weeks' studio time, and I'm going to write the songs on the boat going over. I'm taking a boat and doing a Bowie. I didn't think anybody travelled on those things any more, which is why I'm going. I think they're scrapping them. All the songs will be written on the boat, so the next album's going to be called "Hello Sailor" — little ditties like "Never Throw Into The Wind" . . . "I was dancing the cha-cha in the ballroom and I chucked up all over the captain" — who said I can't write lyrics? I haven't done it yet, actually. Every time I pluck up the courage to write something it just sounds like a heap of crap. "Solar Prestige A Gammon" was my idea. I love it, because I always suggest things that Bernie Taupin's going to get knifed in the back for.'

Now I knew the interrogation was a flop. How can you grill a mug who just talks you to death? I hadda do something — fast. 'Get serious, kid,' I told him. 'Give us what we want and I might untie one of your hands.' I cut him loose and he winced as the circulation started coming back. The clock was ticking and I knew Webb was on her way, so I put two slugs through the clock to stop that goddam ticking that was getting on my nerves and driving me crazy. As the smoke cleared I hit him with another question. 'Rock and roll today,' I said, bitterly, 'has a history, a tradition. It has set itself precedents. It no longer can claim the freshness and naïvety that was its hallmark even as far back as the dawn of the sixties. Whaddya gotta say to that, punk?'

'It was completely spontaneous and naïve, y'know? Things weren't done for a purpose. Now everything's calculated, and management says, "You must do this, you must wear that, and you're not doing any interviews because you're going to do a moody for six months." People didn't do that in the old days because they were just in it for the fun. Everybody would get in one big coach and just drive around. You don't get that any more, because it's all egos and moodies and managers and solicitors and accountants.'

The guy was loose. He even owned up that 'Jolene' by Dolly Parton was Bernie Taupin's favourite record of all time, which made me feel a little better about Bernie Taupin. For that we try and get the heat off him for a little while. 'In fact, Bernie's gone over to the States to meet her and Lynn Anderson.'

But, hell, we want the real stuff. The secrets. And I was gonna get them even if I couldn't leave anything behind. I hauled out the Luger again and tapped it meditatively against the top of his head. 'I'm dying of cancer and I've only got one lung,' he whimpered. Not good enough. 'People go through my trash cans for my old shoes and glasses and Rolls Royces.' Better. 'Are you horrible to your roadies, Elton?'

'I love them,' he smirked. 'I don't tie them up and beat them or anything. They tie me up and beat me. That's why I love them. No, I'm very nice to my roadies. Just the other day I gave one of them a winegum.

'I like your initials,' he said suddenly. He was raving again. That cheap truth serum never works. 'In fact, I love initials. I'm Elton John T.O.T. – tired old tart. Also W.I.N.O. AND J.U.N.K.I.E. The Strawbs are obviously on drugs – their last album was called 'Hero And Heroin'. And look at Quaalude Quaye – he's gone to America, actually. It's the best thing for him. He can play with musicians like Phil Upchurch. Send him back to Nigeria, that's what I say. We've got enough of 'em over here as it is.'

'Why not record a reggae band?' I asked just to calm him down.

'Yeah, I met Judge Dread at a football match and he said he had some really good stuff. So I bought an ounce. Watford scored as well. The whole team . . . reggae's great. That's the sort of stuff we would like to have put out. Have you seen any good bands lately? I saw the Band of the Royal Scots Guards recently and they were really good. No feedback or anything. No problems with the PA — great for open-air gigs. Why don't The Lovin' Spoonful get back together?'

'Well, The Fudge are back together,' I said feebly. He's out-babbled me. 'That means Jeff Beck's looking for a band again.'

'All existing musicians had better go and hide if Jeff's on the prowl,' he said. 'He's a really nice guy, though. We nearly worked together, actually rehearsed for a week at Camden Town Hall. He actually approached us and asked to join, before we'd had any success in the States. We were still playing places like the Speak-easy. I was totally mind-boggled by the whole thing. This was just after he'd had that two-year lay-off. We had rehearsals which went fine, but he wanted to chuck out my bass player and drummer, and things would've disintegrated and I would have ended up as Jeff Beck's pianist. He said, "Seeing as how I've got a big name in the States, I'll take 90 per cent and you and the rest of the lads can have 10 per cent between you," and that put us off a bit. But he's a nice guy. I always say hello to him everytime I see him, and he still cleans my shoes every day.

'The funny thing is that we were still being managed by Dick James at the time, and we sat in his office and said, "We got this chance to go with Jeff Beck, it'll mean five or ten thousand dollars a night" and Dick said, "Listen, if you play the Troubador in LA you'll be earning that much in two months, I guarantee it." And we said, "Dick, you fool, these things take time." And then in two months' time we're in the States earning five thousand a night — I just didn't believe it. Dick was right. He qualified for the Treasure Trail and so did we. And look where it got us.'

The time was drawing near, and there wasn't much time left. Stevens had gotten me a delay, but Julie Webb and the Homicide Squad were closing in. I only had time for one more question. 'What,' I said quietly, though my guts were beginning to churn, 'made you the star you are today, Elton?'

He grinned up at me. I don't know how he managed it, but he smiled through the blood on his lips and whispered, 'Vitamin E. Quaaludes. Heroin. Plus sexual intercourse with sheep.'

Then Webb arrived. The rest you know.

# Lee Hazelwood: 'Poet, Fool Or Bum' (Stateside)

*NME*, 13 July 1974

Bum.

# Frank Zappa: 'Frenk! Frenk! Ees Aynsley playeeng?'

*NME*, 5 October 1974

WHY is Stephen Stills not smiling?

To be more precise, why are those noble, rugged features sporting an expression roughly equivalent to that of a man whose ankles are being attacked by a flotilla of evil-minded piranhas? Why, for that matter, is he wearing a green velvet jacket?

Why – if you really want to get down into the meat of the matter – is he present at Frank Zappa's tenth anniversary party in this ludicrous Paris nightclub – especially since when he once got up to jam with The Mothers, the band went into their parody version of 'Suite: Judy Blue Eyes'. You know – the one with the jokes about Elliott Roberts' big bank book and Joni Mitchell's autographed picture and Crosby flushing his stash down the john. And what about those 'three unreleased recordings of Crosby, Stills, Nash and Young fighting in the dressing-room at the Fillmore East' on The Mothers' 'Fillmore East/June '71' album?

Never mind. Stephen Stills is here and that is all that *really* matters. C'mon, Stephen. Get up there and play the drums. This is gonna be a *great party*. After all, didn't Zappa stalk over to our table and say, 'Herbie set all this up. Blame him'? Didn't Herbie Cohen, Zappa's manager, say that he saw rehearsals that afternoon and that it was gonna be *really weird*? Didn't the guy from

61

Warner and his Brothers say that this whole deal was costing no less than – wait for it – £30,000?

So who are all these people present to help Francis Vincent Zappa (or 'F.Z.' as he likes to refer to himself these days) celebrate ten years of Mothering? Well, some of them are movie people'n some of them are *fashion* people'n some of them are from the French rock press'n some of them just seem to be the type of liggers who show up at parties in fancy duds and cluster in corners murmuring. 'Yes, but is Bianca coming?'

Frank, are you kidding? Who you jivin' with that chic debris? I mean, could you have ever taken Jimmy Carl Black or Ray Collins to a party like this?

Herbie was right about the show. It is *weird and a half*. The place is called the Alcazar, and the evening's entertainment is a kind of acrobatic-musical-sexual-satirical cabaret with a cast of thousands. Every so often the waiters – all nattily accoutred in 'DiscReet' T-shirts – quit hauling round the champagne and bound onto the stage for a quick chant and prance. Meanwhile, the regular cast – who seem able to switch make-up and set within seconds – scamper through a succession of sketches, parodies and musical production numbers. An angel flaps around for a few seconds and vanishes, an aerialiste does a few swift undulations around a trapeze, Mae West, The Andrews Sisters, Barbra Streisand and Sylvie Vartan are mimicked, and the whole thing is spiced up with *plenty of tit*. Periodically a sign reading 'Welcome Zappa' is flashed overhead. Suddenly, with the velocity of a striking poodle, Uncle Frank himself is on the stage, looking more scarecrow-orientated than ever, his hair longer than it's been since 'Hot Rats' days, dipping and wheeling through a deadpan tango right there with the cast.

So get up, Stephen! Play the *drums* already!

Eventually, of course, it all arrives at the big finish (whose name, naturally, is Oscar) and Frank, sneer at a rakish angle, descends smoothly from the ceiling in a setting that would have made Busby Berkeley ejaculate over the boards.

Chicks in scanty arrangements of sequins and feathers posing all over the place – guys in scanty arrangements of sequins and feathers posing all over the place – animals in scanty arrangements of sequins and feathers posing all over the place – Stephen Stills in a scanty arrangement of . . .

It sho' hadda lotta class.

... Which is considerably more than anybody could say about the Palais de Sport on a drizzly Friday afternoon. For a start, the place is ringed with cops. Cops by the vanload, exuding enough Gallic cool to freeze an eskimo's nostrils, cops standing around looking vaguely menacing and firing off fusillades of dirty looks at the scruffy hordes who're already hanging around outside. On a nearby wall is defiantly emblazoned 'Music populaire – music libre', and at a recent concert at this selfsame hall there was a riot of fairly impressive proportions, firebombs were chucked in through windows and a couple of people got offed.

Still, who's going to leap a barrier and fight their way past security guards to get their hands onto Frank Zappa's bod? This concert costs 30 francs, which is roughly three quid, and even by soundcheck time the faithful are already there.

The only trouble is that the soundcheck ain't. The gear was six hours late attempting to struggle its way through customs, and the band end up frantically pitching in and setting up their own stuff while the roadies set up the mixer and cart the PA onto the stage. Even F.Z. himself can be seen on his knees sticking gaffers' tape onto the wires leading from his pedals to his amp.

Let's leave Frank sitting on a box near his Marshall cabinet and take a look around the stage. That sensuous figure in the black T-shirt and white pants gonging experimentally on a marimba could surely be none other than Ruth Underwood, wife of the celebrated saxophone whipper-outer and currently appearing in The Mothers without her old man.

Key quote: 'Ruth is a-*mazing*. When Jean-Luc Ponty and her ol' man Ian were in the band she felt overshadowed by those cats. Now she's makin' those cats look *saaaaaad*.' – Napoleon Murphy Brock, later that same night.

Napoleon Murphy Brock? Who, you may well be asking, is Napoleon Murphy Brock? Get this, NMB is the black guy over there with the saxophone and the flute and the moustache. He is The Mothers' latest lead singer, and Frank discovered him in a Hawaiian nightclub leading a Top 40 soul band. At the end of the set, Napoleon was summoned to the presence.

'I said, "Who is Frank Zappa?" They told me he was the leader of The Mothers. I said, "Oh, *right*. He's the guy who has his picture taken sittin' on the toilet."'

63

So Frank told Napoleon that he'd like him to join The Mothers and leave the following week on a European tour. Napoleon turned him down because he and his group had been booked into the nightclub for another seven weeks and told Zappa to call him when he got back. He ended up joining the band, playing sax and singing backup on 'Apostrophe' and graduating to lead singer of the touring band.

So that's Napoleon. He will be back later on in the show, ladies and gentlemen. Behind drums is Chester Thompson, about whom little information is currently available. Relevant piece of information: in the previous incarnation of The Mothers, there were two drummers. The other, Ralph Humphrey, proved superfluous.

Next exhibit is Tom Fowler on bass. With his medium-length hair, floppy moustache and nondescript clothes, he's a little short of visual thrills, but he pegs down the bottom end as cute as you please. Next along is George Duke, who's been a Mother on and off for three or four years and has a couple of solo albums on the jazz charts. He's now playing synthesizer as well as clavinet and electric piano, and he's also doing a fair bit of singing and dialogue in addition to his other duties.

Then there's ... well, there's that skinny guy with the silly moustache who composes all this foolishness, and has just basked in the warmth of a Top Ten album, namely 'Apostrophe'. It is possibly the smallest touring line-up that Zappa has ever led, a mere spindly six pieces. The previous line-up also boasted an extra drummer, Don Preston, a rhythm guitarist, and two more horn players. This version is playing essentially the same parts, but it sounds a lot cleaner and less cluttered.

Anyway, Frank is just beginning to get the sound he wants out of Chester Thompson's drums when the Visigoths descend screaming from the mountains. Migawd, they've ... *let the kids in.* Right in the middle of the soundcheck.

Of course, one of them zooms right down to the front and starts leaning over the barriers shouting '*Frenk! Frenk!*' at the God-mother, who is sitting on his box puffing morosely on a Winston, doodling on his guitar and no doubt wondering what a person such as himself could say to a vegetable. 'Frenk! Frenk!' the young fellow howls in irresistibly piteous tones. 'Ees *Aynsley* playeeng?'

Frank gives him the old headshake routine and he wanders away looking all disconsolate and gets down to the evening's real heavy business, which consists of getting blasted. Honestly, kids, I cannot recall ever having seen (or smelt) so much cannabis being consumed at an indoor concert in all my entire chickenscratchin'acetastin'motivatin' life. The air was thick with the reek of the foul stuff. All over the place, the delicate, soothing sound of Zappa shouting at his sound engineers was drowned by the insistent rustle of cigarette papers. Even after the band had sorted out their sound and quit the stage, the auditorium was periodically briefly lit by a cigarette lighter cooking up some hash. Behind me, one little devil was snorting an illicit substance. Either that or he had a filthy cold and should have stayed home in bed taking aspirins.

A li'l ol' lady comes trotting by with a tray fluting, *Chocolats! Chocolats!* Halfway down the front row she passes this scraggy-looking guy who closely resembles the 'John Wesley Harding' period Dylan. His pitch is 'Hashish! Hashish!' The number of stops he's making at 100 francs a time show that there's clearly money to be made in this field of endeavour by an enterprising young man with his wits about him.

What makes the whole deal so delightfully incongruous (apart from Zappa's widely publicized loathing for all drugs except Winstons, coffee and saxophones) is that police cordon around the hall. Outside, the fuzz in force. Inside, kids jumping up and down gleefully waving chillums. Dashed clever, these Frogs.

Cutting all this acute sociological observation stuff short, let's flash forward to the Actual Performance and zero in on a tune entitled 'Approximate'. 'It is called "Approximate",' announces Frank in his most pedagogic manner, 'because while the rhythm is specified, the notes are not. It will be performed for you in three sections. The first with instruments, the second with the human voice and the third with the human foot.'

He is as good as his word. After a moderately deranged performance of 'Approximate' (assuming that that was what it in fact was), Fowler and Brock stashed their axes and approached the microphone. 'Come up front, Ruth, and let the people get off on your vibes,' commanded Zappa, his moustache twitching ferociously in the cool night air. (My theory is that a breeze was blowing from the audience towards the stage and that Zappa was unintentionally getting stoned, but that's as may be. 'Get down, Ruth!' Ms Underwood complies smilingly, and then the ensemble runs through the piece vocally. They then return to their instruments and perform it again, this time in complete silence.

This was one of the few incidences of yerractual Mothers craziness that took place in the set. Of course, there was Zappa's ballet with Brock during 'Redonzo'; a graphic demonstration of the mating habits of a small cowbell (wielded by Ms Underwood) and a large one (wielded by F.Z.); a demonstration of how F.Z.'s characteristic style of conducting can gradually inflate itself into a full-blown Mime Sequence (see Broughton E., Bowie D., Marceau M., etc.); and a continuous stream of visual jive from the extravagant Brock to keep things from getting too serious. F'rinstance, at one point Zappa announced that George Duke would play a piano solo, at which point Duke launched into a monologue about a one-night stand with a Voodoo Queen, embellished with assorted snorks and cackles from the synthesizer.

Apart from hot flushes of 'Dog Breath', 'It Can't Happen Here' and a few other choice goodies from the olden days, the set principally consisted of the kind of stuff that Zappa's been serving up on 'Apostrophe', 'Over-nite Sensation' and now 'Roxy And Elsewhere'; i.e. jokey little songs with lyrics about dirty feet, Sears ponchos, dental floss, phoney gurus and mistreated arctic fowl, set to a kind of souped-up 'Hot Rats' instrumental sound and garlicked up with loads of guitar solos. Brock's manic saxophone, stylized soul vocals and demented stage capering serve to lighten things up slightly, and as long as he's involved Zappa could well write some slightly heavier songs. As it is, F.Z. seems way too firmly stuck into his current little niche for comfort.

Apart from his recent little contretemps with the Massed Promoters of London, Zappa is: (a) ignoring most of the rest of the rock world ('I only listen to rock and roll records for purposes of research. Black Sabbath have one song that's real good. It's called "Supernaut". I also like Harry Chapin's "W.O.L.D.", and Mott The Hoople have three songs on their last album that I like a whole lot'); (b) unhappy with the rigmarole of having to talk to dumb journalists who don't know what 12-tone is, can't read music and don't even know how wide recording tape is; (c) at work on a new and unspecified movie project and (d) still dressing funny. Over supper, he was treated to the uncommon spectacle of three journalists all trying to conduct different kinds of interviews. There's an amiable young fellow from the *Evening News* asking questions like 'Do you consider yourself to be an anarchist, Frank?' and yours truly getting all historically orientated and trying to ferret out bits of interesting info about past aspects of Motherlore. As a result the conversation gets irreparably fragmented.

Hey, Frank – how's project XS going? You know – that satirically orientated heavy metal glam band that Mike Des Barres was talking about some while back?

'That project has been cancelled ever since that guy started talking about it in the press.'

Michael, what hast thou wrought?

'He was talking about doing an album and a tour before I'd even auditioned him. I just heard about him from his girlfriend and talked to him on the phone, and it was a really dumb, punkish thing to do to start talking about it. Anyway, that project has now been dropped.'

Whew.

Other tidbits unearthed during the rest of the conversation will be incorporated into a fairly extensive programme of Zappa features planned by the author in conjunction with Ian MacDonald and presented for your reading pleasure in the near future, so for the time being let us return to Napoleon Murphy Brock, who's sitting in a hotel room clutching a glass of vodka and orange juice discoursing on the True Zappa.

'Everybody thinks that Frank Zappa is really way out there, but he ain't. He's just totally down to earth. You know that song "Stinkfoot"? It's just . . . you know that when you're wearing a pair of tennis shoes, no air gets into them and when you take 'em off people just go, "What is *that?*" That's all that that song is about. To understand Frank, you just have to go for the simplest meaning in any lyric and you'll be right there.'

Flashback to the previous night's party and Zappa explaining the absence of Ruth Underwood by informing the assembly that 'Ruth's back in the hotel in the bath with her legs up against the wall.'

'What I *meant*,' elucidates Zappa at the supper-table, 'was that Ruth's *mind* was in the bath. With its legs apart.'

# Alex Harvey:
# 'Ah wuz framed'

*NME*, 19 October 1974

'THE situation is this. My life's ambition would be to get to the point where if somebody came up to me an' smashed me in the side of the face, I would have the strength and the bottle and be big enough to turn my head and say, "Have another go."'

'I've done it already . . . a couple of times.'

How did it feel?

'Glorious. I did that once with a kid that I could have *destroyed*. Big boy; strong, angry . . . wi' his bird, and he smashed me. He was wide open. His kidneys were hanging all over the place, his balls were everywhere. Without any undue sweat, I coulda made it very painful for him. Didn't. Felt proud. When I was much younger I took a coupla liberties, busted a few guys and felt good. But what have you got? You've got a geezer lyin' on the ground clutching himself, crying, mouth all bloody, in pain . . . and you're sayin', "I'm Leonardo da Vinci and this is my handiwork. There's a guy lyin' there, God, and I'm big and brave. I won." There's no glory there. None.'

Alex Harvey has a problem. It's a problem that many other bands would be overjoyed to have, and many more are currently courting it. Put simply, the problem is that the Sensational Alex Harvey Band's street-gang persona has actually convinced too many people.

It's left them convinced even after the show's over, when the kids are catching that last tube home. Things have reached the pitch where Alex is having to undermine his act by telling the audience that the Harvey team are not a violent band.

Can there really be such a thing as *too much credibility*?

Clearly so, but along the way Harvey's band have gone from Marquee level to Rainbow level in two years, from if-this-one-don't-make-it-the-next-one-will reviews to more than comfortable sales for the new album – all achieved for a variety of reasons.

Like the band play good and look good; like the fact that Alex Harvey will do just about anything legal that he can think of if it'll get the audience off; like the fact that they just naturally have a knack of vibing into things that their audiences can identify — plus the big one, the killer, the $64,000 bonus point: they come on like they mean it.

Even when Alex does his Mickey Spillane routine or sings about Sergeant Fury, then it's an honest fantasy, the fantasy of a real person who's letting his Walter Mitty out for a trot around the stage, and not just the latest instalment of somebody's pose-of-the-month club.

But when Harvey puts on his leather jacket and busts through his polystyrene wall to announce that he was framed, *no one believes him.*

The character he's playing when he sings that song is so patently a villain (an incompetent clown of a villain, true enough; but a villain none the less) that his protestations of innocence are merely comic. Sure he did it, man, just look at him. No way he was framed. And at a time when rock and roll is as much fantasy fodder as it is anything else, right the way from Harvey as gangboss to ELP as prototypes for the New Cybernetic Technological Man, face value is what makes it.

The Harvey audience after the London Palladium show the other week was strange as hell. It isn't often that you feel a genuinely violent aura from a British audience. 20,000 New York kids squashed into Madison Square Garden for Alice Cooper or Humble Pie is one thing, and the worshipful messianic hysteria of a Bowie gig is another, but there's an intensity and tension at a Harvey gig which is sump'n else again, a whole other ball game. If Alex's crowd control instinct wasn't so sharp, things could very well get chaotic.

Still, that's getting a trifle morbid. It ain't happened yet, and if A. Harvey Esq. has anything to do with it, it never will. Harvey ain't a hard nut. He has been, and if he wanted to he could be again, but getting pegged as one pisses him off.

'I reckon it's all related to sex. Stickin' a bayonet into somebody, or shootin' someone with a Spandau, is the same thing as taking a woman to bed. For one kind of mentality, copulation an' liquidation are both different ends of the stick. Most people who wanna be a hard nut just for the sake of it are terrible lays. I've had some of their women and it turns out like that. They have to prove they're *men*, when they don't have to. Who wants to *prove* it? It's like the geezers who have to find queers and bash them. In my family there's a couple of mercenaries – fought in the Yemen and the Congo . . .'

On which side?

'Money. They have this thing about being a man of arms. On the street where I was brought up, a hard nut was what everybody wanted to be – a hard case. People'd say, "He's a hard citizen" and that was like sayin' he's top of the pops, man. That was the ultimate. My grandfather wasn't like that. He was a pacifist in the First World War, and he was in the same cell as Shinwell – who later became Churchill's Minister of War. Both of them were conscientious objectors at the same time. Ain't *that* a turn-up? I often wish I'd picked his brain more, because he was a clever man. He once told me that when he was inside they hosed him down and his friend died – whether they killed him or not is beside the point – and this Special Branch sergeant bust all his teeth out with a cane. I was about fourteen or fifteen when he told me that, and I was *boilin*'. He said, "Don't you realize, that man didn't *understand*." But when he left the prison, that man came up to him and shook his hand and said, "You're a man!" Prison guards and policemen and soldiers deserve more sympathy than anybody else.'

Talk switches to the Windsor festival, and the recent débâcle there. Harvey can't get over the fact that 'the young policemen – kids of twenty or twenty-one – looked so happy.

'Music has got to have something to do with it. The powers-that-be originally didn't want rock to be a Power. Whether you like it or not, anybody who's involved in rock and roll is involved in politics. Anything that involves a big crowd of people listening to something you say is politics. Mebbe politics is out of date. Politicians don't know a *light*! See these men – I don't dislike them – but when I see these poor men, Wilson and Heath, walking about and blustering and saying, "We'll do this and we'll do that" with their silly suits on – they're a hundred years out of date. They've got nothing to do with what's going on.

'I'd rather see Ian Hunter in charge of the lifeboat, 'cuz at least I can trust his motives.

'Their ideas of what people are – especially young people – is absolutely nowhere. How dare they set themselves up and tell me – and I'm nearly forty – that they know how to conduct my life.

What they've got in their minds is an old form of government that used to work when we could send a gunboat up the river and put down the darkies.

'I don't think it's possible now for any human being to be in charge. Look at poor Nixon; he ain't the only one. I reckon the only way it can be done now is something along these lines: get a computer, and instead of voting, everybody gets a list of ten priorities. Check 'em off in order and feed 'em into the computer and let it work it out.

'How many leaders were there in history who got it right? I love history — it's my complete absorbing hobby. Two things I found out from studying history. Nobody ever won a war. A hundred thousand dead at Waterloo. No glory in that. Nobody needs that.

'There was a great thing happened in 1967 — flower-power. The media rubbed that out. Julius Caesar said it, "Divide and conquer."'

Half past four in the morning in a hotel room in Bradford. Harvey's drinking vodka. Despite dire warnings from S. Pokesman (played tonight by Simon Puxley) about how nobody ever sells out Bradford and how it was generally one of the all-time horrible gig situations and how no one ever sold out Bradford and couldn't I make it to one of the other gigs and a whole bunch of stuff like that.

What actually happened was that Alex and his cohorts packed the place out and pulled two encores with no trouble at all. The SAHB's set is always fresh and alive, because Harvey is a compulsive improviser. While the sequence and structure of the set remains constant, he can never resist the temptation to throw in a new schtick of some sort. During the Mickey Spillane bit in 'The Man In The Jar', he puffed theatrically on a cigarette; a chance conversation with the author over dinner resulted in a new verse about Linda Lovelace being inserted (if you'll pardon the expression) into 'Sergeant Fury'. The fact that the show is never performed by remote control helps keep it all plugged in to Main Audience Outlet.

In particular, Harvey's curtain-raiser is his masterstroke. Hands clasped behind his back, features contorted into that *beezzarre* snarl/grin of his, he saunters out into the spotlight like some psychotic ringmaster and calmly announces the band, who then

71

slip onstage and paste the living crap out of 'The Faith Healer'. In terms of pacing, staging and dynamics, it's one of the slickest things currently happening on the British rock stage.

Only one false note is struck, both musically and ideologically, and that is when the band perform Alice Cooper's 'School's Out'. After concentrating exclusively on the personality of Alex Harvey (or, to be fair, the collective personality of the SAHB), it seems an unnecessary and in fact outright unpleasant mental wrench to suddenly have to think about Alice Cooper.

On a more visceral level, the song seems out of keeping in terms of Harvey's own philosophical position. Alice Cooper operates on the basis of the old paradox: 'You can't believe anything I'm saying because I never tell the truth.' Which means that if the statement is true, then by making an accurate statement he's contradicted himself, and if he's lying, then he's telling the truth, in which case he's lying. Dig it? Everything that Cooper does is filtered through the psychotic, completely unreliable Cooper persona, and therefore any position that he happens to take up is admittedly a pose and/or a fraud.

Therefore, the quite serious anarchistic/revolutionary sentiments of the song are defused by the fact that Alice Cooper's singing it, and we all know what a liar Alice is. But when Harvey — who Means It and is Committed and has Integrity and Credibility 'n' all that hoopla — sings it, then its philosophy has to be taken seriously. And while he's probably agreed wholeheartedly that the educational system of this country is totally screwed up, I don't think that he'd consider blowing up school buildings any kind of viable solution.

I've just spent several paragraphs discussing Alice Cooper in what's supposed to be an Alex Harvey piece, which illustrates fairly basically why he shouldn't be playing 'School's Out'. Still, the band play it okay and kids really dig it, so, if so desired, file under 'pissing-in-the-wind'.

'Framed' and 'The Man In The Jar' are by now time-honoured Harvey set-pieces, but Alex pulled off some sort of masterstroke on 'Anthem', the encore. As the band settle down into the repeated melody line, Vicky Silva, a small, elfin lady in a satin dress trots out onstage and starts singing along with it while Alex prowls the stage, arms extended and raised in his best 'Next' album cover pose. Dry ice begins to seep from the sides of the stage and . . . are you ready for this? . . . two pipers in full regalia wander out and join in. The audience sway entranced along with it all and Alex climbs up on top of a monitor speaker and blissfully conducts it all along. A *coup de théâtre* of massive proportions. Excelsior, Bradford.

And up in the hotel room, Harvey reverses the flow of the discussion. 'You tell me this. Answer a question for me, now. For a while, I thought that I represented a kind of uncle/father/big brother figure to a lot of these kids. Now I don't know . . . if I knew, I'd be able to do it better. I'm show-business conscious, you know that? What are these kids getting out of me? I don't lie to them. I don't tell them I'm twenty-eight or thirty-four – I'm thirty-nine, I'll be forty next birthday. *So what do I represent?*'

So it goes at five in the morning. And, incidentally, it says a lot about Alex Harvey as a human being that he both admits to being uncertain and is prepared to ask. Most rock stars would just tell you what they're about and expect to be taken at face value.

So what *does* Harvey represent? First of all, he's – as he makes no attempt to conceal – old enough to be the father of most of his fans, and to many of them he's the first member of his generation who's made the slightest public attempt to understand them and sympathize with them. Also, he makes no concessions to chic. He doesn't hang out with Andy Warhol, he doesn't hang out with Elizabeth Taylor. His persona is wholly Street. His turf and the audience's is one and the same.

Of course, qualities like this can't exist in a vacuum. Without a kick-ass rock and roll band, a bunch of fine songs and Harvey's faultless instinctive showmanship, none of it would be happening. After all, a rock audience's first and most essential motivation for paying out its shekels is the desire to rock and stomp 'til midnight and just righteously get off.

Right from those early Marquee days, Harvey did just that. Even before he met up with his current band, he'd play the *NME* Free Nights at the Marquee in late '71 and early '72 with just a rhythm section and get more and more people in each time. Then he met Tear Gas, a Scots 'progressive' band (remember 'progressive music'? Oh, well) and The SAHB was born. Started out playing the clubs, outgrew them, moved into the halls. Played the London Palladium. They must be doing something right.

So now kids are showing up to gigs in striped T-shirts just like his – a distinct recognizable Alex Harvey costume, and it's dead cheap and looks natural on just about anybody – and shouting, 'Alex! Alex!' and when he scuttles up onto that platform over the drums, whips out that spray-can of black paint and lovingly inscribes 'Vambo Rool' on the brick-look wallpaper that covers the polystyrene, the reaction from the audience is astounding. It isn't so much that they cheer, it's the sudden release of collective tension, the instant identification.

To put it as crudely and basically as possible, what Alex has done has taken the show to the audience. For better or for worse, he hasn't so much created some huge, epic super-spectacular and laid it on a stage before them as built his whole show around them. We see Alex living through his life in the street environment, grooving on his fantasies of gangster movies, comic-book heroes and – in the extraordinary production number of Fred Astaire's 'Dancing Cheek To Cheek' that they performed at the Palladium – Hollywood musicals. *That* is what 'The Impossible Dream' signifies in the environment that Harvey built for it. To live the street life and still survive both physically and spiritually – is this an Impossible Dream?

Alex Harvey shouldn't be singing 'School's Out'. Alice Cooper should sing 'Vambo Marble Eye'.

# George Harrison: 'Ding Dong' (Apple)

*NME*, 14 December 1974

SOME people are born dull. Some achieve dullness and others have dullness thrust upon them. I should imagine that some of you have already perused the lyrics of this trite little ballad, as presented in Harrison's ad. last week. Repetitive, you may have thought. Blindingly uninspired, you may have murmured to yourself. Well lemme tellya – until you've actually sat in the presence of this horrific object, you ain't heard n-n-nnuthin' yet. I have rarely heard a drabber melody, a more vacuous set of lyrics, a cornier production, a more lacklustre vocal or a less inspired song concept. No matter how twee McCartney became, how dumb Ringo seemed or what a Kozmic Klutz Lennon made of himself, no other ex-Moptop has ever sunk to these depths. It is quite possible that many people will find 'Ding Dong' spiritually uplifting. It is possible – nay, probable – that this hideous piece of garf will become a big hit.

# Albert King: 'I Wanna Get Funky' (Stax)

*NME*, 15 February 1975

'I WANNA Get Funky' is the best album I've heard all year.

If you want to get technical, that makes it the best album I've heard in six weeks, but the principle remains the same, i.e. it's great.

It's generally accepted that Albert King's last worthwhile album was 'Live Wire/Blues Power', which was six or seven years ago.

It's taken all this time for him to achieve a genuine return to greatness, masterminded by the Stax backroom mob and aided/ abetted by The Bar-Kays, The Movement, Hot, Buttered And Soul, The Memphis Horns, The Memphis Symphony Orchestra and a genius rhythm guitarist named Donald Kenzie.

The way he's done it is to achieve the best synthesis of modern smoothie soul and rough-edged urban blues that I've ever heard. It pulls off everything that B.B. King has been attempting on his last eight albums, and indeed represents the finest progressive statements in the blues field since B.B.'s 'Thrill Is Gone' five years ago.

He's used most of Isaac Hayes' musicians on this album, and adapted many of old chromedome's techniques, but by singing in time-honoured A. King fashion and playing his usual fluid, sweet-biting, thrifty guitar, he's totally altered the context and the perspective.

For a start, he makes 'em all jump a hell of a lot more than Big Ike ever did, and despite the plush 747 arrangements and deluxe production, he still keeps the mood way down in the alley.

Probably the album's most totally captivating moment is on a reworked version of his 1965 R&B hit 'Crosscut Saw' (the arrangement of which was lifted by Electric Flag for their version of Howlin' Wolf's 'Killing Floor' and Led Zep for 'Lemon Song').

He kicks it off *à la* seventies, switches halfway through to the original arrangement, blows a few choruses of exquisite guitar and then switches back. Real memory lane stuff for R&B freaks with memories that go back further than Barry White.

The track that could be a disco breakout if it gets the plays is 'I Can't Hear Nothin' But The Blues', the album's most moving selection and the ultimate justification, if any were needed, for the whole project.

King's singing is genuinely poignant, his guitar playing is a triumph of combined emotion, precision and timing, and the arrangement contrives to be sumptuous without ever relying on overstatement.

There's all kindsa stuff along with all of that; the mesmerically swaying title song, an instrumental with spoken jive called 'Flat Tire', an almost excruciating but saved-by-the-bell exercise in White/Hayes mumbling territory entitled "Til My Back Ain't Got No Bone', and several other hunks of marrow-enriched wonderment.

The dearth of good blues albums released in recent years has been exceeded only by the profusion of lame soul albums, so it's doubly pleasurable to be treated to a record that makes out just fine in both leagues. Allow me to recommend 'I Wanna Get Funky' without any reservations whatsoever.

The cover, by the way, depicts Albert wreathed in pipe-smoke and sporting a mammoth pair of headphones, calmly picking away at an upside-down Strat, which seems to have replaced the Gibson Flying V that he's been toting for the last fifteen years.

He doesn't have to sing 'I Wanna Get Funky'. He just *is*.

# LaBelle:
# 'Voulez-vous coucher
# avec moi ce soir?'

*NME*, 8 March 1975

'THE re-vo-lu-shun . . . will *not* be televaaaaaazed,' declaims Patti LaBelle, staring into the audience from the stage of the Congresgebouw in The Hague.

An audience which, due to Holland's large West Indian community, is almost one third black and duded up to the nines in a credible reproduction of American superfly street chic; an audience pulled in by posters emblazoned with the enticing legend 'LaBelle – Voulez-vous couchez avec moi ce soir?' and by the fact that 'Lady Marmalade', the song that contains that line, is number one in Holland.

Patti sends a quick searchlight glance raking around the theatre, hand on hip, taunting half-smile, head on one side checking out the machine-gun rattle of the congas behind her to make sure the accents are coming together right. Fourteen years on the road and enough dues paid for any sixteen people you care to name, doesn't miss a trick. Deep breath.

'You will not be able to stay *home*, bruthaaaaa . . .' Taunting inflection on the last two words. 'You will not be able to plug in, turn on and cop out, you will *not* be able to lose yourself on scaaaaaag, because the revolution will not be televaaaaaaazed!' She turns her back on the audience and struts towards the back of the stage into a storm of drums, congas and bass as Sarah Dash, glossy-faced, bare-stomached and silver-winged, moves forward to knife home the next line.

Once upon a time, it was Patti LaBelle and The Bluebelles in beehive wigs and evening gowns, playing 'Somewhere Over The Rainbow' and 'Danny Boy' for peanuts, living off one hit ('I Sold My Heart To The Junkman') in the jungle-telegraph network of scuzzy soul clubs known as the 'chitlin circuit'; getting treated like animals in the South; ripped off, pissed off, crapped on, spiralling perpetually downwards over years and years of playing nonsense music that they didn't care about; sitting still for all kinds of jive, getting older and getting nowhere: unplanned obsolescence and a palpable stink of futility and uselessness. Ultimately, neither cared about nor caring.

Now it's 1975 (okay?) and Patti LaBelle and The Bluebelles, losers, are now LaBelle, winners, the salvation of those of us who've been estranged from soul music by years of drowning in Philly soft cheese, or Barry White-ed into indifference, and the darlings of the chic gay crowd who think they're absolutely *divine* because they may be women but they know how to *dress*.

LaBelle don't play nuthin' but hard core soul and rock and roll. They preach a gospel of re-vo-lu-shun and funky sex in voices that drip neon pussyjuice and incandescent silver sweat, and they put on a glittery theatrical show that instantly negates any charges of effeteness or pusillanimity, simply because the energy level is so goddam high that LaBelle could light up half of London during the next power cut simply by hooking up a mike to the generator and singing into it.

In other words, they got themselves a thing going, Jack!

That's what they are. Who they are is Patti LaBelle, Sarah Dash and (fanfare please, maestro!) Nona Hendryx.

Patti's the lead singer, one of those fire-breathing motor-cycle black madonnas who're proving that the dominant energy in current black music is coming from the women. When she's not LaBelle-ing, she's Mrs Patricia Louise Edwards, mother of a two-year-old child and wife of a Philadelphia schoolteacher who gets well uptight when referred to as 'Mr LaBelle'.

'He ain't hangin' on my coat-tails — no way. All he's hangin' on to are my good vibrations (*sotto voce*) and some of the bad ones, too.' Patti digs being Mrs Edwards, but she also digs being Patti LaBelle. She ain't jive, but she knows how to.

Moving left across the stage, we find Sarah Dash, who is — you should pardon the expression — a rilly wonderful human being. Quiet, self-contained, amiable, seemingly unscathed by the decade-plus of horrible treatment that she went through in LaBelle's previous incarnation, totally open, v. trusting. She's the one who sings the high backup parts. Introduced on stage as 'silver throat', when she puts her head back and really opens up her throat, you get notes so brain-frazzlingly pure that you can almost

78

see them shining out of her mouth as if she had a spotlight in her larynx. Charm incarnate, girl next door.

Then there's Nona Hendryx. Visually, she's easily the most stunning member of LaBelle. Classic eyes-and-cheekbones face, slightly buck teeth, pendulous lower lip. Onstage, she wears the most outrageous clothes. Against Patti's straightforward thigh-boots and jump-suit and Sarah's Hawaiian-influenced hula-dancer drag, Nona wears a white cat-suit with a sequinned triangle at the crotch – symbolic pubic hair – and as the final weird-me-'til-my-back-ain't-got-no-bone touch, a pair of silver handcuffs dangling at her belt.

Nona also writes songs, and her material makes up two thirds of the group's act. Her songs are voraciously, aggressively sensual, bursting at the seams with energy. Nice chunes, too (although 'Nightbird', possibly her most celebrated song, uses the first few bars of Neil Young's 'Don't Let It Bring You Down' as its springboard). Though she's the least interesting vocalist of the three, she probably contributes more than either Sarah or Patti to the basic conceptual architecture of the band.

Which is as good a place as any to haul Vicki Wickham into the picture. Tall, bleach-blonde, high-energy, English accent with American usage, she first encountered the girls (then including ex-Supreme Cindy Birdsong) in their previous incarnation when they came over to do *Ready Steady Go*. Ran into them again in 1970 in the States when she was working for Buddah, and got the transformation going by taking over as their manager, gradually metamorphosing what seemed like a thoroughly obsolete and washed-up girl group into the absolute outside edge of wild-eyed kamikaze glitter-soul: everything that a seventies soul act should be.

Hence LaBelle. It's taken five years or so under the new regime just to get it this far, with four albums on three different labels. It took a year just to get out of the old Patti LaBelle and The Bluebelles Atlantic contract.

Then they junked the wigs and gowns and got into denims and Afros, made the 'Moonshadow' album for Warners, moved to RCA for 'LaBelle' and 'Pressure Cookin'', and finally ended up with 'Nightbirds' on Epic, and we're more or less up to date; which brings us back to the Congresgebouw, and the Dutch West Indians and like that.

*

First of all, LaBelle's band wander onto the stage and play about ten minutes of mechanized funk. The house lights remain on, the audience guzzles away at ice-cream and beer, and roadies scuttle on and off.

The band's only honky, bassist Hector Seda, wanders out to the lip of the stage, connected to his amp by a too-short curly lead, like an astronaut space-walking away from the mother-ship. The band funk away rather remarkably until Kaptain Keyboards (Bud Ellison) leans into his mike and echoes a 'Right now at this tahm' routine and announces 'Sarah Dash . . . Nona Hendryx . . . Patti LaBelle . . . LABELLE!!'

WHOOM! On they come: Patti in a big silver jacket that sticks out at the back and gives her a rather unfortunate resemblance to a duck, Sarah in her Venusian go-go dancer outfit and Nona in a weird skin-tight silver effort that's ridged from crotch to neck and looks like the belly of some unearthly insect.

On the first number, the sound is fairly catastrophic and the lighting is something of a non-happener. In fact, the dominant effect is that of three hyperactive silvery figures scampering all over the stage playing hide-and-seek with the beat.

However, together it all cometh on the second number. Patti discards the jacket and the assembled company launches into a gorgeously intense funkification of Speedy Keen's 'Something In The Air', with some thrilling trade-offs between Patti's raw-nerved lead and Sarah and Nona's ethereal backups on the 'right nows'.

Just as you're settling into the groove – the soundmen have cleaned up their act considerably by now – the percussion switches into a hell-for-leather ride as Patti swaggers to the mike and peers out into the audience.

'The re-vo-lu-shun . . . will *not* be televaaaaaaazed . . .'

Which is more or less where we came in, with the inspired imagination-powered pole-vault from 'Something In The Air' to Gil Scott-Heron's 'The Revolution Will Not Be Televized' (originally performed by The Last Poets). The girls trade off stanzas, advancing to the mike, laying down a fast curve of street jive and then going back to struttin' while the band get their fingers into the meat and start stroking. It all builds up to a climactic point with Patti back up front.

'The revolu-shun will be no re-runs, sistahs 'n' bruthaaaaaaaaaaa' (her voice rising implacably in an impossible siren screech until a jerk of her hips cuts off the music).

'The re-vo-lu-shun' (mocking stage whisper) 'is goin' be laaaaah-hve' (pause) 'right now, right now . . .' and it's back into 'Something In The Air' for a stunning climax, with Patti lying on the stage and launching into a little homily about how noddin' out and sittin' on yo' ass ain't gettin' nobody *no* place — and out. Killer city. That duff opening is thoroughly eradicated.

From there it's into 'Are You Lonely', one of Nona's heaviest and most powerful songs; a superlative version of The Stones' 'Wild Horses'; plus this and that and then — off. House lights up. More beer, more ice-cream.

The reason for the break is that there's more costumes to be worn for the second half, but the transition is poorly handled. The only alternative would be to have the band playing for ten or fifteen minutes, but that has, according to Vicki Wickham, been attempted and discarded. So there's an intermission. Ho hum.

Meanwhile, back on stage, the band are doing another warm-up, only this time there's a strange object vaguely resembling a black Christmas tree parked behind the drums. Another five minutes of miscellaneous funk which gradually turns itself inside out and becomes the intro to 'Nightbirds', then the voice of Sarah Dash is heard floating around the theatre for a full couple of minutes before the Christmas tree suddenly turns around and reveals itself as Sarah.

Scarcely has the applause for this particular little *coup de théâtre* died down when a red light goes on at stage right, backlighting some kind of peacock-feather arrangement that hauls out a mike and starts singing like Nona Hendryx, and the two of them bounce the song around for a while until a third ostrich descends from the ceiling via some complex hydraulic set-up making Patti LaBelle noises.

By now things have risen to a pitch of sufficiently high fever quotient to pop the mercury out of any but the most stoical of thermometers. The three voices are dancing all over each other and the band is *cookin'*, but unless 'I think I'm stuck!' is part of the lyric of 'Nightbirds', then Patti's having herself a little bit of a problem. However, she soon gets free and joins Sarah and Nona up front.

From then on in there ain't no holding 'em. They power their way through the rest of their set (all of which apart from 'Something In The Air', 'The Revolution Will Not Be Televized' and

'Wild Horses' is from 'Nightbirds'), transmitting sheer energy by throat-power alone, though they don't exactly stand still while they're doing it. The band do their stuff and that's it. They don't blow it at all, though Seda's strolls to the front of the stage just look dumb when the girls are on, particularly when he nearly bumps into Patti.

When they do 'You Turn Me On', they stay with the 'I come like the pourin' rain each time you call my name/keep doin' what you're doin', what you're doin'' bit, just repeating it acappella until it becomes a sexual mantra of almost epic proportions. From there it's into a hammer-and-tongs version of 'Lady Marmalade', with a beautifully jive ending.

'Does everybody know what "voulez-vous coucher avec moi, ce soir?" means?' asks Patti, with a 'the devil made me do it' gleam in her eye.

One totally crazed black guy one third of the way back starts howling, 'Yeah! Yeah!'

'If there's anybody who *don't* know what it means,' she continues, 'I think I'm gonna have to do me some *educatin'* here. Now, does everybody know what it means?'

The Totally Crazed Black Guy abruptly changes his mind and yells, 'No! No!' Patti calls him up to the front and . . . well, you don't really want to know what happened next, do you?

Anyway, right now about this tahm, we come to the spot in our show where we get down and do the funky interview. Dateline: Hotel Pulitzer, Amsterdam. Timeline: around 11 a.m. on a Monday morning. Condition Line: grotesquely hung-over. Your reporter is in such a thoroughly hideous state that he doesn't trust himself to rub up against anything foodier than a large glass of orange juice.

'It was hard for me to make the change, but it was inevitable because it was necessary.' That, by the way, is Patti talking about The Change. 'We were going nowhere fast, because we were doing the same thing over and over. We started getting a lotta calls to do rock and roll revival shows.'

It was that, finally, that drove home to Patti and the girls that they had to do something fast, because working revival shows is a tacit admission that you peaked a long time back and that your only value is nostalgic.

'It's healthy the way it is now, because before it was nothing. You didn't know what you were singin' about, you were just singin' a pretty tune.'

The key to the change, really, is something that Sarah had said over supper the previous night, in answer to a question about whether her views had changed when the band reshaped their act. 'I always felt the way I do now,' she'd replied. 'It's just that now I can express it.'

A lot of that expression derives from the songs supplied to the band by Ms Hendryx. Hit it, Nona! . . .

'I was writing for about six years. We only recorded one or two of my songs, and I wasn't really writing about what I'm writing about now. I wasn't writing about the things around me, the social and political things that happened. Then Sarah and Patti started taking an interest and suggested that there might be something there worth working on.'

The change took a lot of people completely by surprise. Club-owners and audiences who'd expected wigs, gowns and 'You'll Never Walk Alone' got jeans, Afros and 'The Revolution Will Not Be Televized'.

'It still hasn't really come across yet like "Lady M" has. They can accept that, but they can't accept that truth about the system and the revolution, but we gon' keep singin' it until they get it . . . right in the *ass*! A lot of people tell you problems, but they don't tell you the solution. We're givin' you the problem *and* the solution.'

Naturally, LaBelle aren't permitted to do 'The Revolution Will Not Be Televized' on TV. Naturally.

Anyway, enough of this. Let's talk about some real stuff. What's with the handcuffs, Nona?

'I forgot the whip.'

Huh?

'Handcuffs? I like handcuffs. I always have. It's just a fetish. I used to ask policemen to lock me up 'cuz I liked the handcuffs. I never had a chance to wear a costume with handcuffs until now. I got to get a new whip tomorrow . . . and maybe a riding crop. I used to have a cat o' nine tails, but somebody stole it.'

Nona looks like she could rhapsodize dreamily onwards into the sunset about chains, whips, handcuffs and other lovin' things, but you don't really want to know about that kinda stuff either, so regretfully we got back to talking about the important stuff like . . .

'The costumes sorta pick up our characters,' muses Nona.

'You'n Sarah can speak for yourselves, but my costume don't pick up *my* character,' interjects Patti. All right, so how does your costume differ from your character?

"Cuz it's *tacky*.' She punches the line across like a vaudeville professional.

'What Nona and Sarah were wearin' ain't. When Sarah took off her cape, everyone just went "Whoooooo!" I took off mine, and they said, "Put it on."' The entire gathering collapses into their toast. Patti rides the laugh until it starts to die down, and then socks the punch line home. "Cuz what I had on was *jaaaaaaave!*'

Back into the toast. 'The object of our show is actually to educate people. To get them next to using their minds, giving some thought about what's wrong in the world and to curing it, to bringing people together. Music shouldn't be segregated. You got R&B, soul, white black music . . . white music is over *here*, black music is over *there*. We only play to one people – all people.

'The costumes are just a come-on, like a glittery sign. Then people read the sign and see what's on it. We're just tryin' to turn people onto stuff that's real, like life in America. It's universal. When I come over here I don't have to tell you to watch out for Nixon and Ford. In London, you probably have to watch out for the Queen.'

Damn right. She keeps breaking milk bottles outside my flat, for a start, and when those Corgis get to cooking . . .

'No, I'm serious. I mean, I don't know about the Queen . . .'

'What she's talking about,' volunteers Nona, 'is America, and America is everywhere. It's universal because you can apply it to every people. Everybody has the same problems. When we're talking about the revolution, we're talking about people being hungry.'

'The system is what it's about,' resumes Patti, 'and the system is everybody and every place. I can warn you about mine 'cuz I live there, but I can warn you about yours if need be. That's what we do, that's what we're here for. To be an entertainer means you have such great access – to TV, to radio, to the stage – and people come to see you. So when they do, let them leave with something.'

84

All in all, it's about time for people to start listening. After all, Sarah's thirty this August and she still doesn't have a stereo that works.

## Randy Newman: The agony and the agony

*NME*, 29 March 1975

'YOU know a fantasy I used to have? I don't have fantasies any more, which is what makes it difficult to write, but when I started making records, what I always wanted was critical acclaim – I could see myself being thought of as a genius and all that shit – and I used to write down what I'd answer for those *NME* Life-Lines. Favourite food, favourite colour, best friend – I used to like seeing that, you know . . .'

Maybe we could resurrect it just one time for you.

'No, I-I-I-uh . . . it was such a pathetic little dream . . .'

What I was trying to figure out was why Randy Newman's jacket pocket was stuffed with Kleenex.

The reason I knew about the Kleenex was that I was wearing the jacket, and the reason that I was wearing it was that the head waiter of the Amsterdam hotel we were staying in wouldn't let me into the restaurant in the jacket I was already wearing. So the guy from the record company went and borrowed a jacket from Randy Newman and his manager, and even though it was nothing grander than a Made-In-The-People's-Republic-Of-China khaki cotton affair with a 'Dark Horse' badge pinned to the lapel, it got me into the restaurant.

Once in, I frisked the jacket and located a huge wodge of crumpled Kleenexes in the pocket. Not just one or two, but a real man-sized fistful. Obviously, someone expected not only to cut himself on the menu, but to spill a full bottle of wine, knock over a couple of prawn cocktails, put his elbow in the cannelloni and catch a streaming cold; all of which fitted very neatly into the way I felt about Randy Newman.

I always visualized Newman as the kind of guy you'd end up sitting next to on a long plane journey. He'd fumble with his seatbelt, drop his book, snore for hours on end, knock over his beer, decide to take a leak, wander up the aisle the wrong way with his shirt-tail coming out, trip over his shoe-laces, end up getting locked in the john and eventually coming out with his flies undone. Mr Average, USA. One natural-born dentist, a real regular Middle American guy. I'd buy a used car from Randy Newman any time as long as it wasn't him who'd used it.

Imagine my shock when I discovered that it wasn't Randy Newman's jacket after all, but his manager's. Randy's was a sleek pearl-grey suede job with shiny buttons, which just goes to show you never can tell.

Randy Newman was in Holland to receive a Gold Disc for 'Good Old Boys', and to do three numbers on a Dutch TV show called *Music All In*, and by early evening the Dutch Rock Press is assembled in the Hotel Amstel waiting for The Star to present himself. The cashew nuts are going down a treat, and the orange juice is proving infinitely more popular than the sherry. The cigars are disgusting, though – the kind that disintegrate in a kind of dry crackle when you try and stub them out. The photogs fiddle with the cameras and cross and uncross their legs, and every so often someone makes a placatory announcement that he's gonna be here in just a *little* while, so we all sit down and wait for The Star.

The Star, however, has just flown in from LA and is feeling terrible. He's exhausted, he feels sick, he hates industry parties – but eventually he mooches into the lift, hunches his shoulders and warily enters the room, every slumped inch of his body radiating de-energization. His hair has been trimmed back from its previous encroachment into the realms of the modish pop star to a short tangle that spills onto his forehead and halfway down his ears. He's a big man, but somehow he doesn't seem like one. He walks with a slump, shoulders rounded and head forward, and he seems self-conscious and ungainly and very, very tired. He shuffles forward uncertainly into a silent storm of flashbulbs and hesitantly makes his way towards the end table, which is obviously The Star's table since it's the only one with a tablecloth.

Immediately everyone crowds around him and starts asking

questions. A few words filter through the restrained hubbub. 'Wellllll – in a way it's cynical . . . James Last . . . I like to have . . . I just wanted to write something about the South . . . "Rednecks" . . . I don't know – do you? . . . I don't quite understand . . . I just – uh – would rather do nothing at all.'

Eventually it gets to be ceremony time, and a Record Company Executive struts forward to lay the Gold Disc For The Latest Album on The Star. 'In recognition of your creativity,' he orates, 've are wery prod to present you vith this for your last album, which I personally think is *excellent* album . . .'

'Aw, thank you,' mumbles Newman, shifting from foot to foot and trying to smile.

'Congratulations on your tremendous . . .'

'I'm very proud to have received it . . .' Outbreak of spontaneous applause as Newman accepts the Gold Disc, holding it most gingerly as if he was afraid of dropping it. 'It's almost like being presented with my own headstone,' he deadpans. The photographers cluster in, imploring 'Smile! Smile!'

'I don't have a smile,' grits Newman, twisting the corners of his mouth by sheer muscle control. 'Say cheese!' trumpets a photographer. 'Cheese,' replies Newman. He is Not Smiling.

Finally, the Record Company Executive grabs Newman in a flying tackle. One arm around the shoulders nearly making The Star drop the Gold Disc, face turned to the camera in a real shiteating grin as the flash goes off, trapping Newman's features in a frozen expression that radiates exhaustion, boredom, repulsion and just a *soupçon* of sudden terror.

Thank you . . . cut. Print it.

A supper had been planned by the record company for 8.30, but Newman takes a sleeping pill and goes to bed. He sleeps badly, and keeps waking up to find out that it's still dark. The following afternoon, he's slumped over a coffee in the cafeteria of a TV studio in Hilversum, hulked grouching behind his shades. An unhappy bear dragged prematurely from hibernation and encased in an LA gentleman-cowboy shirt and a pair of faded jeans. The shirt is buttoned almost all the way up to his neck and the tail is coming out at the back.

He's jet-lagged out of his brain by the twelve-hour flight from LA, and tomorrow he's going to have to do it all again. Unfortunately, he won't get much of a chance to rest up from all of that, because he's got a gig to do.

'The one that I'll be doing in a few days will be the last one for the foreseeable future. I just haven't been paying attention. I don't think the audiences have noticed much, but I've been making mistakes that I've never made before, and . . . you know, when it doesn't mean anything to you any more – the laughter and the applause – it takes you down all around. I think – it affects your whole emotional range. If you can't appreciate something that's obviously gratifying, then it isn't worth it. You know. But I'm about done anyway. I've done all I can do . . .'

Crumpled in a chair like some kind of denim turtle, he emanates an almost frightening aura of tiredness. He's got bags under his eyes big enough to stash a complete set of Yes albums in and his skin is pasty and flaccid. You almost feel guilty taking up his time by talking to him, using time that he could have spent sleeping or something. Doing up a whole gang of vitamin pills, maybe.

'. . . at the moment. Guess I could make another record or something.'

It's gotten to the point where he'll switch off his mind in mid-concert to think about something and by the time he zeroes back in on what he's doing – sitting up there on a stage in front of a few thousand raptly listening people – he's played three songs.

We sit and talk and I ask all kinds of things-to-ask-Randy-Newman type questions along the lines of how do you do *this* and what did you mean by *that* and your attitude to this is *what* and so on, and he stumbles through answers that he's not really thinking about. It's not that he's being snotty or unobliging; it's simply a matter of tiredness. The poor bastard's out on his feet and I'm asking him for detailed information about his creative processes and his motivation and all kinds of detailed junk . . . really felt bad about it.

And this simp from a radio station slides in under the pretext of 'just taping for a couple of minutes'. Once he's got Randy trussed up, though, he reveals his true plan: he wants to do an hour-long special with Randy introducing his own selections from his work. Something like compiling your own Greatest Hits album, writing your own liner notes and reciting the whole thing . . . and all at two minutes' notice.

Newman takes it gamely, though. He gets out a piece of paper and a pencil and starts laboriously scrawling out notes. Like a schoolboy, he pulls up his turtle-shell shoulders around his ears and screws up his mouth, blinking. Wearily, he starts into talking about 'Rednecks'. After a couple of minutes, the radio guy discovers that his tape is twisted and that he'll have to start again.

'That song, "Rednecks" . . .'

'Er – could you introduce yourself?'

Newman sighs and licks his lips. 'This is Randy Newman. This is Randy Newman. That song, "Rednecks" is the first . . . that I wrote . . . for the album that ultimately became "Good Old Boys" . . . and at the time I had no intentions of making a specifically Southern album . . . or a concept album . . .'

He speaks as if the very act is painful to him. His voice always sounds rusty, but now it sounds like Hal from *2001* beginning to run down, like ancient chains red and flaking with rust being hauled around some pivot. And there's the radio station guy with his big microphone in his hand poised to catch every word, leaning forward attentively; every inch the perfect interviewer, head cocked to one side as the tired bear opposite him creaks into his machine.

'. . . but after I wrote it I felt that I ought to develop it a bit more to explain the song.' He pauses. The interviewer gazes blankly at him and Newman gazes blankly back. 'I'd written songs before that were kind of *ambiguous*, and I thought this one might be misunderstood by some people at least' (his voice has blisters on its feet) 'so I wrote another song to explain the first one and that was "Birmingham".'

A real professional link job. 'And then I had it, this character who was . . .' Mr Radio interrupts. 'Sorry, could you say, "And that was 'Birmingham'"?'

'That was "Birmingham". Uh – I wanted to write about the industrial South, a city that has kind of a bad reputation. I wanted to write about a character who was very proud of where he was living. After I wrote that' (he hauls himself through his rap with the unwilling dutifulness of a man jogging in the snow), 'I believe that the next song I wrote was "Marie".' Pause. 'That was "Marie".' (He's learnt the ground rules.) 'And – uh – the song I had on there "Wedding In Cherokee County" was originally – what I originally wanted to do was write an Albanian anthem. I was kinda interested in Albania, having absolutely no allies in

89

the world any more, right next to Russia always yapping at her and calling them running dogs. So I tried to write an Albanian anthem – "*white moon shines on the goat herd*," and so on – but it wasn't working. Sounded like "Back Home Again In Indiana", and so I ended up writing this thing and called it "An Albanian Love Song" and I just changed it to North-Eastern Alabama. And there it was.'

'About some of your *older* material?' murmurs Mr Radio in the diplomatic tones of an expensive specialist making a house call on a rich patient and checking out the symptoms. 'And about zer *bladduh?* . . .'

Newman peers at his scrap of paper. 'Lessee . . . "Sail Away" . . .'

'And also tell something about your early life, how you got into zer businesss,' prompts Mr Radio. Newman's looking positively groggy, more owlish than ever. 'All right?'

'I'm not all right, but okay,' mumbles Newman with as much amiability as he can summon. He runs through an account of how his uncles Alfred and Lionel Newman wrote movie music and how his father got him classical piano lessons from age seven. 'I started writing songs when I was . . . sixteen, I believe, and this was at the urging of Larry Waronker whose father was in the record business, and I did. I took them to a publisher and he signed me up for three dollars a month or something. People there at the same time were Leon Russell and David Gates, P.J. Proby and Glen Campbell, Jackie De Shannon – and what we tried to do was write follow-ups for people who'd had hits of some kind. We were spectacularly unsuccessful. We were a kind of poor man's Carole King and Barry Mann and Neil Sedaka. Ultimately, people started to say that I should try and record, which I resisted . . . for a while.'

By some unholy effort of will, he seems to have forced his system to work, and he's beginning to warm to his theme and sound almost animated. '. . . as I've resisted doing almost everything that I ever have done. I signed with Warners and did my album . . . *an* album around '68/'69. I always used to complain about the records that people used to make of my songs and I figured that I shouldn't be able to give myself that kind of an out any more; it was too easy just to sit back and complain without doing anything about it . . . so now I could mess my songs up myself.'

He does a little spiel about 'Sail Away', and remembering the rules, climaxes with 'That was "Sail Away"'. '"Yellow Man" is kinda the same type of song . . .'

Newman explains Newman before your very ears. Wonder how Dylan would sound doing the same thing? Maybe Mr Radio should try and get him to do it.

'How many more do you want? "Lonely At The Top", "Suzanne", "Kingfish" . . . yeah, I can always talk about that. "Lonely At The Top" I actually wrote with Frank Sinatra in mind. I've always been interested in the kind of thing people who are very successful . . . it's always been humorous and unsympathetic to me when they whine about how miserable they are . . . and I thought that it would be nice for him to do a song like that, not that he embodies that attitude or anything – Frank, if you're listening out there. I don't think he ever saw the song, but I was doing an album with Barbra Streisand once – she was doing some of my songs and I was playing – and I wanted her to do it, but she said that people would think she meant it.

'"Suzanne" was written after I talked to Jimi Hendrix' – he pronounces the name very carefully and distinctly – 'I've always been a great admirer of – I *was* a great admirer of Jimi Hendrix, and I knew he was in town, and I wanted him to play on the "12 Songs" album, and so I wrote "Suzanne" with that in mind. We somehow didn't get together on it because he went to Hawaii or something. It's kind of a diseased love song about an inept potential molester, but here it is.

'I don't sound too lively, do I?' he asks wryly. 'What else was on "12 Songs" that I could talk about?' he asks the reporter, who is slumped on a nearby couch decaying almost visibly. '"Have You Seen My Baby",' I suggest. 'Was that on "12 Songs"?' mutters a rather puzzled Newman. '"Burn Down The Cornfield", "Mama Told Me Not To Come",' I reel off. He seems to remember the album at last. 'I didn't really want to record "Mama Told Me Not To Come", I never liked it anyway; I think I was probably wrong about that because I'm not always the best judge of my own work, but "Three Dog Night" did it and it was a big hit in America. They changed it around a bit, made kind of a hook out the title, but anyway this is my version of it . . .'

He's finally through with it all, and even records a trailer for the show. 'Hello, this is Randy Newman. I hope you'll be able to listen to me today at five o'clock . . . thank you. *Thank you?*' he repeats incredulously. 'Do people still say that?' Exit Mr Radio.

Newman thinks back to the party. 'It wasn't so bad. Look . . .' he stares helplessly and silently for what seems like a couple of minutes, 'it would have been rude to be disdainful of it or not to . . . I was hoping I was looking like I was happy. I wasn't because I was so tired, maybe, but I was glad to get the gold record . . . and glad they're that interested and . . . look, it's a very unusual situation for a yuman being to be in. Unusual for me, you know? But the worst things of that type that I have been in were in England. Theeeeee *worst*. Those goddam buffets with the promotion men and their wives and their wives' sisters and friends. Those are *deadly*. When I *die*,' he's working himself up now into a gentle man's rage, 'that's what my hell will be like – an English industry promotion party.

'They don't care if you're there, you know. Those have been some of the worst things that've ever happened to me. They're worse than in the States. I haven't had one in the States for years,' he adds parenthetically. 'I won't let 'em do it, and I'm never gonna do another one there, but this was relatively painless. I would not want to display my basic ingratitude . . . but I always try to remember that it's better than working. I was really dreading coming over here, making that plane trip, and getting all dislodged by the time and everything . . . but I was reading this book at the time about Livingstone, and in it, it tells about his African journeys. Two thousand miles at a mile a day through eight feet of muddy water . . . terrrrrrrible! And I thought what the hell, sit first class on the plane, big deal . . .'

In the studio, the orchestra is running through its paces. Like all TV studio orchestras, it's made up of a few young guys who look like they play jazz or rock for fun and do this for the money, and a bunch of elders who've probably been playing in TV orchestras ever since TV was first invented. The set is Late Tack: all cushioned bays for the studio audience and plastic light banks. They rehearse the *Music All In* signature tune and a very large black lady named Veronica Vee runs through 'The Lady Is A Tramp'.

Eventually the compere, a balding man with thick sideboards

and a beige turtleneck, announces 'Rendi Newmann' and The Star shuffles warily towards the piano. A camera hurtles down upon him like some maddened vampiric tank, but he shoulders his way to the piano, and as he sits down behind it the photographers move in, zapping him with flashes, totally blocking him from view. Over on the monitor, a cameraman gets a focus on Newman's defiant, suffering potato face as he rolls perfunctorily through 'Political Science', looking and sounding more laconic than ever, swallowing his words like pills as he sings them.

Without a break he sings 'Birmingham' as the lighting men go through their paces, and then asks, 'Where's the conductor?' Said individual manifests himself and Newman launches into 'I Think It's Going To Rain Today'.

As the rehearsal ends, the last I see of Randy Newman is behind one of the backdrops as he sits, head in hands, next to his manager. He drops his cigarette to the floor and unconsciously rubs the sole of his shoe over the butt over and over again until the shreds of tobacco are spread all around his foot, until it's completely and utterly crushed.

# Patti Smith:
# Down in the scuzz with
# the heavy cult figures

*NME*, 7 June 1975

CBGB is a toilet. An impossibly scuzzy little club buried somewhere in the sections of the Village that the cab-drivers don't like to drive through.

It looks as if the proprietors kick holes in the walls and piss in the corners before they let the customers in: fo' the *atmosphere*, you dig. None of the low-budget would-be elegance of Max's Kansas City in the final agonies of its death throes, but carefully choreographed movie-set sleaze.

The audience, who consist mainly of nondescript urban hippies, a smattering of heav-vy street bro's, rock intelligentsia and the occasional confused tourist, are revelling in the tack and basking in their own hipness just for being there.

Tonight, y'see, is Patti Smith and Television, two of the most droppable names of the New York rock circuit.

Patti Smith is a Heavy Cult Figure, who attracts the Cool Four Hundred, and Television are still on the verge of becoming Heavy Cult Figures, which is even more attractive.

The fastest and most concise way to describe Television is that they're New York's equivalent to The Feelgoods.

They're a lot younger, perform original material and Tom Verlaine, the leader, was evidently severely traumatized by Lou Reed at an impressionable age; but, outside of the obvious cultural differences between the Manhattan and Canvey Islands, the similarities are astounding.

Both bands play chopped-down, hard-edged, no-bullshit rock and roll, totally eschewing the preening Mickey-Mouse decadence that poleaxed the previous new wave of NY bands.

Television don't dress up and they don't even move much.

The rhythm guitarist is spraddle-legged and blank-eyed, chopping at his Telecaster like some deranged piece of machinery, braced so that he can lurch in any direction without falling over. He's wearing a Fillmore East T-shirt, which is the ultimate in dressing down.

The bass player wears his shades on every other number, and Verlaine, frozen-faced and zombie-eyed, alternately clutches his mike stand with both hands and blazes away at off-balance methedrine speed-fingers lead guitar marathons on a gold-topped Les Paul.

Television are a total product of New York, but like The Feelgoods, they embody both the traditional and the revolutionary, and they represent an escape from the roller-coaster to oblivion into which rock is currently straitjacketed — i.e., an *imaginative* return to basics — and what they lose to The Feelgoods in energy and pacing they gain in imagination.

That a band like Television are currently happening and that people are listening to them is indisputable proof that rock is a hardier beast than much of the more depressing evidence would suggest.

Which brings us, quite logically, to Patti Smith, who has Just Signed A Big Contract and is therefore about to be massively publicized and fed into the star machine.

Right now, though, she and Television are still on display fairly regularly to anybody with three or four dollars to hand over as CBGB's price of admission.

Her performing environment is a stage smaller than Greg Lake's carpet, which places her less than two feet away from the nearest customer and gives her less than a foot's height advantage. The lighting is, to say the least, rudimentary.

Which means that, in a club like CBGB, the tricks of the trade that the big guys use to duplicate or replace real charisma are technically impossible, and so the act either has to do it all by themselves or else it doesn't get done at all.

Patti Smith has an aura that'd probably show up under ultra-violet light. She can generate more intensity with a single movement of one hand than most rock performers can produce in an entire set.

On the face of it, it's an unlikely act to team with a chopped-hog hell-driven rock band like Television. A lady poet, backed by a band who don't even have a drummer, sounds like an improbable expression for any kind of definitive rock consciousness. But Patti Smith is in the rock and roll market-place and she knows the ground rules. More important, she knows how it works.

She's an odd little waif figure in a grubby black suit and black satin shirt, so skinny that her clothes hang baggily all over her, with chopped-off black hair and a face like Keith Richards' kid sister would have if she'd gotten as wasted by age seventeen as Keith is now.

Her band (Richard Sohl on guitar and bass, Lenny Kaye on guitar and a kid known as D.N.V. – an abbreviation of 'Death In Venice') play like a garage band who've learned a few thirties licks to go with the mutated AM rock.

She stands there machine-gunning out her lines, singing a bit and talking a bit, in total control, riding it and steering it with a twist of a shoulder here, a flick of the wrist there – scaled-down bird-like movements that carry an almost unbelievable degree of power, an instinctive grasp of the principles of mime that teach that the quality and timing of a gesture are infinitely more important than its size.

Her closing *tour de force*, an inspired juxtaposition of 'Land Of 1,000 Dances' with a rock-poem about a kid getting beaten up in a locker room, was undoubtedly the most gripping performance that I've seen by a white act since the last time I saw The Who.

For the duration of her set that night, Patti Smith embodied and equalled everybody that I've ever dug on a rock and roll stage.

Whether her records will be any good or not (or for that matter, whether Television will be able to get it down on record) is another kettle of swordfish altogether.

All that really needs to be said is that watching Television and Patti Smith that evening was one of the most exciting rock experiences that I've had for a long, long time, and that both acts have something that rock and roll desperately needs.

One more thing. In the audience at the Alice Cooper gig in Detroit was a chick done up exactly like Patti Smith. Something's happening.

# Paul McCartney: 'No, not really in a way actually as it happens'

*NME*, 26 July 1975

VENUS and Mars are late.

The sandwiches don't care, though. Even though they're the same day's vintage – fresh, soft white-bread triangles housing excerpts from what was once a proud, regal salmon – the effects of being stashed in a direct line with brilliant sunlight has crisped and dried them to the point where this premature ageing process has reduced them to the approximate consistency of the kind of sandwiches that get exhumed from six days' burial in the less congenial kind of pub.

The wine is warm and overly sweet, but this matters even less to Venus and Mars than the terrifying fate that has befallen the sarnies. After all, Venus and Mars are lunching – not wisely but well – and the state of the nation sandwich-wise is of purely academic importance.

And the sun shines bright on the old Greek Street home of McCartney Productions, and everybody is waiting for Venus and

Mars to get back from lunch so that they can Talk About The Album — The Album being 'Venus And Mars', the successor to the platinum-plated throne of 'Band On The Run', the most successful and one of the best pieces of product to emanate from anybody who used to be in The Beatles.

The result of a sojourn in N'Orleans recording in the very famous Allen Toussaint's very famous studio, 'Venus And Mars' is . . .

. . . a terrible album.

Let's have a quick wander around the perimeters and check out the architecture while we're waiting for the deities (in their civilian identities of Paul and Linda McCartney, ordinary everyday popstars-next-door) to choke down their coffee and amble back to the office.

'McCartney can make albums like "Band On The Run" any time he wants to,' claims a former associate of the Wings operation. '"Venus And Mars" is what he's actually into, though. He likes writing songs for his kids.'

Up until the arrival of 'Band On The Run' in the latter months of 1973, the prevailing assessment of Monsieur McCartney was that he was the possessor of a 'basically bourgeois talent' — which meant that he was essentially uncommitted to rock and roll, was irremediably cutesy-pie, played and composed music with an unforgivably low *cojones* quotient, wrote songs that begged for Andy Williams to cover them, wimped around all over the place with a wife who seemed to have even less musical credibility than her fiendish Oriental opposite number, allowed an overwhelming facility for pleasant melody and easy-going charm to degenerate into vacuous glibness, angled his music at the mums and dads, came off poorly in comparison to the gritty honesty and commitment of John Lennon, the uplifting spirituality of George Harrison (or what looked like uplifting spirituality at the time) and the cloddish charm of Ringo Starr (from whom nobody expected anything better than cloddish charm anyway), was a swot and a teacher's pet and a soppy sneak who didn't even *pretend* to relate to a seventies which had taken him at his word about doing it in the road.

The grouchy spoilsport who'd dragged the hallowed name of The Beatles through the courts . . .

Paul McCartney was Infra Dig. Paul McCartney was Terminally Uncool. Paul McCartney was Right Out.

'Eastman is an *animal*! A fucking stupid middle-class *pig*! I wouldn't let animals like that near me!' – The Dummy John Lennon, 'Magical Misery Tour' (from the National Lampoon's 'Radio Dinner' album).

Yeah. That was the camel that broke the straw's back.

John Lennon married a Japanese avant-garde artist several years his senior, who was Third World and far out and had credibility even though hardly anybody either liked her work or understood it.

Paul McCartney married a blonde All-American goil from a wealthy family whose papa was popularly supposed to be Eastman of Eastman Kodak even though he was a lawyer whose pre-Deed Poll (or Yank equivalent) name had been ... Epstein. Ha ha. Cosmic irony.

Lennon made all the right noises and McCartney made all the wrong ones. John Lennon was Right On and Paul McCartney ... well, it was clear that even though he'd been one of the king architects of hippie, the boy was a closet straight who couldn't wait to kiss the revolution goodbye and scuttle back to domesticity.

Still, he kept trying.

He put out a pro-IRA single at approximately the right time (i.e. before everybody wised up about the IRA), got banned by the BBC to take away the saccharine aftertaste of the miserable string of bubblegum singles that he and Linda were foisting on an admittedly uncomplaining mass market (by far the most embarrassing of which was 'Mary Had A Little Lamb'), had the fortune/ misfortune to get busted for dope smoking/growing/holding every third week, and finally put together 'Wings – which was, I'm told, a fairly creditable rock and roll band live.

Their principal exercise was a mammoth tour of Europe (during which Macca got himself – you guessed – well and truly busted because someone had sent him some D-O-P-E through the mails) which roughly coincided with the self-immolation of John Lennon's musical/political credibility via the sublimely fatuous 'Some Time In New York City'. At this time, Wings included, alongside Paul'n'Linda, Denny Laine on git-tar, Henry McCullough on another git-tar and a moustachioed Yank drummer named Denny Seiwell.

The album that followed in the tracks of this epic jaunt was 'Red Rose Speedway', which was judged quite good at the time.

Time passes.

Seiwell and McCullough travel on, and Laine and the McCartneys bop off to Lagos to record their next album. Amidst mucho hi-jinx, 'Band On The Run' emerges unto a suitably impressed world, and anti-Macca canards are dissipated like wet farts in a strong wind.

'Band On The Run', y'see, is perhaps the ultimate maximization of McCartney's post-Beatle potential; which is to say that it exploits to the utmost his gift for melody and his not-inconsiderable expertise with sound while minimizing his penchant for cheap sentimentality.

Featuring some of the most thoughtful and intelligent pop synthesizer work within living memory, a succession of solid melodies, the occasional flash of genuine inspiration and a virtuoso production, 'Band On The Run' was hailed by myriad writers (including your humble present chronicler) as some kind of kozmik *meisterwerk*, even though in retrospect it seems that it came on that way in contrast to the limp asininity of all the then-currently new ex-Beatle products ('Mind Games', 'Living In The Material World' and 'Ringo', to be precise).

Still, let us not be uncharitable to 'Band On The Run'.

While the lyrics preclude it from truly epic status, it was undoubtedly about 4,000 per cent better than anything that anybody at the time considered McCartney capable of producing.

Suddenly Paul McCartney was the golden boy again. Lennon had OD'ed on dumb politics and ingrown ego, George Harrison's prissy holier-than-thou chunderings had gotten righteously on the collective wick, Ringo was solidly into his role as rent-a-looning-companion and all-purpose klutz . . . and simpy bourgeois Macca had pulled off an excellent album.

Oh, the weeping and the wailing, the recriminations and the tears! *Oy Gevalt*!

It was an event of almost morality-play proportions, a triumph of decency. After years of taking shit from everybody for being a square and a Blue Meanie, vindication had arrived with a surprise knockout in the twelfth round. McCartney proved that Nice Guys didn't have to Finish Last; that you could be a Kleen Kut Kid and a scholar and a gentleman and still make a decent album.

And then he coasted; peeled a couple of tracks off the wad of tunes on 'Band On The Run' and slapped them down on the counter reincarnated as hit singles, took life easy, brought in Jeff Britton (karate heavy and ex-member of The Wild Angels) to play drums and Jimmy McCulloch (former boy genius of Thunderclap Newman and Stone The Crows) as lead guitarist, took life easy, made a couple of pleasant but dull singles with his bro' Mike, took life easy, made a couple of pleasant but dull Wings singles and set off to New Orleans to cut a new album, etc. etc. . . .

. . . which is where things start getting heavy.

'Venus And Mars' is not only one of the worst albums I've ever heard from a so-called 'major artist', but it's also the most decadent. Sure, it's got nothing to do with heroin or homosexuality or make-up or any of the other stuff that we used to think of as being 'decadent' when we were young(er) and dumb(er) back in '72, but it goes much deeper than that.

'Venus And Mars' is a symptom of decadence because it is the product of a considerable talent in an advanced stage of decay. It is totally lacking in either true beauty, true strength or true innocence; offering in the stead of these qualities – qualities which one could quite reasonably demand from the work of an artist of Paul McCartney's eminence – a vapid, shallow prettiness which is ultimately more saddening than the work of even the dumbest no-hoper.

It's the whole lilies-that-fester syndrome: basically, nobody gives a shit if someone they've never heard of unloads a turkey because it's just another bad album. For someone of McCartney's level/status/importance to deliberately trivialize his talent is something of a blow.

The band don't help much, either. Jimmy McCulloch just keeps his head down and blasts away with some decent guitar whenever he gets a chance; for which he really cannot be blamed. I mean, he's probably totally overawed by working with P. Mc – and besides, who the hell expects Jimmy McCulloch to have to carry a Paul McCartney album?

Denny Laine remains as self-effacing as usual, Linda is – well, Linda – and Joe English just plays drums.

Mostly, it's gloopy ballads and pop songs slightly below the ingenuity and creativity level of the average Wombles single interspersed with McCartney speciality pieces like 'You Gave Me The Answer' which is music-hall rooty-toot in the well-worn 'When I'm 64'/'Honey Pie'/'Your Mother Should Know' tradition, only less palatable than any of its predecessors.

There's the incredibly patronizing 'Rock Show' with its oblique references to dope, Jimmy Page, and 'long hair at Madison Square', plus the reactionary nose-upturning at the excesses of '72 glamrock – and played so totally limpwristedly as to turn whatever satirical edge the song may originally have had straight back onto its creator. And this from the man who parodied John Lennon so accurately less than two years ago on 'Let Me Roll It'.

The only even remotely acceptable piece on the whole album is 'Letting Go', a lightweight exercise in pop Stevie Wonder. Much has been made of the inclusion of the *Crossroads* theme, which fits in alarmingly well with the general artistic and intellectual tone of the album. Later on in the proceedings, you'll hear from P. Mc's own mobile, well-shaped lips exactly what he thought he was doing by including it, but Clue Number One is that he's undoubtedly delighted that the show has subsequently adopted his version of the tune.

I bet Paul McCartney really *likes Crossroads.*

Understand me: I'm not putting McCartney down for aspiring to lower-middle-class ideals either in his life or his music. I'm not putting him down for attempting to produce light, innocent, pretty music, either.

Demanding absolute purity of attitude and total devotion to duty from musicians is pointless and obtuse, since musicians ain't no way saints or perfect human beings, and it's totally useless to castigate McCartney – or anybody else – just for being himself.

There's nothing wrong with innocence, even though it's pretty damn scarce these days. A great deal of the most valuable contributions to rock thus far have fallen into precisely that bracket: the *innocent* celebration of California hedonism and the consumer ethic that made the early work of The Beach Boys so heartbreakingly wonderful, the *innocent* street macho of Eddie Cochran, the *innocent* search for good times and political consciousness of The MC5, the *innocent* frustration of early Who, the *innocent* good-natured humour of The Lovin' Spoonful – and especially the *innocent* joyfulness of classic Beatles.

What I *am* castigating McCartney for is *knowingly* and deliberately aiming for the effect of innocence by creating simpering, empty music that substitutes saccharine for honest sweetness, crassness for innocence and prettiness for beauty, for selling himself short by refusing to extend his talent past the area of glib facility, for taking the easy way out – ultimately for not realizing that, with talent, comes the responsibility of using it to its utmost.

Venus and Mars are all right – Jack.

So I sit there in the offices of McCartney Productions watching Denny Laine and Jimmy McCulloch clowning around, and I flip through magazines and think about the weather and my phone bill and the goddam sandwiches – everything but what I'm going to say to Venus and Mars when they côme back and whether I'm going to tell McCartney right up front how much I hate his album (and by extension him for making it) and if so, how.

It ain't easy, troops, because I'm as full of Beatleawe as the next bozo who was eleven when 'Love Me Do' came out and who queued up for two and a half hours to see the very first showing of *A Hard Day's Night* when it came to town and saved up for two months to buy the albums etcetera etcetera. Fill in your own Beatle memories and dilute to taste.

Meeting Paul McCartney is still a hell of a big deal even though it's for the second time. The first time was just after 'Band On The Run' came out and there was no problem there because I'd liked the album – but now?

These things are sent to try us.

Well, eventually he and Linda arrived and said hello very jolly and amiable, and we retired into the next room to do the interview.

Conspicuous by his absence was *NME*'s Living Legend Of The Leica, Joe Stevens, who'd been designated to record the occasion on film. It appeared, see, that Linda had taken some very cute shots of the group a few days earlier and had decided that it would be very groovy if all the music papers used them to go along with their interviews.

So she instructed Wings' publicist, Tony Brainsby, to call all the music paper photographers and tell them not to bother showing up. It apparently never occurred to her simply to send her photographs along and let the various editors decide what they wanted to use in their papers: hers versus the staff photographers' competing on pure merit. But then it's much easier to get photos published if you make sure that nobody else has any up-to-date material. Nice one, Linda!

McCartney cuts an almost studiedly inelegant figure in a built-for-comfort ensemble of jeans, waistcoat and white shirt, complete with an artful dusting of stubble. If you saw him in the street you'd think he looked a lot like Paul McCartney, but . . . nahhhh, it couldn't be him. Could it?

He accepts a cigarette, rips the filter off it and bends into the lighter flame. After he's done this a few times you automatically tear off the filter before handing him the next cigarette.

That week the old Apple building had come down, and for want of anything better I mumbled something about whether he'd had any sentimental pangs about the demolition of that particular symbol of our collective misspent youth.

'Not Apple, really because it went a couple of years ago really.'

I had to restrain myself from counting the 'really's.

'. . . because it went a couple of years ago really, just hangin' on with people wondering what to do with it, y'know.'

I decide to switch to the 'y'know's.

'This is just the official closing down. It's just like recording a record, y'know, three years ago and it's finally released, y'know.'

Pause.

'No, y'know, it just wasn't working, y'know, and you can't keep it goin' if it's not happenin'. So . . . no, I don't have any pangs. It's all cool, y'know? The relationship with the others is the only kind of pang I might add, and we're all cool.

'We're all friends and stuff.'

Yeah, well, ex-Beatle relations *are* much better than they have been.

'Yeah, sure.'

Pause.

'No, not really in a way actually as it happens.'

(Note to the more easily confused reader. Mr McCartney's initial response to the author's statement was indeed, 'Yeah, sure. No, not really in a way actually as it happens.')

He continues:

'. . . because it never was that bad. Y'know. It's just that there

103

was a big press skirmish and everyone – particularly John – flung a few words around, and there was a bit of a number, but that actually kind of blew over in about a month and we were already kind of speaking to each other and chatting and stuff.

'Y'know. There you go.'

But surely the dominant impression was that the Fab Four had been at knife-point for two years.

'Yeah, it looked like that. But you see, there was a lot . . . I mean, I don't really want to get into it, but there was a lot of sort of business stuff rather than kind of knife-point between the four of us.

'There was a lot of knife . . . knifing y'know. There was a few baddies in there for a while, y'know, and that's why it really looked kind of bitter for a while, but it wasn't that bitter between us, y'know. I say it's really nice and friendly now.

'So I say I don't really want to go with it, because it's really old news for me . . .'

This can't go on much longer. Sooner or later I've got to ask him about the album. I took my mouth in both hands and asked The Question.

'The – uh – logical thing to ask about next is the "Venus And Mars" album.'

'It's a new record.'

Smart-ass.

'New LP released soon. What do you want to know about it?'

Box clever. If there's one thing I've told you time and time again, it's *box clever*. Watch his left – it's the one he holds the razor in.

'It's very much lighter and simpler than its predecessor . . .'

'Is it?' *Mein Gott* – the Macca Shuffle, already.

Try again.

'It doesn't have as much attack as "Band On The Run".'

Christ, somewhere in the Grand Interviewer's Lexicon (or even in the *Necronomicon* of the mad Arab Abdul Alhazred) there must be a diplomatic way of saying 'Your album is so godawful I wouldn't use it to line a budgie cage even if I had a budgie,' but I couldn't think of it.

What can a person such as myself say to a . . . to a . . . to an ex-Beatle who's just made a crappy album?

Luckily, he weighs in with something before I collapse in a

mummified heap of stick-like, withered brown limbs on the icy flagstones of the crypt . . . sorry, on the lush carpeting of the floor of the warm, sunlit room.

'Oh well, y'know, I mean the funny thing about that is it's that that is so much down to people's opinions, y'know. I'd take it up to Liverpool, y'know, to play it to a few people up in Liverpool and they said just the opposite.'

Must be something in the drinking water down there.

'They said, "Awwwww *man* I 'aven't heard you singing like that for years; it's got much more attack, much more bite . . ."'

Or maybe it's industrial pollution in the atmosphere.

'I don't myself think it's lighter. It might be . . . I dunno.'

Yeah, but surely 'Band On The Run' made gestures in the direction of being a rock album . . . whereas this is just . . . an easy listening album?

'Yeah. Some of it is, yeah. I mean, you've got a couple of tracks that aren't. You got . . . "Call Me Back Again" on the second side isn't easy listening.'

Damn right it isn't.

'And you've got "Letting Go". And "Rock Show" is kind of . . . hardish.'

'It sounds like David Essex,' I mutter, temporarily forgetting about my non-aggression policy.

"Rock Show"? Geddoudovit. Who has *NME* sent along, ladies and gentlemen?' he declaims into the microphone of my cassette machine, nesting cosily at his elbow.

'He's been out all night, he's stoned out of his brain, he doesn't know what's go . . . No, it doesn't sound like David Essex to me, but thank you for the compliment.'

*Whew!* A biting attack!

Might as well carry the fight straight to the enemy.

'It sounds to me as if there are a couple of parodies on it. "Old Egypt" had a couple of T. Rex touches in there . . . thought you might be getting satirical again?'

'Oh no. I'm not satirical, I'm . . . er . . . I wasn't into that.

'Y'know what you think an idea's come from and where it's come from, it's never the same thing, y'know. People get the records and read in things and I just think of a few words and a couple of tunes and go and record 'em, y'know. I definitely didn't think it's T. Rex or I'm doing a David Essex or anything.

105

'As far as I were concerned, it's just me doing it and – uh – it might turn out sounding like that. I see your point – *almost* – but I'm not going to concede the point, ladies and gentlemen, and thank you.'

Tricky question time. 'Why did you record the *Crossroads* theme?'

'It's a joke.' Blimey. 'It's after "Lonely Old People", you see, they're kind of sitting there in the park saying "Nobody asked me to play?" It's a kind of poignant moment' – he switches into announcerese for the last two words – 'and then there's a little break and then *Crossroads* starts up and that's very . . . it's lonely old people, y'know, it's kind of just the kind of thing that lonely old people watch.

'It could just as easily have been *Coronation Street*, but we knew the chords to *Crossroads*. No, I just thought that it would be just nice to do it.

'The thing is that for people who haven't heard it and don't know the whole *Crossroads* thing, like Americans, like a fellow who was helping me arange this stuff, he just thought it was just a lovely tune.

'He thought I'd written it.

'He just thought it was a beautiful little tune, and it is. I quite like it as tune, y'know, the *Crossroads* thing. It fitted. Originally it was just a joke, but as it got recorded, it ended up as . . . less of a joke.

'And I just wanted to see Tony Hatch after he realized that we'd recorded one of his numbers on our new album. I want to tell him, and there's a bit about Jimmy Page, and I wanted to tell *him* before anybody else told him. In "Rock Show" there's a line about "what's that he's rolling across the stage/It looks like the one used used by Jimmy Page/Like a relic from a different age". '*Per*sonally' – he stomps the first syllable like a bass drum pedal – 'I was just thinking of a nice old amp and the people in the audience are saying "that's an AK300. Wowee, it looks just like the one used by Jimmy Page."

'And he was the only guitarist who rhymed with "stage". John Cage? Not the same.'

I figured it was about time to bring up that line about 'scoring an ounce'.

'"*Tension mounts/Sometimes you score an ounce.*" You see? The references are always there. Slip 'em in. This is what I feel' (Pythonesque).

Very neat, squire. Very subtle.

'We-e-e-el,' self-deprecating aw-shucksing, 'I liked it. It *is* about a rock show, and that is part of it all, so I thought . . . y'know, I like to slip those in just so that it's not so . . . *respectable*. If you know what I mean.'

Aha. I knew we'd start talking about dope sooner or later.

'Talking of being respectable and not being respectable, do you think there's any significance in the fact that you've been busted a quite inordinate number of times? Do you think Somebody's Out To Get You?'

'Na-a-a-h. I don't at all. It's basically because it's like . . . we don't really think it's a crime, and so we go about it as if it isn't.

'Unfortunately some people think it is, and go about it as if it is, so if you're hauled up by a highway patrolman in LA and he smells a bit in the car, he doesn't think that it's just an innocent little thing that's not going to harm anyone. He thinks of it as the whole dangerous what-is-this-depravity scene, y'know.

'I think it's as depraved as booze, which I think is . . . *slightly* depraved, but a lot of things are *slightly* depraved.'

But howcum Certain Bands can go on the road with enough cocaine to fill Brian Wilson's sandbox, but poor ol' P.M. gets slugged every time for tame stuff like the killer weed? Isn't it just a *little* bit paranoid?

'It's just one of those things. Just the luck of the draw. I don't think it mounts up to any kind of conspiracy. I don't think like that. I don't believe there's that goes on.

'Maybe it does, y'know, and if it does it doesn't matter. As long as *I* don't think it does, I'm cool.

'The only really unfortunate thing about it, really, is that it starts to get you a reputation as a kind of druggie. The only thing about is that it is really only a kind of minor offence. It isn't something we take too seriously, and of course the press image is really far worse.

'"Linda Gets Busted For Drug Smuggling", and all it was was that someone was trying to send us stuff through the post as a friendly gesture. It's not that cool, I know that, but our thing is by no means as bad as it sometimes looks. It doesn't bother me too much.

'We're not serious drug addicts or anything. We just try to keep it quiet and not get into it a lot, because even talking about it in this interview is like adding to it. In fact, I don't take drugs at all. I categorically state – are you getting all this, tape? – that I do not take drugs.

'The fact is that it's illegal, and if a thing's illegal you're liable to get caught doing it and that's sort of all there is to it really. I don't really like to go on about it. It's not important.'

The conversation trotted around the room a couple of times, nodded off for a few minutes and surfaced, via an alarmingly devious route, at the prospects of Live Wings Over The White Cliffs Of Dover – a British tour, in fact.

'We're rehearsing at the moment with our new drummer, the fellow who drummed on the album. He's called Joe English. We're just rehearsing – or *practising*, as Pete Townshend would say – and as soon as we've learned enough numbers and get it together, we'll . . . tour.

'Hopefully Britain – I'd love to do Britain first, y'know, see how it goes. Everyone's keen to go and play, everybody feels like it, everyone's pleased with the LP. We're just rehearsing, learned a few numbers – learn a few more and then we'll rock off on tour.'

It'll be more than two years since the last Wings appearance in Britain.

'Something like that. I don't keep count of things like that. I feel that making a record is almost like playing live, anyway. It's just going and doing *something*. Doesn't really make much difference to me, though I suppose it does to you or the punters.'

S'pose it does at that, Paul.

'. . . Because it's the time they get to see you and stuff.'

An associate enters the room to enthuse about the latest bunch of pictures. He reserves particularly warm approval for one set of group shots. 'Everyones's so *happy* and *smiling*!' he coos.

They start to discuss which shot should be used for the cover of something or other before McCartney snaps, 'Well, we'll talk about it in a sec, because he's got his tape running.'

I felt the mantle of E. Howard Hunt descend about my shoulders.

'Besides, *NME* must take precedence over such mundane matters.'

He returns to the conversation and we bitch a bit on the disgusting state of British radio, which is the first topic on which he's felt like expressing a clear-cut opinion. Eventually he decides that though it could be a lot better, it could also be a lot worse.

'The Bay City Rollers — I think that's all good, that stuff. I like those bands for the younger kids. I would not want to force on the younger kids *good music*. It's like me dad forcing on me *good music*, y'know; his idea was a tenor, y'know, a beautiful tenor voice but I used to think, "No, he sounds like he's strangled."

'I'd like to hear Elvis much better, or someone *I* thought had a good voice, y'know. I don't feel that you have to tell everyone, "This is good and The Bay City Rollers are rubbish." I think they're a good group for what they do, I even like the *Osmonds* for what they do.

'I mean I know there's this kind of it's dreadful like uncool to even kind of . . . y'know, you wanna laugh at that them sort-of-thing, 'cause you know sort of what it is; it's a bit teenybop and stuff.

'I think, well great, y'know. It's only the people of ten years ago laughing at The Beatles when The Beatles first came out, y'know. It doesn't mean to say that 'cause they hadn't got brilliant music . . . but it's only my opinion or our opinion, because a lot of people think their music *is* brilliant, and there's nothing you can do about it. You can't go about saying, "No it isn't, it's rubbish."

'I think it's great. I mean, if that's what the kids want to listen to and that's what they want to play and they get it on doing that, well, I say good luck to 'em, y'know.

'They just wanna bop, y'know; good on 'em. Little Mary fell in love with Donny Osmond about a year back when everyone did, and what she liked about him was that when he'd sing a song on television, she'd say "He loves me, doesn't he, daddy?" She'd have this thing that the feller singing was singing just for her, and all girls — well, little girls — love that.

'That's always been a big part of music — Elvis, Beatles, y'know. The Stones are still kind of . . . y'know . . . it's the kind of romance thing still. There's still a kind of playing-to-chicks thing that if you took it away, you'd lose half of the whole music scene, y'know.'

*

He goes on to state that even though there's a lot of rubbish in the chart, there's also a lot of good stuff.

'You always get that – I mean, there was Ken Dodd's record a few years ago which suddenly got *huge* and everyone said, "Oh blimey."

'But good luck to him really, y'know.

'If people like it and they want to go out and buy it, well, that's it. I'll tell you when I'd think the charts were in a state: when there was just *nothing* in the charts.'

Strong measures are clearly called for.

What gets you pissed off these days?

Time comes to a standstill. Caught in a frozen moment, an infinite silence fills the room. P. Mc knits his brow. The receptionist knits half a bedsock.

Time passes.

Eventually, McCartney delivers judgement.

'I really can't think of one,' he muses. 'I know I've got them. Mmmm . . . I don't know really. I really can't think of anything particularly. It's a good time for me. There's probably a few somewhere. Something silly like the milkman didn't arrive for three days . . .'

Enter, in a clap of thunder, Linda McCartney. McCartney appeals to her to think of a few things that irritate him. 'Common Market . . . very major. British television, British radio, British taxation . . . another bummer. They're going to lose all their –'

'Right, we got it,' cuts in McCartney. Linda instantly lapses into respectful silence.

He delivers a short set speech about what lunacy the Common Market is.

'We don't like the Common Market . . . *I* don't like the Common Market.'

'*I* don't like the Common Market,' pipes up Linda.

'Linda doesn't like it either,' continues McCartney, and carries on with the political science. 'On to taxation – very quickly – the British government are making it very difficult for a lot of kind of big earners for Britain like Elton John, Rod Stewart, myself . . . y'know, a lot of people . . . making it very difficult for them to stay in England, because basically you get . . . if you earn a pound, they get ninety-eight pence of it and you get to keep two. And that's . . .

'And that's demoralizing.

'You just think, "Oh, *bloody 'ell* – it's just too much. Some feller somewhere is takin' all of that out of my pound."'

'And not giving it back to the people either,' quoth Linda. 'It's not like –'

'It doesn't look like because of it everything's going much better,' continues McCartney.

He doesn't seem to have any qualms about interrupting Linda whenever she attempts to say anything, and it doesn't seem to worry her too much.

'So I say they're starting to force people out, which then gives you the problem that all that money then isn't coming into England and all the recording studios in England, people can't use 'em 'cuz they've gotta record out of the country, so it gets . . .

'That's why people record out of the country a lot of the time.

'So things like that, I think maybe if they were just a little more reasonable on the tax they kind of took something like *half* of it off you, which is bad enough, then at least people would be able to live with that and would be able to stay and kind of keep the money coming into the country. It just doesn't seem very wise to me to punish everyone to the extent that they gotta move, 'cuz then it means that everyone's moving out.

'It's – uh – the blues drain or somethin'.'

Well, now you've got an American visa, how about pulling up stakes?

'No. I live in England, and I just like living here. It's a nice place.'

'I would never move because of money,' interjects Linda. 'I would never change my life because of money. Ever. If I like a place –'

'Yeah, well,' declaims Macca. 'Y'know, that's the idea is just that, well, y'know that we like to live here and wouldn't like to be forced out because of –'

'BUT!!!' yells Linda and they attempt to shout each other down for a few seconds before McCartney triumphs and continues.

'But it'd be great if the government . . . you go to Nashville and there's a hurricane warning on the telly. Every two hours there's a big hurricane and you suddenly get the feeling that your roof's gonna get blown off.

'You go to Los Angeles and there's an *earthquake* warning, and the tremor rate and the . . . on the . . . *thing, y'know* . . . the

111

whassitcalled ... the Richter Index or something they got out
there: "It's so-and-so today and it looks like we're gonna explode
today, folks," and you suddenly think "Oh God, at least old
Britain doesn't have hurricanes and earthquakes!"'

Ah, so *that's* why we shouldn't have gone into the Common
Market.

'... and when we got back here after America, I really felt
wow, at least the ground doesn't move under your feet ... I like
the British people. I think they're the salt of the earth. Very good
people, y'know. I like American people too' (quick glance at
Linda) 'but I *prefer* ...'

No holding Linda now, gang. She's determined to articulate
more than seven words this time before Big Mac steamrollers her
with any more folk wisdom.

'No, but I know ... yeah ...' (must run in the family) 'but in
New Orleans, we met *real people* ...'

That's as far as she gets. Macca crunches in with:

'Down to earth ... hangin' out, yeah.'

And they croon to each other about *real people* for a while
before McCartney weighs in with a pronouncement that really
sums the whole thing up:

'England is England and Britain is Britain and there's something special about it for me. There's just something it has that
... I mean, you get a day like today, a lovely day in the city, it's
just good and everyone comes out in their frocks and stuff and
*weeeeeey* and it's ... yeah, it's that one again and it's lovely,
y'know what I mean?

'Can't beat it.'


At some earlier point during the proceedings, McCartney had
burbled something about a 'hip government'. Where does he
think such an implausible beast will come from?

'Well nobody knows, do they?' he says, casually obliterating
something that Linda is trying to say at the same time. Howcum
she hasn't bonged him with a tambourine by now?

The end part of her comment emerges, while McCartney is
drawing breath, as '... smoking too many cigarettes and doing it
like ...'

'Like lawyers and solicitors,' McCartney continues smoothly,
'and accountants ...'

112

Linda: 'Have you *seen* them?'

'. . . it's all like a boardroom, the whole thing.'

Linda: 'They're nothing like *ordinary people*.'

'You need sort of a man of the people,' quoth Macca sagely. 'Y'know, you need like . . .'

Linda: 'Abraham Lin . . .'

'. . . one of these backwoodsmen who comes out of the people and says, "This is not good enough!" There's a lot of common sense, *I* think . . .'

Your turn, Linda, he's pausing for breath again.

'I think that this generation that's in government now is an *older* generation, and as it changes because *we're* different than the last generation, and finally there's going to be someone in power from one of the generations who's kinda *loose* and who's thinking more about philosophy of life –'

'*Quality* of life and how to make people enjoy it.'

'. . . about *living*,' declaims his spouse, 'I was just saying to Paul – this is funny,' she asides, allowing P. Mc to come back with:

'Because that's the way to get people *working*: get them to enjoy life.'

'. . . we should get back to . . . we should be ripping down the factories – *employing* people to rip down the factories and then employing them to plant *food* – we're going to have a food shortage soon, which is *ridicul* –'

Very sorry, Linda, but your time's up, and it's back to Paul now, who's got something that he's really aching to get off his chest.

. . . Paul?

'And the funny thing is that it looks like that may be what everything . . .

'I mean, if this goes on like we're saying it's going on, it looks like that might be kind of the thing, y'know, that the only way back to kind of away from the kind of crazy 1984 thing would be that that goes so far that the planet can't support it, and everybody really literally has to start ripping 'em down. I think that there's kind of enough common sense flying around among *ordinary people* . . .

'I think there's more than there's ever been, y'know, what with television and education and all that stuff. I think there's an awful lot of common sense among . . . just *people*.

'I think they've got very . . . I always remember when I was kind of a kid kind of thing, knowing that governments always underestimated people, and people were a lot hipper than governments and things gave them credit for. I still think it's there, y'know, and I think the government has to kind of try its way and it's not gonna work and Harold Wilson's gonna try and get everyone Socialist and it's not gonna work, but that's not really quite what Britain wants. Margaret Thatcher's gonna try and get everyone Tory, but that's not quite what everyone wants and the Liberals are gonna try and go up the middle . . .

'There's a lot of people going back to . . . there was a thing also a few years ago, d'you remember? — there was a feller said that in the future in a certain year we were all gonna have just one square yard of land.'

He pauses to let the impact of his words sink in.

'*Each*. I can't remember much about it, it was just all about everyone standing around having a square yard of land each. But if you fly over America you see all the towns huddled around a little river or lake somewhere. And then you see masses of . . . millions of acres of desert and things and so it doesn't really seem to me that we're all going to be huddled on one acre somewhere.

'Maybe the cities are going to get very huddled. In which case they're going to have to spread out a bit.

'I don't know . . . it's their problem, anyway.'

'Back to basics,' says Linda, ever the practical one.

'Yeah, back to "Venus And Mars", lads. Tell us about your album.'

'Oh, all right,' says Paul.

# Bruce Springsteen: Man, myth or monster?

*NME*, 11 October 1975

*SPARKS fly on E Street . . .*

The further west you get the worse off you are without a car.

In Houston, Texas, if you ain't got wheels you are one hundred per cent screwed; you mooch down the street past the massage parlours and churches kicking at abandoned beer cans and looking for a place to eat after midnight (room service cuts off at 12, y'see).

You mooch along until you find a drive-in diner with a vaguely surreal patio full of hacked and crumbling white plaster tables and chairs, where they give you a free milkshake (chocolate, strawberry or vanilla) if you order the steak sandwich.

So you go ahead and order it and you find out why the 'shakes are free (they're god-awful is why) and you sit there and smoke a cigarette in the wild spooky Texas night and start thinking about Bruce Springsteen.

Ninety minutes earlier, you'd been in the Music Hall, a 4,000-seater Houston hall where the aforementioned Spruce Stringbean had played the second of two packo-sellout gigs.

You know what happens at certain gigs when you're sitting there and you hear someone blissfully clapping time impossibly close to you and you look down and find that it's you? The Springsteen gig was one of those dream gigs when a performer schleps his reality and his environment onto the stage with him and manages to interlock his universe with his listeners.

After seeing Springsteen you realize that his records are dumb and irrelevant; forget 'em, they're trash, they're a shadow show in a distorting mirror, and he's not really there at all. It's possible to hear his records and hardly dig him at all; it ain't possible to see his show and walk out quite the same.

I mean, the cat is *good*.

Let's you and me check out some charts. In the latest *Cash Box* Top 100 albums Bruce's new album 'Born To Run' is in at number ten (with a bullet of course). Last week it was at thirty-one and the week before that it wasn't even in the goddam shops. His two previous albums, 'The Wild, The Innocent And The E Street Shuffle' and 'Greetings From Asbury Park NJ', are at eighty-five and 100 respectively. Also with bullets.

Let's try *Billboard*. There we find 'Born To Run' at eight (*with* a bullet) up from eighty-four on its second week on the charts. The other two albums are bulleted at ninety-eight and ninety-nine. In *Record World*, the new album is at three up from ten, while the oldies are in at 113 and 123.

The weird thing is that neither of those first two albums even made the top 200 when they first came out. In its first six months, 'Greetings' sold all of 50,000 copies, which for America is a rotten sale.

It was even money that CBS were going to drop Springsteen when Clive Davis fell, because he was a rookie act with a flop album who'd been one of Clive's pet prodigies. Still, a few folks in the company thought the boy was really something and hung in there, and now the CBS people are portentously intoning stuff abut how Brucie's too big to do any but the most carefully selected interviews and no, you can't take any off-stage photos. Sorry.

Pure '72 Tony DeFries.

Anyway, for those of you who simply remember Springbruce as one of the '73 class of new Dylans, it's Fax Time on WNME. Springsteen is a twenty-five-year-old bona-fide street-punk from Freehold, New Jersey. Freehold is just down the road from Asbury Park, a real under-the-boardwalk street paradise full of clubs, pinball arcades, beaches and hotnight streetcorner Americana of all descriptions. Asbury Park is Springsteen's sourcepoint: an environment that he re-creates in the riotous R&B punk ballet of his stage show.

Really, it's *that thing* that makes the difference between his records (which don't make it) and his stage show (which does); on record he comes on like some kind of sensitive singer-songwriter with a mental block about ever leaving anything at all out of a song. Good idea, bad idea, no damn idea at all, sling it in, man, it'll fit. Except that the good lines were so good that it left a bad taste in the ear when they were juxtaposed with the bad ones.

The songs on the new album are a lot more tasteful, but the ponderous mock-Spector arrangements are from hunger.

The trouble was that the quality of Springsteen's best work made it mandatory to judge the rest of his work by that standard. Yer average turkey rock act can be patted on the back if it manages to haul one good song out of the garbage heap of its regular output, but when Springsteen was goood he was so good that he made you hate him for not being that good all the time. Just as it was impossible to take the more outrageous claims of his supporters seriously when sitting at home checking out his records, it was likewise impossible to write him off.

I mean, new Dylan, new Schmylan; I get uptight when I hear *anyone* touted as the new *anything*. It's one thing to say that someone occupies an equivalent position to some famous biggie in terms of the context of today's music scene, or whatever, but whenever I hear that 'new Beatles/new Dylan/new Stones' jive I hang up and walk out.


So I was pissed off with Springsteen right up front because of the outrageous disservice that his more vocal admirers were doing him, saddling the poor kid with a label that he just couldn't live up to, no way. Plus it didn't even sound as if he was trying to live up to it in the first place.

The strongest vibe that I got off Springsteen's records was that he was the best new white R&B voice/musical identity that I'd heard in a long time. And I was blown over when I saw him live and discovered that the aspect of his work that had impressed me the most was, in fact, the deepest and most central core of his work.

Let's get to it: Springsteen has the finest understanding of black music – not just the sound of it, but the philosophy and ethics of the modern R&B show – of any white act since the J. Geils Band.

He also has stage presence like only a handful of seventies acts have it – Bowie, Patti Smith, Bob Marley, Brilleaux/Johnson, LaBelle, Alex Harvey (curiously, The SAHB display an instinctive grasp of the philosophy of R&B choreography even though they don't play no R&B). Plus he's got a great voice and a kick-ass band.

*

117

Anyway, he comes on stage slouching and bowlegged and akimbo in jeans and leathers, wispy beard and pirate earring, and the first thing is that I'm surprised by how *small* he is. He does 'Incident On 57th Street' all alone at the centre mike with just his piano player Roy 'The Professor' Bitten, and he's doing an excellent impersonation of a cat who's all limbs that he doesn't know what to do with.

His feet shuffle, his face screws up like an old glove, he doesn't know what to do with his hands, he twitches. Then the band come on and their presence seems to give him confidence and he sneakslides into his stylized strut where street body movement extends into the dancing zone.

The song is 'Tenth Avenue Freeze Out', off the new album (the album version reflects the Springsteen stage vibe far better than most of his recordings, incidentally). By now he's got one of those po'-boy slouch caps hanging off the side of his head, and he's well into his definitive onstage characterization: sassy street dude deluxe in his tennis shoes laying down his jive and talking trash on the corner, all good peer group stuff, working off of the two main guys in his group (known, quite logically in terms of Springsteen's Asbury mythology, as the E Street Band).

The ones I'm talking about are Miami Steve (guitar), a sharp-lookin' mofo in a cream gangster suit, who used to play with Springsteen in his New Jersey bar band days, and Clarence Clemons (saxophone). Now Clemons is not only the cat whose musical contributions invariably kick the numbers into overdrive, but he's Springsteen's most effective visual foil onstage.

He's a huge black Man-Mountain, magisterially duded up in a white suit, hat and shoes, and I think they use ultra-violet lights on him to let him gleam spookily through even when the stage is at its most dimly lit.

He looks like the living incarnation of R&B, does Clemons. If you want a perfect indication of what R&B means to its most devoted white enthusiasts, all you need is a picture of Clarence Clemons. He looks just like you always wished King Curtis did.

And in terms of the theatre of Springsteen's show, whenever he and Clemons give each other five or fall into a snatch of soul dancing or bump into each other, it's as if the Great Spirit of R&B was smiling on this white-punk upstart from under the board-walk.

118

Clemons is a mainman; he plays hot, raucous, steamy R&B tenor the way it was meant to be played. Springsteen says, 'Clarence plays the notes you want to hear,' and he's dead-on right.

Springsteen pulls off his first real and deadly *coup de théâtre* early on in the set, during 'Spirit In The Night' (a song from 'Greetings' and still one of his best), taken kinda looser and shakier than before.

Springsteen works the front of the stage when he comes to that slowed-down last verse, sitting there dangling his legs off the edge, and as he comes to the line '*Ran into the lake in just his socks and his shirt*', he changes '*lake*' to 'pit' and — *kthunk* — right on the word 'pit' he drops down into the photo pit (which doesn't actually have any photographers in it, just a coupla black cops looking totally confused).

The words '*in his socks and shirt*' come with agonized slowness from nowhere — no one can see him, where the hell did that sonovabitch get to? — until you see fingers clawing at the other lip of the pit and arms reach down and haul Springsteen up until he's perched on the edge right up against the front row.

He turns his head and peeks over his leather shoulder with a real sly '*Heyyyyyyyyy*, man' street grin, and wriggles out of the front row's clutches, drops back into the pit and hauls himself back onto the stage just as the band rampages back into the chorus with Springsteen wildly strutting back and forth across the stage.

Man, did they love that bit! Springsteen isn't — yet — the kind of act who needs to be afraid to go right down into his audience, as opposed to giving them that tantalizing handtouch that's the rock and roll equivalent of the limp-fish wave that the Queen gives the plebs during state visits.

It's a nice little populist touch, a seventies visual-aid version of those horrible 'Hey-man-we're-all-one-man' raps that turkey hippie bands used to lay down during the more excessive moments of the sixties, but it was done with flash and stagecraft shrewdness of the kind that — it needs to be said again — are more common to black acts.

When Springsteen is at his best he's funky and when he's funky he's at his best.

Believe it.

119

When he does a classic oldie, like 'Pretty Flamingo' played cool and sweet and steady he snaps it straight into his own mythology.

He prefaced it with a long rap about how he and Miami Steve useta lounge on the front porch with their guitars and watch this chick sashay by; and even though everybody there knew that Springsteen hadn't written the song (at least, I hope they knew), it had become his by osmosis; it clearly existed as part of the same cultural universe as his own songs, came from the same place.

The absolute highest moment of the set was 'The E Street Shuffle', which expanded outwards from the bubbling, snappy disco item that it was on the album to a whole ballet street parable.

It started out with Springsteen draped against a mike stand with his cap askew on his head (the cap was almost visual code that he was gonna be at his most theatrically *street*), reminiscing about his early bands down in Asbury Park, New Joisey, and the clubs that he used to play, like the Student Prince, and how his band couldn't get work because they played Chuck Berry and R&B instead of Top 40 and Vanilla Fudge.

. . . And how he and Miami Steve started out with a ten-piece band and gradually got down to a five-piece because people kept drifting away as the money got worse.

He and Steve mime bopping down the street wondering what their band lacked and then you see the gigantic figure of Clemons looming out of the darkness just outside the spotlight.

They quiver and quake in awe, all with a running commentary from Springsteen (who, incidentally, is a great raconteur) until Steve and Clemons do a slow-motion soul-slap. And at the precise moment that their hands meet over Springsteen's head, he drops into a crouch and whispers, '*Sparks fly on E Street . . .*' and it really is one of the all-time magic moments, bettered only by the bit where Springsteen drinks from a paper cup and flips it over his shoulder without a backward glance *and it lands right side up.*

Bruce Springsteen's been playing in bar bands since he was fifteen. He knows every bar band trick in the book, all the old rock-'em-sock-'em scams that you have to use to draw the patrons' attention out of their glasses and onto the stage. If you can really and truly pull that one off in the bars, then you're gonna go great in a concert hall, where the audience already has its attention focused on you.

Springsteen's totally hip to that. Apart from the two numbers ('Thunder Road' from the new album, which acts as a breather about halfway through his set, and the aforementioned 'Incident On 57th Street') that he performs with only piano accompaniment, he never lets up on his audience, never stops working the hall, makes sure that there's always something cooking onstage, no dead space at all.

It's pure comin'-straight-atcha-look-out stuff, the purest assimilation and distillation of the styles and ambience of timeless uptown-Saturday-night classic R&B that I've seen from any white act since the heyday of J. Geils.

Whether lease-lending from Chuck Berry's 'Come On' with 'Backstreets' or Bo Diddley on 'She's The One' or playing a searingly sweet Albert King 'Ain't No Sunshine' intro to 'Kitty's Back', Springsteen has a totally sure command of his idiom.

He presents a perfect white interpretation of black music for white people, which ties up perfectly with his articulate-punk persona, as per all those CBS posters of Brucie standing lonesome in the street with a beat-up pair of sneakers dangling from the head of his vintage Fender Esquire (a perfect punk guitar, by the way; a Les Paul would look far too serious-musicianly for a punk image).

The only trouble with the whole trip of Springsteen as ultimate punko deluxe is that his portrayal is too detailed and his songs are too sentimental and too articulate (cf. John Lennon's remark about how you could always recognize an actor because of the way their faces moved). Real punks are more like The Ramones or Television: they're so snotty that they couldn't even give a shit about whether you really consider them to be *real* street punks or not.

Plus they write in platitudes, which is great, because the last thing on their minds is getting poetically agonized about their punkhood. Springsteen provides such a finely detailed larger-than-life portrait of a punk that he overkills his own verisimilitude.

In a way, the street-rock of Springsteen is the exact polar opposite of the street-rock of Lou Reed. Reed presents himself as having gone through so much as to have become totally deadened to everything — cocooned so smoothly in his insulating smack bubble that he's an utterly dispassionate observer of everything that passes before his senses, detached to the point where all perspective vanishes and all events are of equal importance (the same trick that Vonnegut pulled in *Breakfast of Champions*, in a way).

Springsteen, on the other hand, lives in the same world, but he attempts to turn the streets and alleys of New York and Asbury Park into a highly coloured, magical wonderland of bizarre beauty and terror.

Where Reed flattens it out, Springsteen imbues it with a vital, three-dimensional life. It's the exact opposite of the jaded I've-tried-everything-twice-and-got-bored-with-it-the-first-time-pass-the-valium school of eleganza sleaze rock, and when that energy is hung off a stone good-time R&B show, then Christ don't it make ya feel good.

That's why the records don't make it. On the records the focus is on Bruce the soulful poet rather than on Springsteen the whompin' stompin' R&B man. On record you can spot every strained lyric, every overblown image, every little error of judgement. Onstage, you just don't give a shit as long as Clemons is honking and Bruce is struttin' and Miami Steve is layin' down that sweet sweet groove.

The trouble with Springsteen's new album is that it sounds as if he'd been told too often how *important* he is and as a result has set out to write *important* songs and make an *important* record. *'It's hard to be a saint when you're just a poor boy on the street,'* wrote Springsteen on his first album, but the converse holds true: it's hard to be a poor boy on the street when the people who surround you are telling you that you're a saint, or at the very least, a big-ass rock and roll star.

The vitality of the whole Springsteen ambience is dependent on his street empathy, and the bigger Springsteen gets, the more he's going to see of limousines and fancy hotels and record company people who fall over themselves to tell him he's wonderful, and the less he's going to see of the environment from which he drains his energy. The benefits that accrue to musicians because of the thing that they do well can all too easily incapacitate them from doing that thing any longer, because it isolates them from the circumstances that made them want/need to do that thing in the first place.

And then they end up playing the part of the person they used to be, playing it parrot fashion as if they'd learned it from someone else's records and videotapes, and as like as not the audiences don't know the difference and couldn't give a shit as long as they get what they came to see, and the record company sycophants and PR people don't care as long as dem ol' units keep getting shipped coast to coast.

Springsteen's probably got a way to go before any of that starts happening to him, but happen it will; both because of the nature of his music and because of the way one or two people in his record company are unintentionally liable to kill the goose that lays the gold albums.

See, Springsteen's early songs were written about his present; his next album will have to be written about his past, because his new present will consist of the rock star life. If he draws on *that*, then we're liable to end up with a clutch of Ian Hunter-type songs about the angst of the rock star, and Ian's already done that number to perfection.

It's a problem that doesn't arise for the likes of, say, Elton, because there's nothing street about him or his show and he certainly isn't presenting himself as a cat off the block.

Springsteen *is*, and soon as he ceases to be a down-in-the-alley dude, he'll either have to become something else or else resign himself to becoming just another elegant phoney.

One of the worries I have about Springsteen is that he may never make the record that hits as hard as his stage show. None of his albums pack more than a flyweight punch, and the only possible reason for listening to any of them is so that you know the songs when you see him – that is, *if* you see him.

The CBS guy was of the opinion that it wasn't necessary for Springsteen to do anything more than a TV special – over which, naturally, he must have 'total control' – and a London show or two.

Playing Glasgow or Manchester is 'not necessary' – just as doing any but the safest patty-cake interviews is 'not necessary'. Just as, if he had a good live album out, listening to any of his studio albums would be 'not necessary'.

Still, you gotta see his show when he brings it over, because Bruce Springsteen and his R&B Punk Ballet Company is one of the best things I've ever seen on a rock and roll stage.

Hey, Bruce – just remember who you say you are and keep yer nose clean. And don't believe more than half of what they tell you.

# 1975:
# A scuzz odyssey

*NME*, 8 November 1975

*BEAT on the brat, beat on the brat, beat on the brat with a baseball bat . . .*

Ladies and gentlemen, The Ramones.

The Ramones are quite ridiculous. They used to play twenty-minute sets because they only had eight songs, but now they're up to forty-five minutes. At one gig they clocked in with twelve songs in twenty-six minutes, instant classics like 'Beat On The Brat' (the complete lyric of which is quoted above), 'Judy Is A Punk', 'I Don't Wanna Go Down In The Basement', 'I Want To Be Your Boyfriend' and many more. Many, *many* more.

Tonight they're playing the Performance Studio on the Lower East Side. You walk up a flight of stairs to get to the Studio, where a sign informs you that it's a free gig, but a three-buck 'donation' is requested, and if you don't pay the 'donation' ya don't get in, capeesh?

However, as part of the deal you get all the beer you can drink (if you're prepared to draw it yourself), and sets by The Ramones and Blondie. You also get the chance to sit through about an hour and a half of fifties tapes memorizing the faces of the other nine people who showed up. This is because Blondie's drummer had to be collected from the airport.

For a while it looked as though there were going to be nearly as many people on the stage as there were in the audience, because the Performance Studio is pretty damn small. I mean, I've been in bigger living-rooms. It makes me remember how disappointed I was the first time I ever went to the Marquee. It was so small and scuzzy, not at all the place of myth and legend that I'd built it up to be all those years, and it came as a shock to discover that a highly touted NY flash like The Ramones would be playing to a total audience of – at final count – twenty-seven people, nine of whom were photographers.

What had happened was that The Ramones – and, by extension, most of their colleagues on the New York underground circuit – had received such a lot of media attention from the NY area rock press that I'd assumed that they were getting to be quite big.

What's actually happening is that New York has a thriving local band scene, and they get coverage in their local rags just as a hot new San Francisco band might get coverage in *Rolling Stone* or a good Detroit band might make it into *Creem* or a pub band with promise might get a little space in *NME* even though they're only playing to a hundred people a night.

Or less.

CBGB, a small club on the Bowery round about the Bleecker Street intersection, is to the New York punk band scene what the Marquee was to London rock in the sixties.

It's where most of the bands do their main gigs and where they hang out to watch and/or heckle (the latter activity a speciality of members past and present of The New York Dolls) their friends and competitors.

So far, the nearest thing to a star to be produced by CBGB is Patti Smith – put it this way, she's the only one out of that scene to have a record deal with a major company – and she was out of circulation around the time I was there because she was closeted in Electric Ladyland with John Cale making the 'Horses' album.

Similarly, Television, regarded by the prime voyeurs on the New York scene as being the Next Band To Happen, were conspicuous by their elusiveness. Having been thoroughly knocked out by them earlier this year, I was hot to see 'em again, but couldn't find head nor hair of them.

Their bass player, Richard Hell, had teamed up with ex-Doll Johnny Thunders to form a new band called The Heartbreakers, and casual chat with the locals revealed conflicting reports as to whether they were actually still together.

Since then, I've heard a privately pressed single ('Little Johnny Jewel Pts 1 and 2' on the Ork label) and a tape. The single is rotten and the tape reveals only sporadic flashes of the power they revealed the night I saw them.

Television are known around New York for their wilful inconsistency (a piece on the band in New York's *Soho Weekly News* by Alan Betrock begins: 'Take two people down to see Television on two different nights and the odds are that they'll return with completely diverse opinions'). And since they still haven't recorded anything impressive (viz. the débâcle of the Eno Tape, a tale of almost legendary status in CBGB annals), it seems unlikely that any of the major labels who've decided that they can get along without Television are likely to change their minds unless a particularly hip A&R man manages to catch Tom Verlaine and his henchmen on a flamingly good night.

The Ramones, though, are a band that the London rock scene could really use. Jeez, I'd give a week's pay just to see them explode over an unprepared audience at, say, Dingwalls. They're simultaneously so funny, such a cartoon vision of rock and roll, and so tight and powerful that they're just bound to enchant anyone who fell in love with rock and roll for the right reasons.

I mean, if you started digging rock because it provided a vital insight into the mood of the times, or because so many rock musicians today are – what you say down there? – *genuinely creative* (you know, like Rick Wakeman or Mike Oldfield), then forget it, Jack, 'cuz The Ramones will just make you whoops your cookies.

The Ramones aren't worried about being genuinely creative, and if you told them they provided a unique insight into anything they'd probably piss on your shoes, and you'd deserve it, too.

They ain't glitter queens. They ain't a blues band. What they do is fire off ridiculously compressed bursts of power chords and hooklines, nuthin' but hit singles or what would be hit singles if there was any justice in this crummy world (well, well, well, take a look arowoond etc.).

C'mon up and meet the boys. That's Dee Dee on bass – he's the one in the black leather jacket, sneakers and torn-up jeans. Over there behind the drums is Tommy, he's the short one in the black leather jacket, beat-up jeans and sneakers. Johnny's the guitar player in the black leather jacket, Captain America T-shirt, torn jeans and sneakers, and the one in the black leather jacket, torn jeans, sneakers and McGuinn shades is Joey. They all claim 'Ramone' as their surname.

Joey Ramone isn't much over seven feet tall. You see this

unbelievably long and thin streak of dirty denim and scuffed leather up onstage and when your eyes get to the top you find out he's slouching. Joey Ramone slouches like a telegraph pole slouches, and what's more he stays slouched. At moments of extreme urgency he performs this strange jack-knife motion with his right leg. It looks as though he's trying to kick himself in the ass.

Each song begins with Dee Dee shouting 'one-two-three-four', followed by a headlong, full-speed rampage around the riff — whichever riff it is. The Ramones not only don't play no drum solos (thank you, Lord) but they don't even play guitar solos — well, maybe one or two, but nothing lasts over three minutes top whack. It's more likely to be two minutes and ten seconds on average. Never more than three quarters of a minute between songs except in cases of equipment failure.

Joey spits out the title of the song, Dee Dee shouts 'one-two-three-four' and they're off again, maybe with '53rd And 3rd' ('*53rd and 3rd waiting for a trick/53rd and 3rd is making me sick*'). They're great.

Coming on alternately like tough kids pretending to be innocent and green kids pretending to be tough, The Ramones are pocket punks, a perfect razor-edged bubblegum band. They should never make an album. They should make a single every week, 'cuz they've already got enough songs to last them for the first six months.

Whether The Ramones will get that chance while they're still young enough to take advantage of it is a whole different thing, though. White hard rock is about the least commercial singles material currently extant in this age of disco tyranny and MOR slop, and The Ramones are a clear case of a product existing well in advance of a market.

Which is probably why at the moment there's no sign of a record deal.

Supporting them, incidentally, on that epic night at the Performance Studio, was Blondie (formerly of decadent Ladybirds-type vocal group The Stilettoes) who's this cute little bundle of platinum hair with a voice like a squeaky bath toy and quite the cruddiest garage-type garage band I've seen since the last band *I* was in (and that band was a fuzz-box pretentioso blues band. This one is just cruddy.)

127

She has what could politely be described as a somewhat suspect sense of pitch, but her charm lies in the fact that she's a kid who's pretending desperately hard to be a star and who's aware of it. Which is why it works at all (apart from on account of she's so gosh-darned cute, gol-ding it); because her act has that home-madish quality.

Sadly, Blondie will never be a star simply because she ain't good enough, but for the time being I hope she's having fun. Whatever her actual age, though, she's spiritually a part of the Great American Nymphet Tradition.

Down at CBGB itself, however, things are cookin'. The place is a lot brighter and cleaner than it was last time I saw it, it's pretty solidly packed out and the jukebox is pumping out classic stuff like The Animals' 'Club-A-Go-Go', Jeff Beck and Donovan's great 'Barabajagal' – definitely the hippest jukebox this side of the Hope & Anchor.

There's a band setting up onstage, and the unpleasant looking guy who looks like Lou Reed wearing one of Wilko Johnson's suits who's shouldering his way past the bar turns out to be the lead singer.

The group are called Tuff Darts. The bass player looks like Peter Tork on speed.

'*I'm so sick 'n tired of the crap I gotta take in this town*,' they sneer eloquently. '*If it don't get no better I swear I'm gonna burn it down.*'

Well, really, boys ... don't you think that's – uh – taking things a little too far? I mean, the state New York's in right now you couldn't even claim the insurance.

Tuff Darts are more like your standard issue rock band, which means that the lead guitarist plays solos and the bass player goes zoom instead of clunk. They conjure up more of a late sixties/early seventies H. Metal roar than the trebly clang of the more early-sixties-orientated CBGB bands, but they sing in the classic acrid whine of the modern-day NY punk, and they look great. Apart from The Ramones, they're probably the best of the current crop.

Tonight they're supporting The Heartbreakers, the first (tadaaaaaaa!) NY punk supergroup, formed by Richard Hell, former bass player with Television, and The New York Dolls'

Johnny Thunders (guitar, vocal and lurch) and Jerry Nolan (drums and sweat-stains).

The line-up is completed by a morose-looking lead guitarist who looks as if his name ought to be Gary, but is more likely to be Albert. They are dreadful. Brother, are they dreadful.

They make their entrances in standard NY punk uniform: black leather jackets, T-shirts, sneakers and jeans. Hell is the sole exception: he's got a short '65-style British moddycut, shades and a crumpled black suit.

Thunders is playing a huge unwieldy Gretsch White Falcon guitar; Hell a Felix Pappalardi-style Gibson violin bass, and the erstwhile Gary (or Albert) an anonymous looking Les Paul. Thunders is, I'm told, a fairly inadequate guitarist at the best of times, but since no one's seen him at anything which could possibly be described as 'the best of times' since the early stages of The New York Dolls it must reluctantly be assumed that the display of minimal ability combined with maximum arrogance that he put on that night is the norm.

'Ooohhh, look! Johnny's taking his jacket off! YUMMMMM!!!' breathes Miriam from Cleveland. Miriam and her sister (and/or best pal) Helen flew up from Cleveland just to see The Heartbreakers, and they weren't disappointed, which either says a lot about Thunders' much-vaunted 'charisma' or for Cleveland — a town where, according to Miriam, there is a group of people who get *NME* sent over to them from England, all have the first Feelgoods album on import and helped break Alex Harvey in that part of the world. Hi there, Cleveland!

The only thing they did all night that got me off was an enthusiastic if undisciplined performance of the immortal Tommy Boyce and Bobby Hart song 'I'm Not Your Steppin' Stone', featured by The Monkees on the B-side of 'I'm A Believer', and that was GREAT because the song is GREAT and therefore any performance of it no matter how otherwise mediocre is GREAT.

The basic trouble with The Heartbreakers is that while Richard Hell was an effective foil for Tom Verlaine in Television and Johnny Thunders more or less functioned in The Dolls, neither of them has either the personality or the talent to lead or co-lead a band, which means that The Heartbreakers are forced to rely on Mach 9 volume and Mach 10 posturing, neither of which are any cure for the summertime blues.

Unless you're from Cleveland.

However, Thunders' ex-Dollhood gives the group a little added *cachet* around CBGB: after all, The Dolls made two albums and toured the world, while most of the other Bowery punk bands haven't even played much outside of New York State and New Joisey let alone Britain and Europe and Japan. So that makes Johnny Thunders a big man and gives him the right to demand to use the back door at CBGB so he doesn't have to walk through the audience like everybody else does.

Meanwhile, over on West 4th Street just past the Bottom Line, the orthodox wing of The New York Dolls (i.e. vocalist David Johansen and guitarist Sylvain Sylvain) are holding court in a video studio and viewing videotape of their Japanese gigs.

Sylvain – if I may call him by his first Sylvain – is wearing a black leather jacket, T-shirt, sneakers and jeans and enthusing about Ibanez guitars. He claims Ibanez make Fender and Gibson copies that are better than the originals. He was particularly fond of their Flying V, which he can be seen playing on the big screen that dominates the far end of the room.

Equipped with an ex-roadie on bass, a session drummer they found waiting for work at the Musicians' Union Hall and a fairly nifty keyboard player, they begin to sound like a fairly enjoyable high school R&B band, though they still indulge in old-style Dolls cavorting which now has a certain endearingly nostalgic quality.

Johansen is slumped up against the wall with his girlfriend Cyrinda Fox (a nice gal from Texas, natch) wearing red pants and boots and an absurd red hat. 'This band is more like me and Syl always wanted the band to be like, but the others couldn't play this stuff. What we did before was a lot of fun, and I think it's great that a bunch of kids like us did that much,' he says.

It's a safe bet that the new-look Dolls (who, at the time of writing, had not yet done any US dates and are – you guessed – currently without a record deal) will not be playing CBGB. According to reports, Johansen considers that The Dolls are too big a name to play CBGB, believing them to be a concert rather than a club band.

Apparently nobody's told him how many foreign tours and hit records some of the bands who play the Marquee have had.

Actually, The Dolls were the most successful of an earlier wave of New York bands, all of whom were firmly attached to the glitter fiasco of a coupla years back. There's a well-known line around to the effect that in those days, 'The hottest band in town were the ones with the highest platforms,' and that's about the way it was.

Now, however, the best of the class of '75, like The Ramones and Tuff Darts are delivering what The Dolls promised to, but didn't.

The last CBGB double bill I saw was Talking Heads supporting Shirts. They're a bit oddball for CBGB in that neither band is remotely in the dominant punk tradition. Talking Heads are seemingly aiming for an effect similar to the early Velvets' more icily restrained material, but their music is too thin and disjointed to make it work.

They've got a lead singer who looks a cross between John MacLaughlin and Bryan Ferry who scratches away earnestly at a big acoustic and a Fender Mustang with a Gibson humbucking pick-up wired in to replace the original top pick-up on account of Fender top pick-ups ain't as hot as their back pick-ups for some reason.

Their bassist, however, is probably the most arresting single figure in any of these bands, with the possible exception of Joey Ramone.

Her name's Martina Weymouth; she wears leather pants, grips her bass like it was the only thing keeping her from drifting out into some weird echoing warp phase, has blonde hair and the most frightened eyes I've ever seen. She plays mean, zonking bass, like the heavier she plays the more secure she is, the less likely to just float away or vanish or something.

Talking Heads' trip just didn't come through for me, possibly because David Byrne was having a lot of trouble with his amp and I couldn't hear the words, but Martina Weymouth ('Rock is no longer a noble cause,' she told the *Village Voice*) is some sort of star and as long as she needs that desperately to keep playing the bass like that, she stands a good chance of being Heard Of.

Shirts were the lead act that night, and they were far and away the most conventionally commercial act in their league. They were oddly reminiscent of the kind of act that CBS were signing in their 'Rock Machine' phase: keyboards, horns, congas, two guitarists and a girl singer.

The latter, Annie Golden by name, works by day in the promo department at ABC Records, and sends out neatly typed handouts on the band to anybody who expresses an interest. They play less interesting music than their colleagues; nohow and contrariwise, they're also the best musicians and, given the non-visionary nature of the average A&R office, far the most likely to get signed and Make It.

Ms Golden, however, is a better-than-average white female rock singer and an energetic live performer (to get academic for a second); and with or without the band someone'll pick up on her.

It would be cruel, though not strictly inaccurate, to remark that if all these bands were doing their scuffling out of Tulipville, Arkansas, no one would ever hear of them (though it would require a major genetic mutation for Tulipville, Arkansas, to produce a band like The Ramones in the first place).

At the present moment, The Dolls and Patti Smith are the only acts to emerge from the seventies New York into the national and international rock market from the New York club scene, though Kiss, Bruce Springsteen, Todd Rundgren and The Blue Oyster Cult all have associations with New York and its immediate environs.

The areas whose bands seem to be judged most appealing by the Yankee rock *lumpen* seem to be the South, Midwest and West Coast.

Basically, it's a tight, thriving community scene, a back-alley off rock's main drag, and CBGB is home turf to a whole host of bands, many more than I had a chance to see (like The Fast and The Miamis – same theoretical basis as The Ramones, I'm told – and The Stilettoes).

The reason that CBGB makes it is that it offers a forum for hopefuls who have something going and plays host to those bands' audiences, not to mention turning one band's audience onto another band and helping to broaden the field. It genuinely – pardon the lapse into '69 London Ladbroke Grove-ese – *provides a genuine service to the community*.

People talk about 'CBGB bands' the same way that they musta used to have talked about 'Max's type bands'. It's one of those rare rock and roll venues which has a character all its own and has taken it upon itself to nuture a specific scene; a specific school of music.

Plus the bucks ain't bad, either. On three bucks a throw and a two-drink minimum, nobody's hurtin'.

The New York bands probably don't play as well as their British counterparts; they're much lower on the conventional virtues and ain't no way as consistent. But there's a kind of spark in the best of them, like Television on a good night (I assume what I saw was a good night) or The Ramones (ditto) or even Tuff Darts (ditto again) that I haven't seen in any post-Feelgoods British bands at all.

What makes them happen is a generally abnormally high energy level, the desire to combine traditionalism with experiment by cutting rock right down to the basic ingredient that made 'em like it in the first place and then rebuilding from there. Maybe they just have a different – and therefore more novel – line in clichés from their British counterparts, but their humour, vitality and simplicity are engaging indeed.

Mostly, they have eschewed blues, country and jazz flavourings: they don't play no folk-rock, jazz-rock, funk-rock, country-rock, glitter-rock or nuthin' like that. They play rock-rock; rock and roll stylized, interpreted, refined according to personal preference and perspective and then fed back into itself.

Maybe the present decade is less of a specific area in its own right than simply a viewpoint from which to reassess the fifties and sixties. Seems that way in New York, because when it comes right down to it, what all of these bands have in common is that they're re-presenting the fifties and sixties in a way that could only be the seventies.

'*In spite of all the amputations/you could still dance to a New York station.*'

Lou Reed said that. Something like that, anyway.

'*I'm goin' back to New York City/I do be-leeeve I've had ee-nuff.*'

Bob Dylan said that.

'Somebody better record these bands (and do it *right*) before they become extinct.'

I said that.

# Lowell George: Willin' at the Watergate

*NME*, 6 December 1975

ONCE upon a time in the early sixties when everybody suddenly started getting paranoid about advertising men, and half the people you met were convinced that the 'Hidden Persuaders' were secretly ruling the world from Madison Avenue, you used to hear this cute slogan attributed to some grey-flannel-suited wolverine Machiavelli from one of the big ad agencies.

This bit of pre-fab folk wisdom went, 'You don't sell the steak, you sell the sizzle.'

The thing is, it ain't that easy to tell where the steak ends and the sizzle begins. Obviously it's the steak that's sizzling, and if you extend the metaphor so that Little Feat are the steak, then the sizzle is what happens when the stocky, bearded guy with the tired eyes standing up front bears down on his white Stratocaster with the metal tube on his finger and makes it sound *just so* . . .

It's a sizzle, right enough. He lays the sizzle simmering and bubbling over the chug of the rest of the band, and when he hits the note, that's when you just naturally get up on yer hind legs and put on your sailin' shoes.

*Ladies and gentlemen, Little Feat. On guitar and vocals, Mr Lowell George.*

Obviously, something had to give sometime.

If the first half of the seventies were delineated by a desire for an excess of posturing and extravagance – a succession of arrogant elitists more concerned with mimicking the worst and most inhuman manifestations of old-style Hollywood stardom – then it was inevitable that sooner or later the whole rhinestoned bubble would burst and leave a sticky mess over the faces of a large number of both its perpetrators and its audience.

Hence the burning question of the moment, asked in the pages of most thinking rock papers and in the homes of most thinking rock devotees: 'Is rock dead?'

If the question is interpreted to mean, 'Is the music (and by extension the makers and listeners thereof) stone kaput?' the answer is obviously, 'Hell, no.'

If it's interpreted to mean, 'Is rock in the process of streamlining itself by shedding a tacky old skin which was draining too much energy from the parent organism?' then the answer is, 'Yes please – and can you put that Little Feat album on again?'

Yes, Virginia, rock and roll is going through a sea-change right now, possibly the most important of its history.

What's happening is that, having neglected Mr Dylan's dictum about not following leaders and watching our parking meters, we went so far in the other direction that we elevated to hero status people who not only didn't deserve it but who in some cases – and five points to anybody who breathed the name 'Springsteen' at this point – are bright enough to realize that becoming a hero may even be against their interests. As a result, many of our idols are constructed entirely of clay, and our parking meters are way, way, *way* overdue, baby; overdue to the point that this whole thing is about to be towed away if we don't get our blind eyes away from the telescope; if we don't stop looking for shooting stars and start taking an interest in what's actually going on a little closer to home; if we don't start listening to what real people are saying about real things through the medium of real music.

*Ladies and gentlemen, Little Feat. On guitar and vocals, Mr Lowell George.*

Maybe the time has come to sacrifice a few of the old gods – the ones who have become either too preoccupied by the circumstances of their godhood, or too debilitated by the stresses and strains of said godhood to be able to remember or act upon the memory of why we made 'em gods in the first place. You know – the ones who're too busy hiding out from taxmen, romancing movie stars, and getting their blood changed to do records and tours and get the crumbling remnants of their music out to the people who save up for the albums and queue three days to get tickets to see 'em onstage on their bi-annual tours.

These people have consciously divorced themselves from us to the point that what they have to say to us don't matter any more. What Mick Jagger thinks about anything is no longer relevant. What Rod Stewart thinks isn't relevant.

So who needs 'em?

Sure, if we're still assessing rock in terms of these screwed-up old dinosaurs and the likelihood of new dinosaurs emerging, then yes, baby, rock *is* dead, and if it means an end to dinosaurs I'll be right up there lighting the first log on the funeral pyre.

But rock manifestly *isn't* dead – and in evidence I'll call Dr Feelgood, The Wailers, Patti Smith, Bob Dylan (a potential dinosaur who, alone among his contemporaries, cared enough to evolve) and . . .

*Ladies and gentlemen, Little Feat. On vocals and guitar, Mr Lowell George.*

Lowell George isn't a star. He's a musician.

You stand in the corridor outside his second-floor room in the Watergate Hotel in Washington DC, and as you prepare to ring the bell you notice a single, solitary squeezed lemon lurking on the carpet. He lets you in, murmurs 'Well, hey' and disappears into the bathroom, and you prowl around for a few moments.

It takes you a few seconds to realize that the two speakers that flank the bed aren't part of the hotel furnishings because they seem to blend in so well with the decor – the same fake grain veneer plastic wood beloved by the Gracious Living Departments of both hotels and electronic equipment designers. There's a box of cassettes – Bach lute music, Ry Cooder, home-compiled bluegrass, The Stones – a folded *NME* by the sofa, a fake *National Enquirer* front page made up by Warners.

Lowell George is Mr Average. He's not a glitter wimp or a cocaine pimp or a street punk; just a stocky bearded guy with an air of bearlike abstracted amiability in jeans, scuffed suede boots, a mauve shirt and a blue V-neck pullover that, if worn by an Englishman, would seem to have space-warped their way straight out of Marks & Spencer.

He offers you a choice of real and fake mineral water, tops it up with ice and half a lemon ('Uhhhh . . . where'd I put that knife?') and we sit down.

Before I can even think 'interview', I realize that we've just spent fifteen minutes talking about a mutual friend and ten minutes discussing the Marx Brothers.

How the hell do you 'interview' a guy like that?

See, when the idea of going to Washington and doing a Little Feat piece came up, I hadn't intended to interview anybody at all.

Little Feat's music always seemed to speak for itself more than adequately and rather than ruthlessly interrogate the creators thereof for musical minutiae and scabrous personal anecdotes about other famous people, it seemed more appropriate to try and just hang out and write a documentary number on the band and their associates.

It didn't work out quite like that because I'd bumped into Lowell George in the lobby and had an incidental two minutes' conversation which convinced me that the guy was so obviously enjoyable to talk to that getting in an hour's gab with him was going to be a pleasure in itself. So I got back in touch with the PR wing of the operation and said that I'd changed my mind, and could they fix up an interview after all. Borrowed a tape machine, fought my way past the maddened lemon in the corridor, rang the doorbell . . . it was quite an adventure.

So at one point we were talking about The Byrds, and how the first two albums are so similar in content, technique and texture that they sound like one album, and Mr George sez: 'The sound was very similar, because the band had not gone through any of the monumental changes that occur when a band gets very successful and everybody gets a big head.

'I mean, that's one of the problems of rock and roll, when a kid of twenty-two or three gets successful and goes to a $200,000 a year place in space and thinks "Shit, I can play the drums and earn $200,000 a year – fuck these guys!" And they go out on their own and they find out that it's all a mistake – ya know?

'What a wonderful industry.'

What about the disassociation that occurs when a songwriter who draws on his environment is pulled out of that environment and placed among the limos, dope, five-star hotels and trashy women of rock stardom?

'Of course. That happens to everybody. Springsteen will write songs about all the press he's got. He's had more press than any living being who hasn't sold a hundred thousand albums ever. It's amazing. Bruce is bigger than a politician. I haven't met the guy and I haven't heard his records, so I can't tell you what's going to happen to him. That happens to me too, but I always have those cheesy Holiday Inns to bring me right back down to earth, and I don't think we'll ever escape them.

'Another thing is that I'm not anxious to play in gigantic halls,

137

which is where we're headed right now. I don't relish that idea *at all*. I'd rather play to three, five, seven thousand people and play for several nights, maybe three nights in a row if we have a huge audience. Play to a small audience where the reality is much closer. You know, where there's still a communication.'

But what happens when the records start breaking big and the record company starts pushing the band to play those bigger gigs and reach more consumers with less outlay?

'It isn't record companies that say that, it's agents and managers. They'd love that to happen because they make more money that way. Actually, it really shouldn't be up to them. It should be up to me, and I'm working on that right now, trying to have it be *my* decision and not be anybody else's. One thing is that I hate to come to a town and be out the next day. You never get to find out about the street and what's going down and if there's a song out there to be written. I mean, *this city . . .*'

Washington. The band's PR say it's their 'home town' (even though they're from good ol' Ho-Lee-Wood, LA, Calif.) and that night at the gig the emcee will exhort the crowd to 'Please welcome home, Little Feat!'

'This city is an amazing place and I love to stay around here, because there's so much great music. It's very provincial. Twenty miles across that river right there is Virginia, where bluegrass music runs rampant in the streets. There's players here that are as good as there ever have been — I can think of two mandolin players that have lived in this town, and a dobro player, Mike Auldridge, who is just unbelievable, the dobro player of all time, and John Starling, a singer-songwriter who lives in the vicinity who is also a doctor. I hate to exclude all that.

'Jerry Garcia, you know, goes out and gets back on the street again, forms another group that is not quite together and has no — an untogether together band — and performs because he wants to get back to the street again.'

I allowed as how I thought that that was great of Garcia, but wished that a few people whose music was closer to my own street would do the same.

'Name one.'

Led Zep?

'I love their music, but their presentation leaves a little to be desired. Also they play a little bit too loud for ten thousand seats.

It's so godawful *loud*. I'd love to hear those guys come out with little cheesy Fender amps in a tiny hall some place under another name, but I reckon they're a little too *advanced* to do that.'

Yeah, but what Zep play *has* to be that loud to provide that overpowering annihilation effect that H. Metal depends on, especially for a band like Zep, who are all about power of various kinds.

'That's a very sexual concept — volume as subjugation of the feminine. I wonder if that's a formula that those folks have arrived at.'

The doorbell rings, and when we resume, Lowell is recounting the tale of a gig at 'a horrible little auditorium in Venice, California', where all the biggies arrived to catch El Feat.

'There was Phantom Fingers — what's his name? — Page; yeah, Plant and Page, that warbler from Australia — what's her name? — Helen Reddy, the Hagar Brothers from *Yee-Haw* (US C&W TV show). We had Ringo — it cracked me up that those people would be concerned about the idiom that we were playing in and concerned enough to go to Venice, California. I was impressed pretty much despite myself.

'We have gathered a kind of what you might call an underground audience which is now above ground. Sometimes the show might not be very good, but it's still because we're six people with six different feelings about what should be played. Sometimes it's on — sometimes we're really great. But it's amazing how overwhelming this whole music thing is, that people should devote their lives to finding out what kind of aftershave Frank Sinatra uses.

'I think the first major music star to gain a gigantic audience was Bing Crosby. Those old musicals were kind of what created this whole massive record market. But now, heavy metal has had its day both in terms of the music and those individuals who deal in that kind of lifestyle. People came to see Joe Cocker because he was gonna throw up on the drummer, and oddly enough he did it almost every night. It was almost like it was a *plan*. Now Joe Cocker doesn't seem to be in mind to plan *anything*, so I wonder who did plan it. Maybe someone puts ipecac in his Southern Comfort.

'We did a coupla concerts with him, and they said, "You haveta play for *fifty-five minutes*. If you go over we're in trouble." And the reason for that was that they wanted to get him on the stage as quickly as possible. He's such a fantastic singer, has such a fantastic style. He does a-*maz*-ing things with his voice.

'Yeah, who knows. Right now it's all going backwards. Pretty soon we'll be back in the swing era. People are saying, "We've had everything else, so . . ." I hate to concern myself with any of that. I'd rather just sit down and write, just try to write a good song, wherever it's supposed to be.

'Something else about what happens when you reach a certain stage: one's life gets so taken up with airports and transportation and getting to the gig on time that there's no time left for writing. Nowadays I'm really screwed to come up with a page of lyrics, which is no fun.

'Sure, when you start to make it you have to lose something, and basically this is a *business* and I realized that none of the people in the business see any reason why you should do it other than to make money. I've realized that and now I have to deal with it daily and now I'm a real negative factor to many of the people who have to deal with the band.

'I will cancel a show – and have – if we're supposed to be opening for a band that I despise. I will not play for them.

'And then I get the office' – here he slips into a classic Lenny Bruce 'agent' voice – '"Hey, whass goin' awn? Yuh cancelled th' gig!" and I go, "Yeah!"'

'They say, "But we gotta get to that town 'n sell re-cuds!" I say, "Okay, here's what you do. Get a bass player and a curtain and I'll stand in back of *you* and *you* do the show." They say, "No, that won't work."

'The logic behind *why* you do it is something that a lotta people forget too early on. I want to try and hold onto it . . .'

*Ladies and gentlemen, Little Feat. On guitar and vocals, Mr Lowell George.*


The Capitol in Washington is a slick 10,000-seater seemingly constructed entirely out of recycled orange peel and old 'Action Man' dolls. The show double-bills Dave Mason and Little Feat as co-headliners supported by Catfish Hodge.

Hodge is from Detroit, the former lead singer of a band called Catfish who had a couple of bombarella albums out on CBS some years ago. He's an enormously fat guy rigged out in wall-to-wall denim and a woolly bobble hat, plus several feet of beard and an acoustic guitar. He goes out for broadmarket appeal by tawkin' about how we wuz all gonna hev ourselves a shit-kickin pawteh heah tonaht and dropping five dope references a second, and the ponytail and lumberjacket element in the audience really dug that.

And then Little Feat were brought on, up in front of a big audience in a plastic hall, and they got it on right from the opening 'Apolitical Blues' (god, who else plays a slow blues with satirical lyrics as an opening number?) right through to the closing percussion shake-it-up of 'Feats Don't Fail Me Now', they were sublime.

Right from percussionist Sam Clayton's screwdriver-jiver gimme-fiver why-ain't-I-with-the-Ohio-Players caperings through to Lowell's almost abstracted *sang-froid*, their very disparity helped maintain the balance, a balance upset only by co-guitarist Paul Barrere's bullmoose parade-ground bellows of ritual invocations like 'Rrrrrock'n'*roll*!' and 'Git *doown*!' which are okay for the likes of Johnny Winter, but seem almost absurdly contrived and affected in the context of Little Feat.

But what made it happen is that Lowell and his boys know what makes it work. They know what sounds good and they *play* what sounds good from an instinctive sense of balance and control. When Lowell sends a lick skimming and sizzling across the chugging, choppy surface of the band's music, he does so simply because he knows that it ought to be there because it's *right*.

And then he comes out and sings 'Willin'', and for the first time since I grew to love that song I realized why.

Ostensibly, the subject of the song is truckdriving, but anybody who thinks that 'Willin'' is just a song about truckdriving probably also thinks that Raymond Chandler's Philip Marlowe books are *about* a detective.

In both cases, subject-matter is merely a metaphor; but whereas Chandler's theme is the hardship and the necessity of being true to yourself in a world where everybody else is simply out for themselves, George's theme in 'Willin'' is life and love of life and the knowledge that both the good times and the bad times come from the same place and that neither one can be denied in favour of the other because they are truly indivisible.

George's protagonist in 'Willin'' has been through it all: he's weather-beaten and bleeding and rootless and he misses his woman, but he's still on his feet and still willin', not out of blind stoicism but out of a serene realization of a fact of life that's been staring us all in the faces since Day One and is there to be built on if we can just bring ourselves to see it.

Listen to 'Willin'' again, listen to the marvellous tenderness in Lowell George's voice as he sings it and think on it next time God catches you unaware with a blind forearm smash and you find yourself hurting.

Right now, too many of the biggies are too concerned with laying their pitiful little problems on us to be able to still say something that can feed back into our own lives and help us share the weight. Neil Young can, Bob Dylan can, but what has *your* local superstar said to you lately?

Lowell George isn't a star. He's a musician.

He's just this bearded guy in California who doesn't look like a leper messiah, who's probably no better in bed than you are, who's a good conversationalist and probably fun to get wrecked with, who isn't a hero and who certainly isn't a Leader or The Future Of Rock, or much of anything except a guy who writes beautiful songs and plays guitar a certain way.

It just seems that rock music is better off in the hands of unassuming guys like Lowell George than with the elegantly and expensively wasted household name of your choice.

After all, he's still willin'.

*Ladies and gentlemen, Little Feat. On guitar and vocals, Mr Lowell George.*

# Black Sabbath: Hammersmith Odeon

*NME*, 24 January 1976

THE bastards weren't loud enough!

Not even halfway loud enough. No right-thinking individual can get off on the Sabs unless they're loud enough to make yer brain cells seep out yer ears and run for cover in the warm safety of your trouser pockets.

You need to feel as if Geezer's sproinging away on the coils of your cerebellum while they're connected up to a light socket, if you wanna get technical about it. Simultaneously Tony Iommi's got to be heaving giant slabs of semi-sentient guitar gunge around just behind your eyelids and Bill . . . well, Bill's probably out the back smashing his way through a brick wall by the simple expedient of hitting it with his head, while Ozzy caterwauls about something or other in a locked basement.

That's the way yer real Sabs conna-sewer likes it.

'Cuz when it *ain't* that loud, it becomes uncomfortably apparent that Black Sabbath are one of the dullest gaggles of clowns ever to haul onto a stage (Ozzy, this means you, *schlubbo*. Do you know what you look like in those trousers?) Luckily I gained access to the photo pit after about twenty minutes of the set and was thus able not only to see the boys close up but to hear the music at a decent volume.

I really enjoyed it after that.

There was some horrible object tricked out like a giant sea-shell with a cross on it behind Bill Ward's drum kit. Their S. Pokesman told me that Bill had recently delivered a jest (larf a minute, Bill is) about how they were gonna sell it to Blue Oyster Cult after the tour, but Blue Oyster Cult are American and therefore have much better props – not to mention better costumes. Just wait'll you see Ozzy's outfit.

Larf? I thought I'd never start.

Lessee now – they did 'War Pigs', 'Children Of The Grave', 'Snowblind', 'Iron Man', 'War Pigs' – 'ang on, I think I've already mentioned that one – 'Sabbra Cadabra' and lots of other good stuff. Geezer and Iommi had the equivalent of six Laney 200-watt stacks each piled up into a neat little battlement across the back of the stage (but it still wasn't loud enough) and Iommi was playing a really nice John Birch guitar with little crosses inlaid on the neck. Couldn't see much of Bill, but he kept knocking his cymbals over so he must've been having a good time.

Once you're in a position to get yer cortex shot, you can just settle down and groove while the band lumber around grinding it out. Occasionally they stop so that Tony Iommi can look pained and blat out one of his patented *fast bits*. The hall-mark of an Iommi fast bit (to use the technical term) is that it doesn't really

143

fit into the band context so 'Sabbra Cadabra' (the number into which it's usually slotted) has to crunch to a halt while he jabbers away at velocity Mark 10 for a few minutes.

Ozzy looks great. He's got this yellow T-shirt with a glitter V on the front and fringes on the sleeves and the world's most ridic trousers. They're tight around the ass (bad move, Ozzy) and baggy round the crotch (no Freddie Mercury I've-got-the-whole-world-in-my-pants tactics from these boys) and show his navy-blue underpants off to excellent advantage. They also clash exquisitely with his knee-length blue platform boots.

All joking aside, folks, I really like the Sabs ('specially when they're *really loud*).

Most people I know who don't like them generally make the mistake of taking them seriously (or trying to) and failing to get off because the whole Sabs trip is so patently dumb. The trick is to regard the whole thing (performance, audience reaction etc.) as a huge joke mounted especially for your amusement and then (provided it's loud enough) you can have a wonderful time.

I mean, what other band can provide a moment when their entire audience howls the word 'Paranoid!' as loud as they possibly can? That's always worth the price of admission by itself.

The food was unspeakable.

# Buffy Sainte-Marie: Never argue with a pregnant Indian

*NME*, 1 May 1976

CARL Perkins looks glazed. Teeth, eyes, toupee, rhine-stoned double-knit denim-look casuals: all veneered with the same hospital-tile finish as the off-white Telecaster that Perkins is manoeuvring through the hordes of ill-matched supplicants cooling their Circle-T brand heels outside Buffy Sainte-Marie's dressing-room.

Past the uproarious hoedown jamming and rebel yells filtering through the door of The Dillards' dressing-room, and the aromatic cloud of smoke and various past and present Wings guitar players in various states of cerebral disrepair floating out of Andy Fairweather-Lowe's, past Murray Kash and his daughter, past a weather-beaten middle-aged man in white Stetson and khaki fatigues announcing, 'Hah, ah'm Jaiff Jaiffreys frum Hewst'n Taixas. Hah're yew dewin'?' to anybody who wanders into firing range, past a security guard who looks like a bit player specializing in Det Sgts in British cop shows, Perkins laboriously insinuates himself and his Tele, a smile nailed firmly around his mouth and his eyes masked with exhaustion and disillusion.

Dig: it's Monday night in the Great Intestine of Wembley Stadium, the third night of the Big Country Thing.

Buffy Sainte-Marie has just ritually murdered the audience with what folks who underwent the Entire Megillah said was The Set Of The Weekend.

Yeah well . . . faster than a speeding bullet, able to leap tall buildings in a single bound, and nothing less than a napalm attack can puncture the mood she creates. Yes, it's Supersquaw, champion of the oppressed, the musical marvel from another tribe who has devoted her life to aiding those in need.

Would you believe she was a-maz-ing?
Terrific?
Exquisitely entertaining?
Fantastically wonderful?
All of the above?
Congratulations. That is the *correct* answer.

Despite an absurd stage set-up that looked like some dimwit attempt to create a wholly abhorrent TV variety-show environment (complete with 'studio audience' cannily placed *onstage* in front of the real audience for handy-dandy instant-access reaction shots to make things easier for the camera crew), a sound mix that cut most of the raunch out of the ballsy rock and country fills laid down by the rhythm section of Jeremiah, her young Florida-based backup band, and a monumentally loopy lighting policy that put full house lights on at the end of each number and occasionally in mid-tune, Buffy put on an all-singing, all-dancing, all-rapping, rock 'em sock 'em hour-plus of everything from 'Until It's Time For You To Go', 'Universal Soldier', 'Soldier Blue' through to 'Native North American Child', 'Now That The Buffalo's Gone', 'Cripple

Creek' and naturally a heapin' handful of her country songs, few of which she gets a chance to play before less specialized audiences.

It was also an outrageously *physical* show; startlingly so in terms of Buffy's increasingly visible pregnancy.

Coming after the numbingly laid-back Andy Fairweather-Lowe (who, to swipe an epigram from John Sebastian, looked 'about as local as a fish in a tree'), things were wide-open for her to lay energy, passion, intelligence, commitment and general *aliveness* on her audience. And, wouldja believe, the Indian really kicked ass on the cowboys.

An Indian on a country show? Buffalo Bill Cody and Kit Carson woulda crapped their buckskins.

After all, the ironies are manifest. Consider: it's a truism that the winning side gets to have its version of the story accepted as the prevailing historical orthodoxy, but it gets heavier when the defeated are unable even to lick their wounds and regenerate their economy and their culture overseas without even a smear of foreign aid as salve to speed up the healing process, but have to live as virtual POWs in the land that was once theirs and watch themselves portrayed as savage, merciless bad-guy primitives in their conquerors' media.

Must've felt weird watching cowboy movies on TV as a kid.

'We-e-e-e-e-ll . . . as a very young kid I was told by my adoptive mother that cowboy movies and history books had very little to do with reality and were a matter of money and political convenience. I was aware of that from a very early age, so I'd go to cowboy movies, and when they got really gross I'd know they were really gross and I'd know *why* they were really gross and I'd be able to back away and not be hurt by any of it. Today, I'm less able to do that, because I don't have anybody telling me where it's at . . . y'know?'

Buffy Sainte-Marie, decked out right nice in embroidered white cotton and feathers in her nightcloud hair, sits in anticipation of a lamb chop and direct occupation of a quantity of orange juice in the dining-room of the Hyde Park Hotel. She's with Sheldon Peters Wolfchild, her old man and collaborator in her current Create-A-New-Indian project (plus your 'umble servant on cassette machine). A head waiter who's a dead ringer for Henry ('Goot

eefnink. Mein famous Infradraw messod could safe *your* contree')
Kissinger has acknowledged, with all the joyous alacrity of a man
who's just sold his nearest and dearest into slavery and gotten
paid off in Monopoly money, that we did indeed have a reservation.

Don't be silly, m'man. All Indians got reservations.

'But even today I can still get involved with good drama, even
at the expense of anything, because that's what art's about. Art is
magic; art knows how to turn off your reality and replace it with
somebody else's. Now, as an adult looking back on all of that, I
get madder and madder, and what I do with that anger is try and
turn it into something every day, because I don't like being
angry, feeling frustrated and futile.

'Indians have changed a lot since I started singing. They've
come a long way. Back then most Indian women had short hair
and bouffant hair-do's and were trying to get jobs as secretaries.
Indian men had short hair and their consciousness was little more
than what The Man told them, but deep down inside there was
such frustration, only it wasn't even recognized. I'd show up and
do a concert and two years later I'd come back and see a different
scene. Times are really changing for Indian people. Consciousness
is going . . . *straight* up.'

With the occupation of Alcatraz being the first media manifestation.

'And of course the affair at Wounded Knee, which most people
have never understood at all, was an attempt by the Sioux people
to impeach an elected official. It's never been told. *That's* what
was going on at Wounded Knee. The Sioux people decided to
impeach an elected official and were not allowed to by the United
States Government – *in writing*.

'The FBI, the CIA, Federal marshals, tanks . . . dum-dum
bullets, which were declared illegal by the Geneva Convention,
were used on American Indian civilians.

'Indian people today are excited, they're encouraged, they're
enthused . . . and greatly hassled. Wiretaps, mail arriving opened,
beheadings . . .'

*Beheadings?*

'Child rape, jailings, our money tied up with bondsmen, lawyers
and judges so that we can't be free to raise the bail money . . .
however, we've come so far in the last ten years, and the reason

147

that they're putting so much pressure on us now is because we're happening. It's not like before. We weren't nearly so hassled fifteen years ago.

'Sheldon' – she inclines her head towards Wolfchild – 'who's a Vietnam veteran and worked as an artist at Walt Disney Studios – what could be more American than that – has the FBI showing up at his place of business asking all kinds of foolish questions.'

'They found my name,' explains Sheldon, 'on a piece of paper that was layin' on the ground on a reservation in South Dakota. They came around and asked me questions for two hours. They asked what my name was doing on a piece of paper on a reservation in South Dakota. How should I know?'

'I sent a tape in to ABC,' continues Buffy, 'just a little cassette for radio stations giving information about Native American history for the Bicentennial; things like "Did you know that the first American to be killed in the Revolutionary War was half-Indian and half black?" . . .'

Crispus Attucks.

'You know that? Most *Americans* don't. Anyway, the tape arrived at ABC totally scrambled – completely unusable. But in spite of all that, what we're doing is . . . one: we're still alive, two: we're still creative.

'Sheldon and I have a company called Creative Native to do things like that tape, mount a scholarship fund to help American Indian kids through whatever school hassles they're having, concerts, benefits, Indian art exhibitions . . . whatever comes up. We were supposed to be teaching history courses this summer, but we're making a baby instead.

'The government is very definitely on our backs, but we're not getting thrown by it. Anybody see the salt?'

The conversation noses past Carlos Castaneda's Don Juan books and the mystical aspects of 'Starwalker', the spine-chillingly incantatory ace taste from the new 'Sweet America' album and various manifestations of pop spirituality.

'Indian religions are really something for anybody who's inquiring into spiritual things. Our religions have been illegal for so long. Some were only legalized in 1960. Some of our people couldn't even vote until 1960. I mean, this is April, the anniversary of the Equal Rights Amendment of 1924, when all people born on

148

American soil were granted citizenship and the right to vote – except for Indians. It was specified that Indians were excluded. Don't ask me why. It just seems that somewhere in a part of the American consciousness that I don't understand lies the idea that Indians are potential traitors to America.

'What you picked up on in "Sweet America" was exactly right. We love our country in a way that George Washington could never guess. Not from a profit motive, not for what we can get out of it, but simply because to us America is an extension of God, yet the Ghost Dance religion, which is like basic Christianity accompanied by Indian dancing and Indian style ... the Ghost Dancers were thrown into a pit and massacred. The Sand Creek massacre was led by a Methodist minister.

'Genocide – *real* genocide – has not been carried out that often in human history, but it was in America.

'As much as I've been around the world, as much success as I've had as an entertainer, as much education as I've had, I'm still surprised that there's such a war on. People don't want to know about Indians. People don't want to see an Indian art show, that there is a government that would want it not to happen. Like a plains Indian of 1860 dancing to God and Christ in the desert, and then the soldiers came ...'

The sentence trails off and her eyes change focus. 'I can't understand it,' she murmurs, half under her breath. 'I ... can't ... understand ... it.' After a few seconds she switches back into the conversation. 'As a modern, contemporary person I know where that's at. I see it in every Indian person. However much we learn and however much we have to give, somebody wants to kill it, and you have to rise above that every now and then, because our generation may be the last that still has a link with our past. So many of our people are dying.'

It seems, though, that there has to be a reconstruction of the cultural link between Buffy's generation of Indians and, say, the generation that saw the first invaders and the first settlers.

'Ye-a-ahh ... I think the same way you do. That's just what we have to do. When Sheldon and I are at home and we're empty, we know how to nourish ourselves spiritually. We know where to go and what to do. It's to do with the ability to open yourself to the things that nourish, and it's in silence – not in the words of the prayer.

'We know how to go to a clean spot and build a fire, burn some of the sweet grass that grows on the plains, and practise our own religions. We're both sophisticated, educated people: I studied Oriental philosophy and Sheldon religions of the world, but we probably have a great deal in common with Indians of 1100.'

But after all that time and all that violence and all that political and cultural repression, how much of that original culture can be salvaged?

'Don't let me mislead you now. There are still some tribes that are still virtually intact, particularly in the Southwest. The plains tribes – my tribe, Sheldon's tribe – really got it, though. I mean, *nobody* survives the American wartime machine. But I know that *we're* surviving, and it's not a question of how much can be salvaged, but a question of how much can be *built*.

'This isn't based on some scholarly Jesuit priest's account of how the Indians were in 1500 and learning Latin to read it and learn how to be a real Indian, because the Indian of 1500 is no more real than the Indian of 1976. Our reality is *right now*. It's got nothing to do with wearing the clothes we wore in 1500. I'm telling you that we're still intact. Some of our tribes are very raggedy, but we ain't gone.'

> *Who's got the rhythm of the universe inside him?*
> *Who taught the pilgrims how to make it in the wild?*
> *Who's got a credit card with old Mother Nature?*
> *Yeah! Native North American Child!*
>
> *'Native North American Child'; Essex Music 1972*
>
> *. . . I know a boy from a tribe so primitive*
> *He can call me up without a telephone.*
>
> *'Moonshot'; Essex Music 1972*

Though an impressive song cycle of Indian-consciousness material has built up over the twelve years that Buffy Sainte-Marie has been recording (the bulk of which have been collected into an anthology album entitled 'Native North American Child' by Vanguard, the company for whom she recorded until a year or two back), it's only with the suite that occupies the second – and far superior – side of 'Sweet America' that she's actually infused Indian musical elements into her compositions.

'That's something that I've wanted to do for a very long time, but I was working in Nashville with a fine producer' – Norbert Putnam – 'and very fine musicians' – McCoy, Buttrey, David Briggs, The Memphis Horns – 'and Norbert has real strong musical ideas. I liked his ideas and he liked my music, but when two strong people meet, quite often something gets neutralized.

'What I'd wanted to do was explore the possibilities of a cross-cultural musical experience – if you wanna use big words to describe it. I wanted to present Indian music to radio listeners – purely, the way I knew it, not like some Hollywood movie. What that involved was that the producer would be open to it, like it and that I would take a band among Indian people to hear Indian music in real situations enough for them to be able to play it without either getting in the way or being intimidated by it.

'So what I did last spring and summer was to take my band to a whole lot of Indian reservations for concerts. It was nice because it meant something to the people on the reservations to be able to hear some live music and it was nice for the musicians because they got to know Indian people and Indian music and they got that feel. Then there was working with Henry Lewy' – who co-produced and engineered the album – 'who's so open to many styles that it became possible. I asked Sheldon and Tony Purley, "Hey, c'mon and sing with me" . . . it was the kind of thing that can't happen in a fine-studio-musician atmosphere no matter how good they are.

'But Henry and the people at the record company who were worried about whether it would sell or not said, "Put all those songs on the second side." Those are all the songs I like. You don't know what it's like to walk into a studio with songs like "Qu'Appelle Valley, Saskatchewan", "I Been Down" and "Star-walker" and just know that they're gonna end up on side two as cuts 4 and 5 . . .

'Crazy old world. Still, it's the only one we got.'

> *Well, my name it ain't nothin' an' I come from Maine,*
> *And I love the rabbits and I love the rain,*
> *I been to China an' I been to Spain,*
> *And I never learned nuthin' at all, except there*
> *Ain't no time for the worryin' blues,*
> *It's a raggedy world an' it's a lifetime-cruise,*
> *It's a little tin dime that you get to spend,*
> *To start it all over again.*

151

*My name it ain't nothin' and I come from Mars,*
*And I love macaroni and I love the stars,*
*I love to float and I love to fly,*
*And I love to see you smile*
*Now I'll never grow up but I'll never grow down,*
*It's a raggedy world it keep spinnin' around,*
*Don't sound like much but it's real, it's true,*
*And there ain't no time for the worryin' blues,*
*NO THERE AIN'T!!!!!*

*'Ain't No Time For The Worryin' Blues'*
*Caleb Music, 1976*

# The Rolling Stones: Too rolled to stone

NME, 8 May 1976

**T**HE nice thing about the law of gravity is that it applies to *everybody*.

Basically, the law of gravity don't give a flying one if you're President of the United States or Princess Anne or Keith Richards or just some schmuck on the street. You mess with the law of gravity, man, you get your centre of gravity at too acute an angle to your feet and bubeleh, sure as bears poop in the woods you're gonna fall on your rosy ass, and that's a fact.

Gerry Ford falls down a lot (maybe he was attempting to walk and chew gum at the same time). Princess Anne got slung off her nag the other week and – *da da ba da daba da da* – Keith Richards, guitarist, songwriter and social arbiter to a whole generation of middle-class drug abusers, skids wildly on the polished, dragon-painted portable stage that The Rolling Stones are using on their '76 Tour of Europe and takes a dive in front of 10,000 earnest young Frankfurters right in the middle of 'Jumpin' Jack Flash'.

152

It don't phase ol' Keith none, though.

Ol' Keith just collects his legs until he's sitting in some kind of weird discombobulated lotus posture variant and continues whacking away at his guitar, not missing a single saw-toothed rusty chrome chord the whole time.

It don't phase Mick Jagger either – Mick Jag-gur *performing* on the ramp that leads down into the audience from stage centre like the tongue on The Stones' logo. Jagger just flounces over to his fallen comrade, his mouth a giant red O like some dumb glossy PVC Claus Oldenburg sofa or something and he bends down oh-so-graceful and he hands Keith his pick – which the maestro has dropped on his journey from here to there – and helps him locate his legs and jack-knife back onto his feet.

*'Falling down gets you accepted'* – Mick Farren, 1976.

Yeah, but Keith Richards don't got to devote one second's thought to what gets you accepted as opposed to what gets you the Cosmic Phooey. Keith, you dig, is one of the ones who get to do the accepting – or, alternatively, to hand out the Cosmic Phooeys to the poor unfortunates who come over limp when measured up to the Big Yardstick.

The Rolling Stones may not be Keith Richards, say the folks who are hip to the finer nuances of these things, but hey, *Keith Richards is The Rolling Stones.*

You know the riffs:

There's the one that goes 'When Keith Richards comes into a room rock and roll walks in the door,' right, and the 'Keith Richards the world's most elegantly wasted human being' which comes equipped with hyperbolic virtuoso prose which attempts to outdo the last writer's description of how utterly, utterly *out of* it and cadaverous Mr Richards looked at the time, and the scholarly bit about Keith's pitiless open-tuned riffing and Newman Jones III and the four hundred and ninety-seven guitars: all of which boil down to a single one-liner terse enough to stick on a telegram and not be hurting when you get your phone bill, and that one goes 'Keith Richards *is* rock and roll.'

Yeah, well, rock and roll just fell on its ass.

In Frankfurt.

Where else?

Anyway, enough of this – *whoooooeeeeeee!* – kandy-kolored

tangerine-flake streamline baby-sitting and down to hard-tack brass-hat fax'n info about what this month's Biggest Fuss is about and what a number of you equivalent to the population of a decent-sized city have sent out up-front bread for a chance to get a brainful of The Rolling Stones' show, 1976 model, as performed before the finest flower of Frankfurt youth at some concert hall I never found out the name of and soon to be on display at Earls Court, an occasion which will mark the first appearance of the Glimmer Twins on the shores of this green and unpleasant land for – *ummmmmm* – two years.

Bill Wyman and Charlie Watts, who earn less than their more charismatic colleagues due to their restricted compositional activities – have been around more recently. In fact, I spotted them at a Heathrow check-in counter last year, and no one seemed to be paying them much mind.

The new Stones' show is prefaced by an admirable cassette tape of exclusively black and mostly pretty tough dirt-yard black music. It's got Bo Diddley doing 'You Don't Love Me', and some Robert Johnson and Earl Hooker, plus some real dirty-ass JA juice, intermingled with some soupy modern falsetto creamy pimp-suit crooning.

The journalistic herd in the cattle-pen press section right under the left speaker banks plays conjecture poker and comes to the conclusion that the drunk-and-dirty-mo'-dead-than-alive stuff was Keith's choice and the well-groomed shot-silk pimpmobile muzak was Jagger's, which is about 50 per cent correct, since we later ascertain that our phantom deejay is none other than Honest Ron Wood, with a few additions made by Big Mick.

The Stones' tradition had always been to have black support acts, the best they could get. B.B. King, Stevie Wonder, Ike and Tina Turner (ITT to their accountant), on a couple of dates even Muddy Waters – who *is* the blues even more than Keith *is* rock and roll – they've all vaulted to white acceptance of varying degrees off The Stones' springboard. It's pretty cool of The Stones to use these acts, 'cuz before they come on their audiences get to see a little bit of where they're coming from and why they got the soul and the balls to consider that there's still some dues to pay.

The Meters, in case they haven't slipped through your screening processes, are Allen Toussaint's house band from N'Awlins: a finger-lickin' tasty funk rhythm section fronted by a rather unfortunate singer/percussionist who, in terms of sinuosity and control, outdances Jagger completely; but in the process winds up so disco prissy that he fails to establish any real individual presence.

However, The Meters' *collective* presence is strong and happy. From 'Fire On The Bayou' through a rock and roll medley and even their slightly over-inflated version of Neil Young's 'Down By The River' (which works great on the verses, but their reluctance to get into any backing vocals blows it on the chorus), they lay it down warm, sweet and twitching.

Guitarist Leo Nocentelli (playing, for guitar freaks, a black Telecaster DeLuxe – the same model that Keith Richards will play later on) proved once again that the most constructive elaborations of the Hendrix legacy are coming from young black guitarists like Sugar of The Ohio Players and LaBelle's current lead guitarist, not to mention Ernie Isley.

The Meters go down okay, but the applause has faded almost before Art Neville has made it into the wings, which means that the audience were into digging them while they were there, but right now it's Stones-time, and nuthin' but nuthin' gets to delay Stones-time.

Not by more than half an hour, anyway.

We listen to The Tape again, and then the lights go down – wheeeeeooooowwww! – a WEA dude comes on to introduce the band – in English, possibly as a concession to the GIs off the bases who make up at least half the audience. You can spot 'em easy. They're the ones with the short hair and the frayed jeans who're looking aggressive and hooking down booze and hash at as frenetic a rate as possible.

The German WEA guy says, 'The Rolling Stones!' like he was about to take his bow after performing some particularly abstruse conjuring trick, and in the dark two shadowy humans with dapper silhouettes move purposefully towards strategic seats behind drum kit and piano.

And then the lights come up and Mick Jagger, Keith Richards and Ronnie Wood lurch onto the stage in a cluster and Bill Wyman, looking timidly rather than satanically withdrawn, beams in to his spot in front of his stack. Wood, cigarette mounted at a jaunty angle, scuttles over to his amp, Keith Richards ruffles his hair and hitches up his guitar, Jagger – wearing a silver leather

155

jacket that looks to be part of David Bowie's 1972 offstage wardrobe — parades around the stage with a gait like his pout expanded into an entire bodily style.

Charlie (ah, Charlie's good tonight, inne? Whaddya mean, scumbag, Charlie's good *every* night) lights the fuse on that snare-bass drum-and-cowbell intro to 'Honky Tonk Woman'. Keith, leaning backwards from the knees, methodically chops out those measured opening chords like each chord was a white line on a mirror, Jagger prowls the stage like he's sniffing each bit of it for a particular odour — like a dog trying to remember just where he pissed the night before — and yep, it's The Rollin' Stones right enough. Know 'em anywhere.

The sound is loud and a trifle frazzled round the edges. Only thing wrong with it is that you can hardly hear the guitars or the vocals. The vocals come up a bit in time for the chorus, Mick and Keith leaning into the mike and Jagger stretching out the syllables like silly putty, rubber notes from rubber lips. '. . . haaaaaaaawonky tonka haawonky tonk-uh waaamaaanuhhhh . . .'

The Great Charlie Watts is playing so clean and crisp and precise that it's almost a shock to pick up on the fact that there's also a ridiculous amount of muscle in his backbeat. Even allowing for the fact that Ollie Brown, a lean black denim percussionist, is whoppin' ass on various passive objects right behind him, it's clear just who's down in the engine room hefting the coal into the furnace.

Next up they do 'All Down The Line' off 'Exile On Main Street', and halfway through someone wakes up behind the mixing desk and cuts in the afterburners on the guitars. It happens in midchord and suddenly a Keithchord comes scything out of the speakers and slices the top of my head off. I suddenly feel that my skull's just metamorphosized into a two and a half minute softboiled egg and that some intensive bastard is about to dig in with a spoon and eat my brains up.

Trouble is, the sound man put so much treble onto the guitars (which, since I was right under an exceedingly musclebound speaker stack, had suddenly become hideously loud) that the music from there on in was reduced to being about as aesthetically pleasing as having some demento engrave the Lord's Prayer on your scalp with a dentist's drill. It was just too goddam loud to make any sense out of, and I speak as a man who once sat five feet away from the stage at a Sabs gig and spent the entire set yowling, 'Louder! Louder!'

It probably sounded great at the back, but from where I was ... look, I'm only telling you this so that you'll realize that all musical judgements contained herein are approximate.

Apart from Ollie Brown, the only other supporting musician (leaving the mysterious Exact Status of Ronnie Wood out of it) was the omnipresent Billy Preston ('Ivories tickled to order; Beatles and Stones a speciality') who, for some reason, appeared minus his mushroom cloud Afro wig and satin and tat.

Messrs Wood and Richards flanked Jagger, looking for all the world like a pair of diseased crows.

They're a remarkably well-matched pair both eyewise and earwise. Eyewise, they were like bookends propping up the Jagger Library Of Poses; and Wood's extrovert contrast to Mick Taylor's studious angelic self-effacing whiz-kid-in-the-shadows-next-to-Bill concentration erodes Richards' previously obvious Number Two Son position. He's taken over some of the backing vocals that used to be Richards', and his cheery scampering about and winning ways with a cigarette butt set off the traditionally limned legendary Jagger and Richards stage mannerisms.

Earwise he works out infinitely better than I'd foreseen (or foreheard). I've heard him play some of the most lamentable guitar known to medical science during his days with The Faces (working, perhaps, on the principle that band and audience alike were too wiped out to know the difference and that nobody cared but a few snotty reviewers who'd get savaged by their readers in the letters pages anyway), but now and then, like on the early Stewart solo albums and the Clapton Rainbow concert and one or two occasional Faces gigs when Rod Stewart's ego and the various consumptions had been kept in check, he'd hauled out some chops that weren't to be coughed over.

Here, operating as an extension of Richards, filling out Rock And Roll Himself's riffs and squeezing curlicues out of the lead guitar tube to put the icing on the cake, he got it on with a ferocious energy and a commendably disciplined and canny channelling of same. Dig: nobody gets fifteen minutes to solo while the rest of the band go off to leak, take a hit, cop a drink or get blown in this band. Nobody gets to be self-indulgent except You Know Who.

*

A while back I was ripped at the zoo and as we drifted through the ape section we saw a gibbon going through its party pieces. Using its tail like a fifth limb, it was swinging around the trees in its romping ground with a kind of insolent facility and grace that said, 'I'm only doing this 'cuz I feel like it, suckers. Any minute now I'm gonna stop and just squat in a corner and you're gonna stand around like dummies and wait for me to do it some more and I won't. So there.'

That gibbon is totally hip to Mick Jagger.

Except that Jagger don't stop. He prowls and struts and minces and flounces like a faggot chimpanzee, his whole body one big pout. His moves are athletic/gymnastic rather than balletic, like a callisthenics programme designed jointly by Lionel Blair and the Royal Canadian Air Force.

He shoulders into Ronnie Wood, limpwrists so extravagantly that the movement spreads right up his arm to his shoulder, and Toms outrageously between numbers, going 'All *right!*' and '*Yeah!*' and 'Sssssssssu-*guh!*' like he was Ike Hayes or somebody.

The only time he stays still is when he sits down behind the electric piano for 'Fool To Cry', one of the four numbers they do off the new album (the others, in case you wanna learn the words in time for Earls Court, are 'Hey Negrita' – so-so – 'Hand Of Fate' – more impressive live than on record – and 'Hot Stuff' – which still sucks on ice).

They do 'Get Off My Cloud', 'You Can't Always Get What You Want', 'Happy' (which Jagger caps with a heavily sarcastic 'Fank you Keef. That wos *great*'), 'You Got To Move' (with Keith standing back to spin out the guitar lines and Jagger, Preston, and Wood clustered round the mikes), 'Brown Sugar' (audience really picking up on the 'Yeah . . . yeah . . . yeah . . . shoooooo!' bits) and an oddly perfunctory 'Midnight Rambler', which doesn't really play tug-o'-war with your nerves the way it oughtta despite the ritual whipping of the stage with the hallowed silver belt and not-quite-dramatic-enough lighting changes.

Still, it was 'Midnight Rambler' which launched the set into second gear, which it needed to, coming as it did after Billy Preston singing 'Nothing From Nothing' and performing a rather undignified Ikettes dance routine with Jagger.

Where it all really cut loose was on the final 'Jumpin' Jack

Flash'/'Street Fightin' Man' medley wherein Keith fell down etc., etc. Richards/Wood doesn't have the crystalline snaky lead/ firing from the hip rhythm purity as Richards/Taylor, but it's so raunchy that if it moved in next door your lawn wouldn't even wait around long enough to die, it'd move to a nicer neighbourhood.

The trouble is that Jagger's cosmic inflation of spoiled brattishness has been so crudely exaggerated that it's stylized itself up its own ass. It's a good show, but he comes on so strong that it just degenerates into hamming.

He plays the spoiled brat much better offstage, anyway.

Well, in my dream he did. Lemme tell you about it.

After the show I went back up to my room and had a smoke. Somebody spoke and I went into a dream. I had me a dream that made me sad about The Stones and the . . .

In my dream, Dave Walters from WEA ushered me and three other rock-press folks into Ronnie Wood's room so that we could like *hang out*. And as soon as I'd been introduced to Mr Wood – who acted pleasant and civil despite my having, in the real world, written some fairly unpleasant and uncivil things about him in the past – we sat down and smoked.

The end of the room we're in is occupied by a sofa, a table, a gang of chairs and a mammoth sound system blasting out Maceo Merriweather, Furry Lewis, Robert Johnson and good reggae. Over at the big table, Keith Richards, who looks – let's just say 'tired' – is giving an interview to a Swedish radio guy.

I'd read in the *Sunday Times* that each Stone received £25 a day pocket money, so after we'd talked blues a little bit, I asked Woody what he spent his on.

'It's more like £350 a week,' he said amiably enough. 'That's just the per diem.'

I discovered that Honest Ron was brother to Art Wood, former leader of the Artwoods, a group who I'd dug when I was fifteen or so and who'd included Keef Hartley on drums and Jon Lord on organ.

A seat at The Captain's Table had fallen vacant, so I annexed it just as Keith started into answering someone's question about why all the stuff on the new album was a year or more old.

'Those were just the dates on which we did the basic tracks,' he

159

articulated carefully. 'There was a lot of overdubbing and mixing later on but there's only so much room for information on an album cover.'

I asked him what happened to the stuff they'd cut with Jeff Beck.

'We didn't do any songs; we just played and sometimes the tapes were rolling and sometimes they weren't.'

So how was it?

Irritable flicker of the eyes. 'You know Jeff. Sometimes 'e was brilliant and sometimes it was rubbish. Ronnie can tell you far more about Jeff Beck than I can anyway.'

Richards assembles refreshments delicately on the table in front of him, emits a resounding *snffff* and leans headlong into the next question which is 'What do you think of groups like Eddie and The Hot Rods and The Count Bishops and The Sex Pistols who are like what The Stones used to be like twelve years ago?'

It seems pretty dumb to ask a cat who ain't been in England for two years what he think of three unrecorded bands who've sprung up in the last six months, but hell, whaddya expect from a dream? Logic?

'I only really listen to black music these days,' says Richards, *snffff*. 'I ain't too interested in white bands who rip off white bands who ripped off black bands.'

Ronnie Wood wanders over and hands Richards a fragment of cigarette packet with something written on it. Richards scans it, *snffffs* it, and looks at me very hard. He also makes no attempt to pass his refreshments around.

That fragment of my conscious mind which is monitoring the dream wonders, 'Is this some masterly demonstration of Zen and the art of Cool Maintenance, or is the guy the most outrageous bogarter in Christendom?'

Keith looks at the note and then back at me.

Though I'm sitting opposite him, in some weird floating dream way I can read the note. It says, 'Keith – do you realize that you're talking to Charles Shaar Murray?' I *must* be dreaming – big rock stars passing notes in class.

We talk a bit about how Albert King's still fantastic but B.B. King's down the pan these days, and then I look up from Number Three and see that Mick Jagger's come into the room, making a

Grand Entrance which unfortunately nobody really reacts to. Sure, I know what Robert Greenfield wrote in STP about how by his mere presence Jagger changes any event that he is present at, but Jagger's coming into this room don't change it none. He just gets the automatic glance that the sound of an opening door and footsteps always gets.

'I read your review, Charles, and I thought it was rubbish,' Keith says suddenly and, staring defiantly around the table to dare anyone to call him out, snarfs loudly. Weirdass dream. Nick Kent told me that when Keith gets annoyed he throws ashtrays.

'Yeah, well,' I say, 'I thought the album was pretty disappointing.'

'Most people liked it,' he comes back. 'Did you write that just to be different, then?'

'Naw, most people I know thought it was dreadful too.'

'Maybe you ought to broaden your circle of acquaintances,' he said.

'Oh, I dunno . . . it's getting broader all the time.'

Damn! I wouldn't *dare* to talk back to Keith Richards like that normally. I'm waiting for him to do something bizarre and heavy and Keithish when Ronnie Wood intercedes:

'There was something in your review,' sez Honest Ron, 'that Keith got really upset about. I can't quite remember what it was, but . . . I'm surprised that he didn't take it up with you.'

From beyond Wood comes a sound exactly like Mick Jagger saying in his 'proletarian' voice, 'Oi fort your review wos bahluddy stoopid.'

Mentally shutting out these disturbing hallucinations within the dream, I carry on talking to Wood.

'OI FORT YOUR REVIEW WOS BLAHHHDY STOOPID!'

Louder this time. Omigawdomigawdomigawd. This is a dream. This is a dream. Even if it wasn't, that bit wouldn't be happening. Do not panic. Think only of yourself. Do . . . not . . . panic.

Jagger gets up and flounces away to talk to Paul Wasserman, a heavy-set bearded very straight-looking American who's doing the tour PR.

Shortly after Dave Walters from WEA comes over to me. He's turned green.

He tells me that Mr Jagger would like me and my fellow rock chroniclers to vacate the premises immediately.

I gather up my various impedimenta like a good boy should.

Dave Walters is back and this time he's colour-coordinated to match Billy Preston's velvet jacket.

'Paul Wasserman's just told me that Mick said that if you're not out in thirty seconds he'll get the heavies to throw you out.'

Dream or no dream, I'm a lover not a fighter. Ultimately, I'd rather be a healthy wimp than an injured punk.

Just past the threshold, Keith appears looking placatory.

'Look,' he says in conciliatory tones, '*Jagger* . . .' he enunciates the name in less than admiring tones, a sort of aw-come-on-you-know-what-he's-like intonation. '*Jagger* wants to go over some songs and rearrange the set. We're probably havin' a party in Bill Preston's room when 'e gets back from eatin' . . . give us yer room number and I'll give you a buzz later on.'

We roll a smoke, light it up.

As soon as it gets to Keith, he says, 'What's your number? 572? Okay, talk to you later,' and vanishes into the room with it. We are left staring at the door.

With that tranquil acceptance of the utterly impossible that accompanies a dream state, I assimilate the fact that Keith Richards, quintessential rock star, cool personified and the idol of millions, has just ripped me off for my last smoke.

Back in the room I started reading my book. And then I took the phone right offa the hook.

Woke up in the morning and then realized that it was only in my dream. God, if only it had *really happened* . . . the night I stoned The Stones.

Somehow, it made all the bread I'd spent on Stones records when I was a kid worthwhile. Somehow. Couldn't quite figure out how, though.

Then, just after I'd checked out, the porter rushed over to the cab and handed me this envelope marked 'Charles Murray Room 572'. Inside was a note scrawled in red felt-tip on a torn-out page of the tour programme.

And this is what it said:

'Dear Charles (The disappointed man):

'Just to say that we hoped you get yourself and your critical faculties safely back to Tin Pan Alley. How come you don't get high? You sure work at it hard enough. That's what London does for you. Enthusiasm = unhip (an equation from the smoke). Did you ever write a review of "Exile"? If you did, and still have a copy, I'd like to see it!

'Anyway, thanks for the number at the door! Come see us in London and we'll get you mighty high (you deserve it; hanging out with neurotic queens from the provinces is gloom by the bucket). I'd love to see a review of your visit to Ronnie's room, now we understand it all. Death to Eddie and The Hotrods!'

It was just signed 'Stones', but that 'number at the door' bit just had to refer to the final encounter with Keith in my dream. But that was impossible unless Keith had had the same dream I had.

After all, I've never even *met* The Rolling Stones. I'm not even sure I've ever been in Frankfurt. Or reviewed a new Stones album. Or even heard about them putting one out since 'It's Only Rock 'N' Roll'.

Look, don't turn me in. I'm harmless. Really I am. I've just got a vivid imagination, that's all. I made all this up, honest. I mean, any fool knows The Stones aren't really like that.

Are they?

Hey Keith . . . we can't go on meeting like this.

# The Sex Pistols: Screen on the Green

*NME*, 11 September 1976

IT'S almost funny. Not quite worth an uproarious explosion of uncontrollable hilarity, but definitely good for a wry chuckle or two when it happens to someone else. Trouble is no one's laughing because all the professional chucklers just found out that the joke's on them.

Any halfway competent rock and roll pulse-fingerer knows that this is The Year Of The Punk. You got Patti Smith doing Rimbaud's-in-the-basement-mixing-up-the-medicine, you got Bruce Springsteen with his down-these-mean-streets-a-man-must-go stereologues, you got The Ramones as updated Hanna-Barbera Dead End Kids, you got Ian Hunter doing I-used-to-be-a-punk-until-I-got-old-and-made-all-this-money, you got everybody and his kid brother (or sister) crawling out of the woodwork in leather jackets trying to look like they were hell on wheels in a street fight and shouting Put The Balls Back Into The Music.

Ultimately, if the whole concept of Punk means anything it means Nasty Kids and if Punk Rock means anything it means music of, by and for Nasty Kids. So when a group of real live Nasty Kids come along playing Nasty Kids music and actually behaving like Nasty Kids, it is no bleeding good at all for those who have been loudly thirsting for someone to come along and blow all them old farts away to throw up their hands in prissy-ass horror and exclaim in a duchessy fluster that oh no, *this* wasn't what they meant *at all* and won't it please go away.

In words of one (or, at the most, *two*) syllables: you wanted Sex Pistols and now you've got 'em. Trouble is, they look like they aren't going to go away, so what are you going to do with them?

Alternatively – ha ha – what are they going to do with *you*?

In a way, it's a classic horror-movie situation. Dr Frankenstein's monster didn't turn out according to plan but he was stuck with it anyway. Professor Bozo opens up a pyramid/summons a demon/ goes up to the Old Dark Mansion despite the warnings of the villagers and gets into a whole mess of trouble. Don't rub the lamp unless you can handle the genie.

The current vogue for Punkophilia and Aggro Chic has created the atmosphere in which a group like The Sex Pistols could get started and find an audience and – dig it – it is entirely too late to start complaining because they behave like real Nasty Kids and not the stylized abstraction of Nasty Kiddery which we've been demanding and applauding from sensitive, well-educated, late twenties pop superstars.

Anyway, time's a-wastin'. Their gig at the Screen on the Green (a fine independent cinema in Islington – plug!) has already started; in fact we've already missed the first band, a Manchester group called Buzzcocks. All kinds of folks in Bizarre Costumes – the kind of clothes you used to find at Bowie gigs before 'e went all funny-like – are milling around the foyer playing the wild mutation. The occasional celeb – Chris Spedding, who has eyes to produce The Pistols, and Sadistic Mika – is mingling.

Up on the stage it's Party Piece time. A bunch of people, including a chick in SM drag with *tits out* (photographer from one of the nationals working overtime, presumably with the intention of selling a nice big fat look-at-all-this-disgusting-decadence-and-degradation centrespread) and a lumpy guy in romp-ers are dancing around to a barrage of Ferry and Bowie records. Every time the lumpy go-go boy does a particularly ambitious move the record jumps. He makes elaborate not-my-fault gestures and keeps dancing. The record keeps jumping.

This goes on for quite a while.

Movies are projected on the screen and someone gets creative with the lights. The area nearby reeks of amyl nitrate.

There is nothing more tedious and embarrassing than inept re-creations of that which was considered avante-garde ten years ago. Someone has obviously read too many articles about the Andy Warhol/Velvet Underground Exploding Plastic Inevitable Show. Andy and Lou and Cale would laugh their butts off. This ain't rock and roll – this is interestocide.

Sooner or later – later, actually – a group called Clash take the stage. They are the kind of garage band who should be speedily returned to their garage, preferably with the motor running, which would undoubtedly be more of a loss to their friends and families than to either rock or roll.

Their extreme-left guitarist, allegedly known as Joe Strummer, has good moves, but he and the band are a little shaky on ground that involves starting, stopping and changing chord at approxi-mately the same time.

In between times, they show Kenneth Anger's *Scorpio Rising*. The Pistols' gear is assembled in a commendably short time with an equally commendable absence of fuss, pissing about and Roadies' Playtime and then The Pistols slope onstage and Johnny Rotten lays some ritual abuse on the audience and then they start to play.

Any reports that I had heard and that you may have heard about The Pistols being lame and sloppy are completely and utterly full of shit. They play loud, clean and tight and they don't mess around. They're well into the two-minute-thirty-second powerdrive, though they're a different cup of manic monomania than The Ramones. They have the same air of seething just-about-repressed violence that The Feelgoods have, and watching them gives that same clenched-gut feeling that you get walking through Shepherd's Bush just after the pubs shut and you see The Lads hanging out on the corner looking for some action and you wonder whether the action might be you.

The Pistols are all those short-haired kids in the big boots and rolled-up baggies and sleeveless T-shirts. Their music is coming from the straight-out-of-school-and-onto-the-dole deathtrap which we seem to have engineered for Our Young: the '76 British terminal stasis, the modern urban blind alley.

The first thirty seconds of their set blew out all the boring, amateurish artsy-fartsy mock-decadence that preceded it purely by virtue of its tautness, directness and utter realism. They did songs with titles like 'I'm A Lazy Sod' and 'I'm Pretty Vacant', they did blasts-from-the-past like 'I'm Not Your Steppin' Stone' (ten points for doing it, ten more for doing it well) and 'Substitute' (a Shepherd's Bush special, that) and they kept on rockin'.

'Should I say all the trendy fings like "peace and love, maaaaaaan"?' asked Johnny Rotten, leaning out off the stage manic-ally jerking off his retractable mike-stand. '"Are you all having a good time, maaaaaaan"?' Believe it: this *ain't* the summer of love.

They ain't quite the full-tilt crazies they'd like to be, though: Johnny Rotten knocked his false tooth out on the mike and had the front rows down on their knees amidst the garbage looking for it. He kept bitching about it all the way through the gig; Iggy wouldn't even have *noticed*. Still, they got more energy and more *real* than any British act to emerge this year and even if they get big and famous and rich I really can't imagine Johnny Rotten showing up at parties with Rod'n'Britt 'n' Mick'n'Bianca or buying the next-door villa to Keef'n'Anita in the South of France.

And if Elton ever sees them I swear he'll never be able to sing 'Saturday Night's All Right For Fighting' again without choking on his Dr Pepper.

# Patti Smith: Open day in Babble-on

*NME*, 23 October 1976

'IT'S like ... I'm not *ever* gonna be a hundred per cent cool, y'know ... I mean, for you to like even *try* to be a hundred per cent cool to me is like just ... a *joke*. I'm never a hundred per cent cool and look how cool *I* am ...'

Patti Smith's movie for the night appears to be *Don't Look Back*. She showed up for the post-gig press and media binge held in the bar of her Amsterdam hotel in full regalia of the 1965 Bob Dylan. Dark suit, white shirt, the *identical* impenetrable heavy-rimmed shades. Now, up in her room finally doing the interview she'd been postponing all day, her voice crackles with exhaustion as she alternates NYC street-sneers and put-downs with long elliptical surrealist streams-of-consciousness (to put it politely), and spaced jive babbling (to not).

She's definitely into her role as Dylan in *Don't Look Back*.

Me, I seem to be cast as the man from *Time* magazine.

'. . . it's like . . . there's no shame in not being cool sometimes, y'know . . . *I'm* often really uncool. Back in the States they call me "winghead" because my hair always . . . didj'ever notice how my hair sticks out?'

'I thought you did that on purpose,' I murmur.

'It sticks out because I'm too spaced out to take care of it. I mean, why do you think they call them "dreadlocks", man? It's all *tangles*, man . . . when you've been on the road a long time you forget what you look like, you enter a kind of monkey stage. I think we're getting to the monkey section of the tour. By the time we get to England I'm really gonna be a monkey. I want to be a really mean monkey . . .'

The gig was at the Paradiso, a converted church near the centre of town. It's the most famous rock venue in the country, undoubtedly the top club/small gig in town.

Like the Milky Way, a more recent and less publicized club with more or less the same set-up, it's renowned for its openly sold dope. Last year at the Milky Way (I ended up there because the Paradiso was closed that night), they'd had giant slabs of hash laid out on stalls so that you could taste and try, buy however much you wanted or could afford, and then wander over to a table and smoke yourself stupid in a paranoia-free atmosphere. Things seem to have tightened up some, though, because we're told that anybody who's buying has to go through some complicated play-acting rituals with the bloke at the pipes-and-skins stall. We're also told to watch out for dealers palming the wares and replacing the package with a seemingly identical dummy or inferior one sneaked out of a pocket. This ain't the summer of love.

There was an ominous crackle in the air. Things had gotten off to a bad start when Patti's piano player Richard Sohl – generally referred to as 'D.N.V.', an abbreviation of *Death In Venice*, because of his resemblance to the young boy who plays Dirk Bogarde's *bête noire* – had dropped out of the tour because of his dislike of heavy-duty touring and large concert halls. D.N.V. had been with Patti longer than any of her musicians except Lenny Kaye, and therefore Andy Paley, a former member of The Sidewinders and a long-time friend of the band, had been drafted in as pinch-hitter, done two rushed rehearsals and schlepped straight off to Europe.

'Andy is real crazy, he's amazing. Amazingly crazy. He was telling me what a good soldier he was gonna be – *left right left right*, y'know – he was gonna be a real fascist – and he's *so spaced out*. You know what he put us through? The first night we're on the road a girl comes into his room to interview him and the only word she knows is "champagne". Then he had a nervous breakdown and heart attack. Every heavy metal record happened to him on this airplane on the way to Hamburg and we had to put him in an audience . . . *ambulance*. Lenny and I had our pockets . . . I had so much hash on me and we were sitting in this hospital with all these people like . . . like *nurses*, y'know? . . . I've never been to a fuckin' hospital, man, I'd rather crawl across the floor a thousand times and bang my head against the wall than go to hospital . . . and there we were in this Nazi hospital in Hamburg . . .'

Everyone seemed tired and on edge. Downstairs in the dressing-room area a young French fan called Claude was sprawled in a chair terminally drunk. He'd been hanging around all day waiting for a chance to meet Patti and the management had let him wait in exchange for a bit of amateur stagehanding. But here he was finally in front of Patti Smith and he was too drunk to recognize her. All he can do is vomit what at first looks like blood but – to everyone's relief – turns out to be wine.

Patti snaps in a one-liner, New York street style – 'Hey Claude, ya want some heroin?' – then genuine concern takes over and she moves in, holding him by the shoulders and talking to him urgent and gentle, close up. His head tilts back and he heaves up some more wine. 'It's okay,' Patti says, 'every man I've ever fucked has thrown up on me at least once.'

Everyone stands around embarrassed. 'It's getting a little bit too real,' someone mutters. Hanging thick in the air is that peculiar mixed reaction people always get when they see someone stripped down and ugly as a result of an overdose of anything – a reaction compounded of more or less equal measures of contempt, repulsion, pity and guilt which tells them that if something drove them to hit a bottle or chemical that hard they wouldn't be presenting a much more admirable spectacle themselves, there-but-for-the-grace-of-God-go-I and don't laugh too hard or crack too wise because next time it could be me alone and incapacitated in a roomful of strangers.

Gradually the fog begins to clear and Claude realizes that someone's talking to him soothingly and wiping his mouth with a damp cloth and that it's *Patti Smith*.

He reacts first with shame at having disgraced himself before her, then anger because he thinks she's laughing at him. He shoves her hard in the shoulder and the manager moves in to restrain him. Patti waves him away and takes Claude in her arms. He begins to cry.

Everyone looks away and then wanders up for the soundcheck. Patti and Pennie Smith (no relation) gently lead Claude upstairs.

The support act for the evening is George Melly and The Feetwarmers. Melly strolls in looking like the Mayor of Savannah in a cowboy hat and an ostentatious check suit. He's chewing a More and leaning on an elegant white cane, which he describes as 'purely an affectation really' when questioned about his health. Someone later, rather uncharitably, ascribes it to gout.

The Feetwarmers, all immaculately costumed in Early Gangster, set up their equipment with a sulphurously phlegmatic profession-alism while Patti and the band and their sound man, Mo, express various differences of opinion. 'It sounds really Mickey Mouse up here,' snaps Patti as the slow and painful process of adjusting each amp, mike and instrument sound winds interminably on. The Feetwarmers seem to regard rock bands struggling to sort out their mountains of gear as being inept, spoiled brats who can't work their own gadgets.

'I'm sorry that we won't be able to stay and see you,' Melly tells Patti urbanely, 'but we have another show to do tonight in The Hague.' Patti tells him sure, she understands, she knows how it is.

By showtime the club is pretty thoroughly packed. Up in the balconies as well as down on the floor, it's like the District Line in the rush hour except that everybody's stoned as fruitbats and the train ain't leaving the station.

Lights go down, roadies loom around with torches, the troops go on to the usual preliminary clang-honk-tweets and then Patti and the band blaze into Uncle Lou's 'We're Gonna Have A Real Good Time Together' as the lights go up. It's a great opener — short, sharp, appropriate without being too obvious. Ivan Kral and Lenny Kaye are already in overdrive on the guitars, Jay Dee Daugherty's lamming into his drums like a crazy man, slipping a hi-hat accent just a whisker ahead of the beat to give it just the right jet-boosting surge with Patti leaping up and down like a demented pogo stick, her flea-market rags a constant blur of motion.

Nice applause. She calls them children of Paradise, tells 'em that she's been 'sampling the local wares. I rilly like think windmills are sooooo *cool*, ya know.'

Puzzled silence. One jovial drunk with the equivalent lung power of a mid-price PA system yells ' "Break It Op!" '

'If you take one part windmills,' says Patti from the stage, 'one part hashish and one part cocaine . . .' ragged cheers of recognition of the key words. The drunk yells, ' "Break It Op!" ' again and then changes his mind. He refills his lungs and bawls, 'Fock! Fock!'

Patti ignores him '. . . you get a rilly great drink.'

They work their way through the set, through a few selections from 'Radio Ethiopia' ('This is from our new album. It's a rilly cooool record with a rilly great bass and drum sound'), a couple of borrowings — a great blasting version of The Stones' 'Time Is On My Side', preceded as always by Patti's 'Tick tock — fuck the clock' recitation riff, and their medley of Lou Reed's 'Pale Blue Eyes' and the Punk Archivist National Anthem 'Louie Louie' — and some of the material from 'Horses'.

Throughout it all our stentorian friend keeps on howling for ' "Break It Op!" '.

'Redondo Beach' is, as ever, talked in. 'Redondo! Beach! Is A Beach! Where! Women! Love Uthaaaaaahhhh! Women!' staccatos Patti then closes in on the mike to make little kissing noises.

They do a fair version of 'Kimberly' — their live performances of it always pall in comparison to the album track, because Kral and Kaye are both on guitar and that magnificent bass line is therefore conspicuous by its absence.

Both because of a basic shift of musical emphasis and in order to take the weight off Paley, the band is much more guitar-heavy than they were the last time I'd seen them. Paley moves to bass for 'Gloria' – Kral sketches in the opening chords on piano and resumes his guitar duties as soon as the song hots up – and plays some guitar on the encores.

Patti has amp trouble during 'Radio Ethiopa' and this only adds to the irritation caused by the audience's fairly subdued reaction throughout the set. By the time the set proper ends she's on the verge of losing her temper and walks straight offstage.

The first encore is the speciality version of 'My Generation' with Kral singing the alternate verses and Kaye taking a nicely over the top bass solo. Patti leaves still simmering, and on her return for the second encore berates those who dwell in the 'false paradise' in a long improvised rhythmical tongue-lashing. She's into a rap about breathing and energy and pyramids and triangles when our friend Break It Op starts broadcasting again. Without even pausing for breath she goes from pyramids and triangles and breathing and energy to 'Fuck *you*, asshole!'

'Do you think you're really cool just standing there going, "blecccchh"?' she snaps. 'I can do that too. Why don't you take your dick out? Gowan *take your dick out*! Or whyncha go home and just say "blechhhhhhh!" in front of the mirror?'

There is silence. Mr Break It Op has subsided.

She gets back into her rap and steers it into 'Land' and finally they really drive it in and drive it home and drive it deep and the people start dancing, but it's too little and too late to effect any kind of major reconciliation.

As the number rampages to a climax, she steps to the mike and rattles off 'Andy-Paley-Ivan-Kral-Jay-Dee-Daugherty-Lenny-Kaye-the-Patti-Smith-Group!', makes a pfui-I-wash-my-hands-of-you gesture and rushes offstage. Her brother Todd, who's working with the road crew on tour, takes her arm and then they vanish.

The audience, probably brought down more by her anger than by any deficiencies in the set, leave quickly and quietly. You can tell that it's one of those occasions where it is definitely not cool to wander into the dressing-room before allowing a reasonable interval of cooling-off time to elapse.

When Pennie Smith and I are finally summoned to join the assembled company, the unspoken feeling enfolding the room seems to be that they'd just blown Amsterdam pretty thoroughly.

171

Whether it was the exhaustion, the residue of various injuries and illnesses, the sound problems, the audience or whatever, it'd been a bad gig. And while an artist of genius who does a bad gig can still be an artist of genius, a bad gig by an artist of genius is still a bad gig.

'So what's your instinctive reaction to a guy in the crowd who yells out?' I ask Patti back in the *Don't Look Back* suite. 'To ignore him or cut him back or what?'

'It's the same as your instinct might be. Sometimes I'll laugh, sometimes I'll tell him to fuck off, sometimes I'll ignore him, sometimes I'll like seduce him to do it more. I'm just reacting. Like I don't have like a stage act – I don't have like a stage *persona*' – she pronounces it *per-son-na* – 'I don't turn on a separate set of reflexes when I get on the stage, I'm the same person I am here. In fact often I'm better here than I am up there, y'know? I know what I can do alone as an artist, y'know, and it's rilly intoxicating and to get up on a stage, y'know, and to try and match that intoxication takes a lot of fuckin' work. A *lot of* fuckin' work. Your head has to be like pounding like inside the belly of a bell, be made of like concrete. But soft, *rubbery* concrete.

'It's just incredible what you have to do and then sometimes you don't even get off because the people are like uptight or they don't understand that they're free, y'know. I don't give a shit what people do. They can say I hate you as long as they say . . . anything, y'know? Sometimes I really dig people who give me a hard time because it's friction but it's *reaction* . . .'

That afternoon we'd all gone down the Flea Market. Patti bought an obviously, blatantly fake US Army shirt. She was wearing an Amelia Earhart flying cap and enormous goggle-like shades.

She delightedly traded insults with a couple of very stoned and extrovert faggots who asked if they could buy Ivan Kral ('I might pick you up if you were alone and wearing different coloured boots') and posed for pictures waving around copies of her three bootleg albums and a Blue Oyster Cult bootleg. (Two out of the three – 'Turn It Up' and 'Hard Nipples' – are actually the same one in different packaging, so be warned. The third, 'Teenage Perversity And Ships in The Night', is the one Patti recommends, anyway.)

The guy behind the stall doesn't understand. He thinks this crazy girl is trying to steal his records. He grabs and shouts. She turns on him.

'*Fuck you asshole* – I'm Patti Smith and this is *my record*! I ain't getting any money for this – I oughtta call the cops on ya . . .'

A pinch-faced customer with horn-rimmed glasses, spots and the kind of short hair that they had before long hair, unhesitatingly sides with the stallholder and grabs the records back. They stare dumbly at this frenzied apparition in the jackboots, flapping khaki coat and shirts, goggles and flying helmet. She turns and stalks away.

'What was so good about the sixties,' she'd said over dinner, 'was that we had so many great dressers to copy. Every time I saw Brian Jones with some new trousers I had to get some . . . I remember I saw a picture of Paul McCartney in some really great striped trousers. He wasn't my favourite Beatle but those trousers were *sooooo* cool that even John had to get a pair. I hitch-hiked into town and I found a pair in a department store and I got them . . . that was such a thrill. I want to do that, I want to provide kids with something cool to copy . . .'

She's had her lookalike phases, her Keith Richards, her Bob Dylan, her Jeff Beck, her Jim Morrison.

'I put in a *lotta* work studying those cats. When you work as hard at it as I did, you really end up getting them *down*. I've been studying a lot of Jeanne Moreau. She is like so *cool*. She is *sooooo* heavy. She's the complete woman . . . complete *anything*, she is just *complete*. I've been looking at a lot of photographs of Brigitte Bardot, too . . .'

In the studio of a Dutch photographer, she asks him what kind of photos he wants. When he shrugs obligingly, she runs through some riffs – he gets the eyebulging speedfreak, the blank arrogant poker-face sneer, the gamine grin, the sexy guerrilla with the army shirt opened at the top to show the tops of her breasts and knotted up over her belly, he gets mock-*Vogue*, he gets wistful-little-girl . . . Riffs.

'So what makes the difference between a really great rock and roll record and one that doesn't happen?' I ask, faithfully adhering to my role as man from *Time*.

'If it makes me feel great ... if it makes me laugh ... like a bubble breaking in my heart. Like a really completely sincere effort to communicate and desire to connect: even if it doesn't totally come into focus the intention is so clear that unless you're a really bitter person you'll open your heart to it and let it reach you.

'See, there's like two different great kinds of rock and roll. There's fascist rock and roll, which is like Bowie and disco and Motown ... y'know, like a metronome. It's rilly great, it's perfect, I mean it gets ya. You can't help but get caught in the groove, y'know?

'The other one isn't really defined; it's like raw energy that you're trying to sensuously and rhythmatically hone – is that the right word, Lenny? Hone? – hone ... you do your honing, get into different kinds of plants, kind of cup-shaped ... more like bell-shaped like tulips ... no, not like tulips but like lilies ... you get into the horn of any flower that has a bell shape and it's a really pleasurable thing ... ya know sound. If you're really relentlessly into something and you're into sound, it gets to the point where it doesn't matter whether you're good or evil or dream or nightmare or whatever, you get into this rhythm of sound and you just *have* to be great no matter who you are. I mean, Karen Carpenter could be great if she'd just loosen up a little.

'It's all there. You just have to be willing to get baptized over and over again. Most people just get baptized once and they think they got everything covered. They know how they're gonna think for the rest of their lives ...'

Do you want to make a fascist rock record?

'I wanna make something like "Station To Station" ... something in as purposive a state as "Station To Station" and as perfect as "Black And Blue". Those two albums are like "Sergeant Pepper" and "Pet Sounds" or something ... and then "Radio Ethiopia" because it's going to be really great. I really love both elements – there's more than two elements, there's three. There's like language which you don't have to deal with – I'd just as soon deal with sound, but when I'm called upon to use language in order to go a step higher or a step further to explore just for the pleasure ... of Man ... is real cool. I forgot where this sentence was going to end ... I had to say "real cool" because I couldn't remember where the sentence should end up...

174

'"Radio Ethiopia" is a lot like Albert Ayler. That's not hard to understand. I don't know what people will think of our record, but how I view it is like . . . the first record was like a little egg, ya know . . . and this one is like a little chick . . . and then the little chick opens its mouth . . . and takes in a little *worm* . . . and gets nourished and gets strong and becomes . . .'

'A *bigger* bird,' croons Lenny Kaye.

## Muddy Waters: Knee-deep in the Big Muddy

*NME*, 30 April 1977

*T*HE *kind of blues I play, there's no money in it. You makes a good livin' when you gets established like I am, but you don't reach that kind of overnight million dollar thing, man . . . no way.*

*If you play nuthin' but blues, it's hard to get big off of it. It takes years and years and still kids come in and go, 'Who he?'*

The kid with the cancelled eyes and the bombsite face has his eye on my bottle of beer. As we stand at the edge of the club watching Johnny Winter leading Muddy Waters' band through the first half of the show, he sees I have my eye on his pipe. We come to a wordless agreement and trade implements. As we swap back I ask him if Muddy Waters has been on yet.

He turns those dented hubcap orbs on me.

'Muddy *who*?'

In the end, I have to ask four people before I finally find one who says, 'No, man, it's just been Johnny and the band on so far.'

Once that's been established and I'm assured that I haven't dragged Joe Stevens, a lady from CBS records, her two kid brothers and a driver all the way from New York City to Willimantic, Connecticut, on a mere wild blues chase, it's possible to relax and take stock of the surroundings and the music.

We're in a sprawling, low-ceilinged wooden building called the Shaboo Inn. Kids from the neighbouring three or four states all converge there – it seems like every under-age drunken driver within a hundred miles is there; damage cases lurching around afterwards slurring, 'Hey, whut city we in, man?', the lot.

It's crowded, smoky, sweatbox hot despite the noisy air-conditioning and there are two small exits – upfront and back-stage –which means that if a fire started in there the audience and bands would have to be sent home in canvas bags and the whole process would take maybe ten or fifteen minutes . . . imagine all those blurred-round-the-edges teenage casualties stomping each other to get at the exits. Jesus, what a mess . . .

As this horrific fantasy subsides, focus in if you will on the band.

Reading from left to right, the first man we come to is Pinetop Perkins, born at Belzoni, Mississippi, in 1913. He's played piano for Muddy since the death of Otis Spann, Muddy's half-brother and the finest blues pianist of his time, in 1970.

Next to him behind the drums is Willie 'Big Eyes' Smith – formerly known as 'Little Willie Smith' – born 1936 in Helena, Arkansas, a former harmonica player who switched to drums in the late fifties because the blues was in one of its periodic doldrums '. . . and harps went out. So I had to look for other ways to keep a job and I learned drums.' He's played with Muddy since the early sixties, thrashing his kit with perfect power and control.

Next up is Bob Margolin, a young bearded white guitarist who's played rhythm for Muddy for three or four years. He keeps his Stratocaster turned well down and he looks unbelievably nervous, even after all this time. His playing is oddly hesitant as if he's perpetually waiting for cues from the older men around him – like James Cotton on harp.

Cotton, born in Tunica, Mississippi, in 1935, is one of the guest stars on this tour. Taught by Sonny Boy Williamson II and Muddy's harmonica player for twelve years, he's led his own band for some time, and it's from Cotton's band that Muddy's borrowed bassist Charles Calmese, the youngest man on the stage, snake-eyed and agile, pumping out time-honoured lines embellished with a few contemporary fillips on a fretless Fender.

Upfront taking care of business in the absence of The Man is a man who could be nineteen or ninety, a long thin streak of Texas white lightning perched on a high stool with a Gibson Firebird in his lap, clad in black velvet and a floppy hat of the same fabric, milky hair pushed back and falling to his shoulders, a face so white that it practically vanishes when he leans into the lights . . . born in 1944 in Leland, Mississippi, Mr Johnny Winter.

Shorn of his rock star accoutrements and 2001-watt monoliths, Winter's put himself back into the College of Musical Knowledge for a post-graduate Ph.D course in the blues from the man who personally tutored the likes of Little Walter, Jimmy Rogers, James Cotton, Junior Wells, Buddy Guy, Mike Bloomfield and Paul Butterfield in the intricacies of their craft, and whose home-study course has benefited − among others − Mick Jagger, Keith Richards, Eric Clapton, Brian Jones, Peter Green, Elvis Presley, Carl Perkins, Bo Diddley, Eric Burdon, John Mayall, Stevie Winwood, Jack Bruce, Jimmy Page, Robert Plant, Jimi Hendrix, The Band, Rory Gallagher, The Feelgoods, Paul Rodgers, Lew Lewis, Rod Stewart . . . let's just say that Muddy's students have, over the years, done him proud.

Like just about every Southern kid, Winter had grown up hearing the seminal rock and country records over the radio and, for him, Muddy was always The Man.

He'd simultaneously paid off a massive musical debt and set himself up for the treat of a lifetime by getting Muddy signed up to Blue Sky Records − his manager Steve Paul's label − and producing/kibitzing/guitaring 'Hard Again', the album which inaugurated Muddy's stay with the company by recapturing the colossal vitality and crispness of Muddy's fifties recordings.

And now he's upfront leading a stellar line-up of three generations of Chicago bluesmen, warming up the crowd for The Man. He's shouting John Lee Hooker's 'Serve You Right To Suffer' into the mike and playing the sweetest, sharpest, saltiest blues guitar you can imagine, expanding the content of the genre without ever breaking faith with its form.

The audience is grooving on it, but they seem a bit puzzled as to why Johnny isn't wearing his satins and jewellery and playing the ferocious death-before-dishonour power-chord rock and roll that's been his major stock in trade in the seventies.

A kid who yells for 'Rock And Roll Hoochie Koo' gets a poised '*Fuck* ya!' gouged into his face, followed by a galloping, hell-for-leather sword-cane version of Elmore James' Robert-Johnson-derived 'Dust My Broom'.

As he kick-starts his solo, his left hand sneaks to his volume control and he's up off the stool and dancing with it now, his face dreamily and serenely abstracted as he switches his butt across the stage. He doesn't do 'Guitar moves'; in fact, it's like he's dancing to the music and he's forgotten that he's got a guitar in his hands and that he's playing, or – indeed – that he doesn't realize that he's off his stool.

He looked like a skeleton dancing in moonlight, answering some unearthly summons.

On this up, he ends the set and calls a fifteen-minute break before The Main Event – and even though sound commercial reasoning dictates whose name is highest and biggest on the posters, there's no question as to whose show it is.

When things reassemble, Perkins, Smith, Margolin, Calmese and Cotton essay an instrumental.

Cotton wails his brains out with a succession of devastating solos, but the stiffness and nervousness of Margolin's playing keeps things fairly earthbound until Winter re-enters, plugs in and starts striking sparks off his guitar. The other musicians ignite and things are burning pretty good when Cotton brings on Muddy Waters.

Muddy Waters was born on 4 April 1915 in Rolling Fork, Mississippi; the second son of farmer Ollie Morganfield, who named him McKinley. In 1918 his mother died, and young McKinley Morganfield was sent to live with his grandmother in Clarksdale, some hundred miles away.

'I was raised in the country, and out there they didn't have no *concrete*, ya know . . . just muddy country roads, and people used to clean their feet off on our front porch. I'd be playing around crawlin' in the mud, probably *eatin'* it . . . and my grandmother started callin' me her little muddy baby.

'I started to play the harp when I was seven. At nine I was *really* tryin' to play. At thirteen I thought I was *good*. The kids I used to sing to would call out "*Hey Muddy Waters play us a piece.*"

'I didn't like that "Muddy Water" thing, ya know . . . I didn't mind my grandmother calling me Muddy, but that whole Muddy Waters thing, I didn't like it. It just growed on me.'

In the latter part of his teens, McKinley Morganfield saw the great Delta bluesman Charley Patton. Patton was nearly thirty years Muddy's senior and impressed him enormously – as he had also impressed a twenty-one-year-old Arkansawan named Chester Burnett, himself later to become a blues legend as Howlin' Wolf.

'I saw Charley Patton in my younger life days – him and Son House, a lot of the older guys. What got to me about Charley Patton was that he was such a good clown man with the guitar. Pattin' it and beatin' on it and puttin' it behind his neck and turnin' it over . . . I loved that, but I loved Son House because he used the bottleneck so beautiful. He was one of the best Mississippi things of the time.

'I think me myself and Robert Johnson got the most out of Son House. Of course Robert he come up so fast, but I had to stay with the Son House single-string kind of thing.'

Muddy had formed a duo with a friend of his, a guitarist named Scott Bohannon. Within a year, though, Muddy had traded in his harps for a guitar, and by the time he was seventeen, he was playing bottleneck leads to Bohannon's rhythm. He'd already known for a long time that he was going to be a professional musician for life.

'I left the home with that when I was a little kid, and ever since I can remember, *this is what I wanted to be*. Something outstanding. If I couldn't make it in music, I'd be a big preacher, a great ball player.

'I didn't want to grow up with no one knowin' me but the neighbourhood people. I wanted the world to know a *lot* about me. I thank my God I got it through . . .'

Throughout his late teens and his twenties, Muddy made his living in much the same way as many other unskilled and semi-educated young Southern blacks: he went to work on neighbouring cotton plantations, but he did better than most, thanks to his musical abilities. A night's music earned him $2.50, as opposed to $3.75 paid for five days' work.

Plus a small whisky still out in the bushes.

Son House, the man from who he learned the finer points of bottleneck guitar and a certain amount of his early repertoire, was a brilliant guitarist who remained in obscurity until tracked down and recorded in 1966 ('Son House, I presume'). Son House taught Muddy some of the songs – and the essentials of the style – of Robert Johnson, undoubtedly the finest country blues singer of all.

*

To say that Robert Johnson was a 'mystery' and an 'enigma' is to understate. No one seems to know where he was born or when, although he must've been around Muddy's age. Nobody knows what he looked like (though he is frequently described as being 'small and dark'), because there are no known photographs of him.

He was a shy young kid who desperately wanted to emulate the older bluesmen and seemed patently unable to do so until he vanished for about six months and then came back the best and most exciting singer/guitarist and composer that anyone had ever heard.

Between 1936 and 1938 he recorded twenty-nine sides for Vocalion Records – all of which are now available on a pair of indispensable CBS albums entitled 'Robert Johnson, King Of The Delta Blues Singers (Vols I & II)' – a blues more supple, driving and achingly immediate than anything existing at the time.

The blues of Robert Johnson represent the absolute artistic peak of the pre-war rural blues: his guitar playing foreshadowed the future of the music, with funky bass-string riffing, vibrant, biting slide counterpoints and powerful, choppy chording that formed the basis of the way the electric blues bands – black *and* white – of the future would balance off lead, rhythm and bass guitars.

He was solidly in the tradition of the Mississippi Delta bluesmen who'd preceded him, but like his spiritual descendants Charlie Parker and Jimi Hendrix, he was just that much further out.

It was his songs, and the way he sang them, that mattered the most, though. Hearing Robert Johnson really drives home why religious folks called the blues 'devil music' and why many musicians from religious backgrounds found the decision to play blues an almost Faustian choice.

Johnson opens a window into an almost apocalyptic world in his blues, a world where he and the devil walk side by side (*'Early this morning when you knocked upon my door/I said "Hello Satan, I do believe it's time to go"'*), where the blues walks like a man and pours down like hell ('Hell Hound On My Trail'), where he's out late at night after redneck curfew ('Crossroads'), and even when the devil blues makes him impotent ('Phonograph Blues', 'Stones In My Passway').

He sings in a voice that sounds like bare trees clutching hopelessly at a grey sky, as if he was running down the road trying not to look at them. Robert Johnson was serving life without parole on Desolation Row before Bob Dylan was even born.

The unnerving suddenness with which he'd acquired his powers and the subject-matter of his songs led many to venture the opinion that Johnson had, indeed, made a Faustian pact with the devil. He died in 1938 – no one quite knows how.

Some say he was stabbed, some poisoned, but everybody agrees that it was in a fight over a girl.

The reason for the mystery is that he was an itinerant musician in a strange town, with none of his friends with him either to prevent or to record the manner of his death, and besides, who cares what happens to a vagrant black in some small Southern town where nobody knows him . . .?

Muddy Waters knew Johnson principally from his records and from what Son House had taught him, but Johnson influenced him enormously.

'I didn't know Robert well at all, because I don't remember meeting him. He was in a little town called Frye's Point, and he was playing on the corner there. People were crowdin' round him, and I stopped and peeked over. I got back into the car and left, because he was a *dangerous* man . . . and he really was *using* the *git*-tar, man . . .

'I crawled away and pulled out, because it was too heavy for me . . .'

The echoes of Robert Johnson in Muddy's first recordings were overwhelming.

Folklorist Alan Lomax recorded him for the Library of Congress in 1941 and again in 1942, both solo and as a member of the Sons Sims Four, a group he played with occasionally.

In his mid-twenties at the time, his voice is considerably lighter and younger than the classic Muddy Waters Voice of his fifties recordings, and the phrasing and intonation are unmistakably derived from Johnson, as is the guitar style.

Muddy's playing and singing carried a solidity and weight that Johnson's perhaps lacked, but similarly the realms of metaphysical terror which were Johnson's prowling grounds were closed to

Muddy – perhaps thankfully, because Muddy Waters is still with us in the flesh, whereas Johnson's presence is ghostly beyond belief.

No mere Johnson *imitator* was Muddy, though, not even then. His sheer warmth, strength and authority completely polarized and redefined even the most obviously Johnson-derived pieces, and he displays thrilling, tantalizing hints of the power that he would unleash on his next foray into recording.

He was absolutely determined that he would record again – and this time see the records released and paid for. The Library of Congress, which treats folk musicians as wildlife specimens rather than artists, never paid Muddy for the recordings until a quarter of a century later, when they were finally released by Testament Records as 'Down On Stovall's Plantation'.

The centre of blues recording was Chicago, which then – as now – boasted a substantial black population.

The industry was undergoing a hiatus at the time, since due to a combination of wartime raw-materials shortages and a massive union dispute, there were no recordings made for several years.

Muddy arrived in Chicago in 1943 – the year after his final session with Lomax – and went to stay with an uncle of his. He got a job in a paper factory, but he soon found himself making more money playing guitar and singing at parties and bars. In 1944 he found that he wasn't loud enough and got himself his first electric guitar.

'It wasn't no name brand electric guitar, but it was a *built-in* electric *git*-tar, no pick-up just stuck on. It gave me so much trouble that that's probably why I forgot the name; every time I looked round I had to have it fixed. Finally it got stoled from me in one of them little neighbourhood clubs, and the next one I got me was a Gretsch, and that's the one I used on all my early hits.'

In 1946, pianist Albert Luandrew – better known as Sunnyland Slim – needed a guitarist for a session he was cutting for Aristocrat Records, a small label run as a sideline by Leonard and Phil Chess, who were proprietors of a bar called the Macambo, and a gentlemen named Sammy Goldberg.

Slim knew Muddy from various jams and gigs, and so he brought him along to Goldberg and the Chess brothers, and they and bassist Ernest 'Big' Crawford cut four sides.

Muddy and Slim each took two lead vocals, and therefore got a single apiece out of it.

On all four of the selections, Slim's piano is the predominant instrument – after all, he was the veteran and Muddy the novice – but the guitar is taut and inventive. Playing, surprisingly enough, without a slide, Muddy reveals himself as a lead guitarist who'd not only refined his existing tricks in the preceding five years, but has also learned an awful lot of new ones. His voice had developed considerably more power and control and the Johnson influences had been almost fully absorbed and transcended.

After one single as a sideman, one as a featured artist and a third where he and Slim shared billing, he was ready to step out on his own.

In 1948, Sunnyland Slim quit Aristocrat.

Muddy, however, was already far more than just Sunnyland Slim's protégé, a fact which he proved with devastating success when, accompanied only by Big Crawford, he cut a version of a song called 'I Be's Troubled', which he'd first cut for Alan Lomax back in Mississippi in 1942.

This time it was called 'I Can't Be Satisfied'.

By blues standards, it was a smash-hit around Chicago and in the South. Almost certainly, it was one of the records that, way over in Memphis, Tennessee, a thirteen-year-old po'-white boy named Elvis Aron Presley must've listened to on the black radio station.

Big Crawford's pumping, punching bass lines presage those which Bill Black was to play six years later when Presley cut his interpretation of Arthur 'Big Boy' Crudup's 'That's All Right Mama', an interpretation which owes much to the pacing and phrasing of Muddy's record.

The record had two major effects.

The first was to persuade the Chess brothers that the harsh, electrified Delta blues was *the* sound. They then dropped the cocktail pop and jazz that they'd been recording and quickly established themselves as a pre-eminent boss blues label.

The second was to make Muddy Waters the undisputed boss of Chicago blues.

He consolidated his success with a series of harder, heavier, more passionate and more electric hits, and began to assemble, member by member, the toughest and most exciting band in town. Muddy Waters' Blues Band was to become, not only the best and most influential band in Chicago, but what was for all practical purposes, the first electric rock band.

His first ally was Jimmy Rogers (sometimes known as 'Chicago Jimmy Rogers' to distinguish him from the white country singer Jimmie Rodgers), a fine guitarist and singer who, like many of Muddy's sidemen, cut solo recordings at Muddy's sessions with the leader backing them up.

'He was playing harp, I was playing git-tar – that was when I got my git-tar stoled. Then he switched over – we went with a guy called Blue Smitty.

'He made a coupla records for Chess, but I don't know if you'd remember him – he played a hell of a good guitar. Me and him played guitar, and Jimmy Rogers played harp: three of us. This lasted almost a year, and then Blue Smitty left us and Jimmy got a job, and this left me by myself.

'I got a guy named Baby Face Leroy (Foster). He played drums and guitar, but he and I was playing git-tars together. Then Little Walter came to play with Baby Face Leroy, and Jimmy was hangin' round. He was a good musician, and I wanted to cut him in with us and make four. So I put Leroy on the drums, Jimmy on the guitar and Little Walter on the harp.'

Marion 'Little Walter' Jacobs was born in Marksville, Lousiana, in either 1930 or 1931.

He played both harmonica and guitar when, barely twenty, he joined up with Muddy's band. He was a more than fair guitarist – as his performances on some of Muddy's records amply testify – but his true turf was mouth harp.

Little Walter is the man against whom all other blues harpists must be measured. Rank him as of equal importance and influence on his instrument and in his field as Robert Johnson, Charlie Parker and Jimi Hendrix were in theirs.

'Before I had him as a harp player he was used to playing on his own. He didn't have very good time, but me and Jimmy teached him that. Plus we taught him how to settle down. He was *wild*, he had to play *fast*! He was always a jump boy, had that up'n-go power. *Lotta* energy!

'He could cool down and play a slow blues, but when he go for himself he play sump'n up-tempo.'

Walter was a renowned hell-raiser, and even after his work with Muddy and his solo records both while he was in the band and after had made him as big a star as Muddy for a while, his wildness and taste for the booze seriously damaged his career.

'He was a great guy. He had kind of a bad temper, but he was a great guy, man . . . and if he wanted to love you he loved you.

'A lot of peoples give him the wrong thing, 'cause he just didn't want to take no foolishness off nobody. A *lot* of people don't want to take no jive from peoples, and he was that type.

'But otherwise, man, whatever he did, he did it to himself.

'He didn't go sticking up nobody or none of *that* jive, but he was a fast boy. People said he drank, but what the hell, *everybody* drinks. I drink too.

'I think he was one of the swellest guys that was ever in the business. And he *did* like me. Awwwwww man, he was another Robert Johnson. It's hard to find them kinds of peoples.'

Charlie Parker, Jimi Hendrix, Billie Holiday, John Coltrane . . .

'Yeah man . . . those guys, you don't run into them too often. They *born* with that. Walter was *born* with what he had and, man, you couldn't take it from him. He could *do* it.

'His mind was so fast he could think twice to your once; that's how he learned to harp so good. Kids are still trying to play like him but they not yet up to the point . . .'

In 1950, the Chess brothers separated themselves from Sammy Goldberg and Aristocrat in order to set up a new operation: Chess Records.

They leased a few masters from the South – among them the records Sam Phillips at Sun made with Howlin' Wolf before he, too, moved to Chicago – but mostly they found all the blues they could handle right there in Chicago.

The Muddy Waters' Blues Band ruled the roost, notching up best-sellers not only with Muddy's own records but with solo records from Jimmy Rogers and Little Walter. Muddy and the band also backed up other artists, notably Sonny Boy Williamson.

In contrast to the rockabilly records that Southern whites were to make in a few years' time – in which only the lead guitar and the echo chambers sounded electric – the Waters band was making an almost totally electric music.

Since its music was an extension of country blues, they used a small number of instruments heavily amplified for maximum cut-and-thrust power, in direct contrast to the big bands which used a large number of acoustic instruments in which maybe only the singer and the guitarists used electricity to cut through the horns.

The drummers thrashed away mercilessly to compete with the cranked-up guitar amps used by Waters and Rogers (Rogers alternated bass and lead parts against Muddy's rhythm and slide, since in those pre-electric-bass days, bass was really only practical in the studio).

Walter's harp was closely miked and gave him a volume, sustain and richness of tone that enabled him to fill the air with the huge chording of a four-piece horn section or else soar like a single alto sax, like a slide guitar or like a voice.

And over the top rode Muddy triumphant, slashing the air into thin slices with bare-wire slide and declaiming his witty, observant and poignant songs with magisterial dignity and savage aplomb.

Rock and roll proper was still two or three years away, but boisterous, rampaging, remorseless electric street music was developing by leaps and bounds in Chicago.

The music's still with us, but, sadly, Little Walter isn't.

He suffered a massive concussion in a back-alley brawl outside a Chicago club where he'd worked one night in 1967. He complained of a headache, took a couple of aspirins, went to sleep and never woke up.

'I was here when rock and roll first came out with Chuck Berry and all of them. I sent him to Chess, told him to tell Leonard Chess that it was me sent him over there. He recorded with the Chicago people: Otis Spann, the drummer Odie Payne, I believe . . .'

Muddy has always been noted for his willingness to advance other people's careers. He not only let Rogers and Little Walter record on his time, but he played on their records, gave them solo spots on his gigs and gave them the benefits of all his experience, musical and otherwise. Many of his former sidemen who now lead their own bands have benefited from both his advice and his object lessons on the tricky art of leading a band.

'Was a lot of changes made when we was goin' through the thing . . . I had a lot of mens in the band. That's why I feels that I did a lot more for blues players than anybody else I know ever lived.

'I taught a lot of people how to do it, I took 'em into my band and I made good blues stars out of 'em . . .'

More than any other single event, it was Muddy's visit to England in 1958 that laid the first foundation stone for the Great British R&B boom of the early sixties.

Earthshakingly loud by the standards of the time (even Otis Spann's piano was amplified), at least one major British jazz critic of the time was so freaked out by the volume of the Waters band (he was more accustomed to the acoustic 'folk' blues of Big Bill Broonzy and Brownie McGhee) that he reviewed the show from the toilet.

It was that visit that inspired Alexis Korner and Cyril Davies to form Blues Incorporated and provide the environment that produced The Rolling Stones, The Yardbirds, Manfred Mann, The Pretty Things and the rest of the Crawdaddy / Marquee school of young white Britblues bands.

It was in that same year that Muddy received the first real answering shout from across the colour line.

'It was when Elvis Presley made a picture with a song had that "Hoochie Coochie Man" beat . . . *ba da da da dum* . . . and I thought, "I better watch out. I believe whitey's pickin' up on things that I'm doin'."'

The song in question was 'Trouble' from the movie *King Creole*.

It was probably Presley's last fling as a hardcore rock and roller, and also the last fling of hardcore rock and roll for a few years.

When the bottom dropped out of hard rock to coincide with Presley's induction into the army, the blues market also contracted sharply. Muddy's coup was to take his band – then consisting of Pat Hare (guitar), James Cotton (harp), Otis Spann (piano), Andrew Stephens (bass) and Francis Clay (drums) – to the Newport Jazz Festival.

From his triumphant performance there, slightly subdued though it was after his experience at the hands of the British jazz critics, came the superb 'Muddy Waters At Newport' album, which introduced him to white jazz fans. He also recorded the acoustic 'Muddy Waters, Folk Singer' album and the Broonzy tribute 'Muddy Sings Big Bill', both of which gained him a foothold with white folk fans.

But nevertheless, his black public was being eroded by the smoother, jazzier 'urban blues' of B.B. King and Albert King, and by the gospel-influenced pop-soul coming out of Motown in Detroit and Stax in Memphis. Both these forms seemed 'classier' to the burgeoning black middle class, who were beginning to find the music of men like Muddy and Howlin' Wolf a little too rough and dirty.

'I'm dead outa Mississippi, the country. I play cotton-patch music, cornfield, fishfry. B.B. and Albert are a different style; a higher class of people'd see them, more middle-class people – in those days, anyway.

'Now you talkin' direct to black, because white people, if they like you, they don't give a damn. I have doctors and everything who come around: doctors, lawyers maybe even a judge slip in there sometime.

'But in those days some clubs would rather have B.B. in there than me, because a more white-collar guy comes in to see him. They'd want to be *sophisticated*, they'd say they don't dig the *deep* blues like me and Wolf were playin' . . . John Lee Hooker, maybe Lightnin' Hopkins.

'What the hell, you can't please everybody.

'What do I care: back when I was playin' for only black I always had my house full, you couldn't even get *in*. I didn't need no guy in the necktie, y'know wh'mean?'

In 1964, Muddy was to begin to reap the harvest of the seeds he'd planted over in England back in 1958.

'Then all at once there was The Rollin' Stones. When they did it, they created a whole wide-open space for the music. They said who did it first and how they came by knowin' it.

'They told the truth about it, and that really put a shot in my arm with the whites. I tip my hat to 'em.

'They took a lot of what I was doin', but who care? The Rolling Stones . . . it took the people from England to hip *my* people – *my* white people – to what they had in their own backyard. That sounds funny, but it's the truth.

'It was The Beatles and The Rolling Stones: The Beatles did a lot of Chuck Berry, The Rolling Stones did some of my stuff. That's what it took to wake up the people in my own country, in my own state where I was born, that a black man's music is not a crime to bring in the house.

'There was a time when a kid couldn't bring that music into a father and mother's house. *Don't bring that nigger music in here.* That's *right*!

'Those kids didn't give a damn what your colour is; they just want to hear the records.

'Then the college kids started comin' to see me in places where I was afraid for 'em even to be there, maybe twelve or fourteen of them a night. I said, "Brother, I hope they can handle this, they don't know where they at. I hope don't nothin' happen to 'em. I hope everybody leave 'em alone!"

'This was before Martin Luther King's thing was happening, and even then they was going to the black places . . . they had more nerve than I woulda had, man . . . I mean, I'm scared to go in some black places myself now.

'All the kids got nerve these days. Me, I don't got no nerve. I'd just rather stay peaceable, sit round and watch my TV and watch my kids grow up. I been through what they goin' through.

'I been in some *baaad* places in my lifetime, but I went through sound and safe. I didn't get nobody and didn't nobody get me. I used to pack *that thing* here . . .' he slaps his hip pocket meaningfully – 'but you don't need that to live.

'I don't think about *that* no more. I goes on havin' a good time, man . . . I get in my car and go to the store . . . I'm having a good time.'

Muddy Waters lives today in a small white wooden house on a quiet street in a suburb of Chicago.

It's only in the last few years that he finally got enough money together to be able to move out of Chicago's ghetto South Side, but when one considers that Muddy Waters is a colossus of modern popular music and that he's been working his butt off as a star performer and recording artist for more than a quarter of a century, the smallness and modesty of his home comes as something of a shock, despite the expensive comfortable furniture, the electronic kitchen and the small swimming pool in the yard.

Suddenly you realize that over those years Muddy hasn't ever seen much of a financial reward for his work. He has little more than any hard-working man coming up to retirement age would have.

Over the years, he's made several stylistic experiments in the hope of clicking with a wider market in the way that B.B. and

Albert have done, but his reluctance to move too far from the music that is his unquestioned forte has resulted in some less than enthusiastic performances on some less than worthy projects.

There was 'Brass And The Blues', a lightly swinging album backing him up with jazz horns, and a pair of horrendous 'psychedelic' albums, 'Electric Mud' and 'After The Rain' ('Chess thought they could make some money off of those and hell, I could use some money too'), neither of which made it either artistically or commercially.

A pair of 'team-up' albums – 'Super Blues' with Bo Diddley and Little Walter, and 'Super Super Blues Band' with Bo and Howlin' Wolf – were better and did better, and in 1969 he teamed up with Otis Spann, Paul Butterfield, Mike Bloomfield, Duck Dunn and Buddy Miles for a superb double album entitled – appropriately enough – 'Fathers And Sons'.

(In the seventies, there was a 'London Sessions' album with Rory Gallagher, Stevie Winwood, Georgie Fame, Rick Grech and Mitch Mitchell.)

It seemed that that was it, except that the following year Muddy was involved in an almost fatal car accident that laid him low for many months.

'I came back good. I came back much better'n I ever thought I would. The public didn't think I'd ever come back as strong as I am now.

'Some thought I'd never play again, because I couldn't even move my fingers, man . . . but I can't play no hour and a half or two hours no more, man. My age is too old for that, I wouldn't even think about doin' that.

'Forty-five to fifty minutes, man, that's enough for a sixty-two-year-old man. I know the kids would love for me to stay out there more . . . I could go on for a few minutes longer but I'm trying to protect this one body. The kids be hollerin' for more all night, but if I did in a coupla weeks I be lyin' on my back in a bed somewhere.

'I'm trying to protect Muddy Waters. You don't get a sixty-two-year-old man out on no stage for no two hours, man . . . you kiddin'?

'The band go out there first and then I do my forty-five, fifty minutes . . . yeah, cool . . . but me go out there for an hour and a half? No way.'

*

Last year, Muddy severed his connection with Chess Records, the company which his success helped to build and with which his name had been virtually synonymous for more than twenty-five years.

His departure coincided with the sale of Chess to the New Jersey-based All Platinum label.

'That be the second time they sold me, and I got tired of being sold to everybody. The first time was when they sold me to a company called GRT, and then they sold me to *another* record company, and I said, "This ain't no good for me. I *quit*." '

His manager, Scott Cameron, went to CBS records, who suggested that he apply directly to Steve Paul's Blue Sky Records, who CBS distributed.

'They said that this label was the *direct* one for me, and it was the one that Johnny Winter was connected up with.

'When they said "Johnny Winter", this was it. I was just thrilled all over, because when I met Johnny a few years ago in Texas, he didn't have the big contract then and he wasn't a big rock and roll star. He was playin' so much of the old stuff . . . all the old blues players like me'n Jimmy Rogers and a lot more, he was playin' all of our stuff.

'I figured that this was the greatest chance, man, of all my days, to get with someone who's still got it, got that early fifties sound.'

Using Muddy's own piano, drums and rhythm guitar plus James Cotton and his bass player and Winter himself, they went ahead to make the album that turned out to be the magnificent 'Hard Again'.

'We tried to keep it down in the fifties style, and I think this is one of the best records I've made in a long time . . . with that really *Muddy Waters* sound. I thought the "Fathers And Sons" was a heckuva good record, but I think this is *the top*. I really do.

'We're trying to get as close to the old sound as we can. We talked to Jimmy Rogers, and he's ready, and maybe on the next one we use Walter Horton' — also known as 'Shakey Horton' and 'Big Walter', another of the great fifties Chicago harps — 'he's an old-timer, and he got some good old sound in his body, plus I'm sure ol' Sunnyland Slim got a coupla sides in him. We're just starting to think about it.'

\*

But most of all, Muddy yields to no one in his admiration for Johnny Winter; the only one of the young blues guitarists who has mastered the guitar styles which Waters and his contemporaries pioneered.

Most of the noted young white bluesmen of the sixties, like Clapton, Green and Bloomfield, took B.B. King as their model, but Winter is the only one who can capture Muddy's own style.

It takes a very careful listen to 'Hard Again' to discern that it's Winter playing those Waters-styled guitar lines and not the old master himself. Waters will hear no criticisms of Winter, not even of his often rather strained blues singing.

'He got a *good* voice on him for a white boy. How the hell you expect him to be able to sing like me?'

Johnny Winter's former colleague Rick Derringer has a few things to say about the Winter/Waters relationship:

'I heard a whole lot of those albums where people like Muddy and Wolf and Hooker were doing the blues with wah-wah pedals, trying to make it a commercial, viable thing, trying to make it sell, but what I liked about Muddy and Johnny together wasn't how good Johnny was playing, but just the fact that when Muddy was on the stage with Johnny he was incredibly alive and aware and energetic . . . he just had to look over and see Johnny there.

'If he could see him, it was great.

'If you ask Muddy, "Which out of the young rock and roll guys turns you on?" he'd say, "My favourite one is that Johnny Winter," and Johnny'd tell you that his all-time *idol* – living, at least – is Muddy Waters. So when they get together it's a real two-way thing. That's why they work good.'

Up on stage at the Shaboo, Willie Smith sets up that two-fisted bump and grind, and Winter and Cotton power the band into 'Hoochie Man'.

Seated centre-stage, plucking casually at a businesslike brown Telecaster, clad in short-sleeved sports shirt and slacks, Muddy declaims the classic braggadocio of Willie Dixon's Chicago anthem with the casual authority of a man who knows that he's not going to be called upon to prove what he sings but is still prepared to back it up every inch of the way.

An all-encompassing boast of mystic, secular and sexual power, he slams home the last chorus with as much zest and vitality and utter conviction that he must've put into his first performances half a century ago back in Clarksdale, Mississippi:

'*I'm here, everybody knows I'm here/I'm that hoochie coochie man, Let the whole damn world know I'm here.*'

And they do. Lord *God*, they do.

And the one black kid in the club – tall, skinny, Afro'ed – is looking at Muddy almost in shock, as if he can't believe that this old man who looks like his grandfather is generating so much power.

When a drunken white boy behind him starts to babble and laugh during the next song, he turns on him savagely:

'Shut yo' white mouth, motherfucker. *This is the blues.*'

For Muddy, Winter must be the ideal sideman.

Whenever the old master needs to take a breath, Winter can take over the vocal for a while, be it 'Mannish Boy (I'm A Man)' or Muddy's time-honoured hard-charging finale number 'Got My Mojo Working'. And yet he never risks distracting the audience from Muddy, he stays on his stool until Muddy gets up and then he gets up too to groove around with him.

The programme includes Muddy standards like 'Honey Bee' and 'I'm A Howlin' Wolf' (an old song of Muddy's that he now sings as a tribute to his old friend, dead this past two years) plus 'Way Down In Florida', from the new album.

It's on this song that Muddy takes his only guitar solo of the night.

The kids at the Shaboo have by now heard guitar players pull out every trick in the book, but the old man has a surprise or two left for 'em yet.

Every time I see Muddy, I'm always taken aback at the sheer savagery of his soloing. I've never heard *anybody* this side of Jeff Beck generate so much attack, so much venom with a guitar.

Listening to Muddy soloing is like getting into a razor fight in the middle of a cloud of enraged napalm wasps out for blood and marrowbone jelly. He just *kills*, and for all his astonishing speed and flair and invention, Winter just can't hit as hard as Muddy.

And that's why we need old masters, 'cuz if younger folk could do just as well then they'd be superfluous, long overdue for rock and roll euthanasia. The reason that Muddy Waters is *still* a great and not just an honoured ancestor, a museum grandaddy, is that *no one can do it like Muddy Waters*.

And somehow I don't think anyone will.

*I ain't no small-timer*
*I ain't no punk*
*My name is Muddy Waters*
*An' I'm the man who put the* unk *into the funk.*

# This sure ain't the summer of love

NME, 9 July 1977

*When one of the booted ladies recognized a promising customer, she used to grab him, haul him into a cab and whisk him off to be whipped. Don't the SA boys do exactly the same with their customers – except that the whipping is in fatal earnest? Wasn't the one a kind of psychological dress rehearsal for the other?*

Christopher Isherwood, Down There on a Visit

Steve Hillage was on TV the other night, filmed at last summer's Hyde Park freebie.

He was singing about 'the love that is all around you' and I just had to laugh because of the blatant incongruity of Hillage's daft – albeit charming and well-meant – hippie-dippie noodlings juxtaposed against the current state of the game: more and more of the players being carried off the pitch with minor flesh wounds.

Rock and rollerball. Damn right this ain't the summer of love.

Right now, rock and roll is under heavier attack than it's been at any time since they fired the starting gun in the mid-fifties. For the first time, a record has gotten to number one in the face of a universal straight-media blank-out on political grounds.

Two members of the band who made that record have been attacked in the street by *citizens*.

The group and their adherents have been the victims of a police riot – sure, the barney between John Rotten's brother and the French photog was the flashpoint, but would the Guardians Of Our Liberties have reacted in the same way if the occupants of the launch had been – say – a bunch of rich tourists who'd had a tot too much to drink?

Effectively, The Sex Pistols are outlaws; they're fair game. If Johnny Rotten had been killed the other week, a lot of people in this country would've just shrugged their shoulders.

In the wake of the attacks on Rotten and Pistols drummer Paul Cook – the fact that anyone could want to beat up a sweet geezer like Paul Cook is simultaneously absurd and horrifying – there've been attacks on TV Smith of The Adverts, Dave Vanian of The Damned, Jean-Jacques Burnel of The Stranglers, Bob Geldof of The Boomtown Rats, *all* of The Boys and their manager, Lee Black Childers, manager of Johnny Thunders And The Heartbreakers – who're currently awaiting deportation, the bottling a few months back of Generation X's guitar player . . . the beat goes on, and it's either something very organized or else the first signs of a mass reaction against punks and punkery that transcends that which can be articulated.

People get violent for many reasons, sure, but there's a complex web of different factors coming into play here.

First of all people get violent when they feel themselves to be powerless; lacking the power either to articulate their rage or to make their feelings, their attitudes or even their existence known in any other way.

Just as graffiti is a message to the world from someone who doesn't have access to public media or the bread to buy himself a legal billboard like the big companies do, street violence is a message from someone whose hatred is consuming to such an extent that he must let it consume its object before it consumes him.

When you are hated by a large amount of inarticulate people who feel that there is no accessible outlet for their feelings and views, then you either have to stay off the streets or learn to live with the fact that at any moment someone – or someseveral – is going to brace you in an alley and take a swing at you. Or worse.

Yet Johnny Rotten isn't the enemy of a suppressed and inarticulate minority; Johnny Rotten – the most prominent and archetypal of punk rockers, musicians and fans alike – is a national scapegoat.

MPs and journalists rail at him, broadcasters refuse his advertising and ban his records, local government odium bars him from public stages . . . and he gets attacked in the street.

The mass of this country's population and the information

195

entertainment complexes that service them haven't *ever* been as scared of a youth-culture phenomenon as they are now.

Teds, beatniks, mods, rockers, hippies, skinheads, glitterkids . . . no competition.

To the outside adult eye, Punk Rock is the weirdest, ugliest, nastiest, scariest, most thoroughly repulsive and flat-out *incomprehensible* variant on the Teenage Wasteland formula they've ever seen. It's certainly the most frenziedly vilified.

Ten years ago, the hippies also rejected the Mum And Dad virtues which Fleet Street and the electronic media seem to regard as the only barrier between us and barbarism, but their rejection was more comprehensible because they actually seemed to be *in favour* of things (i.e. Free Love, Stop The War, Legalize Dope, Abolish Money, A Better World For You And Me Tra-La, etcetera, etcetera).

Punks, on the other hand, represent Teenage Frankenstein Unleashed at his most destructive and unreasonable: rejecting it all with a snarl.

Grown-ups – at least – understood that in their strange way, hippies were having a lot of fun.

Every hippie, it was secretly suspected, had turned his brain into rainbow custard with the aid of a whole battery of psychedelic drugs; plus there seemed to be a whole lot of screwing going on all over the place, and if there's one thing Fleet Street understands it's chicks with their tits out and a great big golden opportunity to condemn people who look like they're having a better time than they ought to.

But – by and large – punks ain't that sexy and they do more booze than anything else (though the *Daily Mirror* discovered The Amphetamine Menace shortly after Keef's trial in Aylesbury) so it wasn't as if they were partaking in Strange Unholy Pleasures that a Godfearing society has no option but to stamp out. They certainly didn't seem to be having a better time than the law allows.

Hippie pleasures were middle-class pleasures: the pleasures of kids who'd have had it made if they only accepted the Best Of Everything that their parents had planned for them. Instead, they dropped out.

Punks are working-class: they don't have anything to drop out *from*.

Hippies rejected society; society has rejected the punks. And society has always hated, suppressed and tried to destroy the people who bear most blatantly the scars inflicted upon them by the system under which they have to live because those scars remind the authorities of their own guilt and failure.

> *I am the world's forgotten boy,*
> *The one who searches and destroys.*
>> *Iggy and The Stooges, 'Search And Destroy'*

The violence of punk rock has shocked this society's most eminently shockable elements precisely because it is simply a gruesome reflection of the violence of society. And as nothing is such an efficient begetter of violence as violence itself, the whole thing is beginning to escalate.

The trouble is that punk violence – like most rock and roll violence – is more of a metaphor than an actuality, but the violence with which it is being met is all too real. In this respect, punks are far more sinned against than sinning, but try telling *that* to the *Sunday Ghoul*.

There's far more of the true dialectic of violence in the stage act of early Who and Hendrix, in The Rolling Stones performing 'Midnight Rambler' or in Alex Harvey's Hitler routine in 'Framed', but somehow that's distanced and presented in such a way that no one who wasn't a flat-out psychotic would take it as an index of the personal behaviour of the artist concerned.

Mind you, there *are* people out there who think that *Coronation Street* is real, and after Michael Winner's *Death Wish* opened in New York, a whole bunch of creeps went out on the streets with guns just like Charles Bronson and started blowing away perfectly innocent blacks, longhairs and Puerto Ricans under the impression that they were vicious evil junkie muggers.

Life is most likely to imitate art, it seems, when art begins to deal with the evil and the grotesque.

Rock and roll is a more influential art form than most in this respect because the artist appears *as himself*. Clint Eastwood appears as Dirty Harry, Christopher Lee appears as Count Dracula: no one believes than Clint Eastwood goes around blowing people's heads off with a ·44 magnum any more than they believe that Christopher Lee chomps on arteries for fun and sustenance

(I've seen him during the day, so I know it's not true).

But Mick Jagger and John Rotten appear as themselves, and therefore the private person is held to be accountable for the activities of the public person, which is why Mick Jagger *frissons* over assassination fantasies in the back of a limousine and good patriotic citizens razor John Rotten on the street.

This kind of thing never used to happen to rock stars.

They might get busted if they were notorious dopers or if they got pissed and drove their cars too absurdly, but their appearance on the street wasn't a cue for retards to come and turn them over.

The reason that most of them can't go out on the street for a drink or to browse around in a bookshop or whatever is that the people who dig 'em would crowd around and follow 'em and make it impossible for them to do what they came out to do.

We have a new kind of rock star now, and – like all other new kinds of star – it arose out of an attempt to break down the star system.

The reason that we *have* a New Wave in the first place is that there were sufficient people who felt bored by and alienated from the traditional occupants of the Rock And Roll Pantheon to form a whole gaggle of new bands and to provide audiences (An Audience?) for them.

The vibe was extremely anti-star for the simple reason that most orthodox rock stars were failing their ethics exam.

Strictly speaking, this wasn't really their fault (though some behaved far more badly than others) simply because stardom is an abnormal condition and it has an abnormal effect on people.

It carries an infinity of temptations: a veritable Pandora's Box of all the things that shy, repressed kids are conditioned to want. Fame, prestige, money, public admiration, all the attention that someone who'd been ignored and put down in adolescence could possibly desire.

Man, stardom blows an awful lot of minds in a lot of different ways: some people turn into rank assholes, others can't handle the pressure and flip out. They get cataclysmically messed up on booze and dope, their work suffers, they get paranoid and go megalonova.

Others step back from the whole thing and try to be anti-star themselves, but it takes a huge amount of charisma to deliberately discard all the appurtenances of stardom and still be a Giant Shadow Hovering Over Our Culture or whatever. Maybe you have to be Bob Dylan to pull that one off.

So it's not surprising that people got pissed off with their Stars, except that it was exceptional naïvety to believe that those folks who hit the Stardom Jackpot wouldn't get affected by it.

Besides, you cannot have mass communication without having stars.

Radio, television, movies, rock and roll, politics and sport alike all create stars by their very nature: stardom is implicit and unavoidable. To talk of destroying the star system is completely and utterly utopian: if you're gonna have movies you'll have movie stars, if you have rock and roll then you're going to have to have rock and roll stars.

If you're a rock and roll success then you're a rock and roll star. The only thing that can be done if the stars aren't carrying themselves the way they should is to register a massive vote of no confidence at the record-shop counter and the club or theatre box office until the recalcitrant star is either induced to get his act together or else is summarily deposed.

If the latter you replace him with somebody else.

Stars are normally created by the people who love them: it's usually the people's affection and respect that makes an artist into a star.

In the New Wave, the amount of mass media attention that has fattened the scene up to the point where national – or even international – stars can come out of it has been almost universally condemnatory. Media that love scandals have turned punk rockers into a national scandal, made them a larger and larger target simply in order to have the pleasure of seeing them shot down.

John Rotten is Public Punk Number One.

His name and his appearance are synonymous – as far as the mass of the population are concerned – with the movement in general. He has been made a star at least as much by the people who hate him and all of what they think he stands for as by those who dig him.

He's the personification of What Is Wrong With This Country,

199

and he's taking his lumps for it in a manner that no rock star before him has ever had to do. Mick Jagger, Jimi Hendrix and all the other Wild Men Of Rock were at least able to get themselves and their music onto radio and television and into the shops and they were able to perform their music live.

Other punk rockers have been able to benefit from the attention that's been focused onto the scene without incurring nearly so much odium. The Damned are in a position to celebrate their first anniversary with a four-night season at a well-known London venue, to give away a freebie single to those who show up and to go on *Supersonic*. The Jam and The Stranglers can go on *Top of the Pops* and get played on the radio.

Obviously, there's nothing wrong with that – but The Pistols spearheaded the whole thing and, being the most prominent targets, have suffered most.

Maybe that's what goes with the New Stardom, and no one can deny that new stars have emerged out of the movement that was to destroy the whole Stardom Scam. Jean-Jacques Burnel, Rat Scabies, Joe Strummer and their peers are stars now, and faced with all the rewards and problems that have always beset stars.

But stardom '77 style means being set up, and Johnny Rotten – more than anyone else – has been set up. Not – as used to be opined – by Malcolm McLaren, but by all the hysterical *Punk Rock Shock Horror Youth Cult Probe* shit that's been peddled by media fools who love nothing better than to create a new target out of the nearest available human material, stir up hatred for and fear of it and then lead the attack.

A bunch of kids, who have committed no crime that wouldn't be excused in others, are now victims at large. Famous and obscure punk rockers alike are now fair game for violent fools whose only means of asserting themselves is to do some damage – and Sid Vicious's pernicious gabble about people who deserve 'a good kickin'' is, I hope, turning to ashes in his mouth after the events of the last few weeks.

Violence does breed violence, and the inability to distinguish between violence as pose, violence as metaphor, violence as theatrical device and the real, ugly truth of the matter is coming home to roost with – may I say it? – a vengeance.

*

It's always been a staple theory among artists and critics that stylized, dramatized violence has a primarily cathartic effect: e.g. the spectacle of Sam Peckinpah movies or Pete Townshend dismembering a Stratocaster exorcizes and relieves the urge for violence in the audience. Kids — it is reasoned — who have witnessed Alice Cooper performing ritual murder and undergoing ritual execution are less — rather than more — likely to indulge in personal violence of their own.

It doesn't seem to be working like that any more. This country is up shit creek at the moment — and it's more the fault of Jim Callaghan and Maggie Thatcher than John Rotten. And the fact that everyone's feeling the pressure right now means that they turn to the nearest available target in the vain and ugly hope that by destroying an irritant they'll somehow make things better and obtain some satisfaction.

It's this blind, maimed rage that made the occupants of black America's urban ghettoes burn down their own turf rather than razing Wall Street to the ground. It's this same thing that makes disenfranchised Teds bottle Kid Reed of The Boys in a bus queue.

For the sake of every last little thing that matters — who gives a shit whether your music is Jerry Lee Lewis or Black Sabbath or Joni Mitchell or The Damned? We are all of us in the same sinking ship, and carving up fellow passengers doesn't achieve any damn thing at all. Are we so colossally screwed up that we turn on each other while Moloch and Mammon carry on unscathed?

Are we going to be so dumb all our lives that we let them get away with tricking us so blatantly?

Are we *really* so easily manipulated?

I quoted Christopher Isherwood earlier on: not because I want to launch into any kind of diatribe about Neo-Nazism (I'm reasonably confident that we're not going to fall for the genocide scam again — touch wood) but because we seem to be misunderstanding the stylized violence in the music.

Life is imitating art, but it's getting it wrong and totally missing the point.

If we allow a situation to develop where Warhol's dictum about 'In the future, everybody will be famous for fifteen minutes' gets twisted into 'In the future, everybody who gets to be a certain kind of star will have the shit kicked out of them for fifteen minutes', then those who hate us will have won.

If we lose our perspective sufficiently to start mistaking the nearest target for the biggest one, then those who hate us will have won.

And if we do not hang together, then most assuredly we will be hanged separately.

Listen. Which side are you on? What do you believe in?

Are you part of the problem or are you part of the solution?

And again: what we gonna *do* about it?

# The Sex Pistols: John, Paul, Steve and Sidney

*NME*, 6 August 1977

THE prosperous cyborgs at the next table in the backroom of this expensive Stockholm eating-place are sloshing down their coffee as fast as they possibly can, with such indecent haste that one plump, middle-aged Swedette disgraces herself in the process. As they vacate the premises, another troupe are ushered in, take a look at the party in the corner and usher themselves out again.

John Rotten – a discordant symphony of spiky crimson hair, grubby white tuxedo embellished with a giant paper clip on the lapel and an absolutely God-awful black tie with orange polka-dots – looks at the departing Swedish posteriors with no little disdain.

'It must've been my aftershave,' he remarks in his fake-out voice, halfway between Kenneth Williams, Sweeney Todd and Peter Cook, and returns to his beefheart fillet, which – much to his disgust – is delicious. He eats nearly all of it and that night he doesn't even throw up.

In Stockholm, The Sex Pistols are a big deal.

'God Save The Queen' is in the Top Ten, just as it is in Norway, where they also have – for their pains – a monarchy. They've been splattered all over the national press in Scandinavia just like over here; more so than any other visiting rock band, or so they tell me, anyway.

It hardly bears thinking about: 'The outrageous young superstar of Britain's controversial punk-rock group The Sex Pistols knocked over an ashtray this morning while having his breakfast. MPs commented, "Is this the kind of behaviour that we want our young people to emulate? We must certainly think carefully about allowing this kind of performer on television." See editorial: page two.' And all in Swedish, too . . .

In general, though, Sweden has been less willing to take John Rotten at his word and identify him with the Antichrist than the good ol' UK. They've stayed four nights in the same Stockholm hotel without any complaints from the management, despite Sid Vicious taking a leak in the corridor because two girls had locked themselves in the bathroom of his particular chamber. When the local equivalent of Teds (a bunch of kustom kar kruisers/ *American Graffiti* freaks known as *raggare*) began harassing the Pistols' fans as they left the gig and, indeed, followed the band and their admirers back to – and into – the hotel, the police were right there for the protection of the people.

I even saw one Swedish copper at the back of the hall on the second gig doing a restrained but joyful pogo to the lilting strains of 'Pretty Vacant'. Can you imagine that at a British Pistols gig – in fact, can you imagine a British Pistols gig at all these days? In Britain, if the police were informed that The Sex Pistols and/or their fans were getting the shit whacked out of them somewhere, the most you could expect would be that they'd show up an hour or two later to count the bodies and bust the survivors (if any) for threatening behaviour.

At home The Sex Pistols are public enemies. In Sweden, they're an important visiting Britpop group. So it goes . . .

Lemme tell you a little bit about Stockholm, just for context and perspective, before we get on to the good bits. They've got the highest standard of living in the world over there – weep, Amerika, weep – with an average weekly wage of £120 and prices to match. A bottle of beer will set you back over a quid a throw, and by British standards it ain't even beer; more like a beer-flavoured soft drink that fills you up and leaves you belching and farting and urinating like an elephant and doesn't even get you pissed.

You can drink twenty quids' worth of the poxy stuff and still go to bed sober, though the O. Henry twist-in-the-tail comes when you wake up with a hangover.

Somehow the idea of suffering a hangover without even having been drunk is peculiarly Swedish.

The natives don't see it quite that way, though. Through some weirdness or other of the Scandinavian metabolism, they get completely zonko on the stuff, with the result that the authorities think that they have an alcohol problem. You can imagine what effect this would have on a bunch like The Sex Pistols, who are pretty fond of their beer. It got so bad that by the end of the tour John Rotten gave up in disgust and started drinking Coca-Cola.

Swedish television is fun, too. For a start, the two channels only operate for a combined seven hours each night, and the programming seems to consist almost exclusively of obscure documentaries and the occasional mouldy old English B-picture. Radio is impossibly dopey – you can't even dance to a rock and roll station, 'cuz there's nuthin' goin' on at all. Not at *all*.

In the discos, they play the same dumbo records that they play in UK discos only six months later, and the girls think you're weird if you don't/can't dance the Bump.

Put it this way: if you think that there's nothing going on in your particular corner of the UK, then there's *double* nothing going on in Sweden. Make that treble nothing. God only knows what the Swedes get up to in the privacy of their own homes to cope with the total lack of decent public entertainment facilities, but it must be pretty bloody extreme.

We thought some kind of oasis had been discovered when we found a late-night cafe that served Guinness.

John Rotten – who is, after all, an Irisher by roots (the rest of the band call him 'Paddy' sometimes) and therefore likes his Guinness – was enchanted by this revelation until we discovered that it was – are you beginning to get the picture now? – a special Scanda variety of Guinness even though it's brewed up in Dublin, and therefore no stronger than the rest of the stuff they have over there.

We ordered up about ten of the bloody things, swilled them down and discovered to our horror that we were all still sober, so we celebrated the fact by doing a burner on the establishment in question and vamoosing without settling the bill. We'd got as far as the car of our self-appointed guide – a Chris Spedding lookalike who runs a punk boutique called Suicide and who calls himself 'the only true punk in Sweden' – before a search party from the cafe catches up with us and hauls The Only True Punk away to face retribution.

At this stage in the proceedings, The Pistols are only three-quarters strong.

Sid Vicious is in London, where he has had to appear in court on charges of possessing an offensive weapon of the knifish variety and assaulting a police officer.

That leaves the rest of the party as Rotten, Steve Jones, Paul Cook, roadies Rodent (borrowed from The Clash) and Boogie, and Virgin Records' International Panjandrum Laurie Dunn, an amiable Australian (stop laughing at the back, there) whose room seems to function as an assembly point. People at a loss for anything to do seem to end up going to Laurie's room as a convenient way of running into other people with nothing to do.

Steve Jones plays guitar. He's been playing the guitar for little more than a year and a half, which would indicate that he's going to be a monster player by the time he's been playing for a bit longer. The reason that he sounds far more professional and experienced than he actually is is that he sticks to what is simple and effective and – within the confines of a hard rock aesthetic – tasteful.

He knows what constitutes a good guitar sound, his time and attack are impeccable, and he plays no self-indulgent bullshit whatsoever.

There are a lot of musicians far 'better' than Steve Jones (in the technical-ecstasy sense, that is) who could learn a lot from listening to him, could remind themselves of what they were originally looking for when they started out and how they lost it along the way.

Steve Jones is the oldest of The Pistols at twenty-two, and his stolid features and blocky physique make him, visually at least, the most atypical Pistol of 'em all. On the first evening he went out to dinner in a Normal Person costume of dark blue blazer,

205

grey slacks and a neat shirt and tie; camouflage so effective that I nearly didn't recognize him when he passed me in the corridor. It was only his fluorescent hennaed hair that gave him away as being a rock and roller.

He's a friendly, relaxed, good-natured geezer; could be anybody you know and like and drink with, could be you.

Paul Cook plays drums, and has done so for three years now. Like Jones, he plays with an ear for what sounds good, a straight-ahead high-powered no-bullshit approach to what he does and no distance at all between himself and his drums.

Again, he's an ordinary guy in the best sense of the term; he was in at the roots of the band when a convocation of kids with heisted instruments were jamming around in Shepherd's Bush; no formal groups, just a bunch of people playing together.

The nucleus was Cook and Jones (the latter then singing as well as playing guitar), Glen Matlock on bass and sundry additional guitarists including Mick Jones (now of The Clash), Brian James (now of The Damned) and Nick Kent (now of no fixed abode).

The Sex Pistols had their dark genesis when Jones, Matlock and Cook got together with Johnny Rotten under the Cupid auspices of Malcolm McLaren.

Since Glen Matlock got the push and was replaced by Rotten's old college (not 'university' – *college*) buddy and neo-bassist Sid Vicious, The Pistols have consisted of two factions: Cook/Jones and Rotten/Vicious.

These factions are by no means opposed or unfriendly or at cross-purposes: it's just that Paul and Steve get up earlier and go to bed earlier (with all that implies) and John and Sid get up later and go to bed later (with all *that* implies): Paul and Steve hanging out together before Sid and John get up and Sid and John hanging out together after Paul and Steve have gone to bed.

John and Sid are the public face of The Sex Pistols: Jagger and Richard to the other two's Watts and Wyman, even though it'd be highly misleading to assume that the creative chores are split that way as well.

Anyway, that's as much background as we've time or need for, so zoom in on the Happy House, a Stockholm club run under the auspices of the local university's Student Union where we're a few minutes early for the soundcheck prior to the first of the band's two nights there.

One thing you have to say for Rodent: it takes a lot of bottle to set up gear while wearing a pair of those dumb bondage pants that strap together at the knees.

Rodent, Boogie and this Swede called Toby (though the band and their own crew call him Bollock-Chops) have just schlepped a massive PA system, three amps, a drum kit and all the rest of the paraphernalia that it takes to put on a rock show up to the second floor of this horrible structure, and Rodent's done it all in bondage pants. He does it the next night with his sleeves held together with crocodile clips. It's a man's life in the punk-rock business. Join the professionals.

Sid Vicious has caused everybody a massive amount of relief by returning from London with the news that he beat the assault rap completely and copped a mere (?)£125 fine for the knife.

How'd you dress for court, Sid?

'Oh, I wore this real corny shirt my Mum got me about five years ago and me steels. I must've looked a right stroppy cunt.'

Oh yeah, we haven't really met Sid yet. He got the name 'Sid' when he was named after an allegedly really foul-looking albino hamster of that name that he and Rotten used to have.

'I hate the name Sid, it's a right poxy name, it's really vile. I stayed in for about two weeks because everyone kept calling me Sid, but they just wouldn't stop. Rotten started. He's 'orrible like that, he's always picking on me . . .'

Rotten: 'Sid's the philosopher of the band.'

Vicious: 'I'm an intellectual.'

Rotten: 'He's also an oaf. He listens to what everybody else says and thinks, "How can I get in on this?"'

Vicious: 'No I don't! I'm a highly original thinker, man, he's just jealous because I'm really the brains of the group. I've written all the songs, even right from the beginning when I wasn't even in the group. They was so useless they had to come to me because of they couldn't think of anything by themselves . . .'

Thank you, boys. We'll be returning to this conversation later, but meantime there's this soundcheck to do and it sounds *terrible*.

The stage is acoustically weird and means that by the time Sid's got his bass amp set up so that he can hear himself the bass is thundering around the hall with an echo that bounces like a speedfreak playing pinball. The drums and guitar have been utterly swamped and everybody has a headache.

The problem is partially solved by the simple expedient of moving the amp forward until it's beside Sid instead of behind him. It's unorthodox but it works and it means that a semi-reasonable balance can be obtained. The sound still swims in the echoey hall and everybody's brought down something – you should pardon the expression – *rotten*.

Outside, a youthful horde of Swedish punks decked out in fair facsimiles of Britpunk outfits are milling around looking up at the window behind which the band and their entourage are lurking.

None of these kids are going to get in tonight, however, because Happy House gigs are mostly for over-twenty-threes only – a fact which causes bitter amusement because it means that the audience is, officially at least, all older than the band.

When the group make a break for it to go back to the hotel, it's Sid Vicious who stays out in the street listening to what the people have to say and assuring them that the band are on their side. He's out there for more than five minutes before he's virtually pulled into the car.

'I don't think we should be playing for them poxy student hippies. I reckon we should tell 'em that we don't play unless they let the kids in – either that or open up the back doors and let the kids in anyway.' In the end, the kids have to wait until the following night when it's fifteen-and-over, but it's not a situation that the band are particularly happy with.

In the dressing-room back at the Happy House a few hours later, John is ostentatiously asleep on a couch, Steve is tuning up his white Les Paul with the aid of a Strobo-Tune (more accurate than the human ear, totally silent so you don't bug the shit out of everybody else in the room by making horrible noises, hours of fun for all the family, get one today!) and Sid is whacking out Dee Dee Ramone bass lines on his white Fender Precision bass.

Sid's musicianship (or lack of same) is something of an issue with some people, so let's say right here that he's coming along pretty good.

His choice of Dee Dee as his model is a wise one, since that's just the kind of clean, strong and simple playing that The Pistols require.

At present, he's using a kind of flailing-from-the-elbow right-hand action that takes far more effort than the notes require, but he keeps time, doesn't hit more than his share of bum notes (not *much* more than his share, anyway) and takes his new-found role as A Bass Player as seriously as he takes anything.

Up in the hall, the student audience is milling around ignoring the reggae that's pumping out of the PA system. There are signs of movement from behind the silver curtains and then they're on, revealed in all their scummy glory.

Rotten's behind the mike, staring out at the audience through gunmetal pupils, mouth tight, shoulders hunched, one hand clamped around the microphone.

'I'd like to apologize,' he says harshly, 'for all the people who couldn't get in. It wasn't our fault.'

And the band kicks into 'Anarchy In The UK', Jones' guitar a saw-toothed snarl teetering on the edge of a feedback holocaust, Sid's bass synched firmly into Cook's walloping drums and Rotten an avenging scarecrow, an accusing outcast cawing doom and contempt like Poe's raven.

There's been a lot of bullshit laid down about The Pistols' musicianship by a lot of people who should know better (but the world is full of people who 'should know better' but never do).

I played 'God Save The Queen' to Mick Ronson when he was over here a little while ago and he looked at me in amazement and said, 'I don't understand why people keep telling me that they can't play! They're fucking great!' And, of course, he's right. They put down a blazing roller-coaster powerdrive for Rotten's caustic vocals to ride and it sounds totally *right*.

Except that there's something wrong. Somewhere along the line the monitors have completely dropped out, and Rotten can't hear himself singing, with the result that he has to shout even louder, his pitching becomes ever more erratic and his throat gets put under more and more strain.

Between numbers, Rotten mercilessly harangues Boogie, who's responsible for the live sound-mix, but there's absolutely nothing Boogie can do. The monitors are completely shot, and they'll just have to be patched up before tomorrow's gig.

Still, The Pistols flail on through 'I Wanna Be Me', 'I'm A Lazy Sod', 'EMI' (by far the best song so far written about a record company), 'God Save The Queen', 'Problems', 'No Feelings', 'Pretty Vacant', the encore of 'No Fun' and sundry others, and it's hard to see how anyone who digs rock and roll couldn't dig The Pistols; while they're onstage you couldn't conceive of anybody being better and John Rotten bestrides the rock and roll stage of the second half of the seventies the way David Bowie did for the first half.

If the last few British rock and roll years have produced a superstar, Johnny Rotten is *it*. And let Fleet Street, the BBC and the rock establishment cope with that the best way they know how, because it isn't just happening, it's already happened. And if the definitive British rock band of *now* feel that they have to go to Europe or Scandinavia or even America just to be able to play in front of people, then there's something worse than anarchy in the UK right now.

'Never are tyrants born of anarchy,' wrote celebrated fun person the Marquis de Sade. 'You see them flourish only behind the screen of law.' And right now in 1977, who's to say he's wrong?

Get up, stand up, stand up for your rights . . . and segue straight into Marley's 'Exodus' pumping out of the sound system of a hideously twee rococo disco deep in the 'eart of Stockholm. It's playing at least twice as loud as anything else that they've played so far tonight, and that's because John and Sid have commandeered the disco DJ's command post and they've found it among his records. They've also found 'Pretty Vacant' and that comes up next . . . even louder.

The following afternoon finds The Pistols' party signing autographs, hanging out, posing and nicking things at The Only True Punk In Sweden's boutique.

The verdict seems to be that everything there is pretty much like SEX was a year or so ago and, in keeping with the celebrated Swedish standard of living, everything is around twice the price that it would be in London. A photographer is on hand to capture the golden moments. Swelling almost visibly with pride, Sweden's Only True Punk unveils with a flourish a deluxe leather jacket that he's ordered up specially for Sid.

Vicious – charmingly clad in baggy pink pants, a floral blouse and sandals with a little pink bow in his immaculately spiky coiffure – takes one look at it and declares it poxy, vile, corny and twee.

Sweden's Only True Punk looks deeply hurt.

Over the other side of the shop, Rotten is trying on a pair of repulsive leopard-skin-topped shoes.

'They're really 'orrible,' he beams. 'I must have them. I could start another absurd trend ... like safety pins.' The way that previous sartorial quirk of his had caught on with The Youth and become an industry virtually overnight is a source of vast amusement to him – as well it might be.

With The Only True Swedish Punk and his girlfriend are two twelve-year-old kids, neighbours of theirs from out in the country, where they live. These two kids immediately latch onto Vicious, and he spends much of his day sitting with them and playing with them and talking to them ... generally keeping the kids amused. He's really great with them ... if you know anyone who's got a pre-adolescent kid who's into punk rock and needs a babysitter, allow me to recommend you Sid Vicious, Mary Poppins in punk's clothing.

The previous night, the air had been thick with rumours that the *raggare* had eyes for trashing, and for the second gig – the one open to the teenage punk rockers – the talk is intensified.

The band's limo – shaddup at the back there! – and the attendant dronemobiles are waved through a police cordon and everyone's hustled through a back door *mach schnell*.

'Get that poser inside!' snaps Rotten as Sweden's Only True Punk dawdles to make sure he's noticed in the exalted company. There's less dressing-room ligging than last time and the band are on fast as shit.

The punkette audience tonight is a lot cooler and better behaved than the beer-chucking beardies who made up last night's crew, and the band feel a far greater kinship to the crowd.

'It's our night tonight!' shouts Rotten as the band crash into 'Anarchy' and tonight his contempt is not directed at the audience but – on their behalf – at a phantom enemy: the crowds of *raggare* who lurk outside the police cordons in their Dodges, Chevies and Cadillacs.

Tonight everything goes fine. The monitors work, the sound's fine and the band relax and play a better, longer set, graced by a couple of additional numbers that they hadn't bothered to get into the night before, including 'Satellite Boy' and 'Submission'.

Next to me, a girl sits on her boyfriend's shoulders, oblivious to the little bubble of blood welling up around the safety-pin puncture in her cheek. After a while, she switches the safety pin to her other cheek so's she can link it up with the chain in her earring. Pretty soon, that begins to bleed too. She doesn't care.

A little way away, another girl has tossed away her T-shirt and is happily bouncing her tits around until her boyfriend wraps his jacket around her; he keeps dancing. She doesn't care, either.

Everybody — band, audience, even the cop at the back — is high as a kite and happy as can be. There's no violence and not a bad vibe in sight; everybody's getting off.

And this is the show that our guardians won't let us see?

Listen, all The Pistols do is get up on-stage, play some songs and get off again. Shit, officer, t'ain't nothin' but a little rock and roll fun; no chicken-killing, throwing of clothes into the audience, nudity, or any of that dirty stuff. No audience manipulation, no incitement.

This is *healthy*, Jack.

The trouble comes after the audience leave; it ain't The Pistols' fault, and there's nothing at all that The Pistols can do about it. We're all upstairs drinking rats' piss when there's a commotion outside and someone reports in with the news that a bunch of *raggare* have just chased a couple of young girl fans and ripped the pins right through their faces to prove what big bad tough guys they are.

Sid wants to go out there and lay into them. Someone else suggests ramming them with the limousine like the cat in the South did to the Ku Klux Klan a while back. Ultimately, there's nothing that can be done except call the Fuzz and feel very, very sick about the whole thing.

So ultimately, why are the various Establishments — governmental, media and even rock and roll — more frightened of The Pistols than of any other previous manifestation of rock and roll madness?

'Because they were all to some extent slightly controlled by the industry,' says Rotten, ensconced with Vicious and Cook in the relative peace and quiet of a hotel room. 'There was always an element of the Establishment behind it, but with us it's totally our own. We do what we want to do and there's no industry behind us. *That's* the difference. *That's* what frightens them.'

'Or rather,' interposes Vicious, 'the industry is *behind* us rather than with us.'

Hey, if the industry's behind you it's got a knife in its hand . . .

'Yeah,' says Sid, 'but we've got a Chieftain tank.'

'They can't control us,' continues Rotten. 'We're uncontrollable. They've predicted all down the line against us, and they've failed. This scares them. They've never been able to do that before. They've always known before that the money would come into it, but they've missed the boat so many times.'

Paul Cook: 'The thing was that everyone in the beginning was so sure that no way was it going to take off. People like Nicky Horne said that they'd never play punk rock and now he don't play nothing but.'

Which is an equally narrow attitude . . .

Rotten: 'If not worse. With us it used to be "They won't catch on because *we're* going to stop it" and there've been a hell of a lot of organizations out to stop us, and they've all failed.'

Me, I don't think The Pistols can be stopped unless the kids are tired of them.

Rotten: 'They're the ones who make all the decisions now. They're the ones that count, and I hope they've got the brains to suss it all out for themselves and not be told by the press, "This band is finished" and then think, "Yes, that's right, they're finished and I'm not going to like them any more. I'm now going to like *this*." They've got to decide for themselves.'

Cook: 'I think it's gone beyond the point where people can be told. They wouldn't play "God Save The Queen" but that went to the top of the charts, and that usually dictates what goes in.'

We talk about The Only True Swedish Punk's boutique, and Rotten opines that places like that should only be there to inspire people to create their own look, and be what they are instead of adopting a ready-made façade. The same dictum, *natürlich*, applies to Moozic:

'That's what music should be about,' says Rotten. 'I get very sick with the imitations. I *despise* them. They ruin it. They have no reason to be in it other than wanting money, which shows. You've got to have your own point of view. You can have an idol, like you may see a band and think, "God, that band are *really fucking good*, I'd like to be like that." So you start up your own band, and then your own ideas come in as well on top of that and you have a foundation. But a lot of those bands don't *leave* that foundation and they stay in a rut and they listen to all the other songs in their morbid little circle and they do rewrites of them. Hence fifty thousand songs about how hard it is to be on the dole.'

'Been listening to The Clash, obviously,' says Sid. 'The Clash only wrote those songs in the first place 'cause of me and 'im [Rotten] moaning about living in a poxy squat in Hampstead. It was probably them coming up there and seeing the squalor we were living in that encouraged them to write all that shit.'

Squalor in Hampstead, the bastion of liberalism?

'Oh no,' says Rotten. 'You shoulda seen it.'

Vicious: 'It was liberal, all right. It didn't even have a bathtub.'

Was there any particular plan or strategy in mind right at the start of The Pistols?

Rotten: 'Instinct. It hasn't really worked out like that. We never sat down and wrote a thesis. There's no rules, and no order. We just do it, which is more to the point. *Do it*, and when you can't do it no more, then don't do it at all.'

Vicious: 'If it requires any real effort, then there's no point in doing it. It should just *come*. If you have to force it, then there's something wrong.'

Rotten: 'Yeah, if you have to sit down in your room and go, "I've *got* to write a song, but *what about*?" . . . that's rubbish. It just comes. It's there.'

Yeah, I know just what you mean, John. Pure, untainted, burning creativity . . .

'Oh *yeah*, man. *Far out*. It's very hard not to run into those hippie bullshit phrases, because some of them were good, some of them actually meant something. It's just a shame that they ruined a lot of 'em with silly ideas about, "Yeah man, I wanna be *free*," which meant fuck all.'

Vicious: 'Free from what they never even said.'

'Course we did, man, free from the same things you want free from: preplanned existences, boring jobs, stifling media . . .

Cook: 'Yeah, but they were like that themselves, weren't they?'

Rotten: 'I can remember going to those concerts and seeing all those hippies being far out and together, maaaaaaaaan, *despising* me because I was about twenty years younger than they were and having short hair. That's when I saw through their bullshit. A lot of punks are like that as well, which makes me really *sick*.'

Cook: 'The only memory of hippies I have was when I was in a park once when we was skinheads and we was throwin' conkers at these hippies and they were goin', "Hey that's really nice, man, I really *love conkers*."'

Rotten: 'Well, that made you a fool then, didn't it? I think they won hands down, because you were wasting your energy and they were laughing at you.'

It may or may not seem ironic now, but when Johnny Rotten was fifteen-year-old John Lydon of Finsbury Park, he was tossed out of school because his hair was too *long*, the old find-out-what-the-kids-are-doing-and-make-them-stop trick.

'Yeah, but when they find out it's always too late,' he says. 'In five years' time they'll have schoolteachers with safety pins in their ears. It's so predictable with those oafs.'

Vicious: 'The definition of a grown-up is someone who catches on just as something becomes redundant.'

The kids Rotten went to school with weren't really into music, 'except the geezers I hung around with. It was in skinhead times and they couldn't understand how a skinhead could like The Velvet Underground. It was quite apt. I went to the Catholic School in Caledonian Road, opposite the prison. What a dungeon!'

Forcefeeding you religion along with the lessons?

'Yeah, it was terrible. They really destroy you with what they do to your soul. They try and take away any kind of thought that might in any way be original. You know when caning was banned? In Catholic schools that didn't apply, because they're not state-run. They get aid from the state, but they're not entirely state-run. I don't know where they get their money from . . . I'd like to know. It's probably some Irish mafia.

'What they try to do is turn you out a robot. When it comes to allocating jobs for a student who's about to be kicked out into the wild world, it's always jobs like bank clerk ... be a railway attendant or a ticket collector. Even the ones who stayed on for A-levels ...'

Were any of the teachers halfway human?

'The ones that were got sacked very quickly. Everything was taught in a very strict style, in the same way that they taught religion: this is the truth, the whole truth and nothing but the truth, and if you don't like it you're gonna get caned. But Catholic schools build rebels: a lot went along with it, but a lot didn't. There was always a riot in religion classes. *Nobody* liked that subject.

'I got kicked out when I was nearly fifteen – fourteen and a half – because I had too long hair. I had *really* long hair ...'

'A balding old hippie with a big pair of platforms on,' sneers Vicious. 'That's what you were. I went to the same college as him ...'

'... to get O-levels,' Rotten finishes the sentence for him. 'I waited a year and a bit because I went on building sites working, and then I went to get some O-levels because I still had it in me that *O-levels were the way to heaven* ... plus I didn't want to work no more. I got a grant. It was very easy. For some reason I always liked technical drawing and geography. At college, I did maths, English, physics, technical drawing and chemistry ...'

Cook: 'I've got an O-level in woodwork.'

Vicious: 'I've got two O-levels ... English and English literature ... and I'm very intelligent.'

Rotten: 'English literature was a joke. I passed that with flying colours without even trying. It was stupid fucking Keats poetry, because I did my English in my Catholic school. They kicked me out halfway through the course because they said I'd never pass, but they'd already entered me, so I went and took the exam privately because I was still entitled to down at County Hall.

'And I passed with an A ... and I went down there with the certificate and showed it to 'em.'

Unlike fellow reggae freaks in The Clash, there's no reggae in The Pistols' repertoire.

'I find that slightly condescending – and that is *not* a slag-off of The Clash. I'm white, and I'm rock. I don't like rock music, but I like what we do with it. How could we sing about "Jah Rastafari"?

Even "Police And Thieves" is full of innuendo, it's about three in one God on the cross and on each side are the police and the thieves: Rasta in the middle. That's what the song implies. It doesn't need to say more, because a Jamaican will know straight away. Besides, I don't like Junior Murvin's voice.'

He's very much like Curtis Mayfield.

'Yeah, very much like Curtis Mayfield.'

And you don't like Curtis Mayfield?

'Yeah, I do. I like the music; there's a different feel about it.'

Do black kids dig your music? Do they understand it as part of the same thing?

'For sure. Where was that gig where a lot of dreads turned up? That was really shocking. I think it was an early Nashville, years ago. There was a few of them at the back, and I was really shocked that they'd be there. I talked to them afterwards and they said, "Understand, just understand, man will understand, mon." You never get any trouble from blacks. They understand it's the same movement.'

Yeah, but reggae singers talk about what they love at least as much as they do about what they hate.

'Don't we?'

Only by implication: in the sense that if it's known what you stand against it can then be inferred what you stand *for*.

'Yeah, but it's the same with reggae. There are so many people who refuse to listen to them: "No no, it's all a big con. All this terrible Jah and Rasta stuff, it's all a big con to make money." There's been loads of reviews . . .

'That one by Nick Kent was just classic ignorance, comparing reggae with hippies.'

Many people like to feel that Malcolm McLaren is in total control of The Sex Pistols: Svengali to Rotten's Trilby. Maybe they feel happier thinking that Rotten's controlled by McLaren, than they do feeling that maybe he isn't controlled at all.

'They need to do that because they don't want to think differently than they already do. They like their safe world. They don't like realizing the way things actually are.'

Cook: 'They fucking do that with everybody. They don't like admitting that anybody actually is the way they are. They always say, "They got it from *them*, they're just like *them*."'

217

Vicious: 'The trouble is that the general public are so contrived themselves that they can't imagine how anybody else could *not* be contrived. Therefore, if you're not contrived, they have to find some way of justifying their own contrivance . . .'

*Ghost voice-over from the past: Jack Nicholson in* Easy Rider *telling Fonda and Hopper: 'They're not scared of you. They're scared of what you represent to them . . . what you represent to them is freedom. But talking about it and being it — that's two different things. I mean, it's real hard to be free when you are bought and sold in the market place. 'Course, don't ever tell anybody that they're not free, 'cause then they're gonna get real busy killin' and maimin' to prove to you that they are. Oh yeah — they're gonna talk to you and talk to you and talk to you about individual freedom, but they see a free individual, it's gonna scare 'em.'*

But I don't tell 'em what my ghost voice says, because that's hippies, and that's past and gone . . . and it was bullshit anyway.

Or so they tell me.

A few more things about Johnny Rotten. When he was eight he had meningitis, and it left him with weak eyes, permanent sinus, stunted growth and a hunched back.

The once-decayed teeth which got him his nickname are held together with steel rods.

The only time I saw him throw up was because his dinner had disagreed with his somewhat unstable digestive system . . . and then some twisto went into the bog after he'd finished and started taking polaroids of it.

He uses foot powder on his hair because it absorbs all the grease. I never saw him hassle anyone who didn't hassle him, and I never saw him bullshit anyone who didn't bullshit him, and what more can you say for anyone in 1977?

'Turn the other cheek too often and you get a razor through it' — John Rotten, 1977.

Still, 1977 is a prize year for violence, and talking about The Pistols nearly always ends up as talking about violence so — in the words of Gary Gilmore — *let's do it.*

'When they push you into a corner like that, what are you to do? You either kill them or give up, which is very sad, because we're fighting people who ought to be on our side . . . or *are* on our side, but don't know it. They say we're using them, but the real people who are using them they don't even know about.'

Vicious: 'We're quite nice friendly chappies, really, but everyone has a beastly side to them, don't they? I can't think of anyone I know who if somebody messed around with them they wouldn't do 'em over.'

Rotten: 'People are sick of being used, but they're now attacking the wrong people, e.g. *us*. When I was a skinhead, everyone I know used to go to the football games, and the match had nothing to do with it. What else was there to do? Disco? The Youth Club? *Talkin' 'bout my generation* . . . there was nothing else except alcohol.'

Yeah, but having a barney with a bunch of people who're there to have one too is one thing, but random picking-on in the streets – like some skinheads used to do to hippies – is a whole other ball game.

Rotten: 'Yeah, but to a skinhead it looked like: "These geezers are having fun doing what they're doing and we're not just because of the way we look, so smash 'em up and stop their fun." It's just like the *raggare* here and the Teds in London, 'cause like I said, when I had a crop and I went to a festival, the reaction I had was terrible.

'Violence is always the end result of nothing to do. And it's very easy, and it's very *stupid*.'

Johnny Rotten is an avid fan of *The Prisoner*, which figures. After all, he's not a number. He's a free man.

And no matter what they put him through, he'll always be a freer man than any of the people who've tried to tear him down.

# Elvis Presley obituary: Rhapsody in blue

*NME*, 27 August 1977

THE death of Elvis Presley was truly the stuff of which nightmares are made.

The first great symbol of rock music as youth-culture jailbreak dying alone of a heart-attack brought on by an over-strenuous game of squash, dying as a sick, obese, tortured hulk, dying lonely, miserable, dope-raddled, dying empty, dying exhausted, dying – finally – as a man who had everything he ever wanted but found it all wanting.

Elvis Presley was a symbol, yeah. He was an icon, he was rock and roll incarnate, he was an idol, he was a hero. He gave the kids a look and a sound and an attitude: he gave us his identity and once he gave it to us he was left with nothing of his own except the useless trash accumulated by millionaires who have nothing but money which can buy nothing but objects.

That was all he had because it was all we could give him: an adulation and an idolatry that dehumanized him, left him as flat and two-dimensional as the Elvis poster on my wall. Just as – to a certain extent – everybody who plays or consumes rock and roll has become something of what Elvis made them, Elvis became what we made *him*.

And once we turned him into a poster, transformed him into effigy, became something new by sucking on his soul, he became a monster: first a young, beautiful and awesome monster, then a bland, castrated monster and finally a hideous, pitiful monster who inspired a mixture of pity and derision and – maybe – a shudder of mortality, a *frisson* of decay.

Dorian Gray for Our Generation. The human poster was gruesome by the end, and much of his pain must have come from the fact that he knew it. If we make a man into a god, he must suffer as a man does, but his suffering must be on a godlike scale.

And how can a man survive the torments of a god and still remain unscathed?

The bloated bulk that was Elvis Presley's body was the outward sign of the death by attrition of Elvis Presley's spirit.

He stuffed himself with food, napalmed his brain with smack and cocaine – even though, true to the dictates of his beloved deceased mum, he kept off smoke and booze, an All-American boy! – surrounded himself with more and more toys; any damn thing to make it stop hurting.

By the time I discovered the superhero of the fifties, he was already the bland-out of the sixties. Everybody knew who Elvis was – he was a likely contender for the Most Famous Person In

The World title even though The Beatles and Stones and Dylans and Hendrixes were making their waves – and, for some, this memory of the golden creature who redefined 'youth' created an indulgence for what Presley was becoming. For others it created contempt.

It seemed that the only one who didn't know who Elvis was any more was Elvis. Obviously you can't be a teenage mutant from outer space/inner Memphis for all your life, but it seemed like a betrayal that Elvis was conforming to the dictates of fifties adult orthodoxy just as a new sixties generation – fuelled on Chess blues, Motown soul and the finest moments of fifties rock – was starting to tear down a new set of barricades.

Elvis the man and Elvis the living tabernacle were slowly beginning to move apart, and when the irresistible force and the immovable object were one and the same, then it is inevitable that something has to give. In the seventies Elvis made his heroic attempt to rejoin his severed selves, to come to terms with the legend, to roll away the stone and become unified once more.

He did the TV special, got back in front of people once more and for a while it was an almost supernatural visitation once more, the resurrection shuffle.

And then the two images separated once more, the man and the god, the flesh and the spirit. Body and soul began to destroy each other.

The man grew ugly, the legend grew tarnished, the god became a joke.

Elvis Presley, ultimately, became the nightmare B-side of the Great Rock Dream. So you wanna be a rock and roll star? So you wanna be Elvis Presley? So you want to be someone who millions of women want to ball and millions of men want to *be*? So you want fame, talent, beauty, riches, admiration, love, power?

*Have* it, baby. Have it with my compliments. Have it and enjoy it and see if it's what you really want once you've got it. The only catch is that once you've got it you can't give it back.

Imagine, then, what Elvis Presley, nineteen-year-old truckdriver of Memphis, Tennessee, would have thought if somehow he could've had some prescient flash of Elvis Presley, forty-two-year-old superstar of Memphis, Tennessee, killing his pain with an obscene blend of cheeseburgers and scag.

If they could meet, the one with everything to come, the other with everything gone . . . would they still know each other?

Stardom kills. One way or another, it wreaks an awful destruction on all but those with the utmost strength and inflexibility and those with the utmost humility and self-knowledge.

And the kind of stardom that was visited upon Elvis Presley was simply more than he could handle. They made him a god, after all, and he was only a man, with a man's strength of mind and body and no more.

Maybe, if he'd been able to see into the future, he'd've preferred to stay a truckdriver. As it was, we turned him into what he became, but *we* didn't have to pay the price.

# Glam rock remembered

*NME*, 8 October 1977

GLITTER is gone and speaking personally I'm delighted because there's never been a rock and roll fashion that has suited me less.

Can you imagine the agonies of embarrassment and rejection I felt when all the skinny exquisites would gather all comers to discuss make-up and *Granny Takes a Trip* clothes while˙ I'd languish alone waiting for the conversation to return to something I could participate in, like women, or me?

Well, during the years of the Glam Scam I felt like the Ugly Duckling and it wasn't much of a consolation to know that some of the people who were right in there with eye make-up, blusher, and multi-level silver boots looked like Christmas turkeys.

There was glitter everything. Glitter rock was the most prominent but there was glitter soul. LaBelle were by far the most convincing but since then every Bootsy somebody wore something silver and sparkled and mirrored – and even glitter folk-rock with Dave Cousins of The Strawbs showing up on *Top of the Pops* with fake cheekbones and the full Bolan routine.

Did you see the suits and the platform boots? Oh dear, oh gawd, oh my, oh my.

Glitter hit rock and roll like an unnaturally luminous tidal-wave and now it's receded, leaving nothing but a sequinned scum over some of the rock that it touched. Some of the things it washed up, to maintain this marine metaphor for as long as possible, have been able to survive without their glistening carapaces – hands up anybody who remembers Queen as the fag-end of glam rock? No? Okay, anyone here remember Jobriath? – and some haven't.

The Stones adopted just enough of it to be able to look cute and contemporary without having seemed to be jumping on anybody else's bandwagon (plus Jagger had been wearing make-up ever since *Performance* was filmed, anyway) and even straight-ahead hamburger'n fries blues rockers like Johnny Winter and his bro' Edgar swamped themselves in rhinestones even though it didn't change their music any. The nice thing about it was that you could be into it on any level you liked: lifestyle, music or just a few cute presentation tricks.

David Bowie developed his particular individual wrinkle-variation out of his science-fiction leper-messiah Ziggy Stardust fantasy and out of his theatrical experience, plus a handful of theories about the Nature of Stardom and how to achieve it in six easy lessons.

Easily the most valid and convincing of the glitter pack, Bowie and the horde of teenage mini-Ziggies who followed him provided the curtain-raiser for punk by – in the words of no less an authority on the subject than Johnny Rotten himself – 'by demonstrating how totally plastic everything else before him had been'.

And, incidentally, he also provided the impetus for kids to dye their hair fantasy colours like blue, green, scarlet and purple – colours that human hair never achieved unaided – to wear clothes based on *Flash Gordon* comics and thirties movies, to be exactly what they wanted to be and screw reality, Jack!

Not since the first heady flights of hippie five years before had kids been allowed to look so bizarre, and where hippies had taken their clothing fantasies from foreign climes and bygone times, Glitterkids looked to visions of other planets and metallic cybernetic futures.

Another Bowie source was the bisexual underground of the Andy Warhol circus. Glitter was about sex, too – any kind of sex you could think of. (Un)fortunately, not everybody had the kind of androgynous beautiful-monster visual that lent itself to the bisexual chic look, which is why there was an awful lot of mutton dressed up as lamb floating around at the time.

And the kids remade-remodelled in the various sparkling images before them: Bryan Ferry and Roxy Music started out with a kind of art school vision of Eddie Cochran in the year 2001 but rapidly sidetracked/sound tracked into a chintzy evocation of thirties/forties movie-star Gatsby-cocktail eleganza that had flat-out nothing to do with rock and roll at all, simply being an extension of the kind of vapid croonarama that made the invention of rock and roll necessary in the first place.

There was room for an awful lot of enigma-variation in the glitter universe: Marc Bolan got into it with a style based on maximization of his original androgynous prettiness, which was very effective as long as his features remained uncoarsened by time and life. By *that* time he was beautiful no longer, but the costumes had become outrageous to the point that they looked absurd on anyone of less than utterly transcendental physical beauty.

Alice Cooper started out with an individual twist on the Frank Zappa theory of full-tilt Mondo Shocko that led first into mock-transvestism (complete with earnest theorizing in the ads for his early albums) then into mock-psychosis followed by mock-Universal Pictures late-night horror-movie gallivantings and finally into pure showbiz. What Cooper did for the mascara business can hardly be over-estimated.

All the above-mentioned had earnest pretensions to Artistic Legitimacy With Capital Letters. Slade, Gary Glitter and The Sweet were content to be Pop (with a capital letter), which meant that they skipped the heavy raps about Theatre Of Cruelty/Theatre Of The Absurd/Everyone Is Bisexual, Maaaan and all the rest of it and simply concentrated on entertainment.

Slade looked glittering and ridiculous just for the sheer hell of it; they'd begun as skinheads, but then saw themselves on television and thought they looked boring so they tidied up their visual stage by stage until by the time they'd finished they looked both further out and more outrageously authentic than most of the Artistic glitter-rockers.

See, their particular way of anticipating punk was to bring the ambience of the football terraces – not to mention a slice of the *population* of the football terraces – in the rock arenas. They had none of the pretentions of Ferry or the delicacy and imagination of Bowie's 'Ziggy Stardust' leper-messiah trip: Slade were raunch and roll and British music-hall; they probably thought Max's Kansas City was in Kansas.

Ultimately they blew it because they had no political/social vision whatsoever – if they'd had the sort of breadth of vision that Mott The Hoople's Ian Hunter had then they might have been a 1977 punk band five years early – and because, like Marc Bolan, they spent too much time unsuccessfully wooing American audiences when they should have been staying at home concentrating on making the kind of dent on the home market that no one could ever have forgotten about.

Thirdly and lastly, their music matured the wrong way: their individuality was dissipated by their eventual growth into the kind of group that originally they seemed like they were set to replace.

Sweet and Gary Glitter were purest meatball: Sweet were an old-fashioned Heavy Metal band nurtured into *Top of the Pops* silks and satins by master pop manipulators Nicky Chinn and Mike Chapman with a string of hits that began with Kasenatatz-Katz-style kiddie-pop based around nursery-school *doubles entendres* like 'Little Willy' and gradually growing into pop Heavy Metal and rather unconvincing Teen-Apocalypse – now mock anthems of unrest and rebellion via occasional near-masterpieces like 'Ballroom Blitz' and 'Blockbuster'.

They wore the full panoply of Bowie-inspired mixtures of silver jump-suits, pancake make-up and long peroxided locks, but they were really cast as a seventies version of Dave Dee, Dozy, Beaky, Mick and Tich when they *really* wanted to be Deep Purple.

But Gary Glitter . . . now he was the ultimate in pop mindlessness, to the extent that you ended up admiring his nerve and trying not to laugh at the sheer absurdity of the visual spectacle that he provided. A massive hulk of a man, all furry torso and spare tyre, round-faced and sweating and did-he-wear-a-toupee-or-not, he looked like a Christmas turkey all done up in Bacofoil and ready for the chef. He made records based around distant distorted guitars, an omni-present electronically compressed drum sound playing a metronomic jackboot tempo and grunting call-and-response vocals based around catch-phrases and even more simple-minded nursery porn than Sweet's records.

He even called his group The Glitter Band, thereby swiping the name of an entire genre. And little girls went apeshit over him: toupee, paunch and all. He looked more like a barman than a teenage idol, but he wasn't afraid to look like a twerp. He looked even more of a twerp than Elton John, another artist with less-than-obvious teen appeal who parlayed his somewhat unlikely appearance into total asset by sheer flash.

Despite a musical classification nearer to Hip MOR than the rest of the artists discussed herein, Elton's stage presentation and manic let's-drop-the-big-one-now clothes sense puts him right in there with the bigtime glitter rockers, all feathers, sequins, gold and silver lamé, multi-storey platforms . . . there wasn't a visual trick going that EJ didn't have in his repertoire.

The interchangeable terms back in the heyday of all this weirdness were 'Glitter' and 'Glamour', the latter generally abbreviated to 'Glam'. What it meant was that what the world needed less of was some guy in a beard standing with his back to the audience playing an organ solo for twenty-five minutes, and what it needed more of was short, sharp attractive-sounding records performed by interesting-looking, visually flamboyant geezers with a different attitude. It was about posters on the wall, singles on the jukebox and that satin top in the window that would, please God, still be there come Friday when the paypacket/pocket money arrived so it could be worn to the Bowie/T. Rex/Roxy Music concert on Saturday.

Plus it was a great parent shocker: is that one with the short hair and the lipstick a boy or a girl? (giggle). Are you *really* going to go out looking like that? But didn't that David Bowie say he was a homosexual? (Is he or isn't he? Well, he is and he isn't.) I've never seen anything like it, have you? (Welllllll . . .)

Glitter had its backfire, especially since it only served to reinforce and emphasize the distinctions between the demi-gods (up there) and the punters. The emphasis on stardom as a way of life was horribly elitist and very destructive, and at least one promising glitter group crashed in flames because they thought they had to behave like stars long before they could physically and mentally handle it, long before they could financially afford it — down to the bottom line — long before theirrstatus as a band warranted it.

In the end it was fun, all that glitters not being gold, but who can afford gold anyway? When it came right down to it, glitter carried with it the seeds of its own destruction, but that's okay too. It was the first real *pop* thing that happened in the seventies and it brought a great cast with it, a cast of geniuses and madmen, poseurs and philosophers, winners and losers, clowns and warriors, stars and fools. All those gleaming turkeys in their joke-shop threads livened things up a lot, and any time there's no room for a phenomenon that gives kids something new to do to keep Queen Boredom at bay, then it's time to hang up the rock and roll shoes and get into stamp collecting.

# David Bowie: Who was that (un)masked man?

*NME*, 12 November 1977

**D**AVID Bowie sits in shadow now, a creature of the grey autumn dusk that seeps through his hotel window. He makes no attempt to fight off the encroaching greyness with electric light; rather he welcomes it, wraps it gratefully around himself, only turning on the lights much later, and then at another's request.

He wears a check shirt and a pair of Levis, his hair is short and sandy; his entire persona untainted by artifice of any description. Distinguishing marks: none.

None save one: his face, the only thing he has in common with David Bowie as he was five years ago when I met him for the first time in the same locale, the Dorchester Hotel in Mayfair.

Then he was the most glittering element in a densely sparkling room; it was a moot point whether he lit the room or the room lit him.

Then he was surrounded by a gaudy cast of freaks and mutants and acolytes: Lou Reed was there, pale and mascara'd, black nail varnish in his podgy white fingers; Iggy Pop in T. Rex T-shirt, wild amusement throttled down into neutral and idling; Mick Ronson and The Spiders From Mars, done up to the nines and seeming vaguely uncomfortable (*I don't think we're in Hull any more, Toto*); Tony DeFries, boss of Mainman, the company that managed Bowie in those days, ebullient ringmaster secure in his pride; Bowie's wife Angie, effervescent consort and queen of the circus.

There was booze flowing and a lot of high nervous laughter; self-consciousness loose like some predatory gas in the room and just about everyone falling victim to it in their own ways – Lou showed his by coming into the room while I was talking to Bowie, kissing him wordlessly on the lips and then making a silent exit – except for Bowie himself, grooving delightedly in this whole absurd Ziggy Stardust spectacle mounted expressly for his benefit. Heady days, you can be like your dreams tonight . . .

The laughter of that party is only in my head now, because David Bowie travels silently and alone now, *sans* entourage, *sans* disguises, *sans* circus, *sans* everything. His only companion now is a harried American publicist, wall-papering the cracks in her schedule by growing ever more officious and mannered.

1972 is five years ago, Ziggy Stardust is a discarded marionette in a trunk somewhere, worlds away, marooned and adrift in space and time, a voiceless, bodiless ghost. His host-body is his own man now, out from behind the beautiful, uncaring mask.

Walking along the silent corridors towards Bowie's room, I was wondering who – or what – would be there to meet me. The last time I'd seen him had been the last day of 1973, and he'd been drunk and snooty and vaguely unpleasant, a game player supreme, a robot amuck and careening into people with a grin, not caring because after all they were only robots too; can trash be expected to care about the welfare of other trash?

Since then there'd been 'Diamond Dogs', the final nightmare of glitter apocalypse; 'David Live', in which the corpse of Ziggy had been reanimated in hell to run through his act one more time; 'Young Americans', a nightmare of a different kind dominated by 'Fame', a ghastly grinning grind in a mirrored disco leering at its own helplessness (*now that you got it what you gonna do with it, sucker?*); 'Station To Station', person-to-person at one remove, desperation as the heart fights a losing battle against the iron in the soul; 'Low', the phoenix subsumed in the ashes of defeat, cryptic messages from the ninety-ninth floor; and finally 'Heroes', and a sense of humanity reasserted, the finest 'modern' record of the year.

Look at it this way, there's an inevitable sense of anticipatory curiosity as you prepare to meet someone for the first time in almost four years. They're different, you're different, everything's different, and you wonder how much has actually remained the same. You can readily imagine the extent to which this feeling is compounded when the person in question is David Bowie.

And now, of course, he isn't a space invader or an alien marooned or a disco puppetmaster or anything else that he's built around himself. He certainly isn't David Jones from Brixton, but he is completely and utterly David Bowie. The divesting of the assorted glib carapaces of the past doesn't mean that he's vanished – though the 'Low' strategy of the politics of self-incarnation seemed that way inclined – as of right now, it seems as if David Bowie has *appeared*.

Of course. And here he is.

He's up out of his armchair and onto the balls of his feet as the door closes behind me.

'Christ, how long has it been?'

'Four years, man,' and set up the tape machine – Bowie attempting to balance the microphone on top of a Carlsberg bottle – and no time to swap small talk because interview time is severely circumscribed, so by the time we've both sat down and Bowie's lit his Gauloise there's nothing to do but pull the pin and get straight into it.

'Where can we start after four years?' he asks. Hell, we can start anywhere; we both know where it'll go . . . why does 'Heroes' – or more accurately ' "Heroes" ' – come in quotes? Are the inverted commas actually part of the title?

'Yeah. Firstly – it was quite a silly point really – I thought I'd pick on the only narrative song to use as the title. It was arbitrary, really, because I could have used any of the songs as the title, because there's no concept to the album . . .'

I'd felt that the use of quotes indicated a dimension of irony about the word 'Heroes' or about the whole concept of heroism.

'Well, in that example they were, on that title track. The situation that sparked off the whole thing was – I thought – highly ironic. There's a wall by the studio' – the album having been recorded at Hansa By The Wall in West Berlin – 'about *there*. It's about twenty or thirty metres away from the studio and the control room looks out onto it. There's a turret on top of the wall where the guards sit and during the course of lunch break every day, a boy and girl would meet out there and carry on.

'They were obviously having an affair.

'And I thought *of all the places to meet in Berlin, why pick a bench underneath a guard turret on The Wall*? They'd come from different directions and always meet there . . . oh, they were both from the West, but they'd always meet right there. And I – using licence – presumed that they were feeling somewhat guilty about this affair and so they'd imposed this restriction on themselves, thereby giving themselves an excuse for their *heroic* act. I used this as a basis . . .'

Therefore it *is* ironic.

'Yes, it is. You're perfectly right about that, but there was no reason why the album should have been called "Heroes". It could have been called 'The Sons Of The Silent Age'. It was just a collection of stuff that I and Eno and Fripp had put together. Some of the stuff that was left off was very amusing, but this was the best of the batch, the stuff that knocked *us* out.'

Do you find that recording in a studio that's right by the Berlin Wall gives you a sense of being on the *edge* of something?

'That's exactly right. I find that I have to put myself in those situations to produce any reasonably good writing. I've still got that same thing about when I get to a country or a situation and I have to put myself on a dangerous level, whether emotionally or mentally or physically, and it resolves itself in things like that: living in Berlin leading what is quite a Spartan life for a person of my means, and in forcing myself to live according to the restrictions of that city.

'It produces very good writing. I've almost taken as much experience as I wanted out of that city.'

So it's time to move, now that other people are writing songs about the Berlin Wall.

Bowie chuckles into his Special Brew. 'Yes, I had noticed that, actually. I haven't yet made up my mind, but I have the choice of two places that I'm thinking of going to. One's Japan and the other's Israel, and I don't know which one's going to win . . .'

The thought of The Thin White Duke in a kibbutz strikes one as being too good a visual to pass up, plus Bowie went through a Japanese phase in '73.

'Yes, I keep wanting to go back there. I think I'll plump for Kyoto, because I want something very serene around me for a few months to see if that produces anything. It is also important to my private life that I go to Kyoto.'

We talk about the Japanese mime/dance/theatre troup Ondeko Za, who'd just completed a run at Sadler's Wells and who Bowie had missed by a day in Amsterdam. 'It sounds like a token show for us lot to have a gander at,' Bowie comments after I've described the show. 'But in Japan – when I was travelling through it – there was an awful lot, particularly in the outlying villages and provinces, of very strange ritual performances that I hadn't seen before. And still, because my knowledge of Japanese is limited – to say the least! – I never really found out from what school it came from, or what its origins were.'

Since the purpose of all ritual must be invocation, what were these rituals designed to invoke?

'Well, a lot of them were from Shintoism, and they talk very liberally about being one of the few countries in the world that tolerate all religions, but you'll only find about three Christians in the whole of Japan. They're *tolerated*,' he laughs harshly, 'but everybody else is a Shintoist, mate! So most of their art forms derive from either that or the Imperial sources. It's very sophisticated, but a bit suspect sometimes . . .'

Yeah, but so's Bowie himself. I think of the koto Bowie plays on 'Moss Garden' from side two of 'Heroes' and his berserk scream of 'I'm under Japanese influence and my honour's at stake' from 'Blackout' on the same album, and reflect that the kibbutzim probably won't be seeing D.B. for a while yet.

So what about China? After all, back in '71, Bowie was something of a Maoist . . .

'Ahhh, that's still there. That place continues to intoxicate me. I got a glimpse of it when I was in Hong Kong . . . it's strange.

There's no wall there, you see. When you move out of Hong Kong into China you *can* just walk over and often you won't get shot at. It's quite feasible to sort of wander into China and just look around, wander around all those villages right near the border.'

Hey, living dangerously is one thing, but recording an album in a situation where one of your musicians was actually liable to get *shot* . . .

A sharp chuckle. 'I never travel with *musicians*. I only travel on my own these days.' A far cry from the times when he wouldn't budge an inch without bodyguard, secretary, personal assistant, travelling companion, hairdresser, PR . . . 'All my travelling is done strictly on the basis of wanting to get my ideas for writing from real events rather than from going back to the system from whence it came. I'm very wary of listening to much music.'

He gestures at the massive, imposing stereo set enthroned on the table by the sofa. 'RCA sent all this stuff over and I forgot to ask them for some records, but by the time they deliver any I'll be gone. It doesn't really follow me around much. Imagine trying to plug one of those in in Bangkok! My drummer insists in carrying one around with massive headphones and wires sticking out everywhere. I don't travel like that. I only have a tape machine to use as a notebook.

'No. *Event, Character, Situation*: they're my preference for the basis of writing. But at the moment, I'm not even really interested in that. I mean, the last two things have made for a complete re-evaluation of my writing style. It had a lot to do with being bored with the traditional things I'd been writing, and with wanting to put myself in the position of having to come up with a new musical language for myself.'

I mention that 'Low' missed me completely.

'Well, I'm not surprised,' he says. 'A lot of it missed me as well. I don't understand it. I don't understand "Heroes" either. It's something that's derived through process and method with absolutely no idea of the consequences and no preconceptions of any kind.'

'Low' had seemed to me to be an album about – and presenting in an attractive light – withdrawal from the world almost to the point of catatonic schizophrenia.

232

Bowie grimaces and clears his throat a trifle ostentatiously. 'There is more than an element of truth in what you say. For me it was very ... I *wanted* to do that,' he interrupts himself defiantly. 'What you've read from the experience of that album is absolutely accurate. I *did* achieve something, because there's very few albums that I haven't experienced at first hand. You can even tell what city I've been in just by listening to the albums.

'I'm *completely* open. I'm so eclectic that complete vulnerability is involved.' You've got no shields, then. 'None at all. I've never developed them, and I'm not too sure that I want to any more only because I'm becoming far more satisfied with life ... my *private* life. I'm becoming incredibly straight, level, assertive, moderate ... very different from, say, two years ago.'

Two years ago you were an uptight game player with a sore nose ...

'Out there on the wall! No, listen, I'd been *exposed*,' he gives the last syllable of the word a savage, ironic twist, 'to a general LA-ism which, quite frankly, I can't cope with. It's the most vile piss-pot in the world.'

LA, I say, is like being trapped on the set of a movie you didn't want to see in the first place.

'Absolutely! It's worse than that. It transcends that. It's a movie that is so corrupt with a script that is so devious and insidious. It's the scariest movie ever written. You feel a total victim there, and you know someone's got the strings on you.'

So why do people build themselves mansions out there? It must be like voluntary self-imprisonment.

'Oh, it is. It's like going to live in Switzerland to look after your tax money, which is the most incredible thing I ever did. I don't *live* there but I stayed there. I don't live anywhere. I have never got around to getting myself a piece of land, putting up a house on it and saying *this is mine, this is home*. If I did that, that would just about ruin everything. I don't think I'd ever write anything again, I must have complete freedom from bases. If I ever had anything that resembled a base – like a flat on a long lease or anything – I felt so incredibly trapped.

'Even if I go away I know that it's waiting for me – more than that, it's like it has me on a string, and it's dragging me back. I don't foresee that I could *live* comfortably in any of the cities I go to. Unlike my managerial predecessor. I'm not investment minded. I still like the idea of making records next to the wall. I think that is what one should do, in my case anyway.'

Returning to the subject of the recent waxings, it seems that 'Heroes' is an attempt to fight back against the state of mind that 'Low' wallows in.

'Do you know something? The hardest thing for me to do is to help you in solving those problems, because all I know is the input on the album. I have as much idea of the − outback?' (he laughs) 'about what comes back off that album as what you do. Eno is the same. Neither of us understand on a linear level what the thing's about, but we get a damn good impression of information coming off those two albums that seems very strong, and that wasn't intentional. The intention was to go in and play around with method and process, but when we'd finished "Low" and "Heroes" what we had in our hands was something that actually does give information.

'If it seems obvious to you, then you've described my state of mind at the time of making those two albums very accurately. That's exactly − on both albums − what I've gone through. "Low" was a reaction to having gone through that peculiar . . . that dull greeny-grey limelight of American rock and roll and its repercussions; pulling myself out of it and getting to Europe and saying *for God's sake re-evaluate why you wanted to get into this in the first place? Did you really do it just to clown around in LA? Retire. What you need is to look at yourself a bit more accurately. Find some people you don't understand and a place you don't want to be and just put yourself into it. Force yourself to buy your own groceries . . .*

'And that's exactly what I do. I have an apartment on top of an auto shop in an area of town which is quite heavily populated by Turks, and I did that for a bit . . .'

Two relevant quotes: the novelist Elizabeth Bowen once wrote, 'Anywhere, at any time, with anyone, one may be seized by the suspicion of being alien − ease is therefore to be found in a place which nominally *is* foreign: this shifts the weight,' which is as good a thumbnail sketch of the obsessive traveller as any I've encountered.

And then there's the character of Herbert Stencil in Thomas Pynchon's *V*: 'Herbert Stencil, like small children at a certain stage and Henry Adams in the *Education*, as well as certain autocrats since time out of mind, always referred to himself in the third person.

'This helped "Stencil" appear as only one personality among a repertoire of identities. "Forcible dislocation of personality" was what he called the general technique, which is not exactly the same as "seeing the other person's point of view"; for it involved, say, wearing clothes that Stencil wouldn't be caught dead in, eating foods that would have made Stencil gag, living in unfamiliar digs, frequenting bars or cafes of a non-Stencillian character; all this for weeks on end; and why? To keep Stencil in his place; that is, in the third person.'

'Ooh, aren't you well read!' mocks Bowie, but his eyes show a flash of recognition. 'I understand that *completely*! I completely sympathize with the man! I know exactly why he did that, I think! So that initial period of living in Berlin produced "Low", which is *isn't it great to be on your own, let's just pull down the blinds and fuck 'em all*. The first side of "Low" was all about me: "Always Crashing In The Same Car" and all that self-pitying crap, but side two was more an observation in musical terms: my reaction to seeing the East bloc, how West Berlin survives in the midst of it, which was something that I couldn't express in words. Rather it required *textures*, and of all the people that I've heard write textures, Brian [Eno]'s textures always appealed to me the most.'

Yeah, but they lack *context*.

'Brian isn't interested in context. He's a man with peculiar notions, some of which I can come to terms with very easily and are most accessible, and some of it is way above my head, mate, in terms of his analytical studies of cybernetics and his application of those things to music and his general sort of fine arts approach. It's something that I've known from way back as a general characteristic of a kind of person that I used to know when I was a lot younger. I find that very *simpatico*. All those crazies . . .

'But I can't really talk on his behalf. We spend most of our time joking. Laughing and falling on the floor. I think out of all the time we spent recording, forty minutes out of every hour was spent just *crying* with laughter. Do you know Fripp? Have you

235

ever spent time with him in a humorous state? He is *incredibly* funny. *Unbelievable* sense of humour. Having the two of them in one studio produces so much random humour — *incredible* stuff . . .

'So anyway, what I'm doing in this wonderful new world of discovery and experimentation is a refocus about what I'm trying to do.'

We talked a little bit about (you should pardon the expression) punk rock and Bowie opined that the worst thing about punk was the way that so many bands were diving gleefully into the category instead of striving to be assessed outside of it.

'That's the worst thing about it. None of them are fighting it; none of them are saying *we are us*. They're saying *yeah, we are punk* and in so doing they're putting a boundary on their writing scope, which is a shame because there could be a real movement of sorts. But you have to let a movement remain as a subculture for a little while and gain some — I'm wary of using the word "maturity" — gain some recognition of its own relationship with the environment that it lives in. That's Eno's Rate of Change; one of his cybernetic things, and it's very interesting.

'People are more interested in the technical innovations as they happen rather than the rate of change *within* where they happen.'

Hence gadget obsession?

'Oh, that's not so bad. I don't mind that. I welcome any new relationship between man and his machine. I think that's very optimistic and very good. The *average* man . . . see, what you've got now is a situation where a hundred years ago the average man could fix anything that went wrong in his home. If it went wrong he could fix it. But how many things does a man have now that are out of his area of knowledge? If his television goes, he has to get a specialist to fix it. He doesn't know his immediate environment. This is because we are put under the impression that we are to accept every new technological achievement that is pushed upon us before we readily understand the last lot.'

What's the last technological innovation that you understood?

'Me? I think the fountain pen. I'm the perfect example of the victim of technology. I think it's disastrous.'

\*

Change of subject. Did Bowie consider that he was being misrepresented when he was tied in with fascism last year?

'What I thought was that I'd made some very trite theatrical observations which in fact backfired. I can't blame the press for that.'

Did you consider it to be a mistake?

'Oh God, yes, but I thrive on mistakes. If I haven't made three good mistakes in a week, then I'm not worth anything. You only learn from mistakes.'

So what were you actually trying to say with all of that?

'It was an immediate reaction to England having not seen it for so long. What I said on the Continent was based on anticipation, and when I got here I thought I'd got it right. I seem to have the knack for putting myself in those kind of dangerous positions. I'd just dried up and I couldn't write anything.'

Do you think that, once again, London would be a place that would stimulate your writing?

'It is a very different London, and that is worth consideration. It's been on my mind the longer I've been here, and I've been coming back for a couple of days at a time just taking tentative looks, but there's so many places that I haven't been to get a vibe from . . .'

There we had to leave it, because Bowie had to scoot off to a screening of a movie to which he'd been invited to contribute the music. In a conversation of such brevity, there were many things left undiscussed: like the involvement between D.B. and The Ig a.k.a. James Jewel Osterberg, the death of Marc Bolan and a relationship that had gone from friendship to feuding to friendship once more, the whole experience of Nicolas Roeg and *The Man Who Fell To Earth*, German *motorik* disco and the Kraftwerk connection, have-you-seen-Ronno and the contrast between Bowie as lone self-sufficient traveller and the man I used to know who couldn't make a move without a court of jesters and retainers and flunkies and gofers, and many more things that'll have to be discussed some other time in the future.

But I do know this much: David Bowie is the one man in rock whose work will, I suspect, continue to fascinate me for the rest of my life, which I won't grow out of even if I stop listening to anything else in the rock field. Sometimes I'll love it and sometimes I'll hate it, sometimes I'll find it infuriating and sometimes exhilarating, sometimes riveting and sometimes incomprehensible, but I can think of no other rock artist whose *next* album is always the one I'm most looking forward to hearing.

# Cher and Greg Allman: 'Allman And Woman' (Warner Bros)

*NME*, 19 November 1977

THERE is schlock and there is schlock. They are both on this album.

First of all, there's Gruntin' Gregg Allman's personalized variety of sullen mushmouth fonky-honky ramblings. Then there's Cher Allman's I'm-too-elegant-to-be-singing-this-song MOR haughtiness. Both represent schlock developed to the point where it almost spills over into the realms of pure tack. Schlock squared. Schlock to the power of *n*.

Still, let's leave the technical jargon out of this. 'Two The Hard Way' is purest California blancmange, as might be expected from an album that has to accommodate two such disparate – uh – *talents*. Gregg has had to tone down some of his customary excesses – no bad thing in itself – but Cher meets him halfway by trying to sing 'soulfully' and the result is musical toothache.

The material isn't to blame. Innocent victims include such classics as Little Milton's 'We're Gonna Make It' (imagine the woosome twosome crooning '*We may not have a cent to pay the rent but we're gonna make it*'), Smokey Robinson's immortal 'You Really Got A Hold On Me', Jimmy Webb's 'Do What You Gotta Do', Jackson Browne's 'Shadow Dream Song' and various lesser chunes. After The Miracles, The Beatles and Laura Nyro/ LaBelle you might've thought that there was nothing more that could've been done with 'You Really Got A Hold On Me', and you'd've been right.

Because of the Allmans' career as stars of stage, screen, courtroom and gossip column, this album commands a degree of public interest totally out of proportion to what it actually delivers musically. Gregg has been through it over the last few years – what with the deaths of Duane Allman and Berry Oakley, the acrimonious breakup of The Allman Brothers Band, the Georgia connection with Prez Carter and his on-again-off-again-on-again marriage to Cher and the Scooter Herring bust, but all this suffering clearly hasn't helped his singing any.

On the cover Gregg and Cher look like a couple of shop-window dummies who've fallen over each other in the display case of some Hollywood boutique.

And the billing! Jesus, at least Sonny Bono gave Cher a name check on the labels of the records, but 'Allman And Woman' is so disparaging that anyone more sensitive than Cher would probably have been quite offended.

The duo's total assets would seem to be one cute navel and three good Hammond organ blues licks. You can't see the former or hear the latter so 'Two The Hard Way' is pretty much a write-off.

One last thing. The album is dedicated to the kids, Chastity and Elijah. When they get old enough to hear this album and realize the kind of people they live with, if Chastity and Elijah got any sense they'll leave home.

# Howlin' Wolf: 'The Legendary Sun Performers' (Charly)

*NME*, 24 December 1977

THIS album's like a rusty locomotive screaming down the track faster than it was ever intended to go: rusted, ragged and rough-edged, but surging with enormous power and providing one hell of a good time for all aboard.

Howlin' Wolf a.k.a. Chester Burnett worked in and around Memphis as a performer and deejay when these tracks were recorded. At first he recorded for Sam Phillips' Sun label, but when Phillips began leasing Wolf's tracks to Chess Records in Chicago things started moving to the point where Wolf up and split to Chicago.

Wolf was with Chess from 1953 until his death in 1976. That's twenty-three years: certainly the most productive years of his recording career. Therefore, it would seem that if Wolf is associated with any label he's one of the Chess pantheon, along with Muddy Waters, Sonny Boy Williamson II, Chuck Berry, Bo Diddley and Little Walter, and that it's more than slightly presumptuous to claim him as part of the Sun Legend.

That's just nit-picking. If bagging him as part of the Sun story means making Wolf accessible to people whose awareness of Sun extends only to their white rockabilly tradition then I'm all for it, because Howlin' Wolf was one of the major music makers of the last quarter-century and this album is a worthy addition to his contributions to the redoubtable Chess catalogue.

In English – this album is a summer lightning sheet-storm; a killer-diller; a Tasmanian gorilla (hi, Anne Nightingale).

Here we go. Cut in '51 and '52, this album includes eight tracks never issued anywhere before, four tracks leased to Chess at the time of recording and four issued on an earlier – and now deleted – Charly album. All told, that's sixteen tracks of Howlin' Wolf. Prime cut, no fat, no gristle.

The only accompanists whose names are known are Albert Williams and Ike Turner (piano on various cuts), Willie Steele (drums) and Willie Johnson (guitar), though on the tracks where the band are unknown the guitar sounds a lot like Pat Hare.

The musicianship is certainly of an astonishingly high standard – in fact, on the basis of this album and two Sun blues compilations that Charly put out a few weeks back, one could make an excellent case for suggesting that Memphis's black bluesmen were several light years ahead of their po' white counterparts in terms of both feel and technique.

And of course there's the Wolf playing stabbing, jabbing, stinging mouth harp and singing in that indescribable voice. Wolf sang like a hurricane filtered through a letterbox; all the power and emotion in the universe crammed into a small space until it sounded almost tinny, cramped and raging.

The music on this album has a loose-limbed, good-humoured swing, it's less claustrophobic and obsessive than most of Wolf's Chess work. One track in particular, 'Look-A-Here Baby', is – wait for it – 1951 fusion music, blending be-bop, country blues and –

via Wolf's sly talk-song delivery – a talkover routine that any dub master would be proud to put his name to. 'You're my colour and you're my kind,' says Wolf softly at the end. Roots, mon!

Elsewhere, there's the slow, scarifying blues of 'My Last Affair' and 'Howlin' For My Baby', music which reminds me why it's the blues I turn to when I feel trapped and beaten. It makes me feel better; that's what the blues is for. Then there's the drink-yo'-whisky-drink-yo'-wine ruff-tuff goodtime music of 'Everybody's In The Mood' . . . blues for dancing, drinking and carrying on.

I really don't know why people haven't made the connection between the blues (black ghetto music from the USA), punk (white ghetto music from the UK/USA) and reggae (black ghetto music from JA). They all do the same things, albeit for different people, and I ain't heard an album in a long time that rams it home like this one does. A fine, fine album wherever you're coming from.

Every home should have one. Don't turn the Wolf from your door.

# *Star Wars*

*NME*, 24 December 1977

NEVER mind the soundtrack album, the badges, the Marvel Comics, the novel, the toy robots, the souvenir poster mags, the soap dolls, the calendars, bath salts, the serializations, the stories-behind-the-filming-of . . . here comes the movie.

*Star Wars* is the only movie I've ever seen which captures the unique feeling of reading comic books while stoned. Figures trudge across a desert landscape lit by two suns, and it all looks perfectly real. Absurd spaceships catch you in their slipstream with a beautiful stereophonic hi-volume *swissssssshhhhhhhhh* (even though there's no air in space and therefore no sound), non-human beings are more effectively realized by make-up and overdubbed sound than in *any* SF movie/teleplay I've ever seen before . . . the sets, the costumes, the weapons, the devices, the effects and – most important of all – the sheer size and scale of the intergalactic conflict depicted in the movie are completely and utterly convincing.

The name of the game, therefore, is Spectacle, Adventure, Fun and (pssssst) Discreet Moralizing. The name of the game is not any genuinely challenging vision of the future (or, by extension, of the present), any character with greater depth than a sheet of medium-grade cardboard (though the two robots and old pros Alec Guinness and Peter Cushing come closest) or any situation that hasn't been a cliché in comic books for twenty years and in science fiction itself for thirty or forty.

Still, I wasn't exactly expecting Mr Lucas and his assorted minions to deliver *Star Wars And Peace*, so I didn't have any expectations to be dashed. After all, it's no worse in this respect than the stuff that DC Comics were peddling up until the late sixties.

What makes *Star Wars* something more than just another schlocko space western with light-sabres instead of knives and blasters instead of Colts is the astonishing authenticity of the environment and the perfect evocation of space. The film induces a willing suspension of disbelief with greater ease and flair than any galactic epic since *2001*, and considering that it uses far more different sets and locations than Kubrick's classic, it is – technologically speaking – a far greater achievement.

Intellectually and emotionally speaking, the comparison becomes absurd, mainly because the philosophical implications are zero. A piece of total escapism, *Star Wars* treats good and evil as complete black/white absolutes. The heroes gleam with saintly righteousness, the villains glower and leer (those who don't wear masks that do their glowering and leering for them, like David Prowse's towering mega-demon Darth Vader) and nowhere is there the slightest evidence of any moral complexity.

Did I say nowhere? Well, there's the hard-bitten mercenary pilot Han Solo (Harrison Ford) who keeps threatening to piss off and leave the good guys in the lurch to save his highly paid skin, but the question isn't so much 'Will Han Solo's better nature take control and lead him to kick in with the heroes?' as '*when* will he?' He's got such an honest face that there's never any real doubt.

No, what we're dealing with here is the stuff of the fairy story: It reminds me of nothing so much as *The Wizard of Oz*. Solo's sidekick Chewbacca the Wookie — a giant furry lion-man — is The Cowardly Lion to the life; See Threepio, the senior of the movie's two robots (the name is a phoneticization of C-3PO) is a perfect Tin Man; and there's even a beautiful (well, fairly beautiful anyhow) princess on a quest. Actually, the movie's male hero — Luke Skywalker, played with terrifying wetness by Mark Hamill — is more like Judy Garland than Carrie Fisher's Princess Leia.

The movie's *deus ex machina* is The Force — which is the power that runs the universe, etc., etc. It's a neutral force, like electricity, and whether it's used for good or evil depends entirely on the leanings of the person in question. A fairly sophisticated concept (not that it has much competition anywhere else in the movie), but again Lucas gives it the most simplistic interpretation possible: nice people do nice things with The Force, horrid people do horrid things, blah-blah. It's all so *simple*. We never find out how a complex personality could use The Force, because Lucas hasn't provided us with one.

Still, if *Star Wars* had been that kind of movie, it wouldn't have captured the mass imagination in the effortless way that it has. The sixties were a time of challenge, and there was an audience for the kind of challenging ideas that *2001* set before us. The seventies are a time of coping with psychic defeats and the deadening of our collective nerve ends, and *Star Wars* is an entertainment built around pure spectacle: it tickles, dazzles and delights the senses while leaving the intellect and the emotions as undisturbed as possible.

Finally, it's disco for the eyes.


# Bob Marley: 'A lickle love an' t'ing'

*NME*, 18 February 1978

ROBERT Nesta Marley resembles a Pharaoh when he turns his head: that profile, simultaneously sensual and ascetic with its abrupt stab of goatee beard, looks like something you'd expect to see frescoed on one of the inner walls of a pyramid.

The woollen snakes of his dreadlocks are crammed into a massive beret of red, gold and green huge enough to hold a year's supply of ganja; he's wearing a pair of pyjamas and leather sandals.

The effect is superficially incongruous but it's nothing to get hung about; he's got a brimming glass of orange juice close to hand and an Eko acoustic guitar leans up against the other bed. He's sprawled out with the utter relaxation possible only to a man who's very fit and very stoned.

Bob Marley is holed up in a comfortable service apartment in Bayswater, London. From the outer room, 'Exodus' plays at a comfortable volume and Marley's companions hold the fort while the ranking dread holds court in the bedroom.

Marley's been compared to everything from a 'black Mick Jagger' (for his charisma, energy and revolutionary attitudes by American rock critics who should know better) to a 'black Cliff Richard' (for his religious proselytizing by a mouthy Irish new waver who should *definitely* know better – right, Modest Bob?). He's also survived an attempt at political assassination – made when his contributions to the election campaign of Prime Minister Michael Manley got too much for his opponents – an all-too-real manifestation of something that, at various times, the likes of Mick Jagger, Alice Cooper and David Bowie have morbidly fantasized about.

He is now an exile twice over: from both his native homeland of Jamaica – where he cannot return because of the danger of another attempt on his life – and from his spiritual homeland of Africa. Still, life and work go on: he's in Britain right now to complete work on his new album 'Kaya', the follow-up to 'Exodus', an album which spawned a mind-boggling triad of hit singles: 'Exodus' itself, 'Waiting In Vain' and 'Jamming', the latter double-A-sided with 'Punky Reggae Party', a New Wave/reggae solidarity song co-written with and produced by Lee Perry a.k.a. Scratch a.k.a. The Upsetter, the man who produced and sponsored The Wailers' work in the period before the original trio of Marley, Bunny (Wailer) O'Riley and Peter Tosh signed to Island.

'Punky Reggae Party' includes references to The Clash, The Jam, The Damned and Dr Feelgood (not groups who one would have thought made up a regular part of Marley's musical diet), as well as the (for Marley) unlikely line 'No boring old farts will be there', so it seemed not unreasonable to open up the proceedings with an inquiry as to how 'Punky Reggae Party' came into being.

'Well, y'know, the punks do a song called 'Police And Thieves' and so the man who produce the song – Lee Perry – him have the idea to do this.'

Why does he think many punk rockers have made the reggae connection?

'Y'mean most musicians tend fe like to have a slight touch of reggae about the place? Reggae is a good music ... *truly*, and musicians like it because you can listen to reggae and know that it is a good music, because if anything wrong with it, a musician supposed to know. The only thing can make it wrong is if someone make a mistake and the producer no cares and let it go on.'

I'm not sure if he's misunderstood the question or if I've misunderstood the answer or both. For some reason we're both laughing. Listen, you mention The Clash, The Damned, The Jam *et al.* on this record. Have you heard them, and what feeling do you get from *their* music?

Back comes the grin. 'From their music? Well, Upsetter write it, y'know. Is 'im write it so is 'im really as have the feeling. 'Im like the punks and if 'im like them then me like 'em, y'know wh'mean? Me an' 'im work *close*.'

Well, that would seem to be that for 'Punky Reggae Party' and hey, I ain't gonna be the one to use a phrase like 'Jah Punk' in this conversation. It seems (thankfully) that Marley isn't either, and that takes us to 'Kaya', the new(est) album.

Earlier in the day, I'd been furnished with a cassette of the first four tracks from 'Kaya' to be mastered and cut. 'Sun Is Shining' and the title track are older songs first recorded by the original Wailers with Lee Perry, and the original versions can be located by the curious and discerning on Trojan's 'African Herbsman' album. The other two tracks on the cassette were 'Is It Love' (the new single) and 'Easy Skanking'.

In fact, I'd been told that most of 'Kaya' was material originally laid down at the 'Exodus' sessions.

'All of it was recorded during that time of "Exodus". What really 'appen is we have all of these songs and to re'earse dem all the while we figure might as well jus' get them recorded. So we record them so we can get them off our heads and think about some other *new* songs, y'know?'

Yeah, but if Marley wants to get to the new songs, why re-record so many older ones? Such songs from the Island Wailers' catalogue as 'Small Axe', 'Duppy Conqueror', 'Lively Up Yourself', 'Trenchtown Rock', '400 Years', 'Night Shift' and 'Put It On' derive from the Trojan years and before. Is it because he hears them differently now?

'Some of them really mean a lot to me, y'know? But them never really get justice like in production, so if you don't do them over them lost.'

By the way, how's your foot? I ask. (Last year Marley had an operation on his right big toe for the removal of a cyst.)

'Yeah, I play some football and get into a hurting. They make a big t'ing 'bout it, but ...' he giggles '... pure skank. Pure *SKANK*. This the year of the punk, y'know? The buoys have a t'ing in their ear and me have a toe ... the year of the punk!'

What does 'Kaya' mean, Bob?

''Erb. Man sometimes seh "kaya" because he sell 'erb in the yard and people seh him can't come in because he sell 'erb so he seh "kaya" or something else he call it. "Kaya" is a favourite name for it.'

Yeah, you have to keep coming up with new names for it so The Man don't know what you're talking about ...

'Yeah mon. *Seen.*'

... 'cause everybody knows what 'ganja' means now.

'Seen.'


Marley's been out of Jamaica for quite a while now, I wonder if he's getting homesick?

'Yeah, me can say me really miss the yout' 'cause me like to have plenty yout' round me, but me not get depressed because me like what I do when me not there. Me really dig it. Me been in Miami a lot, but the weather wasn't good for Miami. When I was there it went down to thirty, but the sun shine every day even when it get cool. Me make a wood fire and it nice. But Jamaica still the best.'

So where's number two?

'Well, Jamiaca number two still. My number one is Africa, with Jamaica number two.'

Africa's something of a sore spot with Marley. Whispers have it that Jah Bob did try to visit East Africa at one point but was refused admittance to Ethiopia. He prefers to say that the time was not right for him to go there.

'I get the urge that the time is right when the yout' unite in Jamaica. *Then* the time is right for Africa. If you go to Africa when the yout' is not unite in a Jamaica then somethin' wrong somewhere. Need to have some kinda *proof* fe walk with. When the yout' is unite in Jamaica then is a nice time fe go to Africa, because then you can say there is example.'

Marley has had to get clear of JA because of the astonishingly heavy situation that his unique position has created for him. It would be impossible, for example, to conceive of a situation wherein a British or American rock star would have to pack his leaving trunk due to fear of political assassination. Indeed, it is virtually unimaginable for any British or American rock and roller to get to a position where he and his work are considered that politically important. So obviously Bob Marley can't stay on the street — not because he's too precious to let his boots touch concrete, but because political guns are out for him.

It's in the light of that that one must ask him if he's changed — inside of himself — because of his success.

'Me change before me can change again. That mean that all of me changes me go through already. This is where me want to be . . . Rasta . . . y'know wh'mean? A yout' go in all directions. Them may change because — y'know — ideas are just ideas, but when y'have a commitment to somet'ing then you can't change just like that.'

One of the entourage comes in with a proof of the 'Kaya' album cover — 't'ank you, skippah!' — the front of which depicts a serene, smiling Marley fronded in leaves, and the back a mighty spliff — along the lines of Yggdrasil, the Tree of Life from Norse mythology — with its roots deep in the earth and its blazing head in the clouds. Be seein' ya down Woolworths with *this* one, dreadee.

Marley seizes on the sleeve. 'This is a spliff . . . a spliff, right? And this is the earth . . . the eart' a smoke the spliff and leaves a come out of the spliff same time . . . and the roots, yeah! Man who make this really 'ard . . . really 'ard worker.'

Hey Bob, while we're on the subject of 'erb, how come you can put away such a colossal amount of the stuff and still manage to

stay upright, let alone play football, put on a dynamite show an'
t'ing? Most people I know wander around in circles with their
eyes crossed and then fall over if they smoke that much.

'T'ing is ... you shouldn't smoke so much. You shouldn't
smoke 'erb like me. You should smoke just a little bit when you
feel like a draw. If it don't make you feel good. One shouldn't
smoke more than ... Smoking's a t'ing like ... if you just start
smoke, you smoke one draw an' it get you high, good? Tomorrow,
you smoke one draw an' it don't get you as high as the first draw
so you automtically take two draw. An' next day you take three
draw until you ready to smoke a spliff, but it shouldn't get to
where you smoke 'til you drop on the ground. That na right.'

He chuckles. 'That na right.'

Marley's albums show a clear continuity – or rather, they have
done ever since he started making albums *as albums* at the
beginning of the Island deal. This progression has become quite
definite, and so – following the clear call-to-arms of 'Exodus' –
what kind of step in the journey does 'Kaya' represent?

'It's like ... you reach a certain spot, right? In your journey,
it's like you're driving down the highway and you reach a rest-
place and you go in and get a cup of coffee an' t'ing and this is
that. Slow down and take it e-e-e-easy ... "Easy Skanking",
y'know. Just take a lickle bit easy right now. You just can't go on
hard all the time ... got to take a lickle bit easy sometime.'

'So this is like a rest ... for some kaya ...'

We both found ourselves saying, 'Stop for a smoke' at the same
time. Marley dissolves into a cloud of laughter and slaps palms,
mutters, 'Raaaaaaaasclaat!'

He collapses in a seemingly endless fit of giggles.

Eventually he regains his composure. 'For the next one we go at it
really 'ard 'cause we gotta make up the energy, make up the
distance. Dem call that "political" but no more. More like just
*natural*, not the love song, more *pure* like "Rastaman Vibration".
Me write them love song sometime but me can't write them songs
all the time because I could just write them every day quick-quick!

'But a love song is really an easy song for us. Go ahead an' tell
a girl seh, "should I leave you or should I come with you?" or
"we had a nice t'ing going which we don't have any more" ...
easy t'ing to write.'

248

Yeah, but *both* kinds of songs are important . . .

'*Yeh mon! Very important!* Album like this, now . . .' he gestures towards the 'Kaya' sleeve over on the other bed, 'you might have a young girl going to school or a young yout' going to school not knowing nothin' 'bout Rasta . . . they might like "She's Gone" from this album, see? If them like "She's Gone", automatically them might like somet'ing else because them have the album . . . and then from the word go they read the word and the word seh "Jah".

'*It never leave.* It never leave any man who hear the word "Rasta". Dem tellya dem *never forgot* that word because y'just don't forgot it. But y'have fe invite. You can't just . . .

'It's not everyone that you could a tell. Men are the same – war. Men do the same – fighting. Men need the same – a lickle love an' t'ing, y'know. Because it is no great pleasure – y'know – to sing 'bout suffering because me no feel like people should a really suffer, and it is not a great thing to sing about suffering, but y'have to sing about it because it a go on.

'I think t'ings a gone improve this year because yout' a gonna be united. Too many things a go on. Too *scatter*. You need fe *unite*. It start a Jamaica, and once it start a Jamaica then it gonna be a full-scale unity all over. God, Jamaica's a hard place to get unity . . . really 'ard. But once it start and get serious . . .

'But Marcus Garvey tell 'em that the yout' gon' come together one day. The greatest t'ing that ever happen to me in my life a happen that I ever know about is that the yout' in a Jamaica seh that they gonna stop kill one another because of *politics*.'

He virtually spits the last word, expelling it from his mouth as he would the taste of some awful evil.

The talk of unity is not mere wishful thinking; a few weeks ago the warring gunmen of rival Kingston ghettoes set aside their difference and called a truce to their political fighting.

'That me live to see the day when them seh that . . . Dem try to kill me before when I seh that. Plenty gunshot come after me because they no want me to see the day when the yout' am come together . . . the yout' in Jamaica say they no fight politics, because it got very *nasty* with machine gun . . . and it just be *yout' an' yout'* who suffer the same thing, so them seh *no more'a dat.* That will be a very great achievement and everybody gon' benefit from it because it gon' be an example.'

Yeah, it's an old situation . . . like in the States, where The Man sends junk and exploitation into the ghetto to keep oppressed people fighting each other and ripping each other off, so that they never get to recognize and fight their real enemies . . .

Marley erupts. *'Seen! Seen! Seen! Seen!* That is what *really happen.* But somebody gon' get wise in the crowd and see it but when dem figure y'have me roun' you for seven years – seen? – and there was a time when they could sent me with the t'ings 'cause I no know. Figure me *right.* But me read in a newspaper seh *this* man gone to war with *that* country and in a next country political t'ings start; man shoot man so . . . it just happen in a Jamaica. Put a man in one place for seven years, he a see it.

'There will come a time when he will look upon it and seh "What *is* this? This man a no try and help me. Him no care if someone a try and kill me or send me to try and shoot somebody." And then the yout' are gon say *no more'a dat.*

'And then the guy uptown really gon' feel it. *Uptown feel it, mon!* Y'know wh'mean?'

Seen, Bob.


I tell Marley about Norman Mailer's famous proposal that disputes between countries – or, more accurately, disputes between *governments* – be settled by single combat between the leaders of those governments, thereby affecting no innocents whatsoever.

Marley is highly taken with this notion.

'Who seh dat?'

An American writer named Norman Mailer.

'If they follow that scale it would be better because the guy who lead a country he would have to be physically fit.' Another explosion of laughter. 'And if him physically fit then automatically him brains and everyt'ing work right, 'cause if him naw fit him brain naw work good. 'Im have to be the President because it gon' be a 'eavyweight world.

'Guy has a gun, and he got a bullet instead of a hit.

'It's really a great idea what 'im [Mailer] seh, but them guys naw do that. Me myself t'ink more that the people can force them to do that if the people get the idea. So much people naw be dead if fe his idea. Naw send the innocent people get dead fe him. Really terrible . . .'

Further discussion of this topic was clouded by considering the consequences of a fifteen-round refereed bout between Jimmy Carter and Idi Amin. I wish I'd thought to ask Marley what *he* thought of Idi Amin, because a lot of Jamaicans seem to dig Amin simply because he's black, holds power and has run a few rings round the bigshot Western countries. However, I'd've thought that it was a bit hard to groove on Big Daddy unless you're into genocide, torture and institutionalized terrorism. Still . . .

'Everybody wan' get rich,' Marley says at length, after we've both recovered, 'because politics is just people wan' get rich.'

No, politics isn't so much the drive for wealth as the drive for power, for the ability to *control* . . .

'*Yeah*. That hurt. T'ing that *hurt*, mon. Really hurt. Seen. Too true. Once you wanna be a politician, man, you don't know what you want to be already.

'Politics is a weird situation. They never give me a chance to try and give some help. All they do is try to kill me, and it slow up the yout'. The plan I have . . . not a plan but . . . ideas me have to try and help yout'. True politics. Politicians naw t'ink clean of no one, 'cause way them think, think everyone think same way, so when plenty yout' come them try an' kill me.'

Did anyone ever catch up with the guys who tried to kill you, I ask. A second later I get wise to myself. *Silly question.*

Marley looks at me pityingly. He shakes his head and laughs.

'Yeah, but surely people must know who they are . . .'

'Well, mon, you know . . . we know is who . . . but even them innocent . . .'

Seen, Bob. The men who pulled the triggers ain't as guilty as the men who pulled *their* triggers.

'That's why Jamaica become such a place. Cannot live in our country, y'have no *protection*. Is neither with Russia nor with America. Is with your own.

'*Rasta*. Rasta say peace an' love an' life. If we ever get guns and rule people an' force an' do dem t'ing, all who have to do with us will seh, "He's not Rasta."

'We seen people who are not Rasta. We seen the terrible things that happen to them, an' we don't want to be one of them people. So when Rasta get strong them try kill the people who have some lickle potentials.

251

'But the yout' will come together, seen? Come together united. Make it much *easier*.'

Summer wouldn't have been summer these last few years without the by now almost statutory Marley concerts. From the Lyceum in '75 (the gig that produced the live album), Hammersmith Odeon in '76 and the Rainbow in '77, they've gotten steadily less enjoyable, not due to any deterioration on the part of Bob Marley and The Wailers, but simply because of the constricting qualities of the latter two venues. Marley sees it in the same way, but cites the high incidence of theft and intimidation at the Lyceum – by what one of our less salubrious national newspapers referred to as 'a gang of Rastafarian youths' – as a reason why he didn't return there.

'If a yout' is weak, an' he not have education, not have education of his *own* ... education cause a lot of problem. Education is good, but they naw teach 'bout the history of their own. Me no come know about *Rasta*, know about *Africa*. Had to search for that *myself*, but they teach me 'bout Christopher Columbus and 'bout Marco Polo. It was hard to learn because that was the teaching that them give, instead of teaching about Africa, Christianity, Africa, Solomon an' David an' show them the way black people used to live, how black people *supposed* to live, how *all* people supposed to live.

'People out on the street them *ignorant*, man! None of them know how to live! Them should really know what is right and what is wrong because to teach them 'bout Marco Polo is not in their culture. Is just a brainwash.

'Alright. I don't say, "Don't teach about Marco Polo." Teach about Marco Polo, but teach 'em of Selassie I too, or Marcus Garvey or some a dem people too. Else people grow up on the street *ignorant*, know nothing about themselves, think them *nothing* because where dem teach 'im learn nothing about 'imself.'

Still, it's good that these things can be taught through music, that people can sing about it ...

'That is the t'ing now where the best thing happens in the music, that people are singing about it, and that is inspiration, because them people naw read naw *book* fe know 'bout Rasta ...'

\*

Round about this point, Bob's concentration (and mine) received an interruption by way of the last of what had been an endless series of peremptory phone calls. When we reconvened, I showed Marley the Stiff Records biro (yeah mon, one a dem bloodclaat promotional devices that record companies lay on Media Folk to make sure that we think of them and their fabulous Artistes and Wonderful Product as often as possible).

This particular doodad is a transparent little number containing a genuine US $2,000 bill. 'Deminted' has nothing to do with the flavour, it means that the US Mint – in their infinite wisdom – decided that for some technical reason, their bills were unfit to mingle with the rest of their product. The bill has, of course, been shredded into confetti to prevent any embarrassment to those of their customers who may not be so discriminating about the more obscure details of a $2,000 bill that someone may be waving in their faces in proposed exchange for some goods or service.

Anyway, I haul this pen out and show it Marley, who is highly intrigued.

'Who the man who put this together??? Two t'ousand dollar bill? Genuine? Yeah mon, this a . . . *raaasclaaaaaaaat*!!!'

He explodes into laughter again.

'If you go to Jamaica, seh "This a two t'ousand dollar bill in here," man put it together. Just seh, "Got a lickle job for you, man, put it together . . ."'

Do you want to keep it, Bob?

'Keep it? T'ank you very much, man.'

He rummages in the brown paper bag next to his glass of orange juice.

'Y'wan' some 'erb, mon?'

Serious t'ing. It's difficult to feel that you've got anything like the measure of a man in a ninety-minute meeting, and God knows that the rock and roll interview isn't necessarily the best framework for that, anyway.

Let's just say that I had these cloudy visions a little while later of me asking Marley exactly how he played his rydim on the guitar and he showed me this lick and then had me try it while he sang along and shook his red, gold and green woolly mushroom in time.

At one point I remember him saying, 'T'ings so good on eart' we send men fe go to moon to see if anybody need any help up there.' Another time he seemed to be delivering this sermon about how men trust doctors too much and God too little.

So Pharaoh, so good.

# The Jam:
# 'All Mod Cons'
# (Polydor)

*NME*, 28 October 1978

THIRD albums generally mean that it's shut-up-or-get-cut-up time: when an act's original momentum has drained away and they've got to cover the distance from a standing start, when you've got to cross 'naïve charm' off your list of assets.

For The Jam, it seemed as if the Third Album Syndrome hit with their second album. 'This Is The Modern World' was dull and confused, lacking both the raging, one-dimensional attack of their first album and any kind of newly won maturity. A couple of vaguely duff singles followed and, in the wake of a general disillusionment with the Brave New Wave World, it seemed as if Paul Weller and his team were about to be swept under the carpet.

Well, it just goes to show you never can tell. 'All Mod Cons' is the third Jam album to be released (it's actually the fourth Jam album to be recorded; the *actual* third Jam album was judged, found wanting and scrapped) and it's not only several light years ahead of anything they've done before but also the album that's going to catapult The Jam right into the front rank of international rock and roll; one of the handful of truly essential rock albums of the last few years.

The title is more than Grade B punning or a clever-clever link-up with the nostalgibuzz packaging (like the target design on the label, the Swinging London trinketry, the Lambretta diagram or the Immediate-style lettering); it's a direct reference to both the broadening of musical idiom and Weller's reaffirmation of a specific Mod consciousness.

254

Remember the Mod ideal: it was a lower-middle and working-class consciousness that stressed independence, fun and fashion without loss of integrity or descent into elitism or consumerism; unselfconscious solidarity and a dollop of non-sectarian concern for others. Weller has transcended his original naïvety without becoming cynical about anything other than the music business.

Mod became hippies and we know that didn't work; the more exploratory end of Mod rock became psychedelia. Just as Weller's Mod ideal has abandoned the modern equivalent of beach-fighting and competitive posing, his Mod musical values have moved from '65 to '66: the intoxicating period between pilled-up guitar-strangling and 'Sergeant Pepper'. Reference points: 'Rubber Soul' and 'A Quick One' rather than 'Small Faces' and 'My Generation'.

Still, though Weller's blends of acoustic and electric six- and twelve-string guitars, sound effects, overdubs and more careful structuring and arranging of songs (not to mention a quantum leap in standard of composition) may cause *frissons* of delight over at the likes of Bomp, Trouser Press and other covens of ageing Yankee Anglophiles, 'All Mod Cons' is an album based firmly in 1978 and looking forward.

*This* is the modern world: 'Down In The Tube Station At Midnight' is a fair indication of what Weller's up to on this album, as was 'A-Bomb In Wardour Street' (I can't help thinking that he's given more hard clear-eyed consideration to the implications of the Sham Army than Jimmy Pursey has), but they don't remotely tell the whole story. For one thing, Weller has the almost unique ability to write love songs that convince the listener that the singer is *really in love*. Whether he's describing an affair that's going well or badly, he writes with a penetrating, committed insight that rings perfectly, utterly true.

Weller writes lovingly and (choke on it) sensitively without ever descending to the patented sentimentality that is the stock-in-trade of the emotionally bankrupt. That sentimentality is but the reverse side of the macho coin, and both sides spell loveless-ness. The inclusion of 'English Rose' (a one-man pick'n'croon acoustic number backed only by a tape of the sea) is both a musical and emotional finger in the eye for everyone who still clings to the old punk tough-guy stereotype and is prepared to call The Jam out for not doing likewise.

Weller is – like Bruce Springsteen – tough enough not to feel he needs to prove it any more, strong enough to break down his own defences, secure enough to make himself vulnerable. The consciousness of 'All Mod Cons' is the most admirable in all of British rock and roll, and one that most of his one-time peers could do well to study.

Through the album, then: the brief, brusque title track and its immediate successor ('To Be Someone') examine the rock business; first in a tart V-sign to some entrepreneurial type who wishes to squeeze the singer dry and then throw him away, and second in a cuttingly ironic track about a superstar who lost touch with the kids and blew his career. Weller is, by implication, assuring his listeners that *no way* is that going to happen to him: but the song is so well thought out and so convincing that it chokes back the instinctive 'Oh *yeah*?' that a less honest song in the same vein would elicit from a less honest band.

From there we're into 'Mr Clean', an attack on the complacent middle-aged 'professional classes'. The extreme violence of its language (the nearest this album comes to an orthodox punk stance, in fact) is matched with music that combines delicacy and aggression with an astonishing command of dynamics. This is as good a place as any to point out that bassist Bruce Foxton and drummer Rick Buckler are more than equal to the new demands that Weller is making on them; the vitality, empathy and resourcefulness that they display throughout the album makes 'All Mod Cons' a collective triumph for The Jam as well as a personal triumph for Weller.

'David Watts' follows (written by Ray Davies, sung by Foxton and a re-recorded improvement on the 45) with 'English Rose' in hot pursuit. The side ends with 'In The Crowd', which places Weller dazed and confused in the supermarket. It bears a superficial thematic resemblance to 'The Combine' (from the previous album) in that it places its protagonist in a crowd and examines his reactions to the situation, but its musical and lyrical sophistication smashes 'The Combine' straight back to the stone age. It ends with a lengthy, hallucinatory backward guitar solo which sounds as fresh and new as anything George Harrison or Pete Townshend did a dozen years ago, and a reference back to 'Away From The Numbers'.

'Billy Hunt', whom we meet at the beginning of the second

side, is not a visible envy-focus like Davies' 'David Watts' but the protagonist's faintly ludicrous all-powerful fantasy self: what he projects in the day dreams that see him through his crappy job. The deliberate naïvety of this fantasy is caught and projected by Weller with a skill that is nothing short of marvellous.

A brace of love songs follow: 'It's Too Bad' is a song of regret for a couple's mutual inability to save a relationship which they both know is infinitely worth saving. Musically, it's deliriously, wonderfully '66 Beat Groupish in a way that represents exactly what all those tinpot powerpop bands were aiming for but couldn't manage. Lyrically, even if this sort of song was Weller's only lick, he'd still be giving Pete Shelley and all his New Romance fandangos a real run for his money.

'Fly' is an exquisite electric/acoustic construction, a real lovers' song, but from there on in the mood changes for the 'Doctor Marten's Apocalypse' of 'A-Bomb in Wardour Street' and 'Tube Station'. In both these songs, Weller depicts himself as the victim who doesn't know why he's getting trashed at the hands of people who don't know why they feel they have to hand out the aggro.

We've heard a lot of stupid, destructive songs about the alleged joys of violence lately and they all stink: if these songs are listened to in the spirit in which they were written then maybe we'll see a few less pictures of kids getting carried off the terraces with darts in their skulls. And if these songs mean that one less meaningless street fight gets started then we'll all owe Paul Weller a favour.

The Jam brought us The Sound Of '65 in 1976, and now in 1978 they bring us the sound of '66. Again, they've done it in such a way that even though you can still hear The Who here and there and a few distinct Beatleisms in those ornate descending twelve-string chord sequences, it all sounds fresher and newer than anything else this year. 'All Mod Cons' is the album that'll make Bob Harris's ears bleed the next time he asks what *has* Britain produced lately; more important, it'll be the album that make The Jam *real* contenders for the crown.

Look out, all you rock and rollers: as of now The Jam are the ones you have to beat.

# *Superman:*
# The movie

*NME*, 23 December 1978

**T**HERE is a peculiar magic about the comic book which, all too often, is unable to maintain its power when removed from the garishly cheap environment of four-colour pulp.

There has never, for example, been a successful cross-fertilization between comics and rock; novels based on comic-book themes have been invariably awful, and TV shows have usually been either patronizingly camp (*Batman*) or reluctant to attempt to capture that elusive atmosphere by adhering too closely to the original format (*The Incredible Hulk, Wonder Woman, Spider-Man*). The end result is usually frustrating, all the more so in the occasional flash of what the show or movie could have been like if they'd had the courage (and the budget) to go the whole way (again, *The Incredible Hulk* is a case in point).

Richard Donner's megabuck epic *Superman* film breaks on through to the other side: it captures the innocence of the comic book by playing it straight. It combines the intergalactic sweep of the imagination and the excruciating down-home corniness that combined to make Superman (and all his multifarious successors and descendants) into the most potent connection with Myth Central that post-war culture can provide.

Moreover, Donner and his writers (*Godfather*'s godfather Mario Puzo and a small army of rewrite men) have – happily – realized that the reason that *Superman* has not only been a stone success in its own right for forty years but has spawned an entire industry has as much to do with the characters as with the action. The prototype superhero and his supporting cast are therefore realized accurately enough to make any longtime comic-book freak feel thoroughly at home (despite the occasional jarring flash of artistic licence, the mythos are, in the main, intact).

Most of the movie's pre-publicity has centred around the participation of Marlon Brando as Superman's father Jor-El, and the fact that Brando knocked down nearly four million dollars for a fortnight's work (is that cleaning up or what?). Before the movie is fifteen minutes old, the planet Krypton has gone for a total burton taking Marlon with it (not to mention Susannah York, clever Trevor Howard, Harry Andrews and Maria Schell) though Jor-El crops up later in electronically reincarnated form.

Christopher Reeve (young person getting Big Break with Plum Role; just praise The Elders Of Krypton that producers Alexander Salkind, Ily Salkind and Pierre Spengler didn't cast John Travolta) doesn't show up until an hour into the movie. The first hour is composed of two prologues (though they're fast and entertaining enough not to seem that way): the first showing a tantalizing taste of Krypton with technowonders-a-go-go and the special effects team going berserk and spending a large small fortune, and the second depicting the adolescence of the super-Moses in the Midwestern bullrushes. The two major ingredients of the mythos – Krypton as technology and myth and Smallville as repository of homeliness and America's idea of its own values – are thereby neatly and imaginatively laid out.

The movie hews to the late forties version of the Superman myth (i.e. that he passed his adolescence incognito and only revealed himself to the world as a fully grown Superman) and Clark Kent, Lois Lane, Jimmy Olsen and Perry White could well have stepped straight out of a late forties or early fifties comic, even though the street scenes give the impression that the film is set in the present day. The Smallville Revision (i.e. that Superman began his career as a teenaged Superboy) is ignored, though Lana Lang (the Lois Lane of his teens, a character brought into being by the Smallville Revision) appears briefly.

The atmosphere of the forties Superman is preserved ideologically as well as visually. 'I fight for truth, justice and the American way,' Reeve announces to Margot Kidder's A-rated and splendidly horny Lois Lane, and – depending on temperament – you either wince or laugh. Unlike the seventies Superman, who suffered from all the angst and self-doubt that has washed over the entire comic-book field since Stan Lee's early sixties innovations in *Spider-Man*, the movie Superman has a clearcut sense of purpose and no conflicts of ideological interests (could Superman have intervened in the Vietnam war or in the Middle East? On which side? Why?). His only contact with the seventies comes when he rushes to a phone booth to change costumes, discovers that it's an open-fronted modern one, shakes his head sadly and ends up doing his Superstrip in a revolving door.

Unlike his predecessors in the role (and Adam West's horrendous *Batman*), Reeve contrives not to look ridiculous in his Superman outfit. The technological credibility of the character is maintained with the aid of extraordinary verisimilitude in the flying sequences (none of the lo-budget cheapnis which marred the *Spider-Man* movie, for example) and no, Vladimir, you *can't* see the wires.

Jarring bits: the big 'S' logo on Brando's Jor-El costumes (maybe it *is* the El family crest or a Kryptonian 'J' but I still don't believe it), Gene Hackman's campy Luthor (straight out of the old *Batman* show, complete with silly wigs and Ned Beatty as a lamebrained assistant – I wanna see the *real* Luthor, bald and nasty – grrrrr), the lazily scripted *deus ex machina* method Superman uses to save California (wish he hadn't bothered – bye bye, Asylum) at the movie's climax, and the sexist running gag about Lois Lane's lousy spelling.

Grooves: the nostalgic opener, the brilliant credits, the hallucinatory, crystalline Krypton scenes, Reeve's slapstick Clark Kent, Margot Kidder's horny, aggressive Lois Lane and the genuine sexual tension between them, Valerie Perrine's New Jersey girl playing at slinky villainess and the genuine visual poetry of the flying sequences.

Comic-book movies can fall between two stools: if they're too faithful people not into comics will just think they're D-U-M-B (everyone's accusing me) and if they're not faithful enough, narrowminded purists like your humble correspondent will be heartily pissed off. This one should strike the first happy medium.

*Superman*'s blend of technology and innocence, imagination and naïvety, sophistication and honesty carries a genuinely enchanting power. I know it's a big-money Warner Brothers Christmas sucker-trap – or rather the adult me is painfully aware of the machinations, manipulations and megabuckbiz aspect of the whole thing, while the twelve-year-old me couldn't give a shit, lost in an old-time sense of wonder and grooving to high heaven.

'Next year: *Superman II*' it says on the end titles. In *Superman II*, our hero faces off against Terence Stamp, Sarah Douglas and Jack O'Halloran as the three Kryptonian villains exiled before the planet goes BLAAAAAMMMMM at the beginning of this movie. You best believe that the adult me and the twelve-year-old me are gonna be there – in the two best seats in the house.

# Mekons/The Fall/
# Human League/Gang Of Four/
# Stiff Little Fingers

*NME*, 31 March 1979

AND the stars look very different today . . .

For all practical rock purposes, we may as well own up that we are now living in the eighties. Just to be arbitrary, let's assume that the fifties began when Leo Fender invented the bass guitar and Elvis Presley plastered his hillbilly leer over international horizons; the sixties began with The Beatles and the seventies opened for business with 'Virginia Plain', 'Ziggy Stardust' and 'All The Young Dudes'.

Sunday's Lyceum gig will stand as a watershed between the seventies and the eighties.

Five bands billed and one opening as an afterthought: some of the audience sniffing around looking for the eighties the way dogs look for bones and some looking for 1977 (if they find it, they pogo; if they don't, they throw things). Some were looking for art, and I hope they found it; some were looking for fun, and I *know* they found it; some were looking for members of the opposite sex (they did okay, some of them anyway); some were looking for booze and drugs, and they got lucky as well.

Everybody found something and if it wasn't what they went out looking for . . . well, ace, shut your face. You want it on a plate?

Openers: heavy men in evening dress mashing down on the toes of the wife's brother's boots and then confiscating his laces on the grounds that he was some kind of aggressive skinhead. Dennis Brown and Dillinger ricocheting round the hall and no white folks dancing. Ahhh, the first bondage pants of spring: one girl wearing so much metal that she drowns out the disco when she walks past.

Endocrine glands get geared up for something and then an unscheduled *hors d'œuvre*: Mark Perry and two colleagues marching to the beat of a different drum machine as Good Missionaries (*not* ATV) attempt to exorcize various demons collected at Greenwich and Derby. Everyone is masked (except the drum machine) and the music is disguised even though Perry's rant is naked and shivering. The first section is inconsequential beyond belief, though the latter half gets almost mesmerizing when a structure is imposed. Most people are puzzled, though some enjoy the tweaks and boings. As The Missionaries make their exit kids turn to each other and murmur, 'Shit, I could do that.'

They are absolutely right. They probably could. Would they want to?

Mekons are next and your reporter (a sixties kid disguised as a seventies oldster and earnestly participating in the search for the eighties) is instantly reminded of a remark recently made by Graham Parker to the effect that a lot of bands nowadays sing very witty songs in Gumby voices and get theses written about them. Mekons are a whacked-out cross between Jilted John and The Rezillos: there seem to be more of them on the stage than there actually are and they jump around like *The Magic Roundabout.*

Their audience rapport is instant and cheery; one of the singers gets more mileage out of blowing an attempt at a James Brown cum Rod Stewart Hot Move with his mike stand than he would've done if he'd brought it off. Guitarist Kevin Mekon similarly gets much mileage out of being unable to get his red Burns guitar to stay in tune. Their killer single 'Where Were You' provokes an outburst of manic pogoing which lasts until the end of the set and earns them their encore in classic style.

Someone somewhere seems to have perpetuated the impression that there is something Arty about Mekons. There isn't. They are Big Fun, and I hope they remain Big Fun even after they've become a proper professional rock band with real Fenders, leads that don't give up halfway through numbers and so on.

Lots of young people seem to have it in for The Fall, and a fair proportion of them were at the Lyceum.

The Fall were by far the most unorthodox band on the bill (i.e. they sounded less like The Clash than anybody except The Human League, but then they're different), since Good Missionaries weren't so much a band as an event or a happening or Art or something like that, and the intolerant boilsuckers who can't see that there's room for more than one sort of rock band made them pay for their daring.

They'd hardly had time to get plugged in before it became blindingly obvious why they'd entitled their album 'Live At The Witch Trials'.

Plastic glasses! Beer cans! Coke cans! Gob! Yep, what we had here was a classic case of remembering those fabulous seventies. The low point of the set was when some spiky psycho leapt on stage and slugged Mark E. Smith (Fall mikeperson) two or three times and then jumped back into the audience before Smith or anybody else had time to ask him to account for his behaviour.

Okay, The Fall are Difficult And Arty, if that's how you interpret attempts to dispense with orthodox rock ideas of what structure and texture ought to be; or alternatively, if that's how you'd describe a band who can't take their music where they want it to go by using the conventional language of rock. The Fall are threatening: not in the conventional tear-ya-down sense, but threatening in that they tell you stuff that you may not want to hear in a manner to which you are not accustomed.

The Fall are not comforting in the way that even the most badass conventional rock act is: The Pistols could be incredibly comforting if you identified yourself with their threat rather than with their targets. Yeah! We're All Punks Together! Bugger the Queen!

This response is not possible with The Fall. Not yet, anyway. Maybe later, when we've all learned the words to the songs and started to dress like them and the people who threw things at them (maybe even the *scheisskopf* who hit Smith) will be *boasting* about having been to this gig. Right now, they are not just alienated from (ta-daaaaaa!) society but from standard rock, and that includes punk.

None of them look like punks, and the punks gave 'em the kind of response that Dr Feelgood used to get from Ted audiences when they were starting out. The worst kind of Teds are stuck in 1957 and yeah, sure, we've all been laughing at them for years, but punks stuck in 1977 (or anyone stuck anywhere, for that matter) are just as bad, and this kind of shit has GOT TO STOP NOW.

If you don't like The Fall, sod off to the bar and get quietly pissed with your mates until Stiff Little Fingers come on in approved clothes and play some approved pogo music. All right, creeps?

Back to The Fall . . . Martin Bramah plays upside-down guitar on a drastically surgeried Fender. All his licks sound to be upside-down as well: high squibbling rat-scratch solos when you'd expect chunky rhythms (enriched with marrowbone jelly) and verse vica. He looks both perpetually surprised and Somewhere Else. Mark E. Smith, who has a Prince Valiant haircut, a maroon shirt that keeps coming out at the back, an indomitably accusing voice and more personal courage than anybody else in the hall that night, kept on 'singing' after a lesser human would've split the stage in either a flood of tears or a fit of pique.

Yvonne Pawlett pats away at her piano and looks shit-scared, as well she might be. Singers and guitarists can *dodge* f'Chrissake, and drummers have kits in front of them, but a small girl behind a small piano is vulnerable beyond belief and Rock Against Sexism does *not* mean that Real Men can now chuck stuff at girls onstage. (Sorry to keep going on about all this, but I was *pissed off* and I still am. Okay?) Her sound is misty and pervasive, gauzy and stinging.

Marc Lacey is huge and stolid and his sound is likewise: bass playing that you could build any kind of edifice upon. Karl Burns' replacement (dunno his name; sorry) kept his head down and the beat in place. The Fall impressed me enormously: haven't learned to like their records yet, but any band this powerful live has to be able to get it down in the studio somehow.

They were the only group on the bill (Perry wasn't billed, remember) who didn't do an encore, but they were the band who deserved one the most.

The glass-chuckers had temporarily exhausted themselves: it wasn't until The Human League bleeped into 'Blind Youth' that the missiles returned.

The League are electronic entertainers from Sheffield, and the only reason that anyone could find them less enthralling than the gargantuanly overrated Suicide is that they don't have any kind of New York Loft/Junk Squalor mystique going for them. Structurally, they are orthodox: it's just that they prefer synthesizers and slide shows to Les Pauls and jumping up and down.

They are Fun rather than Art (the barrier is artificial but let's talk in those terms for the benefit of glass-chuckers everywhere), performing The Righteous Brothers' 'You've Lost That Lovin' Feelin'' almost properly and seguing ridiculous transcriptions of Gary Glitter's 'Rock And Roll' and Iggy Pop's 'Nightclubbing' together for their encore.

The Fall used conventional instrumentation (guitar, bass,

264

drums, keyboards, singer) to produce unconventional music; The Human League use unconventional instrumentation (synths, drum machine) to produce what is basically rock esperanto. They got a good ride from the audience in exchange for a good gig; they were hugely enjoyable and will Go Far.

Four bands into the night and my ears were beginning to go.

The Gang Of Four leapt onstage with Fenders at the ready to perform the most conventional rock music thus far. The singer windmilled his arms and shouted, guitarist Andy Gill ran about and waved his guitar and the rhythm section hammered away. They exist on a jagged line drawn between Pere Ubu and Wilko Johnson with a few reggae detours when they swopped instruments: Gill played drums and the drummer came upfront to blow some melodica in an earnest approximation of Augustus Pablo.

They were fine, and the pogoers loved 'em (if anybody threw anything I was in the bog at the time), but definitely late seventies.

This ain't even approximately doing them justice, but as noted above, my perceptions were pretty blunted by that stage. I'd like to see 'em again when not on a mission to find the eighties, 'cause they're a good contemporary rock band with nary a hint of Arty Pretension or elitism to be found anywhere about their persons.

Finally . . . the moment you've all been waiting for . . . STIFF LITTLE FINGERS!!!

Yep, present and correct: drum risers, expensive guitars, leather jackets. Success, success, success, does it matter? It's invidious and shameful to dump on a band because you don't dig the way some of their punters behave (the Sham trap beckons: please put your foot in here) but there was complacency in the air this night. Jake Burns could've told off the kids who'd mistreated The Fall and he didn't. Wasn't his fault, but Fingers have paid enough dues for two dozen bands and they should know that it's too late to stop now.

Apart from the token democracy of sticking Burns at the side of the stage (if a geezer sings lead and plays most of the guitar solos he deserves to be where more of the audience can see him), it was conventional Punk Heroic: leatherjacketed agitpop, rama-lamafirebomb.

Sod the eighties: it was a Clash-surrogate late seventies punk gig by the end.

Again, I'm allowing what happened to The Fall to sour my reactions and I shouldn't be taking it out on Stiff Little Fingers. If I'd arrived just as Gang Of Four went on, I'd probably have had a whale of a time, because Stiff Little Fingers are – objectively speaking – a hell of a band with power, courage, conviction and skill.

But I saw them play like Heroes and get received like Heroes and something was wrong, because the band who had showed the most real heroism (quiet, with a small 'h') got bottled off the stage and didn't get to do the encore that – in real terms – they'd earned.

For a band to make easy gestures to an audience who only want to make easy gestures back is the most suspect device in rock, but there's no way a band can break this deadlock without either sabotaging their set or else playing Deliberately Difficult music, which puts us right back where we started, breaking our balls on the Art/Fun fence.

The seventies are going to have to learn to cope with the eighties the same way that the sixties learned to cope with the seventies (remember 'boring old farts'? If you threw a glass, check yourself out very carefully) and the fifties had to cope with the sixties and everybody had to learn to cope with rock and roll when it started in the first place.

We've still got a long way to go.

# The New Barbarians: 'What town are we in?' 'What song are we playing?'

*NME*, 26 May 1979

Awwwwww *mama!* I wanna tell ya 'bout Texas radio and the big beat.

You step out of the airport in Dallas and straight onto hot concrete looking for a cab and there's this big green Ford that looks like it lost a fight with a steamroller sometime around the years that Chuck Berry got slung inside for statutory rape. Up comes the driver, a huge beefy bespectacled man nudging into his mid-forties: he walks like Bo Diddley, don't need no crutch. Throws your stuff in the back, gives it the gun and the big green Ford lurches through the weave of roads and tunnels leading onto the expressway that takes you into Dallas, the Kennedy-snuffing capital of the world.

The heat in New York is humid and it steams you: in Texas the heat is dry and it bakes you. Inside the big green Ford, everything is cool. My man Bo punches his radio and out comes *soul music*, amazing pounding emotional dance music, blowing hot to the heart and cold to the bone. Bo flashes a grin wide as his radiator grille, all gold and ivory and tobacco. 'Out here in Texas,' he says, 'you can get yourself some *faaaaaahn* weed. Hey.'

There's a spliff in his hand. Yank-style: tiny, tight and white. On him it looks like a toothpick. 'None for me,' he says, 'I prefer to wait till I'm off-duty 'cuz it screws up mah *drahvin'*. But y'all go right ahead.'

Just below knee-level, right by the gearshift, is a mess of skins and clips and a small bag of pot. Hospitality, Texas-style. He asks what we're doing in the state and I tell him we've come to see Ron Wood.

Not a flicker.

Ron Wood of The *Stones*. He relaxes.

'Ah hey, The *Stones*. Yeah, they cool. I tellya who I saw a while back who was outasite: Wings. You know them?'

Meanwhile the soul station has got its fingers into Donna Summer's 'Hot Stuff', the hot dry highway has faded into a blur. 'You can hear some good blues 'roun' here – Lowell Fulson, he lives 'roun' heah sumplace, but I tellya what I really dig: country an' western music, Merle Haggard and Charlie Pride . . . who was that cat that recorded "When I Need You"? Leo Sayer? Yeah, he's outasite too . . .'

The night's gig is in Houston, right at the other end of the state. However, for this leg of the tour, Ron Wood's touring group The New Barbarians (a name donated to him by Neil Young, high on the list of anticipated superstar guests who never show up) are domiciled in Dallas, at the Fairmont Hotel. Going to stay at the Fairmont is not so much like going to stay in a hotel as moving into a new neighbourhood. It makes any Hilton look like a greasy boarding-house in Doncaster. Air-conditioned to the *nth*

267

degree of frosty elegance, chandeliered, plum plush, huge enough to cover a full city block. Al Martino singing in the bar for the last night of a two-week residency. This is *elegance*, Jack. Makes you *sick*.

Anyway, this is where the Barbarians are stationed. The deal is as follows: at some unspecified time the band haul themselves out of their pits, do whatever is necessary to get themselves ready to do what they do. Then they spill over the lobby in a flurry of scarves and shades and guitar cases and lean blonde girls who make the Texas businessmen with the briefcase phones drinking and talking business in the bar stare. Then they step into the limos and cruise to a private airfield where their chartered jet is waiting. They climb into the jet where the stewardesses say 'Far out' to anything anyone says to them and no one has to *ex-ting- wish cigarettes and othah smoking mateeriahl* during take-off and landing and you can eat the chicken salad or the roast beef cooked right there in front of you by a nutter in a chef's hat. At the other end they disembark into another bunch of limos, or maybe it's the same limos and the same drivers, who the hell can tell, and they gas the suckers up and whizz them straight into the back of the hall, behind the stage, where they can hear Keith Richards' reggae tapes, ricocheting around the building and the anticipatory bullfight cheers from the kids as each record ends before they disappear down a long grey corridor and into the band room where the hopefuls cluster outside for the forbidden glimpse of gods at rest and play. Then when they're all tuned up and ready they run down the grey corridor and the stage goes dark and the roadies who've been grooming the amps and dicking around with the lights get into position and the yell goes up till it shakes the building and the Voice Of God declaims, 'Ladeeeez 'n' gentlemen, THE NEW BARBARIANS . . .'

All right. The New Barbarians is the Ron Wood tour. The object of the exercise is two-fold: to do some dates to promote this album that honest Ron's made to inaugurate his new solo deal with CBS Records, and also to give the two members of The Stones with the most insatiable appetite for gigging and playing and jamming and having fun something to do while Jagger hides out from Bianca's lawyers and the main corporate edifice – a cultural institution known as The Rolling Stones – starts to think about its next album and tour.

The New Barbarians are six: there's honest Ron outfront to carry the weight on guitar and vocals (and mouth-harp and pedal steel and tenor saxophone, but that's another matter). Behind the drums is Joseph 'Zigaboo' Modeliste of The Meters, the New Orleans funk axis who've supported The Stones on two tours and who form the nucleus of Allen Toussaint's operation. Almost hidden by the keyboards rig is Ian MacLagan, tiny and dapper, hair rinsed grey, veteran of Small Faces, The Faces and the last lot of Stones activities, an ex-mod to the back teeth. Looming over a tiny Alembic bass, meet and greet Stanley Clarke, a lean towering young Jumpin' Black Flash, and the acknowledged king of fusion bass (unless you count Jaco Pastorius as a fusion bassist). Bobby Keyes, a Stones regular for most of the seventies and the pride of Lubbock, is blowing his golden saxophone.

Lemme see. We left anyone out?

Keith Richards and Ronnie Wood pop out of their respective limo doors virtually simultaneously. Ronnie Wood looks just like Keith Richards but Keith Richards looks just like Mick Jones.

Wood is jaunty and bouncy. He looks as if the world's sleekest, blackest hedgehog is sitting on his head. Richards' face is white and expressionless. The milling throngs of musicians, ladies, drivers, assistants, liggers, under-assistant West Coast promopersons and whatnot part like the Red Sea to let them through.

Mick Jagger is nowhere in evidence. Bob Dylan is somewhere else entirely. Neil Young is probably asleep. Joe Walsh may not even be present in spirit. Jeff Beck, Jimmy Page and Eric Clapton show neither hide nor hair nor guitar pick. All the 'guest star' buzz, carefully denied and eschewed by those connected with the tour but well in evidence and certainly not hindering the sale of a ticket or three, is carefully weighed and judged to be so much catcrap. Still, it's buzz and you can't knock it. These venues they're playing are *big* suckers and this tour ain't exactly costing fourpence to put together and a seat sold is a seat sold is a seat *sold*, Jack. Can you dig it?

This is bigtime rock and roll, USA. This is not half a dozen guys crammed into a dying transit wiping motorway grease off their chops and trying to decide whether they can afford to buy new strings *and* get pissed tonight after the gig. This is big business and it moves sweet and sleek as a whisper down cool grey air-conditioned corridors from late afternoon to early morning.

269

Right here on this baking airfield, the entourage is out of the air-conditioning for the second of six moments of its day. The first was when they left the hotel to get in the limos. The third will be when they make the lightning transfer into the second set of limos up in Houston. The next will be when they climb out of those limos and into the plane after the gig, and then – wait a second, got to figure this out – ummmmmm – when they get *out* of the plane and into the next set of limos, and finally they'll have to leave the cars and get into the hotel. Then it's cool canned air scented with ice cubes and plain sailing all the way.

The reason for all this farting about is v. simple. The Barbs ain't playing Dallas, and nobody except a few real hip people even know they're there. Meanwhile, all the kids in Houston are going totally pineapples because they think that somewhere in their town, Keith Richards, man, is holed up in a room with Tibetan prayer shawls over the lamps and Rasta posters all over the wall and all sorts of amazing far-out scenes are going on all over the place and there's cocaine and blowjobs and weirdness and if they comb Houston and harass all the desk clerks in all the major hotels someone will finally break down and admit that yes, Keith and Woody *are* there and yes, Mick Jagger *is* with them – sharp intake of breath, *wow* – and the room number is 821 and there's a party going on and all you have to do is get in there – shit, man, everybody knows what goes on around a Stones tour, which is what this almost is seeing as how it's Woody's tour and Keith's with him, and *please* mister if you know where they are you won't regret telling me . . .

That's what Sonja thinks, anyway. Sonja's from Georgia originally and she says she's only seventeen and she's just *crazy* about the Stones and she looks like a rock-and-roll fourteen-year-old designed by a committee of *Oui* staffers. Makes you feel like a real asshole to have to tell her that sorry, the tour's staying in Dallas and Jagger ain't there at all.

So this way, The Barbs get to keep all the Sonjas and the ones who aren't even cute and, worst of all, their male equivalents the hell out from under their feet. The time when these guys wanted to drown in Sonjas is long gone. The amount of publicity that Richards has had over that bust in Toronto has been so ludicrous that, by contrast, going out on Woody's tour is almost like going into hiding but just the same the name of the game is P-R-I-V-A-C-Y and plenty of it.

So Sonja's little tanned shoulders droop and her little fantasy is shot to shit but even if she was in Dallas and she'd made it up to Keith's Room it wouldn't be what she expected. Still, later for that even as Sonja walks dejectedly back towards her seat, 'cuz the lights are going down and the yell goes up till it shakes the building and the Voice Of God declaims, 'Ladeeeez 'n' gentlemen, THE NEW BARBARIANS . . .!'

Simultaneous action: everybody in the hall climbs up on their hind legs, waves their fist in the air and bellows. Security men fan out and motion kids back to their seats in a show of force that keeps everybody docile without any visible aggro. Modeliste climbs up behind the drums, MacLagan slides in behind his Hammond/piano/moog set-up. Keyes ambles over to his mike, horn at the ready, bottle of Bourbon clamped firmly in his other hand. Stanley Clarke, bass tight to his chest, prowls in front of his amp like some impassive panther. In his black leather pants he looks like some parallel-universe version of Phil Lynott.

Ronnie Wood comes scampering out with his silver guitar. White shirt open at the neck and tie askew, white towelling jacket, red knee boots and impish grin of a favourite bantamweight contender making an entrance on the night that Norman Mailer is going to see him take the title. Exuberantly running on the spot, fists in the air, his angular face contorted into comic aggression, he is an appealing figure: friendly, self-mocking, energetic. No matter how flash he dresses and how much he poses, you just *know* that Ronnie Wood is all right.

Wander through all the rock and roll sleazepits in all the rock and roll cities and you never hear anyone telling you that Ronnie Wood is a bastard. Post-punks who resent Jagger because they think he's a jetset poseur or Richards because they see him as a millionaire junkie who walks his way out of busts that would have put ordinary citizens away for most of the eighties . . . they still check Ronnie Wood from back when The Faces were still accepted as a people's band by *everyone*.

Remember him then? Capering about like a naughty kid caught with a cigarette behind the bike sheds on the run from the school caretaker. Like back at the first live all-star *Tommy* at the Lyceum all those years ago when it was as solemn as the opening of Parliament until Rod Stewart swaggered on to do 'Pinball Wizard'

271

and there behind him, tagging along like the kid brother you just couldn't bear to leave behind ... guess who? An oily clamped into his chimp-grin, hair miraculously on end, was Woody, scampering exuberantly to an amp. You couldn't hear anything he played, but he looked like the gatecrasher who's having more fun than anybody else at the party.

His entry into The Stones has lightened up the texture considerably. The Mick Taylor phase of The Stones was the period when Jagger and Richards became the visible *gestalt* of the band. Anybody with more than half an eardrum could tell you that The Stones would have great difficulty sounding like The Stones if Charlie Watts decided to hang up his rock and roll sticks and Bill Wyman isn't exactly a klutz, but though Taylor supplied skill, intelligence and feel he had less personality than the average chair.

So between them Mick and Keith supplied the fantasy: love-and-joy-and-loneliness-and-sex-and-sex-and-sex-and-sex plus booze-and-pills-and-powders plus please-allow-me-to-introduce-myself and it's-a-gas-gas-gas and world's-most-elegantly-wasted-human-being and all the rest of the bullshit, while Taylor melted into the rhythm section and tossed out his swampsnake leads and the legends cavorted out front.

Woody's entry into the hallowed unit dispelled a few of the shadows. His good-natured cockiness let fresh air into corridors still paced by spectres of Meredith Hunter and Brian Jones, of tales about knives and pool-cues and drowning, of Hollywood and the Riviera. Honest Ron, the human face of The Rolling Stones!

'I suppose I seem more accessible,' he says later that night. He attempts to open a bottle of beer on the edge of a table and succeeds only in tearing a giant chunk of wood out of the unoffending piece of furniture. He looks up with the expression of comic dismay with which he customarily greets his unsuccessful attempts at little public bar macho stunts. 'That's 'cos I *am* more accessible. I mean, Mick and Keith are founder members and it's all been going on for much longer for them. The pressure is much greater for them, so it's all much easier for me . . .'

Onstage, he completes his lap of honour but the cheers he garners for this display of unselfconscious cheek are as a damp fart to what happens when Keith Richards, one sinewy fist clamped around a bottle of Rebel Yell bourbon and the other hefted skywards, strides to the front of the stage, spectral but solid, wasted but not weary. Foppish no longer, his unassuming yellow shirt, black jacket and blue jeans spell out that the pomp and circumstance of The Stones have been packed up in mothballs for tonight, but that aspect of Keith Richards which exists both within and without the context of The Stones is what's important.

Stage centre, there's the three-headed mike stand that first saw service at the Kilburn Gaumont gigs that promoted Wood's first solo project 'I've Got My Own Album To Do' way back when he was still in The Faces. Immediately stage right of the mike is a music stand – most incongruous – loaded with set-lists, key lyrics, mouth-harps, slides, cigarettes, picks and the like. Woody dances out front, counts four and kicks into Chuck Berry's 'Sweet Little Rock And Roller'.

The sound is full and relaxed. It isn't pompous overblown stadium rock and it isn't razor-edged British R&B, but it has that perfect combination of ease and power, lurch and balance, that characterizes what is meant when the term 'barroom rock and roll' is used as a compliment.

Clarke and Modeliste lay down a taut, sleek backbeat that gives the guitars just enough slack for them to take chances with the rhythm, but not so much that the chances don't all pay off. Wood's guitar sound is thick and distorted, Richards' pithy and thin. Between them, they stretch the beat like elastic and then tighten it up again. MacLagan tinkles and splashes, Keyes honks like a wild goose with catarrh. It's a groove.

Listen, whatever you think of these guys and the way they live – and it's worth remembering that they've been at it so long that they genuinely don't know how to do it any other way – they didn't get where they are just by having good haircuts and hanging out with Margaret Trudeau and Truman Capote. They're capable of more than just going through the by-now traditional, choreographed, institutionalized ritual of a Stones show. Three-quarters of the way through the show – I reckon it's when Richards stumbles upfront to dip and stab his way through his first solo of the night – I decide I'd rather be seeing The New Barbarians than a Stones show just because it's fresher, looser and almost completely unpretentious.

273

Most of the material is drawn from one of three main sources: material from Wood's new album 'Gimme Some Neck' and its predecessors 'Now Look' and 'I've Got My Own Album To Do', deepdown blues like 'Rock Me' and 'Worried Life Blues' and Stones numbers. Richards and MacLagan hold down most of the backing vocals, with Richards getting a fistful of numbers of his own to sing.

For one of Richards' vocal numbers, 'Let's Go Steady', Woody dumps his guitar in favour of the tenor sax that's been his pride and joy since Christmas. 'Variety you want? Variety you get!' he announces to the audience, rubbing his hands. A present from his girlfriend Jo Howard, the sax used to belong to Plas Johnson, and Wood blows simple but precise triplets alongside Bobby Keyes as Richards delivers a strained but effective fifties gospel blues ballad vocal.

Then it's switcharound time again as a roadie brings out a pedal steel guitar and Keith ducks around behind MacLagan's piano as the diminutive mod moves to the organ for the stone-country 'Apartment 109'. The Texas kids lap it up. Sheeeeeeet! Yeee-haw!

Neither Wood nor Richards have ever been renowned for sterile perfection. The dynamic between them is always subject to the moment: when everything's clicking, they are the epitome of the swagger and stab that two meshing rock and roll guitars can muster; when the wires get crossed they sound like a fight in a scrapyard. They're having persistent tuning problems and amp buzzes anyway: the best guitars, amps and roadcrews that money can buy and they've still got problems.

Richards in particular is goofing out more than any other big-time guitar player. Even when they're laying down a 'Jumpin' Jack Flash' encore sharp enough to perform open-heart surgery with, he still slides up to a climactic chord and misses it by a good three frets. For the intro to 'Rock Me', he takes a slow 12-bar chorus by himself to introduce the riff, and he misfrets notes, strings fall off his fingers.

He does everything but drop his pick, and stares down the audience as if he's daring someone to make something of it.

On the blues numbers, Wood fishes out a mouth-harp and blows squeaky, tooling Jimmy Reed-style blowing-and-bending figures, a change from the Little Walter/Sonny Boy Williamson/

Junior Wells style favoured by most white blues harpists. It bears the same combination of diffidence and flash that marks almost everything he does.

It's the blues numbers and the funkier pieces like 'Infekshun', 'Am I Grooving You?' and 'I Can Feel The Fire' that prove the most combustible. For a start, Clarke and Modeliste get a chance to step out some and the cool, deadly ease with which they negotiate the more complex rhythms is splendidly counter-balanced by the sharp, rough, bourbon-soaked guitars. At one splendid point, Wood – dashing around the stage like a demented parrot on jetskates – ends a solo with a screaming high note so off-key that it's hardly in the same galaxy as the rest of the tune and Clarke puts his head on one side and goes 'Whew!' and Wood cracks up . . .

Gotcha!

'Am I Grooving You?' fades into Clarke's showpiece: Bootsy Collins meets Sly Stone meets Jimi Hendrix inside Phil Lynott's leather pants: 5,000 watts of skinny soul. It takes him about 90 seconds to pulp the entire audience. He picks the riff from Curtis Mayfield's 'Pusherman' in sing-song harmonics (Wood skipping out from the back, where the white boys are taking a breather sip and smoke, to double up the riff on harp to soak the hall in a breath of country blues) and then pounds his bass to a paste with dazzling speed runs and remorseless rhythm figures. He then crosses the stage to do it again, takes his ovation, grins in his beard and steps back to let Modeliste demonstrate a dozen differ-ent ways to play the same beat in the space of little over a minute and then everybody comes back refreshed.

'Contrary to what you've heard,' shouts Wood, 'there ain't no one here but us chickens. There are no special guests tonight . . . except you lot!'

The roar he gets for that demonstrates that no significant proportion of the almost-but-not-quite sold-out house could give a shit, even during The Stones numbers. 'Who The Fuck is Mick Jagger?' is the message stretched out across the girl photog's T-shirt, and even when Keith kicks-starts 'Honky Tonk Women', dragging out the chords so long you think the beat just *has* to fall apart (but it doesn't), no ghosts walk.

Purists may get disapproving and wonder if Ron Wood has the *right* to sing 'Honky Tonk Women' or 'Jumpin' Jack Flash', but hell, man, Johnny Winter and Peter Frampton both did 'Jumpin' Jack Flash' and *anyone* has more right to do 'Jumpin' Jack Flash' than Peter Frampton. Plus things start getting silly when Stones fans start getting protective about 'Love In Vain' cuz I'm *sure* they checked with Robert Johnson first . . .

The New Barbarians show is rough, warm, human, good-humoured, energetic, unassuming and strictly life-size. When you see it, you ain't staring at something gigantic and far away. It's not as spectacular and legend-soaked as a Stones show, but it has a warmth and humanity and friendliness that will never waft off a stage that has Mick Jagger on it and THE ROLLING STONES on the poster outside. Whether you still believe in the great Stones myth of The Greatest Rock And Roll Band In The World or whether you see them in the post-punk light as a bunch of poncy smacked-back old jackoffs, they can never be just a rock band playing for your pleasure and theirs. The New Barbarians can. That's the difference.

'That's partly why I'm becoming an American citizen,' explains Ronnie Wood. The show's long over, the jacks are in the boxes and the clowns should have gone to bed but they haven't: they're up in Keith's room. As 'Gimme Some Neck' blasts out of Wood's sound system and a thickset denimed lump of Texan muscle called Rob jerks around the room bellowing along with the album . . .

Wait a second. I've got to tell you about this guy.

Rob's eyes bulge behind his glasses and his face goes red. His short curly blond hair is in total disarray. Like Bobby Keyes, he went to the same school in Lubbock, Texas, as Buddy Holly, though they weren't in the same year. What makes Rob a footnote in rock and roll history is that when Buddy got snuffed, young Rob was the cat who inherited Buddy's record collection. Still got 'em at home now.

He leaps up to Wood and grabs Honest Ron's slender white hand in his own huge calloused sausage fingers and pumps along with the record, bellowing lyrics and bourbon at Woody, who is jerked in and out of his seat like a puppet. They hug. Rob lurches off on another tour of the room.

Wood shakes out a Marlboro, tosses it in the air and attempts

276

to catch it in his mouth to regain his composure. He misses completely, tries again and this time almost swallows the damn thing. He pulls it out of his mouth and lights it. Luckily, it's not too damp to burn.

'It's weird, but if I'm an American citizen I'll be able to spend more time in England. I really want to, because London's my fuckin' home, but what with the tax and all . . .'

I ask him what he thinks about Thaatchi and he winces.

'Maybe it'd be better for the country if all the prodigal sons could come back there and spread their money around and try and help out some of the people who the government won't be helping out, bring some of the money back home . . . that doesn't make much sense, does it?'

Keith Richards takes much of the New Wave's resentment of The Stones' role pretty much to heart, and seems in turn vaguely resentful of that attitude to The Stones: a kind of I-died-in-the-war-for-you-and-now-you-hate-me-you-ungrateful-jerks viewpoint. How does Woody feel?

'Well, I do feel a little hurt by it, but not as much as Keith because of his being a founder member. I'm still a bit new, so I don't maybe feel quite so isolated, but I don't know . . . maybe it's what I deserve.'

Who do you like out of the newer bands?

'It may sound corny, but I always liked The Sex Pistols,' he says, a trifle ruefully. The Pistols were the first band to take a massive swing at The Stones, but by order of the unacknowledged kinship that links all British rebel bands no matter how much Jagger and Lydon would deny it, The Stones and The Pistols are karmically related, sons rebelling against fathers.

Richards' attitude to punk is more combative, more competitive. Unlike Wood, he feels personally challenged by the whole thing. In the plane on the way back from Houston, me and Joe Stevens were sitting in the front compartment shooting the shit when up comes Richards, barefoot, white-faced, rumpled, hair spun out like black candy-floss, eyes ringed with exhaustion, one leathery fist still clamped around his bourbon. He looks me up and down, checking the threads (black suit, white shirt, black tie red sneakers, shades, short hair).

'Hello, Charles,' he says flatly, voice simultaneously dry, crisp and slurred, 'what are you going to do now that punk is dead?'

My gorge rises. It's one thing to discuss whether punk is dead when you live in Britain and check the scene, but what the hell right does Keith Richards have to say that from where he sits?

So we start in on that, and I tell him that punk didn't just mean punk bands and nihilism, it meant throwing the gates wide open for any sort of band that wanted to play and could do something that means something to kids and that it ain't just stuck in '77 but it's progressing in all sorts of directions. I start talking about The Human League and Stiff Little Fingers and Magazine, f'chrissakes.

'Ah,' he says, 'but progressing used to mean something different, didn't it? Who's that band who sound like The Doors? I hate them. Progressing used to mean Yes and Genesis and all that lot. What's Public Image about? Johnny Rotten or Lydon or whatever you call him . . . I like him, but that single's just a Byrds guitar sound, innit? And whether you like 'em or not you've got to admit that McGuinn and those guys do that better than anybody . . .'

He makes much more sense talking about blues — Buddy Guy and Junior Wells were supposed to be jamming with them in Chicago, but Buddy was driving up from New Orleans and missed the gig even though Junior got up and blew a few — and reggae.

He turns me on to radio station WLIB in New York, which serves the Caribbean expatriates among the black community and plays music from Trinidad and Jamaica and if you tune in to them you can hear Culture and Spear and Isaacs right there in the heart of Babylon. 'If a good pre is on sale in Kingston on Monday it'll be in the shops in New York on Wednesday and I'll have it Friday,' Keith announces.

'One of my proudest moments was introducing Stanley Clarke to Robbie Shakespeare and Zigaboo to Sly Dunbar backstage at Madison Square Garden.'

He unbends considerably when I tell him how important reggae is to the new bands, just like blues was to The Stones when they started. He checks Gregory Isaacs and Spear something fierce, and regards 'Money In My Pocket' as 'pretty lame as Dennis Brown records go'. He's had a pad in JA since '66, and he's been hip to reggae for well over a decade, so it ain't like the cat has no ears left or anything. It's just that I regard the scene in the UK as being exciting and valuable and I'm annoyed that he doesn't. What happens is that at different times, he and MacLagan and Wood all latch me and stare at me penetratingly as if they were asking something important and say, 'Tell me . . . whaddya think of The Police?'

Stanley Clarke is adapting to the loose-knit, high-energy music of The Barbs with *élan* and aplomb. He's well and truly turned onto reggae and he's even checked a few punk bands. 'What I like about them, I guess, is that there're so *many* of them. What music needs is musicians and the more people there are playing, the better it is.'

So how'd a man of Clarke's background get involved in this?

'Well, I'd been playing a few tours with Jeff Beck and a British drummer named Simon Phillips, and I wasn't doin' anything because Jeff has a few things to tie up before we play again. I know Ronnie real well because he'd come to see us a lot, and when he called up I figured this'd be more fun than takin' a holiday.'

Clarke doesn't feel anything incongruous about going from super-fusion music to Wood's warm, sloppy rock and roll.

'It's a looser feel and higher energy, but I ain't a *jazz* bass player. I'm a *bass* player. They're real good to play with.'

Modeliste is Wood's favourite drummer after The Great Charlie Watts, who played on every track on the album except for the single, Bob Dylan's 'Seven Days', on which Mick Fleetwood does the duties. If the album has a Stones feel to it, it's not so much Wood who provides it, though his guitar playing is well in the tradition: nor is it Richards, who only plays (and then fairly unobtrusively) on two of the tracks. It's Watts, and 'Gimme Some Neck' is another tribute to his genius as the unchallenged chairman of the board of rock and roll drummers.

Wood is explaining how he wormed the song out of Dylan when they were both down in Miami for an Eric Clapton album. 'I've always had a lot of front with Bob ever since he came to the party for my first solo album in New York. He was the first to arrive, and no one recognized him at all. He was all wrapped up and he looked greasy and he sidled up to me and said, "Heeeeeeeeeey, man, I really dig your album." [Wood's Dylan impression sounds like anybody else's Dylan impression, but at least it's authentic.]

'I just went *huh*? Since then, he's always been really nice. If I call his office, he calls me back in five minutes, like when I had to call to get the words for "Seven Days" out of him.' He giggles. 'I've got more front than Harrods, I have!'

Rob comes up and tells me that he'd rilly 'preciate it, cousin, if he could wear my red sneakers for the rest of the night. He asks my room number and says he'll have the sneakers outside my door at 8 the next morning. Unfortunately, we take the same shoe size, so we swap – after all, he's an old schoolmate of Buddy Holly's and he's built like a brick shithouse.

There goes the phone! The voice on the other end crackles even though there's no static. 'This is Keith, man,' it sez. 'C'mon up to my room. All the heavies are here and we're havin' a party. Five minutes?' It's his third call. Woody says Keith wants to be interviewed as well, which is fine, because with a bit of luck he may be loaded enough for me to ask him how he got out of Toronto.

Keith's room is a floor above Woody's. On the wall are photos of The Barbs, of Peter Tosh. A Rasta flag the size of my living-room floor and a beautiful pencil drawing of a Rasta child nestle by the Playmate Of The Month. A tape of the night's gig roars out of a huge cassette player. The place is strewn with empty bottles and loaded people. Bobby Keyes is in a bad mood and his wife is talking to him slowly and intensely. Suddenly he chucks a piece of toast at Wood as a particularly hot slide lick comes up.

'That means I played a lick he wishes *he'd* played,' explains Wood. Airily he flicks a Marlboro butt in the general direction of the potted plant in the corner. It falls a good eight inches short and starts burning a hole in the carpet. He looks ruefully about him, scuttles over, picks it up and puts it in an ashtray.

Richards is methodically turning the room upside down. He's looking for a bag of Jamaican 'erb which he has misplaced and he's gonna find it if it takes all night. He keeps rolling the sleeves of his T-shirt up over his shoulders as if the touch of the fabric is unpleasant to him. Swigging his bourbon, he rummages through yet another suitcase.

Rob comes bounding up to me, pointing angrily at my sneakers. 'These dayim thangs is hurtin' mah ankles!' he says as if I'd deliberately pulled a dirty trick on him. We change back.

Found it! Richards holds his bag of grass proudly aloft, stumbles towards the corner sofa and hauls out his skins. Rob plumps himself down right next to Richards, who looks about him as if he's only just realized where he is and then passes out, cheeks drawn, mouth open, eyes shut.

Rob helps himself to the grass and he and a bunch of gigantic cowboys (members of the Dallas Cowboys football team, as it happens) begin getting wrecked.

Grab grab grab. Richards is schlumpfed out in a corner while a bunch of people he hardly knows ring room service on his tab, smoke his dope and make free with his room. It's a while before anyone gets on the case and then Wood begins clearing out the jetsam and getting Richards revived.

He says he'll ring me if Keith is fit to talk when the room's been cleared. He doesn't, so presumably he wasn't.

Before they make *who* run?

Next morning, I'm trying to find the soul station that we heard in the cab and the sucker is *hiding*. So you make do with the regular stations and evolve a system whereby you switch channels any time they play Olivia Newton-John. There's a New Barbarians commercial which mispronounces two of the names and plays 'Seven Days' and 'Jumpin' Jack Flash' as background. When 'Jumpin' Jack Flash' was cut, Brian Jones was still alive and Ron Wood was playing bass in Jeff Beck's band.

One more channel and suddenly Jagger's voice fills the room as 'Sympathy For The Devil' spills out over Dallas . . . '*who killed the Kennedys when after all it was you and me?*'

Awwwwwwwww, *mama* . . . Texas radio and the big beat . . .

# John Cooper Clarke: Motormouth

*NME*, 7 July 1979

JOHN Cooper Clarke is telling a joke.

'There are these three fellers, see, all lined up to apply to join the Foreign Legion. The third one is the actual geezer we are concerned with on this occasion, though. Anyway the first one goes up to the recruitin' sergeant, who asks him, "Why do you want to join the Foreign Legion then?"

"'E says "I've just been 'urt in love and I can't bear to even look at another woman."

'"Oh well," says the sergeant "you certainly won't get to see a lot of women here. Go over there and collect yer ammunition."

'Then it's the second one's turn and 'e goes up to the sergeant and the sergeant asks 'im why 'e wants to join the Foreign Legion. "Well," says the second bloke, "I just fancy the idea of killin' people."

'"Well, you'll be onto a good thing 'ere," says the sergeant, "we kill quite a lot of people fairly regularly as it 'appens. Nip over there and collect yer ammunition."

'Finally, our 'ero gets 'is turn and the sergeant asks 'im what 'is motivations are for chusing this particular mode of employment an' 'e says, "I 'ate Arabs."

'"Well you're in luck then," says the sergeant, "I was just telling this other feller 'ere that we get to kill loads of geezers 'ere in the Foreign Legion an' it just so 'appens that most of 'em are Arabs. Go over there an' pick up yer ammunition."

'So they're all wawkin' through the fortress like, and suddenly this lookout up on a tower yells, "The Arabs are attacking! The Arabs are attacking!" Our 'ero swings up his gun and 'e shoots the lookout dead. The sergeant grabs our young friend by the throat an' screams, "What the bloody 'ell did you do that for?"

'So 'e looks the sergeant straight in the eye an' says, "If there's one thing I 'ate more than an Arab, it's a grasser."'

John Cooper Clarke is bounding on stage at Manchester Free Trade Hall, a cavernous building steeped in musty Victorian municipality, a room dusted with hard work and religion. It is Manchester's principal venue, a hall which has played host to the likes of 10cc and Black Sabbath and David Bowie in its time, and now the headlining attraction is a man whose job it is to stand on stages armed with nothing but a microphone, a jug of vodka and orange juice and two plastic carrier bags stuffed with notebooks and scrawled sheets of paper.

He is not a singer, though he has been known to declaim in different keys when the occasion demands it. He is not a rock musician by trade, though he has been one in the past and owns a Fender Telecaster and holds a Musicians' Union card which lists his instrument as 'drone guitar'.

He operates in a nebulous territory bounded by four corners: the points of his compass are poet, comic, musician and author. You could say he is an entertainer, and certainly none of the people filling between half and three quarters of the Free Trade Hall's seating would gainsay you. Laugh? Thought they'd wet themselves.

Hometown night! A lifetime's worth of dues and time to pay off. Tonight Johnny Clarke, local character made good and gone national, takes his nationwide tour to the biggest venue on his old turf. From the interval spots at years of folk and jazz and pub and punk gigs to the main attraction at the Free Trade Hall: success, success, success (does it matter?). There're a regiment of friends and acquaintances on the guest list and a journalist and photographer in tow to record the occasion. Three days later, a squib will appear in the rumours and speculation section of a London-based rock paper not renowned for encouraging either its staff or its readers to develop any discernible capacity for thinking in the abstract: a paragraph to the effect that the local hero returned from London to bomb on his old turf. They didn't know (or care) that Johnny Clarke still lives in Salford in a flat above a chemist's shop 'with an aroma of strange and wonderful pharmaceutical concoctions on the stairs'.

John Cooper Clarke is being asked how local tradespeople react to his newfound status as a celeb: 'Me greengrocer sells me rotten spuds. 'E thinks I can afford it.'

John Cooper Clarke is late on stage tonight in Manchester. He had arrived at the stage door in a cloud of well-wishers who had ambushed him in the streets as he stalked from where his

283

manager's car was parked outside the journalist's hotel just after the first of his two support bands had left the stage. Once ensconced in his dressing-room, attacking the vodka and picking incredulously at a display of salads and cold meats, he had discovered that a vital carrier bag full of stuff had been left in Didsbury, where his manager/producer/bass player/chaffeur Martin Hannett a.k.a. Martin Zero maintains a desirable residence. A cab was dispatched to collect and deliver the bag — how many rock gigs have been shoved onto the back burner while a fast car noses dark streets to Pick Up Something In A Bag For The Band? — while, onstage, Joy Division ram dark slabs of organized noise at the audience as a scarecrow singer moves like James Brown in hell.

Acid rock a decade or so on. It is whispered that acid enjoys considerable allegiance from a lot of the young postpunks in Manchester. As the bassist triggers a synthesizer and a skin breaks on the snare drum and the band's sound begins to resemble Awful Things carved out of smooth black marble, who could argue?

John Cooper Clarke is vibing up. He goes to the toilet a lot and returns with his hair more conscientiously erect than before. It is parted at the side like a black lace curtain to reveal an ear peering surreptitiously at the world. A tiny crucifix hangs where the coke spoon used to be. He is asked why. 'I gave up coke for Christ,' he offers. Strands of grey are beginning to appear in his hair. He has a slight cast in one eye.

John Cooper Clarke appears in a cold oval of light stage centre. The effect is comic. The stage has been built for choirs and brass bands, political meetings and rock shows, and across its vast acreage stalks a skinny streak like some elongated insect on its hind legs, carrier bags stuffed with plunder, a mutant centipede who's just looted 1966. The only non-vocal sounds to be heard are the rhythmical *splatsplatsplat* of his spearmint gum and the shuffle of his olive-green Chuck Taylor basketball shoes on the boards.

He pulls the top section of the microphone stand to the horizontal, sights along it, mows the audience with hi-octane verbiage like he owns the world's first automatic-fire blowgun. A Ramones approach to poetry. Wham bam up an' at 'em Sam! 1-2-3-4!

'Ere 'e cums naow!

'Gabardinangusatthemagazinerackviewsthasituationfrumtha-
frontothebacknawbuddyzlukinatthamanwithamacstickitraghtback-
onthastackJACK!!!'

Clarke's onstage declaiming voice resembles that of an auction-
eer with a grudge against the world and a sneer as permanently
attached as a scar. He sprays the audience with words and saliva,
revving up while he chews his gum right into the mike and runs
on the spot like the Health Fanatic himself, heart, lungs and brain
working overtime and getting paid off in adrenalin. His offstage
conversational voice is slow and muted, words rolled round mouth
and cortex, savoured for resonances and ambiguities and then
allowed to drip from his nose and run down his shirtfront.

His vowels are in an uproar. The 'e', 'a' and 'i' sounds slash like
razor-edged frisbees; the 'o' and 'u' sounds boom and reverberate
like someone yelling down a corrugated-iron tunnel. He plays his
accent like a virtuoso, moves like a shadowboxer, bopping and
dodging and weaving to avoid blows, punching with his mouth,
leading with his nose, a voice-triggered pneumatic drill buzzing
into your brain.

John Cooper Clarke is asking someone if he goes too fast on
stage. 'I s'pose I do, really, it's embarrassing to think about so I get
me 'ead down and rush. I'm used to werkin' in clubs and not in sit-
down places and you have to assume that the audience has a short
attention span. That's not to underestimate 'em or say they're
stupid 'cuz when I'm in clubs I 'ave a short attention span too . . .'

Running on the spot, ticktockticktock. Ruffle through the carrier
bag, find the notebook, hit the vodka and give us another one just
like the other one, do. He has three repertoires which overlap
briefly: a stage repertoire, a studio repertoire and a load of other
stuff: crime novels, a semi-fictional autobiography entitled *Ten
Years in an Open-Neck Shirt* which is slated for publication
sometime soon. The stage repertoire is hi-impact, rhythmical,
packed with dense twisting internal rhymes, compressed, compact
imagery, elbows to the rib, kicks to ankle. Satire, scatology,
painless social critique, honed and polished.

John Cooper Clarke is living on his wit.

'ToofattafucksorryboutthatgottaSCROtumwiyeredwitha-
THUUUURMO-STAT . . .'

Nonstop. Rapido rapido. Don't let 'em get bored ferchrissake. Poems, jokes and banter jostle like compartments on an InterCity 125; epigrams and sardonic couplets, metaphors juxtaposed like sleeping partners in an arranged marriage flash by like telegraph poles, two images together make a third thing, bigger and different.

Detractors claim it's doggerel ('his imagery is terribly gauche, darling, and what he's doing is *so* old-fashioned') or accuse him of being an intellectual Jasper Carrott or – worst of all – of *not being rock and roll*. Ask him if *he* thinks it's rock and roll and he laughs helplessly and says no.

John Cooper Clarke is being asked to define rock and roll and his relationship to same.

'Electric guitars, bass and drums ... not too much goin' on across the beat. My relationship with rock and roll is like Lenny Bruce's with modern jazz – I like the clothes and attitude.' He remembers groups in which he used to perform, operating guitar rather than microphone, but writing the words, one in which 'we had two riffs: Bo Diddley an '''Igh 'Eel Sneakers''. We could do 'em at two speeds, fast an' slow, which gave us four options.'

He recalls The Vendettas: 'Me cousin Sid was the singer, because they told me I sounded too nasal. Sid 'ad a sort of raspy quality to 'is voice, an' 'e sounded somewhat redolent of 'Owlin' Wolf. Nowadays everybody's got an electric guitar – people have bloody guitars cummin' outer their ears – but then there weren't that many people playin'. The lead guitarist got engaged an' I was stuck with all these lyrics ...'

Clarke vaguely recalls that there was one 'about a man who sold 'ats', but none survive to the present day. He is deliberately vague about dates, and particularly vague about the age of some of his material. Gabby Mancunians recall him performing some of his current stuff several years ago, but ask him when The Vendettas were performing and he'll just say, 'the sixties'. Push him a bit and he elucidates: 'the late sixties'.

So whatchareckon to the Rock Biz then John?

Shrugs. 'Water off a duck's back, reely.'

But it is your new home now, innit?

'I 'aven't moved in yet. I been round to put up some wallpaper, but I 'aven't moved in.'

There's methedrine his madness. John Cooper Clarke is cranked up really high as he slams through 'Twat', a stream of sustained invective and distilled hate. The effect is somewhat akin to having someone piss on your shoes for five minutes. 'Lahk a dose of scayybiz ai've got yewoondermaskin/yew maike lahfa feeehrytail GRI-IH-IH-IH-IMMM!' He attacks as only the defenceless can: the only craft more vulnerable is that of the improvising comedian and Clarke knows it, which is why he eschews onstage improvisation.

'Y'mean like stream-of-consciousness . . . or unconsciousness? Naw, it could turn out to be reely borin'. I'd rather werk on the stuff at 'ome. Besides, if you improvise in public you tend to reveal a lot, and I'm not particularly fond of barin' me soul.'

Why not?

'Well, I read rather too much Mickey Spillane.'

Squelchsquelchsquelch goes the gum.

'Lakadeathattaburthdehpahty/yewspoilahhhlthafuun/ lakesuukdanspattouttsmaaaaaatieyou'renawyuset'ennywun . . .

Still, Clarke's got one in the book that has 'Twat' beat all hollow for sheer vituperative power. Like John Lydon, Elvis Costello, Bob Geldof and many others both more and less eminent in and out of rock, JCC is a sufferer from what we doctors generally refer to as A Catholic Education, and 'Limbo', which can be found on the 'Walking Back To Happiness' live album, is the case history.

'The school was run by nuns. The 'ead one was about ninety. She used to wear these black Wulewerth's plimsolls and you'd only 'ear 'er cummin' because she 'ad this pair 'a scissors on a long string tied round 'er waist . . . to break the embarrassin' silences. You'd 'ear this terrifyin' scraaaapin' sound an' you'd knaw she was sumwhere nearby. We never found out what she used them for.

'Me dad was in the Communist Paaty. I went to that school at the insistence of 'is sisters – I blame it all on me antie, actually. I was like 'is 'ostage to 'eaven: lemme in or the kid gets it.'

So it was Catholicism at school and Communism at home?

'Naw, not reely. 'E didn't push it nearly as 'ard as they did.'

John Cooper Clarke is knackered. He's in the living-room of Hannett Towers in Didsbury, slumped out by the gas fire in a room painted like a block of Neapolitan ice-cream and filled with records, tapes, electronic gear and well-worn furniture. Martin 'Zero' Hannett is playing through a Phil Spector tape and Clarke is musing sleepily on his need to change his name on account of the 'John Cooper Clarke' moniker having been already nailed down by an already registered member of Equity.

'What's this other John Cooper Clarke like? I dunno. I 'aven't checked him out yet. I could change me name to TV Lounge, reckon, or Richie Valence. Can you 'ave dead people? Buddy 'Olly, Winston Churchill . . .'

The JCC tour of the UK doesn't exactly carry that marauding-army-of-rock-and-roll-gypsies-come-for-your-daughters-and-your-money vibe. It's more a three-people-in-an-estate-car sortathingy: Clarke, Hannett and the latter's girlfriend Sue. Hannett wears Oxfam-shop, post-punk threads, shades, no socks and long curly Ian Hunter hair. He describes his multifarious functions by pointing to his spindly ward and announcing 'I'm his mother'. He vibes with Clarke, fights a losing battle against the Punk Poet's peerless propensity for Losing Things (those precious carrier bags, for example, and the olive-green sneakers that went AWOL the following night in Newcastle, never to return). Hannett supervises the wordslinger's career progress, writes, arranges and produces all his music, plays the bass in The Invisible Girls, Clarke's studio band, which is slowly evolving into a stage band for future use. He also makes toast: the power behind the throne.

He's even diversified by producing legendary fun people Magazine for their next single. His conversations with Clarke are cryptic, semi-coded-semi-clear and hilarious to the participants. Clarke shacks on Hannett's couch when – for any reason – he can't make it back to the flat over the chemist's in Salford. But Hannett is El Zonko – almost – as he occupies the couch for easy access to the tape deck. That leaves the cushions for Clarke. The shades are off and the slur is more pronounced. He begins to doze off, mumbles in his sleep, then wakes himself up.

His albums haven't been released in the States, but they might be. CBS's New York office is manifestly confused by the product they keep getting from London, as was aptly demonstrated by the sizzling acumen with which they assessed the first Clash album. Still, come hell or high water, America is getting the JCC experience, maybe in August.

'I'd like to do New York solo,' Clarke murmurs, 'I believe a

meaningful tour of key laundrettes is bein' seeriously mooooted.'
He pronounces it 'muted' and the ambiguity is pleasing. On first
hearing of 'I Wanna Be Nice' from the 'Disguise In Love' album,
it was difficult for southern-jessie ears to discern whether Clarke
was saying 'Better look elsewhere' or 'better luck elsewhere' until,
by a process of rigorous analysis, it was determined that if it had
been the former it would have come out as 'better luke elsewhere'.
Ambiguities of Pinteresque proportions abound.

A discussion had been taking place in which Clarke had opined
that he felt more sympathy for Carl Jung than Sigmund Freud
(two singer-songwriters currently signed respectively to Warners
and Arista) because 'I'd rather not believe that everything can be
reduced to sex', when it was idly raised that a considerable
amount of Pinter's dialogue resembled the recorded conversations
of chronic schizophrenics.

Clarke is a devotee of Pinter's work, and quotes from it
extensively. (He also has large chunks of the work of Damon
Runyon committed to memory, and Runyon's prose sounds extraordinarily comfortable when rendered in Clarke's lugubrious,
sardonic Salford tones.) He begins to enthuse about Pinter's *No
Man's Land.*

'It's basically about this poet called Spune who finds 'is way
into this rich old geezer's 'ouse. This rich old geezer's got these
two incredibly sinister bodyguards, real psychos in their way.
This geezer was the last person you'd expect to 'ave two psycho
bodyguards: 'e was all doddery with a horrible propensity for
fallin' over. Everybody's drinkin' all the time. Then this geezer
called Foster, who's the more sinister of the two bodyguards
because 'e's more affable, comes in an' 'e says, "Pheeeeeeew,
what a day. Taxi drivers 'ate me. They 'ate me. What you
drinkin'?"'

'Then Spune tells Foster about this paintin' which he was goin'
to do but 'ad never got around to actually doin' an' 'e says, "I was
sat outside this cafe by this river where a man 'ad caught a fish.
Three children were lookin' at the fish talkin' among themselves
about what kind of a fish it was. A travellin' salesman walks in
and there's a guy leanin' against the bar whistlin'. I was goin' to
call it 'The Whistler'. Would you 'ave understood why I'd've
called it 'The Whistler'?"'

'Andy Foster says, "Well I may not have understood it, but I would've been grateful for it. A good work of art tends to move me. I'm not a prat, y'know." You should read that. You can read it in an hour, and then you'll read it again and again. I try and see as much of his stuff as I can, especially on TV. It adapts so well to TV. His basic premise – well not 'is *basic* premise, but one of 'em – is that every sentence has at least twenty-four meanings. Any sentence that anyone can write can immediately be taken in any one of twenty-four ways.

'It's a very sound approach. All 'is plays have dead realistic dialogue where sumbody says sumthing and the other person isn't listening properly or doesn't hear it right and comes back with a really incongruous answer, and so on.'

Ever written any plays yourself?

'No, but I'd like to.'

Any acting?

'No, but there's only one sort of part I could play. I'd always be typecast.' He pauses a beat, awaits the raised eyebrow, and when it comes, he smirks and drawls, 'Juuuuuuveniles.'

Up onstage at the Free Trade Hall, Clarke's breath comes in short pants and then goes home to change.

'AhcantogbakterSALfordthacoppersgotmemaaaaaaktenterthadaraaaaagonanexitJohnnyClaaakeTA!' and he's off, carrier bags in one hand, glass in the other, slipping and sliding on the polished boards. The Amazing Talking Man! He's mowed 'em down, kept them 'angin' on 'is every WERDlike for overanower, made 'em laugh, made 'em think (maybe), hit 'em in sore spots, tickled 'em in sensitive ones. For his first encore, he gives them 'Beasley Street', a massive epic delivered at dead march pace, bleak, grim and evocative, not entirely devoid of humour but definitely short on the cheap, easy laughs that he's been accused of perpetually seeking, not revved-up cranked-high heads-down entertainment but an inkling of what lies behind the jokey façade, a taste of the kind of material that Clarke had kept up his sleeve while doling out the tasty *hors d'œuvres* that cinched the rep.

And he has 'em. Cold. It's the payoff for all the failures, all the brush-offs, all the dismissals, all the years as a printer's assistant or a night watchman or an assistant to a man whose job it was to photograph wounds for an insurance company, all the years on the Nat King Cole, all the times he's dodged bottles and glasses and veg and other sundry missiles or been booed and roared off stages . . .

When did people stop throwing things at you, John?

'When I started getting in't music press. That should give you some sort of idea of your readership! I did Glasgow Apollo with Be Bop De Luxe . . . it's the biggest venue on the circuit int it. Glasgow Apollo, It 'olds 3,800 people and *they all hated me*. They all started to shout the moment I came on. I didn't get a *werd* out. They got a fifty-foot-'igh stage so you got more in common with the people in the balcony than the wuns in the stalls. I just stood there for about four minutes and looked at them. Imagine that: 4,000 people all loathing me at once. It was one of the most muving experiences of my life. I was muved very efficiently. I just said, "Let's call it a draw." I come in by the frunt daw an' went straight out by the back.

'I'd give anything to be able to relive that.'

John Cooper Clarke is asking a question.

'This is a thing I always ask people: if you 'ad to make luve to an animal, what would it be? Something out of the human realm of existence. Not larger than an elephant and not smaller than a guinea-pig. As sensuous or as ridiculous as you like, though I reckon that people who would do it with a guinea-pig are basically very sadistic people.

'Pandas eat a lot of fruit, and they'd be extremely comfortable . . . if you *'ad* to, but in my more *dynamic* mudes I would like to fook a giyant sea bird that upon climax would drop me into a placid ocean where I would be immediately digested by a huge translucent fish and then deposited upon a desert island paradise . . . unscathed.

'A surprising number of people get very flustered and refuse to answer this question at *all*.'

What method of psychological analysis does Clarke use to codify and interpret the answers he does get?

'Well, it's really pretty basic. Anyone who'd fook a guinea-pig is definitely not to be trusted.'

John Cooper Clarke is asleep now, head thrown back to the ceiling. Random images are floating up from his brain, a brain crammed with Pinter and Lou Reed and Dylan and Magritte and *Coronation Street* and Burroughs and Warhol and Runyon and

Italian futurist poets and Man Ray and Spillane and uncounted hordes of made-for-TV horror films and Chandler and Len Deighton and Brion Gysin: all the stuff that boils up like bubbles of marsh gas from the plastic carrier bag full of diamonds and trash that does duty as his cerebral cortex, the source point for the automatic writing with which he's currently experimenting.

Head thrown back like the corpse he'd like to play in movies, a series of cameo roles in which he floats face down in rivers, falls off balconies and tumbles out of closets at detectives' feet, always billed 'and featuring John Cooper Clarke as himself' ... he's sprawledoutflatonnisbackJACK!

But the motormouth keeps on going, far below the discernibility threshold. He regains consciousness long enough to retail an anecdote about someone who always speaks French in his sleep before he's away again, curled up by the gas fire.

Hush, hush, whisper who dares. John Cooper Clarke is saying his prayers.

## Ian Dury And The Blockheads: Hammersmith Odeon

*NME*, 18 August 1979

'GOOD evening! I'm from Essex ...'

Hammersmith Odeon is soft and warm, awash with beer and love. The Ianduryandtheblockheads Experience is well under way: funk, farts and folk wisdom. Across the stage the ensemble are strung out in a wavy line playing plasticated pinball music, rocking and bouncing like champs.

Davey Payne looks like a punk Dr Who and sounds like a flock of enraged geese. Mickey Gallagher sits inside his suit and goes *wheeooop wheeooop*. Chaz Jankel keeps his hat on his head and his cards close to his chest. Charley Charles puts the fear of God into his drums and makes sure that whatever it was they did to offend him, they certainly won't do it again. Norman Watt-Roy resembles Mick Jones with jaundice and makes his bass go *boing*; and John Turnbull looks normal and demonstrates without the faintest shadow of a doubt his unalienable right to own so many guitars.

Add up the figures in the left-hand column and the digital readout says that describing The Blockheads' music as 'compulsively danceable' would be only slightly less inane than complaining about the shortage of good pubs in the Gobi Desert.

In other words: a wonderful band (in case you couldn't tell).

From the one-two Sucker-punch curtain raiser of 'Wake Up' and 'Clever Trevor' through to 'Lullaby For Franci/es' and the band walking off a houselit stage while Andy Dunkley spins a biscuit and gives the congregation their marching orders, the Ianduryandtheblockheads show was as cuddly and heartwarming an experience as any reasonable person could demand for their ackers.

And that was the bloody trouble!

Since 'New Boots And Panties' became 'the working man's "Tubular Bells"', Ian Dury has been adopted as some sort of mascot, as treasured and beloved an emblem as a battered teddy bear with a ripped ear and scorch marks on its fur. Qualities for which Ian Dury is loved: all-round strike-a-light chirpiness, acute observation, assimilation of the common parlance (which, of course, lays him open to all the boring old gags about who's-more-working-class-than-who-then), his deft wit and sleight-of-word, his beery anthems, his winning streak of danceable fluff singles, his warmth, his compassion, his excellent band!

So his shows are comfy and furry, all hands-knees-and-whoops-daisy and jolly good fun, and it's a telling demonstration of the way audiences take what they want from bands and leave the rest at the side of the plate. In a way, it parallels the way that the harsh urgency exhibited by The Boomtown Rats when they were dodging hails of sputum in crappy clubs gradually got eroded as the records sold and they became stars. On Dury's first major outing in his current incarnation back in Live Stiffs days, his show was riveting because it balanced the cheerful and the macabre, the sweet and the savage, the darkness and the light. Dury was a genuinely awe-inspiring figure, a victim taking his revenge, a vision of terror as well as delight. In terms of sheer emotional power and impact, he took on Elvis and The Attractions and beat them hands down.

The success he received was nothing less than his due. For his courage and his humour and his wit and his acuity, he was duly rewarded and recognized. No problem!

But now Ian Dury is a family entertainer. A *great* family entertainer beyond a shadow of a doubt (I ain't knockin', y'understand), but a family entertainer none the less, putting on a show where everything is flattened down in one dimension: that of bawdy warmth and cosy sentimentality.

The balancing factor of darkness and terror is all but gone as even songs like 'Plaistow Patricia' and 'Blockheads' itself (key example, that) have become cuddlycosynice by dint of sheer familiarity and repetition. As has most of Dury's show.

Keen amateur environmental semanticists will have clocked the most. Apart from the evergreen and utterly wonderful 'Sweet Gene Vincent', the most authentically affecting moments in the show were the darkest.

First there was 'Waiting For Your Taxi', an insidiously chilling exercise in mounting menace wherein Dury is impaled like a broken moth at the centre of rapiers of light beamed from all corners of the stage, a horrific allusion to the Union Jack for which kudos are due to the fighting chaps. Why won't the taxi come? What are the consequences of its non-arrival? Is it, in fact, a taxi at all? Why are you staring at me like that?

And the real *tour de force* comes with 'Dance Of The Screamers', far and away the most magnificent Dury opus thus far.

Here his compassion blends with anger rather than sentimentality, and rather than congratulating his audience, he reminds them that just because they've taken one victim to their hearts doesn't mean they're entitled to pat themselves on the back for the rest of their lives, because this society is full of people going under for lack of love and support.

Here, for once, Dury doesn't just twang your heartstrings with a chuckle and a grimace, he hangs a sixteen-ton weight off 'em and then fires it out of a cannon.

However, the echoes of this harrowing moment are swiftly dissipated by a return to jollity and the *de rigueur* volley of Oy-Oy! call-and-response routines.

There is a massive audience for the type of stylized music-hall funk he can churn out with seeming effortlessness and he can stick with that for as long as he wants and people will sentimentalize him and love him and all will be tickety-boo. Alternatively, he can take a step back and delve into the darkness which is the true source of his power and bring sweetness and light back from that.

Both asthetically and commercially, the latter option is the tough one. Songs as heavy as 'Dance Of The Screamers' are hellishly hard to write (involving as they do no little psychic strain) and equally hard to take if you're just out for beery bawdry, but they're the ones that count.

I think it's time Ian Dury started shaking up his audiences again.

# Boomtown Rats: The Rat who would walk on water

*NME*, 20 October 1979

AUTUMN: a light drizzle is falling on Edinburgh. It lacks forty minutes of midnight and most good citizens are abed.

A few of the populace wander through the dampness, languidly travelling from here to there. On Princes Street, a knot of noisy young men search for a taxi, periodically collaring passers-by and interrogating them as to the whereabouts of an establishment known as the Astoria Club, where at this very moment Wilko Johnson's Solid Senders are filling a room with harsh incantatory R&B voodoo.

The tallest of the party is getting spiritually prepared for the midnight chimes which will unofficially announce the commencement of the twenty-seventh anniversary of his birth. He has, however, soundchecked his birthday by erroneously announcing it twenty-four hours prematurely, thus ensuring two nights' worth of free drinks, and only a phone conversation with his girlfriend in London has brought this mistake to light.

Fuelled on Pina Colada and a plate of spaghetti and insulated against the damp in a garment which could only be described as a windcheater, he perceives another potential source of vital information, approaches him with a gait halfway between a shamble and a lope, asks the way to the club.

And – just like a B movie – the light hits the shambler from the darkness full in the face, and his victim turns round, checks the thick hair, the face slightly too loose for the skull, the lanky frame, the pyjamas under his closest companion's trench-coat . . . and his mind's in sync like clockwork and he gestures down the road with his thumb and says in the most perfectly pinched and pawky Edinburgh voice that any film-maker could possibly want:

'Ah doan leike yer reicuds tha' much, but the club's doon theire.'

Sha lala lala lala la la. Happy birthday, Boomtown Bob!

Fact: any way you want to slice it, pal, The Boomtown Rats are probably the biggest group in the UK right now. Normally, statistics relating to mass consumer spending are only fit to line your lunchbox. By now, most people who follow these things have long lost count of the number of movies that are supposedly the greatest success in the history of the commercial cinema, and the number of recording artists who have been touted as the biggest, fastest sellers of all time is probably astronomical. As ever, the Americans are the worst offenders in this respect: who can be bothered to whip out the calculators and work out whether The Bee Gees or Boston or Frampton or Fleetwood Mac or The Knack or whoever had the most impressive sales figures?

It's the silliest spin-off rock and roll brag-match of all: my sales are bigger than your sales! Worse, it encourages people to hero-worship execs and accountants as well as players. If the imaginary guitar was this much of a blight, are we ready for the imaginary calculator?

So there are three kinds of falsehoods: lies, damn lies and statistics and we're hip to all that, but that still leaves us with the fact that The Rats have had two number ones on the trot, that their tour sold a quarter of a million tickets nationwide in one day (work it out: that's an average of 10,416,666 tickets an hour. See what I mean about statistics?) Their last single did Ireland's national drink honour by nudging 'Mull Of Kintyre' out of the *Guinness Book of Records*, and as Bob Geldof took great pleasure in informing Paul McCartney, 'We didn't need fokkin' bagpipes to do it with, neither.'

The Rats' third album, 'The Fine Art Of Surfacing', comes out in a week or two, and will probably bring more statistics in its wake. Maybe *Sun* readers prefer Abba and Wings; maybe *NME* readers ballot in The Clash as the main squeeze, but until it's wrestled out on a formal basis with some long-term institution from the days of The Rats' sixties youth, it comes back to our Fact: The Boomtown Rats are currently in charge.

Go see The Rats and you find yourself without landmarks. Anyone accustomed to consuming music tribally will be astonishingly confused, because there's no clear-cut grouping at all, no neat punks/mods/skins/dreads/metazoids polarization. Outside Newcastle City Hall, the girls wait patiently to leap on Bob Geldof or Johnny Fingers in that no-man's land between door and coach. Inside you find everyone from the tough, crusted punk diehards with the zips and the clips and the chains and the Sid slogans whitewashed onto the back of the Lewis Leather right through the pop kids and the older hey-we-know-about-music crew ... and grannies, and people who've never seen a rock show before in their lives.

'Some of them,' Geldof is explaining somewhere, in a hotel room or in a taxi or a coach or a restaurant or on the street, anywhere people talk, 'have never been to any kind of gig in their *lives*, man. I had this theory and one night I thought I'd check it out so I asked, "Hey, don't be shy now, who's never been to a concert before?" and quite a few put their hands up. They'd seen us on TV, and come along to see *Top of the Pops* live . . .'

ACCESS ALL AREAS is what it says on Bob Geldof's backstage pass, and thus far in the game he's well on the way to achieving just exactly that thing in terms of – what's that charming expression – *market penetration*. All across the board, The Boomtown Rats are the pick to click. First New Wave band on the playlist. First New Wave band on *Top of the Pops*. First New Wave band with a unilateral number one single ('God Save The Queen' didn't top *all* the charts).

Whether you regard those as achievements or evidence of selling out and/or terminal blandness decides which side of The Rats' fence you're on.

It also says that whether you attribute The Rats' success to cunning, manipulation, exploitation and marketing or to suss, energy, instinct and equal dollops of raw talent and sheer brass neck is ultimately immaterial. What it comes down to is Bob Geldof and Paula Yates making the front page of the *Evening Standard* just for showing up at the *Quadrophenia* premier, or Geldof getting a round of applause in Newcastle just for taking his jacket off, or Geldof's slow leer and fast mouth front and centre on a TV screen, or yet another smash single that artfully bestrides inspiration and scam, or Johnnie Fingers signing his seventeenth autograph of the day before he's even properly awake . . .

What it comes down to is TOP BAND. The Clash have the guns, but The Rats have the numbers.

And once you step out of the immediate environment of the band and their followers, a world in which cute eerie Johnny Fingers, shy shaded Gerry Cott, bouncy little Pete Briquette, rough red-eyed Garry Roberts and sensible immaculate Simon Crowe all carry their weight, play their part and make up irreplaceable portions of the whole Boomtown Rats thing, once you get into the outside worlds where television is real . . . then the man with the numbers is Bob Geldof.

'Obviously to a large extent people consider it to be a one-man affair, which it really isn't,' Geldof is saying. He is sprawled out on a hotel bed contemplating a melting glass of Bacardi and coke. He has three more hours of being twenty-six left to go.

'I could pull out endless examples . . . I'm the most garrulous. I represent and articulate a lot of what they believe. I might say something and Garry or Gerry might not agree and we'll argue over it and in that sense I would not presume to speak for them, but in a larger sense the sentiments are the same. They'll argue with you in pretty much the same way that I would argue with you. We were friends before the band because we shared common interests and when you've shared a friendship for a long time you share ideas. I just did the talking because I was the most gregarious and garrulous and had the habit of talking in one-liners like the person sitting opposite me . . .'

CUT AWAY: Geldof in a hotel lobby recounting the tale of the time that – in jocular mood – he regaled the audience at the New York Palladium to a comparison between the creative powers of Bruce Springsteen and The Rats which found little favour on 2nd Avenue. 'When we said that thing about Springsteen . . .'

Gerry Cott, sitting opposite Geldof, raises his eyebrows sufficiently for them to be visible above his shades. He waggles them slowly and deliberately. '"When *we* said that", Bob? Did Pete and I say that?'

*

298

CUT BACK: 'It wasn't something that we considered or developed. To a certain extent it was foisted on me because once I started mouthing off about all and sundry people kept wanting more interviews with me as opposed to interviews with Fingers, say. They consider that they are far more likely to get something which is good copy from me than from Garry or Gerry or Pete or Simon, which isn't necessarily the case . . .'

CUT AWAY: Garry Roberts out to lunch, jammed into a hotel room which — support band blues — houses all of Protex, the Belfast band who're supporting The Rats on tour. Also present are Briquette, Fingers, Cott and lots of tapes and whisky. As Ian Hunter bawls out his deep concern about something or other over howling Ronson guitar and a drum sound that would make Phil Spector blow up his mixing desk, Roberts intones: 'I don't give a fuck whether I get my name in the papers as long as it's spelled right.'

JUMP: a rainy afternoon in Newcastle. On the second day of a two-day stand at Newcastle City Hall, The Rats are splitting up to undertake specific, pre-gig responsibilities. Fingers, Briquette, Cott, Roberts, Crowe, guest saxophonist Dave McHale and the crew pile into the coach and head for the soundcheck while Geldof goes up to his room to get changed and watch *Star Trek* while waiting to go to the BBC's Newcastle studios to do a quick interview. He wears grey-blue baggy jeans, an old grey windcheater, a late-model Rats T-shirt and a red bandana and as the camera focuses in on him for the trailer, the media effect is readily apparent.

Science! Geldof's hair, skin and clothes take on brighter and more interesting hues as the engineers adjust the colour. Even without TV make-up, Geldof takes on a slight glow. While they do the 'laterionintheprogramme-we'll-be-talking-to' bit, he ruffles his hair, grins, sulks and then comes back down to wait for the interview proper and have a quick drink. He tells the TV guys about the rise of the independent labels, retails a scabrous, surreal anecdote about a night spent in Zurich in the company of H.R. Giger, the artist who designed *Alien*, fields their earnest what's-the-answer-then-Bob probes with firm politeness, tells a couple of jokes, climbs the stairs again to do the real thing, dances through it without raising a sweat, charms everybody stupid and cabs it to the gig in time to eat spaghetti backstage with the crew and the rest of the band.

'He's a genius!' enthuses a soldier on the train whose other faves include Ritchie Blackmore and Derrick Harriott. 'Magic!' says the cab-driver, who doesn't buy records any more but listens to what his niece brings round. 'Oh, he's so big-headed,' says Shelley, a lean lively blonde girl who sings with a Newcastle punk band called Screaming Targets. Bob Geldof is called upon to have an opinion about everything, and just about everyone with more than a passing interest in today's vital, bouncy, alive pop scene has an opinion about Bob Geldof.

Talk to insiders with grudges and you hear that Geldof has OD'd on media, that he's gone Hollywood and is now completely unbearable, that he's planning to dump The Rats and go solo . . . well, if I'm any judge of anything at all then all that is nothing but fifty-seven varieties of bullshit. Bob Geldof is no more unbearable than he was two years ago, which means that he's still the same rapid, forceful, generous, ruthless, amusing, infuriating parcel of contrariness, charm and ego that he was a year and a half ago. He's wiser and warier now, a lot more skilled and a lot more paranoid, but . . . anyone who thought he was an asshole or a charlatan back then will undoubtedly consider themselves vindicated. Anyone who got on with him and instinctively liked him then (and I'm *that* soldier) will have found no reason to modify that judgement.

So is he the same as when he began?

'What we were talking about earlier – the ACCESS ALL AREAS aspect of the dream – I still want that. In those countries where we haven't done it I still feel this . . . *need* . . . to do it as I did here at the beginning. I feel driven to maintain what we've got, and I still feel a keen sense of competition. Everything to me is potential competition and must be viewed in that light.

'I don't know if I have any more ambitions, but I have a lot of dreams. Ambitions are things you'll probably attain; a dream is something that you hope you'll attain. An ambition is more readily definable than a dream, a dream has a nebulous quality. If your ambition is to get to number one, when you get there you've achieved that ambition. I don't think the dream that I had at the beginning has been attained, but a lot of the ambitions have been.'

How much of what's happened for The Boomtown Rats has been the way you thought it would be?

'All of it, and I wouldn't change any of it. In retrospect, I was very much aware of what I was going into, probably because of having worked on the papers. I'm certainly not disappointed. It's all turned out just as brilliant and as wonderfully exciting and as challenging as I hoped it would be. I'm coming out the other side a little dented and a little depressed about various things occasionally . . .'

CUT AWAY: rust never sleeps and neither do telephones. Geldof had heard on the wire – London calling – that The Rats' reviews had been a trifle uncomplimentary, but a slap in *Sounds* perused before the Newcastle gig had led to nothing more than Geldof mock-ordering the band, light and sound men 'More cock-ups tonight, please. We're too slick. Let's have duff sound, duff lights, naffo playing and street credibility.' However, the following day en route to Edinburgh, an *NME* had materialized on the coach and he read it over my shoulder, looking alternately at it and away like a kid at a horror movie.

He looks up then and catches sight of the headline on last week's *Live!* review. '*When you get rich and famous you can afford to shit on the fans,*' it says. Even without looking around I know he's seen it, because a barrier slams down and the chatty, playful, argumentative Geldof I'd been sitting beside is transformed into a deflated, wounded creature I'd never seen before. He wraps the hurt round him like a blanket, solidifies it into a cave. He draws his legs up until his knees are at chin level, then clasps his head in his hands. Half to me, half to himself, half out of the window, he hisses: 'When . . . will . . . I . . . learn . . . to . . . keep . . . my . . . fucking . . . mouth . . . shut? WHEN? Ahhhhhh, Jazus . . .'

He turns to me, maybe seeing me, maybe not. 'It was a *joke*, man. I said it like . . .' He switches into a ludicrous American radio voice, the phoniest voice imaginable.

'"Heeeeeey! When you get to be rich and famous you can afford to shit on your audience!" It's an old Steve Martin joke . . .'

Steve Martin is a person of the comedian persuasion who is considered amusing by Americans and persons who have spent much time in the land of the dollar.

'No one could possibly think that even for one second I could have . . . when will I fucking learn, man!' A bleak vista opens up before him: a year, two or three years maybe, of having to explain away that quote, a one-off joke delivered in what he felt was the most blatantly obvious manner. He appears near tears. I feel like The Compleat Schmuck.

Look. Geldof is my friend — I hope he is, anyway — and when a person you consider to be a friend is in distress or pain and depression, then your instinct should be to steam in and offer what crumbs of consolation you can: aid, comfort, whatever. Right now, I'm the enemy. Whatever has been done to Geldof has been done by me and mine. Under those circumstances, comfort is an insult.

The silence is horrible. All the palling around of the morning and the night before seems a ghastly joke. Fingers spots his frontman's distress and aims the coldest of gazes. It is nearly twenty minutes before Geldof speaks again. At this point, no formal interview material has been taped and the whole thing begins to look doubtful. 'You'll have to bear with me,' Bob says flatly. He gazes pointedly out of the window.

Later, Geldof pulls me aside and asks me to forget his little outburst. 'It's like Jimmy Pursey on a bad day,' he murmurs, a trifle embarrassed. Lots of people feel that Geldof is an arrogant, self-important clown whom they'd like to see taken down a peg or two. I have, and I never want to see that again.

CUT BACK: '. . . a little neurotic, more neurotic than I was before. It's all so public when you achieve those ambitions and you've got so much to live up to constantly; that's the only pressure that I could really do without. But then again it's healthy . . . I suppose.'

Earlier on during the coach ride, once Geldof had regained his equanimity, he'd explained that the reason that he'd blitzed the media, gone on every TV show that would have him, talked to every paper that was interested, was that he wanted to avoid the growth of any mystique, to allow familiarity to breed . . . not contempt, of course, but safety. A state whereby people could be as familiar with him as they were with their friends, whereby Bob Geldof would be no big deal, whereby he would be believed when he said something he meant, indulged if he got silly, understood if he took the piss.

On tape, the same topic: 'A lot of people won't accept the demystification theory. They'll think it's bollocks, but believe it or don't believe it, that's what I thought would happen. People must be so sick of seeing me by now on TV or reading about me or just constantly being exposed to me. I thought that after a certain point it just appears normal that there is this kind of growing media stature, but after that point it works against itself. I can walk through Clapham and people just go, "'Ello Bob". If you don't ponce about in limos ... I don't make a point of walking through the fokkin' West End, but if I have to get to the Marquee I'll take the tube and walk. There are no riots in the street, but people come up and ask for autographs – and I wanted that accessibility, so that people wouldn't be afraid to come up and chat. I thought that was healthy.

'It wasn't any big crusade, any great plan to demystify as such, I just never saw any necessity to become a Rod Stewart or a Rolling Stone or a Beatle. The Beatles probably couldn't go out on the street without being seriously mobbed, but I figured that if I shot my mouth off constantly people would get tired of seeing me . . .'

Yeah, but if that backfired they could also stop coming to Rats gigs.

'That's a risk you have to take. They kept telling me I was getting overexposed, that it was too easy to get to me.' He lapses into the American Bullshit Voice. 'Hey! Don't go down to the radio stations, don't go down to the TV stations. Create some mystery, Bob . . .'

After the Newcastle gig, The Rats put in an hour talking to fans, and two more hours with any fans who make it back to the hotel, though they sneak away from the bar for an hour to consume coffee, sandwiches and sixties poprocksoul hits from the jukebox. Gerry Cott, the shyest Rat, is desolated because his main stage guitar, a custom-built Aria, has been ripped off from the dressing-room.

Cott is, perhaps, the perfect antithesis to Geldof. Where Bob will stick his hand out and introduce himself to anybody in the room whom he wants to meet, Cott is almost painfully restrained with strangers. The last time he conquered his inhibitions was in Liverpool, when The Slits were playing Erics, and Cott rushed straight round to see them after The Rats had finished their own gig. Finding that he'd enjoyed what he'd seen, he'd gone backstage to offer his congratulations and got cut dead by Ari for his pains. After all, The Slits are Artists and they couldn't compromise their fabled integrity by hobnobbing with one of those pushy paddies from *Top of the Pops* come down to patronize them.

Thus it was when Bob was celebrating his birthday at the Astoria in Edinburgh, Gerry hung back in the bar rather than come down to Wilko's dressing-room with Geldof and Briquette. Cott had idolized Wilko since The Rats started in Dublin as Feelgoods copyists, and it wasn't until a wild-eyed Wilko arrived at The Rats' hotel demanding bitter lemons and company that Cott got himself introduced and was happy at last, as happy as he is playing his guitar in front of the giant electronic backdrop that Geldof thinks looks like a hi-tech version of the frame from *Jailhouse Rock* and which other people think looks like expensive megalomania.

The gig went off like clockwork: there was something drastically wrong with the event, and it wasn't The Rats' performance. Rather it was that The Rats were trying to be a punching, jostling, all-action rock band with a high-energy low-bullshit presentation (apart from the set, which is at least democratic in that it dwarfs all six of them impartially), but the audience were − ahem − in a different space. They were in a *Top of the Pops* star space, punks and Grannies alike. They applauded the removal of Bob's jacket, submitted with warmth and good grace, enjoyed themselves and went home. The great gigs happen when the passion of the performer is met and matched by the passion of the audience, but while it was a loving and acquiescent audience, it was not a strong audience. Their response was soft, and sitting amongst them halfway back was like being at the movies.

'*You can get it if you want it and you need it bad enough*,' sang Geldof, "*cause you're young and good-lookin' and you're acting kinda tough . . .*'

Ay! And what then?

'There must come a point when people get sick of reading about you, but this seems not the case. We've had this kind of quasi-Ratsteria shit, which is flattering up to a point, but then I didn't think it would occur. I worked consciously to deflate that, to show that it was *no fokkin' big deal*, it was just six guys up onstage playin' instruments, and that is *it*. I realize that a big part of the fairy tale is the projection of that dream: there you are onstage and you exist because they allow you to exist and by the same token they're the projection of *our* fantasies. And of course they're shouting and rearing and that was part of the fantasy, part of the dream. They're clapping you and your songs; they know the words. I defy anyone not to be flattered by that.

'But I always thought that we neutralized idolatory to a tremendous extent by talking at a normal conversational level without going [into American Bullshit Voice] "Heeeeyyyy! Alri-i-i-ight! Rock and *roll*!" and all that shit, you know?'

Geldof's rep as Grand Manipulator is another Rataspect that's more than a little overblown. 'I Don't Like Mondays' was originally written as a reggae number, and gradually mutated into its present form over a lengthy series of rehearsals and demos. And even then . . .

'I thought "Mondays" was a B-side. I just couldn't hear the hooks. I couldn't hear the hooks on "Rat Trap" either. I don't know why that was number one.'

Much has been made lately of Geldof's reaction to what he considers to be the overrating of other artists like Bruce Springsteen, The Clash and The Jam. What *that's* down to is that he considers that their work gets taken seriously while The Rats' isn't, that their mystiques reinforce their work instead of devaluing it.

'I read,' he will expound heatedly, 'that Springsteen brought his kid sister and his fokkin' mother onstage with him. Can you imagine what they'd say about me if I brought mothers and sisters onstage at Rats gigs?' It's like he wants to be taken as a Serious Artist despite his unwillingness to take himself too seriously, like he wants to be believed even when he's insisting on not being believed. Discuss an aspect of one of his songs and he'll do it in detail, singing the words to you in taxi or bar or street, clicking his fingers.

'I remember saying to you that I thought I had maybe fifty more years on average, and that I didn't believe that there was very much after that. So if you take that as your viewpoint, it stands to reason that you're going to push your life to the limits . . .'

In rock circles, remarks like that are normally just a glib rationale for taking too many drugs.

'I don't mean that! I mean trying to push yourself and your abilities to their extremes. I don't mean drug excess or booze excess and hastening your end, I mean testing your capabilities as a human being. If you've only got those few years to do it in, you have to go at breakneck speed, which is maybe a pessimistic point of view because any minute a guy could walk in with a gun: bang! Instant wipeout. I'm preoccupied with the romanticism of death, the finality of death . . .'

What's so romantic about death?

'"*Dead lovers don't have nothing but a certain desperate sense of style*" . . . I always wonder how I'm going to die. Will I go quietly in my sleep, will I get mangled by a car and lie there screaming or maybe it'll be some cancerous thing. It's going to happen and it's final. I'm not concerned with immortality, because if I believed in the Catholic concept of eternity I'd be so frightened that I couldn't handle it. Immortality doesn't bother me. If people have forgotten about "I Don't Like Mondays" two weeks from now, *no problem*. I've never considered immortality in terms of rock and roll. I don't think rock songs should be remembered. It's a twentieth-century art form, it's here and then it's superseded. Immortality doesn't interest me. I'm purely concerned with the here and now. I reckon that if you're aware that you've only got a few years to do it, you end up with a fairly pessimistic viewpoint about most things. I've got fairly gloomy ideas.

'That could be absolute bullshit, but I've had to rationalize it in those terms. I'm just preoccupied with . . . death, which is very Woody Allenesque. Some people would think I'm trying to jump on some standard psychological bandwagon, but it's not true.'

That ain't the side of Bob Geldof that crops up on the chat shows, though.

'When you're not actually consciously thinking about whatever it is that drives you, then you . . . I can't see a contradiction, because like I said, I want to push this lifestyle to its limits, which would fit in with me being this so-called outrageous person, but I don't think I've ever been outrageous in my whole fokkin' life. I'm a *reasonable chap*. I have to reason things out with myself until I'm blue in the face. I'm Mister Liberal. I got a fokkin' shitty review and instead of wanting to hit the guy I think *God, he's right. Why did he think that? Lemme think back. "Mondays" was a hit. Why was that?*

'I suppose it was the way I was brought up. I do and say things very impetuously, which I know I will live to regret, but that's what I think so I'll say 'em anyway. People think I'm fokkin' outrageous, but I'm not! I'm Jack fokkin' Average!

'We got to be a successful band and I got interviewed because they thought I could string two words together and that is it, but I'm no more outlandish or outrageous than any Jack Average.'

Then there's the other side of it: the ones who don't think you're outrageous think you're too safe and cuddly. I mean, Jagger never got accepted that quick by the media.

'Well, in those days he couldn't have been acceptable because there were no standards for that sort of acceptance, but they humour my so-called outrageousness because I put it in a way that seems reasonable. I'm acceptable to them because I can pull figures. I'm aware of that and I will use it and they will use me. You scratch my back, I'll claw yours. I'm more than willing to go along with that, because I can use that and I dig being on TV. I'm at a certain level for some shows, and more than that they can't have it.

'They don't think of it in terms of what I spend most of my time doing, i.e. writing songs, rehearsing them, recording them, performing them. They just think [he switches to American Bullshit] "Heeyyyyyy! Bob Geldof! Lead singer of The Boomtown Rats! Per-son-aaa-lit-tee! Let's get *him* on the show!" Being on TV is not what I *do* . . .

'There's the desire not to be this huge star, and on the other hand I enjoy the trappings, getting into discos free, because I'm not so removed from the normal that I don't get a buzz out of that. I'm not so cool yet that I haven't lost that.

'I wish sometimes that I had.'

Fame fame fame faaaaaame. What's your name?

For The Rats, it's only the UK that had totally toppled. In Europe and America, they're still fighting for a foothold. Geldof bookended the Springsteen furore by slagging Aerosmith at some awful California fest and totally pissing off all the Aerosmith fans, which had CBS execs turning pale: '"Errhhh, *Bob* heh, heh,"' he mimics gleefully. '"I reckon we just lost another market there."' CBS have contrived to lose 'I Don't Like Mondays' in the radio shuffle, and on their next American tour The Rats are going to have to bust their balls not just to satisfy demands but to create them. Over there, they're still fighting and that's really what Geldof does best.

But what happens if Europe and the States fall on the same scale as the UK? What if that hunger to win audiences over is slaked?

'Then it just comes down to the joy of writing songs and performing. That's what you have when you start, and hopefully even when there are no more worlds to conquer, that's what you should always have.'

And Bob Geldof becomes twenty-seven on a bouncing dance floor in Edinburgh, listening to the blues.

Happy birthday, Boomtown Bob. They say that there's no such thing as a sane star and the only guesswork you have to do is diagnose the exact method of going funny in the head that the artists in question has chosen, but Geldof's in better shape than most. He *is* the same as when he began, and we even managed to get through all of this without once calling him Modest Bo—

Rats.

# Guy Stevens: 'There are only two Phil Spectors in the world and I am one of them'

*NME*, 22 December 1979

*THEY rushed down the street together, digging everything in the early way they had, which later became so much sadder and perceptive and blank. But then they danced down the street like dingledodies, and I shambled after as I've been doing all my life after people who interest me, because the only people for me are the mad ones, the ones who are mad to live, mad to talk,.mad to be saved, desirous of everything at the same time, the ones who never yawn or say a commonplace thing, but burn, burn, burn like fabulous yellow roman candles*

*exploding like spiders across the stars and in the middle*
*you see the blue centrelight pop and everybody goes*
*'Awwwwwww!' . . .*

*Jack Kerouac,* On The Road

*He's in love with rock and roll, WOOAAHHHRLD!*
*He's in love with getting stoned,*
*WOOOAAAHHHRLD!*

*The Clash, 'Janie Jones'*

*With Guy Stevens it was very, very special, because if it*
*hadn't been for him seeing that glimmer of whatever that*
*I certainly wasn't aware of, I'd still be workin' in the*
*factory right now.*

*Ian Hunter*

*Guy Stevens? Forget him. He's had it.*

*A Music Industry Figure*

Take a deep breath and you could recount the Guy Stevens story in one sentence.

Kingpin mod deejay at the Scene Club in '64, Our Man In London for Sue Records, the legendary soul label, first house producer for Island Records where he signed and produced Free and Spooky Tooth as well as inventing Mott The Hoople, discoverer of The Clash after a long time in hibernation and now finally producer of their new album 'London Calling', the man who got Chuck Berry out of jail in 1964, the man who supplied The Who with the compilation tape that gave them most of their early pre-original material repertoire, the man who introduced Keith Reid to Procol Harum and generated 'Whiter Shade Of Pale' only to fail to get them signed up and then had to stand by and watch them sell 90,000,000 copies for someone else, the man who smashed up every piece of furniture in a recording studio to get the performance he wanted out of the group he was recording, the man who Mick Jones of The Clash still thinks is responsible for getting him fired from his first real band, the man who heard Phil Spector rant about how it was him, Phil Spector, who *first* discovered The Beatles, the man who . . .

Guy Stevens, with the rolling, popping, bulging eyes of a veteran form speedfreak, the boozer's lurch and slur, smashing through or falling over every obstacle between him and the *perfect* rock and roll record, the *ultimate* rock and roll record, the *final* rock and roll record, the *next* rock and roll record . . . be that obstacle human or inanimate, himself or something else. Staggering, screaming, crying, flailing, laughing, Guy Stevens arouses pity, terror, admiration, revulsion, contempt.

In 1971 they wrote him off as a hopeless loser, a man too far gone into the depths of alcoholics' perdition to be of any use to himself or anyone else again.

And now, in the closing weeks of 1979, Guy Stevens is back in the charts. It is – as they say – a mighty long way down rock and roll. The inevitable corollary is that it's an even longer way back up again. Guy Stevens has been to hell and back.

'What happened was I was living in a one-room no-water flat in Leicester Square and playing records for Ronan O'Rahilly – later of Radio Caroline – down at the Scene Club. I had an R&B night every Monday, and a lot of people like The Stones and Animals used to come down . . .'

Guy Stevens is ensconced in a taxi heading for a friend's flat, where our interview is scheduled to take place. He had arrived at the *NME* offices half an hour late and roaring drunk, his hand lacerated and bleeding following some sort of incident with a glass door. Apparently, the prospect of being interviewed – at once exhilarating and terrifying – had sent him down to the pub as soon as it opened. He is fifteen years away in time, back when Mod really was mod, back when Guy Stevens had a direct line to R&B central.

'I got all my records mail-order. You sent 'em the money and got the records back within seven days from Stan's Record Store in Shreveport, Louisiana, USA, and it's right down deep in Tennessee . . .'

Wait a second, Guy. How can it be in Tennessee if it's in Louisiana?

'Well, it's somewhere around there. It all started for me when I was eleven years old and the first record I ever heard was "Whole Lotta Shakin' Goin' On" by Jerry Lee Lewis and that was the end of my school career. What I did was to start this thing at school where every boy in the school had to pay me a shilling a week – that's 5p – to be a member of my rock and roll club, and I chose the records. We had "Peggy Sue", "That'll Be The Day", Larry

Williams' "Bony Maronie", all the hits of the time, Jerry Lee Lewis' "Great Balls Of Fire" . . . and I got expelled for it eventually.

'So I was expelled at fourteen, and I went to work for Lloyd's, the insurance brokers. They thought I was kinda funny. By '63 I had all these records that I'd imported from Stan's Record Store in Shreveport, Louisiana, right? . . . And Peter Meaden came round one night. He was the bloke who formed The Who, and he arranged to bring them round one day with their manager, Kit Lambert.

'And they were really weird. They just stood there. My wife, who I was then living with – we're separated now – made a cup of tea for each one of them and they *still* stood still. I played 'em "Rumble" by Link Wray and put it on a tape for them – because by then I'd built up this enormous collection and Steve Marriott and everybody used to come round to get material.

'So The Who were there with Kit Lambert, and he offered me a fiver to make a two-and-a-half-hour tape for them, because Townshend hadn't started writing and they had no material to play on stage. So I played 'em all James Brown stuff, "Pleeeeeeeeeeease Pleeeaaase Pleeease" . . .' Hair flying, right there in the cab, Stevens becomes James Brown. 'And I played 'em "Rumble" by Link Wray, which was *the* classic Pete Townshend record, which he'd never heard before.'

Stevens' mouth begins to emit gigantic, grinding guitar chords and odd flecks of spittle. Demonic possesion by a guitar.

'So Townshend, Daltrey, Entwistle and Moon sat there for three hours drinking tea looking like little schoolboys and my poor wife was going, "Would you like another cup of tea" and they're saying, "Uh . . . well . . . um . . . ah . . . dunno," and I'm playing the records going, "Jesus *Christ*! WAKE UP!" I was going through my cabinet where I had all my singles, I had *every Motown single*, *every Stax* . . . I went to Stax in Memphis in 1963 and they said, "It's just a record shop." I said no, no, you've got a studio and they say, "We're just a record shop." So I went behind the shop and there was the studio where Booker T made "Green Onions". The whole lot, Rufus Thomas . . . and it was the size of this taxi we're sitting in now.'

One visualizes a younger Stevens, mod suit, hair cropped short, ranting and screaming at the bemused counter assistant at Stax, or a young, shy Who clutching cooling teacups while this *maniac*

jumps up and down, hitting them with soul music and screaming . . .

'And at Stax I said to them in 1963, "Don't you understand the
importance of what you're doing?" I can't tell you enough . . .
they were *nuts! They thought the record shop was more important
than the studio!*'

The whole industry thinks shops are more important than
studios, though.

'Well, if they think filing cabinets are gonna sell records, then
they'd better start selling them now. Records sell because they are
made by dedicated people who love to sing and love to play, and
that's what it's about. The record companies are full of people
who are either secretaries, hangers-on or people who don't know
anything about music all thinking, "Well, it's better than working
in a bank."'

From deejaying, scene-making and propagandizing blues, soul
and rock and roll, Stevens moved to operating Sue Records as
part of the then fledgling Island label. From living off what he
made from selling Scene Club tickets at Piccadilly Circus tube
station, he graduated to a £15 a week salary from Island. From
label administration to production was only one band away.

'What happened was that these guys came down from Carlisle
in a van in '65. They were called the VIPs, later to be known as
Spooky Tooth, and they were all nutters, all complete maniacs,
and they ambushed Island Records at the same time as I did. I
was always at total war with Chris Blackwell [then – as now –
Island's headman] and . . . I can't put him down in a nice way,
really. He was always a millionaire dilettante: he had a million
anyway so he didn't need to bother, but I never knew this. I had
just started the Sue label, and I got Charlie & Inez Foxx, I got
James Brown, I got a hell of a lot.

'Sue was formed by a guy called Juggy Murray in New York,
and he started the label with Charlie & Inez Foxx's "Mocking-
bird"; that was Sue 301. I went over to get a record called "The
Love Of My Man", which nobody has covered, and I hope Elkie
Brooks isn't listening. "The Love Of My Man" by Viola Kilgore.
Unbelievable. Un-be-*liev*-able. Blitzkrieg, out the window, number
one, *easy*. He owned the copyright. Chris went over and offered
him $500. Juggy wanted half a million. It got to three in the

American charts; if you check back you'll find it. One of the greatest records I've ever heard in my life.

'I wanted it to be on Sue. The main thing was that I wanted everything good to be on Sue. I wanted *Bob Dylan* to be on Sue. That was why I started importing records for Island with David Betteridge [now a CBS high-up] and Chris. And it nearly bankrupted Island.'

By now we're established in a luxurious flat belonging to a friend of Guy's. We're drinking coffee and brandy, except that Kosmo Vinyl – acting as Guy's part-time minder on behalf of The Clash – is surreptitiously filching Guy's brandy glass every time it's refilled and drinking it himself. Guy doesn't appear to notice, since every so often he is allowed to take a sip.

We're in '67 now, discussing the first Traffic album 'Dear Mr Fantasy', the getting-it-together-in-a-cottage-in-the-country one with the ghost on the cover. 'I did that cover! I went down to the cottage in Berkshire with them, I did the cover, I did *everything*! It sounds terrible to say all this . . . maybe I should say nothing. What do you want me to say?'

'Tell 'im the facts, Guy,' interjects Kosmo from across the room.

'Steve Winwood asked me to come down, said, "I want you to produce Traffic and live with us." So I went down there and it was a bit fairytale, a bit weird. There were some very weird things going on. They were smoking a hell of a lot, and each one of them would come out and say to me, "Oh God, I can't go on with life" and all this. That was Jim Capaldi. Then Steve Winwood would come out with, "I can't cope! It's all gone too far! It's all too much! We've had a hit single! Oh God!" And then *Chris Wood* started going, "Oh God! I've had enough!"

'I said, "Hang on, I've just heard this from three people! What *is* this? Have you all learned it off parrot fashion or what?" I was down there with all my belongings, all my records and everything thinking "Jesus Christ, they're all going *mad*!" And what they were all going mad over was Steve's girlfriend, but that's definitely another story . . .

'But the worst thing that happened between me and Blackwell was the "Whiter Shade Of Pale" incident. He had it on his desk for a week! What happened was this boy I knew called Keith Reid came into the office with these words he'd written. He worked in a solicitors' office for £4.50 a week, and he brought in these words which were vaguely Dylanish, and I told him the words were great and suggested that he got himself to a good songwriter.'

Reid ended up with Gary Brooker and Procol Harum. Chris Blackwell turned the result down, and when it was finally issued elsewhere, it made number one in two weeks flat, became one of the biggest records of '67 and still sells astronomical quantities whenever it's reissued. Guy Stevens had a nervous breakdown.

At the same time, Guy's massive record collection was stolen from his mother's house in 1967, and – to add insult to injury – the thief sold them all off for ninepence each (that's old money. In contemporary currency that would be 3.75p each. Weep!).

'The guy didn't know what he was selling. I had every Miracles record. Every Muddy Waters record. I had every Chess record from 001. Listen! I was at a session with Phil Chess in 1964 with Chuck Berry when he was doing "Promised Land" and "Nadine". I was at the session! I was taking photographs! I got Chuck Berry out of prison! I put tremendous pressure on Pye Records, who had Chess and Checker over here, and the head of the company at the time was Ian Ralfini.

'I put pressure on him to get "Memphis Tennessee" released as a single. It was out as a B-side, with "Let It Rock". They taped all the Chuck Berry tracks *off my records*! Not from master tapes but from my records! I mean, I may have spat on them or something. You never know what happens, do you? Now you'll know that if your old Chuck Berry records jump or something, it's probably me spitting on them.

'The first thing I actually produced was with Spooky Tooth. It was called "In A Dream" and it *built up*. All my records build up. Have you noticed that? Now, what I've done with the new Clash album is I've made 'em actually *play* a bit. I hope that's no offence to anyone . . . they haven't turned into Andy Williams or anything. Actually, I could do a really good Andy Williams. You wanna hear an Andy Williams impression?'

Guy lurches to his feet, something like a slow-motion film of somebody falling over projected in reverse. He approaches the white piano in the corner of the room, punches out a horribly discordant introduction to 'Moon River', saunters to the centre of the room and collapses into a paroxysm of mock sobbing. He chokes out an anguished monologue about Claudine Longet and the death of the ski instructor and then returns cautiously to the sofa.

'That's it. Ask me another question. Now the thing is that these blokes – Spooky Tooth – came down from Carlisle in a van, and they were *incredibly heavy*, both physically and because they were all taking about 500 blues a week. I loved them. I thought they were incredible and I took Blackwell along to see them. "Spooky Two" was *the* album. The mixing on that was incredible: that was my engineer Andy Johns. I don't know what happened to him. He's still alive, but he's in America.

'Andy – if you're listening – please come home.' Stevens lurches closer to the cassette microphone and raises his voice. 'You can work with anyone here at any time, but' – confidentially now – 'don't get messed up like you did before.'

And then came Mott The Hoople, and that story starts 'in Wormwood Scrubs. I was doing eight months for possession of drugs and I read this book called *Mott The Hoople* by Willard Manus. I wrote to my wife and said, "Keep the title secret." She was my ex-wife, or separated wife, I don't know what they call them, and she wrote back, "Are you joking? *Mott The Hoople?* That's ridiculous!" Anyway, when I came out of prison Island re-employed me at £20 a week – I went up a fiver – and I've got to admit that Mr Betteridge came and picked me up from the gates of Wormwood Scrubs.

'And then I wanted to have a pee, and he said, "Fuck that, have a pee if you want one, but I'll be two miles down the road." I said, "Wait a minute, I just got out of *prison*! Show some sensitivity, for fuck's sake! I don't even know what roads *look* like any more." So I went for a pee and he drove off, and then finally he said, "Oh, I didn't know you were following us." I only found them because my wife was waving her arms out of the window and yelling . . .'

Memories cascade out of Stevens, virtually unchecked. He is obviously pissed and ranting, but there is something eerie about his conversation: he appears more medium than raconteur. His voice undergoes startling changes; one moment almost precise, the next moment so alien that it seems as if he is maintaining his grip on the art of speech only by a conscious effort. He recalls

Janis Joplin telling him at the Albert Hall that she was going to overdose within a year. 'She was the kind of girl who would walk into a bar and just *take over the whole bar*. She'd walk up and . . . "Awwwwwl raht! *A-whoooooo's* gonna bah me a *drank*? A-whoooooo's gonna bah me 'nother drank? Whooo's gonna bah me 'nother *double* drank?"

'Janis Joplin I loved. I loved her music and since her death I've felt funny and tortured about it. If I'd tried . . . when I get really sad I cry at home and play that second track off "I Got Dem Ol' Kozmic Blues Again Mama".'

He also remembers a pre-Yardbirds Eric Clapton, dragged up to Guy's den and finding Freddie King albums blaring out at him while Guy banged a hammer on the floor and screamed 'Play, Eric! Play!' while the young fellow tried to hide in a corner.

He moves on to chaotic Mott The Hoople sessions where studios were reduced to rubble.

'I never hit a microphone. Everything else I destroyed. Why? ANGER! I'm just a very angry person. When a group's been sitting there for two weeks without getting anything done, you've got to . . . lemme tell you about Hunter. The first time . . . I love the fact that he came from a wife and three kids in Archway – changing buses twice – to get to what he thought was some dodgy demo session. He didn't know what it was going to be. The guy at Regent Sound just told him that there was some bloke rambling on about Jerry Lee Lewis and Bob Dylan.

'Ian had a cold and a headache, but he came down and he played "Like A Rolling Stone" and I stopped him and said, "That's it. You're hired. Come by the office tomorrow and pick up your fifteen quid with the rest of the band." He asked what the band was called and I told him Mott The Hoople. He went, "*Whaaaaat?* Mott The *What*?"

'He came in the next morning and got his fifteen quid, and then he finally believed. I'd organized everything, set it all up. There was no embarrassment. The only thing I'd like to say on my behalf is that I think David Bowie scored most of the credit rather than me. I'd chosen the name, found the band – because they had to be right, I'd auditioned over seventy bands in a year.

'I knew they had to be right, have the right attitude. Then I saw these blokes lugging an organ up the stairs, and they were really *lugging* this fucking great organ up the stairs. It was *enormous*, a Hammond C3 the size of a piano, and I thought, "I don't care what they sound like. They've done it. *They got the organ up the stairs.*"

'What happened was that I made five great albums for Island with Mott and luckily David Bowie picked up on them. That was great. I was really pleased. He saved their lives.

'The actual incident that happened . . . you know "Ballad Of Mott The Hoople"? Well, they disbanded in Zurich, they just said, "Well, see ya when we get off the train." Bowie had heard about this, and he'd based most of his rock thing on Mott, all his rock artistry and all his rock vision. I think if he'd been Ian Hunter, he'd have loved it.

'The real trouble with Ian, though, is that he takes himself so seriously. He takes himself *much* too seriously.'

Today, Guy Stevens says, 'I never really recovered from Mott The Hoople.' Ask him about the period between 'Brain Capers' (his last Mott album) and 'London Calling' and his reply is simply, 'You're asking about a very mixed-up period of my life.'

He refocuses. 'I never really got over working with Ian Hunter. You've got to realize that . . . I think Chrysalis Records are doing a great job, signing him up and . . . the trouble with Ian is really . . .

'HE-E-ELLLLP!' A comic wail of distress masks the real one effectively enough for the conversation not to be derailed.

'Listen, The Clash are really great to work with. I found 'em in '76. I produced demos of the first album, "White Riot" an' all that. This character called Bernie Rhodes who owned a garage in Camden Town and happened to live opposite where they rehearsed . . . I was living near there at the time and I wandered in. They were doing "White Riot".'

He launches into his own impromptu performance of the song, spittle flying, hair bouncing, eyes bulging. '"WHITE RIOT!! WANNA RIOT! WHITE RIOT! A RIOT OF MY OWWWW-WWN!" And I just thought "Right! RIOT! RIGHT! RIOT! Let's gooooooh!"'

'And then Bernard got *very tricky*.'

The conversation then saunters into the minefield of The Clash's financial history, a topic over which a discreet veil should be drawn. Suffice it to say that anyone thinking that The Clash's popularity and influence has created a proportionate bulge in their bank accounts is suffering from severe delusions. If anyone's 'turning rebellion into money', it certainly ain't The Clash.

Which is why we find The Clash in a room in a West London office building winding down after a business meeting. The previous day the 'London Calling' video had been shot in the Battersea drizzle, and an evening's rehearsals have just had to be cancelled because their equipment is still waterlogged and as such unfit for immediate use.

Their single is out and warmly received. Everyone who's heard the album thus far thinks it's marvellous, so everyone's telling their Guy Stevens stories.

Joe Strummer looks like a Ted on his way from a building site to an oldies shop hot on the trail of Jerry Lee Lewis out-takes. Paul Simonon looks like The King Of All The Rudies. Topper Headon looks like a punk rockaaaahhh. Mick Jones looks like Al Pacino in *The Godfather*.

'I well remember searching through all the pubs in Oxford Street looking for him,' Strummer recalls. 'I found a row of blokes sitting slumped over the bar staring in their beer. I looked down this row and I spotted him because of his woolly hat. I went up to him and tapped him on the shoulder, he looked round and it was like son-finding-father in one of those corny films. He looked up at me and said, "Have a drink."'

'He had a few rucks during the sessions,' Mick Jones chips in. 'He had one with Mister Oberstein [Maurice Oberstein, big boss man at CBS] where he lay in front of Mister Oberstein's Rolls Royce. He had fights with Bill [Price, engineer of That Ilk] ... why'd he have a fight with you?' he calls over to roadie Baker Glare.

'He threw something of mine across the room,' elucidates Baker.

'We highly recommend him to *anybody* who wants to make a record,' announces Strummer.

'There was this big pile of chairs,' reminisces Jones, 'all stacked up on top of each other like at school and he rushed out during a take and grabbed for the top chair and they all started to come over, so he pushed them back, then went for the top one, pulled it down and *smaaaassssshh*! Then he says, "I'm Guy Stevens and this is what I do ... especially when I'm thinking about my mother" and then he starts behaving ... *eccentrically*.'

During the sessions, Guy would periodically phone Ian Hunter in the States for pep talks. Guy was telling Hunter that he couldn't go on, and Hunter would tell him to stop pissing about and get on with it. He would hang off the hallway phone for hours while The Clash worked in the studio.

'We paid for the calls. We paid for his minicabs as well. He brought in about a year's worth of minicab slips – every minicab he'd taken since the fifties. We'd told him he could have minicabs in and out, so he brought all these other ones in. One day he hired a bodyguard . . .'

The bodyguard eventually turned out to be a cab-driver who'd come in to get paid when Guy didn't have the cash. He ended up staying at the session for eighteen hours.

The Clash received considerable opposition from CBS when they proposed to use Guy Stevens. 'They hate his guts! They said they wouldn't use him again until he was *bankable*. We plan to use him again, and we're going to get all of CBS's acts to use him. We're gonna make him their house producer.

'It gives me heart when Guy tells us about his business history,' continues Strummer. 'At least there's someone around who's as bad as us if not worse. All the dreadful, life-wrecking things that've happened to him . . .'

Jones: 'His presence in a studio definitely makes all the difference. It's like all the mess goes to him like Dorian Gray's portrait or whatever. All the messy sound goes and it becomes *him*, and what's left on the tape is . . . clarity.'

Strummer: 'People tend to be afraid of him because he's off the wall, to put it mildly. And they should be. There's a little bit of an act in there, but it's not entirely an act. It puts a lot of people off. They just think, "Christ, get this man home."'

Jones: 'But even when he's unconscious he can still recite his address.'

Apart from applying time-honoured Guy Stevens production techniques such as the Mott furniture-smashing standby . . .

Strummer: 'He invented some new ones for us. Like pouring beer into the piano to make it sound better . . .'

Jones: 'Like blowing the desk up. Like hitting the guitarist with a ladder. All these I could take, but not pouring beer into the piano. I nearly killed him.'

Strummer: 'When he poured beer into the TV *I* nearly killed 'im an' all. Lucky there were no Space Invaders about or he'd'a done *them* and then Paul would've killed 'im.'

Jones: 'He's obsessed with Liam Brady and Arsenal. He always wears his scarf and on the way to every session he goes and stands in the middle of Arsenal football ground and pays the cab to wait for him. And nobody in the group supports Arsenal.'

The Clash unhesitatingly recommend Guy Stevens. Strummer pronounces him 'the ultimate cure for musical constipation'. How would they react to the dictum — oft-voiced by such worthies as PiL and The Stranglers — to the effect that all record producers are parasites.

Strummer grins broadly. 'They should try him. They've never met a parasite like this one before!'

And the room explodes into laughter.


It has been ten days since the first interview session with Guy Stevens. Then he had arrived at *NME* blind drunk and bleeding. Now, he turns up punctual and sober. The shilling-sized flakes of dandruff in his hair have been washed away. He is wearing new sneakers. Suddenly, he's a hero. Suddenly, everyone loves him. He is in ecstasy.

'I'm buying some new jeans as well! I was tremendously unpopular at CBS until this record went in the charts. Now it's "Hel-*lo*, Guy!" They've all cooled out!

'It's been tremendously refreshing working with The Clash. They've changed a *lot* since I first knew them in '76. Joe is great, because he always puts you straight if you're out of order. The whole thing happened very naturally. It just *worked*.'

Throughout his entire involvement with rock and roll, right from that first Jerry Lee Lewis flash more than twenty years ago, Guy Stevens has been lurching and screaming after one thing, one great blinding, deafening rock and roll epiphany.

'Well, the best way of explaining that would be . . . there's a quote from Jack Kerouac's *On the Road*, quite early on — about page seven or so — something like "All my life I've been chasing after people who are mad, mad to talk, mad to play . . ." People who *want* to. And I suppose that applies to rock and roll. I was eleven when I heard "Whole Lotta Shakin'" and I was never the same again. That intensity of feeling. I've seen performances by Jerry Lee Lewis that were just *unbelievable*. It was when he was at his most unpopular, 200 people in a 2,000-seater, and he played his *heart* out, and that's always stayed with me.

'That electricity, that manic intensity. It's a kind of madness, not a "mad" madness . . . but like Dean Moriarty and Sal Paradise. Chasing, *chasing*. I've always felt that way about making records. Making a record is an event. Big letters: AN EVENT. It's not just "another session": I *hate* people with that attitude. It's electricity. It's *got to be*.

'It may be hard for a company like CBS to accept a concept like this, but I could quite well *die* while making a record. *It's that important.* That's why – if it came to it – I could produce *anybody*.'

Right now, Guy Stevens is out of the dumper with a vengeance. The plan now is to get rid of the booze problem and take advantage of his redeemed credibility to make a lot more records.

'I can't very well afford to take out a small ad in the classifieds, so . . . you couldn't print my phone number so that people can get hold of me, could you? It's 699-4999. Ask for Guy.

'Record production a speciality.'

# The Ramones:
# The return of the
# thin white mooks

*NME*, 2 February 1980

**1  2  3  4**

4-5-6-7!

All-gud-creetins-go-ta-heavun!

The Ramones, however, go to Shepperton via an Indian restaurant in Staines. In their *Old Grey Whistle Test* dressing-room, the only sign of an imminent Ramone visitation is a roadie earnestly breaking in a set of new strings on Johnny Ramone's Mosrite guitar in the midst of a cloud of aromatic smoke that wreathes the huge Music Man amp like mist around Mount Olympus.

Downstairs in the icy barn that houses the studio – like two rehearsal rooms backed onto each other – roadies and technicians mill and Anne Nightingale frets.

The following day, The Ramones launch their 'End Of The Century' tour in Brighton. Tonight, however, they will loom out of the nation's TV sets like some vision of backstreet eruption played for laughs, like four supporting characters from John Rechy's *City of Night* as interpreted by Hanna-Barbera.

They will play 'Rock 'N' Roll Radio' closely followed by 'Rock 'N' Roll High School'. They will demonstrate their capabilities as an example of what Theodore Sturgeon described in *More Than Human* as *homo gestalt*: a group consciousness in which the whole is the sum of parts that would be virtually non-functional if separated. Taken individually, The Ramones would simply be four New York mooks, indistinguishable – except for quirks of construction – from any other similar creatures. Together, they are unique, unmatchable, irreplaceable.

Here they are, wandering in. Four Beatle haircuts (circa 'Revolver'), four shiny bike jackets, four pairs of faded jeans, four pairs of sneakers. Bluff Marky, sullen Johnny, amiable Dee Dee, shy Joey; brudders in all but blood.

'People useta ask us if we really were brudders,' Joey will murmur on a later occasion. His voice is unbelievably reedy and nasal, his intonations as slouched and contorted as his body. 'We'd always say, "No, we're not, but don't tell anyone." And they'd go, "Oh! Okay, your secret is safe with me."' His voice emerges from the side of his mouth, through curtains of hair. If he were not a Ramone – a Ramone, after all, being a creature who, in rock mythology at least, is unable to decide which sneaker to put on first in the morning without at least five minutes' hard thinking – he might be considered the possessor of a fairly dry wit.

Dee Dee is small, trim, muscular. His conversation is amiable and goofy. Ask him how long he and his brudders have been over here and his features – New York rough-hewn offstage, oddly Oriental on – lapse into an expression of comical confusion. 'Uhhhh . . . I dunno. One day? Two days?'

Dee Dee corresponds most closely to the popular received impression of A Ramone. He is da brudders' Real Punk in the pre-Pistolian sense of the word. He's the street fighter, the ex-junkie, the one with the military fixation which asserts itself in alternately comedic and gruesome manifestations throughout their recorded history (his father was a serviceman stationed in Berlin, where he spent his first fourteen years). He's the one who gets in trouble.

322

'Just last week I was on the subway and this guy comes up to me and says, "You Dee Dee Ramone?" I say, "Yuh" and he just goes BAM! Hits me. Well, I took him straight out, but he had this real big guy with him, an' if *he'd* waded in, it woulda bin all over for me, man. I would not be here wid ya now.'

Dee Dee took a bad shot in the ribs, though, and so he removes his T-shirt to bind the painful area with rock's all-purpose adhesive and universal panacea: gaffa tape. Spectators wince at the thought of what it will be like having to remove it.

Johnny is the practical Ramone. At soundchecks, Johnny's in charge and he works with the PA crew to get the Ramones sound together, painstakingly winding the amps up until the guitar stacks are ringing with harmonic overtones, teetering just on the safe edge of a feedback holocaust, putting Dee Dee through his bass paces until the bass stacks produce a humming thump rather than a dull thud. Marky and Dee Dee run through a couple of numbers – Ramones in dub! – in the midst of a cold, empty Brighton Top Rank. In the toilet, two members of The Boys – support band for the tour – are engaging in a petty squabble.

As the extraordinary strains of 'She's The One' ricochet around the building, Joey mooches across the floor like a crippled stick-insect. He wears a hooded red sweatshirt in place of the standard leather jacket – the leather only comes out when he's Ramoning in public – and his freakish frame locomotes with difficulty.

His height is uncertain – beyond the simple designation of 'very tall' – because of his slouch. His legs bend at the knees whether standing or walking and expand to hips which are seemingly wider than his shoulders, which in turn slouch until he resembles one of those old-fashioned street-lamps which curl and droop as if the weight of the lamp itself was too heavy to bear. His limbs begin to wave and stretch in some obscure form of callisthenics as Johnny takes the stage, gazes about him with an expression of confused hostility and unleashes a savage burst of rhythm guitar that strafes the room like a submachine burst. Everyone falls silent.

Despite Marky's careful, solid drumming – as an ex-member of Richard Hell's Voidoids, he has chops which Ramones music never calls upon – Johnny is The Ramones' most remarkable instrumentalist. He drives his guitar like a racing driver, piloting around the chord changes like Jackie Stewart round a hairpin bend, maintaining that constant, deadpan roar so earnestly mimicked in every '77 garage band. It's the musical equivalent of Buster Keaton's poker face, never changing or altering whatever the circumstances, but providing a constant that *seems* to change with the context.

It's a style and approach that is unutterably perfect within its place in The Ramones' noise, and which would be totally inappropriate anywhere else. If The Ramones had never existed, there would be no band for whom Johnny could possibly play the guitar. If Johnny had never existed, The Ramones would never have the right guitar player. For an instant, one almost believes that there is a benevolent force ordering the universe.

Past the discarded bag from the Indian takeaway, Joey approaches the stage. For a second one believes that he will simply stand up straight and *step* onto the stage – the man is after all, a giant; albeit an extremely sickly one – but he elects to heave himself onto the platform, an ungainly tangle of limbs.

The return of the thin white mook. Suddenly, one catches a glimpse of Joey Ramone as a schoolboy, towering, tottering, helpless.

As he finally gains the stage, his girlfriend Linda watches him with pride. She is small, blonde and fizzy: hyperactive, grinning. She fusses over her lanky, ungainly boyfriend, indulges him, nurses him, showers him constantly with affectionate abuse. The previous evening, he had mentioned that New York rock club Hurrah's had been redecorated 'with TV sets all over the walls like sump'n out of the Bowie film. I thought it was real futuristic.' She'd howled at that, never let him forget about it.

'*Real futuristic????* Two video monitors on the walls? Very good, Joe. Real futuristic!'

Now Joey looks out over Brighton Top Rank, with its stylized tack-SF trimmings and he can see her mouthing, 'Real futuristic' at him. He bawls through the mike a few times, Dee Dee bawls 'Wanchewtreefaw!' and The Ramones crash straight through five numbers like The Hulk through a brick wall.

The air is filled with a peculiar magic. Not having seen actual Ramoning for many months, doubt had entered the picture: a nagging worry that The Ramones had been merely an infatuation, that changes in the musical weather had somehow created an immunization to Ramone Fever, that it would seem dumb and shallow and dated, something that could be outgrown. One had feared that the subtleties that had been perceived in their Ramonic fervour and monomania would evaporate, leaving only a sterile racket.

No way, effendim. Within seconds, it seemed that the entire world was reverberating to a sublime noise both crass and sly, both overwhelmingly traditional and revitalizingly perverse, a cruelly devastating parody of rock and roll that exalts the original even as it demolishes it, then lovingly reassembles the pieces almost in the right order, then kicks it over again only to rebuild in yet another subtly altered sequence.

'There are specific ways of taking it,' intones Joey as he wraps himself around a T-bone steak which will later give him such intense stomach cramps that he will be virtually unable to sing on-stage for several minutes that evening. 'And it's not all meant to be taken at the same level. Some of it's meant to be taken humorously, some of it isn't. It's not quite that . . .'

'Clear-cut?' offers Linda.

'Yeah, yeah.' Joey brushes off the interruption with the implication that the prompting was unnecessary. 'There are a lot of different stances to be taken. A lotta people say it's all cartoon, but it's not. *Some* of it, but . . . a lotta people think what we're doing is very simple until they try to do it, try to play it or really get down to trying to understand what it's all about.

'At one time, everybody was saying, "Oh, that's easy. I could do it, anyone could do that" until they actually tried it. They couldn't do it, y'know? All the bands tried to copy it – our style – but it doesn't sound the same either. But it's meant to be taken at different levels, but the mass majority isn't getting the point. Whether they like it or dislike it, they're missin' it.

'The people that do understand us really *do* understand us. The people who don't understand us should maybe listen to something a little more . . . *obvious*.'

Onstage at Brighton, The Ramones *are* obvious. It's the first night of the tour and the monitors are out to a month of Sunday lunches. Any band that operates at as thunderous an onstage volume as da brudders (three Marshall 100-watt stacks for Johnny with a fourth over on Dee Dee's side of the stage, two Ampeg bass stacks for Dee Dee with a third over by Johnny's amps) is totally dependent on monitors to keep them all in touch. Without that vital link, they play on guesswork: sloppily and tensely.

Their irritation and discomfort is compounded by the fact that their concentration is continually disrupted by showers of phlegm from the faithful and – to add insult to injury – when they encore with 'Do You Wanna Dance' the power goes off halfway through the song. They carry it through on charisma and solidarity, but it is the kind of Ramones show that one would not want on a bootleg.

Backstage, Dee Dee is furious.

'We're gettin' big in the States now, an' we don't haveta come here. It costs us money to come here an' play, ya know?' he declaims, banging one fist on his knee to make his point. 'But we like comin' here an' we want to come here, because we'll never forget that it was the British who took us in first and that we had fans here when we were still playin' to thirty-five people back home. But I'm twenty-eight years old an' a grown man an' I don't like bein' spit on!

'Back home, that's fightin' talk, spittin' on someone. You spit on me in the street an' I'll kill ya. That's showin' contempt for someone, spittin' on them. Do The Clash get spit on?'

He deflates slightly when informed that, yes, The Clash do still get spat on and, no, they don't like it one little bit better than he does.

One week later in Aylesbury Friars, The Ramones redeem and are redeemed. The deejay informs the audience that The Ramones will be very unhappy Ramones if they are spat on and they in fact cop less gob than The Clash did when they were there.

I'd taken my cold to Aylesbury to see if it would succumb to intensive therapy and, of course, it does for over four hours, which renders The Ramones a superior panacea to Night Nurse. The Aylesbury set was cretin heaven.

From Joey's opening announcement of 'It's true . . . we *are* The Ramones' to the final encore, from '*Hey ho let's go*' to '*Gabba gabba hey!*' Ramone Fever spreads like wildfire. Once again, all thoughts of The Ramones as good-fun-in-'77-but-hopelessly-outmoded-now-poor-dears are banished to the outermost darkness where discarded theories lie in dolorous heaps, whimpering to themselves. And if you've got a minute, I'll tell you why.

\*

Much of classic UK punk was initially constructed partially in The Ramones' image. The volume, the pace, the simplicity, the (apparent) nihilism, the leathers and the sneakers were all poured into the cauldron and adopted along with the sartorial, musical and conceptual contributions of The Pistols and The Clash, but the satire and soppiness that went along with the other Ramone ingredients remained unique (The Undertones copped the teenage wimpiness, true enough, but it's somewhat cloying when isolated from the mock aggression and the whackiness).

Where Britpunk singers roared and sneered, Joey Ramone remained wistful and innocent, elegant in his very clumsiness. Their interests and preoccupations — not to mention stylistic devices — coincided with those of what later became 'punk', but The Ramones themselves remained *sui generis*, a law unto themselves. They copped a righteous roasting for not conforming to the exact, specific requirements of punk dogmatists and ideologues, but hey! tough cookies; The Ramones don't conform to anything much except the demands of Ramonehood. When they first reared their mookish heads in Manhattan way back in punk prehistory, they weren't anything except Ramones (though one critic did describe them as 'Semi-glitter' at the time), just as they aren't anything except Ramones now. It's just that the world seemed to catch up with them back in '77.

Now half the bands who copied them way back then have moved on to discover themselves, and the ones who are still copying them are the ones who are trapped, because they never understood what made The Ramones what they were in the first place. The Ramones defy logic and custom as much as ever. They even defy the laws of geometry: their angle on rock is simultaneously obtuse and acute, and that *is* impossible. Ask any mathematician and he'll work it out with a pencil.

Of course, The Ramones couldn't just become Ramones. First they had to invent themselves. As a piece in *Rolling Stone* revealed a while back, Joey Ramone was once Jerry Hyman, just as Dee Dee was Derek Colvin and Johnny was John Cummings. Their parents were interviewed: The Ramones were displeased.

'They put ya down for years and then they get in the article,' complains Dee Dee. 'When we play Atlanta my fadder comes to see us — "That's mah boy up there" — but now what I get is, "How come ya ain't made it yet? How come ya ain't had a

327

number one rekkud? How come ya ain't as big as Kiss?'' No more about the parents!'

Johnny and Dee Dee had attempted to start a band as early on as the early Beatle days when the British invasion hit. 'We went out and got guitars, but we couldn't play 'em. We couldn't play any of the songs, so we forgot about it,' confesses Johnny with a hint of a smile.

'Bein' in a band was just somethin' we'd fantasize about,' offers Dee Dee. 'But you just end up gettin' bad grades in school, your folks get mad atcha 'cuz you make so much noise in your room . . .'

So the future Ramones joined the lumpen New York rock audience, standing on line at the Fillmore East swallowing up the sound and fury of sixties rock. They still speak in respectful voices of The Vagrants, the New York band led by Leslie West before he took his gargantuan bulk to Mountain, of Young Rascals and Vanilla Fudge (the Italo-rock figureheads of NYC), of Jimi Hendrix.

But then rock went down the dumper in the early seventies, and they got their kicks from Slade and T. Rex and early Bowie and The New York Dolls . . . and then Johnny and Dee Dee bought new guitars and started again.

'"Ramone" was like short for all those unpronounceable Italian names,' mumbles Johnny through a steak, 'and we thought people shouldn't haveta tax their minds to remember your last name as well as your first name, so we all had the same last name.'

Different friends were brought in on different instruments – Randy California of Spirit had been in their school as a kid, but he quit long before he would have had a chance to become Randy Ramone – and the brudders tell suitably embroidered tales of trainee Ramones who'd run screaming naked into the street after rehearsals ('He's working in a button factory now') or who'd had to leave to continue his course of ECT. Initally, Joey'd been the drummer.

'Yeah, yeah, right,' interposes Joey in improbable nasal tones. 'I was a regular Keith Moon. A King of Rhythm. I just had that beat, ya know?' But Joey became the singer, and Tommy Erdelyi – namechecked onstage by Joey as 'the late Tommy Ramone' – came in on drums.

While allowing that 'Tommy was a good producer – he got that raw sound down real well', no present Ramone has a single good word to say for the tiny pockmarked one. They were not amused by the fact that he'd gone around claiming to have written most of the material and invented the entire Ramone concept. 'He was a creep, ya know?' mutters Joey through his nose. 'I hated his guts. When he left he told everyone that without him we wouldn't know what to do'n' we'd be lost and we'd break up. Now we're doin' better than ever.'

'The group woulda broken up if Tommy *hadn't* left,' interposes Dee Dee.

'Ya oughtta hear his demos,' continues Joey. 'He's making a solo album. I think he wants ta be the next Steve Forbert. But we were called The Ramones 'n' everything before he ever came along. Ya know what? When he quit playin' the drums he wanted to play lead guitar. He told John that we were gonna have two guitars from here on.'

Tommy gets sole credit for having written 'I Wanna Be Your Boyfriend', the first great Ramones teendream ballad, a tradition since built into a succession of tearful confections scattered around the landscape of the subsequent albums. 'Great song,' he whines. 'Shouldabinnahit.'

That's the story of The Ramones' musical life. *Great song. Shouldabinnahit.* When the cover photo for 'End Of The Century' was delivered, Sire Records in the States told them 'This is the first real cover you've given us.' On this cover, The Ramones appear *sans* leathers in colour-coded T-shirts; black for Dee Dee, yellow for Joey, red for Johnny, blue for Marky. After all those album sleeves which sent hundreds of bands off to buy leathers and find brick walls to lean against, *this* is a 'real cover'? Pshaw!

Now the radio stations aren't afraid of them any more. 'We're still wearin' leathers on the record, though,' Dee Dee states helpfully.

Ramones music *is* dead simple ... if you happen to be a Ramone. To other people, it's either so one-dimensional that it's totally devoid of interest, or else a series of endless urban catacombs filled with contradictions, trapdoors, farce, ghoulishness, self-pity. To The Ramones, it's exactly what rock music is supposed to be: all the bits they like with all the other bits left out.

The very first Ramones song ever written, 'I Don't Wanna Walk Around With You' (composed by Johnny and Dee Dee on the afternoon that they bought their instruments), fell foul of this fate. The song in questions goes:

> *Wantchewtreefawww!*
> *I don't wanna walk around with you,*
> *I don't wanna walk around with you,*
> *I don't wanna walk around with you,*
> *So why'd'ya wanna walk around with me?*
> *(Oh oh oh).*

> © *1976 Taco Tunes,*
> *Bleu Disque Music (ASCAP)*

That's it. That's the whole song. The copyright people claimed it was only a fragment. R.D. Laing should have been so lucky to have written that.

Life in The Ramones goes on. They made a movie, which was dreadful, and they don't defend any part of it in which they do not appear or perform. The reason that *Rock'N'Roll High School* is a screaming yellow zero is that it falls into precisely that trash-aesthetic crevasse that The Ramones vault so effortlessly: it is neither bad enough to be laughed at nor good enough to be enjoyed. The makers substitute shoddiness for suss: they continually hedge their bets and peak nervously over their shoulders.

There is no point where the movie stares the audience straight in the face and demands that they make an actual decision about the merits of what they are doing. There is nothing in it to be either understood or misunderstood. The trashiness is not a stylistic device employed for the love of it, but a snivelling cop-out for ineptitude. Dee Dee will – in another context – cite the American deejays and music biz flotsam who describe any group who are inept as 'punk rock', but that is precisely the kind of thinking employed in the movie – that a film becomes 'trashy' or 'punky' simply because it is bad, and that on these grounds it is not only excusable but somehow even praiseworthy – and thereby The Ramones are damned by association, through no fault of their own.

Helplessly, Johnny cites several moments in the original script that utilized The Ramones to fuller and more effective extent; moments which were either never shot or else edited out. 'It was like they were afraid that they'd weaken the movie if they used us too much.'

330

Instead, they concentrated on the plot: a plot so feeble that it should have been simply waved at the audience, subjected to hoots of mirth and then booted into the middle distance. Still, it was a movie and The Ramones wanted to make a movie and no one else was offering them one.

At least da brudders are doing better on vinyl than on celluloid. Phil Spector played Biggest Brudder on 'End Of The Century', an epic confrontation between the *idiots-savants* and the ageing *enfant terrible*, and the wonders of Spectorscope transform them into giant Ramones in an alley the size of the Grand Canyon, Johnny's guitar taking on the rumbling weight of an entire battalion of cellos. No guns were pulled during the session, and an atmosphere of sweet cooperation overhung the proceedings.

'He wasn't telling us what to do all the time or nothin',' reminisces Dee Dee. 'We had a rehearsal where he came along and we played him all the songs, and we doubled up on the bass and drums as well as the guitars. You know that first chord in "Rock 'N' Roll High School"? He worked on that one chord for ten hours straight. I couldn't take it. I phoned up my mother and said, "Ma, I can't take this no more. I'm not suited for this life." '

The album delves back into Ramones lore by reintroducing Jackie and Judy from the first album's 'Judy Is A Punk' on 'The Return Of Jackie And Judy', reprising the old 'Havana Affair' with 'This Ain't Havana' and including – for the first time – a version of 'Chinese Rocks', a song Dee Dee wrote back in his days as a junkie. When performed by Johnny Thunders' Heartbreakers, the song was an obnoxious hymn of praise to the nastiest drug in town, and in those days – with Dee Dee's addiction still an uncomfortably recent memory – da Brudders had virtually disowned the song. Why, then, are they playing it now?

'We heard a lotta groups playing it, and it all sounded like a bad imitation of The Ramones,' Dee Dee explains. 'I wrote the *whole* of that song. Richard Hell just wrote the riff in the middle – Thunders and Jerry Nolan had *nutt'n* to do with it – and Hell had nutt'n to do with the lyrics or the construction of the song. We just took it back.

'An we don't glorify shootin' dope. The Heartbreakers were proud of bein' junkies, but when we do it it's just a straightforward account of what an addict's life is like, and then it's over an' we're onto somethin' else. Shootin' dope's a lifetime thing, but you can't sniff glue for more than a few months.'

Why not?

'Because yer hair falls out and you can't do nutt'n' 'n' then ya *die*. When we wrote that song "Now I Wanna Sniff Some Glue", it was like an obvious joke, because no one we know sniffs glue, 'cuz that is the most uncool thing you could possibly do. And then when we did the song there were all those kids sniffin' glue in Scotland or sump'n and they blamed it all on us. It was nutt'n ta do with us.'

It's Dee Dee's upbringing as an army brat in Germany which is responsible for the heavily satiric militaristic streak in The Ramones' presentation. 'We told people that we were real disappointed at bein' rejected for Vietnam and they t'ought we were bein' serious. We were all too young for Vietnam an' if we weren't we woulda bin drafted. There's this band in New York called Shrapnel and they're all about seventeen and they wear army uniforms and play from behind sandbags. Nobody takes *them* seriously.'

Later on, Joey gives me a copy of Shrapnel's single. The song titles are 'Combat Love' and − out-Ramoning The Ramones − 'Hey'.

'Militaristic? Well, we're a team, a squad, a force. It's not like there's some big rock star up dere or nutt'n with his backup band. We're a team.'

Marky Ramone, the newest acquisition, is part of the team. 'He was more of a Ramone in spirit than Tommy ever was. He had his own leather jacket'n'everything. He was . . .' Joey's mouth twitches at one corner . . . 'one of us!'

'Gabba Gabba weeeeeee 'cceptcha! Weeeeeeeeccceptcha! one of us!'

Leaning against the back wall at Friars, your correspondent is revelling in a little taste of rock and roll heaven. Despite Joey only singing half of 'I Wanna Be Your Boyfriend' because of the aforementioned stomach cramps, tonight The Ramones are in full flight. Each 'Wanchewtreefawwwww!' and each headlong rush into the next Ramone epic is whipped out like some audacious feat of conjuring or gymnastics, trucked out with an innocent glee − betcha didn't think we could do it again, huh? JUST WATCH! − and pride and enjoyment.

Little bits of Ramone magic − like the way Johnny's thunderously over-amped guitar creates so many overtones on 'Rock 'N'

Roll Radio' that you'd swear there was an organ in somewhere. Like the way Joey even tries to jump around like his more athletic colleagues and of course it's ridiculous, but it's great that he's enjoying himself enough to try. Hey ho! Let's goooooooohhh!

And 'Rock 'N' Roll Radio' pulls a couple of strokes that a group more selfconscious would never have dared to try: the threat of apocalypse slipped in and stated so directly that you could miss it completely, the goofy nostalgia, and the lines: *'Do you remember lying in bed/with the blankets up around your head/radio playing so no one can see?'* It may just be an imminent second childhood, but no rock band ever asked that question before, and no rock band ever made me remember doing just that thing. Rockin' rock and roll radio! Let's gooooohh!

For this and much else . . . in many ways, sure, you're right. The Ramones *are* dumb. But they're dumb in a more communicative, expressive way than anyone else, and musicians far more versatile and songwriters far more 'articulate' have expended all their hard-won skills and failed to say and play one tenth as much. The fashions which they helped to create may be dead, their old imitators may have either moved on or else run aground, but The Ramones simply ramone on, one of a kind, a law unto themselves. Nobody does it better? Nobody does it, *full stop*.

Or like Dee Dee as he clambered onto the coach after the Friars gig, while Johnny went to sit up front and watch the road and Linda wrapped Joey up in a blanket: 'When we got all our reviews 'n I read what the writers had ta say about us I wondered whether we were wastin' our time. Like maybe there was sump'n *wrong* wit' us. Ya know? Then we get up onstage and we rock out an' I know there's nutt'n wrong wit' us.

'Nutt'n!'

Nutt'n can stop the Mooks Of Earl. Play it again, bruddas. An' again an' again an' again.

Wanchewtreefawww!

# Let there be light (entertainment)

*NME*, 1 November 1980

SOMETHING is going to have to be done about *Top of the Pops*.

Your correspondent is, of course, well aware that sensitive people everywhere have been complaining about *Top of the Pops* since the mid-sixties. It also goes without saying that there are many ills troubling Western civilization which are – in real terms – far more harmful than one crappy pop show.

However, since its return to the home screens following that six-week break caused by the technicians' strike, *TOTP* has been given a new format which indicates that our masters have developed some new theories concerning the role which this beat music stuff should play in our lives.

Traditionally, the *TOTP* format was always simple and straightforward. A selection of musical performers with records currently enjoying public favour would flit across the screen introduced by a DJ whose function was to grin, demonstrate his masculinity by leering politely at the tame go-go dancers and assure us that every record in the chart was great. If the DJ kept the verbal down to manageable proportions, the floor manager kept things moving and the chart was healthy, *Top of the Pops* was capable of being almost good fun.

At one point – in the early stages of the dispute – it actually got excellent. All it was at that time was a series of videos linked by titles and the occasional voice-over. BAM BAM BAM: rockin' rock and roll radio, only visual. It actually worked.

But then – like the bad fairy in the pantomime – came the new format. This time, the DJ was supplied with a host of rent-a-celebs, strolling on with their shit-eating grins to read greetings and wisecracks off cue cards, swap limping badinage with the host and whack in hefty plugs for their latest records/movies/TV shows. There was a 'pop news' section, again merely a series of plugs. The other week, Dave Lee Travis prowled through a set liberally decorated with automobiles, all of which were meticulously mentioned by name.

At times, there are so many grade B celebrities plugging their goods that the musical performances seem fewer and further between, separated and spaced by the ludicrous blather that represents Light Entertainment: the kind of thing that can only be justified by the curious theory – which programme planners actually appear to hold – that well-known people popping up for a few seconds and mentioning their latest consumer durables constitutes a spectacle which fascinates the viewing public.

It seems faintly incongruous to start coming on precious about a pop show which has always conspired to present beat music as tacky and trivial and – indeed – lots of the stuff *is* tacky and trivial. However, it's mostly tacky and trivial on its own terms, which are still a good few jumps away from the cosy bubble in which British variety television goes about its business. However, the new-style *Top of the Pops* has gone so far towards comfy parental television to be almost indistinguishable from *Blankety Blank* (which follows it on Thursday nights) – except for the fact that there's no groups on.

Who gives a flying one? When I was a progressive music-type elitist hippie snob – up until seven weeks ago or whenever it was – it was always an article of faith that *Top of the Pops* was a shower of shit, but once the singles chart brightened up and opened out after punk, *TOTP* became a hell of a lot more fun than *Old Grey Whistle Test* (at that time still surfeited out with Proper Musicians With Beards and sensitive Californian types being fawned over by Spineless Bob Harris).

*TOTP* was based on the singles chart, which meant that all of a sudden you could see Pistols, Buzzcocks, Jam, Costello, Dury, Rats and all sorts of interesting 1977-type people right there on chummy, boring old *TOTP*. Right now there are still interesting people gatecrashing the singles chart and getting on *Top of the Pops*, but it's getting harder and harder for them to get a lick in edgeways between all the faded celebs trooping on and off selling their shoddy products. There are less records featured now than there were before. And performances are being trimmed (do you detect a note of paranoia here?).

It is a truism that television does not know how to deal with popular music, always preferring to steer it into the general domain of light entertainment. I have nothing against light entertainment – I am possibly the only British-born contributor to this paper who is prepared to place hand on heart and state that he thoroughly enjoyed *The Blues Brothers* – but what 'light entertainment' means to controllers of UK television is celebrities helping each other plug products, join the charmed conspiratorial circle, and pretend that nothing's wrong. Everything is super. Your movie is super, my record is super, her show is super, his book is super.

So now the studio audience throw balloons and ribbons about to all the super records and applaud all the super guests to the echo (on cue). Where pop (or rock or beat: choose your own euphemism) parts company with 'light entertainment' is that the music does not (should not) pretend that everything is super. The world in which we live collapses apace and the best of our new music faces up to this, either explicitly – by singing about it – or implicitly, by dancing in a manner that suggests that one dances in the knowledge that dancing is not everything.

It is this knowledge that *TOTP* – deliberately or not – is seeking to hide from us. By reducing everything to the level of the TV variety show where everybody knows and is prepared to cover up for everybody else, it steers our music into a backwater where it can do no harm. A Weller or a Bowie is rendered neutral in such a setting.

Context is important: the frame is capable of altering or distorting the picture. Our musicians paint pictures of the world; *Top of the Pops* puts these pictures in a frame which says it doesn't matter.

In a week when Kelly Marie and The Nolans and The Dooleys rule or some TV baritone in a toupee and a facelift gets a totally gratuitous spot, it seems hard to believe that things could ever be any other way. But when a 'Going Underground' or a 'Love Will Tear Us Apart' or something of a similar excellence can be swallowed up in this morass, then one feels cheated.

Sure, they'll give us 'our' music – in measured doses chosen by them – and that's supposed to make it all right when they place it in a context which removes the meaning that made us want it in the first place.

Same time next week then? Super!

# John Lennon and Yoko Ono: 'Double Fantasy' (Geffen)

*NME*, 22 November 1980

IN the cocoon, something stirs. John Lennon – one of the people who used to be in The Beatles, a group reckoned to be hot socks when I was a kid – and Yoko Ono break a five-year recording silence to announce that everything in their garden is wonderful, but wonderful. For people imprinted with the passions and preoccupations of the Beatle Years, the release of 'Double Fantasy' is of necessity An Event, though maybe not a happy one. Everybody else: straight to the next review, please.

Lennon and Ono appear on the cover clamped in a passionate embrace, resembling nothing so much as the Streisand/Kristofferson *Star Is Born* clinch. The album celebrates their mutual devotion to each other and their son Sean to the almost complete exclusion of all other concerns. Everything's peachy for the Lennons and nothing else matters, so everything's peachy QED. How wonderful, man. One is thrilled to hear of so much happiness.

Criticism along orthodox social-realist lines may seem boorish and pompous: after all, anyone can make a record about anything they wish, and if the Ono Lennons find their own domestic and parental bliss to be the only worthwhile subject for their music, then they are perfectly within their rights to finance their next decade with an album that deals purely and simply with their own highly finite universe. The trouble with music that is self-centred to the point of utter solipsism is that one cannot criticize the art without also criticizing the life on which the art is based.

So the Lennons choose their roles and play them to the hilt. John croons his love for his son on 'Beautiful Boy', apologizes to Yoko for ever having been horrid to her, expresses his devotion as debasement. He is besotted and abject (the old bugger still has a wonderful voice, by the way).

On 'Watching The Wheels', he explains that he's perfectly happy not giving a shit about either the rock business or the world events that inspired him to produce 'Some Time In New York City' and that astounding series of late- and post-Beatle solo singles of the early seventies, but by coming out of retirement and releasing an album, he's 'playing the game' whether he admits it or not. Anyway, let's waste no more time on John Lennon. On this showing he can get back to the kitchen and mind the kid and the cows, because all the most interesting material on 'Double Fantasy' is Yoko's.

She answers hubby's 'Beautiful Boy' with her own 'Beautiful Boys', a tripartite essay which devotes its first verse to young Sean, its second to Big John and its third to all the male egos which run the world at the expense of their own and everybody else's humanity. Her verse about Lennon demonstrates that her love and admiration for her husband are considerably more clear-eyed than his for her: he writes about her as an omnipotent, benevolent life-giving Natural Force: she writes about him as a gifted human who is still a child (he says the same thing of himself in another song). Yoko is Mom to both of them: she jestingly depicts herself in just this all-powerful Supermom role in the joky, Nilssonesque 'I'm Your Angel'.

Yoko Ono's entry into rock in the early seventies was heavily attacked by most mainstream rockcrits of the time because even by the eclectic standards of post-hippie art rock her music sounded totally unrocky. In the eighties – post-Slits etc. – her music sounds vastly more modern and considerably more interesting than Lennon's. In particular, 'Kiss Kiss Kiss', 'Give Me Something' and the freezingly eerie 'Every Man Has A Woman Who Loves Him' – an ode to Romantic Destiny, would you believe? – are easily the album's best moments.

Still, Yoko's vision is by no means unflawed. To say the least, anyone who can seriously serve up a song entitled 'Hard Times Are Over' is being a trifle subjective. For those of us still to make our first million, hard times are only just beginning.

'Double Fantasy' is right: a fantasy made for two (with a little cot at the foot of the bed). It sounds like a great life, but unfortunately it makes a lousy record. Still, who said that rock stars – and Lennon is one of those for life whether he wants it or not – were under any obligation to provide record buyers with anything 'useful'? Of course they're not, but people like Paul Weller do so whether there's an obligation or not.

That's why I look forward to a Yoko Ono solo album, why I wish that Lennon had kept his big happy trap shut until he had something to say that was even vaguely relevant to those of us not married to Yoko Ono and why I'm pissed off because I haven't heard the Jam album yet.

Now bliss off.

# Shout! The True Story of the Beatles by Philip Norman (Elm Tree); John Lennon: 1940–1980 by Ray Connolly (Fontana)

*NME*, 4 April 1981

TELL me the story of The Beatles again, Daddy. Tell me about John at art school as a short-sighted Ted and how he first met Paul (who could play 'Twenty Flight Rock' properly), how George was this funny little kid who hung about with them and who no one took seriously. Tell me about Pete Best who got slung out and Stu Sutcliffe who died (but who couldn't really play the bass) and about all those wild nights in Hamburg, *please*, Daddy.

Tell me about how they met Brian Epstein (who had dramatic ambitions and really loved John) and how they got turned down by Decca. Then tell me about how they became the biggest stars the world had ever known. Please, Daddy. I know I've heard this story so many times before, but I always sleep better after I've heard the story of The Beatles . . .

To paraphrase the great Samuel K. Amphong: why is Beatles book? The greatest (rock) story ever told and told and told and TOLD. Every so often it crops up again – thank you, Mark Chapman, you've certainly helped a lot of people sell a lot of THINGS – embellished with a few new details. Philip Norman retells the chalice-in-a-palace legend; Ray Connolly dismisses said anecdote as apocrypha. Like all good bedtime stories, the legend of The Beatles is subject to endless embellishment; every time it

goes round again someone comes up with a couple of new anecdotes to liven up the well-worn tale.

Norman's book — which is by far the better of the two —
actually tells the reader more about John Lennon — but then The
Beatles' story was always more John Lennon's than anybody
else's. Mr Norman certainly has his knife well into Paul McCartney
all the way through the book, which suits this reviewer just fine,
and who can resist a wave of genuine revulsion when we learn that
the first words of the fourteen-year-old Macca, upon learning of
his mother's death were 'But what will we do without her money?'
or that when he was upset with his parents, he would sneak into
their bedroom and put imperceptible rips into their lace curtains?
I mean, what a . . .

Look: all the great rock stories are tragedies. The Beatles' story
was a tragedy even before the hideous, melodramatic climax of
the Lennon shooting. Even the ones that don't climax with death
(Hendrix, Morrison, Joplin, Pistols) climax with slow decay, lost
opportunity and broken promises. I saw The Who on television
last night, and that's the tragedy of a ghastly marriage from which
no one has the courage to walk out. Forgive The Beatles: they just
didn't know any better. How could they? What happened to them
had not happened to anybody else before except Elvis, and look
what happened to him.

As for Beatles' biographers, they have no such excuse for
telling that same old bedtime story all over again to the same old
crew of big babies. In other words:

> *. . . because the story's a saddening bore,*
> *And I've read it ten times or more,*
> *It's about to be writ again . . .*
> *And Lennon's on sale again.*

© *David Bowie: 'Life On Mars' 1971*

# The Police:
# 'Ghost In The Machine'
# (A&M)

*NME*, 3 October 1981

**O** STING, where is thy depth? And whoever suggested that it was necessary or desirable to plumb it?

The Police have run a fair old racket on the world since 1977, when their collective stock was so low that the idea of The Police ever becoming massively popular was only fractionally less ludicrous than the notion that Adam And The Ants could do likewise. Through deafening storms of approbation in every country in the world where Coca-Cola is sold, three well-padded albums and enough decent singles to fill most of one side of a greatest hits album, Sting – The Most Beautiful Man In The World – steps forward to answer that vital question 'Who's your favourite philosopher?'

Well, Lynn Hanna gave the game away completely last week, and the answer must have come as one hell of a shock to the Watsonian Behaviourists in The Police's audience. One imagines a contest somewhat akin to a cross between the Deputy Leadership and the Oscars: Bette Midler rips open an envelope and announces, 'The winner is ... *Arthur Koestler*!' as B.F. Skinner, lips trembling, complexion ashen, does his best to applaud like a good loser should while choking on the fact that the new Police album will not be entitled 'Beyond Freedom And Dignity'.

To support the weight of their current subject-matter, The Police have come up with A New Sound: they've ditched the sharp, cool interlocking fragments of texture and rhythm with which they pioneered New Wave in America and created a sonic blancmange involving hundreds of guitar-synthed, effects-ridden Andy Summers overdubs, a lot of saxophones and several harmonizing Stings. They now sound like a cross between The Bee Gees and a reggaefied Yes which I'm sure everybody will agree is one hell of an advance. Only Stewart Copeland's clattering, bustling drums – as audaciously busy and showy as ever – hew to the

341

original blueprint, and Copeland is consistently the most interesting player throughout.

The album's best moment comes halfway through the second side with 'One World', a swaggering upful call for unity which almost certainly meets with Miles Copeland's full approval. Even there, Summers' guitar sound is muffled and spongy, but the song's feel and sentiment carry a genuine warmth which is unambiguously appealing.

Its worst arrives at the end of the first side: The Police unveil *their* version of 'Demolition Man', the song that Sting wrote for Grace Jones. This rendition of the song pretty much *is* a 'walking disaster': Summers plays an extended Heavy Metal solo all the way through the song, and . . . well, I thought my razor was dull until I heard the bass line.

Everywhere else is blancmange (maybe a better title for the album would have been 'Blancmango De Trop', which would at least have preserved conceptual continuity with their first three efforts): whether Sting's being 'sexual' on 'Hungry For You', metaphysical on 'Spirits In The Material World' or concerned and aware on 'Invisible Sun', he and his colleagues combine a woolly sound with woolly thinking to minimum effect. Even when they briefly return (via a song for which Stewart Copeland wrote the music) to the punky-trash vein which they mined before the Big Skank hit them, 'Rehumanize Yourself' – the album's second-best track, as it happens – is still weighed down by too much paraphernalia.

It's all good humanistic stuff and if rock bands are going to push their favourite philosophers I'd take a reggae-ish pop band promoting Arthur Koestler over a pomp(ous) HM group pimping for Ayn Rand any day of the decade. The fact remains that – as far as this particular listener is concerned – 'Ghost In The Machine' is AMAAAAAAAAAZINGLY DULL. Sting is obviously a decent, intelligent chap and if we were debating politics and philosophy I'd probably find large areas of agreement with him, but dull music with worthy sentiments attached is, ultimately, no more rewarding an aesthetic experience than dull music with foul sentiments.

Koestler's book is available in a Picador edition for considerably less than the cost of The Police's album.

# Alex Harvey, 1935-1982: The faith healer

*NME*, 13 February 1982

*GOOD evening, boys and girls. My name is Harvey* ...

I long ago lost count of the number of times I heard that introduction during the first half of the seventies. The Sensational Alex Harvey Band were one of the craziest, most honest, most creative and most courageous bands of their time, and also the most public and best-known phase of the career of Alex Harvey, the man who won a Tommy Steele rock-alike contest in Glasgow in the mid-fifties and thereafter dubbed himself 'The Last Of The Teenage Idols'.

Alex Harvey died last week. There's a news story with the facts elsewhere in this issue, but now I want to remember Alex Harvey as I knew him and I want you to bear me witness. If you knew him too then you'll know that what I say is true, and if you didn't then I wish you had.

I remember him like this: after a sold-out Rainbow show where the SAHB were received – *totally* received – by an utterly open audience, Alex was hunched over in a corner, desolated. There was a post-gig party going on all over the balcony, and Alex was convinced that he hadn't communicated what he wanted to communicate to the audience: the gig had been a 'success', but Alex felt he hadn't done what he wanted to do. In fact, he had: the reaction from the audience had been as honest and enlightened as the band's performance, and he finally allowed himself to be convinced of this. 'But I don't *ever*,' he insisted, spacing the words out very calmly and very definitely, 'want to hear that Harvey was great if Harvey was shit. If I'm shit I want to *know* about it.'

I remember him like this: in Miami, Florida, the day after the band's truck – containing all their instruments and equipment and costumes – was ripped off from outside the hall where they'd played, Alex was running around a dolphinarium in T-shirt, shorts and cowboy boots admiring the most intelligent species on the planet. He only alluded once to the disaster. 'I wouldn't'a minded,' he announced, 'but I had a coupla *Sergeant Fury* comics lyin' around in that truck.'

And I remember him like this, too: a small, solidly built, black-haired man with rough, seamed features, gapped front teeth, eyes both piercing and amused and a grin that hit his face like an earthquake. He had the kind of voice that most English people would consider to be archetypically Glaswegian, and he embodied warmth, compassion and an all-consuming interest in and concern for other people. He was also one of the least bitter people I have ever met.

What showed most about Alex Harvey the performer was his very real devotion to his audiences. He would go to any length to enlighten and to entertain, and − as his notion of theatrical presentation developed from a few simple costume changes and bits of business to complex arrangements of props and gadgets − his work was never bombastic and never attempted to substitute extravagance for genuine communication. Time after time, he would exhort his audiences to avoid both private and institutionalized violence − 'don't make any bullets, don't buy any bullets and don't shoot any fucken bullets' − and to behave responsibly towards each other and their environment − 'don't piss in the water supply'.

His work derived from a variety of sources: his own experience of growing up in a decaying inner city, the music which he had discovered in his early teens and identified with so thoroughly (the music of artists like Billie Holiday, Jimmie Rodgers, Charlie Parker, Django Reinhardt, Elvis Presley, Howlin' Wolf, Hank Williams, Big Bill Broonzy and Little Richard), and a rich vein of fantasy. He loved *King Kong* and *Treasure Island, Sergeant Fury and his Howlin' Commandos* and *Tarzan, Frankenstein* and *Rio Bravo*, Dashiell Hammett and Marlon Brando. In concert, he would demand, *'Let me put my hands on you'* and − in character as The Faith Healer − he would provide a series of Saturday morning serials that took what was going on outside the cinema into account.

He could appear as Vambo, the graffiti-spraying Robin Hood of the tenements, as the piratical narrator of 'The Tomahawk Kid', as the trench-coated private eye trapped in the bewildering case of 'The Man In The Jar', and − probably most memorably − as the doomed *Wild One*-style hoodlum of 'Framed,' a number which eventually developed into one of the most highly charged set-pieces on the British rock stage.

Originally, he would appear as the Brandoesque biker villain implausibly claiming to have been stitched up, punch his way through a fake brick wall at the back of the stage and — by stuffing a stocking-mask into his mouth — transform into the Brando of *The Godfather*, still pleading his innocence. As the piece changed over the years, Alex took it to the furthest extreme by doing the number as Adolf Hitler, a confrontational reaction to the early signs of the increasing threat of the bonehead Right.

Yet Alex was not only effective when working with his props and costumes. Before the formation of the Sensational Alex Harvey Band, I saw him work supported only by a bass player and a drummer, and he was excellent. And even with SAHB, two of his most effective performances utilized no elaborate devices; they achieved their impact simply because Alex Harvey had the insight to locate the central core of the song and the passion to get him to that core.

His performance of Jacques Brel's 'Next' is purest bravura, and it works precisely because Harvey reduced the distance between himself and the song to nothing. He became the song, was utterly present in the song and, by doing so, pulled the listener right in there with him. He did the same with 'Delilah', the old Tom Jones chestbeater, by forcibly entering the song and demonstrating exactly what it was about: murder and sexual jealousy, something squalid and vicious and utterly unworthy of glamorization.

It is a familiar truism to say of performers that there was no pretence or artifice about them, but in the case of Alex Harvey it is totally appropriate. When he told his audiences that he loved them they believed him, and the reason that they believed him was that they knew it was true. He commanded the same kind of love, trust and respect that Ian Dury does, the kind that comes from a relationship with the audience that is based on honesty. During the period of Alex's greatest popularity, he did not just provide an escape from everyday existence through dem ol' rock and roll fantasies, but he depicted and celebrated that existence and the process of that escape, and the relationship of one to the other.

Prior to the arrival of punk, Alex and his band enjoyed the

closest relationship with the urban realities of the UK of any of their contemporaries and competitors. The SAHB foreshadowed punk, welcomed it and broke up with its arrival.

The two greatest contributing factors to the decline in Alex's fortunes over the last five years were the death of Bill Fehilly, his long-time manager and close friend, and a severe back injury during a tour which rendered him immobile and in great pain for quite some time. Bruised and debilitated both emotionally and physically, he never quite regained his full powers. He formed a post-SAHB band which made one patchy album for RCA which was redeemed by two astonishingly powerful tracks, and had returned to low-key touring during 1981.

What comes most often to mind when thinking of Alex Harvey is his warmth, his humour, his compassion and his seemingly endless capacity to give. It's foolish to talk about his quarter-century in music and his long service to rock and roll as if it was a spell in the army or a lifetime job in an insurance company.

Alex Harvey started in music in the fifties as 'Scotland's Tommy Steele', he formed a band that backed visiting American stars from Vincent and Cochran to John Lee Hooker, he played nightclubs and musicals and finally got to be famous, and the whole time he just gave and gave and gave. Whenever he was in someone's company, he gave himself unreservedly to that person. When he was in front of an audience he gave himself unreservedly to that audience. A faith healer indeed.

His death comes ten years after that of his younger brother Leslie, the lead guitarist and founder member of Stone The Crows, a soul-influenced early-seventies band featuring Maggie Bell as lead vocalist. It was after Leslie died of electrocution onstage that Alex marshalled his full artistic and personal resources to go out and *really* do it, to express that dream he had of rock and roll, not as the sad and discredited thing that it sometimes seems to be, but as something as rough and warm and wild and generous as he was himself.

Alex Harvey was my sergeant. I never met anyone quite like him and I never will again.

# John Lee Hooker, Bobby 'Blue' Bland, B.B. King: Talkin' blues

*NME*, 5 June 1982

*LISTEN to the blues! Listen to what they're saying to you . . .*

The blues speaks haltingly at first, haltingly and quietly in a darkened room. The curtains are drawn to shut out whatever passes for daylight during a dull noon hour in Hammersmith, and a battered guitar case decorated with stickers leans up against one wall.

John Lee Hooker is stretched out in one of the twin beds, his head propped up against a pair of pillows. He seems very small and frail, almost shrunken; it is as if he had once been bigger, much bigger. He is wearing a black satin shirt open over a blue vest, and his fragility is offset by a stylish, globular pot belly. He is unwilling to talk for more than half-an-hour.

> *John Lee Hooker: born 22 August 1917 in Clarkesdale, Mississippi, the son of sharecroppers, and one of eleven children. He learned to play guitar starting with plunking a strip of rubber nailed to a barn wall. At fourteen, he ran away to Memphis and worked his way to Cincinnati and finally to Detroit where his musical career took off and where he made his first records. For a variety of labels he cut a bewildering profusion of tracks, scoring biggest with 'Boogie Chillen', 'I'm In The Mood For Love', 'Crawling King Snake', 'Dimples' and 'Boom Boom'. Toured Britain in the early sixties and became a firm favourite among white blues fans, making inroads into the American rock audience in the late sixties.*

His voice is deep and quiet and hesitant: he has the strongest, thickest Mississippi accent I've ever heard. He talks about his early music.

'The first record I made in Detroit was for a company you

would never have heard of: "Guess I'm Alone" on Staff Records. That was my first little record; it was a small little company just around the community, it didn't get anywhere but just around town, to Ohio and places like that. Then I went to another label and met Bernie Besman . . .'

Bernie Besman recorded Hooker, entranced by his combination of rural 'downhome' style and ragged, clamorous urban intensity. He cut some of the most vital post-war blues tracks with Hooker, and they sold hundreds of thousands of singles. He also decided that his cut of the cake was insufficient, and – not content with paying himself as producer and label boss – took half of the songwriting credits as well.

'He didn't write *anything*! He got into a lotta trouble for that,' Hooker adds, not without an air of quiet satisfaction. 'Now we got that squared away so he's no longer on them songs. After I started getting really big, his label couldn't handle it so they leased my masters out to Modern Records.'

And that put him in some of the fastest R&B leagues of the time. Modern Records – which also incorporated the Crown and Kent labels – could boast the likes of B.B. King and Bobby Bland as leading rookies, and label boss Larry Bihari, like his opposite number at Chess Records in Chicago, was leasing masters of the likes of Sam Phillips as well, channelling blues from all over the country through their LA outlet. Out of all his work, Hooker expresses greatest fondness for his early sides: those and an album he cut in 1970 with Canned Heat, whose outstanding vocalist/guitarist/harpist/pianist Alan Wilson committed suicide before the album's release.

'He was the man. He was *the person*. He could play *anything*, and after he dropped out that band never was the same. He knowed my music like a *book*. He were really outstanding . . .

'What I'm doin' now is . . . I haven't been with a record company in a long, long time, but I just recorded a brand new album. What we doin' is goin' to find a company to lease the master to. It's a really good album, we planned it really good, all new stuff on there. My partner, he's in Vancouver, Canada . . . you probably heard'a Vancouver . . . an' he sent out a lotta letters to a lotta companies an' he gotta lotta respond. We lookin' to un*load* this album on some company, an' it shouldn't be hard to do. Everybody know who John Lee Hooker is: everybody know what I do. It's the same kind of thing, but it's uptempo, it's a more modern sound . . .'

So how does John Lee Hooker check for the modern sound? How does the master of downhome react to soul?

'Awww . . . soul I even hate to talk about, y'know? I don't put it down, but it just ain't my kind of music but if kids like it that's OK with me. I listen to mainly blues an' I like some of the hard *good* rock. I likes *solid* rock, sump'n with a good beat to it. I like the uptempo stuff, but it got to have a *feelin'*, ain't got to be just a bunch of noise. And I likes some good jazz too . . . but the blues is my bag. That's the only music that I *love*.'

John Lee Hooker's music has stayed essentially the same throughout his recording career. He has presented himself in a variety of contexts, but *he* has remained constant to the harsh, droning modalities of the earliest Delta blues. He is a mere seven or eight years older than B.B. King, but musically they are separated by an entire era.

'Others have changed. Me, no. I ain't changed. I don't wanna change. I *could* change. I could go into disco . . . I can play it, but I don't wanna play it. I don't *feel* it. I got one record on the new cut where I did it just to try it out, called "I'm Jealous". It's got a disco beat to it. I did it 'cause we finished recording an' we run out of things to do on it and so we just jammed it out. Maybe it could be somethin' big, y'know, but I'm so into the blues, I don't care who change, I don't care who go for the big money, I'm gonna do what I like an' what I feel. I *feel* what I do.

'An' I'm doin' really good, I ain't hurtin' for money. I got that. A *lot*. I done invest my money in real estate, I got about five homes in the States. I could retire and never do it no more, but I love it too much. This is my life, y'know . . . Things I like to do when I ain't workin': I love baseball, that's my hobby, an' cars is my hobby. I love drivin' new cars, I just got me the new Mercedes. You know the 360SL? I got a new one for '82, it's one of the *best* cars made. That's what I like in life: cars, baseball and I likes *ladies*,' he chuckles loudly, 'but I guess everybody do.'

The phone rings. Hooker is informed that he is about to be photographed and hops spryly out of bed. He zips up his pants, buttons his shirt, claps his hat onto his head. He says his health is real good these days, it's just that he gets awful tired sometimes.

*

And the blues speaks warmly but carefully in a rich, furry voice. In the ante-room of a suite, cartons of Alpine cigarettes and a selection of white polyester suits are strewn around. A bedroom is through *there*. The walls fail to mask the sounds of afternoon television and a tenor saxophone player running through his scales.

> *Robert Calvin Bland, better known as 'Bobby Bland' or 'Bobby Blue Bland': born 27 January 1930, in Rosemark, Tennessee. Moved to Memphis in his mid-teens and joined The Beal Streeters vocal group, which also included B.B. King, Rosco Gordon and Johnny Ace. He recorded for Modern and worked for B.B. as driver and valet, but didn't commit himself to music until after he came out of the army. Until 1961 he and Junior Parker toured as 'Blues Consolidated', but since 'Further On Up The Road' (1957), his first hit, he was a regular in the R&B charts. Neither a songwriter nor an instrumentalist of any distinction, he is purely a vocalist, and as such is probably the finest singer to come out of the post-war blues.*

They don't call him 'Big Bobby Blue Bland' for nothing: Bobby Bland is *enormous*. He is about six foot three and solid, not the amiable butter-ball of his early photos, and not the ingenuous smiler of those early days, either. His face is lined, his eyes are wary and watchful, his exquisitely manicured fingers flash with heavy jewellery. His hair is neither in the extravagant conk of the fifties, nor the natural of the late sixties and the seventies, but long and straight, down over his ears, framing his forehead.

'I would not like to be classified as just a blues singer, because I do a variety of lyrics on the ballad side, but we do just about whatever comes along. When I first started listening, it was blues strictly, then spirituals – I am a Baptist – and then I started listening to Tony Bennett and Nat King Cole, Andy Williams and people in that line . . . more softer stuff. Nat was one of my great admirers . . . I really idolized the way he took his lyrics, his diction and his softness.

'And I listened to country and western, whatever had a story. In my early days I did the harsh blues kind of thing, but I really wanted to do the softer stuff. Sometimes I like to go back to the roots of things, get a good blues lyric going and see what I can get out of that, but mostly it's mellow. I like Nat because he had that velvet voice. Basically, I like to have that good story and I've had a lot of good musicians and good writers. I like anybody who has that good story for me to tell.'

Bland had made his debut with Modern, but after his service stint he ended up recording for Don Robey's Houston-based Duke Records, ending up with ABC when that conglomerate bought Duke in '74.

'I'd done a lot of odd jobs. I specialized in parking cars in this garage and before that I was a grocery boy. I'd always wanted to sing – I sing all the time – but I never thought that I'd get into this particular thing that I have today.

'I'd always wanted to sing, but I had been singing spirituals because the background was a church background, basically. It wasn't that big a switchover, because the blues and spirituals have the same sort of phrasing, and you just sing "baby" instead of "My Lord". I don't see anything *wrong* with singing the blues: I just don't put the two together. I'm just as much a believer today as I was before I knew anything about the blues. I serve The Lord in whatever I am doing, but I wouldn't put the two together. I believe in doing one thing at a time. I did a spiritual album before the last one called "Ain't God Something?" and I can relate to that: he *is* something.'

Bland first met B.B. King when the older man came to Memphis from Mississippi and scored his slot on radio station WDIA.B.B. combined singing and deejaying and 'being the kinda fellow that he is, always willing to help someone out', he let the young Bland sing a number or two on his show. Bland had known King from his records before they actually met, and his admiration has remained undimmed over the years.

And who else does Bland check for vocally?

'I get a lot of pointers from different people, diction-wise or phrasing-wise. Nat King Cole, as I said, for that softness, Perry Como for the old standards, because he shows no strain whatsoever when he's doing a song . . . Andy Williams and Tony Bennett. But I had a lot of idols when I started: Joe Turner, Lowell Fulson, Jimmy Witherspoon, Roy Brown, and for today . . . well, B. is one of my favourites. But for soft music, it's got to be Como, Brook Benton, those kind of people. I like Earth Wind And Fire, I listen to War . . . *"you got the pow-weeerr"* . . . but I'm not really into groups.

'I also like country and western. I did a country album a little while back but they told me it was too bluesy. It didn't do any good because of the way I was doing it, I don't know, but *I* thought I did it just the way I do everything else because I couldn't be just a plain country singer. I was *raised* around country music in a little placed called Rosemark Tennessee, and all you could get on the radio at night-time was Roy Acuff, Red Foley, Eddie Arnold, those type people. I think Kenny Rogers is doing a beautiful job as the new singer in country and western.

'Blues and soul ... I don't see how you can define them ... I think they are just one and the same. They are about facing the facts and seeing that things are as they are ... if there is something that you can do about it, then you better try, and if it doesn't work out then you had better just chalk it up to experience if it's not in your favour. That's what it's all about. I find myself weighin' things, because there's always two sides to everything, two different approaches or whatever. It's like havin' a good woman. You got to cherish her, you got to try and see things how she sees them, and feel what she feels ... I call that facin' facts.'

Probably the most oft-heard criticism made of Bland is that his show is heavily Vegasized: that he is verging on MOR. Well, he's no Vic Goddard, but when the moment comes it's definitely an album of standards. What else would you expect from a hard-core Perry Como fan?

The blues speaks in an animated, precise, warm tone which masks what sounds like real fatigue, in a bright, airy room with cases of flowers, bowls of fruit, packages of albums and a bottle of whisky carefully distributed over the furnishings, B.B. King is being interviewed by two journalists at once. Short and stocky, but drastically slimmed down from his last visit here, he holds court in every sense of the word.

> *Riley B. King, known as B.B. King: born 16 September*
> *1925, in Indianola, Mississippi. He was born on a*
> *plantation, and when he was four his parents separated.*
> *He went to live with his mother, but rejoined his father*
> *at nine when his mother died. At eighteen he quit*
> *plantation work to hitch to Memphis, where he played at*
> *parties and on the streets. His first singles, cut in 1949,*
> *were hits and he had already made a local success as a*

*deejay. He criss-crossed America endlessly in twenty*
*years before he was discovered by the white rock audience.*
*Since then he has become universally accepted as the*
*most prominent and respected blues singer in the world*
*and probably the most influential electric guitarist alive*
*today. He has played all over the world – including in*
*the Soviet Union – and is an Honorary Doctor of Music*
*at Yale University.*

B.B. King's belly occupies the no-man's land between his blue slacks and his safari shirt, his glasses have a discreet BBK on one lens and his hair is impeccably styled into wet-look curls.

'I've always wanted to go to Greece,' he is telling a Greek writer. 'And it always seemed like something happened, I was never able to go.'

The other writer asks him about the 'incredible enthusiasm'. 'Last night was a first for me,' B.B. King proclaims, 'because I've never sung on the same bill as Bobby Bland and John Lee Hooker before, *ever*. We didn't discuss last night who was gonna come back onstage at the end and so the joke was on me because I planned to surprise everybody, the audience as well as Bobby and John – 'cause we really didn't plant nothin' – and I was the one who was surprised because John was not there when I called him. I felt that *history* was made, because even in the States this has never happened before.'

My turn comes up. B.B. had been up until 5.30 that morning, and had spent the day doing a series of gruelling radio interviews, with the result that – despite the extremely professional face that he was putting onto everything – he was absolutely knackered.

I tell him he looks tired.

'Well, this is very important to me. I want all my fans, or anybody's who's interested, to know anything that they might want to know about me. Who knows? Someone in this big . . . metropolitan . . . might want to know just the thing that *you're* going to ask, and if that's the case, I'd like them to know.'

And the weird thing is that he is utterly convincing. That – coming from most other people I've interviewed – would sound like the most horrible, creepy, self-serving bullshit, but from B.B. King it means just what it says. Just as his personal warmth cuts through any showbizzy soft soap onstage, his integrity and courtesy are beyond doubt when you talk to him.

So I started out by asking for his opinion on Charles Sawyer's recently published biography of him. 'Let me say it this way: Charles Sawyer is a good friend of mine, and when he was getting ready to do the book – he asked to do it about ten years prior to that – he said, "What I want to do is write about B.B. King the man, not the musician. I wanna write about you," so I said, "Fine, as long as there's truth in what you write I won't fight you." And I haven't found anything that he wrote that wasn't true.

'There's a few things in there that I would probably not have wrote if I'd been doin' it myself, but there's nothin' there that I'm ashamed of. And he did a *lot* of research. There's things in there that he brought up that I was in error about. I'm happy about it.'

In the book, Sawyer states that B.B.'s ambitions were to record a country album, an album of standards, a big band album and a tribute to Louis Jordan. Is his latest, 'Love Me Tender', the first in that masterplan series?

'Right, it is. I don't know about the ones to follow, but I feel that this is the greatest thing that I have ever done or put together. It just came together so well.'

It certainly emphasizes how many changes have occurred since you first started recording.

'Everything has changed since that time. The music . . . exposure have changed because there are many, many more radio stations today that will feature various type of music – and some blues. Instruments are easier to come by today than they were when I first started. It was hard for me to get a good guitar, but now you can go into a pawnshop or any place and get a good guitar for not a lot of money. Electronics have really become a thing of the future, the computers around now can see a sound and tell you exactly what it is. It may not be able to create it because you have to have a person to do that, but all of this is available. When I was a kid I never used to know the word "computer" because the word was not needed. All of these things have made music change.

'The world is constantly progressing, and you've got to do the same to stay alive and be around in that world.'

Bobby Bland told me earlier on that country music was always around for black people in the South.

'I heard it long before I heard a radio, because in the Delta there was poor whites just like there was poor blacks. They would sing country music and we would sing it too: we called it "the white man's blues". We can sing theirs just like they can sing ours – same difference, but everybody sings gospel.

'Learning to play guitar I used to order books teaching you to play, and the books would have musical notation teaching you where to put your fingers, and this was always done to a country song. I learned to read music and to play like that long before I could play "Three O'Clock Blues" [his first hit, scored in 1952] because there was no blues written down.

'I was well aware of country music at the time, then, just like I was of gospel. It's been in my head all along. I just didn't choose to continue it.

'I don't know which of them albums I'll do next. That's gonna depend on the trend of the music and how the company sees the next album. But at the moment my health is good – I feel real well – and I don't feel in no big hurry to try and finish those other special albums off before I pass on.

'What I wanna do is stay within the trend of the mainstream of music today, but don't get me wrong. I don't want to be too mod. I don't want to get creative to the point where I'm doing something for '92. I want it to be something that people can live with *now*. I don't want it to be sophisticated to the point where it ain't B.B. King – I want it to *be* B.B. King, and I ain't forgettin' my roots of "Three O'Clock Blues". I ain't *never* gonna forget that, but nor do I want it to be as it was then. I don't want to make another "Three O'Clock Blues" for '49, but if I can make a "Three O'Clock Blues" for '82.'

You sounded then as if you were just really *in that moment*.

'I can't be like that now. I'm concerned now about many things now, but then I was only concerned with what I was doing *then*. I didn't even really give a damn if *no*body liked it. But then I started to think, "No, you're *not* the greatest. No, you're *not* the only one that can do it. No, there are *many* people that can do the same thing if not better."

'That I thought later, but *then*, I thought I was one of the greatest singers around, man! I never thought I was the greatest guitar player but ... *that's* when you start to practise. That's when you realize there's a lotta guys out there, buddy, that can do *exactly* what you doin' ...

'But they can't be you! That's the only consolation. They can be good, they can be *better*, but they cannot feel what I feel. *No one knows what I feel . . .*'

No one feels what the Blues Boy feels. It is possibly very easy to attack – from a white rockist standpoint – what the bluesmen do these days, to attack them as a gang of old Vegas showbiz copouts. Joe Strummer does, and I know what he means, but I disagree with him: their journey from the depression in the Delta to the success they have today – small as it is compared to the success achieved by, say, Olivia Newton-John – is a longer journey than anybody reading this paper can possibly have taken.

No one knows what the Blues Man knows: you never get out of these blues alive.

## Black Uhuru: 'What's up, Ducks?'

*NME*, 3 July 1982

*IT seems to be incontrovertible that someone said that he was the way, the truth and the life. And in that capacity he promised that whenever two or three people were gathered together in the name of the Way, the Truth and the Life, there 'I' am in the midst.*

*Even if we do not know the way or cannot believe that there is a way, even if we don't know the truth or don't believe that there is the truth . . . if in the name of these matters we still come together, then 'I', which is not the hallucinations we have inside each of our sacks of skin, is in our midst.*

*That seems to me a most profound proposition.*
*Dare I believe it? Dare I not?*

*This book* [The Facts of Life] *is haunted by the question: What is the correct way to live? When I put this question, through an interpreter, to a reputed saint in Kashmir, said to be over 100 years old ( he looked like an ancient bird ), the instant answer, through the interpreter, was:*

*'Let your heart be like the sun, Shine alike on everyone.'*

*Whence did he derive this knowledge?*
*Or was it mere opinion?*

R.D. Laing, The Facts of Life, *Allen Lane, 1976*

*I and I was granted to drink from the fountain of life*
*I God will make I hold tight*
*I and I knee will not wobble . . .*
*There is a way that seemeth ight to man*
*But in Jah Jah sight it wrong . . .*

*Michael Rose*

Even the whores in the cars are staring. A few streets down from the Place de l'Opéra, just around the corner from the Olympia, Black Uhuru are striding through a Parisian early evening, cutting an effortless swathe through air like silk laden with the indefinable and unique odour of the centre of Paris: a scent of fresh coffee, baking, a touch of brandy and the sour edge of piss.

Step it up *proud* nuh. Up ahead goes Michael Rose, sulky and withdrawn in his grey track suit, locks tucked up in his cap, thoughts tucked up . . . could be anywhere. Getting dragged out before showtime to have his picture taken was not on *his* agenda. Puma Jones sets her own pace, checking the elegant clothes in the windows; she is, if not the last word in chic, certainly one of the next-to-last, but Duckie Simpson is the one whose carriage and presence alert passers-by to the fact that something unusual is going on.

Duckie Simpson founded Black Uhuru. Onstage, he is the least conspicuous member of the group, off to one side carefully stepping in place, joining Puma Jones in those high pure sore-throat harmonies backing and framing Rose's exhortations. But here in this street – or anywhere – his personal authority is unquestioned.

Tall and rawboned, bearded and imperious, he swaggers along in his tall hat and welding goggles, a man confident that he is himself more formidable than anything which could block his path or anyone who might say him nay.

As they pose for Anton Corbijn's camera, the entire street focuses in on them. There is half-suppressed nervous laughter from a family climbing into their car, and Simpson (breaking off from attempting to crack Corbijn's lens with a ferociously dread stare) dramatically whips off his hat. His locks slowly unfurl in the evening breeze: they are not neat braids that fall smoothly to the shoulder, but a defiant growth like swamp roots or antlers.

Dread flash 'im locks an' a weak heart drop, as the saying goes.

On the way back to the concert hall, a young woman detaches herself from the crowd. She is locksed, wears a red, green and back tam and her eyes are shining. She comes over to Simpson, falls into step.

'Good ... ol' ... Ducks,' drawls Michael Rose sardonically. 'Blood ... *claat*!' But by the time the convoy reaches the Olympia and heads backstage, it is Rose who is holding her hand.

Outside the Olympia, Black Uhuru's congregation assemble. Everywhere, giant images stare down from above endless rows of movie houses: even the West End of London is sadly underprivileged cinema-wise compared to this part of Paris. The cafe provides a perfect vantage-point to observe the crowds milling about and then filing in: they are almost exactly what a Black Uhuru audience would be like anywhere in Britain, which is to say one part hip and forward white youth to two parts blacks, half of who – at least – are Dread. The faces of three decades' worth of French stars encircle the foyer bar: the beer goes down and the smoke comes around.

The hall itself is packed solid: it enfolds you in red velvet heat and darkness, sweat and smoke and bodies and talk. The band appear onstage as if deposited there by the power of a single thought, lick into the rhythm of 'Guess Who's Coming To Dinner' and suddenly the music is *inside you*. You have not *heard* it, it has not come forth and *surrounded* you: it is as if you have breathed it in.

There is much talk of 'rhythm' and 'dancing' around: they are long-standing, well-established buzzwords. I have, in my life, heard a lot of rhythm, but the beat that this particular ensemble lay down is like nothing else you can name, the hardest sound I have ever heard musicians produce on a stage.

Check these men: Sly Dunbar is behind the drums, his mournful countenance set in an expression of fierce concentration, peering out over his translucent red, green and gold tom-toms while he generates that flickering hi-hat pulse with one hand and lays down the crispest, most definite, most *unanswerable* two-and-four in the world on the snare with the other.

He has Robbie Shakespeare there with him on one of those

slimline headless Steinberger basses. Head down, fingers working overtime, Shakespeare lives up to his name: his bass *shakes* the hall like some impending earthquake, like the subterranean pulse of an entire planet. If you saw Uhuru at Wembley with The Stones, you got some idea of what's going on, but the PA system hasn't been *made* yet that can let everybody in a stadium that size hear Robbie Shakespeare's bass the way it's supposed to sound. When linked up with Sly's drumming, it's supposed to evoke an irresistible natural force, to create a description of the force of creation itself – in other words, Rastafari.

On top of that, you get direction and embroidery from percussionist Sky Juice, guitarist Darryl Thompson – a tall New York dread with a baddest-brother-on-the-block style – and Bubbler on the keys. And then there's Uhuru: Puma Jones in the middle twisting and chanting, the magisterial presence of Duckie Simpson in place on the periphery and Michael Rose singing, stepping and invoking over his half of the stage.

The Black Uhuru experience is dazzling, militant as all hell and – as you might say – *hard*.

It is in every sense of the word: hard as in tough, hard as in difficult, hard as in ungiving. It is the kind of hard that equates softness with weakness: it is all power and tension, all statement. They don't let up for an instant, even in the less militant tunes like 'Sinsemilla' or 'Sponji Reggae': the mood is confrontational and the word is straight Rastafari.

After a particularly electro-convulsive burst of rhythmic daring from Sly and Robbie, the man from Island Records gets sufficiently into the spirit of the thing to voice a long shout of 'Mmmmmmurdah!', which, after all, was exactly what happened – in a strictly non-metaphorical sense – when Black Uhuru played the Rainbow last July.

'Murder' is a reggae buzzword these last few months, disquietingly enough: it means that something or someone is really *serious* ... because murder is the most serious thing there is. Isn't it?

And Black Uhuru are a serious business. Put it this way: they are not noted for their levity.

The Holiday Inn in the Place de la République is – praise Jah – far more like a French hotel than it is like a Holiday Inn. It says

'Holiday Inn' on the marquee and on the towels and on the bills and in a few other places, but it isn't *really* part of the ubiquitous chain of prefab bolt-holes.

In the foyer: excitement! Sky Juice the percussion player has been the victim of a little Parisian skank. The waiter who brought him his breakfast charged him cash for it at double the customary rate and then stuck the item onto his bill as per normal. The normally ebullient 'Juice is raving:

'Cho 'im t'ief me money man! Mek me see 'im now! Raasclaat *t'ief* man!'

Denise Mills, Uhuru's manager, is not particularly sympathetic. Tall, blonde and devastatingly matter-of-fact, she might seem to be an incongruous occupant of her particular role seeing as how she is (a) female, (b) white and (c) an employee, albeit a senior one, of Island Records. Standing by the desk going over the bills, she tells Sky Juice in briskly callous tones that he's had it, but miraculously the guilty waiter is produced, Sky Juice's 80 francs reappear and all is declared quits. It's a fair cop, but the hotel doesn't seem to feel that the waiter has in any way stepped out of line. He tried on a legitimate skank, got caught and that was that.

On the coach, the company settles in for the drive. Curtains are drawn to keep the French countryside and the stares of the curious where they belong (outside), and the smoke of the herb where *it* belongs (inside). No one talks much, and the order of the day appears to be to get as charged as possible and watch videos: the Kampuchea concerts and an extraordinarily violent Vietnam movie, *The Boys in Company C.*

Darryl Thompson rags Denise Mills about the foul and filthy eating habits of the British with special reference to that vile concoction the steak and kidney pie ('You mean you people actually *eat* that shit?'), and Puma Jones shows off an ornamented biro that she has bought as a souvenir of Paris. Some of the crew doze in the bunks at the back of the coach, and Sly Dunbar keeps a lonely vigil in a back seat, abstaining from the herb ('It just slows me up, makes me want to go to sleep') and tapping out variations to the rhythms that crop up on the video, The Clash and Matumbi seemingly meeting with the most approval.

It is a common fallacy that hanging out with Jamaican performers is a sure way of getting ganja'ed out into the middle distance. This is not, in fact, the case. It is not until your presence has been accepted to some degree that any herb will be offered, and it was quite a few hours into the journey that Puma Jones passed me the back end of the spliff that she'd been smoking. The strength and purity and general *ital* nature of this spliff was such, though, that instead of promoting the likelihood of a conversational break-through, it rendered me incapable of any coherent speech or coordinated action until we were off the coach and onto the boat heading for Albion.

Slowly and purposefully, the party headed for the restaurant, where it speedily became apparent that the relationship between the band and the waiters was not going to be a cordial one.

The Uhuru party order the cream of tomato soup, but Duckie Simpson, eyes blazing, demands that it be made *without cream*. The waiter replies, more than a little superciliously, that cream-of-tomato is 'just an expression, *sir*' and that no actual cream was included in the finished product. Simpson and Rose therefore consented, albeit suspiciously, to consume the soup.

But worse! When it arrives — after protracted delays — it is stone raasclaat cold. Both sides rest on their dignity. The waiter civilly agrees that it *is* cold, gives the tableful of Rastas a filthy gaze and returns very rapidly indeed with fresh bowls of piping hot soup. The game continues throughout the meal. Guess who's coming to dinner? Natty dreadlocks.

Is Black Uhuru achieving what you want to achieve?

'Not yet . . . not at its fullest,' Michael Rose allows. 'This is not about success, this is about free the people mind. The youth-dem got no idea of what they got to deal with. Them live with certain t'ings — Babylon system — and them can't stand it no more. So when them listen to reggae music, reggae music free them mental-ity, open them mind. It take so much of a control over them that even you yourself will ask why. The rhythm *niiiice*, yet the reality that going across, them can't see within it. We travel, because you are limited, and when you travel you get more experience, you get more *open* . . .'

Are the people who're coming to see you receiving what you want to communicate to them or are they just enjoying the show?

'*Bot*'. Them enjoy themselves an' yet they would like to know what's going on, what the lyric is saying.'

What do you want to give to people who come to see you?

'I want to give them the knowledge of what have to be heard: there is *fire* this time. Jah seh 'im shall return as a conquering lion. He was before as a lamb to slaughtah – seen? – so in this time . . . the conquering lion. The youth must know themselves. There is too much fightin' an' war . . . them thing so *unnecessary*. You can't do much . . . but once you retoon to the 'eart, there is enough food there to feed everybody, but as long as you 'ave first class and second class barrier, there will always be war.

'What purpose you think you are living for?' Rose challenges suddenly.

'You can tell me!' His voice rises tauntingly.

I live to do my work and to do what I want without creating pain or suffering for others, to make sure that no one suffers because of me. That a good enough purpose for you?

'*Yeh mon*. But there mus' be someone to pray to. You must know Jah . . . seen? You must know what is right. There are two things in this world, good and bad. One has to deal with the goodness. I and I proud to see so much people coming across. We do not force our music on anybody: you listen an' you tek it for your own. That is its *purpose*. We do not force it on you. If you listen and you are pleased . . . it is up to you. Your own opinion. It is for everyone who wan' hear it.

'We want to help a lot of people, but we don't 'ave enough money. We were wondering if *you* could help out and lend us some.'

You're welcome to my debts.

'I and I know that if this album sell platinum there are a few things that Black Uhuru can do. We can build a studio in Jamaica, 'ave the right amount'a instruments and equipment and everything *right*, get the bes' sound and start record some youth. There is a lotta talent in Jamaica goin' to waste because producers just hustling an' singers are afraid to work wid dem. For "Love Crisis" [Black Uhuru's first album] we never get paid yet. I am angry with them bad producers, but Sly and Robbie 'ave experience. They know the business, they know one mus' give an' take.

'When we firs' start to record with Sly an' Robbie, we didn't get no advance or nut'n like that, but one mus' give an' take. They fin' the rhythms and we sing. They book the time . . . we jus' go in and sing and them find chords and record, a bit of genius work, but it no matter to me. Could sing to a piano or anyt'ing . . .'

362

Rose dismisses any question concerning the respective merits of the various Jamaican governments of the last few years. Since Black Uhuru became a touring band, he has chosen to live in New York City rather than in JA.

Does it seem that nothing can come out of a political system which can help people?

'Help *people*, yes, but can't help me.'

It is time for embarkation cards to be filled out, and Rose catches sight of Puma's special Parisian biro. 'Me wan' borrow that thing,' he cajoles.

'Naw, me buy it special for me sister,' she ripostes, but she knows it isn't going to end there. Rose has picked it up to fill out his own card. 'If you holds it you gwaan *keep* it.'

'Naw, *lose* it man,' his tone simultaneously wheedling and peremptory.

'Yes man,' she retorts sharply, casting an eye at my cassette machine, 'don' mek me argue over the tape . . .'

At this point I look out of the window and catch sight of an inscription bearing the name of the boat in which we are travelling. The symbolism is marvellous . . .

Because *The Spirit of Free Enterprise* brings Black Uhuru to the White Cliffs of Dover . . .

Duckie Simpson has just swaggered through customs with the air of a man who is by definition illegal and is daring somebody to do something about it. His passport is in order, his work permit is cool and his herb . . . well, Jah protect and guide, y'know? He is intrigued by the book I am carrying – R.D. Laing's *The Politics of Experience* – and declares himself to be an enthusiastic and voracious reader.

'I read *everything*, man . . . war, politics, sex, revolution, comics . . . all knowledge is written down there waiting to be found. Everything that has been known has been written down somewhere by somebody, all wisdom there, man . . .'

Beneath his fearsome façade, Duckie Simpson is the most spontaneously warm member of the trio. On the boat, Michael Rose talked to me because he was supposed to. On the bus, Duckie Simpson talks to me because he wants to. He started the group, but he has always subordinated himself to more flamboyant frontmen, like Rose and his predecessor Garth Dennis.

'Me never see myself as a lead singer. Me more prefer to sing harmony, like 'ow me see lead singing is that a lead singer must be outstandin' and very strong. When I'm singing harmony I can sing a high pitch, but when I'm singin' lead I can't do that. I just don't know why, seen? I just can't get certain sounds out of me unless I hear other people singing, so I'm just a born harmony singer. Maybe sometime in the future I'll try to do a lead on a song but now I'm strictly harmony.'

And when you write a song you think in terms of Michael singing it?

'Maybe if I was singing it would turn out different, but the way Michael sings . . . Michael is a very *militant* reggae singer and so like you got to give 'im militant stuff. He can 'andle it more. For instance, give 'im a love song, it be difficult for 'im to 'andle . . .

(Rose had told me, earlier on, that, 'The only level I check is the militant level.')

'The song that means most to me Michael wrote is "Utterance": it is like a Rasta anthem to us. What a joy to hear sounds of a Rastaman . . . in Jamaica, when we were kids, our parents would tell us that the Rasta is a black heart man, that they steal you away and cut your heart out. Dreadlocks used to have to live in the woods an' hills, because in the city they would just run you down, an' my mother would tell me to be careful of those guys. But I started hanging out with them anyway, an' it was a joy to hear what they had to say. You're on the outside, but when you start hanging out with them, you are surprised to find that they're very intelligent.

'I was twelve-plus, thirteen when I start check wha' gwaan with Rasta. My mother had died and there was no one to tell me what to do. I hadda aunt, but she wasn't sayin' very much. I don't listen to what people say, y'hear that?'

Before it is time to go, Puma shows me a collection of Haile Selassie's speeches, delivered to the League of Nations when he was seeking aid against the Italians. Beautifully eloquent, totally founded in common agreement, the very voice of sweet reason itself . . . Selassie continued to ask *why* were all agreements for mutual aid seemingly null and void when the plaintiff was Ethiopia: words to break your heart, Jack.

Finally, there seems to be some understanding and an air of relaxedness: Duckie looks at me and says, 'Where we come from,

is hard. If you jump on a bus, the conductress will curse you
before you even do anything. Do you understand me? This is just
the way we are . . .'

Until the cool-out towards the end, travelling with Black Uhuru
had been an instructive but moderately unpleasant experience.
The atmosphere stopped short of hostility, but there was a tension
and pressure that Black Uhuru just seem to generate around
them. Militant . . . yeah. They are the hardest of the hard, the
toughest of the tough, and as long as Sly and Robbie are with
them to lay down that beat, they're the best band this side of
Aswad.

But – the question is begged – is sheer hardness enough? After
all, the harder they come . . .

# Kurt Vonnegut: 'Ugh! Ugh! Uggle-uggle-uggle!'

*NME*, 26 March 1983

IF anyone ever plays the part of Kurt Vonnegut in a
movie, it would probably have to be Walter Matthau.

It could quite easily be Matthau's sourmashed features crouch-
ing behind Vonnegut's tobacco-bleached moustache, Matthau's
towering height contorted into an apologetic slouch in order not
to embarrass or slight his more stunted brethren, Matthau's drily
nasal tones emerging as if through an intensely convoluted series
of pipes and tubes.

Matthau would probably have a field day with Kurt Vonnegut's
laugh. When some aspect of the ironies of human existence
tickles him beyond endurance, his body literally creases up and
his face begins to resemble a large, moustachioed grape. Each
paroxysm of laughter is separated from the next by a racking,
rattling cough which makes you want to count the cigarette butts
in his ashtray and wonder surreptitiously if he's going to have a
heart attack or cough himself to death right there and then.

365

Saying something funny to Kurt Vonnegut, therefore, carries with it an awesome responsibility. Who would wish on their conscience that this most thoroughly likeable man of American letters keeled over on them without even so much as a 'So it goes'?

So it goes.

Kurt Vonnegut is an American writer in his early sixties who, starting out from a background in engineering and anthropology, made an early reputation in science fiction before becoming one of the very few authors in that field who create a genuine reputation outside it. For sentimental reasons, specialist shops like London's Forbidden Planet still carry complete sets of Vonnegut's work even though their SF content over the last dozen years has been negligible.

A humourist whose principal subject is tragedy, Vonnegut made his first major impression on the literary mainstream with *Slaughterhouse-5*, a fictionalization of his experience as a prisoner of war in the bombing of Dresden during World War II, an event in which 135,000 people died.

Dresden had no military significance whatsoever, and its destruction did not shorten the war or hasten Hitler's defeat by so much as a millisecond. With a few science-fiction interruptions fulfilling the same function as the clowns in Shakespearean tragedy, *Slaughterhouse-5* made Vonnegut's reputation.

'The Dresden atrocity, tremendously expensive and meticulously planned, was so meaningless, finally, that only one person on the entire planet got any benefit from it,' he wrote when the book was reissued in a deluxe edition in 1976. 'I wrote this book, which earned a lot of money for me and made my reputation such as it is. One way or another, I got two or three dollars for every person killed. Some business I'm in.'

He was once accused of selling sugar pills with a bitter coating: sentimentality disguised as tragedy. In Vonnegut's novels, the characters are almost invariably helpless; they are in thrall to history, to their culture, to the chemical activities of their metabolisms. They are the victims of accidents; they are as helpless as the 135,000 who died in Dresden. Vonnegut himself only survived because a collapsing building served to protect him from further injuries.

In his new novel *Deadeye Dick*, his protagonist's life is utterly dominated by the fact that – at the age of twelve – he was cleaning a gun which he impulsively fired, killing a pregnant woman miles away. This character's father was the man who befriended Adolf Hitler in Vienna when the little shithead was a starving painter, and by giving him a coat and buying one of his paintings enabled him to survive long enough to screw up the lives of millions.

So it goes.

The universe, says Vonnegut, is like that. More and more people fall over bigger and slipperier banana skins: no blame.

At the same time, his essays, speeches, interviews and reviews – as collected in his two anthologies of miscellania *Wampeters, Foma and Granfalloons* (1975) and *Palm Sunday* (1981) – have relentlessly demanded from those in authority the kind of responsibility for their actions that they so patently fail to show. His opposition to Nixon during that worthy's term of office was – in true Vonnegutian fashion – both admirable and pointless.

As Vonnegut himself ruefully pointed out, every major literary figure in America was on the record against Nixon, and – until Watergate broke – it didn't do a damn bit of good.

Still, as one of Vonnegut's most celebrated recurring characters, Eliot Rosewater, stated in *God Bless You, Mr Rosewater,* 'Goddamit, you gotta be kind.' Vonnegut's entire body of work, fiction and non-fiction, is dedicated to the proposition that we must recognize and respect the dignity of our fellow humans, and – in doing so – create an end to loneliness.

This tall, rumpled, chain-smoking humanist does not like doing interviews.

'An interview is 180 degrees away from what a writer customarily does, and it quite often depends on the attitude of the interviewer. If some very young person attempts to perform surgery on me and get out of me quickly something that I am having difficulty getting out slowly, then I'm in trouble. I'm used to preparing my words very carefully before they go into print, having them pass through several hands: an editor, my wife and all that, to get it exactly right.

'I've said all *sorts* of things with cameras and tape recorders running that I don't believe at *all* . . . this whole trip to England is completely uncharacteristic. I don't do interviews any more in the United States, and I don't lecture either. Here I'm doing both at the behest of Tom Maschler, who's head of Jonathan Cape [Vonnegut's UK publishers] and a very good friend of mine. With someone like that, any reasonable request becomes a categorical imperative. I have no such friendship with any publisher in New York.' A shrug.

In one of his essays, Vonnegut casually referred to George Orwell as 'a man I admire more than almost any other', but he has written no longer and more elaborate testament to Orwell than that, and neither does he intend to.

'He has been so well represented by himself that there is almost nothing that I could add. If he had been a dramatist, say, then there would have been some point to writing an essay on him, but it would be very hard to bring anything new from the outside to what a journalist is able to say about himself. There is very little more to say about him, except by his wife or maybe by some very close friends. I appreciate him tremendously, I would love to have written what he had written. I would love to have been him . . . I wouldn't like to die as he died, though.'

What does Vonnegut feel that his appreciation of Orwell has contributed to his own work?

'A natural harmony . . . I am from fairly well-to-do circumstances, marginally well-to-do circumstances, and grew up with the same puritanical beliefs that he had, that people with advantages should serve the less fortunate . . .' he launches into a preliminary splutter of laughter, catches himself and continues . . . 'if I had been eight years older I would have been old enough to go to the Spanish Civil War, and I hope that I would have done. What the boyish part of me responds to in him is the spirit of his departure for Spain, not his disillusionment. What thrills me is his going to work in Paris as a dishwasher and then coming over here and finding out what it's like to be a hobo.

'I like that. That's exciting. It's a little like *Treasure Island* or something like that, a wonderful boys' adventure. I have a little of that left in me, and as far as the disillusionment goes . . . sure, disillusionment is boring. I prefer Koestler for disillusionment. I would like to read Orwell for the romance and Koestler for the disillusionment.'

Unlike Orwell, who used common material for both fiction and essays but kept the two rigidly separated, Vonnegut has gradually stripped away so much of the apparatus of the novel from his work that the distinction is rapidly collapsing. How much of that apparatus has to stay before the novel actually becomes an essay?

'Well, I suppose it would be perfectly all right if the thing *did* transform itself into an essay halfway through as long as it made sense as a whole work of art. This is an adventure for me: I have no idea as to what's been causing these changes. I certainly haven't planned each book, but part of it must be my sense of being well-known. People recognize me and this entitles me to a certain degree of familiarity. It's the sort of thing that happened to a great actor like John Barrymore, who became so colourful that it didn't matter a damn what play he was in.'

Like Orwell again, you have become your own most finely delineated character.

'Yeah, well, I would hope so, but that's simply one way of writing. Just as I am tall, and as my eyes are a certain colour, this seems to come naturally. It was some sort of genetic change, not something I planned as a matter of policy.

'What psychiatrists have found – those who've dealt with a lot of writers – is that they can't guide it at all. Sure, they can shape a story or edit it . . . I have taught some – sure, I know it's a joke to teach creative writing, but it can be done – and talking about what I do for a living as a trade, I know that once you've got about seventy-five pages, a book will start making demands of its own, and if you give in to those demands it's been my experience that you have demands and that a book has demands and if you average them out then you will wind up with something which can be contained in an eggshell. Then everything needed for nourishment will be inside of this case, and you bring up a subject and finally the book will insist on amending or refuse to accept your character.

'You have to be *alert* to the needs of your book. One thing I know too is that my intelligence is a new part of the brain very deeply submerged under the old brain and separated by a layer of *fat*.' He punches the last word hard, and grins through his cloud of smoke. 'And every so often, some of this comes through and you see how smart you can be when those messages get through. I want to go to a *surgeon* and have that barrier *slit*' – he leans forward, fighting off an irresistible attack of mirth – 'because *sometimes* . . . I am so *smart*' – he begins to splutter – 'that it's almost *un-be-liev-a-able* . . .'

I will now attempt to let you know what Kurt Vonnegut's

laughter sounds like. The nearest approximation I can provide is this:

'UGH! UGH! UGGLE-UGGLE-UGGLE! Splork! Ahhh! Phwerg!'

Recovering: 'Ordinarily, I lead a rather clumsy life and conduct clumsy conversations but sometimes, boy! It's like I can draw on someone else who's smart, and I think that's the case with Bobby Fischer. The reason that he hides away from everyone is that he doesn't have that layer of fat. As you get old, of course, that layer of fat seals over.

'I think there are only three kinds of prodigies in our civilization: in music, chess and mathematics. It's well known that if you don't get a Nobel Prize in physics by the time you are thirty-five you are *never* going to get it. This is all intuition, but I think the finest work of writers is done in their mid-twenties, customarily. D.H. Lawrence, Hemingway . . . their early short stories are much better. Before they got their maturity, their experience, the stories are *stunning* . . .'

He shrugs again. 'Then they got a little *heavy* . . . but I'm not alarmingly intelligent like Bobby Fischer's alarmingly intelligent or D.H. Lawrence was alarmingly intelligent. If I'd been scary like that, then my career would have shown a steady growth pattern in a society like this. Mind you, if someone had bought stock in me when I was starting . . . the people who published my early work ran no risk, because I was a science-fiction writer and any science-fiction book in paperback – no matter how lousy – sold 95,000 copies. There were 95,000 people who'd buy it no matter what it was, and they could scarcely *read* . . . uggle-uggle-uggle . . .

'What mattered was the cover, and covers on science-fiction books were virtually interchangeable. If you wanted to sell books you'd use a woman or a swastika. At the same time, an exactly equal number of books about cowboys sold. I could have swung the other way, maybe . . . but that has died.'

Vonnegut has been, in the past, quite exceptionally scathing about SF. Has nothing in the field met with his approval?

'There are several great books, but you have to wade through a lot of awful stuff to get there. It was always my complaint from the beginning as a little kid before I started to study physics and chemistry . . . I had contempt for science-fiction writers because they were so ignorant about science. In the thirties, authors of science-fiction thrillers wouldn't know *beans* about science, and I've been impeded in my reading of it by lousy science.

'But planetary literature is being born. We have had great artists like Shakespeare and Goethe who have been important to the whole planet, and it is no longer enough that literature should simply refer to England or France or Germany or America. All that is falling away, because the basic political unit that we have to recognize now is the *planet*. Planetary literature still has to outgrow its early habits. People are so *impatient*! My God, the new theatrical season is nearly half over and we haven't yet got one *great play*! Maybe there won't be one all year! Maybe nothing will happen in the eighties!

'With planetary literature, people will become less and less ethnocentric. It's an ethnocentric little cottage industry with people going haywire scratching out these little stories and putting together a crew with one Scotsman and one Eskimo and one Malaysian and one Chinese and so forth. The world is getting better and better. More and more people are realizing that what is under attack is Earth.'

For Vonnegut, there is no distinction between defending Earth and dumping nukes.

'We have got to get rid of the damn weapons,' he says unequivocally. 'These poisons weren't on Earth until we manufactured them. If God did not see fit to include such ghastly poisons in such hideous concentrations in nature, then how can we? I've got one friend – a cousin who worked on the hydrogen bomb – and he's of the opinion that the planet is *already* poisoned. You do not need an explosion. You do not need a war. The planet is already contaminated.'

Well, thanks, Kurt. You've really made my day.

'Well, I try to spread a little joy. Uggle! They drew a map of Three Mile Island – that plant in Pennsylvania that had blown – they still haven't been able to go right in there. They drew a map of where the winds would've carried this stuff, and they got this wedge-shaped mass of desolation. If it'd hit New Jersey, the whole state would've been unfarmable for 900 years. I think this is why we have a more generalized protest in the United States than I've perceived here or anywhere else. We want to get rid of all the poisons, hence the enormous support.

'It's the top priority for all the environmentalists in the States. Mothers all want clean air and water for their kids. All the Catholic bishops in the United States took an anti-nuclear stance.'

In Vonnegut's books, nobody is ever responsible for anything. Nothing is ever anybody's fault. In the universe as Vonnegut perceives and depicts it, can we be anything more than at the mercy of Forces Beyond Our Control?

'No . . . what is insane is our culture, and people don't yet understand that they can redesign their culture. They haven't even been taught this in school! The thing that I would teach in the first grade is cultural morality and how arbitrary most cultures are for nationalistic reasons or reasons of self-defence. We're told we've got to cling to this culture because it's the very best one, but look how easily Hitler overhauled the old culture of Germany in a matter of . . . hell, two years. From 1932 to 1934.'

He is seized by fit of coughing.

'People sometimes find me – *splurgh!* – intolerably – *blaaagh!* – sentimental – *flurgle!* But I have been mistreated by my fellow man so rarely, and every time it has been not because it was in that man's interest to hurt me, but because the culture demanded it. It was a cultural idea of manliness which slugged me, for example. A soldier will shoot a man because culturally that is what soldiers are supposed to do. People have their brains wrecked by what doctors prescribe and they are just ridden by their cultures. My mother's brain was wrecked by sodium amytal.

'In my new book *Deadeye Dick*, a young kid, twelve years old, shoots a pregnant woman at a distance of a few miles by pulling a trigger on a whim. His father's a gun nut because a display of masculinity is culturally demanded of him. *There's* the evil.'

I ask Kurt Vonnegut what he thinks the worst things in our culture are and he says racism, poverty and loneliness. I ask him what the best thing is and he says cellophane cling-film. Uggle-uggle-uggle!

In the seventies and thus far into the eighties, Kurt Vonnegut's best work has probably been the essays in his two anthologies. His new novel *Deadeye Dick* is probably his most dashing and inventive performance since *Breakfast of Champions*, but his contribution to this culture has been unique and valuable. He is one of nature's favourite uncles.

And I'm still worried about his cough.

# J.G. Ballard:
# Waiting for the
# silver coconuts

*NME*, 22 October 1983

'BECAUSE of the media landscape which we inhabit and the way in which external reality is almost completely a fiction manipulated by someone else ... because we were living inside this enormous *novel*, one could begin to judge external reality almost as a work of art, a very *sinister* work of art, a rather sinister novel very like a nightmare. The sort of distinction that Freud made between the latent and manifest content of a dream, one now has to apply to external reality.

'What *is* going on?'

Beneath the shade of a pair of very fine silver-foil coconut trees, J.G. Ballard sits in his study most days of the week, exploring the last truly alien planet: this one.

External reality in this particular case is a broad comfortable street in Shepperton, not far from the Dream Factory and designed to look like either a set for a suburban sitcom or a deluxe practice track for learner drivers.

It seems highly appropriate to find science fiction's darkest, most authentically disturbing dreams welling up here, where Normality is writ so large as to be utterly surreal.

The dreamer himself is as effectively camouflaged.

It would be tempting to extrapolate Ballard from his books and deduce a gaunt, quiet man resembling a cross between William Burroughs and H.P. Lovecraft as portrayed by Peter Cushing, a man whose eyes are forever fixed on distant beaches where deserted buildings crumble, or else scanning the skies for dead astronauts and satellites chattering obliviously to no one.

A poetic ghoul looking forward to his final peace: to be attained when the world is under 200 feet of water, burnt to a crisp by the sun, battered by massive winds. Probable hobbies: comparing photographs of differently produced fatal injuries, inventing new ways of torturing his characters.

The actual Ballard is, of course, nothing of the sort.

He is a smooth, ellipsoid being, simultaneously rumpled and suave, a porpoise masquerading as an English gentleman. Ballard would not seem remotely out of place deputizing for Ian Carmichael in the Paul Masson California Carafe commercial, or delivering lines like, 'Of course there's absolutely no possibility of letting him live' over a glass of sherry in a British spy film.

He is charming and voluble; enthusiasm dances perpetually behind his eyes. The ideas with which he works create the enthusiasm that fuels his work. His dooms are always blessings in disguise.

His terrain is space: the space between the ears is the space in which his characters are lost. His landscapes are the landscapes of the world we live in, transformed by our own perceptions and by the illusions fostered upon us by people who are themselves deluded, who no more understand the dreams in which they live than they do the ones in which they trick others into living.

From the humid, hothouse dream of *The Drowned World* to the impossibly violent sexual psychosis of *Crash!*, from the bejewelled allegory of *The Crystal World* to the cold, Burroughsian matter-of-factness of *The Atrocity Exhibition* and through the astonishing short stories that he has written continuously since 1956, Ballard is science fiction's most brillant and most unorthodox writer.

As *Star Wars* and sword-and-sorcery dominate the bookstalls, Ballard is still asking the $64,000 Question, the Big One . . .

'What is going on? What *The Atrocity Exhibition* was about was the way that the media landscape has created something very close to a gigantic art gallery with a lot of very lurid paintings on exhibition – this was in the sixties – and the way in which psychopathic strains which are normally either ignored or suppressed were beginning to *use* the media landscape to express and reveal themselves.

'It's still going on, but one saw it particularly in the seventies with the TV coverage of the Vietnam war, and the reduction of all events to pure sensation . . .'

Ballard's analysis of the external world led him into areas which shocked the delicate sensibilities of the mainstream SF world.

When US writer/editor Harlan Ellison was commissioning his anthology *Dangerous Visions*, which was designed to break every

SF taboo in the multiverse, Ballard submitted as his entry *The Assassination of John Fitzgerald Kennedy Considered as a Downhill Auto Race* and his US agent was so appalled that he never even forwarded the story to Ellison in the first place. Ballard blamed Ellison for chickening out, and the resulting misunderstanding remained uncleared for some time.

'I can speak as somebody who has run up against this throughout his whole career: the *enormous* conservatism of science fiction. I mean, here's a medium which you would think would be devoted to change and experiment. In fact, the majority of its writers, especially American writers, are *extremely* right-wing. Some are *paranoid* in their right-wing beliefs. Not just their political views, but their attitudes on race and sex are extremely conservative.

'It's always been a failure of SF that it's never been able to cope with sex. One good thing about the New Wave that sprang up in the early sixties – it was primarily a British phenomenon; Ellison and [Samuel R.] Delaney came much later – was that the British writers wanted to talk about sex in a free and adult way. American science fiction just couldn't cope.

'But if you go back to this idea of the gigantic novel in which we are living, it is not just the psychopathic strains – or the bizarre and maverick strains – which are surfacing, but the whole core of what people want to do with their lives. What you see is a whole mass of private mythologies wriggling their way up to the surface and finding expression.

'If one assumes – as I do – that in the future every home will become like a TV studio in which one is simultaneously writer, director and star of our own show ... what is life? What is our existence except *our own show*? That home movie that we all live inside ... it's already started to some extent. It won't be like *Crossroads*' – his smooth features produce a startlingly wolfish smile – 'it'll be more like *Eraserhead*.

'It isn't necessarily a frightening or even a corrupt future which lies ahead, but it may be one that is truer to our own selves, and I think therefore it is to be welcomed. At a time of transformation and change, like the seventies – which were a major time of change, *much* more interesting than people give 'em credit for – you get a bridge, a zone of transit between one time and another.'

\*

'What about my trees?' he gestures at his towering silver companions. 'They represent my Gauguin phase, my South Sea Islands phase. That high Mylar gloss, that techno flash, is what I want from the South Sea Islands.

'When I think of the South Sea Islands — which I often do, and I've written about them — it's those World War II runways, completely *abandoned*, running away into the dunes, where technology meets possibility and vast Pacifics of the imagination lie ahead, pointing towards those Mylar trees in a small suburban sitting-room.

'I love those trees! I'm just waiting for the silver coconut to pop out.

'If, like me, you're depressed about the future of this country — which I am because of my three kids and the world they're going to grow up in, particularly when North Sea Oil runs out as it's started to do, and things *really* get tough here and the seed corn laid down by Thatcher comes up as armies of warriors with swords, with whatever political conflict lies in store for us — then the only hope of any radical change does lie with the young. There's no question about that.

'Once you reach thirty — and please don't take this personally — one does tend to get locked into The Mortgage, to get more conservative and more restricted in your freedom to dream. You end up gathering baggage around you, standing in the airport of life surrounded by all these suitcases, *worrying* about the excess baggage fees. That's a fact of life, and it's a great shame.

'I've watched this happen within my own field, within science fiction. Yesterday's radicals often become today's conservatives, and don't want today's radicals at any price. It's why something like SF is probably going to be a one-generation phenomenon rather like classic Hollywood was — in age-group I'm talking about — say from Isaac Asimov to Michael Moorcock. Moorcock's younger than me, and he's not strictly speaking an SF writer any more . . .'

Ah, but who *is* these days? Ballard himself certainly isn't.

'I *am*! Of *course* I am! I'm practically the only one left!

'*Star Wars* isn't science fiction. It's pure space fantasy, which has nothing to do with SF. The great authority which SF had in the 1940s and fifties and even before that was that it opened a window onto the immediate future, with a cautionary view. Its claim to being taken seriously was that it was looking at the immediate future.

'If you look at the American magazines like *Astounding, Galaxy, If, Fantastic Universe* and [the British] *New Worlds* of the fifties and the novels written by their authors, there was an enormous amount of straightforward cautionary fiction looking seriously at a changing world. All those stories about the dangers of nuclear war and overpopulation, the threat posed by computers ... that was classic fifties SF. Giant advertising corporations and their threat to freedom as in Frederick Pohl, the effects of pollution, what television would do to our lives ... science fiction was looking seriously at the near future and holding up warning signs, but now it's abandoned that, and I find it deplorable.

'American SF in particular has veered right away from that into fantasy. It's ignored the immediate future; it's no longer interested in what *may* happen. In fact, this terrible thing has happened: if you now write fiction that concerns itself with the near future – or with the future at all – then it is no longer by definition SF.

'When I started writing SF twenty-five or thirty years ago, the biggest problem that you faced as an SF writer was writing about the present day. To set a story in the present day immediately created problems of unease with the editors. They would ask, What *is* this? Are you trying to write mainstream fiction and slip it into the SF format? Listen, Jim, science fiction is about two things: the far future and outer space, and if you don't write about those two things then it's not SF.

'Now the reverse has come. If you want to write about the future, and to write a genuinely cautionary tale about the next ten or fifteen years' trends and what you and I have been talking about – Thatcherism and the rest of it – you would find difficulty in being accepted and having that accepted as science fiction. Whereas if you write a complete fantasy, a bit of deeply nostalgic medieval futurism perhaps set in the distant past as *Star Wars* is set, nothing to do with the world we inhabit ... that is what commercial SF, sadly, has become.

'It's a damn shame. SF has got to look at the present and the near future again, but that's my bias. I consider that I am a classic mainstream SF writer who is interested in the near future.'

But mainstream SF now is stuck at rocketry and sword-and-sorcery.

'But that's America! That's escapism. That just reflects America's own problems with itself. It can't *face* anything. It couldn't face Vietnam, it couldn't face Watergate, it cannot face the fact that America is a largely corrupt society. *That* is why Americans have turned to fantasy.'

In last week's *NME*, Maxim Jakubowski took an entirely well-justified poke at the ludicrously reactionary selection made by the Book Marketing Council for their 'Venture Into Science Fiction' promotion. Ballard is in substantial agreement with Jakubowski's view – and with similar opinions voiced by your humble servant – but he is considerably less miffed at being represented by his first real novel than many might expect.

'Even though *The Drowned World* was written over twenty years ago, it should be put in its context as the *first inner-space novel*. "Inner space" was the flag which I nailed to my mast, and *The Drowned World* – written in '62 or whenever it was – is *literally* the first inner-space novel. Up until that point, catastrophe stories were being done on a very literal level, as adventure stories, but the psychological adventure became the subject-matter for me.

'If you look at the Book Marketing Council's list, you'll see that John Wyndham's *Day of the Triffids* is there. Now it's a fine novel, a classic example of the English kind of Home Counties catastrophe fiction, a very polite society where all kinds of private obsessions are kept firmly buttoned down and people struggle together in the face of an external threat as they did during the Battle of Britain, or as we're led to *believe* they did during the Battle of Britain.

'My novel turns all that upside down. The hero *embraces* the catastrophe as a means by which he can express and fulfil his own nature, pursue his own mythology to the end, whatever that may be. He can accept the logic of his own personality and run that logic right down to the end of the road. That's a different approach. That's what *The Drowned World* is about. That's what nearly all my fiction is about.'

This theme is reiterated most frequently in Ballard's first quartet of novels.

*The Drowned World* was preceded by *The Wind From*

*Nowhere*, a pallid dry-run which Ballard these days disowns so completely that it does not even appear on official lists of his complete works, and succeeded by *The Drought*, which was a far more competent performance though derivative of its great prototype, and the extraordinary visions of *The Crystal World*, which restated the crucial motifs in a new and entrancing variation. *The Crystal World* was written entirely under the influence of alcohol, as was most of *The Atrocity Exhibition*, which heralded Ballard's second major phase: that of his preoccupation with cars, dead celebrities and the media landscape.

Following the horrific exorcism of *Crash!* (the most grisly novel about cars and sex ever written) and *Concrete Island* (in which a businessman's car goes off the road at a motorway junction leaving him trapped in a plot of wasteland with no way of contacting the outside world), Ballard moved into his third and current phase, where the earlier themes are re-examined against a background of contemporary mythology.

His fascination with images of desolation goes back to his childhood, which was, to say the least, somewhat unusual.

He was born in Shanghai in 1930, and lived there until he was fifteen, serving two and a half years' internment by the Japanese during the war before finally arriving in his parents' homeland in 1946.

'I would guess that a large part of the furniture of my fiction was provided ready-made from that landscape: all those barren hotels and deserted beaches, empty apartment blocks ... the whole reality of a kind of stage set from which the cast has exited, leaving one with very little idea of what the actual play is about. All of that comes straight from the landscape of wartime Shanghai, and remember that the war there started in '37 when the Japanese invaded China and ringed the international settlement where I lived. After Pearl Harbor, they took over the city and we were interned.

'Even after the Nagasaki and Hiroshima bombs, the war still went on for another month for us. The Americans were still miles away ...'

How did Ballard, interned in his camp, first hear about those bombs?

'In a very confused way,' he sighs. 'Some people there thought that they had seen the Nagasaki flash. We didn't even know that the war had ended until at least a week after it *had* ended. There was a long interregnum, because the Americans were still across the China Seas, and the Nationalist Chinese forces were still a long way away, and around Shanghai there was an enormous Japanese army, something like two million Japanese soldiers on mainland China by VJ Day, and many of them planned to fight on.

'I think it's got to be accepted that it was only the atom bombs on Hiroshima and Nagasaki tilted the balance of their minds in favour of surrendering. There were certainly many members of the Japanese High Command who wanted to fight on, who wanted to defend the home islands to the last piece of sukiyaki. It was a very confused period, and I think a large part of my fiction comes out of that.

'Something like *The Drowned World* comes straight out of that landscape: flooded paddy fields with apartment buildings in the distance rising out of them which I used to watch from my camp every day, that sun, that very hot sun . . . not *The Crystal World*, now. That's another kettle of fish.

'*The Drowned World* is about time past, biological memory, the sources of the psyche deep in the buried levels of the spinal column, whereas *The Drought* is my image of what the future is going to be. I see the future as very *lunar*' – his voice crackles as he masticates the word – 'very *arid*, very . . . *static*, sudden tremors and harsh black and white shadows, bursts of sensation like signals reaching a cathode ray tube from a crashing airliner or from a distant galaxy.

'It seems to me that we are re-creating around us something of the physiology of a very lunar world, rather cold, affectless – to use a favourite word of mine – lacking in feeling, but perhaps expressing feeling in a different way, which is what I'm trying to get at in books like *Atrocity* and *Crash!* Certainly the early stuff came out of a Chinese landscape.

'After *The Atrocity Exhibition*, I embarked on a series of urban disaster novels set in the present: *Crash!*, *Concrete Island* and *High-Rise*, all of which are concerned with the alien of the urban landscape, which we must embrace.

'In *Concrete Island*, the hero – having spent the whole book trying to escape from the Island – realizes that in fact he has fulfilled himself on the Island and should stay there, which is a kind of metaphor for reconciliation, the kind of reconciliation which we all have to make with our own selves and with our own limitations. All my heroes are trying to break through all these layers of enamel which society and social conventions paste over us.'

Like many SF writers, Ballard's interest in the new technology is on a basically theoretical level. No such vulgar thing as an electric typewriter sullies his desk, and he certainly doesn't have a home computer.

'I'm interested in all that stuff,' he muses, 'but I like to keep it at a distance. I recognize an element of that conservatism in myself, and I think it's partly an age thing. It takes a while, once you're over the age of forty, to readjust yourself to a radical change.

'Things like electric typewriters with built-in memory which are supposedly there to aid and assist writers merely serve to intimidate and depress. I have enough problems without having to cope with that, and as for word processors ... the editing function on those is so laborious.

'And we are living in a culture of surfaces, where style is more important than content. I am a very old-fashioned writer in the sense that my stuff is very carefully architected and I rely on a strong story. Take *The Atrocity Exhibition*: there are very strong stories buried in all that non-linear paragraph-by-paragraph stuff.'

J.G. Ballard is an oddity in modern letters: he stands for the essentially subversive power of the imagination. I like a good modern nursery story as much as the next superannuated media child, but when pap dominates to the extent to which it so demonstrably does in most contemporary fields of artistic endeavour, then it becomes necessary to send for a man like Ballard, the Samaritan saboteur of inner space.

'In a radical view of the world, and assuming that the role of the imagination is to reorder reality in a way that makes a little more sense and tells the truth about ourselves and shows us some kind of possibilities of what our lives could be ... if that's the job of the writer, and it always has been, then the whole modern school of American fiction has produced nothing that remotely compares with Burroughs. His work seems as fresh and exciting and as absolutely radical as ... as it ever was. It takes its place alongside Swift, Lewis Carroll, Rimbaud, Kafka ... the radical reshapers of the imagination, of all the possibilities of our lives.

'There seems no point in writing unless you're going to do that.

'I know that's kind of an unpopular viewpoint in these safe, dull, conservative times, but it's one that I've attempted to cling to. We're in an era where the role of the writer – or the poet, the painter, the musician, the film-maker – is to offer reassurance, which is a great shame.'

Ballard certainly doesn't peddle the conventional form of pulp reassurance, which is that everything will come out comfy despite the odd catastrophe here and there, that things will remain fundamentally the same.

His vision is only comforting in the sense that it demonstrates that there is nothing to which we cannot adapt once we realize that there is no distinction between it and us. That's comfort?

It is utterly appropriate to number Ballard among the true contemporary radicals of the imagination, to mention in the same breath as Burroughs or Genet or Carroll or Rimbaud. His best work is simply a new way of looking at the world.

Somehow, I don't think he'd be too surprised if that silver coconut *did* finally emerge by his typewriter one morning.

# Sly and Robbie: In search of the lost beat

*Vogue*, September 1982

ONCE upon a time, musicians sought the Lost Chord. So many of them were eventually discovered that rock musicians got confused and decided to make do with a basic fistful that could be fitted together *ad infinitum*, while their colleagues in the more rarefied zones declared the entire structure of Western harmonic theory to be utterly null and void and took off into the stratosphere unencumbered by such obsolete baggage. Nowadays, those of a questing disposition slake their thirst for travel, novelty and adventure by hunting bigger game. Every week there are new sightings, new claims. Everybody wants to find the Lost Beat.

Some find it ricocheting around the baking asphalt pavements of New York, rattling out of giant portable radio/cassette machines as the hard, elastic bounce that goes with rapping, break-dancing, video arcades and fantastic, baroque spray-can art. Some hear it sanded down and gloss-varnished in the uptown discos, rubbing shoulders with the cracking, flamboyant sound of the Latin sound, *barrio salsa*. Some listen to the African pop which has been moving in from Nigeria, from Zaire, from Cameroon, from Senegal, from Congo – a light, dazzling beat so trickily graceful that it almost dances for you – or to the galvanic irresistable surge of the traditional Burundi drumming which formed the basis for entire shelvesful of last year's hit singles.

And if that isn't enough, there's always the Caribbean and a revitalized calypso tradition spearheaded by the funked-up variant known as *soca* . . . and, of course, there's still reggae, the most crucial rhythm of the last ten years. Jamaican music has cracked white showbiz on a variety of levels: Prince Charles gravely shakes hands with dreadlocked Rasta musicians from Birmingham at a charity show, The Police conquer the USA with their watered-down dub, Third World skip from reggae to disco and collide with Stevie Wonder coming the other way. Martyred Bob Marley's sunny, defiant grin still flashes from the unlikeliest shop windows, and TV commercials and theme tunes quite often attempt to cop a little lilt and bounce with a touch of reggae drumming.

The reggae beat comes from the bass and drums. More so than in any other form of contemporary music, it's the foundation which counts. The most influential bass-and-drum duo of modern reggae were Aston 'Family Man' Barrett and his brother Carlie, who played with Bob Marley throughout the seventies. But even as early as 1975, a newer, hotter sound was coming up from under. 'Outta dis rock/shall come/a greener riddim,' prophesied the dub poet Linton Kwesi Johnson, 'even more dread/dan what/de breeze of glory bred./Vibratin violence/is how wi move/rockin wid green riddim/de rout/an dry root out.'

That 'green riddim' (rhythm) was first heard to its fullest advantage on 'Right Time', a 1975 hit for a popular Jamaican vocal trio called The Mighty Diamonds. The song was brilliant, but its effectiveness was as much due to the rhythms as it was to melody or lyrics. The bass was simultaneously menacing and warm, rumble and pulse, and the drumming was flamboyant and martial, keeping a steady, solid beat while overlaying it with continuously changing variants. The musicians responsible were bass player Robbie Shakespeare and drummer Lowell 'Sly' Dunbar.

Within weeks, every drummer in Kingston was trying to play like Sly Dunbar, and – more important – every producer was attempting either to hire Sly or to find a drummer who could deliver that Sly rhythm. Sly had the perfect qualities: he could hold a beat as reliably and unshakeably as the great Carlie Barrett, he was as tricky and slippery and imaginative as Kingston's other great session drummer, Leroy 'Horsemouth' Wallace (who starred in the film *Rockers*, in which Robbie Shakespeare had a bit part), and he had more creative imagination than either. Today, Sly and Robbie are far more than a reggae riddim section. When they are not recording for other people's sessions, they are working for themselves, either producing for Island Records or for their own Taxi label. They have been in the studio with everybody who matters in reggae – Gregory Isaacs, Dennis Brown, Bunner Wailer, Burning Spear, Rico, Culture, Mikey Dread, I-Roy – cut superb soul and disco with New York session singer Gwen Guthrie, worked with rock-oriented performers as diverse as Joe Cocker and Ian Dury, participated in a legend-shrouded session with Soul Brother Number One James Brown. They are as sought-after as producers as they are in their instrumental capacity; they have propelled their protégés Black Uhuru to the forefront of the contemporary reggae scene by the simple expedient of producing and arranging their records to the highest possible standards and by consenting to tour with them only. The only way to get to experience Sly and Robbie playing live is to see them with Black Uhuru. And 'experience' it is: when heard properly, a Sly and Robbie riddim is felt as well as heard, it can make your entire body into a loudspeaker.

What made Sly and Robbie a by-word among people who didn't necessarily follow the reggae scene was their work on Grace Jones's 'Warm Leatherette' album in 1980. A Jamaican-born model whose work had shuttled her among the fast elites of New York and Paris, Grace Jones's musical aspirations required a genuinely international sound. Island Records' boss Chris

Blackwell took Jones to the company's studios in the Bahamas and teamed her up with Sly and Robbie. Together, they created a music capable of framing the icy hauteur of Jones's delivery: a blend of New York fashion funk, Continental electronic *motorik*, or machine-noise to evoke industry, Jamaican dub and an eerie gauzy romanticism that came from everywhere and nowhere.

I meet Sly and Robbie on Black Uhuru's tour bus, nosing through the French countryside with the curtains drawn, an oblivious, autonomous capsule of Rastafari insularity. Sly and Robbie refrain from smoking the Holy Herb: Sly claims that the 'erb slows him up. His countenance seems perpetually mournful, permanently set in the hangdog expression that stares out of the sleeve of his current solo album 'Sly-Go-Ville'.

By contrast, Robbie Shakespeare's features seem fixed in an expression of perpetual serene, beatific ecstasy – a big, solid man in loose fatigues. When Sly and Robbie talk, their answers are strictly business. *Musician* business. They play with Black Uhuru, the most militantly Rasta band in all of reggae, but they do not introduce the subject of the iniquities of Babylon, unprompted.

They met, they say, on a session for producer Bunny Lee and clicked instantly. They both cite the legendary Barrett brothers as inspirations, Sly also claiming allegiance to the late Al Jackson, drummer with the sixties soul band Booker T & The MGs while Robbie pays tribute to Lloyd Knibbs, bass player with a Jamaican studio band of similar vintage, The Skatalites. They adopt an amused, diplomatic attitude to the perennial topic of the feelings of the black artist whose work is diluted to vast profit and acclaim – by white imitators. 'Some of them white musicians have a good feelin', and any man who plays reggae helps reggae,' says Robbie.

Dunbar and Shakespeare plan to move their way into African and *soca* rhythms, all of which they mastered in the cabaret and hotel bar bands in which they cut their musical teeth.

Sly has just ordered one of the new-style all-electronic drum kits – as used by Spandau Ballet and Japan – and the pair of them know exactly what sessions they're doing for almost the entire year. Is there anybody they would particularly like to work with in the future? They smile. 'Oh, anybody,' says Robbie. 'We'll work with anybody. Anybody who's got a good tune . . .'

# AC/DC: HM Photo Book
## by Chris Welch (Omnibus);
## Deep Purple:
## The Authorised Biography
## by Chris Charlesworth
## (Omnibus)

*NME* 3 March 1984

THERE is a certain morbid fascination to be enjoyed in flipping through books about bands to whom you never voluntarily listen(ed). Questions arise: why do they pull faces like that? Why do they wear such terrible clothes? Why is this man showing his bum to an audience?

If they're AC/DC it's because they're NOT POOFS, and they've got bloody huge amplifiers to prove it and they drink a lot, so that's that. As well as large numbers of photos – predictably enough – the book contains a rhapsodic retelling of the band's highly riveting history written by Chris Welch, a man who has never forgiven punk rock for distracting attention (even for a second) from the music he likes. It ends with a stirring statement to the effect that AC/DC represent all that is most wonderful and enduring in the human spirit. Cheers!

Chris Charlesworth's book tells – in quite astounding detail – the story of a bunch of musicians who got together, started a band and eventually got very successful even though they kept falling out with various singers and bass players and then replacing them. Finally the guitarist left and the group was never the same after that so they broke up completely. (Right, now you know how it ends, so you don't have to read it.)

The Deep Purple story, especially when told in pictures, demonstrates that their career coincided exactly with the least stylish period in British rock. I don't think there has ever been a pop biography that depicts its protagonists in such horrible clothes, or one which shows them getting uglier in such a short period of time. Ian Paice, the Purple drummer, joined the band as a startlingly pretty youth who could have made a fortune as a teenage idol if he'd been a singer, and left it a fat old man.

Still, who cares, man, THAT'S ROCK AND ROLL INNIT! HAR HAR HAR!

# Bruce Springsteen: 'Born In The USA' (CBS)

*NME*, 4 August 1984

IN Bruce Springsteen's 1984, America – the original big country where dreams stay with you – has contracted; it is now a very small country indeed.

The Great American Highway which Springsteen used to celebrate so feverishly now leads nowhere at all but to another place where things are no better. He no longer proclaims that *there's magic in the night*: the nights are plainly as dead as the days.

From the cranked-up romanticism and defiance of 'Born To Run' nearly ten years ago to the deadpan acoustic recital of defeats and disasters that made up 1982's 'Nebraska', Springsteen's chest-beating and myth-making has given way to a Reaganomic realism that is sobering rather than intoxicating.

The title tune rings like a blow or a curse: Springsteen sings the whole song like a man at the end of his tether and Max Weinberg's snare cracks like a whip the length of a city; when he plays a roll it sounds like collapsing (old) buildings.

Springsteen's protagonist is raised in a small town, gets into trouble, goes off to fight in Vietnam where his brother dies, comes home and can't find work. Dead end: *'I'm ten years burning down the road/nowhere to run ain't got nowhere to go/ Born in the USA/I was born in the USA ...'* The land of the free? *Tell* me about it. When he sneers: *'I'm a cool rockin' daddy in the USA'* you don't believe it any more than he does.

It sets the tone for the whole album. No one spits in the face of the badlands any longer: the badlands didn't even notice. The old cast of street rats and soulful gangsters made their rebellion back in 'Born To Run' and 'Darkness On The Edge Of Town' and it made no damn bit of difference at all.

'*Well maybe we could cut someplace of our own with these drums and these guitars,*' he remembers wearily in 'No Surrender', but the song – and album – has more to do with the question *what do you do the morning after your final defeat?*

Springsteen's characters are married, in their mid-thirties and dealing with parenthood and recession. Maybe the narrator of 'My Hometown' is The Magic Rat ten years on from 'Jungleland' abandoning his dreams of moving out and moving on, initiating his own son into the same lifestyle that he once swore he would escape.

There is refuge in love and the dance, but it is shortlived and hollow: the single 'Dancing In The Dark' (Springsteen's concession to nasty modern pop) is yearning but hollow: you know it won't work out. In 'Cover Me' he blends Talking Heads proto-funk with minor-key blues and some wrenching Albert King-style guitar in an affecting plea for emotional security, but ultimately 'Born In The USA' contains no easy answers.

When one is this thoroughly caught up in the quicksand of society, there are only two escape routes: through what for want of a better term one might call mysticism or through the direct route of political action whereby you agitate, demonstrate and do everything you can think of to change the world around you and create a more life-enhancing environment. Springsteen's characters (and presumably Brucie himself) seem unprepared to take either route, which leaves them up to their necks in good ol' Amerikaka.

No one's going to get high on fantasy or rebellion from listening to 'Born In The USA'. There are no moments of delirious abandon here; the music is as dry and contracted as the state of mind it describes.

It is very rare to see an artist take a clearcut choice between selling his audience the same old bullshit that he knows they love, and telling them the truth even if it means letting go of stuff that sells.

By abandoning all that 'rebel triumphant' blabber'n smoke, Bruce Springsteen displays the kind of moral and artistic integrity that rock music rarely shows any more. The power of 'Born In The USA' is less flashy and less intoxicating, but it is far more real than the power of Springsteen's early work; this is the power of an artist telling the truth.

## David Byrne: The talking head of Talking Heads

*NME*, 8 December 1984

*You may find yourself . . . the leader of a rock band (of sorts)!*
*You may find yourself . . . starring in a movie of that band's performance!*
*You may find yourself . . . in a foreign country, staying in a fine hotel and talking to people about that band and that movie!*
*And you may ask yourself . . . well, how did I get here?*
*And you may ask yourself . . . what do I do now?*

*Watch out! You might get what you're after.*

David Byrne, the talking head of Talking Heads, is one of pop music's stranger creatures.

This is readily apparent when watching him perform: his on-stage demeanour is hugely unsettling: nervous mannerism writ large, one long twitch.

Odd things keep happening to his body. His arms and legs move seemingly without conscious volition: he gazes down at them in horror. He speaks in tongues – a process alluded to in the title of Talking Heads' last studio album – and produces some of the most peculiar vocal noises in popular music.

In 'Psycho Killer', the first great Talking Heads song and the opening number in the *Stop Making Sense* concert film, Byrne sings '*I'm tense and nervous and I can't relax*'.

When he sings it, no one doubts him.

*We dress like students, we dress like housewives.*

Talking Heads are the staying-power champs of New York City's class of '75.

389

They came out of CBGBs, Hilly Kristel's Bowery snake-pit, alongside Television, Blondie, The Ramones, Johnny Thunders' Heartbreakers and the Patti Smith Group, and, though hardcore looks like bringing Da Brudders back strong, it's fair to say that Talking Heads have outlasted and outcreated their one-time peers.

Even then, Byrne and his crew were somewhat strange. They eschewed both the old and new models of rock flash; the standard stadium crap and the proto-punk rebel styles, and they all seemed absolutely terrified.

At that time, Talking Heads were a trio — Byrne singing and playing guitar with Tina Weymouth and Chris Frantz in the rhythm section — and they looked like emotionally disturbed preppies, frightened pigeons in a den of cats. Their music was as wildly incongruous as their appearance: a giddy blend of folk-rock and white soul.

Midway through the performance, Byrne broke a string on his only electric guitar and no one ever made more of a display of changing it. The set ground to a halt and Byrne, his spidery limbs contorted in an agony of embarrassment and clumsiness, seemed to be changing the string in slow-motion, face frozen, eyes staring.

Nine years later, the *New York Times* is hailing Byrne as being 'in the forefront of young American composers'. He scores ballets as well as racking up hit singles and is generally big potatoes. Talking Heads, augmented from the basic quartet by an ever-changing gang of stellar funk sidepersons, frame his anguished yelp with a dense, polyrhythmic wash of sound that's still one of America's most stimulating rock noises.

*I'm just an ordinary guy . . . burning down the house.*

Byrne is installed in a very comfortable suite at the Hyde Park Hotel, equipped with a video and a stack of tapes, including *The Evil Dead*. On a darkening Thursday afternoon. Byrne almost seems part of the encroaching shadows.

In black slacks and shirt with immaculately polished black shoes, he dresses to emphasize his prodigious gawkiness. The slicked-back hair is now neatly trimmed and brushed forward. Despite his cordiality, he evinces an air of abstraction.

He is not, however, a werewolf. I know this because his eyebrows do not meet in the middle. Not quite.

*This is the meaning of life . . . to tune this electric guitar.*

Byrne remembers the broken string incident at CBGBs all those
years ago. He recalls dragging the incident out as long as possible
to get more time onstage. Then, as now, Byrne's philosophy was
that everything that happens onstage is part of the performance.

'The prevalent attitude seems to be, look at this bit but try to
ignore what's going on over there and try to ignore what you're
seeing in the wings. Look at the fact that I've got a nice haircut
and a good tailor, but ignore everything else: like the fact that I
can't move.

'*Stop Making Sense* isn't so much a film about the band as a
film about that performance. It's like doing a film of a play rather
than a documentary about a theatre company.'

Unusually for a concert movie, *Stop Making Sense* includes no
footage of the band arriving at a hall, no cute 'spontaneous'
conversations in the dressing-room, and hardly any shots of the
audience going wild over the band. Its sobriety and absence of
*rockumentary* trappings is an integral part of the way that director
Jonathan Demme visualized the movie.

'Our hope was that, through the way it was filmed, you do get to
know the personalities of the band members and the various
people who play onstage as they're introduced, and that Jonathan
would cut to them when they're doing something that reveals
their personality rather than when they're doing something flashy
like a solo. You think of them as people rather than as . . .
something else.'

Byrne's speaking voice is quiet and oddly quavery. He looks
away as he speaks, and his limbs assume odd, contorted shapes as
he speaks. Even answering fairly routine and unintrusive questions
seems to be painful for him.

Why am I tormenting this poor man? Byrne makes me feel as if
I am poking him with a pointed stick.

The structure of *Stop Making Sense* is unusual (returning to
business): it opens with Byrne arriving on a totally bare stage
clutching an acoustic guitar and a ghetto-blaster.

The blaster blares out a beat-box backing tape to which Byrne
performs a solo 'Psycho Killer', and gradually the musicians join
him. First Tina Weymouth strolls on to play some bass on

'Heaven' and technicians wheel on keyboard stands and the drum kit for Jerry Harrison and Chris Frantz. As the set progresses, backdrops fall into place and the full band assembles.

Was the set/movie structured for visual or musical reasons and was the order of songs intended to provide a cumulative build-up of information?

'Well, I think it would've been unsafe to end with a ballad or something no matter how good it looked. In retrospect, Jonathan pointed out that there was some kind of psychological development going on. My character is kind of thrown into this situation and is a little bewildered by it – angst-ridden or whatnot – and gradually comes out of that until the end where he is eventually united with the other performers and comes out of that. He becomes a more comfortable human being and so it has a happy ending.'

When the percussion break occurs in 'Psycho Killer', Byrne is almost buffeted around the stage by the punishing beat-box track; acted *upon* by the music rather than moving it.

'That's what happened the first time I heard it! I'd programmed the drum machine and put it on cassette and played it for the first time in rehearsal, and I'd forgotten where the little drum breaks were, so every time they occurred it was a kind of surprise. It felt like I was being constantly surprised by this thing.

'A lot of the time it feels like that to me: that even though a song might be of my own, or our own, making, when it's performed onstage it's done to me or I'm being swept along by it. It's a pretty good feeling: that it's all being almost forced upon me. It makes it easier than having to get into it myself.'

How does Byrne feel when he watches himself? What does he think about *that* person?

'Most of the time I feel like I'm getting into another character, though he does have a lot of elements of my own. That's pretty comforting to watch, because it's like watching somebody else. The moments when I drop out of character and start floundering are the most uncomfortable to watch.'

Do characters suggest songs or vice versa?

'In the recent past it's been the music first and that has suggested a lyrical attitude, but before the attitude of the character or the words came first. Now I'm back to that, so it's almost as if someone else is writing the song.

'Often I'm surprised, and that's my favourite part of it, when I come up with something and I don't know where it came from.

'There's an old one called "Electric Guitar" and I'm *still* not sure where that came from. I scribbled part of it down when we were touring in a station wagon and read it to the band, and we all got a big giggle out of it, but I was real excited because I didn't know where it came from or what it represented.

'There's that song on "Remain In Light" called "Born Under Punches" . . . that was real spontaneous, just improvised in the studio . . . spontaneous emissions.'

Are there aspects of Byrne's character which don't surface in the music?

'Oh, yeah. My political views are not very . . . um . . . so . . . lately I did some posters for the election and I found that that was a much more comfortable outlet. Maybe each aspect of my character has its own ideal medium for expression.

'It's assumed that a lot of musicians are speaking for someone else — speaking for the steelworkers or for the underprivileged — whereas a lot of musicians are privileged people.

'I find that it rarely works, except in the case of someone like Robert Wyatt. When he does it I find it pretty touching, in a way. They're definitely political sentiments that he's expressing, but he does it in a way that's so personal. It's an intense personal emotion that's being expressed which happens to be of a political nature.'

In that filmed performance, did Byrne feel 'present' the whole time?

'It's a funny feeling: that I can feel like I'm there, that I know where I am onstage, whether my shoes are tight, or in the middle of singing a song I can know what the next song's going to be. And at the same time, I'm *not* aware of that; I'm totally subsumed by what I'm doing. It's a nice place to be: kind of two places at once.'

What's the most satisfying part of Talking Heads? Is it that feeling of being subsumed?

'That's a good one. I think another one is probably to do with the reason why anyone performs onstage or creates anything, that you have something to say or to do and you want to get it before people. It's a great feeling.

'Even if they don't like it, it's a great feeling just to put it out and be heard. Even when I don't feel like doing it, it only takes two or three songs and then the music just takes me over again.'

David Byrne loosens up as the conversation goes on and the shadows draw in. He no longer fiddles with his shoelaces, and he starts to laugh more and more.

He's found a way to utilize shyness and awkwardness, so much parts of him, by dramatizing them in his performance as he enacts his symbolic journey from the bare wires and raw nerves of 'Psycho Killer' through to the healing and redemption of 'Take Me To The River'. He even makes ironic references to his being 'angst-ridden' here and there in the conversation.

You can't be angst-ridden all the time, David. Do you wake up angst-ridden every morning?

'No, uh . . . most mornings I feel fine. Just fine.'

## Billy Idol:
## 'Rebel Yell' (Chrysalis)

*NME*, 28 September 1985

MAD Max's underwear, Elvis's sneer, Eddie Cochran's vowels, Iggy Pop's jacket. At least he invented his own haircut. (*Actually, he borrowed it from Joe Brown – Ed.*)

## Steve Van Zandt:
## Anti-Apartaid

*NME*, 7 December 1985

SOMETHING nasty has been smeared across the inscription on the plinth supporting the giant bust of Nelson Mandela that stands proudly on guard outside the Royal Festival Hall on London's South Bank. Ken Livingstone frowns, walks over to the statue and begins to try and scratch off the offending gunk.

A few feet away, Little Steven – Steve Van Zandt, formerly

known during his lengthy sojourn with Bruce Springsteen's E Street Band as Miami Steve – huddles into the leather coat with the skull-and-crossbones buttons, and prepares for a lunchtime photocall for the launch of 'Sun City', the massive all-star anti-apartheid project designed to demonstrate that there are some things from which even big-time pop stars will refuse to make money.

Billed to join Van Zandt and Livingstone for the photo session by the statue are Bishop Trevor Huddleston, the founder of the Anti-Apartheid Movement and the man who bought Hugh Masekela his first trumpet, and Liberal leader David Steel. Van Zandt, a slight, piratical figure swathed in scarves, chats to the towering bishop as Livingstone makes wry little remarks about 'new forms of GLC street entertainment' and inquires if David Steel is coming. The woman from Anti-Apartheid opines that this is unlikely. Of course! The Liberal Party will always send its good wishes and then not show up.

As the photographers move in, Huddleston asks the shivering guitarist, 'How did you get caught up in all this, then?' Van Zandt rolls his eyes. It is clearly a long story . . .

'I guess I've been aware of it for four or five years,' he explains a few hours later, his voice slurred with fatigue from a day that started at 5 a.m., after two hours' sleep, 'but I didn't start looking at it until about two or three years ago. I decided to write about it as soon as "Voice Of America"' – (his last solo album) – 'was finished during the winter of '83. South Africa wasn't exactly getting much attention then – I couldn't find a *word* about it. This news blackout now has *really* taken things off the front pages, hasn't it?'

So Van Zandt went over to South Africa to check things out for himself. 'I always do a lot of research before I write something, and no matter how many books I read and people I talked to I couldn't quite get a grip on South Africa. I couldn't understand it, ya know, and I felt that if I was gonna write about it I had to go, so I went down there and it was really as shocking as you may have expected it to be. When you're *there* and you see it . . . it took me a few weeks just to discipline myself enough to get anything done. You just can't function.

'I started mostly in Johannesburg, which is where the meetings

395

were. I wanted to meet the members of the black community, to get a feel for who they are and what they want. I went to Cape Town and Pretoria and out into the country, I went into Soweto at night, which is technically against the law. The violence had just started, but it hadn't reached Soweto yet. There were people getting killed every day: the war was *on*, you know . . . and what really made the experience surreal is you go to the black township where there's the obvious poverty and that vibe of imprisonment and the violence beginning, and then ten miles up the road you go to the white neighbourhood and there's not a *sign* of anything wrong . . .'

The same geographical and psychic distance that divides the South Bronx from the Upper East Side, or Brixton from Park Lane?

'I think you're right. One of the points of this record, and one of the points of focusing on South Africa, is hopefully to make us see ourselves a little more clearly. The racist problem, and bigotry in general, is just getting worse in America, and I think it's also escalating here as well.'

It follows, therefore, that launching a major propaganda offensive against apartheid must have upset quite a few people. How much opposition was there for Van Zandt's project?

'The main opposition always comes from the establishment themselves in the music business. Nobody particularly encourages people to talk about reality. Five or six companies turned us down . . .'

American labels turning down something with Bruce Springsteen on it? That practically counts as treason . . .

'That shows how controversial this is in America. Nobody ever thought it would be played on the radio at all. The concept of a political record doesn't exist really in America: not *this* specifically political, and one that is openly critical of the Reagan administration. I guess in a way you can't blame them, but I've always felt that there's got to be a place in our society and a place in our business for this kind of record. If rock 'n' roll is *just* entertaining, then it's only using ten per cent of its potential.

'Escapism and that *background music* kind of thing became the norm somewhere along the line. Because Reagan quoted Bruce that time – which was an incredible joke in America, the guy obviously going for cheap applause and everybody laughing at him because he picked the wrong guy – I saw editorials in Europe saying BRUCE IS RAMBO and all this. I mean – writers, journalists! Reagan, everybody knows he's clinically insane, but when the journalists didn't bother to read the words of "Born In The USA" – that really worries me. Another thing is that the Left and the liberal press as well as the Right come out attacking the concept of artists doing some of the things they've been doing this year. As long as artists stay home and spend their money on a Rolls Royce and eat cocaine all day, nobody's gonna criticize 'em, but when they come out and do something they get criticized. We're in a *very strange* period of time.

'I always tell people, "Well, if you ever miss the fifties, this is it." But things are changing, I think, this year. Really, I feel it. I don't think "Sun City" could even have been released last year, considering how everybody ran from "Voice Of America". They wouldn't even play it on the radio.'

Van Zandt is adamant that the duty of artists to speak up for their beliefs has never been greater. 'When I mention racism and bigotry, it's not just blacks, though believe me that *is* getting worse. A guy named Albert Turner is on trial in Alabama: he's involved in voter registration and he was too successful. It's as simple as that. When you have Louis Farrakhan [the separatist Muslim leader] drawing 25,000 people a night it's an indication of something. When you have a whole new wave of anti-semitism and of course the ongoing tragedy of the American Indian – an exact parallel of the situation in South Africa – and no one quite focusing on it, plus we have a government taking backward steps trying to get rid of affirmative action . . . you can see on the horizon another catastrophe of our own in the making.'

He does feel, however, that the current wave of social concern in the musical community is more realistic, more practical and ultimately more *useful* than the imprecise, inflammatory rhetoric of the 'revolutionary' late sixties. 'I think we are in a new era where hopefully we'll learn from the mistakes of the sixties. The ideals of the sixties were fine, but it's clear that peace 'n' love are not going to cure the world. People are being more mature about what we're setting out to accomplish. The whole drug culture, which was so integrated with all those social concerns in the sixties and which helped burn things out . . . you don't see that now. I can't think of one artist I know involved in political or social concerns who does drugs.

397

'The multi-artist events are good: I think they've all accomplished something, but more important than that, I think individual artists are going to begin to integrate their social concern with their own individual work. Maybe only a couple of tunes on an album or a minute during a concert, but it should be a normal part of our business. Not *oh God*, it's another of *those*, get me some more *background music* . . .'

Steve Van Zandt is a very brave man. If you think it's difficult being a self-identified artist/activist here, you should check out the USA: a country with more ostriches per head of the population than anywhere else in the world. What Van Zandt has pulled together here with his 'Sun City' album and single is the most profoundly dissident project involving major pop artists in all of contemporary entertainment. Transcending the cosy apoliticism of the famine appeals, 'Sun City' is even more of a specific indictment of the neo-colonial profiteering of Western Europe and the USA in South Africa than the (also excellent) Wyatt/ Dammers 'Wind Of Change' single. It also has a beat that can demolish small buildings and everybody from Miles Davis to Ringo Starr, from Lou Reed to LKJ, from Grandmaster Melle Mel to Joey Ramone, from Bob Dylan to Bob Geldof.

And it should also have you.

# I fought the biz and the biz won: Punk ten years on

*NME*, 1 February 1986

BEFORE we get started, let's try a little game. Using the multiple-choice options provided, complete the following quotations:
(1) 'COS IIIII WANNA BEEEEE . . .
(a) Madonna
(b) On TV
(c) Anarcheee
(d) Very rich and famous

(2) STEN GUNS IN . . .
(a) Hammersmith Palais
(b) Rome airport
(c) Ulster
(d) Knightsbridge
(3) SEX AND DRUGS AND . . .
(a) Rock and roll
(b) Ronald Reagan
(c) Working out
(d) Unemployment
(4) I DON'T WANT TO GO TO . . .
(a) Hollywood
(b) Chelsea
(c) The DHSS
(d) The MTV Awards

OK? Well, how did you do? For the record, the 'correct' answers
are (c), (d), (a) and (b), but that's not the point; all the other
answers are correct too.

Ten years on from its inception, the songs that punk sang ring
truer than ever – the first Clash album is, if anything, a better
description of '86 than '76 – but nobody whose record sales are
sufficient to please their bank manager is singing them.

The record industry which the punk activists sought to demolish has both the artists and the audience locked up tighter than
ever. We're so pretty, oh so pretty . . . VACANT.

The blank generation is here: ten years late, it's true, but it's
here. Is is too late to say this isn't what we ordered?

So what was punk, anyway? You're liable to get very different
answers from British and American participants. The US answer
would be something along the lines of: punk originated among the
CBGB club-goers and performers in New York City from '74
onwards (Ramones, Television, Patti Smith, Blondie, Talking
Heads) as an alliance between the kids-just-wanna-have-fun crowd
and a gang of art-rockers suffering from the doomed-young-poets-
in-romantic-squalor syndrome. Unlike hippie art-rock, which
sought to loosen, elaborate and expand rock, this mob were
minimalists who chopped it down and tightened it up. Then the
Brits got hold of it and fucked it up with *politics*, man.

399

Brits will tell you that Malcolm McLaren, Bernie Rhodes, Jamie Reid and a bunch of their friends invented it, created The Pistols and The Clash out of thin air and went around upsetting everyone with funny clothes and haircuts and violence and swearing and swastikas and that apart from Iggy and The New York Dolls none of the Americans were really punks at all but morons and (ptui!) *artists*. Plus it was a WORKING-CLASS movement swelled by a horde of kids who had all been driven simultaneously crazy by tower blocks, the Welfare State and boring jobs, maaaaaaan.

Yes yes yes, but what was it, who did it and why? Well, leaving out the Americans as much as possible (let 'em do their own retrospectives if they can be bothered), it was an alliance of convenience between two groups of people who all had a vested interest in blowing away the unbelievably boring and flabby mess into which white rock music had declined.

There were the Art Statement crew from Worlds End (McLaren *et al.*) who wanted to shake things up and make money and considered the best way to do it was to reawaken the Disruption Factor in rock, and then there were the sharper and more abrasive faction of the post-Feelgoods pub rock crowd loosely grouped around Jake Riviera, Dave Robinson, Nick Lowe and Stiff Records. Punk itself embodied the tension between the anarchists and the rock fundamentalists: those who wanted to make rock and roll exciting and worthwhile again and those who simply wanted to destroy it. Both factions had fun, both factions made money, and in the long run both sides lost.

Another strong bonding factor between the punks (Clash, Pistols, Generation X, Damned, Jam, Banshees, Buzzcocks and the fifteen minutes brigade like Sham 69, The Lurkers, The Drones, The Nosebleeds and so on) and the New Wavers (Costello, Dury, Police, Boomtown Rats) was their hatred for the seventies consensus. God knows that the seventies pop scene was, with a few notable exceptions, no more worth defending than the Wilson/Callaghan Labour administrations which fell to Thatcher's hardnut right-wing fundamentalism in the Westminster equivalent of Oi, but a look back at the obsession with dole queues which was a hallmark of both punk rock and Tory propaganda makes it almost seem like a time when people didn't realize how much worse things were going to get.

Punk was, after all, the time when Bob Geldof launched his

career by sneering *'Don't give me love thy neighbour/don't give me charity/don't give me peace and love and the good lord above/you only get in my way with your stupid ideas.'* Now here we are in a decade in which virtually everybody is 'Lookin' After Number One' and Geldof has demonstrated what can be released in a human being by the desire to sell something more important than their own personality. Paul Weller used to wind people up by threatening to vote Tory, and he is now Britain's most prominent overtly Socialist musician. And The Pistols . . . well, they wrote the final chapter in the Swindle by going to court and walking off with all Malcolm McLaren's money, and who this side of Hollywood can restrain a smirk at *that*?

Punk, like its ancestor Hippie, came out of the industry mincer with its flavour reduced to a simple equation – shorter hair, shorter songs, brighter clothes, snappy graphics – and its roughage – genuine rage, chainsaw noise, political suss – deftly removed. It spawned a few minor fads, like Power-pop, Mod and 2-Tone, and then ran out of steam around the time that pop manufacture became extremely expensive and Fairlights and megavideos became the tools of the trade. The Biz didn't like explicit politics or even explicit emotions, and the audience didn't like roughness and conscious amateurism, so what was left was a blend of spiky haircuts, skinny ties and pink socks tied to machine-tooled, tidied-up variations on standard pop formats. *They think you're useless and so you are, PUNK!*

Yet even though it failed to change the world, as canny observers and those not susceptible to ODing on wishful thinking always knew it would, punk had a hell of an innings, and its effects were not entirely cosmetic. For a start, it provided an entry for the young: before punk, I only knew three or four professional musicians who were younger than I was at the time, which was twenty-five, f'Chrissakes! This quintessential 'youth music' was monopolized by older people and though the likes of Ian Hunter and Alex Harvey (both even older than the norm) had a far better handle on what mattered to the youth than most, they were the first casualties once the real thing arrived.

So punk let youth back into pop: it also allowed women onto the stage as instrumentalists because just about everybody was starting out from a position of equal ineptitude (except those who

401

could play and kept quiet about it in case it damaged their punk cred; there was nothing around as laughable as The Police trying to play like punks) and so many of the traditional snobberies didn't apply. Women with guitars and basses, from Chrissie Hynde to Tina Weymouth, became a fairly unremarkable sight: X-Ray Spex and The Slits may never have gone platinum, but they cleared the way for Raincoats, Bodysnatchers, Belle Stars and Amazulu alike.

Thirdly, punk's chosen black music was reggae, which unlike the blues which had inspired the sixties stars, was played by local blacks who were the punks' contemporaries. Punk adopted reggae and brought it home for tea, and even though the death of Bob Marley prevented the process from its ultimate culmination, the effects of that alliance are punk's third great contribution.

And finally, there's the music. Over the last few days I've listened to everything in the house that brings back memories of the punk years and a ridiculous amount of it still sounds wonderful. The Pistols' sulphurous disgust, the slurred hiss of air past Joe Strummer's speed-rotted fangs (now replaced, of course), the Wilko/Townshend clangour of Paul Weller's guitar and the tuneful challenge of his best songs, the breathy savagery of Costello, the remorseless powerdrive and geeky ambiguity of The Ramones, the teeth-bared sass of Pete Shelley, the Dickensian tension between the chilling and the uproarious that wafts off Ian Dury's best records and the hundreds of one-offs by everyone from Jilted John to The Members . . . white rock music has never sounded so good since, and – even though this remark will not exactly add to my status around the *NME* office – there's no one around or upcoming who can hold the proverbial candle to those bands now.

Because, you see, we can't go back. Every damn thing that's happened in pop since 1945 has been re-re-re-revived, and punk is now just another ready-to-wear option in the Great Youth Culture Collection. Times are too hard now for anybody to seek to glorify or romanticize poverty, and most people would rather be seen as more prosperous than they are, rather than less. Hippie and punk both tried to change the way pop is produced and consumed and both left the industry stronger than before. If pop is ever going to claim that subversion is once again on the agenda, it is going to have to be very convincing – and it is also going to have to gather some measure of popular support for such a thing from an audience whose needs are more efficiently serviced than ever before. Both seem equally unlikely.

> *It's gonna come along, pass and drop. When it all started*
> *I was amazed, I never saw any movement move so quick,*
> *right, tremendous potential. All the kids caught onto*
> *something, they got onto an idea. They felt it and then*
> *they got into the clothes – same old story – got into the*
> *music – same old story – and they said 'fuck' and spit on*
> *TV – same old story. Then what? Nothin', right?*

> Don Letts interviewed in Sniffin' Glue, *January '77*

Same old story, Don? Yeah, it's a B-A-D joke. The punchline is this: most people don't want things changed to any fundamental degree, but they do like a little bit of excitement now and again.

> *The new groups are not concerned*
> *With what there is to be learned*
> *They got Burtons suits – huh*
> *You think it's funny*
> *Turning rebellion into money.*

> The Clash, *'White Man In Hammersmith Palais'*

P–U–N–K . . . R.I.P.

# Miles Davis: 'Tutu' (Warner Bros)

Q, November 1986

IN direct contradiction to the popular misapprehension that old age brings with it stagnation, rigidity and general hardening of the creative arteries, Miles Davis and his great contemporary B.B. King both demonstrated in their London shows last year that for them passing sixty means an increased sense of playful confidence, a willingness to take chances born of the knowledge that they long ago proved everything they have to prove. If King has aged like Olivier or Gielgud, Miles has matured like Picasso:

ornery, cantankerous and utterly unselfconscious, doing whatever he pleased and prepared to try anything.

Occasionally, critics and fans complain that Miles doesn't make records like he did in the fifties and sixties. Why should he? He made stacks of records in the fifties and sixties, most of them are still available, and in the unlikely event that anybody has every single one of them and still wants more, then Wynton Marsalis will be glad to oblige. Miles's new album – his first for Warners and producer Tommy LiPuma, with George Duke and master bassist Marcus Miller providing the backup, the arrangements and most of the tunes – is superior to anything since his 1980 comeback with the possible exceptions of last year's 'You're Under Arrest' and the live double 'We Want Miles', and sets him up to work his magic on some of the hardest, most galvanic grooves of this most groove-oriented phase of his career.

Davis's own 'Splatch' is a ferocious, hustling go-go with Miller slapping his bass like he had a grudge against it and Miles snaking his way in and out of the Synclavier explosions. No matter how simple the chord changes, he always creates a melody line which saunters into unexpected harmonic regions, as on 'Don't Lose Your Cool', built on a churning dub foundation which does a better job of ripping off Sly 'n' Robbie than those worthies do themselves these days.

. Scritti Politti's 'Perfect Way' – originally slated as the title tune – soon settles down as a punishingly taut computer-funk jam, and 'Tutu' itself is an ominous, majestic ride from New Orleans to Compass Point. The closing 'Full Nelson' is perhaps the most pleasant surprise: it cops such a tight, authentic Prince groove that it almost doesn't matter that Miles's proposed collaboration with His Purple Pygmyhood didn't happen. The title is a triple-entendre, alluding simultaneously to Prince (Nelson), (Nelson) Mandela, and to 'Half Nelson', a tune Miles cut with Coltrane in the fifties.

A couple of the ballads are flawed by some overenthusiastic applications of synthetic strings, but it's a comparatively minor lapse of taste. Miles's performances on 'Tutu' are so finely detailed that fresh nuances appear on each successive hearing: maybe he don't make records like he used to in the fifties, but NOBODY makes records like this. Except Miles Davis.

# Paul Simon:
# 'Graceland' (Warner Bros)

*New Hi-Fi Sound*, November 1986

DESTINED to become one of the all-time classics of AOR, Paul Simon's 'Graceland' bears both sweet and bitter fruit. Recorded in Johannesburg, London and New York, all but two of the basic tracks feature South African musicians – the other two were cut with Los Lobos and Rockin' Dopsie and The Twisters – and it continues Simon's flirtation with ethnic music, after his forays into Colombian and Jamaican sounds.

Whatever his lack of sensitivity in other areas – and we'll get to that later – Simon cannot be accused of anything other than the slightest lapses in musical taste. He's evidently listened long and hard to the music of the townships and black churches of South Africa, and has made some wise musical choices. 'Graceland' bounces along on rootsy, incandescent beats and textures which display the kind of vitality and honesty which most Western pop abandoned long ago, with guitars, drums, accordions and basses combining and re-forming in intricate and dazzling patterns. His choice of Dopsie and Los Lobos as the only indigenous American musicians to lay down the extra grooves is also right on the money: their music has the same folk integrity as the South African band, plus – of course – accordions.

I've never heard South African music by South African musicians recorded to such a high standard, either. Simon has done his own production, aided and abetted by the eternal Roy Halee, and guests like Adrian Belew, The Everly Brothers, Ralph McDonald and even the appalling Linda Ronstadt are combined with the original tracks in a manner both smooth and seamless.

Every groove is a small miracle; 'The Boy In The Bubble' rocks like a township version of Dylan's 'Subterranean Homesick Blues'. 'Diamonds On The Soles Of Her Shoes' drowns you in a tidal wave of voices; 'You Can Call Me Al' is merely one of many showcases for the extraordinary bass work of Baghiti Khumalo; the title track is a country *tour de force* embroidered with the shimmering pedal steel of King Sunny Ade's slide wizard Demola Adepoju. 'I Know What I Know' suffers from ridiculously over-processed drums (keep the goddam folkies away from the Synclaviers; they get drunk with power), but it's a rare indiscretion. Judged on purely musical and technical criteria, 'Graceland' is one honey of an album; and every bit as impressive on LP as it is on the compact disc.

Lyrically, it is less successful. Set against music as powerful, energetic and evocative as this, Simon's wispy voice and New York solipsism sound almost ludicrous. Hearing lines about sitting in a taxi discussing a friend's breakdown or – my favourite – 'She said don't I know you from that cinematographer's party' creates a sense of massive dislocation. It's almost as if some prankish hip-hop DJ has scratched dialogue from a Woody Allen movie into the middle of an Earthworks compilation. His gift has not entirely deserted him, though: 'The Boy In The Bubble' is as close as he ever comes to addressing the political situation in South Africa (in other words, the day-to-day lives of black South Africans), and 'That Was Your Mother' – the Rockin' Dopsie team-up – is warm and witty as well as being righteous zydeco fun. 'Graceland' – as any fule kno (*sic*) – is the name of Elvis Presley's Memphis mansion, and Simon's title track extends the metaphor of the name, and Presley's own mystique, to considerable effect. That's the tune with The Everly Brothers on, and its opening line alone is almost worth the price of admission: 'The Mississippi Delta was shining/like a National guitar/I am following the river/down the highway/through the cradle of the Civil War'. That, friends, is just lovely.

Considerably less lovely, though, is Simon's refusal to address the political consequences of his choice to record this album in Jo'burg. (Those of you who believe in keeping politics out of sport can stop reading here: those who believe that it is impossible to keep politics out of anything to do with South Africa, carry on.) Simon refused to participate in Miami Steve's Artists Against Apartheid project 'Ain't Gonna Play Sun City' because 'it named names'; he appears here as a musical sanctions-buster. It *is* possible to record South African musicians without setting foot in Botha-land; Hugh Masekela regularly does so perfectly adequately in his very well-equipped mobile studio just over the border in Botswana, and the standard is excellent.

To select an analogy which I hope Simon will find offensive: wouldn't you think that there was something wrong with a musician who went to record in Berlin with Jewish musicians in the 1930s, and didn't only avoid the subject of Nazism in his lyrics, but also managed to write a voluminous and scholarly sleeve-note which never managed to allude to the system which was crippling the lives of all those wonderful musicians? An irresistible vision of Simon arises in the mind: a nice, decent, sweet-voiced, shy American tourist in a check shirt wandering around some exotic bazaar peering at all the wares on display, murmuring 'Gee, that's neat — I'll take six,' and then whipping out an American Express card.

The question of how to maintain lines of cultural communications with black South Africa while ostracizing the almost inevitable middleman is a thorny one, and many individuals who are more politically aware than Simon have found themselves in dispute. Simon's position is simply a cop-out.

All actions have consequences, and Simon appears oblivious to the implications of his. Suffice it to say that he has indeed made an excellent album; one which I hope will help alert pop and rock audiences to the splendours not only of South Africa, but of all the music from the African sub-continent. If his social and political awareness were as highly developed as his musical awareness, and his lyrics were a touch more outward-looking, 'Graceland' would have been one of the most remarkable musical accomplishments of the year. As it is, it's a fine record, but sometimes when I listen to it I think of black children dying of malnutrition in one of the richest countries in the world; of the hordes of dead whose funerals are forbidden by law; and of Nelson Mandela rotting in jail simply because he wants for his family and his people nothing more than what we expect by right for ours. Then, for a second or two, I feel a little queasy.

# Prince:
# 'Sign O' The Times'
# (Paisley Park)

*Q*, May 1987

PRINCE wears many faces, sings in many voices and is the seeming master of virtually every instrumental and production style of the post-war pop menu. Like Bruce Springsteen, Madonna and Michael Jackson, he is one of the few pop stars to attain true iconic significance in the eighties, but though Jackson has worked his particular magic by straddling (and annihilating) barriers between male/female, black/white and pop/soul dichotomies, Prince has turned those blends from milkshakes to cocktails with the 100-proof infusion of his furiously tender and endearingly narcissistic emphasis on sexuality. And – unlike Jackson – Prince is his own Quincy Jones, his own Greg Phillinganes, his own Rod Temperton and his own Eddie Van Halen. Whether fronting a live big band and out-JBing James Brown with every hot move in the book or holed up in his studio obsessively multi-tracking instruments and vocals into the night, Prince himself is the whole show. Whether it's masturbation or not, it works.

His current trademark sound is the one inaugurated on 'When Doves Cry' and done to a turn on 'Kiss' and 'Sign O' The Times', the lead-off single for the new double album of the same name: a huge, empty landscape bounded by computer drums and containing little more than a bass line, a few keyboard textures, the odd guitar fill and whichever of Prince's voices he feels like using at the time. It might be a languorous Sly Stone drawl or his patented Curtis Mayfield/Smokey Robinson falsetto or a multi-tracked host of others, but as one of James Brown's MCs might say, he comes from *all* sides on this one.

Like most double albums, 'Sign O' The Times' has its share of filler. 'The Ballad Of Dorothy Parker' is not – as you might be forgiven for assuming – a tribute to the famous New York critic, wit and short-story writer, but a Sly-ish fantasy encounter with a sexy waitress ('Do U want to take a bath?'), 'Play In The Sunshine' is old-time rock and roll fluff with a demented slide-guitar eruption out of Muddy Waters via Johnny Winter, and 'Hot Thing' is a lascivious funk throwaway. However, the good stuff is easily in the majority and it's pure, vintage Prince: sweet, greasy and *baad*.

The album's packaging is adorned with hearts, crucifixes and what Americans think of as a 'peace symbol' (CND emblem to us Brits): an extension of Prince's frequently preached position of public and social responsibility combined with reckless private hedonism. The AIDS era doesn't seem to have put the little chap off his favourite subject: nookie. In 'Slow Love', a string-and-horn-laden ballad reminiscent of Sly's 'Hot Fun In The Summertime', he wants to do it S-L-O-W; on 'It' he wants to do It all the time (complete with Kiss-style drums), on 'If I Was Your Girlfriend' he starts out wanting to be the receiver of girlish confidences and help his beloved choose her clothes but ends up trying to drag her into bed just the same, and on 'Adore' he gets so worked up with passion that he fissures into an entire vocal group. When he reaches 'U Got The Look' (the most likely choice for a follow-up single, complete with Sheila E's drumming and percussion and a screaming synth solo as well as some of the biggest, baddest drums on the whole album) he's ready to collapse writhing on the floor as soon as she walks in the room.

Elsewhere we find Prince fronting The Revolution on 'It's Gonna Be A Beautiful Night', for a live-in-Paris funk workout that'll have dancers gasping, synthing up old-time sixties soul-stomp sounds on 'I Could Never Take The Place Of Your Man' (which climaxes with Jimi Hendrix guitar chops and blare of feedback) and borrowing liberally from George Clinton for the groove and rap of 'Housequake'. Like Larry Blackmon's Cameo, Prince has both the sophistication and the chops to grab some of the most tried-and-trusted elements of traditional rock, soul and R&B and, by combining and recombining them in startlingly new juxtapositions, to place them on the line right at the cutting edge of the funk – that edge where it slices straight into the soft white gut of pop.

'Sign O' The Times' is good fun, good music, good sex and good politics. Prince may be nuts, he may be madly egocentric, domineering, snotty and a classic example of the Short Man Syndrome, but his hot streak shows no signs of cooling off. What's more, he's just made what will almost undoubtedly turn out to be one of the very best records of 1987. U should B ready 2 go 4 it.

# Culture Club: 'This Time' (Virgin)

*Q*, May 1987

THE ambition of any sensible modern pop group should be to score fast, split young and leave a good-sounding Greatest Hits album. Culture Club managed all of that and more, batting out a succession of warm, catchy and ingenious hit singles amidst flurries of delightfully absurd media capering and cavorting. In the autumn of 1984, it was impossible to find a cab-driver in all of New York City who didn't have an opinion about Boy George. 'A man dressed up as a woman!' growled one specimen straight from Central Casting. 'That's adult entertainment. I wouldn't let any teenager of mine go and see a show like that!' That kind of publicity money can only hope to buy.

Of course, the Culture Club saga collapsed under the weight of an unlistenable third album, which just about corresponds to the way that 'This Time' runs out of steam halfway through the second side, but while they were hot they made exemplary pop singles: easily outclassing the Durans and Spandaus who were their principal competition at the time. They stole with both hands, gleefully and unashamedly thrusting huge chunks of Motown, reggae, calypso and even country into the cauldron, blending everything from Judd Lander's mouth-harp on 'Karma Chameleon' and 'Church Of The Poisoned Mind' to the synthesized steel drums of 'I'll Tumble 4 Ya' into their sound, and keeping Helen Terry poised to leap into action whenever someone pressed the Aretha button. Plus, of course, everything was wrapped around George's voice, as thick, rich and comforting as a bowl of hot soup. Naughty but nice, weird but cuddly, Culture Club were the ultimate in safe sex. And all this without ever making a decent video!

'This Time' contains every Culture Club tune you ever wanted to hear, including 'Miss Me Blind', 'Time', 'It's A Miracle', 'Black Money' and 'Do You Really Want To Hurt Me', alongside a few that nobody in particular wanted, like 'The War Song'. As such it is definitive, rendering all the band's previous albums totally obsolete. I can't say I'll miss 'em blind – they outlived their usefulness fairly thoroughly before going their separate ways – or that a possible future regrouping will necessarily be a cue for any noticeable degree of public celebration, but when they were good they were very, very good indeed. What more can you ask of a pop group?

# Terence Trent D'Arby: Yeau!

*Q*, September 1987

'**I**'M very, very self-critical. I'm very critical of others, but I'm also very critical of my own work and there's no one that could possibly put more pressure on me than me. *No one.* And for that reason I'm not worried about it . . .'

Terence Trent D'Arby is explaining how he feels about the tidal wave of superlatives applied to him and his work both by the press posse and by the artist himself. As a result, the self-styled 'genius' can never be judged according to whether he's *good* – or even *very good.* With this level of rhetoric raging about his immaculately braided head, Terence Trent D'Arby has to be *superb* – or else he is nothing. Isn't this a trifle dangerous? Doesn't D'Arby ever look down and see the abyss yawning beneath him?

'. . . Because this interview hasn't gone like the standard interview, I'm taking this slightly seriously. I take 95 per cent of most journalists with a grain of salt because I've done it myself, and I can*not* take most journalists seriously. Because I read, and because I'm a fan, I know what most people like to read. People are *bored* with Lionel Richie going "I-love-everybody-peace-on-earth-we-are-the-world . . ." – *fuck that!* People *love* bastards. People love a loveable rogue. I'm a fucking rogue! All the world loves a clown, all the world loves a *bastard.*

'And – look, I figure even if I fall completely on my face, which I won't, and somebody picks up an old copy of the *Melody Maker* three years from now and they're sittin' on the toilet and they open it up and laugh at it, at least it served a purpose.

'And I'm not worried about it detracting from my music, 'cause when I'm creating I'm as serious about it as I could possibly be. After it's finished and I know my ass is covered I can then start playing a game. If I was insecure about it then I would be very, very afraid to walk that tightrope without a net, but my music is the net, and I can fall onto that. The worst that can happen is that I'll learn my lesson, shut the fuck up, make records and not open my mouth too much. But I'm an extremist.

I'm a Pisces, and *we do not like lukewarm shit* ... when Muhammad Ali fought, just as many people paid to see him lose and get knocked on his ass as came to see him win. But they *came*, and they paid the fucking ticket.

'Look . . . fair enough, yes, I was hyped. I was hyped! Plain and simple . . .'

Terence Trent D'Arby seems like something invented by three rock critics on the phone. Young black American, pretty enough to stimulate salivation in the most hardened female hacks and capable of evoking everybody's favourite vintage soul stars – Al Green, Stevie Wonder, Sam Cooke, Otis Redding, Michael Jackson – with the merest contraction of his larynx. He has the perfect background, too: raised in a severe Pentecostal church family, son-of-a-preacher-man and a gospel-singing mother, moved from Manhattan to Florida to Chicago and finally to New Jersey. Attended a school for gifted children, studied journalism, wrote a column for a Florida newspaper, boxed to Golden Gloves standard, joined the army. Got sent to Germany with Elvis Presley's old regiment, went AWOL to sing with local bands, quit the army, acquired a German manager and ended up in London where – tricked out in the finest of London street fashion, signed to CBS and produced by Heaven 17's Martyn Ware – he becomes the London rock scene's favourite adopted black American son since Jimi Hendrix and takes up a virtual residency on the last weeks of The Tube. Highly articulate, enormously well-read and gifted with an awesome knack for self-promotion, he is soon on the cover of just about everything this side of a packet of condoms, racks up a perfect two-out-of-two-score in the Top 10 and shows every sign of going nova any second now. *Perfect*. Or is he?

The young genius seems to be going through a carefully rehearsed fit of the sulks. His braids are pulled severely back, except for one single solitary specimen hanging coyly over his face from under his oversized po'-boy cap, and due to a bad attack of hay fever he is looking positively greenish, though this could simply be the afternoon sun bouncing off the green tablecloth and the twin bottles of Perrier set out before him. He slouches downstairs to get made up, a process which takes nearly half an hour. Eventually he bounces back up, his voice preceding him. 'I hope you're ready for this, 'cause we gonna talk some *serious* bullshit.'

We start out chatting politics. He fires questions at me – why did the Labour Party lose the election so thoroughly, what do I think of Neil Kinnock's Presidential-style campaign – and speedily demonstrates an unusually firm grasp of the ins and outs of British politics for an American. His own politics are vociferously Socialist, and he loathes and despises his native land.

'If you have a heart, a slight bit of suss and a humanitarian conscience, you can't help but come up with an alternate view of what goes on in America. I've never ever felt right about that. That's why I'm here. It's got fuck all to do with music or the amount of competition, it's just that from a very early age I always knew that there was somewhere better where I could fit in without compromising who I was or the person I was trying to be. The American Dream has a great price, and I just had to get the fuck out. What does it profit a man that he gain the whole world but lose his own soul? It says that somewhere in the Bible, I think. How much will I prostitute myself for my art? A bit, but there has to be a cut-off point. To become yet another safely emasculated black *thing* . . . I'd rather die than be that.'

Would it kill you to be Freddie Jackson?

'Yes. It should kill Freddie Jackson to be Freddie Jackson. Look . . . see . . . from an early age I just felt slightly off-kilter. I have to think it's a certain amount of destiny, that something was preparing me to go the fuck somewhere else and try to bring a breath of fresh air to the scene. Freddie Jackson is probably very happy being what he is and I don't begrudge him that, but I couldn't be that and since Freddie Jackson's doin' it there's no need for me to fucking do that. With that mentality I couldn't say anything that would offend anyone – let's see, yuppie-speak – damage the units that I could possibly be shifting.

'When people ask me if it's very important for me to crack America, well, yes and no. I would find it extremely challenging to attempt to do it on my terms, but if I couldn't do that I'd really rather just leave it the fuck alone.'

D'Arby's accent slides around a lot as he speaks: from Tri-State to Florida to black North London complete with West Indian vowels, from the pulpit – with flights of hypnotic preacherese interlarded with occasional Biblical allusions – to back-alley cussing worthy of Run-DMC. He says fuck more often than anybody else I've ever interviewed, and that includes Bob Geldof and The

**413**

Sex Pistols. Like his singing, it demonstrates his near-effortless gift of mimicry.

I suggest that he has applied a very similar strategy to that employed twenty years ago by another ex-army musical maverick, Jimi Hendrix, who escaped the constrictions of the US scene by relocating to England, trashing the local competition, reinventing himself and returning in triumph to his homeland less than a year later. 'I was asked that last week: do a lot of black American musicians come here because it's easier to make it and there's less competition? It's that very capitalist mentality: what possible reason could you have for wanting to escape the land of milk and honey? Well, the honey is not as sweet as people think it is and the milk's gone fucking sour. Yunno? I don't *need* that shit. For an artist to create to the best of his ability, he has to feel a sense of synchronicity with his surroundings. I feel I'm as good as fucking *anybody* in the States, and I have nothing to run away from, but as a person as well as an artist, I've got to live and I've got to walk the streets. I don't like the vibe I catch when I walk the streets in America, so why should I put up with it if I can find somewhere else where I can eventually raise kids or whatever?

'When I was brought to Europe by the army, immediately I felt more comfortable as a person in Germany than I did in the States, which as a black was quite odd, and I felt that was a sad indictment on the place which I had come from. But if I wanted to be serious about my work, the only places it made sense to be were London and New York, and New York was out from the beginning. London was the only possible choice.'

Before CBS eventually bit, D'Arby was turned down by a fair selection of record companies. Both Island Records and its dance music subsidiary 4th & Broadway declined to get involved, as did WEA and London. 'The guy from London I think literally threw the tape out of the window and said, "I don't need this shit. The last thing I need is another Michael Jackson or a second-rate Prince impersonator" – and practically nothing was changed from demo form to what you hear on the album.'

Ah yes, the album concisely entitled 'Introducing The Hardline According To Terence Trent D'Arby'. No Terence Trent D'Arby interview would be complete without a hymn to 'The Hardline'. When people were accusing Terence of being the subject of what he describes an 'incredible massive mega-selling job' from CBS, he stayed cool. 'I knew that round the corner was coming this album, there would be eleven songs that would prove — even if you didn't like the tunes — that you have to take this guy seriously, that you have to give him the credit for making the most original, or freshest album this year. I say that because basically Prince still made a Prince album and I think it was overrated myself. I'm still a massive fan and I still think he's a genius, but it was overrated. They have to give me credit for not playing the same production games, the same "let's get seven producers in and give 'em one for the rock market, one for the MOR market, one for the yuppies, one for the street-cred crew . . ." *Fuck that!* At the end of the day, I think anybody who completely slags it off will look like a fool to someone who has a bit more suss. I just don't think you can. Being moody, sometimes I hear it and think it and think that it isn't as good as I thought it was, but other times I listen to it and go *YES*! I've delivered the goods and fuck anybody who doesn't agree with me.

'I didn't try to play safe with this album, but I did try to do it as chronological as possible.'

Huh?

'It came to a certain point about a year ago, for example, when every song I wrote after that I would not on principle put on the first album because I want there to be an idea where if I do subsequent albums the person who supports what I do feels growth, sees growth, and it may be naïve but I felt that if I just took the *best* songs you would not see a pattern of development.'

So no fretting about the second album syndrome . . .

'Well, if I should do a second album . . .'

What do you mean *if*? Surely you have a contract to record at least eight albums.

'Well, fuck it. People can't *make* you create, but if it should be done then the second album's already written, and I'm starting to think about the third. I had to know that I will not suffer from the second album syndrome, and now I'm secure in my knowledge that the second album will be more adventurous and better than the first — if I should do it. I could easily have a second career as a quote-unquote *songwriter* and the publisher's always bugging me about . . . but I wouldn't want to do what Prince does, give songs away. Even before the album came out I was offered production jobs for other people, but where a lot of successful black acts fail is that as soon as they start getting production offers, they see the money and the points ... by their third album, they're *wastin'* themselves 'cause what else have they got? They given away a lot of good stuff. I think a lot of it has to do with the romantic image of the artist as well. I'd just rather my stuff go to *me*. If I don't want to use it and somebody else wants it, they can take from my B-sides. My publisher says, What makes you think people want your B-sides, if they're not good enough for you? but I say, Well, they'll come around. Give 'em about a year, they'll come back around and start turning over rocks. There are things I could do for other people – I come up with a lot of very easy tunes which could be hits and I wouldn't want to waste my time on 'em. But I'll throw 'em the *crumbs*. I'll take the *meat*.'

At this point you could be forgiven for wondering whether a man who genuinely believes in himself and the merits of his own work would need to bellow the odds *quite* so loudly. 'The Hardline' is a fairly reasonable album – four good tunes, including the singles – but it hardly represents any major artistic breakthrough, any redefinition of the soul/rock boundary lines. Terence Trent D'Arby may winge about yuppies and the capitalist mentality, but 'The Hardline' is shaping up to be one of this year's hip releases among the upwardly mobile, because of the rebel-chic cachet D'Arby has earned by the fairly reliable stratagem of playing the radical black man around a few impressionable white reporters who are thrilled that a real American black person has come to London to give their scene the stamp of his approval. He also says the kind of things about mainstream black entertainers that most rock critics feel but are too shy to say in case anybody thinks they're racist. Like so:

'I don't care about the States if it means I have to compromise, but I *do* care if it means I can do exactly what I want to do, because it's such a chance to blaze through all that fog and all that puritan haze and all that *bullshit* they goin' through, and just shake fucking shit up. The attitude I'm showing over here would definitely raise some bristles over there, because black male acts are far, far too apologetic.'

Larry Blackmon of Cameo doesn't seem too apologetic to me.

'Well, at the same time, Blackmon isn't *massive*. Look, any black act in the States who has been massive quote-unquote mega-

416

crossover success has had to emasculate himself to some degree. Lionel Richie, well . . . Prince has had to play the bisexual image, cast aspersions as to his dominant heterosexuality. Jackson's had to be asexual, Vandross couldn't possibly offend anybody, George Benson . . . it's like in the contract, it certifies them to a free plastic surgeon visitation, guarantees them a make-up artist at all times to lighten 'em up for photographs if you sell more than two million albums, and these guys wouldn't do or say anything which would lose 'em *one* record sale. What do I care about insulting someone in Iowa that I don't even know? Should I surrender my free will and submit my personality so that I don't offend someone that I don't even know?

'I will not have my balls cut off. I'm sorry, but I need them – they come in handy at times – and I don't want to be like everybody else. I *want* that controversy.'

Run-DMC have a fairly threatening presence, haven't had their skins lightened and sold well over four million copies of their last album.

'. . . to 95 per cent urban kids. I'm trying to prove that you can sell records, be a massive crossover success without chopping off your dick! That is what has happened to every massively successful crossover act! Like Jake Riviera said, you infiltrate and you double-cross. It might be a bit difficult for me to infiltrate and submerge myself and then burst out later, 'cause I just couldn't stand the period of time when I might have to hold my tongue. I'm no fool: I obviously wouldn't say on nationwide TV that I thought America was racist, sexist, homophobic and violent if they asked me why I left . . . I would just say America wasn't a culture I felt comfortable in, too many things wrong, and I'd rather be in a place where I could feel comfortable with who I am, but anybody with any *brain* would understand what I'm trying to say.

'So if making it there means having to be yet another Gregory fucking Abbott, then I'm sorry. I have no great need to rebel against anything in Britain, because your pop scene has traditionally been littered with loons and eccentrics . . . fine! I fit here, but since I'm an American person even though I'm a British act, there is a very, very large buzz going around in the States about me. I have to go there in September, and in January I have to spend four months there on the road, and I'm really not looking forward to that *at all*.

'But I do look forward to looking them in the face after the way they've been placated and catered to and just treat them with contempt if need be. A heckler jump up in the audience or whatever, I'll just tell 'em to *fuck . . . off*! Get the fuck out if you don't like it! And they just ain't used to being talked to like that. Half of them will just boo, but that's *fuel*. I *like* that. They don't forget you that way.

'Have you seen the album? The finished artwork? I don't thank anybody, no seven producers, I don't thank God. I can envision some young white girl's father telling her to take that poster down, because I will leave no doubt! I am a fucking heterosexual! I'm not homophobic, I have no problem with that, but I'm not fucking homosexual, I won't even *begin* to make 'em think I'm a homosexual in order to placate your paranoias that you impress upon your daughters and your sons . . .'

In his mind, D'Arby is no longer in North London doing an interview. He is addressing the Washington Wives and the Parents Musical Resource Council on nationwide television, making Ollie North look like a shrinking violet by comparison.

'. . . that's *your* fucking problem! You get people asking questions like, Don't you feel you have a responsibility to children? I have *fuck all* responsibility to your kids! If I'm doing something that they can't handle or you can't handle, you set them aside. I'm just a reflection of life. I like kids fine, cool runnin's. If I'm around them I try not to say too many "motherfuckers", but that's not my problem to raise anybody's child in society. And having said that, I shall now take my make-up off . . .'

And this is where we must regretfully take our leave of Terence Trent D'Arby for the time being. He is a likeable young hustler, spectacularly full of shit but extremely good company none the less, still obsessed with his native land and the living mirror image of all the American hangups he has come here to escape. He regrets, he says, that he is still an American citizen: he's looking into applying for Irish citizenship. But he has this nightmare where he is trapped and running from door to door, and every time he wrenches one open he finds Uncle Sam behind it sneering *nyah nyah nyah, you can't get out*.

What we don't know is whether, in his nightmare, Uncle Sam is black or white . . .

# *Maus: A Survivor's Tale*
# by Art Spiegelman
# (Penguin)

*Q*, September 1987

THE Holocaust still blows a chill graveyard wind over our century and our future, assuming we have one. The notion of one's genes being *in themselves* an automatic death warrant is something that the human mind should not be able to contemplate but history tells us that it indeed has, and possibly will again. Different people cope with this fact in different ways: for cartoonist Art Spiegelman, the solution was to create Maus, the story of his father Vladek's life in Poland before and during World War II.

The method Spiegelman has chosen is one that has recently been relentlessly trivialized and exploited by Steven Spielberg in his movie *An American Tail*: he has re-cast the events in funny-animal form, though despite their heads and tails, his characters enact genuine history. The Jews are mice, the Nazis are cats, the Poles are pigs, but his intent is as serious as Orwell's was in *Animal Farm*.

Each chapter of Vladek's narrative is framed by visits from his son Artie the cartoonist, who serves as witness to his story and foil for a cantankerous old man's irritability. Spiegelman's difficulty in understanding and relating to his impatient, cranky old father serves as counterpoint to the remorseless horror of Vladek's unfolding autobiography. He is a born hustler, and as the power of the Nazis grows ever stronger, his only hustle is his attempt to keep his family alive and together. To this end, Vladek applies all the ingenuity and energy he once applied to dealing in black-market goods.

Maus, originally serialized as inserts in Spiegelman's avant-garde graphics magazine *RAW* ('The Magazine That Lost Its Faith In Nihilism'), is the first of two volumes. This one ends at the gates of Mauschwitz, and in the second volume (which Spiegelman estimates will take him 'between two and eight years' to complete), Vladek and his wife make their descent into the final horror.

The notion of doing the Holocaust as a comic book may be considered as a breach of Good Taste's final frontiers, but the simple cartoon device dislocates the assumptions which we bring to events almost too awful to contemplate. It is ironic that many people will be more moved by the fate of a family of cartoon mice than by the discarded remains of human beings, but Maus is one of those cultural events which, by the sheer fact of its existence, expands a genre which previously would have been too small to contain it.

# The Gospel According to Miss Ross

*Q*, October 1987

'I'VE been here so many times before,' murmurs Diana Ross as she sweeps, surrounded by a clucking entourage, through the foyer of the EMI Records building in Manchester Square, a vision of cool elegance in her black-on-white embroidered Afghan coat, 'but I can *never* remember how to get here.'

This, in itself, should not be a problem. Nobody in Diana Ross's position needs to remember how to get anywhere: it is the responsibility of others to deliver the star to the designated locations at the appointed times. However, Diana Ross has been coming to Manchester Square – on and off, admittedly – for nearly a quarter of a century, ever since The Supremes made their first trip to the UK in 1964, back in the days when EMI were Motown's British distributors.

Then she was the littlest Supreme, the one in the middle who opened those big eyes wider and wider until millions drowned in them as she mewed her songs of devotion, dependence and disappointment. Now she's a showbiz institution, a reigning diva ... and a woman with a mission. She is, she says, sick of being regarded as simply a 'glamour queen' or a pop singer: Diana Ross wants to educate the youth of today in the glorious history of R&B and its invaluable contribution to the popular music of the world. Her new album 'Red Hot Rhythm And Blues' is but one aspect of this strategy; there is also a TV special (as yet unscheduled for British screening) and – further ahead in the future – maybe even a book.

But first there is a caveat from her publicist: there is to be none of that gossip column stuff. Diana Ross is – visibly – pregnant, but any reference to this condition will constitute grounds for instant termination of the interview. Similarly, questions relating to the contents of *Dreamgirl: My Life as a Supreme* (the recently published memoirs of Diana Ross's former colleague Mary Wilson) are definitely not on the menu; its portraits of Ross as manipulative power-gamer and its unveiling of veritable hampers full of dirty linen in the Motown family place it squarely in the 'no comment' zone.

Which is something of a pity, because Diana Ross's career has rarely been less than tempestuous. Her record sales have fluctuated drastically, with dramatic dips almost invariably followed by peak smashes like the 1980 Chic-produced 'Diana' album, complete with hit singles 'Upside Down', 'I'm Coming Out' and 'My Old Piano', speedily followed by a noisy public falling-out with Nile Rodgers and Bernard Edwards over some last-minute remixing after they had delivered the tapes. Her last hit was with Barry Gibb's calculatedly nostalgic 'Chain Reaction', which drew heavily on her old Supremes sound and stayed at number one for three weeks, but failed to stimulate huge sales of its accompanying album. Her blockbusting performance as Billie Holiday in *Lady Sings The Blues* – in many ways the finest achievement of her career to date – was followed by crushingly mediocre appearances in *Mahogany* and *The Wiz*.

For whatever reasons, a reputation as a prima donna of the first water has surrounded her as tenaciously as the (never substantiated) rumours of drug addiction, and the absurd suggestion that she is Michael Jackson's mother. She has had a brief affair with Kiss's rather unsavoury front man Gene Simmons – he of the ten-inch tongue – hired Andy Warhol to do one of her album sleeves, and (in a sequence diplomatically edited out of the Motown 25th Anniversary TV special a few years ago) pushed and shoved Mary Wilson out of the spotlight and snatched a microphone from her former partner's hand. A proposed benefit concert for a children's playground in New York's Central Park went badly awry when, after a rainstorm necessitated a rescheduling, a bunch of kids from the uptown projects terrorized the crowd and the New York Police Department demanded $650,000 for additional policing. The organizers claimed that – despite the sale of film and video rights to the show – it had lost money and no donation would be made. This caused such a furore that Diana Ross ended up handing over a quarter of a million dollars from her own pocket.

At her last London concert at Wembley Arena, she entered into a public altercation with her sound crew and – before a shocked crowd – kicked several monitor speakers offstage before flouncing off for an unscheduled intermission. Clearly, being Diana Ross is not easy, which is why her publicist is at pains to emphasize that it has been a sizeable coup to persuade her to do interviews at all, and it is crucial that she is not upset in any way.

So we'll leave all that to the popular prints, and join Diana Ross amongst the salmon sandwiches and the pitchers of that really *nice* apple juice with the actual slivers of fruit-pulp floating in it as we discuss something she rarely talks about: music.

'It started with that album I did with "Why Do Fools Fall In Love". See, those are the songs I grew up with and I think this generation that I see in my own children – I have a fifteen-year-old and my husband's son is eighteen – really enjoy these things. It's like a circle and a cycle, and you wonder how they get to hear them. It's almost like a cult thing. My husband's daughter, fifteen years old, is running around singing "Mr Lee".'

'Mr Lee' is, of course, the old Bobbettes tune featured in the movie *Stand By Me* – any fool knows that – and it's one of the oldies reworked by Ross on the new album.

'That's one of the reasons I went in and recorded it, because it tickled me so much that I asked her how she knew it, and of course it was *Stand By Me*, right? She has no history of these songs. They just like them, and as I travelled in Europe I found that everybody liked them and now America's picked up on them again. When I did "Why Do Fools Fall In Love" I also did "Rescue Me", the old Fontella Bass song. These are things I grew up with and I have an experience of them, and I realized that a whole generation did not know where they came from, the source or origins of these songs.

'For me I like music, *period*. I really like songs from operas, but my origins, my growing up as I start to really look back, it came through – and my kids wouldn't even know this – it started through what is called in America R&B. Now R&B really meant black music, but it's not what identifies black music today because there's many white artists, European artists, that sing R&B, so it's changed its emphasis. It's not about black artists – exactly. It's really quite a story. It's a musical tree that I'm talking about, and I've spent a lot of time on it.'

*Tell* me about it. She laughs prettily, shaking her exploded mane. 'I'm not an authority on this, but I made a lot of assumptions that the music we are working and performing today, its origin stems all the way back to slavery. The children of slaves and slave-owners and the music moved its way north and kinda spread out and turned into more *gospel*, and another spin-off was then *jazz*. Gospel was basically message music during slavery, but it also had to do with the instrumentation. The drums first were like a means of communication, and as it moved forward you saw the adding of different instruments. It was this wild frenzy – oh jeez, I'm jumping all ahead,' she interrupts herself crossly, 'but it's this incredible tree. Gospel spun off to soul and there's artists like Aretha, who's really a soul artist.

'And then for a moment there people got confused about what is soul, because they thought The Supremes were singing soul. They called us soul singers and I remember trying to describe what soul meant to me and I said, Well, it means that you have to sing with a lot of *feeling*. I was really just a teenager then . . .'

The Supremes were always a pop group, and to have expected them to sing with that get-down gospel fervour was almost a stereotype of what black people were *supposed* to be like . . .

'But it's so interesting to me because then there was jazz, which took on a totally different improvising kind of thing, and then there was the people who covered jazz, in other words the technical kind of people. All that stuff is a combination of what we are doing now, for example what Anita Baker is doing: she's really an instrument. She sings like a saxophone. For me, after singing music for twenty-seven years and finally taking the time to look at what does my voice represent, where it comes from, what I am about . . .'

Well, your voice has changed over the years . . .

'I hope so!' She bursts into a peal of laughter.

You couldn't have taken on an Etta James song like 'Tell Mama' back in the sixties.

'Well, let me tell you I grew up listening to all Etta James's songs. The first performance I ever did in front of a mirror closing myself up into a room so that no one would ever see me was singing along to Etta James's album. Now even though I could never sound like her or *belt* like her – I had her on my TV special too, by the way, she's *faaaaabulous* – from the time I first started singing before I was sixteen, I wanted to perform but I hadn't gotten with Motown yet. People think my music career started when I got to Motown, but I had been singing since I was a kid. My upbringing was singing in my mother's choir in church even though I wasn't the kind of singer that had this range of expression that could go from *hoooooooo. . .*' she attempts to demonstrate an Aretha scream. It doesn't really happen '. . . and all that thing. I wasn't really like that. My voice was more sensitive, and a lead voice, but the things I did in the choir had more to do with storytelling. So that's part of who I am: my motivation always came from *caring* and *loving* and all that, this expression of *feeling*.

'It's not like you're just singing words. You're not a mechanic or a technician, it comes from somewhere, and I usually select songs that have meaning to me. "There Goes My Baby" was one of the first songs as The Supremes – we were The Primettes, actually. . .' (The Primettes were the girl-group affiliate of a Detroit male vocal group called The Primes, who eventually mutated into The Temptations.) '. . . then we won a contest in Canada and that was one of the songs we sang, along with a Ray Charles song called "Night Time Is The Right Time", and I used to sing the high part. Each of the songs have a real special memory for me. "Mr Lee" I grew up with and my step-daughter liked it so much; "Selfish One" by Jackie Ross was another one, always reminded me of "My Guy" that Mary Wells had out at the time. The album was fun, because I had listened to some interviews from Mick Hucknall and he talked about the rhythm and blues artists that he had admired, and I got in touch with him, said what kind of album I was doing and asked him if he wanted to write a song for me.' Hucknall ended up contributing a song called 'Shine'.

Ross worked on 'Red Hot Rhythm & Blues' with producer Tom Dowd, the former Atlantic staff engineer and producer who recorded a staggering proportion of the selections on the Atlantic R&B box. 'I had gotten to the bottom line where I wanted to do a *rhythm and blues* album and I found Tom Dowd and I *love* working with him.

'It was a chance to throw in the names of all the people I admire; I threw in Aretha Franklin, James Brown and so on. It was exciting for me because I haven't ever had the opportunity to really . . . artists know each other, but they never get the chance to show each other how much they admire each other's work. I might run into Tina, you know, but we only talk for *seconds*. You never get a chance to talk about the things that have made a difference in your career.'

She is intending to see Tina Turner's Wembley show the following night: I recommend that she gets there in time to see her opening act, Robert Cray.

'Oh, I think he's . . . is this the jazz guy?'

No, Robert Cray the blues singer.

'*Oh*! Are you *kidding*? He's *faaaaaabulous*! He's *wonderful*! Ahhhh! There's something about him in his physical that reminds me of Billy Preston . . .'

Well, he's thinner than Billy Preston.

'Oh well, Billy has *gained* a little . . . he is really good. I tried to get him for one of *my* shows before he got so popular.'

So how does Diana Ross feel about the resurgence of interest in the golden years of soul and the early days of Motown?

'Most kids that I know are really interested in music background: they know who the drummer is even though they've never seen him, or who your git-tar player is on the album.' She lowers her voice to impart the next revelation. 'I went on a promotional tour for the album in America, just within the company, all the different RCA branches and so on . . . and I would talk to people who'd been working on my records for years and they didn't know how a record is produced. When I would write on an album that I produced something, they'd ask, What do you do as a producer? What does that mean you do?

'I say it means that you find the musicians, select the songs and sit in there for *hours and hours in the studio*! If you're real forceful you get up there and press little knobs and things yourself! You trust your ears and you sit there through the mixing and it's *hours*! A lot of people don't know that. They think that you walk in, sing your songs, walk away and that's it. Well, it's not like that.'

Isn't that how it was back at Motown?

'We had three incredible producers then, you know, Lamont Dozier and Eddie and Brian Holland, so they take a *lot* of cred. And at the time I couldn't say that I knew anything about it. I went back to Motown to see that little four-track studio again, and . . .' Her voice drops to a dreamy whisper.

'Berry [Gordy, Motown boss and founder] has very little to do with it, but his sister Esther Edwards has made sure that it's still there. When I visited I was so worried that the place was going to catch on fire that I asked Mrs Edwards if she could get some sprinklers in there because they got old pictures that will never be duplicated, they got old costumes, the studio's still there, they got our old sheet music still up there on the piano. I think The Four Tops went and did a TV special from there.'

It was not until Diana Ross portrayed Billie Holiday in the *Lady Sings The Blues* biopic that many people considered her to be an artist or performer of any substance. Interpreting a programme of Holiday's best-loved songs and playing two-handed scenes with the likes of Richard Pryor, she showed capacities undisplayed before – or since. She even wrung plaudits from critics as tough as the *New Yorker*'s legendary movie pundit Pauline Kael, but her subsequent film roles (in *Mahogany* and *The Wiz*) were considerably less impressive and since then *nada*. Why did this once promising movie career falter? For the first time, her complacency seems to dissolve.

'Something happens sometimes when you get things too soon,' she begins slowly. 'The Academy Award nomination frightens you for what comes next. You wanna make the right choice and you get too picky about not making a mistake and then the space is gone. It's not that I haven't worked on my film career because what I've done is started my own production company to find the script that would be the right thing for me to do. At the same time there's something about movie work that forces you to be away from music, so each year I would say my foundation is my music and I'll stay with my music and if a wonderful script comes up then I'll do that . . . I didn't just want to do *black product*, ya know? I wanted to do something which didn't just stick me in a

426

mould again. Then there was a lot of people's life stories which kept coming in, just biopics, which kept coming up and still keeps coming up, but something new, something wonderful, something modern, something which has comedy and music ... they just were not offered to me, and that's the truth.'

She brightens up again returning to the subject of her new R&B crusade. 'You see all these programmes about music and they talk about rock'n'roll and just drop in the black performers as an *influence*, and the truth is they're the originators. I went through a lot of film archives for my TV special and I found this little black-and-white spot of Fats Domino, and The Platters and all the vocal groups and I found out how rap songs today really started way back then. It's just so exciting for me, all this research. I thought maybe I should do a documentary and write a book, because I gathered so much information, went to antique shops looking for old 78s ... it's all part of me now, because now I know what it is.'

It may seem incredible that it's taken until now for Diana Ross to get interested in the history of her music, to read books like Leroi Jones' *Blues People* and Arnold Shaw's *Honkers and Shouters*, but as she explains, 'You've been watching this music since you were very young, but I was in it and people were asking me *what kind of music do you sing Miss Ross*? and I had to figure out what I got from my parents and what was happening to others while I was singing. I worked shows with Otis Redding, but I never quite figured out what kind of music he was doing or where he got it from. It was just part of who we were. When I was reading, I was discovering that record companies were looking for white artists who had the feeling of black artists, but it wasn't until much later that I worked out that Berry Gordy's intent was to find black artists who had a commerical sounding voice that no one could tell was black or white. And I realized that many of the albums that came out of Motown in the early sixties had no black faces on the cover! Did you know that? I didn't know that! I wasn't even *aware* of that! Berry wanted to appeal to the masses, to cross the lines, so he wouldn't even put blacks on the covers!'

As part of her grand continuation of black musical history, Ross has LL Cool J guesting on that TV special. 'I created a fictional character, kind of like Alberta Hunter only not her – I played Alberta – I was sitting in my dressing-room watching

427

Diana Ross on television, and this old woman is saying' – and here Ross transforms for a second and damn right she can act – '"Yeah, I used to do that. I remember the thirties and forties" and then you go back into her memory and you see Little Richard playing a preacher doing "Ninety-Nine And A Half Won't Do". LL Cool J comes up later; he was *so sweet*. But he has this thing he does and I had to tell him, You just can't do that on television! 'Cause he kept grabbing his . . .' (she mimes the action on her own body and lowers her voice as she does so) '*balls*. I had to keep saying I don't think ABC will allow that. He'd be singing and moving around and then grab and I'd be yelling, *Wait! Cameras! You can't do that on television*! But they were so sweet and they were real gentlemen. I met Run-DMC because I hosted the American Music Awards, and that gives me the opportunity to stay in touch with all the new acts . . . I'm just in *love* with Whitney Houston. She represents what I think I represent . . . and she's young.'

She has even unbent sufficiently by the end of the interview to confess that she is pregnant. Diana Ross is exceptionally likeable when she relaxes, and it only emphasizes how rarely in her professional career she's had the opportunity to do just that. It's almost as if she's been there so many times before, but she can never remember how to get there.

## Tina Turner: Flying down to Rio

*Q*, April 1988

THE biggest football stadium in the world is the Maracana in Rio de Janeiro: a big game such as a World Cup Final can pack 120,000 revved-up Brazilians into the terraces and balconies, no problem. Over the past few years, it's become accustomed to playing host to pop shows as well: this is where Frank Sinatra made it into the *Guinness Book of Records* for assembling 152,000 people into the biggest audience ever attracted by a single performer. At 9.45 p.m. on 16 January, 1988, this record is a quarter of an hour away from becoming ancient history. Ol' Blue Eyes' big score is about to be trashed by a forty-eight-year-old woman in a wig.

Not just *any* forty-eight-year-old woman in a wig, either, but one who less than seven years ago had been abandoned by the music business as dead meat. While the 400 percussionists of the Beija Flor samba school – the winners of Carnival '87 – thunder an accompaniment to a thousand-strong carnival parade and the laser display on the 200-foot-high screen next to the giant inflatable Pepsi can flashes dancing Pepsi bottles, Wrangler logos, the Brazilian flag and a cartoon samba dancer doing things with her hips that are impossible for real people even in Brazil, a sweatily enthusiastic crowd of 180,200 get ready for the main event. Over the stadium, somewhere in that hot dark star-pierced sky, hangs the phantom presence of 26 million US and Japanese TV viewers ready to be hooked into Rio by the Home Box Office satellite dead on 10 p.m.

Any residual memory of the opening act – a hideous local combo named Zero, who sound as if they've never heard any music in their lives apart from Simple Minds, though somebody might have told them about INXS – has long been wiped out. The audience – happy, perspiring and eager with anticipation – is overwhelmingly young, which is hardly surprising since over 40 per cent of Brazil's 122 million citizens are under sixteen.

Now Neguinho da Beija Flor is singing over the drums, the green, gold and orange parade has almost completed its lap of honour, an immense Pepsi balloon is batted from hand to hand, something like 70,000 stiff cardboard fans bearing the star's image and the sponsors' logos are spun high into the velvety air. Then the chanting swells, chanting as perhaps only Pele and the heroes of Brazilian football have heard, chanting that concusses the ear like massed bass-drums: 'TEE-*NAH!* TEE-*NAH!* TEE-*NAH!*'

Of course! This crowd is not here to see Michael Jackson, or David Bowie, or Lionel Richie or any of Pepsi's other troubadors. For that matter. they're not here for Madonna, Prince, Whitney Houston or Mark Knopfler, either. What they're here for is mounted in a carnival float just shimmying up to the edge of the stage, snakehipping the mesmeric oval of *rebolou*, the classic samba move. And as the satellites haul in their millions and the percussion that's been rolling and thundering for so long comes to a sudden, jarring STOP . . .

Two things happen. A nation with 365 per cent inflation and an average weekly wage of under £20 moves a step further into the international leisure marketplace. And the woman recently referred to in the *Grimsby Evening Telegraph* as 'the raunchy-thighed grandmother' struts grinning to a stage-centre epiphany, into international live-by-satellite showbiz heaven. 'Owl-*raht!*' whoops Tina Turner.

Behind her, on a set which resembles a Cecil B. DeMille Roman temple constructed out of stainless steel, several men in rock and roll clothes busy themselves with guitars, drums and keyboards, cranking out a Stones-clone thump and grind. Pixie boots flashing, fringed-suede miniskirt swirling, she does that bad boogaloo over to the mike just like Joe Tex as the band steamroll remorselessly into 'Addicted To Love'. In high school, Tina Turner always got straight A's for drama and gym. And she's still getting them.

The Break Every Rule tour seems like it's been going on for years. This is because it *has* been going on for years. It started in January '87 and doesn't finish until the 28 March 1988 show in Osaka, by which time Tina and her team will have played 230 concerts to something like 3,500,000 paying customers in twenty-five countries. Some of the shows have been mega-events like this one – in Brazil's industrial capital São Paulo (the third most densely populated city in the world) she hosted an intimate little gathering for 102,000 people – and others, in areas like the US Midwest where even crossover black acts aren't that welcome, were mere 5,000-seaters, but the tour is still the most protracted farewell trek in pop history. Last Tango or Long Goodbye, it puts the capstone on twenty-seven years of The Road.

Break Every Rule is an extravaganza in every sense of the word. That massive set took a week to move from Buenos Aires to São Paulo, and it will remain in Brazil: a farewell gift from Tina's manager Roger Davies to promoter Manoel Poladian. There are duplicates already built and ready to roll into action in Japan, Australia and the US. It is also an uncommonly strenuous tour: the temperature in the stadium is in the low 80s even at night; under the lights it's over a hundred. Not for nothing are the band 'encouraged' to put in gymnasium time at every stop: for three successive nights Turner whipped her band and crew through gruelling soundchecks and dress rehearsals. Breaking the show up for TV transmission meant rearranging the programme and adding a few numbers – like 'Help' and Pete Townshend's 'Acid Queen' – to the set. The band are fifteen to twenty years Turner's juniors: she drove 'em 'til they whimpered and John Miles – yes, *that* John Miles, Music-was-my-first-love, the Alan Parsons Project and all that, who's been piano man and chief backing singer for the tour – had to chip in and point out that if *she* could do it, so could they.

But do they love it? The crowd roar and whoop their approval of each *coup de théâtre*: the shimmying samba line – a riot of feathers, sequins and sweat – who invade the stage during 'Typical Male', the hydraulic platform which raises Turner fifteen feet in the air on a column of smoke during 'We Don't Need Another Hero', the positioning of saxophonist Deric Dyer on a precarious platform 200 feet up as he blows the solo on 'Private Dancer' (the song which has become to Turner what 'My Way' is to Frank Sinatra), the explosive firework display which supercharges the revved-up climax of the old Ike 'n' Tina arrangement of John Fogerty's Creedence-era 'Proud Mary'.

They are learning to love Anglo-American rock and roll. Domestic product still accounts for 60 per cent of Brazilian record sales (as far as such things can be tabulated without an official chart), but the imported stuff is beginning to catch up as more and more foreign rockers come visiting. Ever since Miles Copeland generated worldwide publicity for The Police by half-filling the 12,000-seater gymnasium of Maracana Stadium and TV producers began to recognize what a photogenic backdrop was available for the Rock In Rio festival, the multinationals have been calling, even though Rock In Rio – the concert featuring Queen, Rod Stewart, Status Quo, AC/DC and Whitesnake, January '85 – lost $11 million. Pop, after all, makes the perfect come-on for famous international brand-names, and if the acts want to be showcased in a part of the world where breaking even without the aid of corporate sponsors is out of the question, then even the most right-on of them have to go along with it. Sting, for example – a man capable of setting *The Guardian Third World Review* to music – had to show up at a press conference organized by Coca-Cola when he played Rio; no Coca-Cola, no show.

And just a few weeks earlier, Simple Minds, Simply Red and The Pretenders had reported for the exotically named Hollywood

Rock Festival only to find that the 'Hollywood' tag was not — as they thought — a gesture towards some received notion of Californian glamour but the name of a brand of cigarette. Thousands of packets were distributed to the predominantly teenage crowd, which was tremendously offensive to militant non-smokers like Jim Kerr, Chrissie Hynde and Mick Hucknall, but if they thought they had any say in the matter they were grievously mistaken. They were, after all, there to sell cigarettes.

Shanty towns and skyscrapers: there is plenty of money in Brazil, but most of it is in the hands of some 5 per cent of the population. A show like Tina Turner's Rio spectacular attracted its massive audience — 40,000 more than Sting's at the same venue — by pegging the ticket prices at the most affordable level of any big-name visiting star ($5 to $20), thereby taking approximately $2 million at the box office. This left a shortfall of a million and a half or so — which is where Pepsi, Wrangler and HBO come in. And all the others.

Roger Davies, the burly, blond Australian who masterminded Tina Turner's upward surge from hotel lounges to multiplatinum celebrity, is sitting in the shade of an umbrella by the hotel pool, overlooking the dazzling white sands of Copacabana Beach. He's none too happy about all the deals that had to be cut to put on the previous night's show. 'Since this was going to be Tina's farewell tour, we wanted to go to all the places we've never been, but . . . it is frustrating to me to see ads for Varig Airlines, Rio Palace Hotel, Wrangler, the scaffolding company, the trucking company, Pepsi, the magazines . . . but that is the only way they can physically do it. In the end you just have to say, "Let 'em put the signs up" because that's what you've got to do. You've got to bite your tongue a little. That's the only way they can come to see us. If you didn't cut deals with everybody it just couldn't happen.

'We were talking about merchandising, but you can't do that. They can barely afford to buy a ticket, let alone a T-shirt.' But they can afford to buy soft drinks. And if any shanty town kid manages to scrape up enough *cruzados* to get his or her hands on such an exotic status symbol as a pair of American jeans, you can bet your last Sam Cooke record that they're not going to be Levis.

Still, the last thing the punters at Maracana Stadium want to think about is the collapsing currency or the debt crisis. They are dazzled by the flash and roar of a state-of-the-art stadium rock show and caught up by Tina Turner's contagious exuberance. Even audiences who are unfamiliar with her legend, who wouldn't know Ike Turner from Lana Turner, recognize instantly that she is willing to work for them until she drops, that she is having the time of her life and that she's an outrageous ham. Even her much-vaunted 'sexiness' and 'raunchiness' are now jokes which she shares with her audiences rather than the grim, obsessive tease of the Ike years.

But after 28 March, all that will be over – and if Tina Turner had her way, it would be all over *now*, the day after Maracana. Because, after that, there's nowhere else to go.

Tina Turner's suite on the seventh and eighth floors of the Rio Palace is whitewashed, wooden-floored, spacious. It's where she's been holed up for most of her Rio sojourn, barring the odd meal at Mr Zee – Rio's top Chinese restaurant – and a couple of photo opportunities on the beach and with the samba dancers of the Beija Flor school who 'jammed' at the show. It's where she's been resting, meditating, exercising and chanting *nyam-mye-ho-renge-kyo* according to the precepts of Nichiren Shoshu Buddhism.

Her voice floats up ahead of her from the lower levels. 'Ber-*NARD*,' she croaks, 'how successful do I have to be in my career before I can stop doing press?' She arrives in her penthouse sitting-room to discover that the interloper is not her publicist, Bernard 'Papa Doc' Doherty, but a Sanyo-toting person from this magazine. As the real Doherty appears, she cracks up: 'Did you hear what I said to him? He said, you don't do press you ain't gonna *have* a career.'

In loose white tank-top and tight black pants, the two main surprises are yes, Tina Turner does indeed look as good close up as on a stage under lights and no, she's not the 'great big woman' of myth but slender, almost tiny. What creates the illusion of size is that huge, leonine bewigged head and her thick, sleekly muscled arms and shoulders. She's still wired from the night before; she can't sit still, continually changes her position on the sofa, drawing her legs up under her, then stretching them out, moving from side to side.

'Well, I'll tell you what it was for me, 28 March will be the last stage performance for me for a long time, maybe the end. A few

433

years ago, I was thinking about Aretha Franklin, and with all the hits Aretha's had, she's never filled a football stadium – not that I know of. And I felt I would sure like to fill a football stadium before I retire. This was a few years ago and it was the time that David Bowie had just filled a football stadium in New Zealand and I wondered what it would be like to play to all those people. Well, I found out last night. I've done it now and I have not left a stone unturned. There's nothing in my career that I can think of that I haven't done, so it's *reeeeaaaaally* a good way to stop. I got that dream. The biggest stadium in the world. *Jeeeeeeez . . .* incredible.'

However, retirement from touring doesn't mean inactivity. 'I'm not that old of a woman yet. If I was in my late sixties I could get into that thing of saying, "Okay, no more *nothing*." I know I'm gonna be busy because I can't be still, but it won't be *this*. I've done *this* now, I did it last night.' She breaks into that patented Tina Turner throaty chuckle: *heh-heh-heh.* 'I could design clothes . . . I could get involved in hair and make up . . . and I want to be an actress.'

So what kind of movies you up for?

'Danger! Excitement! Action! I like the Harrison Ford things, I like the Sigourney Weaver movies, I like being the villain and all of that. I like comedy, but it would have to be *action* comedy like Aykroyd. What's that thing he did, *Ghostbusters*? Like that. It's a comedy, but it's *action* and it's *fun* and it's *silly*. I'm not turning down anything like that. I've done videos and commercials, and they're like small movies. Movies are just a bigger scale, that's all.

'It's gotta be the action and the crazy things right now, because I've got to live through that villain type of craziness, being part man and part animal. Grace Jones is doing the same sort of thing I want to be doing, but Grace is not *nearly* as physical as I want to be. I want to ride the horses, drive the cars and fall off the cliffs. Aunty Entity [Turner's role in *Mad Max Beyond Thunderdome*] was not as fierce as I wanted her to be. I wanted her to go back into the trunk and pull out the clothes that she was wearing when she built that city, because she built *herself* up from nothing and she definitely wasn't wearing that chain dress and those high-heeled shoes.

'You got to get that *edge*; you got to hold the people's attention. I've seen a lot of bland movies – *yawn*, people fallin' asleep. I don't want you falling asleep in *my* movies, I want to keep you right there wondering what I'm gonna do next.

'I'm real open to being *directed*. I think that's all I'll always need; a really good director.'

*A really good director*. When Tina Turner has been successful, that is exactly what she has had. The Tina Turner of the sixties and early seventies – the demonic, voracious man-eater – was Ike Turner's invention: one based simultaneously on Ike's understanding of what would fire up both the chitlin circuit and the white rock audience, and on his own fantasies. After all, Ike had to be the *baddest*, and any woman publicly identified as his also had to be the baddest. Her director now is Roger Davies, who found her hauling an overblown caricature of the old Revue round hotel lounges and Vegas rooms, persuaded her to dump the whole act and start again with a stripped-down, heavied-up rock and roll band.

So is the 'new' Tina Turner Roger Davies's creation? The question makes Davies slightly uncomfortable. 'Maybe there is a little bit of truth in that … there was a lot of the music on "Private Dancer" which she didn't really like, to be honest, and she'll tell you that herself. But I said, That's the direction we have to go in. I know you want to do an AC/DC album, but we're not ready for that yet. If Tina had a choice, she'd do a real hard rock, heavy metal album. I don't mean bang-your-head-against-the-wall stuff, but real *good, pumping* stuff like early AC/DC.

'Tina and I, we've worked as a *team*. Her attitude has always been that she's hired me to be her manager, and if she doesn't listen to me, what's the point in having me? It's all very well saying that I've done all this for Tina, but whatever I've set up for her she's been able to pull off, because when you know you've got someone with the talent and professionalism to back it up, that helps. Obviously, I've given her a lot of direction and she's listened, but she's got the talent and she pulls it off. She never ceases to amaze me. She's so professional, she's got the stamina and she works *so hard*.

'We are at a burnout stage now, and we're very aware of that. We've been doing this for seven years, and we've got to call a halt, give radio programmers and the public a break. There's going to be a double live album coming out and then that'll be *it*, we won't do another album for at least two years.'

435

And the movies?

'Well, that's what she wants to do. She knows it's going to be hard, but there's not a lot of parts out there for black women. We've had hundreds of offers of stereotyped black hooker roles, but we're looking out for something better.'

'I need that suspense,' Turner continues, 'because I need to be in suspense. It's like my stage performance: you start getting bored and you need to move a little *up*. It's got to be the same in my movies.'

So how does Tina Turner stay interested over a long tour, cranking out the same show over and over again?

'The people keep me interested because they haven't seen it. Let me just tell you something: my psychological approach to that is that I've got a good show. This show works. I'm not going to take a chance on changing it around just because I could get bored with it. I love being there in the lights and the clothes, being there for the people. I would have retired *way* long ago, after "Private Dancer", but there was a demand and I felt obligated to the people. I'm there to perform that music that they bought, because they didn't have to buy it. It's for them. Sure, it's great if you love it and you want it for yourself . . . wonderful, you really got it made then. But I've got past the stage of it being for me. I been doin' it for twenty-seven years.'

Turner and Davies concur that when they released 'Private Dancer', the most they aspired to was to sell half a million copies and maybe go gold. Instead, they ended up selling over 10 million copies. 'I had all the Ike and Tina records that went gold in one section of my house, and then just before my success I moved 'em all to one corner of my wall. The wall went from *here* to *there*, and I thought, well, the rest of my career I'll probably fill this wall: one here, one there. Two months later, the single of "Let's Stay Together" became a hit and I put it up; all that big space and one little bitty thing hangin' there. Ego, right? All this is mine. Then the next time I went home there was another gold one that I'd kissed with my big red lips . . . and now that wall is *packed*, they're stacked on the *floor*. I've had to take some to my mother's house, they're *everywhere* . . . but it means something to me because I went out on my own. I tell you, I hung all that stuff and then I just sat and *watched* it for awhile . . .'

So why, out of all the greats from the Golden Age of R&B, has it been Tina Turner who's beome an eighties megastar? Why not, say, Martha Reeves or Wilson Pickett, both of whom had more sixties hits than she did. Turner and Davies asked the same question a couple of years ago when they flew The Wicked Pickett to London to guest in the TV special which curtain-raised the Break Every Rule tour. Pickett cussed Tina out for not giving him the star dressing-room, and for only featuring him on three songs. On the night of recording, Pickett entered into such an intimate relationship with a bottle of Jack Daniel's that he was unable to perform. Tina paid him his full fee and had him driven straight to the airport. He ended up being easily the baddest person on the plane back to New Jersey. Davies, who'd considered offering to manage Pickett and see if he could pull off the same trick twice, was not impressed.

'Most of 'em don't have good management,' says Davies. 'Most of those black acts are still living in the sixties. Pickett still thinks he's a superstar. Those acts grew up in that chitlin circuit and they're still in that mentality, but Tina fell in love with Europe when she toured here, and she wanted to live that way. I don't want this taken the wrong way, and Tina can explain this better than I can, but she's not a typical black person. She's a determined person. If an act had success and has a chip on his shoulder and is bitter, there's not a chance in hell they're gonna do it again. She wanted this success *desperately*. She wanted to prove to herself she could do it.'

When things go wrong for Tina Turner, she assumes it's because she's not working hard enough. Then she works harder: it's why she stuck to Ike Turner long after somebody else would have called the cops or a lawyer. The woman is a bulldozer in human form: she can get anywhere as long as someone's pointing her in the right direction. That was Davies's job; to handle the steering. As a practising Buddhist, Turner chants several hours a day to put herself in tune with the harmony of the universe. When that is achieved, the Protestant work ethic takes over.

'We're talking about magic here. People say, *What have you done, Tina Turner, in the fifty years of your life, to keep people interested?* It was done by contacting something in *here*. I'm not talking about *ree-lid-jahn*; I'm talking about doing things ree-lid-jahs-ly.'

Yet Turner still remains unsatisfied in one crucial area: her music. She doesn't like it. 'I have earned the title Queen Of Rock and Roll, but I don't have a rock and roll record out. I never liked singing R&B. In high school I was singing ballads and, believe it or not, a little bit of op-e-ra. When I first saw Ike Turner's band I loved the music but I hated the words. I was one of those *school* people, and Ike was a street person. I was very sporty and into basketball, and he was nightlife and writing about nightlife things, and I couldn't relate to that because I wasn't living it, and I was not interested in singing about that. So I was turned off for a lot of years of singing what he was writing. Then I realized I was involved after all, and that I *was* singing about myself. Oh, *shit*! *YEEUUCH!*

'Then I was listening to Mick Jagger singin' "HONKY TONK WO-MAIN" and Rod Stewart singin' "HOT LAIGS!" and Elton John with "PHILADELPHIA FREEEE-DUM" and Bowie singin' about I don't know *what* but it *felt* right. I was thinkin' WHOOOOH! SHIT! *This* is what I want!'

But they were copping it off black music . . .

'I don't care *what* they was coppin'! The words were right! It was the *emotions* that was copied! They were copying the emotions that black people were putting into their music, but they were writing about wonderful fun things . . . 'n' stuff. Even the sad songs were not depressing, they were just sad. I knew the difference and I knew I was not singing what I wanted to sing. I am *still* not singing what I want to sing. I wish I had a string of hits about *this* long for those people. That's how you get the people *moving* like Jagger or Bowie – with songs they can relate to.

'I just think R&B is depressing. I wanna be *up*! I don't wanna be down here . . . I always knew I wanted to be rock and roll. I have a little problem with Rog sometimes; he'll bring something in and say it's commercially good music, and I'll say *I need some live show songs!* I have to reach back and borrow "Dancing In The Dark" from Bruce or "Legs" from ZZ Top or something because I haven't actually made that album of show songs.'

As well as the movies – including a biopic in which TT herself will not appear – future projects include two more books, sequels to *I, Tina*, written in cooperation with the *Rolling Stone* journalist, Kurt Loder. 'It was necessary for Kurt to write it because I was writing about somebody else, and you cannot just take one person's word. I could not expect anyone to believe me writing about Ike without someone to do the research and talk to other people. The next book will be me writing, I'll start with the things that he didn't write and tell about the music business and about health and how you look . . . that'll be a short one. And then, the spiritual book comes up. By then I'll have the words to write about the subconscious mind and about how we in the Western world are not really in tune with how you get things done spiritually, about how it comes out of *you* and not what the preacher tells you. That'll be the serious one, but in between there'll be one about the junk, the shit stuff. Women want to know about all that crap. But we're talking about stuff to do in my sixties . . . and I haven't even gotten into my fifties yet.'

That evening, there is a victory party. It is held at one of Pele's homes, a penthouse apartment high over the Avenido Atlantico overlooking Copacabana Beach. The great man himself, never one to neglect a good photo opportunity, dropped in for fifteen minutes to pose alongside Tina and her latest stack of gold and platinum discs. On arrival, percussionist Steve Scales — the self-appointed party animal of the tour, whose job it is to keep everybody entertained — becomes impatient at the crush by the lift, and leads a select party to the service lift, intending to gain admittance that way. 'Niggers *always* know how to get into a party,' he snorts, reeling off his best Eddie Murphy impression. 'Fuck all that *front door* shit.' Unfortunately, the door to the service lift remains resolutely locked — even with Scales beating out his hottest conga parts on it — and everybody has to redescend to the lobby and go up the *proper* way.

The band seem simultaneously euphoric and uneasy. Three of them — guitarist James Ralston, drummer Jack Bruno and bassist Bob Feit — have been with Tina since Davies took over; saxophonist Deric Dyer — who is not a name session man like Scales, Miles or guitarist Laurie Wisefield — dreads the end of the tour and a return to the scuffling life. He'd been shuttling between cabaret and the dole when he auditioned just for the experience; he couldn't believe his good fortune when he got the job. Come April, he's going to be looking for work again.

The party is otherwise not without incident. Turner, ensconced in a corner with her champagne and her precious metal discs, holds effusive court. A luminary from a major Brazilian magazine shows up with a somewhat out-of-order photographer who nuts one of the roadies, a spectacle captured by James Ralston's portable video camera. A slight breeze ruffles the musicians' trademark rock and roll haircuts; slightly permed, clipped short around the ears and long and flowing at the back. The Tina Turner adventure is coming to an end. What comes next? Well, John Miles is planning another crack at the Great Solo Album gambit, and if he likes the demos, Roger Davies is considering getting involved.

But all that is still in the future. Tonight, everyone hangs over the balcony enjoying the spectacular views of a spectacular city and parties all the way to the airport, ready for the next show in Hawaii.

And when the tour's finally over, Tina Turner will have a holiday. She will redecorate her home in Los Angeles, and buy a new one in the South of France. She will wear all her *nice* clothes – as opposed to her stage and street wear – and travel the world. She will visit Egypt and India, see the pyramids and tour the great art galleries of Europe. She will dress for dinner, and at home she will fall asleep on her couch if she wants to. She will live the life of a rich lady, just as she always wanted, back when she was a kid and went to the movies. She will live like Jacqueline Onassis, only on her own money.

It has been said that she is not so much an artist as a performer. This is undoubtedly true. What is also true is that she is a *great* performer, one who virtually transcends taste. Taste, indeed, has never been her strong point, which is why she has always been guided by the taste of others. But – what the hell. Give the lady a great big hand. She has, after all, earned it. Miss Tee-nah Tur-nah!

# Tina Turner: 'Tina Live In Europe' (EMI)

*New Hi-Fi Sound*, June 1988

THE quick review for the busy hi-fi fancier in a hurry: if you've seen Tina Turner in an arena or stadium and you had a good time, then you've just found the tour-souvenir package of your dreams. Well over two hours' worth of all the songs you like, it'll turn your room into an idealized Wembley Arena (i.e. without those abattoir acoustics) and – what with the guest appearances from David Bowie, Robert Cray, Eric Clapton and Bryan Adams (well, maybe not Bryan Adams) – it's probably more exciting than the night you went, despite the lack of dry ice and leather minis.

If you've never seen Tina Turner or don't particularly like her, forget it: 'Tina Live In Europe' is a party to which you haven't been invited.

The longer and more elaborate review for the hi-fi fancier on the bus: 'Tina Live In Europe' is more than just a left-over chicken-leg-and-bottle-of-white-wine from one of the longest retirement parties in popbiz, but it's 'more' in terms of scale rather than substance; a box of chicken legs and entire crate of wine. The quantity – on the CD edition, anyway – is certainly generous; you get twenty-eight tracks lasting almost 130 minutes, plus a fat little booklet containing an intimidatingly endless list of tour dates, a thankyouthankyouthankyou gush from La Turner herself, and masses of photos of people you don't recognize 'looning about' in exotic locations, wearing funny hats and pulling faces at the camera. Dudes on the road! Rock & Roll!

The music's pretty much along the same lines; Turner and her various extremely competent stage bands flip from reggae to rockaballads to sixties soul to modern dance-pop with practised, digital ease, except that most of it ends up as obvious stadium rock.

Loud, stodgy, dense and emptily spectacular, constructed from broad strokes and simple gestures, stadium rock precludes the kind of intimacy possible in club, hall or studio, Springsteen and U2 notwithstanding.

Audiences become faceless both to each other and to the performer, and this music sounds that way. The operative word is inflated; a quiet moment in a stadium show becomes simply a caricature of a quiet moment, and the end result is bathos.

Her theme song, 'Private Dancer', becomes something very odd in this context, an ageing hooker's lament transformed into a triumphalist anthem, as silly and tawdry and melodramatically self-serving as 'My Way' in suspenders.

Mind you, nobody in their right mind goes to a stadium show by anybody except Springsteen – or buys a live album of stadium music (ditto) – in order to experience anything other than the delights of sheer spectacle and a few good stunts.

True, you can't see the sax player blowing the 'Private Dancer' solo from a perch high above the stage or La T herself delivering 'We Don't Need Another Theme Song From A Mad Max Movie Thank You Very Much' from a hydraulic platform wreathed in dry ice, but the cavernous sound and barely restrained hysterics of the performance imply these visual theatricalisms as thoroughly as could be desired.

Where 'Live In Europe' is at its best is at the opening of Side 3 (or Disc 2, depending on format). Here, TT whizzes through a medley of Wilson Pickett hits with fair simulation of the dizzy, sweaty glee of The Golden Age Of R&B, bringing on Robert Cray to duet on '634-5789', and following up with a – don't all faint at once – genuinely soulful and moving Otis Redding-styled reading of Sam Cooke's secular-gospel Civil Rights anthem 'A Change Is Gonna Come', supercharged with a spikily lyrical Cray guitar solo which is, in its way, a small masterpiece.

Her other guests fare less well; on 'Tearing Us Apart', Eric Clapton demonstrates that the on-off switch on his chorus pedal is permanently jammed in the on position, and David Bowie is in full crooner mode for 'Tonight' and a mini-medley of Chris Montez's 'Let's Dance' and his own megasmash of the same title.

Bryan Adams, on the other hand . . . jeez, what a multitude of sins can be committed in the sacred name of rack'n'rowl.

The old Ikanteenuh hits like 'River Deep, Mountain High', 'Proud Mary' and 'Nutbush City Limits' have all seen (and heard) better days; 'River Deep' is taken at an unconcerned snail's pace while 'Nutbush' is sped up to such a febrile, overheated tempo that the groove is trashed. 'Mary' comes out best, though John Miles's backing vocals are no substitute for those of Old Steel Nose. The new stuff sounds pretty much like the studio versions only a tad longer, and tricked out with lifelike stadium reverb. Owlraht?

Tina Turner's best qualities are her eagerness to entertain (she'll do a good, professional job even if she's bored rigid; who could ask more of a plumber?) and her sheer vulgarity. Vulgarity – of both the straightforward and pretentious varieties, and you'll find both here – can often be a highly refreshing alternative to failed art, and at its best so are parts of this album.

At its worst, though, it's simply tedious bombast with no redeeming qualities, and you'll find plenty of that, too. In other words: good value for Tina Turner fans.

# Gilbert Shelton:
# Skint, squalid and hammered
# to the eyeballs

*Q*, July 1988

DONCHA just *hate* 1968? Haven't you had about as much as you can stand of Jerry Rubin, Harold Wilson, Tariq Ali, Chicago, Paris, Vietnam, LSD, LSE, LBJ, Richard Neville, Timothy Leary and The Grateful Dead? Haven't you sworn an oath on a stack of Cream and Jefferson Airplane records to boycott Channel 4 for life and permanently banish the phrase '20th Anniversary' from your vocabulary? Well, there's more to come before you can breathe that final sigh of relief and declare the whole ghastly exercise null and void: 1988 marks a full two decades' worth of the one hippie institution which might easily have been predicted to expire with the passing of its era. That's right, you guessed it – *The Fabulous Furry Freak Brothers*!

It was twenty years ago today – give or take a month or two – that a twenty-nine-year-old Texan cartoonist named Gilbert Shelton, previously most notable for his creation of the grotesque superhero parody Wonder Warthog, introduced readers of an underground rag entitled, surprisingly enough, *The Rag* to a trio of reprobates whose only object in life was to get as ripped as humanly possible and stay that way in perpetuity. There was taciturn, gangling, cynical Freewheelin' Franklin with his walrus moustache and cowboy hat, bespectacled fuzzball Phineas who – if he hadn't been so phenomenally addled – would probably have qualified as the brains of the operation, and greedy, scatterbrained, bone-idle Fat Freddy, not to mention Fat Freddy's scheming, malevolent cat. Together they have remained, skint, squalid and hammered to the eyeballs, twenty years of social change and approximately 10 million copies of assorted Freak Bros books and comics later, in fact. Tony Bennett of Knockabout, Shelton's UK distributor, claims that a Freak Brothers anthology was the first book ever sold in a Virgin store.

Curiously enough, despite two decades of relentless over-consumption they don't look a day older than they did on that historic occasion when Fat Freddy spent the trio's last sixty bucks on what he claimed was a giant magic marijuana seed. It's enough to make a reformed druggie spit: by rights, Freddy, Franklin and Phineas should be in jail, in a bin or overdosed in an alley somewhere by now, but they lead charmed lives, protected by a little bubble of sixties innocence, still aroused from their stoned stupour only by the perpetual need to hustle enough money to pay the rent, buy food or score yet more dope.

So who's buying all these Freak Brothers comics, books, badges and T-shirts? Surely there can't be that many sixties burnouts still unyupped enough to want to carry on reading about these three degenerates and their scabby pet? According to Bennett, the age range of the Freak Bros' clientele stretches from fifteen to fifty, 'from the old locos you'd expect to fifteen-year-olds at boarding school'. Since Knockabout appears to have made it its life's work to keep representative of HM Customs plentifully supplied with the works of Gilbert Shelton's illustrious contemporary Robert Crumb – who, despite a reputation as one of the greatest living American cartoonists and his status as the subject of an admiring BBC Arena documentary profile, is unable to have his work imported into the UK – the company virtually owes its survival to the Freak Brothers. 'They've burned the Crumb books that the BBC showed on TV,' says Bennett. 'We literally wouldn't be here if the authorities decided that they didn't like the Freak Brothers.'

Gilbert Shelton himself lives in Paris these days: he quit the States swearing never to return as long as Reagan was still President, but he found himself enjoying Europe so much that he'll probably stay for the foreseeable future. He is amazed as anybody that his scuzzball creations are still around, having survived from their Texan origins through Shelton's relocation to San Francisco in 1970, two years after the original Haight-Ashbury bohos declared the Official Death Of Hippie. He attributes their almost supernatural longevity to the original strip's wide dissemination through the UPS (Underground Press Syndicate) and the subsequent repackagings via Rip Off Press, the publishing co-op he founded. 'They're not that tied to current events,' he says, 'and like the Marx Brothers, there are three of them who don't resemble each other. They're based on true-life incidents, genuine urban experiences. Even the cat is based on an ill-behaved orange tom that used to belong to a friend of mine in LA.'

But – gulp – aren't the Freak Bros a *bad example to youth*? Isn't this promiscuous druggery a trifle counter-productive in the Just Say No era? Both Shelton and Tony Bennett disagree vehemently. 'They've never been an advertisement for people to take drugs,' claims Bennett indignantly. 'They're always hungover or getting evicted or ripped off.' 'As a kid, I used to enjoy humour based on alcohol and drunkenness long before I ever started to drink myself, but it's a sign of the times,' says the author, 'that the Brothers are now spurning hard drugs and sticking to smoking grass and drinking beer.' The latest Freak Brothers epic *Idiots Abroad* does indeed support Shelton's contention: even though our three heroes' cavalcade of international mishaps is launched by their decision to go to Colombia to buy an entire bale of killer weed, Shelton and his co-author Paul Mavrides keep the Freaks in such hot water that they only get their grubby little paws on a spliff two or three times during the book's ninety-page span. What keeps the narrative going is what has, in fact, kept the strip itself in existence for all these years, the characters themselves, and Shelton's unrivalled comic flair.

'Gilbert Shelton is simply an excellent cartoonist,' says Britain's comics guru Alan Moore. 'The best of the original underground cartoonists with the possible exception of Crumb. He has a strong grasp of traditional cartoon values: simple, accessible story-telling and immaculate slapstick timing. The Freak Brothers are classic comedy, like Laurel and Hardy or Chaplin, and they're a more lasting tribute to the sixties than the real sixties people. After all, they're still here and the counterculture isn't.'

Shelton has fond memories of those early years. Like many of his contemporaries, he participated in the headshop and dancehall culture of the time – where most of the original underground comics were sold – drawing posters for the legendary Vulcan Gas Company club, including several for Johnny Winter. 'He was great,' sighs Shelton, 'definitely the best act ever to play the Vulcan Gas Company.' He is fairly sceptical, though, about any possibility of a resurgence of the heady days of the Haight. 'You've got to remember that property in the Haight-Ashbury back then was amazingly cheap. When we started the Rip Off Press, we were able to rent an empty warehouse with thousands of square feet of space for only $250 a month. Real estate values are so inflated now that it would be impossible for any artists or musicians with as little money as we had then to get the premises to do the work.'

Almost all of Shelton's work – the collected *Freak Brothers*, *Fat Freddy's Cat* and *Wonder Warthog* – is still in print, which goes a long way towards offsetting the fact that he isn't what you might call a fast or prolific worker. The ninety-page *Idiots Abroad* was originally published as three separate comics, each almost a year apart, and a complete set of the Freaks' adventures – *Cat* apart – add up to only slightly more pages than, say, Alan Moore and Dave Gibbons' *Watchmen*. One additional source of income for Shelton has been selling movie rights for the Freaks which invariably lapse before any movies are actually produced, the last of three customers being Universal Pictures. 'I'm not a steady artist,' he says with a self-deprecating shrug which is almost audible over the phone.

Shelton is no great admirer of the current comics scene, still heavily dominated by superheroes, though he speaks very warmly of Gilbert and Jaime Hernandez, his old oppo Robert Crumb and Brummie madman Hunt Emerson. And Fabulous Furry Freak aficionados of all ages and predilections will no doubt be delighted to hear that Fat Freddy and Co. will be around for as long as Shelton himself is still able to hold a pencil. Dope, it seems, will still get you through times of no money better than money will get you through times of no dope.

# Robert Cray:
# The Torment of Young Bob

*Q*, November 1988

IT'S hot and sticky in Atlanta tonight, ladies and gentlemen, and, on the stage of a miniature amphitheatre set in the grounds of a large, verdant and elegantly landscaped park, Young Bob is suffering the torments of the damned.

You shouldn't feel too sorry for him, though: Young Bob is not a nice man. He is a voyeur and a blackmailer: one time he was watching his neighbour woman who didn't bother to draw the blinds on her bedroom window and he saw her fooling around with another man while her husband, was away. So what did Young Bob do? He went and told her that if she didn't want him to tell her husband just exactly what was going on, she'd better take care of him too. He's a liar and a betrayer as well: when his best friend Sonny came back from Vietnam cripped and blind, Young Bob was right in there with Sonny's wife. Young Bob can't resist playing in the dirt no matter what it costs him or anybody else.

Yet none of this makes him happy: he is consumed with regret and guilt even as he adds new notches to his guitar, and women don't seem to treat him any better than he treats them. They play around behind his back, fob him off with lies. This one bitch, she even stole his credit cards. Sometimes he passionately swears that he'll mend his ways, or that he'll never get caught up again, but he does. He always does.

Young Bob lives out in the psychic badlands, in emotional minefields where anything or anyone can blow up in his face. It is literally *blues noir*: like the world of James M. Cain or David Goodis or Jim Thompson as wired for sound by Albert King or Otis Redding, a long dark night of the soul where it's always 3 a.m. Deceit, suspicion, loneliness and guilt are the compass points of Young Bob's world. You wouldn't wish it on *anybody*.

Especially not a nice guy like Robert Cray.

As it happens, your actual Robert Cray is keen to disassociate himself from the excesses of his alter ego's behaviour. 'Young Bob is almost like a third person. He's the *other* character, but we do pick out some of those songs according to how they relate to my personal life,' he will explain. 'Nowadays, a lot of things have changed, because I'm pretty much a one-person guy, you know. But there was a time in the past when I used to have a lot of girlfriends and whatnot when I was on the road. There was one song called "Divided Hearts", that was almost like prophecy or a soothsayer or something, because the song saw something happening to me long before it actually *did* happen. And it's a painful thing to be living that, now. But . . . God, after the last week or so things are getting better in my relationship.' His relief is almost palpable.

Sid The Sexist with a Strat he's not.

In terms of the mythology implied by their lyrics — love is hell and the only possible roles are those of tormentor and victim — The Robert Cray Band are, to quote bassist and founder-member Richard Cousins, 'semi-well-adjusted: all of us identify with the characters in the songs. We actually *like* the songs.' It is therefore appropriate that part of the reason keyboards operator Peter Boe — a wiry, Ray-Banned ex-bebopper with a jazz-club tan — accepted the offer of a place in the band was as a means of making a fast getaway out of Portland, Oregon, after a particularly acrimonious break-up with his girlfriend of the time. Those cheatin' and lyin' songs — which make up a trifling 99 per cent of the band's recorded repertoire — are central to Cray's notion of What The Blues Is All About.

'It is very much a *band*,' insists Boe, 'but in terms of it being a product of one specific person's vision of the emotional content of the music, that would be Robert's chief contribution — outside of the fact that when you see the band you see him out front singing and playing. It's very important to him, and all the rest of the guys keep that in mind when they write.'

Cray is in no doubt whatsoever about what he wants: 'The term "blues" specifically connotates a sad song: flat, right out. Lyrically, it has to be a sad song in my book. Macho songs I don't consider blues tunes even when they're sung by so-called blues singers.' Love songs, apparently, don't qualify either. 'If a guy's happy,' says Cray, extremely firmly, 'he ain't got the blues.'

Still, he enthusiastically quotes a new song by master bluesman John Lee Hooker. Along with George Thorogood and various others, Cray has guested on the great man's forthcoming album, and one song Hooker cut with Carlos Santana has caught his imagination. '*Blu-u-es*,' he sings, in admiring mimicry of Hooker's vibrant baritone, 'is a *healer*.' It's the other half of the wondrous equation of the blues: a sad music which makes you feel good.

The Robert Cray Band is seven days into a sixty-date world tour that visits the UK in mid-October. By half past nine, a dawdling dusk has finally cooled off Chastain Park, much to the relief of a few thousand Atlantans in abbreviated leisurewear, but the emotional temperature is inexorably rising. Robert Cray is immaculate in his black chinos and a shirt like a neon fruit salad as he bears witness to Young Bob's agony, but Young Bob is down on the killing floor.

Each song is another heaped spoonful of soured passion and love in vain, all set to the taut, ominous, rolling rhythms of his band. His mellifluous, haunted voice is answered, taunted and challenged by another; this one higher, nasal, more edgy. When Cray's hands tear at the sparkle-finished Stratocaster around his neck it blurts out what the singer cannot bring himself to say; an unfettered voice from the unconscious.

The Robert Cray Band is simultaneously a showcase for a performer of exceptional individual gifts, and an interdependent *band* in the sixties sense of the word, a self-contained R&B workshop in which six individuals – the four musicians and their producers Bruce Bromberg (who writes as 'D Amy') and Dennis Walker – collaborate. 'Everybody knows when they present songs what will be used and will not be used,' Cray explains. 'Even though it's taken a while, everybody's looking in the same direction, because I am out there singing the songs. Everyone's known me a long time. We've spent a *whole* lot of time together.'

The danger of repetitiousness or over-refinement doesn't worry the band at all. 'I don't think there's any limit on how far we can go with what we're doing,' Cray asserts. 'There's always a different way of telling a story that's about your personal situation.'

'If you distil the lyrical content of those songs,' says Peter Boe, 'down to the most common denominators, you could probably sum the entire thing up in a paragraph. In that respect, it's a challenge to come up with original, fresh, contemporary variations on that theme. Maybe we'll have to widen our scope eventually.' For the time being, though, it is that challenge which Boe finds stimulating: he cites Stravinsky's claim that he wrote best within established perimeters. In one sense, when you pick up a new Robert Cray Band album, you know what you're going to get: mid-tempo cheatin' songs in minor keys paced by the odd gospelly ballad; but then most conventional-wisdom answers to the 'Why Robert Cray?' question are as simplistic and misleading. It is one thing simply to say that Robert Cray is a bluesman (though, of course, he is) or a sixties soul disciple (even though he is that, too) who fortuitously arrived at the right moment to fulfil a latent public need for a polished young R&B nostalgist. Such theories might account for a small, cultish success, but they collapse in the face of the kind of widespread acceptance achieved by 1986's 'Strong Persuader' and which 'Don't Be Afraid Of The Dark' is already poised to eclipse. The songs are far too near the emotional knuckle to function comfortably as retro-nuevo muzak, and Cray himself is too much his own man to serve as anybody's generic anything. A better answer is deftly encapsulated by Tim Kaihatsu, who is better placed than most to assess such matters, since he is in the band but not of it: he is a San Francisco-based guitarist and critic who augments The Robert Cray Band in performance, and he profiled Cray five years ago for *Guitar Player* magazine. For him, it's utterly straightforward.

'Robert is the best of our generation,' he explains, looking round to make sure that his subject is not in earshot. 'He is the best singer, the best guitarist and he looks good on television.'

Young Bob is in purgatory, but Robert Cray is in the pop charts: 400,000 copies moved across the counter in its first week of US release, sending 'Don't Be Afraid Of The Dark' straight in at a more than respectable number 40 (in Britain, sales of 60,000 registered at number 13, which, apart from anything else, gives you a fair idea of the relative state of each country's record industry). Young Bob thrashes in the icy wastes of hell; The Robert Cray Band surge across the country in an air-conditioned tour bus with a painting of Elvis Presley on the side. Young Bob is The Sultan Of Gloom; Robert Cray is a very happy man. Like Uncle John in Little Richard's 'Long Tall Sally', 'he says he gets the blues but he has a lot of fun'.

Beaming, he strides into the bar of one of Atlanta's favourite rock and roll hotels to celebrate high noon with his first beer of the day. The Tower Place's Savannah Room restaurant and Beauregarde's Retreat Bar are positively swarming with rock and roll types: Joe Cocker and his band will be playing Atlanta the following night, and members of his band and crew – including T.M. Stevens, the blond-maned funk-rock bassist who was in The Pretenders for a hot minute around the time of the 'Get Close' album, and saxophonist Deric Dyer, more or less fresh from his stint with Tina Turner – are fairly regular fixtures. Cocker's opening act, America, best known for the mawkish early seventies hit 'Horse With No Name' (once described by Randy Newman as 'that song about a kid who thinks he's taken acid') are also somewhere around: their tour bus bears the self-deprecating name-tag 'Nobody You Know', implying a certain crisis of confidence. There is even a rumour that B.B. King has checked in, though nobody has seen him.

On a massive TV screen above the bar, George Bush chunters on about how Dan Quayle didn't burn his draft card (he was all in favour of the Vietnam war as long as he didn't have to fight it himself); in front of Cray, next to his pack of Marlboros, is a pair of those deluxe Ray-Ban shades with the leather trim. 'We call 'em *Cray*-Bans,' he deadpans, chasing the line with a swallow of Heineken. The band don't exactly have an *endorsement* deal with Ray-Ban, just as they don't exactly have a deal with Nike footwear, but just the same, they now get 'em free. As indicators of recognition by a public wider than a devoted coterie of R&B casualties, free basketball boots and sunglasses are almost as eloquent as chart placings, royalty cheques and gold and platinum albums to hang on the wall. Don't laugh: for Pacific Northwest rhythm 'n' bluesmen in their mid-thirties who've been scuffling since their late teens, these things mean a lot.

Especially when it takes fifteen years to achieve what seems to everyone else to be an overnight success and then it comes so suddenly that Robert Cray himself actually owns little more than a few guitars, a record collection, some clothes, a scrapbook of memorabilia and a bed, the latter leant up against a wall in the closet of a friend's house. Richard Cousins, Cray's best friend, fellow army brat and constant sidekick since the formation of the first Robert Cray Band in 1974, is in a similar situation with but a single exception: he doesn't own a bed. In fact, they've been living out of suitcases for so long that Cousins literally cannot remember the last time he paid any rent.

'America's premier rhythm and blues attraction' have reassembled in Atlanta after a fortnight's break from their combined US-and-world tour, where they had finished with gigs in Rio de Janeiro and São Paulo, Cray flying in from California, where he's considering spending those new bucks on a home – if they ever let him off the road long enough to look at some. Peter Boe has been hometowning with his parents, while drummer David Olson, a bluff, stocky good-ol'-boy who is both the band's sole married member and the only one with the distinction of a permanent address, was beamed down from Syracuse in upstate New York.

Cousins spent his holiday in Jamaica – circumstances which manifest themselves via a straw hat which looks as if it was only obtained after a vicious tussle with a horse, plus a discreet patina of Rasta patois – and his sandals are practically falling off his feet. The only other shoes he has are the cowboy boots he wears on-stage – or, as he puts it, 'at work' – and they're too hot to wear in the heatwave which is wreaking havoc with most of the USA. When the tour reaches New York, the band are due for a raid on Nike, so if the heatwave holds out, Cousins plans to barefoot his way across America.

The two old buddies are an unlikely pair: Cray dignified, relaxed, equable; Cousins ebullient, extrovert and – not to put too fine a point on it – noisy. 'Someone's got to be the clown in the band,' he suggests, in the tones of one who finds the role reasonably congenial. Indeed, in every band someone's got to be Ron Wood, and in this one it's Richard Cousins. He has that mournful but mischievous expression which is as mandatory for the would-be Woody as the tendency to scamper around the stage, sliding up next to anybody whom he feels needs geeing up. If Cray provides the band's drama and focus, it is Cousins who gives them spirit and spark.

The night before the show, a midnight rehearsal is called at a studio some forty minutes' drive outside the city centre. Two weeks off have blunted the band's edge; not to mention the fact that they've just taken delivery of a new stage set: twin six-foot risers for Boe's keyboards and Olson's drums, with Kaihatsu and Cousins stationed beneath them and Cray at stage-centre. Departure has been delayed and delayed again while everybody waits on Kaihatsu, who is suffering from a recurrence of the arthritis developed as a high-school and college athlete – somewhat aggravated after Bill Gardner, the band's tour manager, accidentally trod on his foot – and has been under doctors' orders in San Francisco. As the party congregate in the bar, the chatter is suddenly obliterated by what sounds like the roar of a wounded mastodon, the kind of guttural, wordless eruption that is the last thing that any peaceful drinker ever wants to hear in a bar. Nervously, heads turn, but it is simply Joe Cocker delivering the punchline of a joke about a Scotsman.

Eventually the guitarist arrives from the airport on crutches, the team pile into a van rapidly followed by two crates of Budweiser, a live James Brown tape is cranked into the stereo and the journey is under way.

The rehearsal room resembles a Fender showroom; virtually everything in the room with the exception of Boe's keyboards and Cousins' amplifiers bears the venerable trademark, which is not surprising since Cray appears regularly in the company's ads. Sparkling new Stratocasters and Jazz Basses are everywhere, though Cray still sticks to the discoloured early sixties guitar he's played for the past decade. Cousins proudly displays a battered vintage Jazz Bass, sprayed a worn-through drop-dead blue. 'Now this is *my* guitar,' he says, 'but the sound guys like me to play *those*' — he gestures towards a pair of brand new battery-boosted Specials — 'because they give a clearer signal.' The funky old standby is packed away again. Kahaitsu gingerly eases himself to rest on an upturned flightcase as he, Cray and Boe confer on a harmonized guitar and keyboard transcription of a horn line on the recorded version of 'At Last'. Beers are popped, roadies and technicians bustle, and the band commence a brisk, business-like run-through of their set for the next night's show. It's late and nobody's energy level is particularly high: no time is wasted on casual jamming or lengthy beer breaks. Cans are swilled at the firing position; chat is minimal.

Even at rehearsal, it is easily apparent that success has changed Robert Cray. In his earliest British concerts, there was a palpable restraint verging on inhibition, a preoccupation with neatness, a degree of reserve which has now utterly melted, replaced by a blazing fervour, an emotional nakedness, a willingness to take outrageous risks with melody and meaning. Cray has never been a theatrical performer like his contemporary Stevie Ray Vaughan and he probably will never be — it is virtually impossible to imagine Cray jumping on his guitar, shaking it against the stage or playing it behind his head or back — but his newly earned status has empowered him to communicate more passionately and directly than ever before. With each run-through, he reaches into new corners of every song, finding fresh nuances, twists and details.

The rehearsal seems like a good job well done — until the van is once again nosing through the darkened roads towards the hotel.

The James Brown tape is playing once again, a little louder this time, and Cousins is in his element.

'Aw, *noooooo*!' he squalls. 'Take that shit *off*! That's *terrible*, man!' The current JB band are hustling through the tunes at a breathlessly rapid clip, and Cousins demands that one particularly hectic riff is replayed three or four times. 'How can anybody play that funky?' he wonders. 'Look, turn this vehicle *around*. This band ain't ready yet. We got some more *work* to do.' Fortunately, nobody takes him at his word. Finally, everybody tumbles gratefully into bed to sleep late and get some rest for the show. Except for Cray himself, that is. His days begin, inevitably, with a string of telephone interviews. After all, he's out front singing the songs.

Flash forward to the show, some twenty-odd hours later. Deric Dyer has brought along his tenor sax and, in a rare break in the storm-clouds of Young Bob's agonized soliloquy, the band is romping through the joyous jump of Jimmy McGriff's 'All About My Girl'. Cray, Kaihatsu, Dyer and Boe toss juke-joint choruses around in a breathless, exhilarating game of musical catch: it is both a demonstration of their capabilities as a conventional blues band and as effective a tension-buster as Boe's solo meditation later. Wreathed in cigarette smoke and wearing a T-shirt emblazoned 'Last Of The Hip White Boys', the pianist takes a contemplative, Monkish stroll through the storefront churches and back-alley piano bars of Young Bob's neighbourhood before the band return. Cray is performing like a man possessed: at least five times he has to change his guitar as his strings snap beneath the pressure. Daringly, he ends with a ballad (the fervid, gospelly 'At Last'), leaving the audience without the traditional release of an uptempo finale. To say the Robert Cray Band's show is 'gripping' would be something of an understatement.

Considerably later, after the air-conditioning of the Elvis bus has been reluctantly coaxed into some semblance of life and the band are trundling off to their next stop in Raleigh, North Carolina, Deric Dyer has finally accomplished the difficult feat of consuming enough American beer to achieve a noticeable alteration of consciousness. He tells a similarly exalted companion that Cray's eminence in contemporary blues is comparable only to that once held by Bob Marley in reggae; it may be *years* before his importance will be fully realized. His companion concurs wholeheartedly.

The tour continues. Tim Kahaitsu retires hurt, under strict medical instructions not even to *think* about rejoining the tour until he is capable of walking unaided. The band play a riotous hometown gig on an open-air bill between Jimmy Cliff and The Grateful Dead, and bemusedly report that they haven't seen so much tie-dye in one place since 1969. They open negotiations to bring the Memphis Horns − the immaculate former Stax brass team featured on their two Phonogram albums − with them to Europe. 'Don't Be Afraid Of The Dark' will probably have gone platinum by the time you read this.

And if anybody's still wondering 'Why Robert Cray?' . . . well, being a more convincing singer than Terence Trent D'Arby and a more eloquent guitarist than Eric Clapton certainly didn't hurt. Neither did a fortuitous resemblance to the young Harry Belafonte, not to mention deluxe photo opportunities like Cray's guest appearances in Chuck Berry's *Hail! Hail! Rock And Roll* movie and Tina Turner's *Break Every Rule* TV special and the opening slot on tours by Turner, Clapton and Huey Lewis. But most important is that unique whiff of ice-and-fire: the heat of sex and rage and the chilly, hellish muck-sweat of guilt and loss. In the world constructed for Young Bob by Cray and his cohorts, there is no way out: even in its lightest moments (the rueful, transparent bravado of 'I Guess I Showed Her' or 'Nothin' But A Woman') it is fundamentally grim. The Dark of which Cray cajoles us not to be afraid is more menacing than anything Bruce Springsteen ever found at the edge of town, or in the dankest depths of his tunnel of love.

'I think there's a little of Young Bob in everybody,' says Richard Cousins. 'At the very least, he is everyone who has ever yielded to their emotions or desires when their brains told them it was not the smart thing to do. Which, all in all, is quite a lot of us.'

# 'The Traveling Wilburys: Volume One' (Wilbury Records)

*Q*, December 1988

ONCE upon a time (1969, to be precise) *Rolling Stone*'s review section carried a hoax review of an alleged supersession bootleg entitled 'The Masked Marauders'. The participants, wrote 'T.M. Christian', included Mick Jagger, Bob Dylan, John Lennon, Paul McCartney, George Harrison, and a drummer as yet un-named', all produced by Al Kooper, who'd coined the term 'Supersession' for his 1968 team-up album with Mike Bloomfield and Steve (later 'Stephen') Stills. The punchline was that, despite the stoned sycophancy of the studiously parodied house style, the album was obviously dreadful.

Jump cut to 1988, and we find two of the Masked Marauders – Bob Dylan and George Harrison – popping up alongside Roy Orbison, Tom Petty and Jeff Lynne; all participants disguised only by heavy shades and silly pseudonyms ('Produced by Otis & Nelson Wilbury; Lucky Wilbury courtesy CBS Records, Inc', etc.), and – believe it or not – the whole scam was cooked up round Dave 'Everybody Knows Dave' Stewart's house. However, this time the punchline is that the album is actually pretty good; apart from anything else, it's the best Dylan album we've had for quite a while. The Big Zim is prominently featured on six of the ten selections (seemingly absent only from Lynne and Harrison's exuberant Beatles pastiche 'Heading For The Light', Orbison's inspired redneck-operatic 'Not Alone Any More', Lynne's goofy rockabilly extravangaza 'Rattled' and the Orbison–Harrison pick-and-strummer 'Handle With Care') and the combination of peer pressure and supportive production appears to have kicked him into overdrive. Songs like 'Tweeter And The Monkey Man', 'Congratulations', 'Dirty World' and 'Last Night' are audacious, evocative and raw-nerved: being in a group, even a pretend one, seems to suit him.

Lynne and Harrison go to town on the production; spraying the album with variations on the Carl Perkins Golden Licks course

456

and almost as many Beatley devices as their 'Cloud Nine' collaboration 'When We Were Fab', not to mention pulling out banks of overdubbed harmonies at the drop of a corduroy cap. They move from rockabilly to mock-ska to 'Revolver' to country-rock ancient and modern, providing each soloist with what he needs. Dylan's music becomes less flinty and austere, Harrison's less flimsy, Lynne's less cutesy and inflated and Petty's less Roger-McGuinn-knew-my-father, plus Orbison gets some backdrops that don't melt into insignificance every time he opens his mouth.

All in all, The Traveling Wilburys' debut exceeds all expectations (albeit expectations lowered by most of the participants' recent track records). Let's hope they do it again sometime, or at the very least that Harrison and Lynne produce Dylan's next album. Docked one star for the strained facetiousness of Michael Palin's Very Silly sleeve note, for not inviting Dave Edmunds and because, after all, they're just a bunch of old rock stars dicking about.

# The Bat Interview

*Observer*, May 1989

SPRINGTIME never comes to Gotham City, but in up-state New York, Bruce Wayne's garden is in full bloom. He inspects his neat blocks of tulips and azaleas as if he were their commanding officer; you almost expect them to salute him. With a grunt of audible satisfaction, the former playboy philanthropist who was once The Batman steers his wheelchair along the path and back towards what a generation of television watchers learned to describe as 'stately Wayne Manor'.

This month, Wayne has two excellent causes for celebration: his seventy-fifth birthday coincides with the expiration of a guarantee of media silence which he signed in 1939. This was part of a licensing deal which gave full rights to the name and persona of his alter ego to a then fledgling comic-book company. 'The Batman' made his fictional debut in *Detective Comics*, issue 27 (cover-dated May 1939), and the rest is history. Well, perhaps 'history' is not quite the most appropriate term. Bruce Wayne was The Batman for a little less than four years, his career as a nocturnal vigilante ending abruptly when a four-storey tumble from a Canal Street rooftop left him paralysed from the waist down. Since then, he has devoted his energies to managing his financial empire, and to cultivating his garden.

Today, Bruce Wayne is a thick-set, balding, bright-eyed man whose vitality and energy make it easy to ignore the chair to which he remains confined; a flowing white beard almost conceals the craggy, square-cut jawline so beloved of successive hordes of comic-book artists. His hands are massive and capable; he removes the cork from his lunchtime bottle of champagne with an easy, practised flick of the thumb. Clearly, he relished this long-delayed opportunity to discuss his relationship with his legendary counterpart.

'I had very little to do with the comic-strip after my initial meetings with Bob Kane and Bill Finger, the original artist and writer,' he says, filling his pipe. 'Part of the deal with DC Comics was that, basically, they could invent what they liked; and they didn't want me looking over the staff's shoulders and making them nervous.' He chuckles grimly; I try to imagine that same chuckle echoing from the shadows of a tenement staircase just before the cowled figure descends upon its prey.

'They were accurate about a few things, at least. I was born in 1914; my father, Dr Thomas Wayne, had been very lucky on the stockmarket when I was two or three, so he retired quite young. We didn't live here, though; this place belonged to my father's older brother,' He sighs. 'And it was also true that both my parents were shot by a mugger when we were on our way home from the movies. I was nine years old and I saw the whole thing. I went to live with my uncle, who didn't have any kids of his own; he died when I was fifteen years old and so I inherited the whole pile, stately Wayne Manor. I was very rich and very isolated. I suppose you could say I grew up a little strange.'

So, did he study criminology and martial arts and work out in a gym for eight hours a day and all the rest of it? Become a great athlete and a master detective? Swear revenge on all criminals? Wayne spreads his hands self-deprecatingly and relights his pipe. 'Well, clearly I didn't prepare myself as thoroughly as I should have done, or else I wouldn't be in *this* [he gestures towards his chair]. I was utterly obsessive; I wanted to protect the innocent and *hurt* the guilty. I mean, really *hurt* them. And I thought it would be easy to tell who was who as it was that night when my parents . . . anyway, yes, I was much given to sitting in here and brooding, and one night in 1933, a bat *did* fly in through my window – that window there, just behind you – and it cast this huge shadow over my desk . . . and that gave me the idea of becoming The Batman.'

So he dressed up as a giant bat?

Wayne looks a trifle embarrassed. 'Well, I did wear the cape and the cowl, but the mask covered my whole face. And I never wore grey tights. You know what New York City's like in winter. I'd've frozen to death in a get-up like that. No, it was a leather jacket with plenty of pockets, and black pants and boots; the cape folded up so I could get rid of it in a hurry. I had to abandon quite a few of them, I'm afraid, and that was a real pain, because I had to make them up myself, and I'd spent too much time studying criminology and unarmed combat to learn much about sewing.'

But what about the 'supporting cast'? What about Robin, Alfred, Commissioner Gordon, The Joker, The Penguin, The Catwoman . . .? 'Whoa! One at a time! Robin . . . he was a *real* disappointment. He was a nasty little brat; caught me changing out of the mask, recognized me from a picture in the paper and threatened to tell the police who I was if I didn't start taking him along. Luckily he changed his mind the first time he nearly got shot, so he was quite happy to quit – especially after I told him I'd take him to the zoo and feed him to the sharks if he ever went to the law. No, I'm *not* going to tell you who he was, so don't ask.

'Unfortunately the comics people decided I needed a full-time boy companion. I ask you, who'd willingly take a kid along on jobs like that, especially dressed up in a red-and-yellow pixie outfit? I always wondered how they thought readers would buy the notion of a New York City court allowing an unmarried twenty-five-year-old to adopt a ten-year-old boy, but I guess the readers were all too young to worry about something like that. Still, I'm not surprised they all thought we were gay. I'm quite pleased that I don't have Robin at the moment; they sent the first one off to college in '69 and now he's in another comic – Teen something-or-other – and they killed the second one off last year. I really got a kick out of that. The number of times I felt like shooting the little bastard myself . . .

'Alfred? He certainly wasn't an old English butler. Alfred was an Italian guy from Brooklyn, and his job was to do the driving, both for me as Bruce and me as Batman. Alfredo drove . . . no, of course it wasn't a Batmobile. They were ridiculous: the one they had in the sixties couldn't do more than 40 m.p.h. with a wind behind it. They had to speed up the film every time. What Alfredo had was a black Ford with fake number plates we got from somewhere and changed every couple of days. Alfredo stayed with me until about eight years ago. No, you can't talk to him either.

'Commissioner Gordon was someone Finger and Kane dreamed up; any policeman who'd make someone like me an honorary member of the department would have been fired in three minutes. I was about as respectable as Bernhard Goetz. The comics people took a lot of flak for making a hero out of a vigilante, which is why they had to clean my image up so much. Suddenly I wasn't carrying a gun. I had this kid with me all the time, I was an honorary policeman . . .' Wayne snorts with laughter and refills his champagne glass.

'The Joker was real enough, though. He was a nasty piece of work, but strictly small-time. He used to rob pawnshops by putting dog shit in paper bags, setting the bag on fire and ringing the bell. The old guys would run out, stamp on the bag, and just as they realized what they had on their shoes he'd whack 'em over the head and clean the place out. The Penguin was just a local thug; they called him Penguin because he had a funny walk and liked fish.'

What about all the high-tech stuff in the Batcave? The Bat-computer, shark-repellent Bat-spray, Bat-plane, Bat-this and Bat-that? 'Are you serious? I'm rich but not *that* rich. Have you any idea how much that stuff would cost? Or how I would get hold of it without being traced? Or what kinds of accountants I'd need to keep it all secret from the tax people and the FBI? Or how I could keep it secret from the accountants? The Batcave was an old barn with a car and a few spare capes in it. The comic people invented all that stuff, and then when DC sold the strip to the TV networks the writers went *crazy*. I tell you I *hated* that show so much. Some of the comics had been bad enough, but suddenly I was a laughing stock. It was then that I stopped thinking of the character as "me" and starting thinking of him as . . . well, "him" How could I be *that*? How could *anyone* be that? That fat guy pretending to climb up the wall with the cameras turned sideways?'

So would he have quit if he hadn't fallen off the roof? 'I was seriously considering it. See, another unbelievable thing about the strip is that even though I terrorize people and' — he smiles ruefully — 'violate their civil rights, it doesn't matter because I'm never wrong. Have you noticed that? In the comics I never harm an innocent person. I'm infallible. Well, I wasn't. I would break guys' arms and pull their teeth out with a rusty pliers if I thought they were lying to me, and at least half the time it turned out they were telling the truth. It got to the point where I was hurting more innocent people than I was protecting, and after the last time that happened I decided I was going to hang up the cape and try and find out who I was. My development as a human being had stopped dead the night my parents were killed, and I was still a hurt, angry nine-year-old in the body of a very rich grown-up.'

So what happened?

'This hooker I was trying to interrogate threw a cat in my face and I fell off the damn roof. End of story.' He shrugs. 'But at least she phoned me an ambulance. Even came to see me in hospital a few times . . .' Wayne's bottle of champagne is empty now; he presses a small desk buzzer and a tall, smiling woman seemingly in her late sixties brings him a fresh replacement, nestling in an ice-bucket. 'Thank you, Selina,' he says as she refills our glasses. He anticipates my next question and waves his pipe at me. '*That* is definitely off limits, I still have *some* secrets.' Steering the conversation back to safer ground, I solicit his views on the current flurry of Batactivity; recent mega productions like Frank Miller's *The Dark Night Returns* and *Batman: Year One* and — of course — Tim Burton's eagerly awaited feature film.

'Oh, I liked those Miller books, and that Alan Moore one about The Joker — *The Killing Joke*. But what I can't figure out is that even though I — *he* — is a different age in each of them, they all seem to be happening in the present day, or near to it. In *Year One* I'm — *he's* — twenty-five, Gordon's nearly forty and all the clothes are modern. The Moore one, judging by how old Gordon and his daughter are, takes place at least twenty-five years later but The Batman is still young, and in *Dark Night* he's damn near as old as I am now – and Reagan was still President. I can't figure these people out. The movie, now, I'm looking forward to that, especially Jack Nicholson as The Joker. At least he doesn't have a damn moustache you can see through the make-up.'

Did Wayne enjoy vigilante movies? Was he a fan of *Death Wish* and *Dirty Harry*? He frowns. 'I hated them. *Hated* them. You see, my Dad always voted Democrat, and the whole business of my charity, The Wayne Foundation, was to aid the victims of crimes and to give support to criminals who'd served their sentences and wanted to go straight. That was as me, Bruce, right? But as The Batman, I felt like a Republican. I guess if I'd seen those movies as The Batman, I would've loved 'em. It was' – he raises his bushy eyebrows – 'a rather strange existence.'

Does Wayne take any interest in the comic-book field outside of those which concern him? Has he read *Love & Rockets*? *Watchmen*? *RAW*? *Maus*? *Judge Dredd*? *Crisis*?

'No, of course not. Are you kidding? I'm seventy-five years old. Why the hell should I read comics? I'm a little disturbed by the fact that *you* do. I've received a very generous royalty from DC all these years, and next week my agreement with them terminates. They help to finance The Wayne Foundation, and that's a far better memorial to my father than leaving a trail of broken arms all over the city.'

Behind me, the door opens again. 'I'm afraid,' says Selina, 'that it's time for Bruce's nap now. I've called you a cab, and it should have you back in the city by four. And Bruce, don't you think you've had quite enough to drink?' She gazes meaningfully at the empty champagne bottle by Wayne's elbow.

'Just one more thing before you go,' says Wayne. He rolls his chair across the room to an ornate Victorian cupboard in the far corner, unlocks the door and produces something which he tosses – with remarkable accuracy – into my lap. It is a mint copy of *Detective Comics*, issue 27, cover-dated May 1939. The metallic ink is still fresh and glowing. On the cover, The Batman has just swung down on his Bat-rope, snatching a gun-toting thug from a rooftop. His cape spreads out behind him, like darkly sinister wings. 'STARTING THIS ISSUE,' trumpets the blurb, 'THE AMAZING AND UNIQUE ADVENTURES OF THE BATMAN!' Selecting a felt-tip pen from a tray on his desk he scrawls: 'To Charlie, Best Wishes, Bruce Wayne – THE BATMAN' across the broad, red band bearing the magazine's title. 'Don't you worry,' he smiles. 'I've got hundreds of 'em. Part of my hedge against inflation.' Selina adjusts the blanket across his lap, and he waves goodbye as she wheels him across the hall.

## Miles Davis: The cat who walks alone

*Observer*, May 1989

'MY thing . . . is time,' Miles Davis says, his parched whisper almost swallowed by the surge and crash of Malibu waves. It is now forty years since the sessions which produced his first masterpiece, 'Birth Of The Cool'; one week since the release of his most recent album 'Amandla'; and three days since his sixty-third birthday. He is attempting to explain to a visitor the criteria he applies when choosing musicians and colleagues. But he could equally be discussing his own astonishing creative longevity – never just surviving shifting styles but confronting them, always seeking and finding new worlds for his stalking, inquisitive trumpet to explore. Miles keeps time; it does not keep him.

Somewhere off the coast road by Malibu, Miles is preparing for a European tour; not by practising on the gleaming red and black metal-flake trumpets resting in inconspicuous corners of the sunlit, high-ceilinged living-room, nor by composing (though a string of scales and chord symbols have been jotted on manuscript paper atop the baby grand next to the exercise bike). In faded blue jeans, mustard yellow leather jacket and a black silk T-shirt, his ageless features framed by a recently acquired ruff of thick black curls which would seem faintly ridiculous surrounding a more wrinkled countenance, he is thoughtfully circling a huge canvas laid out on a table, his collaborator Jo Gelbard watching his every move.

He sketches an outline with a heavy crayon, she follows his shapes with a brush, filling the areas he indicates with colour.

Then Miles seizes a brush, linking two previously unconnected sketches with a long, lean curve of blue. The last canvas, still damp, hangs over the doorway. Miles's signature bears an uncanny resemblance to Chagall's. A massive television blasts an afternoon soap opera into the crisp sea air as Miles and Gelbard prowl the borders of their new creation, launching occasional stabbing forays into its heartland. A comparison between the unencumbered line of his approach to both trumpet and brush provokes him to observe that, 'anything looks like a face if you just put the eye in'.

Miles's painting is more than simply a nice hobby or a chance to ego out by slapping his own artwork on his record sleeves. His canvases sell for between $10,000 and $15,000: producer Quincy Jones has just bought ten of them – which has caused Miles something of a severe diplomatic problem. 'Lionel Richie was over last night,' he explains, 'and I had a big one like this, only yellow, which I'd promised to Lionel, only Quincy just bought it. So now I got to get it back.'

'I'll get it back for you,' says Herman Leonard. 'I'll call Quincy today.' Today Miles is reunited with Leonard, the outstanding post-war jazz photographer, for the first time in more than twenty years. A near-contemporary of Miles, Leonard first photographed him in 1948. Sources close to Miles, as the saying goes, have warned that he is unlikely to be forthcoming about his past; unwilling to discuss anything that happened longer ago than last year. 'Miles,' they say, 'is only interested in the present and the future.' Nevertheless, Leonard's presence seems to unlock something in Miles; any self-consciousness about reminiscing evaporates almost instantly.

'Seems like if you finish somethin', then everybody else knows it's finished. In other words, *you're* no secret to *me*. What we do today, we don't have to do tomorrow. We don't even *think* about tomorrow. I was tellin' somebody that the other day; they say that's *existentialism*. I say, well, they probably copied that off of me. You know I used to go with Juliette Greco? Well in '49 we used to go to a place together with Boris Vian and Jean-Paul Sartre. I couldn't speak French so I didn't know what they were sayin', but we were like *that* together. Can you imagine, someone knockin' on your door that you love and you're in a different country?' As he talks, he continues to track his muse around the table. An eye appears, followed by a distinctly Greco-like cheekbone.

'She has different expressions on her face than an American woman; she had the prettiest mouth . . . and nose. But the next time I saw her, she'd had her nose cut off. She told me: "You might not recognize me the next time you see me." She called me up when she was in New York City. I say: "Why?" She say: "I had my nose cut off." I say: "Why?" She say: "Darryl F. Zanuck told me it'd look better when I photograph." Juliette was the prettiest woman I'd ever seen − since my mother − but when she cut off her nose, her beauty just stopped. *How* can a man tell a woman she's got to have her nose cut off? It's about *going where you want to go* in showbusiness.'

In his earliest days as a musician, Miles Davis could well have cut off *his* nose; succumbed to the temptation of attempting to change his musical personality according to passing dictates and prejudices. In the music populated by big men with big sounds, he was a small man with a tight, lonely sound. When the acknowledged master of contemporary trumpet was Dizzy Gillespie, Miles soon abandoned any attempt to match Diz's flamboyant virtuosity and florid, high-register improvisations. He was ill at ease in the instrument's stratospheres and uncomfortable with the speed and volume demanded of fledgling beboppers. But instead of admitting defeat, he cultivated the emotional power of this thin, piercing tone and honed his melodic sensibility to a single, luminous nerve.

For Miles, ever less became ever more. His trumpet became the most eloquent voice in jazz: a vehicle for an unmistakeable musical personality which juxtaposed the toughness and cool of a Bogart with the jaunty melancholia of a Chaplin, shot through with the keen sense of irony common to both. 'You don't have to play all those notes,' he once said. 'You just have to play the pretty ones.'

Between the late forties and the late fifties he had proved his point many times over, whether contrasting his spare, burnished line with the volubility of saxophonists with the dreamy, insolent facility of Charlie Parker and the harsh urgency of John Coltrane − or slithering through the scented landscapes and lush undergrowth of the late Gil Evans's orchestral masterpieces like *Porgy and Bess* or *Sketches of Spain*. For the past twenty years he has gleefully grappled with the electric tonalities of funk and rock, absorbing songs or ideas from James Brown, Sly Stone, Michael

Jackson, Jimi Hendrix and Prince, and whoever's in the charts this week. Wherever he goes he is irreducibly Miles.

Yet he has always been a leader who never looks back to see if anybody is following him. His 1970 'Bitches Brew' precipitated a wave of so-called 'fusion' bands, most of which were led by musicians such as Herbie Hancock, John McLaughlin, Chic Corea and Josef Zawinul, all of whom had graduated from his sixties bands and sessions but, through it all, Miles has followed his own nose. He is the cat who walks alone.

'Music and art?' he muses, paintbrush in hand. 'They're one and the same. It's about *composition*. If you can do this you can do *anything*. You just have to know when to start and stop, or when to move on to something else. You have to have that instinct. You have to . . . ohhhhhh, *shit*!' Miles has just slapped his hand squarely into a freshly painted triangle of yellow. As he steps back, Gelbard moves in to check the damage: nothing that can't be whited out. Miles curses under his breath and disappears in search of paper towels.

He returns, wiping his hands. 'Gil Evans used to ask me, "You can be playing a whole number – chords, breaks, everything – but have you thought about the tempo?" Every time he would do this – "*What's the tempo?*" When we did *Porgy and Bess*, we would get into serious shit – I mean real *serious* shit – about this. His face would change. "*What tempo is it?*" All the time I'd been playin' in tune, but . . . see the tempo is the *whole thing* in music. *The whole goddam thing.*'

He beckons to his visitors and begins to lead them down the winding path to the sea. Since he began dividing his time between his long-term base in New York City and his settled home in California, his inner metronome has readjusted itself. 'I love the pace, and so many of the best musicians are out here. Michael Jackson is here, Quincy Jones is here, George Duke, good writers like El DeBarge. Half of one of my best bands are out here: Herbie Hancock and Wayne Shorter. I have two full wardrobes so whenever I want to be in New York City I can just walk out the door.'

The dry, sunny California climate is also good for Miles's health. An excruciatingly painful hip injury caused his temporary retirement in the latter half of the seventies. And a hip replacement in 1979 left him with a limp. Two decades of strenuous boxing workouts have left him stiff with arthritis, and in the last few years he has begun to develop diabetes. Yet even these ailments have not aged him; he appears less like a sixty-three-year-old than a young man to whom something terrible has happened. With a hoarse, sardonic chuckle, he describes a visit to his Chinese doctor. 'He takes my arm like this' — Miles reaches out and lightly takes hold of my wrist — 'and he say, "How-long-you-play?" I say two and a half hours. He shakes his head and says, "You-have-heart-attack!"'

He treats his frailty as no more than an irritant: his legs have healed sufficiently for him to ride the horses he keeps at a nearby stable. 'I couldn't drive my Ferrari for a long time,' he says, 'but I went back to New York to see my doctor and he said, "Oh by the way, you can drive now." So I went home and called him and said, "Can I ride horses too?" He said yeah. 'Cause both ridin' and drivin' is *here*.' He sinks into a crouch and slaps his thigh. It is the same stance he adopts when his playing is at its most intense.

However deeply involved Miles Davis is in his painting (and it is not altogether certain that his artwork would fetch such high prices were the signature less distinguished), his first and most passionate love is his music. Specifically, making music in concert, where he still produces the most astounding musical transitions from his band with a single keyboard chord, a blast of his trumpet or even merely a flick of the hand or eye. He is a master bandleader, an art in which he admits no living peers other than James Brown and Prince. His enigmatic signals are, he says, mainly memory-joggers for his band. 'The band might forget something,' he says, 'and that one chord might just be able to help 'em remember. Or the drummer or the keyboard might be too loud and I might have to bring one of 'em down a little.'

Miles has always directed his concert and studio ensemble this way — from his post-bop days to the electric fury of the seventies and early eighties. Yet his most recent records 'Tutu' (1986), the *Siesta* soundtrack (1988), and the current 'Amandla' are prepared for him from the ground up, high-tech style, by multi-instrumentalist, composer and producer Marcus Miller, who was the first bassist in Miles's post-1980 comeback ensemble. How does he feel about working with the machines?

'Marcus does that. I don't have anything to do with that stuff.

He's a *genius*, he gets a great sound. We have sections that we play in, and sometimes he'll say, "Play open [unmuted] horn here!" and I'll say, "Yeah, yeah, open horn," but I can't play open horn unless it sounds just right. Trumpeters are funny like that. They ought to say on the product that this record is only a *guide* to what you will hear in person.'

So, ultimately playing live is the most important thing?

'Yeah . . . you can't use the same tempos live that you do on a record. It's got to be faster live. You've got to get the people *up* when they come to hear you.'

Though he has never exactly disguised his views – his straight talk on racial injustice caused a minor furore after an early-sixties *Playboy* interview – Miles is no activist. However, the titles of his recent albums, and brooding sorrow and anger of much of their music, are clear indicators of one area of overriding concern. 'You know this new record? It's called "Amandla". That means *freedom*. That's all I can do, to say "freedom" for Africa, for South Africa. "Tutu" was to say, "we know what you people are goin' through", this is to say we know what they got to do now.' Similarly, revelations concerning the pollution on Malibu Beach have brought environmental issues almost to his back doorstep.

'The worst of the pollution,' he points up the beach, 'is up there. But . . . what the *hell* is this?' With distaste, his toe probes at something washed up at his feet; a stinking mass of odd-looking seaweed tangled with the rotting bones of a small fish. He shakes his head and trudges on.

Both *Siesta* and 'Amandla' are dedicated to the memory of the late Gil Evans, who orchestrated *Birth of the Cool, Porgy and Bess, Sketches of Spain* and *Miles Ahead*; the only man for whom Miles would break his dictum – inherited from Coleman Hawkins – never to play with anyone older than himself. 'Amandla' is richly imbued with Evans-derived textures and colours; a musky, intoxicating distillation of Ellington and Debussy.

Evans died a week before the two veteran warriors were to embark on their most ambitious joint voyage: 'Tosca', with Evans's arrangement and Miles as featured soloist. To record 'Tosca' was Miles's most dearly cherished project, but the notion was so utterly personal to the two of them that the original dream was never to be fulfilled.

'He was touring in Europe a few years ago,' Miles says at

length, 'and on Friday all the arrangements for the band were stolen. You know what that means? *Every* part for *every* musician in *every* tune. And you know what Gil did? He locked himself up in a hotel bedroom, and he wrote them all out again. His eyes were poor too; he had to do it like this.' He mimes, holding up a piece of paper to his eyes and scribbling on it. 'He worked through the weekend, and on Monday they played. That's the kind of guy he was . . . But Gil is with me. He's in my mind. I can tune in on him and I know just what he'd say.'

For a second, a tear seems to gleam in the corner of his eye. Maybe it was the wind, maybe it was just my imagination; because Miles Davis doesn't cry – except through his horn.

Upstairs, Herman Leonard presents Miles with a belated birthday present – a copy of his book *The Eye of Jazz* (Viking Penguin). 'Look at my *book*, man!' he says proudly, pulling out enlargements of his haunting portraits of Duke Ellington, Billie Holiday, Fats Navarro and Charlie Parker. Miles exclaims softly over each one. Eventually he produces a gold marker and signs his double-page spread in Leonard's personal copy of his book. 'To Herman,' he scrawls. 'The best, Miles '89.'

Outside, the Rolls Silver Wraith sits in the shadow at the back of the garage while, a few feet away from the Everlast punching-bag and the basketball hoop, a gleaming silver-blue Ferrari (licence plate MILES 22) basks in the sun. It isn't going anywhere, though; its battery is flat. That's something that'll never be said of its owner. After all, Miles's thing is *time*.

# Madonna: Our lady of hard work

*Daily Telegraph*, 22 July 1990

ON Madonna's earliest tours, she was faced with one singularly knotty dilemma: the sheer physical effort of performing her strenuous dance routines while singing live meant that the quality of either the singing or the dancing would inevitably suffer. Which should it be? Five years ago, she took what was undoubtedly the correct decision in terms of the priorities of the youthful, video-trained audience she then had: she concentrated on the dancing. The vocals were breathless – no *Dick Tracy* pun intended – and often tuneless, but the show *looked* perfect.

Nowadays, Madonna is considerably more resourceful. The chiselled, diamond-hard physique cultivated by her obsessive workout programme isn't just for show: she now has the stamina to sing and dance simultaneously, which is just as well as her current audience is considerably more sophisticated and demanding. This weekend at Wembley Stadium, in what was easily the most theatrical show of a most theatrical year, she provided the answer to another question: what happened to all those post-*Hair* attempts to fuse rock music with the Broadway-style musical? Most of the well-known stabs at bringing rock to the musical theatre have been artistic – if not always commercial – failures, but the process has now been reversed: the major rock-tour spectaculars, like those of Michael Jackson, Prince and Madonna herself, have brought the technology and theatricality of the Broadway stage to the rock arenas and stadia. With its dozen-strong dance troupe, set-piece dialogues, elaborate costumes and multiple sets, including a *Metropolis*-style futurist nightmare, a cathedral, a harem and a thirties nightclub, Madonna's 'Blonde Ambition' is a Broadway musical in all essentials except for its lack of a plot. Backed by an extremely professional band – bassist Daryl Jones is an alumnus of Miles Davis's group, lead guitarist Carlos Rios created the lovely solo on Lionel Richie's otherwise insipid 'Hello' and rhythm guitarist David Walker played on The Jacksons' 'Victory' tour – Madonna not only performed most of her hits, but rammed home their subtexts.

Sexuality was most definitely on the agenda. 'You never really know a guy until you ask him to wear a rubber,' she teased an audience the youngest of whom have probably never even *seen* a condom. Madonna gave the audience as much crotch-grabbing and cussing as any male rap or heavy metal act: 'Like A Virgin', slowed down and given a musky mock-Arabic harem ambience, was bumped-and-ground out on a red velvet bed which rose hydraulically from the centre of the stage; 'Material Girl' found both star and backing singers in curlers and dressing gowns; and for the show's most charged moment – a medley of 'Like A Prayer' and 'Papa Don't Preach' – the cathedral set appeared complete with candles, crucifixes and a confessional booth. A book could be written on the subject of rock's famous lapsed Catholics (like Marianne Faithfull, Dusty Springfield, Bruce Springsteen, Bob Geldof, Johnny Rotten and Madonna herself), and this section of the show has provoked Catholic bishops to threaten her with excommunication. It is difficult to imagine how anyone whose parents named her 'Madonna' could avoid religious imagery; but Madonna Louise Ciccone has built her work around a reconciliation of Catholic guilt and the Protestant work ethic. James Brown used to call himself 'the hardest working man in show business', but nobody around today works harder than Madonna. Even Prince can stand still and play a guitar solo when he needs to catch his breath.

So, finally, is Madonna a negative role model for teenagers? Of course not. She preaches safe sex and hard work: what could be more responsible than that?

# Parting Shots

SOMETIME in late 1960, when I was nine years old, I persuaded my father to invest the substantial sum of ninepence – that's old money: three-quarters of a shilling, which was itself a twentieth part of a pound – in a *Superman* comic-book. On the back cover was an advertisement designed to involve young Americans in a programme of door-to-door selling of seeds; success in this juvenile branch of venture capitalism would entitle the more entrepreneurially gifted tots to a selection of Valuable Prizes, one of which was something called an Elvis Presley Guitar. The accompanying illustration depicted an extravagantly bequiffed youth in brightly coloured clothing gyrating frantically behind an acoustic guitar. Intrigued, I asked my father – naturally, the fount of all wisdom in worldly matters – who Elvis Presley was. '*Ach,*' he replied wearily, 'some idiot from America.'

A seed was duly sown, but not the sort which the advertisers had in mind. Elvis Presley – as I soon discovered after interrogating those of my schoolfriends who were, unlike myself, blessed with older sisters – was a 'rock and roll singer'; further research revealed that 'rock and roll' was the designation applied to those records played by Derek 'Uncle Mac' McCulloch on *Children's Favourites* (BBC Light Programme, between 9 a.m. and 9.55 on Saturday mornings) which I actually liked. Between the endless repetitions of 'Sparky's Magic Piano', 'The Runaway Train', 'The Bubble Car Song', 'The Little White Bull', 'The Ugly Duckling' and an appalling piece of pre-pubescent innuendo involving pink and blue toothbrushes, there were wonderful outbreaks of thundering drums, clanging guitars, honking saxophones, pounding pianos and exuberant voices: coded messages from the badlands beyond the constricting borders of childhood and suburbia, fragments of information about the implied freedoms of teenhood and the big city. That, I decided, was where I belonged; I felt like a displaced person, unaccountably misclassified as a suburban English child when I was really an urban American teenager.

Immediately, I began saving my pocket-money to buy records, though I didn't really know which ones I wanted and ended up with an impressive collection of representative works by Cliff Richard & The Shadows, Billy Fury and Elvis Presley, though Elvis records like the soundtrack from *G.I. Blues* were, for some unknown reason, much less exciting than the earlier ones in the Older Sisters' collections. The acquisition of these records was in itself an act of profound optimism, since we didn't have a record player (such an artefact only arrived in 1962, as a reward for passing the 11-plus). Until then, I was reduced to visiting gramophone-equipped neighbours with my record collection clutched hopefully under my arm, and once my welcomes inevitably wore out, I began stopping total strangers in the street and asking if I could bring my records around to their houses.

Gradually, I learned more about this disreputable music to which I had accidentally become addicted: it was a music sufficiently new and unfamiliar to teach fresh lessons with each successive wave of musicians. My tutor was Penny Marsden, an Older Sister who lived on the corner of our street; just as I discovered The Beatles she taught me about The Rolling Stones and the exotically named blues singers from whose music theirs was derived. By judicious use of my parents' library tickets and a junior librarian who would allow me premature access to the adult section of the library, I began to read about this thing called The

Blues, and thereby discovered — to my horror and revulsion — that this wonderful music was a by-product of slavery, repression and racism. The passing of almost three decades has not blunted the impact of that discovery: it was my earliest and most profound lesson in the intimacy of the relationships between history, politics, culture and entertainment.

My next revelation came from the same source; no sooner had I become — at thirteen — a Born Again Bluesman than I was introduced to the work of Bob Dylan, and through him learned that pop was not only born from the interaction between people and events, but that it could discuss those interactions in terms which were simultaneously simple, passionate and poetic. The inevitable tensions between the political conservatism which I had inherited from my parents and the messages contained in the music to which I devoted all those waking hours not required by school eventually erupted at the end of the sixties when — buoyed by the ripples of the Vietnam war and the black revolt in the US and spurred on by Jimi Hendrix, who became my hero the moment I first saw him on television — I became a would-be psychedelic revolutionary without ever having been a Socialist. Literary influences accompanied the musical ones: I devoured the works of James Baldwin, Norman Mailer and Tom Wolfe and discovered, to my glee, that America was not only producing music, but writers like Lester Bangs and Greil Marcus whose obsessive phrasemaking mirrored my own obsessions, and since my typewriter proved less stubbornly recalcitrant than my guitar, I began to formulate my own approach to fusing these twin concerns.

Wolfe's chameleonic assumption of the inner voices of his subjects, and the near-ventriloquism of his use of those borrowed voices, both struck resonant, reverberant chords in my as-yet untuned sensibility; the apocalyptic language used by Mailer — particularly in *Miami and the Siege of Chicago* — to describe political rallies and riots provided a perfect vocabulary for describing concert audiences; Baldwin's virtuoso assimilation of both literary and street language slid another fragment of my jigsaw into place, as did William Burroughs' junk-sick dadaism. Nik Cohn, in *Awopbopaloobop Alopbamboom*, validated my own perception of pop as both epic and silly, and Dr Hunter S. Thompson's manic voyages convinced me of the value of speed — in all senses.

Answering the ad which eventually led to participating in the *Oz Schoolkids' Issue* was my first attempt to contact that magical world where Things Happened. As a result, I met people who actually did the things I'd spent my adolescence reading about, and clumsily set about attempting to do them myself, as well as worming myself into print via any publication which would have me. Conscripted into the ranks of the freshly remodelled *New Musical Express* alongside various like-minded souls who had followed similar routes, I finally found a platform from which I could translate a private agenda into a public one.

By then, I knew that pop music should, first and foremost, be exciting, but that it could also deliver considerably more than a quick kick. I knew that it was not monolithic in style or content or constituency: that it represented the input and articulated the fantasies of people from no one class or race or nationality. I knew that, sooner or later, it had to have some politics: though not all the time, and not necessarily those which would benefit any of the self-serving hacks and bullshitters who periodically offered themselves up for election. I knew that pop didn't so much love *having* money as it enjoyed *spending* money: that things like shoes, shirts and haircuts were both utterly trivial and vitally important; indeed, that their triviality and importance were inextricably linked. I knew that pop was both about asserting your identity and about reinventing it if the identity with which you started out was unsatisfactory — what, after all, were Bob Dylan, David Bowie, Johnny Rotten and Prince if they were not inventions? — and that pop also involved not only a conspiracy between high-life and low-life to destroy the bourgeoisie, but a conspiracy by the bourgeoisie to penetrate the mysteries of the proletariat and the aristocracy.

Most of all, pop was about teens and twenties: I knew this for a fact before I was ten, and I learned it all over again from a very different perspective when I reached my thirties. Pop was — in stereotype, at least — about being young, living fast and having no regrets, and this proudly proclaimed youth-fascism was only possible because pop-as-we-know-it was itself young. I was born three years before Elvis Presley cut 'That's All Right Mama' and Ray Charles recorded 'I Got A Woman', and pop reached its teens not long after I did. Pop is now nearing forty, and so am I.

In the process, it has become institutionalized; before punk rock arrived in '76, I only knew three professional musicians who were younger than I was. (For the record, they were Gary Moore, first encountered with a shortlived Irish trio named Skid Row; Eddie Jobson, then a keyboard-and-violin child-prodigy in Roxy Music; and the late Jimmy McCullough, who'd played with Thunderclap Newman at the tender age of fifteen and ended up with Paul McCartney in Wings.) For one moment, punk slashed pop in half and piled the musical rubble of the previous twenty years into a makeshift Berlin Wall between the young and the recently young; but once the wall came down it was replaced by a combined museum and shopping mall. The sound of young rock bands earnestly pillaging the sixties is only occasionally drowned by the sound of rap posses sampling the seventies.

Now, fortysomething pop is fun for all the family and ancestor-worship rules. The very fact of pop's longevity has of necessity neutralized much of its allure: it is no longer a strange and wonderful apparition, but part of the furniture. As such, it is by no means utterly barren: after all, we have had motion pictures for most of this century and still good movies are made; we have had literature of one sort or another ever since we became recognizable as a species and still good stories are told. It is simply this: once the simple *fact* of pop was wonderful, just as the *fact* of film or radio or television or fiction itself was in itself miraculous.

Much of the material collected in this book is fuelled by that sense of wonder, and by the anger I felt when that sense of wonder was abused by musicians willing to sell their audiences short, or by audiences willing to let them do it, or by entrepreneurs willing to exploit both. Sometimes I felt that I was taking on the musicians on behalf of their audiences; sometimes that I was taking on the audiences on behalf of the music; and sometimes the music industry on behalf of all of the above. Always, I felt that it was necessary to take on pomposity (my own as well as that of others) on behalf of my readers: if my work wasn't entertaining, I figured, it would never even be read.

And somewhere along the way, long after I gave up on pop as a substitute for literature, or folk wisdom, or political discourse, or even as a communications switchboard for an international peer group, I discovered much to my relief that I still enjoyed it as music. I also came to terms with continuing to write about it.

475

Writing about pop as fortysomethinghood looms no longer strikes me as something disgraceful. After all, perfectly respectable adults continue to earn perfectly respectable livings writing about wine, cheese, sport and gardening: and by comparison a field which still nominally straddles sensibilities as disparate as those of Kylie Minogue and NWA – or New Kids On The Block and Lou Reed, or Eric Clapton and Public Enemy, or Madonna and Billy Bragg – still retains enough contradictions and anomalies to remain interesting.

Aaaaaanyway – that was then and this is now, except that 'now' is unable to sever its umbilical connection to 'then' and that somewhere in the space–time continuum 'then' is still an inseparable functioning aspect of 'now'. In other words, I was so much younger then, but I'm not too sure that I'm very much older than that now.

Charles Shaar Murray<br>
Up against a deadline<br>
London, 2 June 1990

# Index

Toussaint, Allen, 97, 154, 270
Travis, Dave Lee, 334
Tuff Darts, 128–30
Turner, Tina, 154, 428–46, 450, 455
Tull, Jethro, 26
Tyler, Tony, 22

Underwood, Ruth, 63, 66, 67

Van Zandt, Steve, 394–8
Vicious, Sid, 200, 205–19
Visconti, Tony, 20, 24
Volman, Mark, 20, 27
Vonnegut, Kurt, 365–72

Wakeman, Rick, 20
Ward, Bill, 143
Waronker, Larry, 90

Waters, Muddy, 175, 177–94, 240, 408
Watt-Roy, Norman, 292
Watts, Charlie, 154, 156, 206
Wayne, Bruce, 457–63
Welch, Chris, 18, 386
Weller, Paul, 254–6, 401, 402
Weymouth, Martina (Tina), 131, 390–92, 402
Who, The, 16, 27, 95, 311
Wickham, Vicki, 81
Williamson, Robin, 23
Williamson, Sonny Boy, 185, 240
Wilson, Alan, 5, 8
Wilson, Brian, 16, 26
Wilson, Mary, 421

Winner, Michael, 197
Winter, Edgar, 10, 33–5
Winter, Johnny, 5, 9–10, 175, 191–3, 408
Wisefield, Laurie, 439
Wolf, Howlin', 239–41, 286
Wolfchild, Sheldon Peters, 146, 148, 150
Wonder, Stevie, 58, 101, 383
Wood, Ron, 154, 155, 157, 158–61, 267–80
Wyman, Bill, 154, 206

Yardbirds, The, 16
Yates, Paula, 297

Zappa, Frank, 7, 41, 43, 61–7, 224